KU-541-672

FIFTH EDITION

# Programming C# 3.0

*Jesse Liberty and Donald Xie*

O'REILLY®

Beijing · Cambridge · Farnham · Köln · Paris · Sebastopol · Taipei · Tokyo

## Programming C# 3.0, Fifth Edition

by Jesse Liberty and Donald Xie

Copyright © 2008 O'Reilly Media, Inc. All rights reserved.
Printed in the United States of America.

Published by O'Reilly Media, Inc., 1005 Gravenstein Highway North, Sebastopol, CA 95472.

O'Reilly books may be purchased for educational, business, or sales promotional use. Online editions are also available for most titles (*safari.oreilly.com*). For more information, contact our corporate/institutional sales department: (800) 998-9938 or *corporate@oreilly.com*.

**Editor:** John Osborn
**Developmental Editor:** Brian MacDonald
**Production Editor:** Sumita Mukherji
**Copyeditor:** Audrey Doyle
**Proofreader:** Sumita Mukherji

**Indexer:** Angela Howard
**Cover Designer:** Karen Montgomery
**Interior Designer:** David Futato
**Illustrator:** Jessamyn Read

**Printing History:**

| | |
|---|---|
| July 2001: | First Edition. |
| February 2002: | Second Edition. |
| May 2003: | Third Edition. |
| February 2005: | Fourth Edition. |
| December 2007: | Fifth Edition. |

Nutshell Handbook, the Nutshell Handbook logo, and the O'Reilly logo are registered trademarks of O'Reilly Media, Inc. *Programming C# 3.0*, the image of an African crowned crane, and related trade dress are trademarks of O'Reilly Media, Inc.

Java™ is a trademark of Sun Microsystems, Inc. Microsoft, MSDN, the .NET logo, Visual Basic, Visual C++, Visual Studio, and Windows are registered trademarks of Microsoft Corporation.

Many of the designations used by manufacturers and sellers to distinguish their products are claimed as trademarks. Where those designations appear in this book, and O'Reilly Media, Inc. was aware of a trademark claim, the designations have been printed in caps or initial caps.

While every precaution has been taken in the preparation of this book, the publisher and authors assume no responsibility for errors or omissions, or for damages resulting from the use of the information contained herein.

 This book uses RepKover,™ a durable and flexible lay-flat binding.

ISBN-10: 0-596-52743-8
ISBN-13: 978-0-596-52743-3
[M]

# Table of Contents

**Preface** . . . . . . . . . . . . . . . . . . . . . . . . . . . . . . . . . . . . . . . . . . . . . . . . . . . . . . . . . . **ix**

**Part I.  The C# Language**

**1.  C# 3.0 and .NET 3.5** . . . . . . . . . . . . . . . . . . . . . . . . . . . . . . . . . . . . . **3**
The Evolution of C#                                              3
The C# Language                                                 4
The .NET Platform                                               6

**2.  Getting Started: "Hello World"** . . . . . . . . . . . . . . . . . . . . . . . . . . . **7**
Classes, Objects, and Types                                      7
Developing "Hello World"                                         14
Using the Visual Studio 2008 Debugger                            18

**3.  C# Language Fundamentals** . . . . . . . . . . . . . . . . . . . . . . . . . . . . . . **21**
Types                                                           21
Variables and Constants                                         25
Whitespace                                                      33
Statements                                                      33
Operators                                                       49
Preprocessor Directives                                         59

**4.  Classes and Objects** . . . . . . . . . . . . . . . . . . . . . . . . . . . . . . . . . . . **61**
Defining Classes                                                62
Creating Objects                                                67
Using Static Members                                            75
Destroying Objects                                              79
Passing Parameters                                              83

Overloading Methods and Constructors ......... 89
Encapsulating Data with Properties ......... 92
readonly Fields ......... 96

**5. Inheritance and Polymorphism** ...................................... **98**
Specialization and Generalization ......... 98
Inheritance ......... 101
Polymorphism ......... 102
Abstract Classes ......... 109
The Root of All Types: Object ......... 113
Nesting Classes ......... 115

**6. Operator Overloading** ........................................ **118**
Using the operator Keyword ......... 118
Supporting Other .NET Languages ......... 119
Creating Useful Operators ......... 120
Logical Pairs ......... 120
The Equality Operator ......... 120
Conversion Operators ......... 121
Putting Operators to Work ......... 121

**7. Structs** .................................................. **127**
Defining Structs ......... 128
Creating Structs ......... 129

**8. Interfaces** ................................................ **132**
Defining and Implementing an Interface ......... 132
Overriding Interface Implementations ......... 147
Explicit Interface Implementation ......... 151

**9. Arrays, Indexers, and Collections** ................................. **156**
Arrays ......... 156
The foreach Statement ......... 162
Indexers ......... 177
Collection Interfaces ......... 186
Constraints ......... 190
List<T> ......... 195
Queues ......... 206
Stacks ......... 208
Dictionaries ......... 211

**10.  Strings and Regular Expressions** . . . . . . . . . . . . . . . . . . . . . . . . . . . . . . . . . . .  **214**
    Strings                                                                    215
    Regular Expressions                                                        229

**11.  Exceptions** . . . . . . . . . . . . . . . . . . . . . . . . . . . . . . . . . . . . . . . . . . . . . . . . . . . . . . .  **241**
    Throwing and Catching Exceptions                                           242
    Exception Objects                                                          252

**12.  Delegates and Events** . . . . . . . . . . . . . . . . . . . . . . . . . . . . . . . . . . . . . . . . . . . .  **256**
    Events                                                                     256
    Events and Delegates                                                       257
    Anonymous Methods                                                          271


**Part II.   C# and Data**

**13.  Introducing LINQ** . . . . . . . . . . . . . . . . . . . . . . . . . . . . . . . . . . . . . . . . . . . . . . . . .  **279**
    Defining and Executing a Query                                             280
    LINQ and C#                                                                285
    Anonymous Types                                                            291
    Implicitly Typed Local Variables                                           291
    Extension Methods                                                          292
    Lambda Expressions in LINQ                                                 297

**14.  Working with XML** . . . . . . . . . . . . . . . . . . . . . . . . . . . . . . . . . . . . . . . . . . . . . . . .  **302**
    XML Basics (A Quick Review)                                                302
    X Stands for eXtensible                                                    304
    Creating XML Documents                                                     304
    Searching in XML with XPath                                                311
    Searching Using XPathNavigator                                             322
    XML Serialization                                                          329

**15.  Putting LINQ to Work** . . . . . . . . . . . . . . . . . . . . . . . . . . . . . . . . . . . . . . . . . . . . .  **337**
    Getting Set Up                                                             338
    LINQ to SQL Fundamentals                                                   339
    Using Visual Studio LINQ to SQL Designer                                   344
    Retrieving Data                                                            349
    Updating Data Using LINQ to SQL                                            353
    Deleting Relational Data                                                   358
    LINQ to XML                                                                363

16.  **ADO.NET and Relational Databases** . . . . . . . . . . . . . . . . . . . . . . . . . . . . . . . . . .  368
     Relational Databases and SQL                                              368
     The ADO.NET Object Model                                                  372
     Getting Started with ADO.NET                                             374

## Part III.   Programming with C#

17.  **Programming ASP.NET Applications** . . . . . . . . . . . . . . . . . . . . . . . . . . . . . . . .  381
     Web Forms Fundamentals                                                   381
     Creating a Web Form                                                      385
     Data Binding                                                             391

18.  **Programming WPF Applications** . . . . . . . . . . . . . . . . . . . . . . . . . . . . . . . . . . .  404
     WPF in a Very Small Nutshell                                            404
     Building the Application                                                 406
     What Have You Learned, Dorothy?                                         419

19.  **Programming Windows Forms Applications** . . . . . . . . . . . . . . . . . . . . . . . . . .  420
     Creating the Application                                                420

## Part IV.   The CLR and the .NET Framework

20.  **Attributes and Reflection** . . . . . . . . . . . . . . . . . . . . . . . . . . . . . . . . . . . . . . .  449
     Attributes                                                               449
     Reflection                                                               456

21.  **Threads and Synchronization** . . . . . . . . . . . . . . . . . . . . . . . . . . . . . . . . . . . .  465
     Threads                                                                  466
     Synchronization                                                          474
     Race Conditions and Deadlocks                                            485

22.  **Streams** . . . . . . . . . . . . . . . . . . . . . . . . . . . . . . . . . . . . . . . . . . . . . . . . . . . .  487
     Files and Directories                                                   488
     Reading and Writing Data                                                499
     Asynchronous I/O                                                         506
     Network I/O                                                              511
     Web Streams                                                              527
     Serialization                                                            529
     Isolated Storage                                                         538

**23.  Programming .NET and COM** ....................................... **542**

Importing ActiveX Controls                                       542

P/Invoke                                                         551

Pointers                                                         554

**C# Keywords** ....................................................... **561**

**Index** ............................................................. **569**

# Preface

In 2000, .NET revolutionized the way we create both web and Windows applications. .NET 2.0 was a dramatic incremental improvement over .NET 1.0. This book covers C# 3.0 and .NET 3.5, and this time we are looking at an even more significant set of changes.

C# 3.0 introduces a new generation of changes to a framework that takes an enormous leap forward, revolutionizing the way we program Windows applications, web services, and, to a lesser degree, web applications.

In 2000, I wrote in the first edition of this book that Microsoft had "bet the company" on .NET. It was a good bet. In 2007, I bet *my* career on .NET by joining Microsoft as senior program manager in the Silverlight Development Division.

Because one way (my preferred way) to program Silverlight is with C#, I have the opportunity to stay very current with this mature yet rapidly evolving language. It is an exciting time for C#; version 3.0 adds a number of tremendously useful features, and the newest edition of Visual Studio makes programming with these features easier than ever.

It is my goal that you'll find *Programming C# 3.0* to be of great use whether this is your first exposure to .NET programming, or you've been at it for some time. I'll start with the fundamentals, and introduce new additions to the language not as obscure add-ons, but as the integrated features that they are.

If you are already a C# 2.0 programmer, feel free to skim through the parts you know. The new features are called out by appropriate headings; you won't inadvertently skip over them. But be sure to reread Chapter 12, and all of Parts II and III.

# C# and .NET

The programming language of choice for .NET is C#, which builds on the lessons learned from C (high performance), C++ (object-oriented structure), Java™ (garbage collection, high security), and Visual Basic (rapid development) to create a language ideally suited for developing component-based, *n*-tier, distributed Windows client and web applications.

C# 3.0 brings greatly enhanced features and a powerful new development environment. It is the crowning achievement of Microsoft's R&D investment. It is wicked cool.

## About This Book

This book is a tutorial, both on C# and on writing .NET applications with C#.

If you are a proficient C# 2.0 programmer, and all you want to know is what is new in C# 3.0, put this book down, buy *Programming .NET 3.5* by myself and Alex Horovitz (O'Reilly), and then read a lot about Language-Integrated Query (LINQ). You'll get by.

If, on the other hand, you want to brush up on your C# skills, or you are proficient in another programming language such as C++ or Java, or even if C# is your first programming language, this book is for you.

Note that for this edition I have been joined by a second author: Donald Xie. Donald and I have worked together on a number of books for the past decade. He is smart, diligent, and careful, and much of the work of this book is his, but *every word* in this book is mine. Donald wrote and rewrote much of the new material, but he did so knowing that I would then rewrite it so that this book speaks with a single voice. I think it is imperative for a tutorial such as this to speak from the mind of a single developer (me) into the mind of another developer (you) with as little distortion as possible.

## What You Need to Use This Book

To make the best use of this book, please obtain the latest release of Visual Studio 2008. Any edition will do, including the Express edition for C#.

For Chapter 16, you will want to ensure that SQL Server or SQL Server Express is installed (it is normally installed automatically with Visual Studio), and you'll want to install the (old) Northwind database that was created for SQL Server 2000, but which works fine with the latest SQL Server editions.

To run the Windows Presentation Foundation (WPF) example in Chapter 18, you'll need to be running Vista, or you'll need to download the .NET 3.5 runtime.

All of this is available on the Microsoft web site, at no cost. Go to *http://www. microsoft.com* and type "C# Express" into the search window. The first or second link should take you to the download page.

The source code for every example in this book is available through the O'Reilly site, *http://www.oreilly.com/catalog/9780596527433*, or through my portal site: *http:// www.jesseliberty.com*. Please scroll to and click on the book site, then click on Books and scroll to this book, and you should find a link to the source code.

In addition, I provide a private, free support forum for all my writing, which you can also access through the portal.

# How This Book Is Organized

Part I focuses on the details of the language, Part II examines how C# supports interacting with data, Part III discusses how to write .NET programs, and Part IV describes how to use C# with the .NET Common Language Runtime (CLR) and Framework Class Library (FCL).

## Part I: The C# Language

Chapter 1, *C# 3.0 and .NET 3.5*
   This chapter introduces you to the C# language and the .NET 3.5 platform.

Chapter 2, *Getting Started: "Hello World"*
   This chapter demonstrates a simple program to provide a context for what follows, and introduces you to the Visual Studio integrated development environment (IDE) and a number of C# language concepts.

Chapter 3, *C# Language Fundamentals*
   This chapter presents the basics of the language, from built-in datatypes to keywords.

Chapter 4, *Classes and Objects*
   Classes define new types and allow programmers to extend the language so that they can better model the problems they're trying to solve. This chapter explains the components that form the heart and soul of C#.

Chapter 5, *Inheritance and Polymorphism*
   Classes can be complex representations and abstractions of things in the real world. This chapter discusses how classes relate and interact.

Chapter 6, *Operator Overloading*
   This chapter teaches you how to add operators to your user-defined types.

Chapter 7, *Structs*
   This chapter introduce *structs*, which are lightweight objects that are more restricted than classes and that make fewer demands on the operating system and on memory.

Chapter 8, *Interfaces*
Interfaces, the subject of Chapter 8, are contracts: they describe how a class will work so that other programmers can interact with your objects in well-defined ways.

Chapter 9, *Arrays, Indexers, and Collections*
Object-oriented programs can create a great many objects. It is often convenient to group these objects and manipulate them together, and C# provides extensive support for collections. This chapter explores the collection classes provided by the FCL, the new Generic collections, and how to create your own collection types using Generics.

Chapter 10, *Strings and Regular Expressions*
This chapter discusses how you can use C# to manipulate text strings and regular expressions. Most Windows and web programs interact with the user, and strings play a vital role in the user interface.

Chapter 11, *Exceptions*
This chapter explains how to deal with exceptions, which provide an object-oriented mechanism for handling life's little emergencies.

Chapter 12, *Delegates and Events*
Both Windows and web applications are event-driven. In C#, events are first-class members of the language. This chapter focuses on how events are managed and how *delegates* (object-oriented, type-safe callback mechanisms) are used to support event handling.

# Part II: C# and Data

Chapter 13, *Introducing LINQ*
This chapter introduces LINQ, a new technology in C# for interacting with data from any data source, including relational databases, XML, files, and other non-traditional data sources.

Chapter 14, *Working with XML*
This chapter is a brief tutorial on XML, the lingua franca of .NET programming.

Chapter 15, *Putting LINQ to Work*
This chapter returns to LINQ and dives deeper into interacting with SQL and XML data in your C# programs.

Chapter 16, *ADO.NET and Relational Databases*
This chapter demonstrates the use of the .NET Framework's ADO.NET object model, designed to provide access to relational data from objects.

# Part III: Programming with C#

On top of the .NET infrastructure sits a high-level abstraction of the operating system, designed to facilitate object-oriented software development. This top tier includes ASP.NET and Windows applications. ASP.NET (with AJAX) is one of the world's most popular ways to create web applications. Although C# is a standalone programming language, it is my premise that the vast majority of the readers of this book are learning C# to build .NET applications.

Chapter 17, *Programming ASP.NET Applications*
This chapter demonstrates how to build an ASP.NET application and use C# to handle events.

Chapter 18, *Programming WPF Applications*
This chapter is a crash course in building a nontrivial WPF application, with a focus on using C# to create event handlers.

Chapter 19, *Programming Windows Forms Applications*
This chapter demonstrates how to build a significant Windows Forms application, again using C# for event handling.

# Part IV: The CLR and the .NET Framework

Part IV of this book discusses the relationship of C# to the CLR and the FCL.

Chapter 20, *Attributes and Reflection*
.NET assemblies include extensive metadata about classes, methods, properties, events, and so forth. This metadata is compiled into the program and retrieved programmatically through reflection. This chapter explores how to add metadata to your code, how to create custom attributes, and how to access this metadata through reflection. It goes on to discuss dynamic invocation, in which methods are invoked with late (runtime) binding.

Chapter 21, *Threads and Synchronization*
The FCL provides extensive support for asynchronous I/O and other classes that make explicit manipulation of threads unnecessary. However, C# does provide extensive support for *threads* and *synchronization*, discussed in this chapter.

Chapter 22, *Streams*
This chapter discusses *streams*, a mechanism not only for interacting with the user, but also for retrieving data across the Internet. This chapter includes full coverage of C# support for *serialization*: the ability to write an object graph to disk and read it back again.

Chapter 23, *Programming .NET and COM*

This chapter explores interoperability: the ability to interact with COM components that are created outside the managed environment of the .NET Framework. It's possible to call components from C# applications into COM, and to call components from COM into C#. Chapter 23 describes how this is done.

The book concludes with a glossary of C# keywords first published in *C# 3.0 in a Nutshell* by Joseph and Ben Albahari (O'Reilly). Whenever you encounter a keyword that you don't recognize in an example, turn first to the glossary and then to the index for further information.

## Who This Book Is For

*Programming C# 3.0*, Fifth Edition, was written for programmers who want to develop applications for the .NET platform. No doubt many of you already have experience in C++, Java, or Visual Basic (VB). Other readers may have experience with other programming languages, and some readers may have no specific programming experience but perhaps have been working with HTML and other web technologies. This book is written for all of you, though if you have no programming experience at all, you may find some of it tough going.

For a deeper exploration of the more advanced C# language elements we introduce in this book, especially LINQ, we recommend *C# 3.0 in a Nutshell*. *C# 3.0 Cookbook* by Jay Hilyard and Steve Teilhet (O'Reilly) contains more than 250 C# 3.0 solutions to common programming tasks you're likely to face on the job after you've mastered this book.

If you prefer a more structured approach to the basics of C# programming, complete with quizzes and exercises to test your knowledge, I suggest you take a look at *Learning C# 2005*, by myself and Brian MacDonald (O'Reilly).

## Conventions Used in This Book

The following font conventions are used in this book:

*Italic* is used for:

- Pathnames, filenames, and program names
- Internet addresses, such as domain names and URLs
- New terms where they are defined

`Constant Width` is used for:

- Command lines and options that should be typed verbatim
- Names and keywords in program examples, including method names, variable names, and class names

*Constant Width Italic* is used for:

- Replaceable items, such as variables or optional elements, within syntax lines or code

**Constant Width Bold** is used for:

- Emphasis within program code

Pay special attention to notes set apart from the text with the following icons:

 This is a tip. It contains useful supplementary information about the topic at hand.

 This is a warning. It helps you solve and avoid annoying problems.

# Support

As part of my responsibilities as an author, I provide ongoing support for everything I write—here's how.

From my portal site:

*http://www.JesseLiberty.com*

Please scroll down to my private web site (you'll see the word Books circled). Clicking on that image will bring you either to *LibertyAssociates.com* or to *jliberty.com* (same site). Click on Books and scroll to this book, where you will find (at a minimum) the source code, the errata (if there are any), and a FAQ (if there is one!).

Back on my portal site, you'll also find a link to my free, private support forum. Please feel free to post questions about this book or any of my writings there. The most effective way to get help is to ask a very precise question, or even to create a small program that illustrates your area of concern or confusion. You may also want to check the various newsgroups and discussion centers on the Internet. Microsoft offers a wide array of newsgroups.

If you have questions about Silverlight, please use my portal to access Silverlight.net or my Silverlight blog; if you have questions about my O'Reilly articles, please use my portal to access my O'Reilly blog, and if you have questions or comments about my politics, please use my portal to access my political blog. Keeping these things separate keeps me sane and keeps my bosses happy.

—Jesse Liberty

# We'd Like to Hear from You

We have tested and verified the information in this book to the best of our ability, but you may find that features have changed (or even that we have made mistakes!). Please let us know about any errors you find, as well as your suggestions for future editions, by writing to:

O'Reilly Media, Inc.
1005 Gravenstein Highway North
Sebastopol, CA 95472
800-998-9938 (in the United States or Canada)
707-829-0515 (international or local)
707-829-0104 (fax)

We have a web page for the book that lists examples and any plans for future editions. You can access this information at:

*http://www.oreilly.com/catalog/9780596527433*

To comment or ask technical questions about this book, send email to:

*bookquestions@oreilly.com*

For more information about our books, conferences, Resource Centers, and the O'Reilly Network, as well as additional technical articles and discussion on C# and the .NET Framework, see the O'Reilly web site:

*http://www.oreilly.com*

and O'Reilly's ONDotnet:

*http://www.ondotnet.com*

# Using Code Examples

This book is here to help you get your job done. In general, you may use the code in this book in your programs and documentation. You do not need to contact us for permission unless you're reproducing a significant portion of the code. For example, writing a program that uses several chunks of code from this book does not require permission. Selling or distributing a CD-ROM of examples from O'Reilly books *does* require permission. Answering a question by citing this book and quoting example code does not require permission. Incorporating a significant amount of example code from this book into your product's documentation *does* require permission.

We appreciate, but do not require, attribution. An attribution usually includes the title, author, publisher, and ISBN. For example: "*Programming C# 3.0*, Fifth Edition, by Jesse Liberty and Donald Xie. Copyright 2008 O'Reilly Media, Inc., 978-0-596-52743-3."

# Safari® Books Online

 When you see a Safari® Books Online icon on the cover of your favorite technology book, that means the book is available online through the O'Reilly Network Safari Bookshelf.

Safari offers a solution that's better than e-books. It's a virtual library that lets you easily search thousands of top tech books, cut and paste code samples, download chapters, and find quick answers when you need the most accurate, current information. Try it for free at *http://safari.oreilly.com*.

# Acknowledgments

## From Jesse Liberty

I want to thank the extraordinary technical editors who worked on this book: Joe Albahari, Glyn Griffiths, Jay Hilyard, Robert McGovern, and Alex Turner. Special thanks go to Ian Griffiths, who provided extensive technical editing and expertise, and is one of the nicest and smartest people on the planet.

This is the fifth edition of *Programming C#*, and too many friends and readers have helped me improve the book to possibly name them all. John Osborn signed me to O'Reilly, for which I will forever be in his debt, and Tim O'Reilly continues to provide an amazing independent publishing house with some of the highest standards in the industry.

And no, the authors don't get to pick the animals on the cover.

A key player in making this book a far better one than the one *I* wrote was Brian MacDonald; he is an amazingly talented editor and a preternaturally patient man. Without his organizational skills, his unrelenting commitment to excellence, and his unfailing good humor, this book literally would not have been possible. I must also heartily thank my coauthor Donald Xie (who helped me discover that although calling Australia by Skype may be free, calling direct for 30 minutes costs $150!), without whom this edition would not have been on the shelves before C# 4.0!

Many have written in with errata large and small for previous editions, and for that I am very grateful. We've worked hard to fix all of the mistakes, no matter how trivial. We've scoured the book to ensure that no new errors were added, and that all the code compiles and runs properly with Visual Studio 2008. With that said, if you do find errors, please check the errata on my web site (*http://www.JesseLiberty.com*), and if your error is new, please send me email at *jliberty@jliberty.com*.

Finally, in many of our examples, we use the name Douglas Adams as a tribute to and with great respect for this wonderful man, who is the author of the incredible five-part *Hitchhiker's Guide to the Galaxy* trilogy (Del Rey), and many other wonderful books.

## From Donald Xie

I really must thank Jesse for teaching me C++ 10 years ago, and for encouraging me to write. It has been a tremendous pleasure working with Jesse. I would also like to thank the dedicated people at O'Reilly: John Osborn, Brian MacDonald, Sumita Mukherji, and the technical reviewers who have worked tirelessly to make this book possible.

# Dedications

## From Jesse Liberty

This book is dedicated to those who come out, loud, and in your face and in the most inappropriate places. We will look back at this time and shake our heads in wonder. In 49 states, same-sex couples are denied the right to marry, though incarcerated felons are not. In 36 states, you can legally be denied housing just for being queer. In more than half the states, there is no law protecting LGBT children from harassment in school, and the suicide rate among queer teens is 400 percent higher than among straight kids. And, we are still kicking gay heroes out of the military despite the fact that the Israelis and our own NSA, CIA, and FBI are all successfully integrated. So, yes, this dedication is to those of us who are out, full-time.

## From Donald Xie

To my wife, Iris, and our two lovely daughters, Belinda and Clare, for your wonderful support and understanding. I love you all.

# PART I

# The C# Language

Chapter 1, *C# 3.0 and .NET 3.5*

Chapter 2, *Getting Started: "Hello World"*

Chapter 3, *C# Language Fundamentals*

Chapter 4, *Classes and Objects*

Chapter 5, *Inheritance and Polymorphism*

Chapter 6, *Operator Overloading*

Chapter 7, *Structs*

Chapter 8, *Interfaces*

Chapter 9, *Arrays, Indexers, and Collections*

Chapter 10, *Strings and Regular Expressions*

Chapter 11, *Exceptions*

Chapter 12, *Delegates and Events*

# CHAPTER 1

# C# 3.0 and .NET 3.5

The goal of C# 3.0 is to provide a simple, safe, modern, object-oriented, Internet-centric, high-performance language for .NET development. C# is now a fully mature language, and it draws on the lessons learned over the past three decades. In much the same way that you can see in young children the features and personalities of their parents and grandparents, you can easily see in C# the influence of Java, C++, Visual Basic (VB), and other languages, but you can also see the lessons learned since C# was first introduced.

The focus of this book is C# 3.0 and its use as a tool for programming on the .NET platform, specifically and especially with Visual Studio .NET 2008.

 Many of the programs in this book are written as console applications (rather than as Windows or web applications) to facilitate concentrating on features of the language instead of being distracted by the details of the user interface.

This chapter introduces both the C# language and the .NET platform, including the .NET 3.5 Framework.

## The Evolution of C#

Each generation of C# has brought significant additions to the language, with a few standout features. Perhaps the most significant feature added to C# 2.0 was Generics (allowing for an enhancement to type safety when dealing with collections). If so, the most significant addition to C# 3.0 must be the addition of the Language-Integrated Query (LINQ) extensions, which add general-purpose data query extensions to C#; though that is by no means the only enhancement to C#.

Other new features include:

- Lambda expressions (anonymous delegates on steroids)
- Extension methods

- Object initializers
- Anonymous types
- Implicitly typed local variables
- Implicitly typed arrays
- Expression trees
- Automatic properties (a small gem)

# The C# Language

The fundamental C# language is disarmingly simple, with fewer than 100 keywords and a dozen built-in datatypes, but it's highly expressive when it comes to implementing modern programming concepts. C# includes all the support for structured, component-based, object-oriented programming that you expect of a modern language built on the shoulders of C++ and Java. Version 3.0 has been extended in three very important ways:

- Full support for LINQ—queries against data are now part of the language
- Full support for the declarative syntax of Windows Presentation Foundation (WPF; for creating rich Windows applications), Work Flow (WF), and Silverlight (for creating cross-platform, cross-browser Rich Internet Applications)
- Many convenient features added to aid programmer productivity and to work and play well in Visual Studio 2008

## A Tiny Bit of History

The C# language was originally developed by a small team led by two distinguished Microsoft engineers, Anders Hejlsberg and Scott Wiltamuth. Hejlsberg is also known for creating Turbo Pascal, a popular language for PC programming, and for leading the team that designed Borland Delphi, one of the first successful integrated development environments (IDEs) for client/server programming.

## C# Features

At the heart of any object-oriented language is its support for defining and working with classes. Classes define new types, allowing you to extend the language to better model the problem you are trying to solve. C# contains keywords for declaring new classes and their methods and properties, and for implementing encapsulation, inheritance, and polymorphism, the three pillars of object-oriented programming.

In C#, everything pertaining to a class declaration is found in the declaration itself. C# class definitions don't require separate header files or Interface Definition

Language (IDL) files. Moreover, C# supports inline documentation that simplifies the creation of online and print reference documentation for an application.

C# also supports *interfaces*, a means of making a contract with a class for services that the interface stipulates. In C#, a class can inherit from only a single parent, but a class can implement multiple interfaces. When it implements an interface, a C# class in effect promises to provide the functionality the interface specifies.

C# also provides support for *structs*, a concept whose meaning has changed significantly from C++. In C#, a struct is a restricted, lightweight type that, when instantiated, makes fewer demands on the operating system and on memory than a conventional class does. A struct can't inherit from a class or be inherited from, but a struct can implement an interface. This book will demonstrate why I don't consider structs terribly important in the world of Generics. The truth is that I haven't put a struct in a program in five years, except to demonstrate how they are used.

C# provides full support of *delegates*: to provide invocation of methods through indirection. In other languages, such as C++, you might find similar functionality (as in pointers to member functions), but delegates are type-safe reference types that encapsulate methods with specific signatures and return types. Delegates have been extended greatly, first in C# 2.0 and again in C# 3.0, first with anonymous delegates and now with Lambda expressions, laying the groundwork for LINQ. We will cover this in depth in Chapters 13 and 15.

C# provides component-oriented features, such as properties, events, and declarative constructs (such as *attributes*). Component-oriented programming is supported by the storage of metadata with the code for the class. The metadata describes the class, including its methods and properties, as well as its security needs and other attributes, such as whether it can be serialized; the code contains the logic necessary to carry out its functions. A compiled class is thus a self-contained unit. Therefore, a hosting environment that knows how to read a class' metadata and code needs no other information to make use of it. Using C# and the Common Language Runtime (CLR), it is possible to add custom metadata to a class by creating custom attributes. Likewise, it is possible to read class metadata using CLR types that support reflection.

When you compile your code, you create an assembly. An *assembly* is a collection of files that appear to the programmer to be a single dynamic link library (DLL) or executable (EXE). In .NET, an assembly is the basic unit of reuse, versioning, security, and deployment. The CLR provides a number of classes for manipulating assemblies.

A final note about C# is that it also provides support for:

- Directly accessing memory using C++-style pointers
- Keywords for bracketing such operations as unsafe
- Warning the CLR garbage collector not to collect objects referenced by pointers until they are released

Here is the word on pointers: you *can* use them, but you don't. They are like hand grenades. You'll know when you need them, and until you do, you should keep the pin in them, put them in your footlocker, and try not to think about them. If you find yourself taking one out, call a friend before you pull the pin; then, run for cover.

## The .NET Platform

When Microsoft announced C# in July 2000, its unveiling was part of a much larger event: the announcement of the .NET platform. The .NET platform was, in my view, an object-oriented operating system in disguise, laid on top of the existing operating system.

.NET 3.5 represents a further maturation of that framework and brings with it new ways to create, well, just about everything, while making nothing you've learned obsolete.

You can still create server-only web applications, but with AJAX, you can add client-side controls (and AJAX provides support for much more, including automatic JSON encoding and decoding). You can still create Windows Forms applications for Windows applications, but you can also create richer Windows applications using WPF, which uses a declarative syntax called XAML (explained in some detail in Chapter 18). That same XAML is used in creating WF applications, which can be used, among other things, as a business layer for your applications.

> For a full exploration of the new .NET Framework, please see *Programming .NET 3.5* by Jesse Liberty and Alex Horowitz (O'Reilly).

In one of the more exciting additions to the Framework, you can now use that same XAML to produce cross-platform (as of this writing, Windows, Mac, and Unix) and cross-browser (Firefox and Safari) Rich Internet Applications using Microsoft's Silverlight.

> For a full exploration of Silverlight, please see my blog at *http://silverlight.net/blogs/JesseLiberty*, and watch for my book, *Programming Silverlight* (O'Reilly), due in 2008.

All of these development technologies can use C# for the programming logic; C# can be the core for all the programming you do across the board in the development of .NET applications from the Web to the desktop, from thin clients to thick, from Rich Internet Applications to web services.

# CHAPTER 2

# Getting Started: "Hello World"

It is a time-honored tradition to start a programming book with a "Hello World" program. In this chapter, you'll create, compile, and run a simple "Hello World" program written in C#. The analysis of this brief program will introduce key features of the C# language.

Example 2-1 illustrates the fundamental elements of a simple C# program.

*Example 2-1. A simple "Hello World" program in C#*

```
class Hello
{
    static void Main(string[] args)
    {
        // Use the system console object
        System.Console.WriteLine("Hello World!");
    }
}
```

Compiling and running this code displays the words "Hello World!" at the console. Before you compile and run it, let's first take a closer look at this simplest of programs.

## Classes, Objects, and Types

The essence of object-oriented programming is the creation of new types. A *type* represents a thing. Sometimes, the thing is abstract, such as a data table or a thread; sometimes it is more tangible, such as a button in a window. A type defines the thing's general properties and behaviors.

If your program uses three instances of a button type in a window—say, an OK, a Cancel, and a Help button—each button will have a size, though the specific size of each button may differ. Similarly, all the buttons will have the same behaviors (draw, click), though how they actually implement these behaviors may vary. Thus, the details might differ among the individual buttons, but they are all of the same type.

As in many object-oriented programming languages, in C#, a type is defined by a *class*, and the individual instances of that class are known as *objects*. Later chapters explain that there are other types in C# besides classes, including enums, structs, and delegates, but for now, the focus is on classes.

The "Hello World" program declares a single type: the class. To define a C# type, you declare it as a class using the class keyword, give it a name—in this case, Hello—and then define its properties and behaviors. The property and behavior definitions of a C# class must be enclosed by opening and closing braces ({}).

## Methods

A class has properties and behaviors. Behaviors are defined with member methods; properties are discussed in Chapter 3.

A *method* (sometimes called a *function*) is a contained set of operations that are owned by your class. The member methods define what your class can do or how it behaves. Typically, methods are given action names, such as WriteLine() or AddNumbers(). In the case shown here, however, the class method has a special name, Main(), which doesn't describe an action, but does designate to the CLR that this is the main, or first method, for your class.

The CLR calls Main() when your program starts. Main() is the entry point for your program, and every C# program must have a Main() method.[*]

Method declarations are a contract between the creator of the method and the consumer (user) of the method. It is likely that the creator and consumer of the method will be the same programmer, but this doesn't have to be so: it is possible that one member of a development team will create the method, and another programmer will use it.

Programs consist of methods calling one another. When a method *calls* another it can pass values to the method it calls. These values are called *arguments* or *parameters*, and the called method can *return* a value to the method that called it; the value returned is called (cleverly) the *return value*.

In fact, to declare a method, you specify a return value type followed by an identifier, followed by a set of parentheses which are either empty or contain the parameters. For example:

```
int myMethod(int size)
```

declares a method named myMethod() that takes one parameter: an integer that will be referred to within the method as size.

---

[*] It's technically possible to have multiple Main() methods in C#; in that case, you use the /main command-line switch to tell C# which class contains the Main() method that should serve as the entry point to the program. This is highly unusual and is put here to silence those who write in to point out edge cases, as well as to convince sensible readers never to read footnotes.

A *parameter* is a value passed into the method. Typically, that value will be manipulated in the method, which may be useful either in that method, or to whomever called the method. It is like handing your shirt, a button, and a needle to a tailor. The needle helps the tailor do the sewing, but the needle is unchanged. If you are lucky, however, the relationship between the button and the shirt is changed when the tailor is done.

Actually, there are two ways to pass a parameter to a method: by value and by reference. If you pass a parameter *by value*, you pass a copy, and when the method is done, the original value (in the calling method) is unchanged. In that case, what you are saying to the tailor is "sew a button like this one to my shirt."

If you pass a parameter *by reference*, you are effectively passing the button itself. When the called method returns, the value you passed in may well be changed (it may be attached to the shirt!).

A method can return a (single) value ("here's your shirt back"). In the case of myMethod, an integer is returned. The return value type tells the consumer of the method what kind of data the method will return when it finishes running.

Some methods don't return a value at all; these are said to return void, which is specified by the void keyword. For example:

```
void myVoidMethod( );
```

declares a method that returns void and takes no parameters. In C#, you must always declare a return type or void.

There are two ways to get around the limitation that you can return only one value. The first is to pass in a number of objects by reference, let the method change them, and hey! Presto! They're changed in the calling method. This is covered in Chapter 3.

The second is to pass in one object, but make that object a collection (clever, eh?). Collections are covered in Chapter 9.

## Comments

A C# program can also contain comments. Take a look at the first line after the opening brace of the main method shown earlier:

```
// Use the system console object
```

The text begins with two forward slash marks (//). These designate a *comment*. A comment is a note to the programmer and doesn't affect how the program runs. C# supports three types of comments.

The first type, just shown, indicates that all text to the right of the comment mark is to be considered a comment, until the end of that line. This is known as a *C++-style comment*.

The second type of comment, known as a *C-style comment*, begins with an open comment mark (/*) and ends with a closed comment mark (*/). This allows comments to span more than one line without having to have // characters at the beginning of each comment line, as shown in Example 2-2.

*Example 2-2. Illustrating multiline comments*

```
class Hello
{
    static void Main( )
    {
        /* Use the system console object
           as explained in the text */
        System.Console.WriteLine("Hello World");
    }
}
```

Using C-style comments also lets you place a comment in the middle of "live" code, as shown in Example 2-3.

*Example 2-3. A comment mid-code*

```
class Hello
{
    static void Main( )
    {
        System.Console.WriteLine  /*("Hello C# 2.0")*/ ("Hello C# 3.0");
    }
}
```

The programmer's goal here is to comment out the old code, but leave it in place for convenience. This will compile, but it is a terrible practice; the code is very difficult to read, and thus very likely to present maintenance problems down the road. The same block of code would be far easier to read written like this:

```
class Hello
{
    static void Main( )
    {
                              /* ("Hello C# 2.0"); */

        System.Console.WriteLine  ("Hello C# 3.0");
    }
}
```

with the commented code above (or below, or to the right of) the live code.

Although you can't nest C++-style (//) comments, it is possible to nest C++-style comments within C-style (/* */) comments. For this reason, it is common to use C++-style comments whenever possible, and to reserve the C-style comments for "commenting out" blocks of code.

The third and final type of comment that C# supports is used to associate external XML-based documentation with your code.

## Console Applications

"Hello World" is an example of a *console* program. A console application typically has no graphical user interface (GUI); there are no listboxes, buttons, windows, and so forth. Text input and output are handled through the standard console (typically a command or DOS window on your PC). Sticking to console applications for now helps simplify the early examples in this book, and keeps the focus on the language itself. In later chapters, we'll turn our attention to Windows and web applications, and at that time we'll focus on the Visual Studio 2008 GUI design tools.

All that the `Main( )` method does in this simple example is write the text "Hello World" to the *standard output* (typically a command prompt window). Standard output is managed by an object named `Console`. This `Console` object has a method called `WriteLine( )` that takes a *string* (a set of characters) and writes it to the standard output. When you run this program, a command or DOS screen will display the words "Hello World."

You invoke a method with the dot operator (`.`). Thus, to call the `Console WriteLine( )` method, you write `Console.WriteLine(...)`, filling in the string to be printed.

## Namespaces

`Console` is only one of a tremendous number of useful types that are part of the .NET Framework Class Library (FCL). Each class has a name, and thus the FCL contains thousands of names, such as `ArrayList`, `Hashtable`, `FileDialog`, `DataException`, `EventArgs`, and so on. There are hundreds, thousands, even tens of thousands of names.

This presents a problem. No developer can possibly memorize all the names that the .NET Framework uses, and sooner or later you are likely to create an object and give it a name that has already been used. What will happen if you purchase a `Hashtable` class from another vendor, only to discover that it conflicts with the `Hashtable` class that .NET provides? Remember, each class in C# must have a unique name, and you typically can't rename classes in a vendor's code!

The solution to this problem is the use of *namespaces*. A namespace restricts a name's scope, making it meaningful only within the defined namespace.

Assume that I tell you that Jim is an engineer. The word "engineer" is used for many things in English, and can cause confusion. Does he design buildings? Write software? Run a train?[*]

---

[*] Apologies to our friends across the pond, where the person who drives a locomotive is called a "train driver" rather than an "engineer."

In spoken English, I might clarify by saying "he's a scientist," or "he's a train engineer." A C# programmer could tell you that Jim is a science.engineer rather than a train.engineer. The namespace (in this case, science or train) restricts the scope of the word that follows. It creates a "space" in which that name is meaningful.

Further, it might happen that Jim is not just any kind of science.engineer. Perhaps Jim graduated from MIT with a degree in software engineering, not civil engineering (are *civil* engineers especially polite?). Thus, the object that is Jim might be defined more specifically as a science.software.engineer. This classification implies that the namespace software is meaningful within the namespace science, and that engineer in this context is meaningful within the namespace software. If later you learn that Charlotte is a transportation.train.engineer, you will not be confused as to what kind of engineer she is. The two uses of engineer can coexist, each within its own namespace.

Similarly, if it turns out that .NET has a Hashtable class within its System.Collections namespace, and that we have also created a Hashtable class within a ProgCSharp.DataStructures namespace, there is no conflict because each exists in its own namespace.

In Example 2-1, the Console class's name is identified as being in the System namespace by using the code:

```
System.Console.WriteLine( );
```

## The Dot Operator (.)

In Example 2-1 the dot operator (.) is used to access a method (and data) in a class (in this case, the method WriteLine( )), and to restrict the class name to a specific namespace (in this case, to locate Console within the System namespace). This works well because in both cases we are "drilling down" to find the exact thing we want. The top level is the System namespace (which contains all the System objects that the FCL provides); the Console type exists within that namespace, and the WriteLine( ) method is a member function of the Console type.

In many cases, namespaces are hierarchical. For example, the System namespace contains a number of subnamespaces such as Data, Configuration, Collections, and so forth, and the Collections namespace itself is divided into multiple subnamespaces.

Namespaces can help you organize and compartmentalize your types. When you write a complex C# program, you might want to create your own namespace hierarchy, and there is no limit to how deep this hierarchy can be. The goal of namespaces is to help you divide and conquer the complexity of your object hierarchy.

# The using Directive

Rather than writing the word System before Console, you could specify that you will be using types from the System namespace by writing the directive:

```
using System;
```

at the top of the listing, as shown in Example 2-4.

*Example 2-4. The using directive*

```
using System;
class Hello
{
    static void Main( )
    {
        // Console from the System namespace
        Console.WriteLine("Hello World");
    }
}
```

Notice that the using System directive is placed before the Hello class definition. Visual Studio 2008 defaults to including four using statements in every console application (System, System.Collections.Generic, System.Linq, and System.Text).

Although you can designate that you are using the System namespace, you can't designate that you are using the System.Console object, as you can with some languages. Example 2-5 won't compile.

*Example 2-5. Code that doesn't compile (not legal C#)*

```
using System.Console;
class Hello
{
    static void Main( )
    {
    WriteLine("Hello World");
    }
}
```

This generates the compile error:

```
A using namespace directive can only be applied
to namespaces; 'System.Console' is a type not a namespace
```

 If you are using Visual Studio 2008, you will know that you've made a mistake because when you type using System followed by the dot, Visual Studio 2008 will provide a list of valid namespaces, and Console won't be among them.

The using directive can save a great deal of typing, but it can undermine the advantages of namespaces by polluting the scope with many undifferentiated names. A common solution is to use the using directive with the built-in namespaces and with your own corporate namespaces, but perhaps not with third-party components.

## Case Sensitivity

C# is case-sensitive, which means that writeLine is not the same as WriteLine, which in turn is not the same as WRITELINE. Unfortunately, unlike in VB, the C# development environment will not fix your case mistakes; if you write the same word twice with different cases, you might introduce a tricky-to-find bug into your program.

> A handy trick is to hover over a name that is correct in all but case and then to press Ctrl-Space. The AutoComplete feature of IntelliSense will fix the case for you.

To prevent such a time-wasting and energy-depleting mistake, you should develop conventions for naming your variables, functions, constants, and so on. The convention in this book is to name variables with camel notation (e.g., someVariableName), and to name classes, namespaces, functions, constants, and properties with Pascal notation (e.g., SomeFunction).

> The only difference between camel and Pascal notation is that in Pascal notation, names begin with an uppercase letter. Microsoft has developed code style guidelines that make a very good starting point (and often are all you need). You can download them from *http://msdn2.microsoft.com/en-us/library/ms229002(VS.90).aspx*.

## The static Keyword

The Main( ) method shown in Example 2-1 has one more designation. Just before the return type declaration void (which, you will remember, indicates that the method doesn't return a value) you'll find the keyword static:

```
static void Main( )
```

The static keyword indicates that you can invoke Main( ) without first creating an object of type Hello. This somewhat complex issue will be considered in much greater detail in subsequent chapters. One of the problems with learning a new computer language is you must use some of the advanced features before you fully understand them. For now, you can treat the declaration of the Main( ) method as tantamount to magic.

# Developing "Hello World"

There are at least two ways to enter, compile, and run the programs in this book: use the Visual Studio 2008 IDE, or use a text editor and a command-line compiler (along with some additional command-line tools to be introduced later).

Although you *can* develop software outside Visual Studio 2008, the IDE provides enormous advantages. These include indentation support, IntelliSense word completion, color coding, and integration with the help files. Most important, the IDE includes a powerful debugger and a wealth of other tools.

This book tacitly assumes that you'll be using Visual Studio 2008. However, the tutorials focus more on the language and the platform than on the tools. You can copy all the examples into a text editor such as Windows Notepad or Emacs, save them as text files with the extension *.cs*, and compile them with the C# command-line compiler that is distributed with the .NET Framework SDK (or a .NET-compatible development tool chain such as Mono or Microsoft's Shared Source CLI). Note that some examples in later chapters use Visual Studio 2008 tools for creating Windows Forms and Web Forms, but even these you can write by hand in Notepad if you are determined to do things the hard way.

## Editing "Hello World"

To create the "Hello World" program in the IDE, select Visual Studio 2008 from your Start menu or a desktop icon, and then choose File → New → Project from the menu toolbar. This will invoke the New Project window. (If you are using Visual Studio for the first time, the New Project window might appear without further prompting.) Figure 2-1 shows the New Project window.

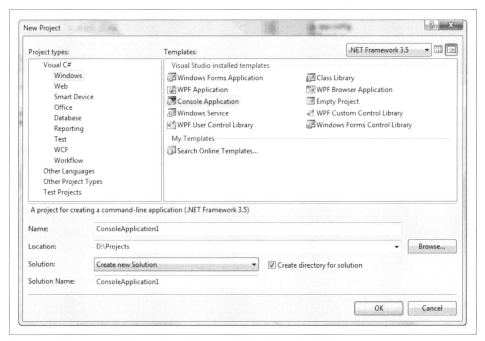

*Figure 2-1. Creating a C# console application in Visual Studio 2008*

To open your application, select Visual C# in the "Project types" window, and choose Console Application in the Templates window (if you use the Express Edition of Visual C#, you don't need to perform that first step; go directly to the console application).

You can now enter a name for the project (e.g., HelloWorld), and select a directory in which to store your files. You may also enter the name of the solution containing the project, and select whether you would like Visual Studio 2008 to create a directory for the new solution for you. Click OK, and a new window will appear in which you can enter the code in Example 2-1, as shown in Figure 2-2.

```
Hello.Program                ▼   Main(string[] args)          ▼

using System;
using System.Collections.Generic;
using System.Linq;
using System.Text;

namespace Hello
{
    class Program
    {
        static void Main(string[] args)
        {
        }
    }
}
```

*Figure 2-2. The editor, opened to your new project*

Notice that Visual Studio 2008 creates a namespace based on the project name you've provided (Hello), and adds using directives for System, System.Collections. Generic, System.Linq, and System.Text because nearly every program you write will need types from those namespaces.

Visual Studio 2008 creates a class named Program, which you are free to rename. When you rename the class, it's a good idea to rename the file as well (*Class1.cs*). If you rename the file, Visual Studio will automatically rename the class for you. To reproduce Example 2-1, for instance, rename the *Program.cs* file (listed in the Solution Explorer window) to *hello.cs* and change the name of Program to Hello (if you do this in the reverse order, Visual Studio will rename the class to hello).

To rename, click on the filename and wait a moment, or right-click and choose Rename.

Finally, Visual Studio 2008 creates a program skeleton to get you started. To reproduce Example 2-1, remove the arguments (`string[] args`) from the `Main( )` method. Then, copy the following two lines into the body of `Main( )`:

```
// Use the system console object
System.Console.WriteLine("Hello World");
```

If you aren't using Visual Studio 2008, open Notepad, type in the code from Example 2-1, and save the file as a text file named *hello.cs*.

## Compiling and Running "Hello World"

There are many ways to compile and run the "Hello World" program from within Visual Studio. Typically, you can accomplish every task by choosing commands from the Visual Studio menu toolbar, by using buttons, and, in many cases, by using key-combination shortcuts.

> You can set keyboard shortcuts by going to Tools → Options → Keyboard. This book assumes you have chosen the default settings.

For example, to compile the "Hello World" program, press Ctrl-Shift-B or choose Build → Build Solution. As an alternative, you can click the Build button on the Build toolbar (you may need to right-click the toolbar to show the Build toolbar). The Build toolbar is shown in Figure 2-3; the Build button is leftmost and highlighted.

*Figure 2-3. Build toolbar*

To run the "Hello World" program without the debugger, you can press Ctrl-F5 on your keyboard, choose Debug → Start Without Debugging from the IDE menu toolbar, or press the Start Without Debugging button on the IDE Build toolbar, as shown in Figure 2-4 (you may need to customize your toolbar to make this button available). You can run the program without first explicitly building it; depending on how your options are set (Tools → Options), the IDE will save the file, build it, and run it, possibly asking you for permission at each step.

*Figure 2-4. Start Without Debugging button*

We strongly recommend that you spend some time exploring the Visual Studio 2008 development environment. This is your principal tool as a .NET developer, and you want to learn to use it well. Time invested up front in getting comfortable with Visual Studio will pay for itself many times over in the coming months. Go ahead, put the book down, and look at it. I'll wait for you.

# Using the Visual Studio 2008 Debugger

Arguably, the single most important tool in any development environment is the debugger. The Visual Studio debugger is very powerful, and it will be well worth whatever time you put in to learning how to use it well. With that said, the fundamentals of debugging are very simple. The three key skills are:

- How to set a breakpoint and how to run to that breakpoint
- How to step into and over method calls
- How to examine and modify the value of variables, member data, and so forth

This chapter doesn't reiterate the entire debugger documentation, but these skills are so fundamental that it does provide a crash (pardon the expression) course.

The debugger can accomplish the same thing in many ways, typically via menu choices, buttons, and so forth.

For example, one wonderful debugging tool is a *breakpoint*: an instruction to the debugger to run your application to a particular line in the code and then stop. The simplest way to set a breakpoint is to click in the left margin. The IDE marks your breakpoint with a red dot, as shown in Figure 2-5.

```
for (int i = 0; i < 3; i++)
{
    winArray[i].DrawWindow( );
}
```

*Figure 2-5. A breakpoint*

Discussing the debugger requires code examples. The code shown here is from Chapter 5, and you aren't expected to understand how it works yet (though if you program in C++ or Java, you'll probably get the gist of it).

To run the debugger, you can choose Debug → Start, or just press F5. The program then compiles and runs to the breakpoint, at which time it stops, and a yellow arrow indicates the next statement for execution, as in Figure 2-6.

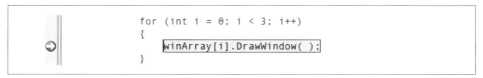

```
for (int i = 0; i < 3; i++)
{
    winArray[i].DrawWindow( );
}
```

*Figure 2-6. The breakpoint hit*

After you've hit your breakpoint, it is easy to examine the values of various objects. For example, you can find the value of the array just by putting the cursor over it and waiting a moment, as shown in Figure 2-7.

```
for (int i = 0; i < 3; i++)
{
    winArray[i].DrawWindow( );
}
```

| ⊟ ● winArray | {abstract_method_and_class.Control[3]} |
| ⊞ ● [0] | {abstract_method_and_class.ListBox} |
| ⊞ ● [1] | {abstract_method_and_class.ListBox} |
| ⊞ ● [2] | {abstract_method_and_class.Button} |

*Figure 2-7. Showing a value*

The debugger IDE also provides a number of useful windows, such as a Locals window that displays the values of all the local variables (see Figure 2-8).

**Locals**

| Name | Value | Type |
|------|-------|------|
| ● args | {string[0]} | string[] |
| ● i | 0 | int |
| ⊞ ● winArray | {abstract_method_and_class.Control[3]} | abstract_method_and_class.Control[] |

Locals | Watch 1

*Figure 2-8. Locals window*

Intrinsic types such as integers simply show their value, but objects show their type and have a plus (+) sign. You can expand these objects to see their internal data, as shown in Figure 2-9. You'll learn more about objects and their internal data in upcoming chapters.

You can step into the next method by pressing F11. Doing so steps into the DrawWindow( ) method of the Window class, as shown in Figure 2-10.

You can see that the next execution statement is now WriteLine( ) in DrawWindow( ). The Autos window has updated to show the current state of the objects.

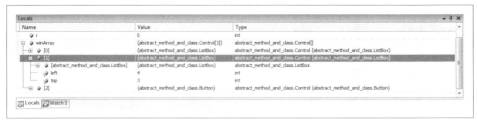

Figure 2-9. Locals window object expanded

Figure 2-10. Stepping into a method

There is much more to learn about the debugger, but this brief introduction should get you started. You can answer many programming questions by writing short demonstration programs and examining them in the debugger. A good debugger is, in some ways, the single most powerful teaching tool for a programming language.

# CHAPTER 3

# C# Language Fundamentals

Chapter 2 demonstrated a very simple C# program. Nonetheless, that little program was complex enough that we had to skip some of the pertinent details. This chapter illuminates these details by delving more deeply into the syntax and structure of the C# language itself.

In this chapter, I discuss the type system in C#, covering built-in types such as `int` and `bool`, and *user-defined types* (types you create) such as classes, structs, and interfaces. I also cover programming fundamentals, such as how to create and use variables and constants. I'll then introduce enumerations, strings, identifiers, expressions, and statements.

In the second part of the chapter, I'll explain and demonstrate the use of flow control statements, using the `if`, `switch`, `while`, `do...while`, `for`, and `foreach` statements. You'll also learn about operators, including the assignment, logical, relational, and mathematical operators. I'll finish up with a short tutorial on the C# preprocessor.

Although C# is principally concerned with the creation and manipulation of objects, it is best to start with the fundamental building blocks: the elements from which objects are created. These include the built-in types that are an intrinsic part of the C# language as well as the syntactic elements of C#.

## Types

Every variable and object in C# has a "type." There are built-in types (e.g., `int`), and you may create your own types (e.g., `Employee`).

When you create an object, you declare its type, and in a statically typed language such as C#, the compiler will "enforce" that typing, giving you an error at compile time (rather than runtime) if you violate the typing by (for example) trying to assign an employee object to an integer variable. This is a good thing; it cuts down on bugs and makes for more reliable code.

In the vast majority of cases, C# is also "manifestly" typed—which means that you explicitly declare the type of the object. There is one exception, which is the use of the keyword var (covered in Chapter 13). In this case, C# is able to infer the type of the object and thus, rather than being manifest, is actually implicit.

Finally, C# is strongly typed, which means that any operation you attempt on any object or variable must be appropriate to that type, or it will cause a compiler error. Once again, this is a good thing; it helps identify bugs reliably at compile time.

In summary, we can say that C# is statically, manifestly, and strongly typed when using most types, except when using the keyword var, at which time it is statically, *implicitly*, and strongly typed!

Key to all of this is that it is always statically and strongly typed, which means that you must declare your types, and the compiler will then enforce that you use your objects according to their declared types, and this is a good thing.

## The Built-In Types

The C# language itself offers the usual cornucopia of intrinsic (built-in) types you expect in a modern language, each of which maps to an underlying type supported by the .NET CTS. Mapping the C# primitive types to the underlying .NET types ensures that objects you create in C# can be used interchangeably with objects created in any other language compliant with the .NET CTS, such as Visual Basic.

Each built-in type has a specific and unchanging size. Table 3-1 lists many of the built-in types offered by C#.

*Table 3-1. C# built-in value types*

| Type | Size (in bytes) | .NET type | Description |
|------|-----------------|-----------|-------------|
| Byte | 1 | Byte | Unsigned (values 0 to 255) |
| Char | 2 | Char | Unicode characters |
| Bool | 1 | Boolean | True or false |
| Sbyte | 1 | SByte | Signed values (−128 to 127) |
| Short | 2 | Int16 | Signed short values (−32,768 to 32,767) |
| Ushort | 2 | UInt16 | Unsigned short values (0 to 65,535) |
| Int | 4 | Int32 | Signed integer values between −2,147,483,648 and 2,147,483,647 |
| Uint | 4 | UInt32 | Unsigned integer values between 0 and 4,294,967,295 |
| Float | 4 | Single | Floating-point number. Holds values from approximately +/−1.5 x 10$^{-45}$ to approximately +/−3.4 x 10$^{38}$ with seven significant figures |
| Double | 8 | Double | Double-precision floating-point. Holds values from approximately +/−5.0 x 10$^{-324}$ to approximately +/−1.8 x 10$^{308}$ with 15 to 16 significant figures |
| decimal | 16 | Decimal | Fixed-precision value up to 28 digits and the position of the decimal point; this is typically used in financial calculations; requires the suffix "m" or "M" |

*Table 3-1. C# built-in value types (continued)*

| Type | Size (in bytes) | .NET type | Description |
|------|-----------------|-----------|-------------|
| Long | 8 | Int64 | Signed integers from −9,223,372,036,854,775,808 to 9,223,372,036,854,775,807 |
| Ulong | 8 | UInt64 | Unsigned integers ranging from 0 to 0xffffffffffffffff |

In addition to these primitive types, C# has two other value types: enum (which I'll explain later in this chapter) and struct (discussed in Chapter 4).

# The Stack and the Heap

A *stack* is a data structure used to store items on a last-in first-out basis (like a stack of dishes at the buffet line in a restaurant). The *stack* refers to an area of memory managed by the processor, on which the local variables are stored.

The *heap* is an initially undifferentiated area of memory that can be referred to by items placed on the stack.

Variables (discussed shortly), whose type is one of the intrinsic types, are usually placed on the stack. Other variables, of types supplied by the Framework or of types you define, are called *objects*, and are usually created on the heap and referred to by a variable on the stack. For this reason, they are called *reference types*.

When a function is called, it is allocated a region of memory on the stack, known as a *stack frame*. This is deallocated when the function returns, and objects that were in the stack frame are said to "go out of scope" and are destroyed.

Objects on the heap are automatically destroyed (known as garbage collection) sometime after the final reference to them is destroyed. Thus, if you create an instance of a user-defined reference type, the variable that refers to it will be destroyed when the stack frame goes away, and if that is the only reference to the object that was created on the heap, it will be cleaned up by the garbage collector.

## Choosing a built-in type

Typically, you decide which size integer to use (short, int, or long) based on the magnitude of the value you want to store. For example, a ushort can only hold values from 0 to 65,535, whereas a uint can hold values from 0 to 4,294,967,295.

With that said, memory is fairly cheap, and programmer time is increasingly expensive; so, most of the time you'll simply declare your variables to be of type int, unless there is a good reason to do otherwise.

When you need to create numbers that represent noninteger values (e.g., 5.7), you'll choose among float, double, and decimal, depending on the size and degree of precision you need. For most small fractional numbers, float is fine.

The compiler assumes that any number with a decimal point is a double unless you tell it otherwise. You must therefore use the f suffix for a float, and the m for a decimal, but no other suffixes are required for other types.

To create a float, follow the number with the letter f:

```
float someFloat = 57f;
;
```

The char type represents a Unicode character. char literals can be simple, Unicode, or escape characters enclosed by single quote marks. For example, A is a simple character, whereas \u0041 is a Unicode character. Escape characters are special two-character tokens that have special meaning to the compiler in which the first character is a backslash. For example, \t is a horizontal tab. Table 3-2 shows the common escape characters.

*Table 3-2. Common escape characters*

| Char | Meaning |
| --- | --- |
| \' | Single quote |
| \" | Double quote |
| \\ | Backslash |
| \0 | Null |
| \a | Alert |
| \b | Backspace |
| \f | Form feed |
| \n | Newline |
| \r | Carriage return |
| \t | Horizontal tab |
| \v | Vertical tab |

## Converting built-in types

Objects of one type can be converted into objects of another type either implicitly or explicitly. Implicit conversions happen automatically; the compiler takes care of it for you.

Implicit conversions happen when you assign a value to a variable of a different type, and the conversion is guaranteed not to lose information. For example, you can implicitly cast from a short (two bytes) to an int (four bytes) by assigning the value in the former to a variable of the latter type. No matter what value is in the short, it is not lost when converted to an int:

```
Create a variable of type short named x and initialize with the value 5
short x = 5;
```

```
// create an integer variable y and initialize with the value held in x
int y = x; // implicit conversion
```

If you convert the other way, however, you certainly *can* lose information. If the value in the int is greater than 32,767, it will be truncated in the conversion. The compiler will not perform an implicit conversion from int to short:

```
short x;
int y = 500;
x = y; // won't compile
```

Explicit conversions happen when you "cast" a value to a different type. The semantics of an explicit conversion are "Hey! Compiler! I know what I'm doing." This is sometimes called "hitting it with the big hammer," and can be very useful or very painful, depending on whether your thumb is in the way of the nail. You must explicitly convert using the cast operator (you place the type you want to convert to in parentheses before the variable you're converting):

```
short x;
int y = 500;
x = (short) y; // OK
```

All the intrinsic types define their own conversion rules.

At times, it is convenient to define conversion rules for your user-defined types, as I discuss in Chapter 6.

# Variables and Constants

A *variable* is a storage location within a method. In the preceding examples, both x and y are variables. You can assign values to your variables, and you can change those values programmatically.

You create a variable by declaring its type and then giving it a name. You can initialize the variable with a value when you declare it, and you can assign a new value to that variable at any time, changing the value held in the variable. Example 3-1 illustrates this.

*Example 3-1. Initializing and assigning a value to a variable*

```
using System;
using System.Collections.Generic;
using System.Text;


namespace InitializingVariables
{
 class Program
 {
    static void Main(string[] args)
```

*Example 3-1. Initializing and assigning a value to a variable (continued)*

```
    {
    int myInt = 7;
    System.Console.WriteLine("Initialized, myInt: {0}",
      myInt);

    myInt = 5;
    System.Console.WriteLine("After assignment, myInt: {0}",
      myInt);

    }
  }
}
```

```
Output:
Initialized, myInt: 7
After assignment, myInt: 5
```

 Visual Studio creates a namespace and using directive for every program. To save space, I've omitted these from most of the code examples after this one.

---

# WriteLine( )

The .NET Framework provides a useful method for writing output to the screen. The details of this method, `System.Console.WriteLine( )`, will become clearer as we progress through the book, but the fundamentals are straightforward. Call the method as shown in Example 3-1, passing in a string that you want printed to the console (the command prompt or shell window) and, optionally, parameters that will be substituted. In the following example:

```
    System.Console.WriteLine("After assignment, myInt: {0}", myInt);
```

the string `"After assignment, myInt:"` is printed as is, followed by the value in the variable `myInt`. The location of the substitution placeholder {0} specifies where the value of the first output variable, `myInt`, is displayed—in this case, at the end of the string. You'll see a great deal more about `WriteLine( )` in coming chapters.

---

Here, you initialize the variable `myInt` to the value 7, display that value, reassign the variable with the value 5, and display it again.

 *VB 6 programmers take note*: in C#, the datatype comes before the variable name.

---

# Definite Assignment

C# requires definite assignment, and one of the consequences of this requirement is that variables must be initialized or assigned to before they are used. To test this rule, change the line that initializes `myInt` in Example 3-1 to:

```
int myInt;
```

and save the revised program shown in Example 3-2.

*Example 3-2. Using an uninitialized variable*

```
using System;

class UninitializedVariable
{
  static void Main(string[] args)
  {
    int myInt;
    System.Console.WriteLine("Uninitialized, myInt: {0}", myInt);
    myInt = 5;
    System.Console.WriteLine("Assigned, myInt: {0}", myInt);

  }
}
```

When you try to compile this listing, the C# compiler will display an error message, as shown in Figure 3-1.

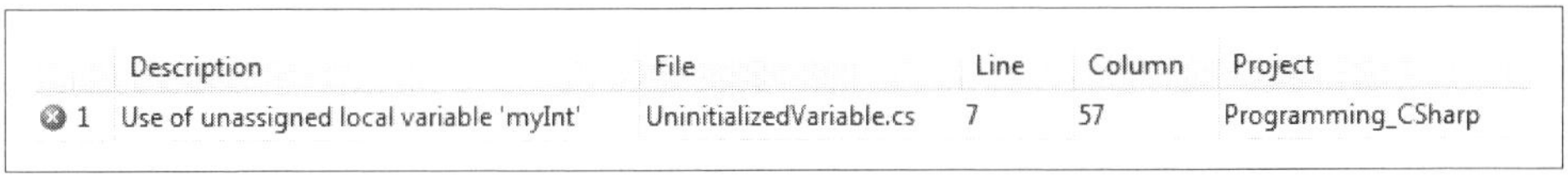

| | Description | File | Line | Column | Project |
|---|---|---|---|---|---|
| ⊗ 1 | Use of unassigned local variable 'myInt' | UninitializedVariable.cs | 7 | 57 | Programming_CSharp |

*Figure 3-1. Error message resulting from using an unassigned variable*

Double-clicking the error message will bring you to the problem in the code.

It isn't legal to use an uninitialized variable in C#. Does this mean you must initialize every variable in a program? In fact, no: you don't actually need to initialize a variable, but you must assign a value to it before you attempt to use it. Example 3-3 illustrates a correct program.

*Example 3-3. Assigning without initializing*

```
using System;

class AssigningWithoutInitializing
{
  static void Main(string[] args)
  {
    int myInt;
    myInt = 7;
```

*Example 3-3. Assigning without initializing (continued)*

```
        System.Console.WriteLine("Assigned, myInt: {0}", myInt);
        myInt = 5;
        System.Console.WriteLine("Reassigned, myInt: {0}", myInt);

    }
}
```

# Constants

A *constant* is an object whose value can't be changed. Variables are a powerful tool, but there are times when you want to use a defined value, one whose value you want to ensure remains constant. For example, you might need to work with the Fahrenheit freezing and boiling points of water in a program simulating a chemistry experiment. Your program will be clearer if you name the variables that store the values FreezingPoint and BoilingPoint, but you don't want to permit their values to be reassigned. How do you prevent reassignment? The answer is to use a constant.

Constants come in three flavors: *literals*, *symbolic constants*, and *enumerations*. In this assignment:

```
    x = 32;
```

the value 32 is a literal constant. The value of 32 is always 32. You can't assign a new value to 32; you can't make 32 represent the value 99 no matter how you might try.

Symbolic constants assign a name to a constant value. You declare a symbolic constant using the const keyword and the following syntax:

```
    const type identifier = value;
```

You must initialize a constant when you declare it, and once initialized, it can't be altered. For example:

```
    const int FreezingPoint = 32;
```

In this declaration, 32 is a literal constant, and FreezingPoint is a symbolic constant of type int. Example 3-4 illustrates the use of symbolic constants.

*Example 3-4. Using symbolic constants*

```
using System;

namespace SymbolicConstants
{
  class SymbolicConstants
  {
    static void Main(string[] args)
    {
      const int FreezingPoint = 32; // degrees Fahrenheit
      const int BoilingPoint = 212;
```

*Example 3-4. Using symbolic constants (continued)*

```
System.Console.WriteLine("Freezing point of water: {0}",
   FreezingPoint);
System.Console.WriteLine("Boiling point of water: {0}",
   BoilingPoint);

//BoilingPoint = 212;

      }
   }
}
```

Example 3-4 creates two symbolic integer constants: FreezingPoint and BoilingPoint. As a matter of style, constant names are typically written in Pascal notation or all caps, but the language certainly does not require this (see the sidebar, "Camel and Pascal Notation").

---

## Camel and Pascal Notation

Camel notation is so named because each word in the identifier is put together without spaces, but with the first letter of each word capitalized, looking like the humps of a camel. In camel notation, the first letter of the identifier is lowercase. Here is an example:

```
myCamelNotationIdentifier
```

Pascal notation is exactly like camel notation, except that the initial letter is uppercase. Here is an example:

```
MyPascalNotationIdentifier
```

---

These constants serve the same purpose as always using the *literal* values 32 and 212 for the freezing and boiling points of water in expressions that require them, but because these constants have names, they convey far more meaning. Also, if you decide to switch this program to Celsius, you can reinitialize these constants at compile time, to 0 and 100, respectively; all the rest of the code ought to continue to work.

To prove to yourself that the constant can't be reassigned, try to uncomment the last line of the program (shown in bold). When you recompile, you should receive the error shown in Figure 3-2.

| | Description | File | Line | Column | Project |
|---|---|---|---|---|---|
| ⊗ 1 | The left-hand side of an assignment must be a variable, property or indexer | SymbolicConstants.cs | 15 | 4 | Programming_CSharp |

*Figure 3-2. Warning that occurs when you try to reassign a constant*

# Enumerations

*Enumerations* can provide a powerful alternative to constants. An enumeration is a distinct value type, consisting of a set of named constants (called the *enumerator list*).

In Example 3-4, you created two related constants:

```
const int FreezingPoint = 32;
const int BoilingPoint = 212;
```

You might wish to add a number of other useful constants to this list, such as:

```
const int LightJacketWeather = 60;
const int SwimmingWeather = 72;
const int WickedCold = 0;
```

This process is somewhat cumbersome, and there is no logical connection between these various constants. C# provides the *enumeration* to solve these problems:

```
enum Temperatures
{
  WickedCold = 0,
  FreezingPoint = 32,
  LightJacketWeather = 60,
  SwimmingWeather = 72,
  BoilingPoint = 212,
}
```

Every enumeration has an underlying type, which can be any integral type (integer, short, long, etc.) except for char. The technical definition of an enumeration is:

```
[attributes] [modifiers] enum identifier
 [:base-type] {enumerator-list};
```

We consider the optional attributes and modifiers later in this book. For now, just focus on the rest of this declaration. An enumeration begins with the keyword enum, which is generally followed by an identifier, such as:

```
enum Temperatures
```

The base type is the underlying type for the enumeration. If you leave out this optional value (and often you will), it defaults to int, but you are free to use any of the integral types (e.g., ushort, long) except for char. For example, the following fragment declares an enumeration of unsigned integers (uint):

```
enum ServingSizes :uint
{
  Small = 1,
  Regular = 2,
  Large = 3
}
```

Notice that an enum declaration ends with the enumerator list. The enumerator list contains the constant assignments for the enumeration, each separated by a comma.

Example 3-5 rewrites Example 3-4 to use an enumeration.

*Example 3-5. Using enumerations to simplify your code*

```
using System;

namespace EnumeratedConstants
{
  class EnumeratedConstants
  {

    enum Temperatures
    {
      WickedCold = 0,
      FreezingPoint = 32,
      LightJacketWeather = 60,
      SwimmingWeather = 72,
      BoilingPoint = 212,
    }

    static void Main(string[] args)
    {
      System.Console.WriteLine("Freezing point of water: {0}",
        (int)Temperatures.FreezingPoint);
      System.Console.WriteLine("Boiling point of water: {0}",
        (int)Temperatures.BoilingPoint);
    }
  }
}
```

As you can see, an enum must be qualified by its identifier (e.g., Temperatures.
WickedCold). By default, an enumeration value is displayed using its symbolic name
(such as BoilingPoint or FreezingPoint). When you want to display the value of an
enumerated constant, you must cast the constant to its underlying type (int). The
integer value is passed to WriteLine, and that value is displayed.

Each constant in an enumeration corresponds to a numerical value—in this case, an
integer. If you don't specifically set it otherwise, the enumeration begins at 0, and
each subsequent value counts up from the previous one.

If you create the following enumeration:

```
enum SomeValues
{
  First,
  Second,
  Third = 20,
  Fourth
}
```

the value of First will be 0, Second will be 1, Third will be 20, and Fourth will be 21.

An explicit conversion is required to convert between an enum type and an integral
type.

## Strings

It is nearly impossible to write a C# program without creating strings. A string object holds a series of characters.

You declare a string variable using the `string` keyword much as you would create an instance of any object:

```
string myString;
```

You create a string literal by placing double quotes around a string of letters:

```
"Hello World"
```

It is common to initialize a string variable with a string literal:

```
string myString = "Hello World";
```

We cover strings in much greater detail in Chapter 10.

## Identifiers

An identifier is just the name the programmer chooses for the types, methods, variables, constants, objects, and so on in the program. An identifier must begin with a letter or an underscore, and remember that identifiers are case-sensitive, so C# treats `someName` and `SomeName` as two different identifiers.

It is normally not good programming practice to create two variables or classes with names that are differentiated only by capitalization. Although the compiler will not be confused, the programmer will be, and the cost of attempting to maintain such a program can be very high.

The exception to this is the common practice of having a member variable (explained in Chapter 4) and a property with the same name, differentiated only by using camel notation for the former, and Pascal notation for the latter.

The Microsoft naming conventions suggest using camel notation (initial lowercase, such as `someVariable`) for variable names, and Pascal notation (initial uppercase, such as `SomeMethodOrProperty`) for method names and most other identifiers.

Microsoft recommends against Hungarian notation (e.g., `iSomeInteger`) and underscores (e.g., `Some_Value`). Microsoft's Charles Simonyi (who was born September 10, 1948, in Budapest) invented Hungarian notation, and it was very useful when languages were limited to a small number of types.

Along with nearly 2 billion other interesting articles, Wikipedia (*http://en.wikipedia.org*) provides extensive articles on Hungarian notation, on Charles Simonyi, and on Richard Dawkins, who holds the Charles Simonyi Chair for Public Understanding of Science at Oxford University.

# Whitespace

In the C# language, spaces, tabs, and newlines are considered to be "whitespace" (so named because you see only the white of the underlying "page"). *Extra* whitespace is generally ignored in C# statements. You can write:

```
myVariable = 5;
```

or:

```
myVariable        =                   5;
```

and the compiler will treat the two statements as identical.

The key word in the preceding rule is "extra" whitespace. Some whitespace is not extra; it is required to allow the compiler to differentiate one word from another. Thus, if you were to enter:

```
int myVariable = 5; // no problem
```

or:

```
int myVariable=5; // no problem
```

both would compile, because the spaces between the identifier `myVariable`, the assignment operator (`=`), and the literal value 5 are "extra." If, however, you were to enter:

```
intMyVariable=5;   // error
```

you would receive a compiler error, because the space between the keyword `int` and the identifier `myVariable` is not extra, it is required.

Another exception to the "whitespace is ignored" rule is within strings. If you write:

```
Console.WriteLine("Hello World");
```

each space between "Hello" and "World" is treated as another character in the string.

Most of the time, the use of whitespace is intuitive. The key is to use whitespace to make the program more readable to the programmer; the compiler is typically indifferent.

 *VB programmers take note*: in C# the end-of-line has no special significance; you end statements with semicolons, not newline characters. There is no line-continuation character because none is needed.

# Statements

In C#, a complete program instruction is called a *statement*. Programs consist of sequences of C# statements. Virtually every statement ends with a semicolon (;). For example:

```
int x; // a statement
x = 23; // another statement
int y = x; // yet another statement
```

C# statements are evaluated in order. The compiler starts at the beginning of a statement list and makes its way to the end. This would be entirely straightforward, and terribly limiting, were it not for branching. There are two types of branches in a C# program: *unconditional branches* and *conditional branches*.

Program flow is also affected by looping and iteration statements, which are signaled by the keywords for, while, do, in, and foreach. I discuss iteration later in this chapter. For now, let's consider some of the more basic methods of conditional and unconditional branching.

## Unconditional Branching Statements

You can create an unconditional branch in one of two ways. The first way is by invoking a method. When the compiler encounters the name of a method, it stops execution in the current method and branches to the newly "called" method. When that method returns a value, execution picks up in the original method on the line just below the method call. Example 3-6 illustrates.

*Example 3-6. Calling a method*

```
using System;


namespace CallingAMethod
{
  class CallingAMethod
  {
    static void Main( )
    {
      Console.WriteLine("In Main! Calling SomeMethod( )...");
      SomeMethod( );
      Console.WriteLine("Back in Main( ).");
    }
    static void SomeMethod( )
    {
      Console.WriteLine("Greetings from SomeMethod!");
    }
  }
}
Output:
In Main! Calling SomeMethod( )...
Greetings from SomeMethod!
Back in Main( ).
```

Program flow begins in Main( ) and proceeds until SomeMethod( ) is invoked (invoking a method is also referred to as "calling" the method). At that point, program flow branches to the method. When the method completes, program flow resumes at the next line after the call to that method.

The second way to create an unconditional branch is with one of the unconditional branch keywords: goto, break, continue, return, or throw. I provide additional information about the first three jump statements later in this chapter. The return statement returns control to the calling method. I discuss the final statement, throw, in Chapter 11.

## Conditional Branching Statements

A conditional branch is created by a conditional statement, which is signaled by a keyword such as if, else, or switch. A conditional branch occurs only if the condition expression evaluates true.

 *C and C++ programmers take note*: unlike C and C++, in which any expression can be used in a conditional, C# requires that all conditional expressions evaluate to a Boolean value.

### if...else statements

if...else statements branch based on a condition. The condition is an expression, tested in the head of the if statement. If the condition evaluates true, the statement (or block of statements) in the body of the if statement is executed.

if statements may contain an optional else statement. The else statement is executed only if the expression in the head of the if statement evaluates false:

```
if (expression)
  statement1
[else
  statement2]
```

This is the kind of if statement description you are likely to find in your compiler documentation. It shows you that the if statement takes a *Boolean expression* (an expression that evaluates true or false) in parentheses, and executes statement1 if the expression evaluates true. Note that statement1 can actually be a block of statements within braces.

You can also see that the else statement is optional, as it is enclosed in square brackets.

 Square brackets are used in the documentation to indicate that the expression is optional. Parentheses (in the if statement) are not part of the documentation, they are actually required in the code.

Although this gives you the syntax of an if statement, an illustration will make its use clear. See Example 3-7.

*Example 3-7. if...else statements*

```
using System;
class Values
{
  static void Main( )
  {
    int valueOne = 10;
    int valueTwo = 20;

    if ( valueOne > valueTwo )
    {
      Console.WriteLine(
      "ValueOne: {0} larger than ValueTwo: {1}",
      valueOne, valueTwo);
    }
    else
    {
      Console.WriteLine(
      "ValueTwo: {0} larger than ValueOne: {1}",
      valueTwo,valueOne);
    }

    valueOne = 30; // set valueOne higher

    if ( valueOne > valueTwo )
    {
      valueTwo = valueOne + 1;

      Console.WriteLine("\nSetting valueTwo to valueOne value, ");
      Console.WriteLine("and incrementing ValueOne.\n");
      Console.WriteLine("ValueOne: {0} ValueTwo: {1}",
      valueOne, valueTwo);
    }
    else
    {
      valueOne = valueTwo;
      Console.WriteLine("Setting them equal. ");
      Console.WriteLine("ValueOne: {0} ValueTwo: {1}",
      valueOne, valueTwo);
    }
  }
}
```

In Example 3-7, the first if statement tests whether valueOne is greater than valueTwo. The relational operators such as greater than (>), less than (<), and equal to (==) are fairly intuitive to use.

The test of whether valueOne is greater than valueTwo evaluates false (because valueOne is 10 and valueTwo is 20, so valueOne is *not* greater than valueTwo). The else statement is invoked, printing the statement:

```
ValueTwo: 20 is larger than ValueOne: 10
```

The second `if` statement evaluates true and all the statements in the `if` block are evaluated, causing two lines to print:

```
Setting valueTwo to valueOne value,
and incrementing ValueOne.

ValueOne: 31 ValueTwo: 30
```

---

## Statement Blocks

You can substitute a statement block anywhere that C# expects a statement. A *statement block* is a set of statements surrounded by braces.

Thus, where you might write:

```
if (someCondition)
    someStatement;
```

you can instead write:

```
if(someCondition)
{
    statementOne;
    statementTwo;
    statementThree;
}
```

---

### Nested if statements

It is possible, and not uncommon, to nest `if` statements to handle complex conditions. For example, suppose you need to write a program to evaluate the temperature, and specifically to return the following types of information:

- If the temperature is 32 degrees or lower, the program should warn you about ice on the road.
- If the temperature is exactly 32 degrees, the program should tell you that there may be ice patches.

There are many good ways to write this program. Example 3-8 illustrates one approach, using nested `if` statements.

*Example 3-8. Nested if statements*

```
using System;
using System.Collections.Generic;
using System.Text;

namespace NestedIf
{
  class NestedIf
  {
```

*Example 3-8. Nested if statements (continued)*

```csharp
static void Main( )
{
  int temp = 32;

  if ( temp <= 32 )
  {
    Console.WriteLine( "Warning! Ice on road!" );
    if ( temp == 32 )
    {
      Console.WriteLine(
      "Temp exactly freezing, beware of water." );
    }
    else
    {
      Console.WriteLine( "Watch for black ice! Temp: {0}", temp );
    } // end else
  } // end if (temp <= 32)
} // end main
} // end class
} // end namespace
```

The logic of Example 3-8 is that it tests whether the temperature is less than or equal to 32. If so, it prints a warning:

```csharp
if (temp <= 32)
{
  Console.WriteLine("Warning! Ice on road!");
```

The program then checks whether the temp is equal to 32 degrees. If so, it prints one message; if not, the temp must be less than 32, and the program prints the second message. Notice that this second if statement is nested within the first if, so the logic of the else is "since it has been established that the temp is less than or equal to 32, and it isn't equal to 32, it must be less than 32."

### switch statements: an alternative to nested ifs

Nested if statements can be hard to read, hard to get right, and hard to debug when used to excess (do not operate heavy machinery when using more than six).

When you have a complex set of choices to make, the switch statement may be a more readable alternative. The logic of a switch statement is "pick a matching value and act accordingly":

```csharp
switch (expression)
{
  case constant-expression:
    statement
    jump-statement
  [default: statement]
}
```

## All Operators Aren't Created Equal

A closer examination of the second `if` statement in Example 3-8 reveals a common potential problem. This `if` statement tests whether the temperature is equal to 32:

```
if (temp == 32)
```

In C and C++, there is an inherent danger in this kind of statement. It's not uncommon for novice programmers to use the assignment operator rather than the equals operator, instead creating the statement:

```
if (temp = 32)
```

This mistake would be difficult to notice, and the result would be that 32 was assigned to `temp`, and 32 would be returned as the value of the assignment statement. Because any nonzero value evaluates true in C and C++ the `if` statement would return true. The side effect would be that `temp` would be assigned a value of 32 whether or not it originally had that value. This is a common bug that could easily be overlooked—if the developers of C# had not anticipated it!

C# solves this problem by requiring `if` statements to accept only Boolean values. The 32 returned by the assignment is not Boolean (it is an integer) and, in C#, there is no automatic conversion from 32 to true. Thus, this bug would be caught at compile time, which is a very good thing and a significant improvement over C++, at the small cost of not allowing implicit conversions from integers to Booleans!

*C++ programmers take note*: because the buggy assignment statement will be caught at compile time, it is no longer necessary to use the counterintuitive syntax:

```
if ( 32 == temp )
```

that was C++'s solution to this problem.

As you can see, like an `if` statement, the expression is put in parentheses in the head of the `switch` statement. Each case statement then requires a constant expression; that is, a literal or symbolic constant or an enumeration. If a case is matched, the statement(s) associated with that case is executed. This must be followed by a jump statement. Typically, the jump statement is break, which transfers execution out of the switch. An alternative is a goto statement, typically used to jump into another case, as Example 3-9 illustrates.

*Example 3-9. The switch statement*

```
using System;
class SwitchStatement
{
    enum Party
    {
        Democrat,
        ConservativeRepublican,
        Republican,
        Libertarian,
        Liberal,
```

*Example 3-9. The switch statement (continued)*

```
        Progressive,
    };
static void Main(string[] args)
    {
        Party myChoice = Party.Libertarian;

        switch (myChoice)
        {
            case Party.Democrat:
                Console.WriteLine("You voted Democratic.\n");
                break;
            case Party.ConservativeRepublican: // fall through
            //Console.WriteLine(
            //"Conservative Republicans are voting Republican\n");
            case Party.Republican:
                Console.WriteLine("You voted Republican.\n");
                break;
            case Party.Liberal:
                Console.WriteLine(" Liberal is now Progressive");
                goto case Party.Progressive;
            case Party.Progressive:
                Console.WriteLine("You voted Progressive.\n");
                break;
            case Party.Libertarian:
                Console.WriteLine("Libertarians are voting Democratic");
                goto case Party.Democrat;
            default:
                Console.WriteLine("You did not pick a valid choice.\n");
                break;
        }

        Console.WriteLine("Thank you for voting.");
    }
}
```

In this whimsical example, we create constants for various political parties. We then assign one value (Libertarian) to the variable myChoice and switch according to that value. If myChoice is equal to Democrat, we print out a statement. Notice that this case ends with break. break is a jump statement that takes us out of the switch statement and down to the first line after the switch, on which we print, "Thank you for voting."

*VB 6 programmers take note*: the equivalent of the C# switch statement is the VB 6 Select Case statement. Also, whereas VB 6 allows you to test a range of values using a single Case statement, C# syntax doesn't provide for this contingency. The following two Case statements are syntactically correct in VB 6:

```
Case Is > 100
Case 50 to 60
```

However, these statements aren't valid in C#. In C#, you can test only a single constant expression. To test a range, you must test each value independently and "fall through" to a common case block.

The value ConservativeRepublican has no statement under it, and it "falls through" to the next statement: Republican. If the value is ConservativeRepublican or Republican, the Republican statements execute. You can "fall through" in this way only if there is no body within the statement. If you uncomment WriteLine( ) under LiberalRepublican, this program won't compile.

> *C and C++ programmers take note*: you can't fall through to the next case unless the case statement is empty. Thus, you *can* write this:
>
> ```
> case 1: // fall through ok (no statement for case 1)
> case 2:
> ```
>
> You *can't*, however, write this:
>
> ```
> case 1:
>   TakeSomeAction( );
>     // fall through not OK, case 1 not empty
> case 2:
> ```
>
> Here, case 1 has a statement in it, and you can't fall through. If you want case 1 to fall through to case 2, you must explicitly use goto:
>
> ```
> case 1:
>  TakeSomeAction( );
>  goto case 2; // explicit fall through
> case 2:
> ```

If you do need a statement, but then you want to execute another case, you can use the goto statement as shown in the Liberal case:

```
goto case Progressive;
```

It is not required that the goto take you to the next case statement. For instance, in the next example, the Libertarian choice also has a goto, but this time it jumps all the way back up to the Democrat case. Because our value was set to Libertarian, this is just what occurs. We print out the Libertarian statement, go to the Democrat case, print that statement, and then hit the break, taking us out of the switch and down to the final statement. The output for all of this is:

```
Libertarians are voting Democrat now.
You voted Democrat.

Thank you for voting.
```

Note the default case, excerpted from Example 3-9:

```
default:
 Console.WriteLine(
 "You did not pick a valid choice.\n");
```

If none of the cases match, the default case will be invoked, warning the user of the mistake.

### Switch on string statements

In the previous example, the switch value was an integral constant. C# offers the ability to switch on a string, allowing you to write:

```
case "Libertarian":
```

If the strings match, the case statement is entered.

# Iteration Statements

C# provides an extensive suite of iteration statements, including for, while, and do...while loops, as well as foreach loops (new to the C family, but familiar to VB programmers). In addition, C# supports the goto, break, continue, and return jump statements.

### The goto statement

The goto statement is the seed from which all other iteration statements have been germinated. Unfortunately, it is a semolina seed, producer of spaghetti code and endless confusion. Most experienced programmers properly shun the goto statement, but in the interest of completeness, here's how you use it:

1. Create a label.
2. goto that label.

The label is an identifier followed by a colon. The goto command is typically tied to a condition, as Example 3-10 illustrates.

*Example 3-10. Using goto*

```
#region Using directives

using System;
using System.Collections.Generic;
using System.Text;

#endregion

namespace UsingGoTo
{
  class UsingGoTo
  {
    static void Main( string[] args )
    {
      int i = 0;
      repeat: // the label
      Console.WriteLine( "i: {0}", i );
      i++;
      if ( i < 10 )
```

*Example 3-10. Using goto (continued)*

```
        goto repeat; // the dastardly deed
        return;
      }
    }
}
```

If you were to try to draw the flow of control in a program that makes extensive use of goto statements, the resulting morass of intersecting and overlapping lines might look like a plate of spaghetti; hence the term "spaghetti code." It was this phenomenon that led to the creation of alternatives such as the while loop. Many programmers feel that using goto in anything other than a trivial example creates confusion and difficult-to-maintain code.

## The while loop

The semantics of the while loop are "while this condition is true, do this work." The syntax is:

```
    while (expression) statement
```

As usual, an expression is any statement that returns a value. While statements require an expression that evaluates to a Boolean (true/false) value, and that statement can, of course, be a block of statements. Example 3-11 updates Example 3-10, using a while loop.

*Example 3-11. Using a while loop*

```
#region Using directives

using System;
using System.Collections.Generic;
using System.Text;

#endregion

namespace WhileLoop
{
  class WhileLoop
  {
    static void Main( string[] args )
    {
      int i = 0;
      while ( i < 10 )
      {
        Console.WriteLine( "i: {0}", i );
        i++;
      }
      return;
    }
  }
}
```

The code in Example 3-11 produces results identical to the code in Example 3-10, but the logic is a bit clearer. The while statement is nicely self-contained, and it reads like an English sentence: "while i is less than 10, print this message and increment i."

Notice that the while loop tests the value of i before entering the loop. This ensures that the loop will not run if the condition tested is false; thus, if i is initialized to 11, the loop will never run.

### The do...while loop

A while statement will never execute if the condition tested returns false. If you want to ensure that your statement is run at least once, use a do...while loop:

```
do statement while (expression);
```

An *expression* is any statement that returns a value. Example 3-12 shows the do... while loop.

*Example 3-12. The do...while loop*

```
#region Using directives

using System;
using System.Collections.Generic;
using System.Text;

#endregion

namespace DoWhile
{
  class DoWhile
  {
    static int Main( string[] args )
    {
      int i = 11;
      do
      {
        Console.WriteLine( "i: {0}", i );
        i++;
      } while ( i < 10 );
      return 0;
    }
  }
}
```

Here, i is initialized to 11 and the while test fails, but only after the body of the loop has run once.

### The for loop

A careful examination of the while loop in Example 3-11 reveals a pattern often seen in iterative statements: initialize a variable (i = 0), test the variable (i < 10), execute a series of statements, and increment the variable (i++). The for loop allows you to combine all these steps in a single loop statement:

```
for ([initializers]; [expression]; [iterators]) statement
```

Example 3-13 illustrates the for loop.

*Example 3-13. The for loop*

```
using System;
using System.Collections.Generic;
using System.Text;


namespace ForLoop
{
  class ForLoop
  {
    static void Main( string[] args )
    {
      for ( int i = 0; i < 100; i++ )
      {
        Console.Write( "{0} ", i );

        if ( i % 10 == 0 )
        {
          Console.WriteLine( "\t{0}", i );
        }
      }
      return ;
    }
  }
}

Output:
0 0
1 2 3 4 5 6 7 8 9 10 10
11 12 13 14 15 16 17 18 19 20 20
21 22 23 24 25 26 27 28 29 30 30
31 32 33 34 35 36 37 38 39 40 40
41 42 43 44 45 46 47 48 49 50 50
51 52 53 54 55 56 57 58 59 60 60
61 62 63 64 65 66 67 68 69 70 70
71 72 73 74 75 76 77 78 79 80 80
81 82 83 84 85 86 87 88 89 90 90
91 92 93 94 95 96 97 98 99
```

This for loop makes use of the modulus operator described later in this chapter. The value of i is printed until i is a multiple of 10:

```
if ( i % 10 == 0)
```

A tab is then printed, followed by the value. Thus, the 10s (20, 30, 40, etc.) are called out on the right side of the output.

*VB 6 programmers take note*: in C#, looping variables are declared within the header of the for or foreach statement (rather than before the statement begins). This means that they are in scope only within the block, and you can't refer to them outside the loop. I cover the foreach statement in detail in Chapter 9.

The individual values are printed using Console.Write( ), which is much like WriteLine( ), but which doesn't enter a newline, allowing the subsequent writes to occur on the same line.

A few quick points to notice: in a for loop, the condition is tested before the statements are executed. Thus, in the example, i is initialized to 0, and then it is tested to see whether it is less than 100. Because i < 100 returns true, the statements within the for loop are executed. After the execution, i is incremented (i++).

Note that the variable i is *scoped* to within the for loop (i.e., the variable i is visible only within the for loop). Example 3-14 will not compile.

*Example 3-14. Scope of variables declared in a for loop*

```
#region Using directives

using System;
using System.Collections.Generic;
using System.Text;

#endregion

namespace ForLoopScope
{
  class ForLoopScope
  {
    static void Main( string[] args )
    {
      for ( int i = 0; i < 100; i++ )
      {
        Console.Write( "{0} ", i );

        if ( i % 10 == 0 )
        {
          Console.WriteLine( "\t{0}", i );
        }
      }
      Console.WriteLine( "\n Final value of i: {0}", i );
    }
  }
}
```

The line shown in bold fails, as the variable i is not available outside the scope of the for loop itself.

# Whitespace and Braces

There is much controversy about the use of whitespace in programming. For example, this for loop:

```csharp
for (int i=0;i<100;i++)
{
  if (i%10 == 0)
  {
    Console.WriteLine("\t{0}", i);
  }
}
```

can be written with more space between the operators:

```csharp
for ( int i = 0; i < 100; i++ )
{
  if ( i % 10 == 0 )
  {
    Console.WriteLine("\t{0}", i);
  }
}
```

Much of this is a matter of personal taste. Visual Studio allows you to set your preferences for the use of whitespace by setting the various options under Tools → Options → TextEditor → C# → Formatting → Spacing.

## The foreach statement

The foreach statement is new to the C family of languages; it is used for looping through the elements of an array or a collection. I defer discussion of this incredibly useful statement until Chapter 9.

## The continue and break statements

There are times when you would like to return to the top of a loop without executing the remaining statements in the loop. The continue statement causes the loop to skip the remaining steps in the loop.

The other side of that coin is the ability to break out of a loop and immediately end all further work within the loop. For this purpose, the break statement exists.

Example 3-15 illustrates the mechanics of continue and break. This code, suggested to us by one of our technical reviewers, is intended to create a traffic signal processing system. The signals are simulated by entering numerals and uppercase characters from the keyboard, using Console.ReadLine( ), which reads a line of text from the keyboard.

The algorithm is simple: receipt of a 0 (zero) means normal conditions, and no further action is required except to log the event. (In this case, the program simply writes a message to the console; a real application might enter a timestamped record in a database.) On receipt of an abort signal (here simulated with an uppercase *A*), the problem is logged and the process is ended. Finally, for any other event, an alarm is raised, perhaps notifying the police. (Note that this sample doesn't actually notify the police, though it does print out a harrowing message to the console.) If the signal is X, the alarm is raised, but the while loop is also terminated.

*Example 3-15. Using continue and break*

```
#region Using directives

using System;
using System.Collections.Generic;
using System.Text;

#endregion

namespace ContinueBreak
{
  class ContinueBreak
  {
    static void Main( string[] args )
    {
      string signal = "0"; // initialize to neutral
      while ( signal != "X" ) // X indicates stop
      {
        Console.Write( "Enter a signal: " );
        signal = Console.ReadLine( );

        // do some work here, no matter what signal you
        // receive
        Console.WriteLine( "Received: {0}", signal );

        if ( signal == "A" )
        {
          // faulty - abort signal processing
          // Log the problem and abort.
          Console.WriteLine( "Fault! Abort\n" );
          break;
        }

        if ( signal == "0" )
        {
          // normal traffic condition
          // log and continue on
          Console.WriteLine( "All is well.\n" );
          continue;
        }


  // Problem. Take action and then log the problem
        // and then continue on
```

*Example 3-15. Using continue and break (continued)*

```
        Console.WriteLine( "{0} -- raise alarm!\n",
        signal );
      } // end while
    } // end main
  } // end class
} // end namespace
```

```
Output:
Enter a signal: 0
Received: 0
All is well.

Enter a signal: B
Received: B
B -- raise alarm!

Enter a signal: A
Received: A
Fault! Abort
```

The point of this exercise is that when the A signal is received, the action in the if statement is taken, and then the program *breaks* out of the loop without raising the alarm. When the signal is 0, it is also undesirable to raise the alarm, so the program *continues* from the top of the loop.

# Operators

An *operator* is a symbol that causes C# to take an action. The C# primitive types (e.g., int) support a number of operators such as assignment, increment, and so forth.

## The Assignment Operator (=)

The = symbol causes the operand on the left side of the operator to have its value changed to whatever is on the right side of the operator. Statements that evaluate to a value are called *expressions*. You may be surprised how many statements *do* evaluate to a value. For example, an assignment such as:

```
    myVariable = 57;
```

is an expression; it evaluates to the value assigned, which, in this case, is 57.

Note that the preceding statement assigns the value 57 to the variable myVariable. The assignment operator (=) doesn't test equality; rather, it causes whatever is on the right side (57) to be assigned to whatever is on the left side (myVariable).

 *VB programmers take note*: C# distinguishes between equality (two equals signs) and assignment (one equals sign).

Because myVariable = 57 (read aloud as "assign the numeric value 57 to the variable whose name is myVariable") is an expression that evaluates to 57, it can be used as part of another assignment operator, such as:

```
mySecondVariable = myVariable = 57;
```

In this statement, the literal value 57 is assigned to the variable myVariable. The value of that assignment (57) is then assigned to the second variable, mySecondVariable. Thus, the value 57 is assigned to both variables.

The value 57 is referred to as a *literal* value (as opposed to a *symbolic* value). A symbolic value is one that is housed in a variable, a constant, or an expression. A literal value is the value itself, written in the conventional way.

You can therefore initialize any number of variables to the same value with one statement:

```
a = b = c = d = e = 20;
```

## Mathematical Operators

C# uses five mathematical operators: four for standard calculations, and a fifth to return the remainder in integer division. The following sections consider the use of these operators.

### Simple arithmetical operators (+, -, *, /)

C# offers operators for simple arithmetic: the addition (+), subtraction (-), multiplication (*), and division (/) operators work as you might expect, with the possible exception of integer division.

When you divide two integers, C# divides like a child in fourth grade: it throws away any fractional remainder. Thus, dividing 17 by 4 returns the value 4 (17/4 = 4, with a remainder of 1). C# provides a special operator (modulus, %, which I describe in the next section) to retrieve the remainder.

Note, however, that C# does return fractional answers when you divide floats, doubles, and decimals.

### The modulus operator (%) to return remainders

To find the remainder in integer division, use the modulus operator (%). For example, the statement 17%4 returns 1 (the remainder after integer division).

The modulus operator turns out to be more useful than you might at first imagine. When you perform modulus n on a number that is a multiple of *n*, the result is 0. Thus, 80%10 = 0 because 80 is an exact multiple of 10. This fact allows you to set up loops in which you take an action every *n*th time through the loop by testing a counter to see whether %n is equal to 0. This strategy comes in handy in the use of the for loop, as I described earlier in this chapter. Example 3-16 illustrates the effects of division on integers, floats, doubles, and decimals.

*Example 3-16. Division and modulus*

```
#region Using directives

using System;
using System.Collections.Generic;
using System.Text;

#endregion

namespace DivisionModulus
{
  class DivisionModulus
  {
    static void Main( string[] args )
    {
      int i1, i2;
      float f1, f2;
      double d1, d2;
      decimal dec1, dec2;

      i1 = 17;
      i2 = 4;
      f1 = 17f;
      f2 = 4f;
      d1 = 17;
      d2 = 4;
      dec1 = 17;
      dec2 = 4;
      Console.WriteLine( "Integer:\t{0}\nfloat:\t\t{1}",
        i1 / i2, f1 / f2 );
      Console.WriteLine( "double:\t\t{0}\ndecimal:\t{1}",
        d1 / d2, dec1 / dec2 );
      Console.WriteLine( "\nModulus:\t{0}", i1 % i2 );

    }
  }
}
```

```
Output:
Integer:    4
float:      4.25
double:     4.25
decimal:    4.25

Modulus:    1
```

Now, consider this line from Example 3-16:

```
Console.WriteLine("Integer:\t{0}\nfloat:\t\t{1}",
  i1/i2, f1/f2);
```

It begins with a call to `Console.WriteLine( )`, passing in this partial string:

```
"Integer:\t{0}\n
```

This will print the characters `Integer:` followed by a tab (`\t`), followed by the first parameter (`{0}`), and then followed by a newline character (`\n`). The next string snippet:

```
float:\t\t{1}
```

is very similar. It prints `float:` followed by two tabs (to ensure alignment), the contents of the second parameter (`{1}`), and then another newline. Notice the subsequent line, as well:

```
Console.WriteLine("\nModulus:\t{0}", i1%i2);
```

This time, the string begins with a newline character, which causes a line to be skipped just before the string `Modulus:` is printed. You can see this effect in the output.

## Increment and Decrement Operators

A common requirement is to add a value to a variable, subtract a value from a variable, or otherwise change the mathematical value, and then to assign that new value back to the same variable. You might even want to assign the result to another variable altogether. The following two sections discuss these cases respectively.

### Calculate and reassign operators

Suppose you want to increment the `mySalary` variable by 5,000. You can do this by writing:

```
mySalary = mySalary + 5000;
```

The addition happens before the assignment, and it is perfectly legal to assign the result back to the original variable. Thus, after this operation completes, `mySalary` will have been incremented by 5,000. You can perform this kind of assignment with any mathematical operator:

```
mySalary = mySalary * 5000;
mySalary = mySalary - 5000;
```

and so forth.

The need to increment and decrement variables is so common that C# includes special operators for self-assignment. Among these operators are +=, -=, *=, /=, and %=, which, respectively, combine addition, subtraction, multiplication, division, and modulus with self-assignment. Thus, you can alternatively write the previous examples as:

```
mySalary += 5000;
mySalary *= 5000;
mySalary -= 5000;
```

The effect of this is to increment mySalary by 5,000, multiply mySalary by 5,000, and subtract 5,000 from the mySalary variable, respectively.

Because incrementing and decrementing by 1 is a very common need, C# (like C and C++ before it) also provides two special operators. To increment by 1, you use the ++ operator, and to decrement by 1, you use the -- operator.

Thus, if you want to increment the variable myAge by 1, you can write:

```
myAge++;
```

## The prefix and postfix operators

To complicate matters further, you might want to increment a variable and assign the results to a second variable:

```
firstValue = secondValue++;
```

The question arises: do you want to assign before you increment the value, or after? In other words, if secondValue starts out with the value 10, do you want to end with firstValue and secondValue equal to 11, or do you want firstValue to be equal to 10 (the original value), and secondValue to be equal to 11?

C# (again, like C and C++) offers two flavors of the increment and decrement operators: *prefix* and *postfix*. Thus, you can write:

```
firstValue = secondValue++; // postfix
```

which will assign first, and then increment (firstValue=10, secondValue=11). You can also write:

```
firstValue = ++secondValue; // prefix
```

which will increment first, and then assign (firstValue=11, secondValue=11).

It is important to understand the different effects of prefix and postfix, as illustrated in Example 3-17.

*Example 3-17. Prefix versus postfix increment*

```
#region Using directives

using System;
using System.Collections.Generic;
using System.Text;

#endregion

namespace PrefixPostfix
{
  class PrefixPostfix
  {
    static void Main( string[] args )
    {
      int valueOne = 10;
```

*Example 3-17. Prefix versus postfix increment (continued)*

```
    int valueTwo;
    valueTwo = valueOne++;
    Console.WriteLine( "After postfix: {0}, {1}", valueOne,
      valueTwo );
    valueOne = 20;
    valueTwo = ++valueOne;
    Console.WriteLine( "After prefix: {0}, {1}", valueOne,
      valueTwo );

  }
 }
}
```

```
Output:
After postfix: 11, 10
After prefix: 21, 21
```

## Relational Operators

Relational operators are used to compare two values, and then return a Boolean (true or false). The greater-than operator (>), for example, returns true if the value on the left of the operator is greater than the value on the right. Thus, 5 > 2 returns the value true, whereas 2 > 5 returns the value false.

Table 3-3 shows the relational operators for C#. This table assumes two variables: bigValue and smallValue, in which bigValue has been assigned the value 100 and smallValue the value 50.

*Table 3-3. C# relational operators (assumes bigValue = 100 and smallValue = 50)*

| Name | Operator | Given this statement | The expression evaluates to |
|---|---|---|---|
| Equals | == | bigValue == 100<br>bigValue == 80 | true<br>false |
| Not equals | != | bigValue != 100<br>bigValue != 80 | false<br>true |
| Greater than | > | bigValue > smallValue | true |
| Greater than or equals | >= | bigValue >= smallValue<br>smallValue >= bigValue | true<br>false |
| Less than | < | bigValue < smallValue | false |
| Less than or equals | <= | smallValue <= bigValue<br>bigValue <= smallValue | true<br>false |

Each relational operator acts as you might expect. However, take note of the equals operator (==), which is created by typing two equals signs (=) in a row (i.e., without any space between them); the C# compiler treats the pair as a single operator.

The C# equals operator (==) tests for equality between the objects on either side of the operator. This operator evaluates to a Boolean value (true or false). Thus, the expression:

```
myX == 5
```

evaluates to true if and only if myX is a variable whose value is 5.

## Use of Logical Operators with Conditionals

If statements (discussed earlier in this chapter) test whether a condition is true. Often, you will want to test whether two conditions are true, or whether only one is true or none is true. C# provides a set of logical operators for this, as shown in Table 3-4. This table assumes two variables, x and y, in which x has the value 5 and y the value 7.

*Table 3-4. C# logical operators (assumes x = 5, y = 7)*

| Name | Operator | Given this statement | The expression evaluates to |
| --- | --- | --- | --- |
| and | && | (x == 3) && (y == 7) | false |
| or | \|\| | (x == 3) \|\| (y == 7) | true |
| not | ! | ! (x == 3) | true |

The and operator (&&) tests whether two statements are both true. The first line in Table 3-4 includes an example that illustrates the use of the and operator:

```
(x == 3) && (y == 7)
```

The entire expression evaluates false because one side (x == 3) is false.

With the or operator (||), either or both sides must be true; the expression is false only if both sides are false. So, in the case of the example in Table 3-4:

```
(x == 3) || (y == 7)
```

the entire expression evaluates true because one side (y==7) is true.

With a not operator (!), the statement is true if the expression is false, and vice versa. So, in the accompanying example:

```
! (x == 3)
```

the entire expression is true because the tested expression (x==3) is false. (The logic is "it is true that it is not true that x is equal to 3.")

## Operator Precedence

The compiler must know the order in which to evaluate a series of operators. For example, if we write:

```
myVariable = 5 + 7 * 3;
```

there are three operators for the compiler to evaluate (=, +, and *). It could, for example, operate left to right, which would assign the value 5 to `myVariable`, then add 7 to the 5 (12) and multiply by 3 (36)—but, of course, then it would throw that 36 away. This is clearly not what is intended.

The rules of precedence tell the compiler which operators to evaluate first. As is the case in algebra, multiplication has higher precedence than addition, so 5+7*3 is equal to 26 rather than 36. Both addition and multiplication have higher precedence than assignment, so the compiler will do the math, and then assign the result (26) to `myVariable` only after the math is completed.

---

## Short-Circuit Evaluation

Short-circuit evaluation allows you to test one-half of an expression and never evaluate the second half if there is no logical way it can matter. In the case of an AND expression, the right half won't be evaluated if the left half is false.

Consider the following code snippet:

```
if ( (x != null) && (x.IsBigAndScary ) )
```

The entire `if` statement is in parentheses, as are the two conditions to be tested. Everything within the outer parentheses must evaluate true for the entire expression to evaluate true, and thus both of the inner expressions must be true for the entire expression to be true. But here is the kicker: the compiler guarantees that it will evaluate these two inner expressions left to right. Thus, x will be tested for null *first*, and if it is null, the second expression will never be tested (which is a good thing because accessing a property on a null object will throw an exception).

This is just like writing:

```
If ( x ! = null )
{
    if (x.IsBigAndScary )
    {
        // do something
    }
}
```

You can also accomplish short-circuit evaluation with an OR expression. In that case, there is no need to test the righthand side if the lefthand side is true because the entire expression evaluates true if *either* side is true. You can thus rewrite your test as follows:

```
if ( (x == null) || (x.IsBigAndScary) )
```

The logic of the first statement was "x must be non-null AND it must be Big and Scary, so if it is null, stop evaluating and don't execute the action."

The logic of the second short-circuit statement is "x may be null or it may be Big and Scary. If x is null we're done, go ahead and execute. If it is not null, go see whether it is Big and Scary, and if it is, execute."

These tests are not quite identical (in the first, you never execute with a null x), but they both protect you from evaluating whether x is Big and Scary if x is null.

---

In C#, parentheses are also used to change the order of precedence much as they are in algebra. Thus, you can change the result by writing:

```
myVariable = (5+7) * 3;
```

Grouping the elements of the assignment in this way causes the compiler to add 5+7, multiply the result by 3, and then assign that value (36) to myVariable. Table 3-5 summarizes operator precedence in C#, listing the operators with the topmost layers being evaluated before the layers that come below.

*Table 3-5. Operator precedence*

| Category | Operators |
| --- | --- |
| Primary | (x) x.y x->y f(x) a[x] x++ x-- new typeof sizeof checked unchecked stackalloc |
| Unary | + - ! ~ ++x -- x (T)x *x &x |
| Multiplicative | * / % |
| Additive | + - |
| Shift | << >> |
| Relational | < > <= >= is as |
| Equality | == != |
| Logical AND | & |
| Logical XOR | ^ |
| Logical OR | | |
| Conditional AND | && |
| Conditional OR | || |
| Conditional | ?: |
| Assignment | = *= /= %= += -= <<= >>= &= ^= |= |

In some complex equations, you might need to nest your parentheses to ensure the proper order of operations. Let's assume we want to know how many seconds a fictional family wastes each morning. It turns out that the adults spend 20 minutes over coffee each morning and 10 minutes reading the newspaper. The children waste 30 minutes dawdling and 10 minutes arguing.

Here's our algorithm:

```
(((minDrinkingCoffee + minReadingNewspaper )* numAdults ) +
((minDawdling + minArguing) * numChildren)) * secondsPerMinute)
```

Although this works, it is hard to read and get right. It's much easier to use interim variables:

```
wastedByEachAdult = minDrinkingCoffee + minReadingNewspaper;
wastedByAllAdults = wastedByEachAdult * numAdults;
wastedByEachKid = minDawdling + minArguing;
wastedByAllKids = wastedByEachKid * numChildren;
```

```
    wastedByFamily = wastedByAllAdults + wastedByAllKids;
    totalSeconds = wastedByFamily * 60;
```

The latter example uses many more interim variables, but it is far easier to read, to understand, and (most important) to debug. As you step through this program in your debugger, you can see the interim values and make sure they are correct.

## The Ternary Operator

Although most operators require one term (e.g., myValue++) or two terms (e.g., a+b), there is one operator that has three: the ternary operator (?:):

   *conditional-expression* **?** *expression1* : *expression2*

This operator evaluates a *conditional expression* (an expression that returns a value of type bool), and then returns the value of either expression1 if the value returned from the conditional expression is true, or expression2 if the value returned is false. The logic is "if this is true, return the first; otherwise, return the second." Example 3-18 illustrates.

*Example 3-18. The ternary operator*

```
using System;
using System.Collections.Generic;
using System.Text;

namespace TernaryOperator
{
  class TernaryOperator
  {
    static void Main( string[] args )
    {
      int valueOne = 10;
      int valueTwo = 20;

      int maxValue = valueOne > valueTwo ? valueOne : valueTwo;

      Console.WriteLine( "ValueOne: {0}, valueTwo: {1}, maxValue: {2}",
        valueOne, valueTwo, maxValue );

    }
  }
}

Output:
ValueOne: 10, valueTwo: 20, maxValue: 20
```

In Example 3-18, the ternary operator is being used to test whether valueOne is greater than valueTwo. If so, the value of valueOne is assigned to the integer variable maxValue; otherwise, the value of valueTwo is assigned to maxValue.

# Preprocessor Directives

In the examples you've seen so far, you've compiled your entire program whenever you compiled any of it. At times, however, you might want to compile only parts of your program—for example, depending on whether you are debugging or building your production code.

Before your code is compiled, another program called the *preprocessor* runs and prepares your program for the compiler. The preprocessor examines your code for special preprocessor directives, all of which begin with the pound sign (#). These directives allow you to define identifiers and then test for their existence.

## Defining Identifiers

#define DEBUG defines a preprocessor identifier, DEBUG. Although other preprocessor directives can come anywhere in your code, identifiers must be defined before any other code, including using statements.

> *C and C++ programmers take note*: the C# preprocessor implements only a subset of the C++ preprocessor and doesn't support macros.

You can test whether DEBUG has been defined with the #if statement. Thus, you can write:

```
#define DEBUG

//... some normal code - not affected by preprocessor

#if DEBUG
   // code to include if debugging
#else
   // code to include if not debugging
#endif

//... some normal code - not affected by preprocessor
```

When the preprocessor runs, it sees the #define statement and records the identifier DEBUG. The preprocessor skips over your normal C# code, and then finds the #if - #else - #endif block.

The #if statement tests for the identifier DEBUG, which does exist, and so the code between #if and #else is compiled into your program—but the code between #else and #endif is *not* compiled. That code doesn't appear in your assembly at all; it is as though it were left out of your source code.

Had the #if statement failed—that is, if you had tested for an identifier that did not exist—the code between #if and #else would not be compiled, but the code between #else and #endif would be compiled.

Any code not surrounded by #if/#endif is not affected by the preprocessor and is compiled into your program.

## Undefining Identifiers

You undefine an identifier with #undef. The preprocessor works its way through the code from top to bottom, so the identifier is defined from the #define statement until the #undef statement, or until the program ends. Thus, if you write:

```
#define DEBUG

#if DEBUG
   // this code will be compiled
#endif

#undef DEBUG

#if DEBUG
   // this code will not be compiled
#endif
```

the first #if will succeed (DEBUG is defined), but the second will fail (DEBUG has been undefined).

## #if, #elif, #else, and #endif

There is no switch statement for the preprocessor, but the #elif and #else directives provide great flexibility. The #elif directive allows the else-if logic of "if DEBUG then action one, else if TEST then action two, else action three":

```
#if DEBUG
   // compile this code if debug is defined
#elif TEST
   // compile this code if debug is not defined
   // but TEST is defined
#else
   // compile this code if neither DEBUG nor TEST
   // is defined
#endif
```

In this example, the preprocessor first tests to see whether the identifier DEBUG is defined. If it is, the code between #if and #elif will be compiled, and the rest of the code until #endif will not be compiled.

If (and only if) DEBUG is not defined, the preprocessor next checks to see whether TEST is defined. Note that the preprocessor will not check for TEST unless DEBUG is not defined. If TEST is defined, the code between the #elif and #else directives will be compiled. If it turns out that neither DEBUG nor TEST is defined, the code between the #else and the #endif statements will be compiled.

# CHAPTER 4

# Classes and Objects

In Chapter 3, I discussed the myriad types built into the C# language, such as int, long, and char. The heart and soul of C#, however, is the ability to create new, complex, programmer-defined types that map cleanly to the objects that make up the problem you are trying to solve, and to use the programmer-defined types that Microsoft has provided in the Framework to facilitate creating applications without having to "reinvent the wheel" to accomplish common tasks such as interacting with the user, databases, web sites, and so forth.

It is this ability to use and create powerful new types that characterizes an object-oriented language. You specify a new type in C# by defining a *class*. (You can also define types with interfaces, as you will see in Chapter 8.) Instances of a class are called *objects*. Objects are created in memory when your program executes.

The difference between a class and an object is the same as the difference between the concept of a dog and the particular dog who is sitting at your feet as you read this. You can't play fetch with the definition of a dog, only with an instance.

A Dog class describes what dogs are like: they have weight, height, eye color, hair color, disposition, and so forth. They also have actions they can take, such as eat, walk, (eat), bark, (eat some more), and sleep. A particular dog (such as Jesse's dog Milo) has a specific weight (68 pounds), height (22 inches), eye color (black), hair color (yellow), disposition (angelic), and so forth. He is capable of all the actions of any dog (though if you knew him you might imagine that eating is the only method he implements).

The huge advantage of classes in object-oriented programming is that they encapsulate the characteristics and capabilities of an entity in a single, self-contained, and self-sustaining *unit of code*. When you want to sort the contents of an instance of a Windows listbox control, for example, you tell the listbox to sort itself. How it does so is of no concern to anyone but the person writing the listbox control; *that* the listbox can be sorted is all any other programmer needs to know. Encapsulation (the idea that an object is self-contained), along with polymorphism and inheritance (explained in just a moment), are the three cardinal principles of object-oriented programming.

An old programming joke asks "how many object-oriented programmers does it take to change a light bulb?" Answer: *none*, you just tell the light bulb to change itself.

This chapter explains the C# language features that are used to create new types by creating classes. It will demonstrate how methods are used to define the behaviors of the class, and how the state of the class is accessed through *properties*, which act like methods to the developer of the class but look like fields to clients of the class. The elements of the class—its behaviors and properties—are known collectively as its *class members*.

## Defining Classes

To create a new class, you first declare it, and then define its methods and fields. You declare a class using the `class` keyword. The complete syntax is as follows:

```
[attributes] [access-modifiers] class identifier [:[base-class [,interface(s)]]
{class-body}
```

 This is a formal definition diagram. Don't let it intimidate you. The items in square brackets are optional.

You read this as follows: "a class is defined by an optional set of attributes followed by an optional set of access modifiers followed by the (nonoptional) keyword `class` which is then followed by the (nonoptional) identifier (the class name).

"The identifier is optionally followed by the name of the base class, or if there is no base class, by the name of the first interface (if any). If there is a base class or an interface, the first of these will be preceded by a colon. If there is a base class and an interface, they will be separated by a comma, as will any subsequent interfaces.

"After all of these will be an open brace, the body of the class, and a closing brace."

Although this can be confusing, an example makes it all much simpler:

```
public class Dog : Mammal
{
    // class body here
}
```

In this little example, `public` is the access modifier, `Dog` is the identifier, and `Mammal` is the base class.

Attributes are covered in Chapter 8; access modifiers are discussed in the next section. (Typically, your classes will use the keyword `public` as an access modifier.) The `identifier` is the name of the class that you provide. The optional `base-class` is discussed in Chapter 5. The member definitions that make up the `class-body` are enclosed by open and closed curly braces ({}).

*C and C++ programmers take note*: a C# class definition does not end with a semicolon, though if you add one, the program will still compile.

In C#, *everything* happens within a class. So far, however, we've not created any instances of that class.

When you make an instance of a class, you are said to *instantiate* the class. The result of instantiating a class is the creation of an instance of the class, known as an *object*.

What is the difference between a class and an instance of that class (an object)? To answer that question, start with the distinction between the *type* int and a *variable* of type int. Thus, although you would write:

```
int myInteger = 5;
```

you wouldn't write:

```
int = 5;  // won't compile
```

You can't assign a value to a type; instead, you assign the value to an object of that type (in this case, a variable of type int).

When you declare a new class, you define the properties of all objects of that class, as well as their behaviors. For example, if you are creating a windowing environment, you might want to create screen widgets (known as controls in Windows programming) to simplify user interaction with your application. One control of interest might be a listbox, which is very useful for presenting a list of choices to the user and enabling the user to select from the list.

Listboxes have a variety of characteristics, called *properties*—for example, height, width, location, and text color. Programmers have also come to expect certain behaviors of listboxes, called *methods*: they can be opened, closed, sorted, and so on.

Object-oriented programming allows you to create a new type, ListBox, which encapsulates these characteristics and capabilities. Such a class might have properties named Height, Width, Location, and TextColor, and member methods named Sort( ), Add( ), Remove( ), and so on.

You can't assign data to the ListBox class. Instead, you must first create an object of that type, as in the following code snippet:

```
ListBox myListBox;  // instantiate a ListBox object
```

Once you create an instance of ListBox, you can assign data to it through its properties, and you can call its methods:

```
myListBox.Height = 50;
myListBox.TextColor = "Black";
myListBox.Sort( );
```

Now, consider a class to keep track of and display the time of day. The internal state of the class must be able to represent the current year, month, date, hour, minute, and second. You probably would also like the class to display the time in a variety of formats. You might implement such a class by defining a single method and six variables, as shown in Example 4-1.

*Example 4-1. Simple Time class*

```
#region Using directives

using System;
using System.Collections.Generic;
using System.Text;

#endregion

namespace TimeClass
{
  public class Time
  {
    // private variables
    int Year;
    int Month;
    int Date;
    int Hour;
    int Minute;
    int Second;

    // public methods
    public void DisplayCurrentTime( )
    {
      Console.WriteLine(
      "stub for DisplayCurrentTime" );
    }
  }

  public class Tester
  {
    static void Main( )
    {
      Time t = new Time( );
      t.DisplayCurrentTime( );
    }
  }
}
```

 You will receive warnings when you compile this class that the member variables of Time (Year, Month, etc.) are never used. Please ignore these warnings for now (though it is generally not a good idea to ignore warnings unless you are certain you understand what they are and why you can ignore them). In this case, we are *stubbing out* the Time class, and if this were a real class, we would make use of these members in other methods.

The only method declared within the Time class definition is DisplayCurrentTime( ). The body of the method is defined within the class definition itself. Unlike other languages (such as C++), C# doesn't require that methods be declared before they are defined, nor does the language support placing its declarations into one file and its code into another. (C# has no header files.) All C# methods are defined inline as shown in Example 4-1 with DisplayCurrentTime( ).

The DisplayCurrentTime( ) method is defined to return void; that is, it will not return a value to a method that invokes it. For now, the body of this method has been stubbed out. The Time class definition ends with the declaration of a number of member variables: Year, Month, Date, Hour, Minute, and Second.

After the closing brace, a second class, Tester, is defined. Tester contains our now familiar Main( ) method. In Main( ), an instance of Time is created and its address is assigned to object t. Because t is an instance of Time, Main( ) can make use of the DisplayCurrentTime( ) method available with objects of that type and call it to display the time:

```
t.DisplayCurrentTime( );
```

## Access Modifiers

An *access modifier* determines which class methods of other classes can see and use a member variable or method within this class. Table 4-1 summarizes the C# access modifiers.

*Table 4-1. Access modifiers*

| Access modifier | Restrictions |
| --- | --- |
| public | No restrictions. Members marked public are visible to any method of any class. |
| private | The members in class A that are marked private are accessible only to methods of class A. |
| protected | The members in class A that are marked protected are accessible to methods of class A and to methods of classes *derived from* class A. |
| internal | The members in class A that are marked internal are accessible to methods of any class in A's assembly. |
| protected internal | The members in class A that are marked protected internal are accessible to methods of class A, to methods of classes *derived from* class A, and to any class in A's assembly. This is effectively protected OR internal. (There is no concept of protected AND internal.) |

It is generally desirable to designate the member variables of a class as private. This means that only member methods of that class can access their value. Because private is the default accessibility level, you don't need to make it explicit, but I recommend that you do so. Thus, in Example 4-1, the declarations of member variables should have been written as follows:

```
// private variables
private int Year;
private int Month;
```

```
    private int Date;
    private int Hour;
    private int Minute;
    private int Second;
```

The Tester class and DisplayCurrentTime( ) method are both declared public so that any other class can make use of them.

 It is good programming practice to explicitly set the accessibility of all methods and members of your class. Although you can rely on the fact that class members are declared private by default, making their access explicit indicates a conscious decision and is self-documenting.

## Method Arguments

Methods can take any number of parameters.[*] The parameter list follows the method name and is enclosed in parentheses, with each parameter preceded by its type. For example, the following declaration defines a method named MyMethod( ), which returns void (i.e., which returns no value at all), and which takes two parameters—an integer and a button:

```
void MyMethod (int firstParam, Button secondParam)
{
  // ...
}
```

Within the body of the method, the parameters act as local variables, as though you had declared them in the body of the method and initialized them with the values passed in. Example 4-2 illustrates how you pass values into a method—in this case, values of type int and float.

*Example 4-2. Passing values into SomeMethod( )*

```
#region Using directives

using System;
using System.Collections.Generic;
using System.Text;

#endregion

namespace PassingValues
{
  public class MyClass
  {
    public void SomeMethod( int firstParam, float secondParam )
    {
```

---

[*] The terms *argument* and *parameter* are often used interchangeably, though some programmers insist on differentiating between the parameter declaration and the arguments passed in when the method is invoked.

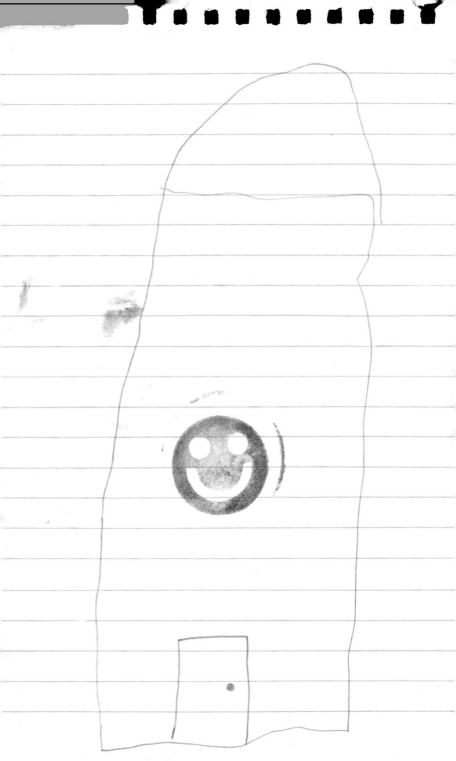

*Example 4-2. Passing values into SomeMethod( ) (continued)*

```
        Console.WriteLine(
          "Here are the parameters received: {0}, {1}",
          firstParam, secondParam );
    }
  }

  public class Tester
  {
    static void Main( )
    {
      int howManyPeople = 5;
      float pi = 3.14f;
      MyClass mc = new MyClass( );
    mc.SomeMethod( howManyPeople, pi );
    }
  }
}
```

The method SomeMethod( ) takes an int and a float and displays them using Console.
WriteLine( ). The parameters, which are named firstParam and secondParam, are
treated as local variables within SomeMethod( ).

> *VB 6 programmers take note*: C# methods don't allow you to declare
> optional arguments. Instead, you have to use method overloading to
> create methods that declare different combinations of arguments. For
> more information, see the section "Overloading Methods and Con-
> structors," later in this chapter.

In the calling method (Main), two local variables (howManyPeople and pi) are created
and initialized. These variables are passed as the parameters to SomeMethod( ). The
compiler maps howManyPeople to firstParam and pi to secondParam, based on their
relative positions in the parameter list.

# Creating Objects

In Chapter 3, I drew a distinction between value types and reference types. The primitive C# types (int, char, etc.) are value types and are created on the stack. Objects,
however, are reference types and are created on the heap, using the keyword new, as
in the following:

```
    Time t = new Time( );
```

t doesn't actually contain the value for the Time object; it contains the address of that
(unnamed) object that is created on the heap. t itself is just a reference to that object.

*VB 6 programmers take note*: although there is a performance penalty in using the VB 6 keywords Dim and New on the same line, in C#, this penalty has been removed. Thus, in C#, there is no drawback to using the new keyword when declaring an object variable.

## Constructors

In Example 4-1, notice that the statement that creates the Time object looks as though it is invoking a method:

```
Time t = new Time( );
```

In fact, a method *is* invoked whenever you instantiate an object. This method is called a *constructor*, and you must either define one as part of your class definition, or let the CLR provide one on your behalf. The job of a constructor is to create the object specified by a class and to put it into a *valid* state. Before the constructor runs, the object is undifferentiated memory; after the constructor completes, the memory holds a valid instance of the class type.

The Time class of Example 4-1 doesn't define a constructor. If a constructor is not declared, the compiler provides one for you. The default constructor creates the object, but takes no other action.

Member variables are initialized to innocuous values (integers to 0, strings to null, etc.).* Table 4-2 lists the default values assigned to primitive types.

*Table 4-2. Primitive types and their default values*

| Type | Default value |
| --- | --- |
| numeric (int, long, etc.) | 0 |
| bool | false |
| char | '\0' (null) |
| enum | 0 |
| reference | null |

Typically, you'll want to define your own constructor and provide it with arguments so that the constructor can set the initial state for your object. In Example 4-1, assume that you want to pass in the current year, month, date, and so forth so that the object is created with meaningful data.

---

* When you write your own constructor, you'll find that these values have been initialized before the constructor runs. In a sense, there are two steps to building new objects—some CLR-level magic that zeros out all the fields and does whatever else needs to be done to make the thing a valid object, and then the steps in the constructor you create (if any).

To define a constructor, you declare a method whose name is the same as the class in which it is declared. Constructors have no return type and are typically declared public. If there are arguments to pass, you define an argument list just as you would for any other method. Example 4-3 declares a constructor for the Time class that accepts a single argument, an object of type DateTime.

*Example 4-3. Declaring a constructor*

```
#region Using directives

using System;
using System.Collections.Generic;
using System.Text;

#endregion

namespace DeclaringConstructor
{
  public class Time
  {

    // private member variables
    int Year;
    int Month;
    int Date;
    int Hour;
    int Minute;
    int Second;

    // public accessor methods
    public void DisplayCurrentTime( )
    {
      System.Console.WriteLine( "{0}/{1}/{2} {3}:{4}:{5}",
        Month, Date, Year, Hour, Minute, Second );
    }

    // constructor
    public Time( System.DateTime dt )
    {

      Year = dt.Year;
      Month = dt.Month;
      Date = dt.Day;
      Hour = dt.Hour;
      Minute = dt.Minute;
      Second = dt.Second;
    }
  }

  public class Tester
  {
    static void Main( )
    {
```

*Example 4-3. Declaring a constructor (continued)*

```
    System.DateTime currentTime = System.DateTime.Now;
    Time t = new Time( currentTime );
    t.DisplayCurrentTime( );
  }
 }
}
```

```
Output:
11/16/2007 16:21:40
```

In this example, the constructor takes a `DateTime` object and initializes all the member variables based on values in that object. When the constructor finishes, the `Time` object exists and the values have been initialized. When `DisplayCurrentTime( )` is called in `Main( )`, the values are displayed.

Try commenting out one of the assignments and running the program again. You'll find that the member variable is initialized by the compiler to 0. Integer member variables are set to 0 if you don't otherwise assign them. Remember, value types (e.g., integers) can't be *uninitialized*; if you don't tell the constructor what to do, it will try for something innocuous.

In Example 4-3, the `DateTime` object is created in the `Main( )` method of `Tester`. This object, supplied by the `System` library, offers a number of public values—Year, Month, Day, Hour, Minute, and Second—that correspond directly to the private member variables of the `Time` object. In addition, the `DateTime` object offers a static member property, `Now`, which is a reference to an instance of a `DateTime` object initialized with the current time.

Examine the highlighted line in `Main( )`, where the `DateTime` object is created by calling the static property `Now`. `Now` creates a `DateTime` value which, in this case, gets copied to the `currentTime` variable on the stack.

The `currentTime` variable is passed as a parameter to the `Time` constructor. The `Time` constructor parameter, `dt`, is a copy of the `DateTime` object.

## Initializers

It is possible to initialize the values of member variables in an *initializer*, instead of having to do so in every constructor. You create an initializer by assigning an initial value to a class member:

```
    private int Second = 30; // initializer
```

Assume that the semantics of our `Time` object are such that no matter what time is set, the seconds are always initialized to 30. You might rewrite the `Time` class to use an initializer so that no matter which constructor is called, the value of `Second` is always initialized, either explicitly by the constructor or implicitly by the initializer. See Example 4-4.

Example 4-4 uses an *overloaded* constructor, which means that there are two versions of the constructor that differ by the number and type of parameters. I explain overloading constructors in detail later in this chapter.

*Example 4-4. Using an initializer*

```
#region Using directives

using System;
using System.Collections.Generic;
using System.Text;

#endregion

namespace Initializer
{
  public class Time
  {
    // private member variables
    private int Year;
    private int Month;
    private int Date;
    private int Hour;
    private int Minute;
    private int Second = 30; // initializer

    // public accessor methods
    public void DisplayCurrentTime( )
    {
      System.DateTime now = System.DateTime.Now;
      System.Console.WriteLine(
      "\nDebug\t: {0}/{1}/{2} {3}:{4}:{5}",
      now.Month, now.Day, now.Year, now.Hour,
        now.Minute, now.Second );

      System.Console.WriteLine( "Time\t: {0}/{1}/{2} {3}:{4}:{5}",
        Month, Date, Year, Hour, Minute, Second );
    }

    // constructors
    public Time( System.DateTime dt )
    {

      Year = dt.Year;
      Month = dt.Month;
      Date = dt.Day;
      Hour = dt.Hour;
      Minute = dt.Minute;
      Second = dt.Second; //explicit assignment

    }
```

*Example 4-4. Using an initializer (continued)*

```
    public Time( int Year, int Month, int Date, int Hour, int Minute )
    {
      this.Year = Year;
      this.Month = Month;
      this.Date = Date;
      this.Hour = Hour;
      this.Minute = Minute;
    }

  }

  public class Tester
  {
    static void Main( )
    {
      System.DateTime currentTime = System.DateTime.Now;
      Time t = new Time( currentTime );
      t.DisplayCurrentTime( );

      Time t2 = new Time( 2007, 11, 18, 11, 45 );
      t2.DisplayCurrentTime( );

    }
  }
}
```

```
Output:
Debug : 11/27/2007 7:52:54
Time : 11/27/2007 7:52:54

Debug : 11/27/2007 7:52:54
Time : 11/18/2007 11:45:30
```

If you don't provide a specific initializer, the constructor will initialize each integer member variable to zero (0). In the case shown, however, the Second member is initialized to 30:

```
    private int Second = 30; // initializer
```

If a value is not passed in for Second, its value will be set to 30 when t2 is created:

```
    Time t2 = new Time(2007,11,18,11,45);
    t2.DisplayCurrentTime( );
```

However, if a value is assigned to Second, as is done in the constructor (which takes a DateTime object, shown in bold), that value overrides the initialized value.

The first time we invoke DisplayCurrentTime( ), we call the constructor that takes a DateTime object, and the seconds are initialized to 54. The second time the method is invoked, we explicitly set the time to 11:45 (not setting the seconds), and the initializer takes over.

If the program didn't have an initializer, and did not otherwise assign a value to Second, the value would be initialized by the CLR to 0.

 *C++ programmers take note*: C# doesn't have a copy constructor, and the semantics of copying are accomplished by implementing the ICloneable interface.

## The ICloneable Interface

The .NET Framework defines an ICloneable interface to support the concept of a copy constructor. (We cover interfaces in detail in Chapter 8.) This interface defines a single method: Clone( ). Classes that support the idea of a copy constructor should implement ICloneable, and then should implement either a shallow copy (calling MemberwiseClone) or a deep copy (e.g., by calling the copy constructor and hand-copying all the members):

```
class SomeType: ICloneable
{
  public Object Clone( )
  {
    return MemberwiseClone( ); // shallow copy
  }
}
```

## The this Keyword

The keyword this refers to the current instance of an object. The this reference (sometimes referred to as a this *pointer*[*]) is a hidden reference passed to every non-static method of a class. Each method can refer to the other methods and variables of that object by way of the this reference.

The this reference is typically used in a number of ways. The first way is to qualify instance members otherwise hidden by parameters, as in the following:

```
public void SomeMethod (int hour)
{
  this.hour = hour;
}
```

In this example, SomeMethod( ) takes a parameter (hour) with the same name as a member variable of the class. The this reference is used to resolve the name ambiguity. Whereas this.hour refers to the member variable, hour refers to the parameter.

---

[*] A pointer is a variable that holds the address of an object in memory. C# doesn't use pointers with managed objects. Some C++ programmers have become so used to talking about a this pointer that they've carried the term over (incorrectly) to C#. We'll refer to the this reference, and pay a 25-cent fine to charity each time we forget.

The argument in favor of this style is that you pick the right variable name and then use it for both the parameter and the member variable. The counter argument is that using the same name for both the parameter and the member variable can be confusing.

The second use of the this reference is to pass the current object as a parameter to another method. For instance:

```
class myClass
{
  public void Foo(OtherClass otherObject)
  {
    otherObject.Bar(this);
  }
}
```

Let's unpack this example. Here, we have a method named myClass.Foo. In the body of this method, you invoke the Bar method of the OtherClass instance, passing in a reference to the current instance of myClass. This allows the Bar method to fiddle with the public methods and members of the current instance of myClass.

The third use of this is with indexers, covered in Chapter 9.

The fourth use of the this reference is to call one overloaded constructor from another, for example:

```
class myClass
{
  public myClass(int i) { //... }
  public myClass() : this(42) { //... }
}
```

In this example, the default constructor invokes the overloaded constructor that takes an integer, by using the this keyword.

The final way that the this keyword is used is to explicitly invoke methods and members of a class, as a form of documentation:

```
public void MyMethod(int y)
{
  int x = 0;
  x = 7; // assign to a local variable
  y = 8; // assign to a parameter
  this.z = 5; // assign to a member variable
  this.Draw(); // invoke member method
}
```

In the cases shown, the use of the this reference is superfluous, but it may make the programmer's intent clearer and does no harm (except, arguably, to clutter the code).

# Using Static Members

The members of a class (variables, methods, events, indexers, etc.) can be either *instance members* or *static members*. Instance members are associated with instances of a type, whereas static members are considered to be part of the class. You access a static member through the name of the class in which it is declared. For example, suppose you have a class named `Button`, and have instantiated objects of that class named `btnUpdate` and `btnDelete`.* Suppose as well that the `Button` class has a static method `SomeMethod( )`. To access the static method, you write:

```
Button.SomeMethod( );
```

rather than:

```
btnUpdate.SomeMethod( );
```

In C#, it is not legal to access a static method or member variable through an instance, and trying to do so will generate a compiler error (C++ programmers take note).

Some languages distinguish between class methods and other (global) methods that are available outside the context of any class. In C#, there are no global methods, only class methods, but you can achieve an analogous result by defining static methods within your class.

 *VB 6 programmers take note*: don't confuse the `static` keyword in C# with the `Static` keyword in VB 6 and VB.NET. In VB, the `Static` keyword declares a variable that is available only to the method in which it was declared. In other words, the `Static` variable is not shared among different objects of its class (i.e., each `Static` variable instance has its own value). However, this variable exists for the life of the program, which allows its value to persist from one method call to another.

In C#, the `static` keyword indicates a class member. In VB, the equivalent keyword is `Shared`.

Static methods act more or less like global methods, in that you can invoke them without actually having an instance of the object at hand. The advantage of static methods over global, however, is that the name is scoped to the class in which it occurs, and thus you don't clutter up the global namespace with myriad function names. This can help manage highly complex programs, and the name of the class acts very much like a namespace for the static methods within it.

---

* As noted earlier, `btnUpdate` and `btnDelete` are actually variables that refer to the unnamed instances on the heap. For simplicity, we'll refer to these as the names of the objects, keeping in mind that this is just shorthand for "the name of the variables that refer to the unnamed instances on the heap."

In addition, static methods may be passed instance members as parameters (or may create such instances themselves within the static method). Because they are scoped to the class, instead of being scoped globally, they have access to the private members of the instances.

 Resist the temptation to create a single class in your program in which you stash all your miscellaneous methods. It is possible, but not desirable, and it undermines the encapsulation of an object-oriented design.

## Invoking Static Methods

The Main( ) method is static. Static methods are said to operate on the class, rather than on an instance of the class. They don't have a this reference, as there is no instance to point to.

 *Java programmers take note*: in C#, calling static methods through instance variables is not permitted.

Static methods can't directly access nonstatic members. For Main( ) to call a nonstatic method, it must instantiate an object. Consider Example 4-2, shown earlier.

SomeMethod( ) is a nonstatic method of MyClass. For Main( ) to access this method, it must first instantiate an object of type MyClass, and then invoke the method through that object.

## Using Static Constructors

If your class declares a static constructor, you are guaranteed that the static constructor will run before any instance of your class is created.*

 You can't control exactly when a static constructor will run, but you do know that it will be after the start of your program and before the first instance is created. Because of this, you can't assume (or determine) whether an instance is being created.

For example, you might add the following static constructor to the Time class from Example 4-4:

---

* Actually, the CLR guarantees to start running the static constructor before *anything* else is done with your class. However, it only guarantees to *start* running the static constructor; it doesn't actually guarantee to *finish* running it. It is possible to concoct a pathological case where two classes have a circular dependency on each other. Rather than deadlock, the CLR can run the constructors on different threads so that it meets the minimal guarantee of at least starting to run both constructors in the right order.

```
static Time( )
{
  Name = "Time";
}
```

Notice that there is no access modifier (e.g., `public`) before the static constructor. Access modifiers aren't allowed on static constructors. In addition, because this is a static member method, you can't access nonstatic member variables, and so `Name` must be declared a static member variable:

```
private static string Name;
```

The final change is to add a line to `DisplayCurrentTime( )`, as in the following:

```
public void DisplayCurrentTime( )
{
  System.Console.WriteLine("Name: {0}", Name);
  System.Console.WriteLine("{0}/{1}/{2} {3}:{4}:{5}",
  Month, Date, Year, Hour, Minute, Second);
}
```

When all these changes are made, the output is:

```
Name: Time
11/27/2007 7:52:54
Name: Time
11/18/2007 11:45:30
```

(Your output will vary depending on the date and time you run this code.)

Although this code works, it isn't necessary to create a static constructor to accomplish this goal. You can, instead, use an initializer:

```
private static string Name = "Time";
```

which accomplishes the same thing. Static constructors are useful, however, for setup work that can't be accomplished with an initializer and that needs to be done only once.

*Java programmers take note*: in C#, a static constructor will serve where a static initializer would be used in Java.

For example, assume you have an unmanaged bit of code in a legacy DLL. You want to provide a class wrapper for this code. You can call `LoadLibrary` in your static constructor and initialize the jump table in the static constructor. I discuss handling legacy code and interoperating with unmanaged code in Chapter 22.

## Static Classes

In C#, there are no global methods or constants. You might find yourself creating small utility classes that exist only to hold static members. Setting aside whether this is a good design, if you create such a class, you won't want any instances created. Mark your class Static to ensure that no instance of the class may be created. Static classes are sealed, and thus you may not create derived types of a Static class. Note, however, that static classes may not contain nonstatic members or have a constructor.

## Using Static Fields

A common way to demonstrate the use of static member variables is to keep track of the number of instances that currently exist for your class. Example 4-5 illustrates.

*Example 4-5. Using static fields for instance counting*

```
#region Using directives

using System;
using System.Collections.Generic;
using System.Text;

#endregion

namespace StaticFields
{
  public class Cat
  {

    private static int instances = 0;

    public Cat( )
    {
      instances++;
    }

    public static void HowManyCats( )
    {
      Console.WriteLine( "{0} cats adopted", instances );
    }
  }

  public class Tester
  {
    static void Main( )
    {
      Cat.HowManyCats( );
      Cat frisky = new Cat( );
      Cat.HowManyCats( );
      Cat whiskers = new Cat( );
      Cat.HowManyCats( );
```

*Example 4-5. Using static fields for instance counting (continued)*

```
      }
    }
}
```

Output:
```
0 cats adopted
1 cats adopted
2 cats adopted
```

The Cat class has been stripped to its absolute essentials. A static member variable called instances is created and initialized to 0. Note that the static member is considered part of the class, not a member of an instance, and so it can't be initialized by the compiler on creation of an instance. Thus, if you want to initialize a static member, you must provide an explicit initializer. When additional instances of Cats are created (in a constructor), the count is incremented.

---

### Static Methods to Access Static Fields

It is undesirable to make member data public. This applies to static member variables as well. One solution is to make the static member private, as we've done here with instances. We have created a public accessor method, HowManyCats( ), to provide access to this private member.

---

## Destroying Objects

Because C# provides garbage collection, you never need to explicitly destroy your objects. However, if your object controls unmanaged resources, you will need to explicitly free those resources when you are done with them. Implicit control over unmanaged resources is provided by a *destructor*, which will be called by the garbage collector when your object is destroyed.

> *C and C++ programmers take note*: a destructor is not necessarily called when an object goes out of scope, but rather when it is garbage-collected (which may happen much later). This is known as *nondeterministic finalization*.

The destructor should only release resources that your object holds on to, and should not reference other objects. Note that if you have only managed references, you don't need to and should not implement a destructor; you want this only for handling unmanaged resources. Because there is some cost to having a destructor, you ought to implement this only on methods that require it (i.e., methods that consume valuable unmanaged resources).

You can't call an object's destructor directly. The garbage collector will call it for you.

---

### How Destructors Work

The garbage collector maintains a list of objects that have a destructor. This list is updated every time such an object is created or destroyed.

When an object on this list is first collected, it is placed in a queue with other objects waiting to be destroyed. After the destructor executes, the garbage collector collects the object and updates the queue, as well as its list of destructible objects.

---

## The C# Destructor

C#'s destructor looks, syntactically, much like a C++ destructor, but it behaves quite differently. You declare a C# destructor with a tilde as follows:

```
~MyClass(){}
```

In C#, this syntax is simply a shortcut for declaring a Finalize() method that chains up to its base class. Thus, when you write:

```
~MyClass()
{
  // do work here
}
```

the C# compiler translates it to:

```
protected override void Finalize()
{
  try
  {
    // do work here.
  }
  finally
  {
    base.Finalize();
  }
}
```

## Destructors Versus Dispose

It is not legal to call a destructor explicitly. Your destructor will be called by the garbage collector. If you do handle precious unmanaged resources (such as file handles) that you want to close and dispose of as quickly as possible, you ought to implement the IDisposable interface.[*] (You will learn more about interfaces in Chapter 8.) The IDisposable interface requires its implementers to define one method, named Dispose( ), to perform whatever cleanup you consider to be crucial. The availability of Dispose( ) is a way for your clients to say, "Don't wait for the destructor to be called, do it right now."

If you provide a Dispose( ) method, you should stop the garbage collector from calling your object's destructor. To do so, call the static method GC.SuppressFinalize( ), passing in the this pointer for your object. Your destructor can then call your Dispose( ) method. Thus, you might write:

```
using System;
class Testing : IDisposable
{
  bool is_disposed = false;
  protected virtual void Dispose(bool disposing)
  {
    if (!is_disposed) // only dispose once!
    {
      if (disposing)
      {
        Console.WriteLine(
        "Not in destructor, OK to reference other objects");
      }
      // perform cleanup for this object
      Console.WriteLine("Disposing...");
    }
    this.is_disposed = true;
  }

  public void Dispose( )
  {
    Dispose(true);
    // tell the GC not to finalize
    GC.SuppressFinalize(this);
  }

  ~Testing( )
  {
    Dispose(false);
    Console.WriteLine("In destructor.");
  }
}
```

---

[*] Most of the time you will not write classes that deal with unmanaged resources such as raw handles directly. You may, however, use wrapper classes such as FileStream and Socket, but these classes do implement IDisposable, in which case you ought to have your class implement IDisposable (but not a finalizer). Your Dispose method will call Dispose on any disposable resources that you're using.

# Implementing the Close( ) Method

For some objects, you may prefer to have your clients call a method named Close( ). (For example, Close( ) may make more sense than Dispose( ) for file objects.) You can implement this by creating a private Dispose( ) method and a public Close( ) method, and having your Close( ) method invoke Dispose( ).

# The using Statement

To make it easier for your clients to properly dispose of your objects, C# provides a using statement that ensures that Dispose( ) will be called at the earliest possible time. The idiom is to declare the objects you are using and then to create a scope for these objects with curly braces. When the closing brace is reached, the Dispose( ) method will be called on the object automatically, as illustrated in Example 4-6.

*Example 4-6. The using statement*

```
#region Using directives

using System;
using System.Collections.Generic;
using System.Drawing;
using System.Text;

#endregion

namespace usingStatement
{
  class Tester
  {
    public static void Main()
    {
      using ( Font theFont = new Font( "Arial", 10.0f ) )
      {
        // use theFont

      } // compiler will call Dispose on theFont

      Font anotherFont = new Font( "Courier", 12.0f );

      using ( anotherFont )
      {
        // use anotherFont

      } // compiler calls Dispose on anotherFont
    }
  }
}
```

In the first part of this example, the Font object is created within the using statement. When the using statement ends, Dispose( ) is called on the Font object.

In the second part of the example, a Font object is created outside the using statement. When we decide to use that font, we put it inside the using statement; when that statement ends, Dispose( ) is called once again.

This second approach is fraught with danger. If an exception is thrown after the object is created, but before the using block is begun, the object will not be disposed. Second, the variable remains in scope after the using block ends, but if it is accessed, it will fail.

The using statement also protects you against unanticipated exceptions. Regardless of how control leaves the using statement, Dispose( ) is called. An implicit try-finally block is created for you. (See Chapter 11 for details.)

# Passing Parameters

By default, value types are passed into methods by value. (See the section "Method Arguments," earlier in this chapter.) This means that when a value object is passed to a method, a temporary copy of the object is created within that method. Once the method completes, the copy is discarded. Although passing by value is the normal case, there are times when you will want to pass value objects by reference. C# provides the ref parameter modifier for passing value objects into a method by reference, and the out modifier for those cases in which you want to pass in a ref variable without first initializing it. C# also supports the params modifier, which allows a method to accept a variable number of parameters. I discuss the params keyword in Chapter 9.

## Passing by Reference

Methods can return only a single value (though that value can be a collection of values). Let's return to the Time class and add a GetTime( ) method, which returns the hour, minutes, and seconds.

 *Java programmers take note*: in C#, there's no need for wrapper classes for basic types such as int (integer). Instead, use reference parameters.

Because you can't return three values, perhaps you can pass in three parameters, let the method modify the parameters, and examine the result in the calling method. Example 4-7 shows a first attempt at this.

*Example 4-7. Returning values in parameters*

```
#region Using directives

using System;
using System.Collections.Generic;
```

*Example 4-7. Returning values in parameters (continued)*

```
using System.Text;

#endregion

namespace ReturningValuesInParams
{
  public class Time
  {
    // private member variables
    private int Year;
    private int Month;
    private int Date;
    private int Hour;
    private int Minute;
    private int Second;

    // public accessor methods
    public void DisplayCurrentTime( )
    {
        System.Console.WriteLine( "{0}/{1}/{2} {3}:{4}:{5}",
          Month, Date, Year, Hour, Minute, Second );
    }

    public int GetHour( )
    {
      return Hour;
    }

    public void GetTime( int h, int m, int s )
    {
      h = Hour;
      m = Minute;
      s = Second;
    }

    // constructor
    public Time( System.DateTime dt )
    {

      Year = dt.Year;
      Month = dt.Month;
      Date = dt.Day;
      Hour = dt.Hour;
      Minute = dt.Minute;
      Second = dt.Second;
    }
  }

  public class Tester
  {
    static void Main( )
    {
```

*Example 4-7. Returning values in parameters (continued)*

```
        System.DateTime currentTime = System.DateTime.Now;
        Time t = new Time( currentTime );
        t.DisplayCurrentTime( );

        int theHour = 0;
        int theMinute = 0;
        int theSecond = 0;
        t.GetTime( theHour, theMinute, theSecond );
        System.Console.WriteLine( "Current time: {0}:{1}:{2}",
          theHour, theMinute, theSecond );
    }
  }
}
```

```
Output:
11/17/2007 13:41:18
Current time: 0:0:0
```

Notice that the Current time in the output is 0:0:0. Clearly, this first attempt did not work. The problem is with the parameters. You pass in three integer parameters to GetTime( ), and you modify the parameters in GetTime( ), but when the values are accessed back in Main( ), they are unchanged. This is because integers are value types, and so are passed by value; a copy is made in GetTime( ). What you need is to pass these values by reference.

Two small changes are required. First, change the parameters of the GetTime( ) method to indicate that the parameters are ref (reference) parameters:

```
    public void GetTime(ref int h, ref int m, ref int s)
    {
      h = Hour;
      m = Minute;
      s = Second;
    }
```

Second, modify the call to GetTime( ) to pass the arguments as references as well:

```
    t.GetTime(ref theHour, ref theMinute, ref theSecond);
```

If you leave out the second step of marking the arguments with the keyword ref, the compiler will complain that the argument can't be converted from an int to a ref int.

The results now show the correct time. By declaring these parameters to be ref parameters, you instruct the compiler to pass them by reference. Instead of a copy being made, the parameter in GetTime( ) is a reference to the same variable (theHour) that is created in Main( ). When you change these values in GetTime( ), the change is reflected in Main( ).

Keep in mind that ref parameters are references to the actual original value: it is as though you said, "Here, work on this one." Conversely, value parameters are copies: it is as though you said, "Here, work on one *just like* this."

## Overcoming Definite Assignment with out Parameters

C# imposes *definite assignment*, which requires that all variables be assigned a value before they are used. In Example 4-7, if you don't initialize theHour, theMinute, and theSecond before you pass them as parameters to GetTime( ), the compiler will complain. Yet, the initialization that is done merely sets their values to 0 before they are passed to the method:

```
int theHour = 0;
int theMinute = 0;
int theSecond = 0;
t.GetTime( ref theHour, ref theMinute, ref theSecond);
```

It seems silly to initialize these values because you immediately pass them by reference into GetTime where they'll be changed, but if you don't, the following compiler errors are reported:

```
Use of unassigned local variable 'theHour'
Use of unassigned local variable 'theMinute'
Use of unassigned local variable 'theSecond'
```

C# provides the out parameter modifier for this situation. The out modifier removes the requirement that a reference parameter be initialized. The parameters to GetTime( ), for example, provide no information to the method; they are simply a mechanism for getting information out of it. Thus, by marking all three as out parameters, you eliminate the need to initialize them outside the method. Within the called method, the out parameters must be assigned a value before the method returns. The following are the altered parameter declarations for GetTime( ):

```
public void GetTime(out int h, out int m, out int s)
{
  h = Hour;
  m = Minute;
  s = Second;
}
```

And here is the new invocation of the method in Main( ):

```
t.GetTime( out theHour, out theMinute, out theSecond);
```

To summarize, value types are passed into methods by value. ref parameters are used to pass value types into a method by reference. This allows you to retrieve their modified values in the calling method. out parameters are used only to return information from a method. Example 4-8 rewrites Example 4-7 to use all three.

*Example 4-8. Using in, out, and ref parameters*

```
#region Using directives

using System;
using System.Collections.Generic;
using System.Text;
```

*Example 4-8. Using in, out, and ref parameters (continued)*

```csharp
#endregion

namespace InOutRef
{
  public class Time
  {
    // private member variables
    private int Year;
    private int Month;
    private int Date;
    private int Hour;
    private int Minute;
    private int Second;

    // public accessor methods
    public void DisplayCurrentTime( )
    {
      System.Console.WriteLine( "{0}/{1}/{2} {3}:{4}:{5}",
        Month, Date, Year, Hour, Minute, Second );
    }

    public int GetHour( )
    {
      return Hour;
    }

    public void SetTime( int hr, out int min, ref int sec )
    {
      // if the passed in time is >= 30
      // increment the minute and set second to 0
      // otherwise leave both alone
      if ( sec >= 30 )
      {
        Minute++;
        Second = 0;
      }
      Hour = hr; // set to value passed in

      // pass the minute and second back out
      min = Minute;
      sec = Second;
    }

    // constructor
    public Time( System.DateTime dt )
    {
      Year = dt.Year;
      Month = dt.Month;
      Date = dt.Day;
      Hour = dt.Hour;
      Minute = dt.Minute;
```

*Example 4-8. Using in, out, and ref parameters (continued)*

```
      Second = dt.Second;
    }
  }

  public class Tester
  {
    static void Main( )
    {
      System.DateTime currentTime = System.DateTime.Now;
      Time t = new Time( currentTime );
      t.DisplayCurrentTime( );

      int theHour = 3;
      int theMinute;
      int theSecond = 20;

      t.SetTime( theHour, out theMinute, ref theSecond );
      System.Console.WriteLine(
        "the Minute is now: {0} and {1} seconds",
        theMinute, theSecond );

      theSecond = 40;
      t.SetTime( theHour, out theMinute, ref theSecond );
      System.Console.WriteLine( "the Minute is now: " +
        "{0} and {1} seconds", theMinute, theSecond );
    }
  }
}
```

```
Output:
11/17/2007 14:6:24
the Minute is now: 6 and 24 seconds
the Minute is now: 7 and 0 seconds
```

SetTime is a bit contrived, but it illustrates the three types of parameters. theHour is passed in as a value parameter; its entire job is to set the member variable Hour, and no value is returned using this parameter.

The ref parameter theSecond is used to set a value in the method. If theSecond is greater than or equal to 30, the member variable Second is reset to 0, and the member variable Minute is incremented.

 You must specify ref on the call and the destination when using reference parameters.

Finally, theMinute is passed into the method only to return the value of the member variable Minute, and thus is marked as an out parameter.

It makes perfect sense that theHour and theSecond must be initialized; their values are needed and used. It is not necessary to initialize theMinute, as it is an out parameter that exists only to return a value. What at first appeared to be arbitrary and capricious rules now make sense; values are required to be initialized only when their initial value is meaningful.

# Overloading Methods and Constructors

Often, you'll want to have more than one function with the same name. The most common example of this is to have more than one constructor. In the examples shown so far, the constructor has taken a single parameter: a DateTime object. It would be convenient to be able to set new Time objects to an arbitrary time by passing in year, month, date, hour, minute, and second values. It would be even more convenient if some clients could use one constructor, and other clients could use the other constructor. Function overloading provides for exactly these contingencies.

The *signature* of a method is defined by its name and its parameter list. Two methods differ in their signatures if they have different names or different parameter lists. Parameter lists can differ by having different numbers or types of parameters. For example, in the following code, the first method differs from the second in the number of parameters, and the second differs from the third in the types of parameters:

```
void myMethod(int p1);
void myMethod(int p1, int p2);
void myMethod(int p1, string s1);
```

A class can have any number of methods, as long as each one's signature differs from that of all the others.

Example 4-9 illustrates the Time class with two constructors: one that takes a DateTime object, and the other that takes six integers.

*Example 4-9. Overloading the constructor*

```
#region Using directives

using System;
using System.Collections.Generic;
using System.Text;

#endregion

namespace OverloadedConstructor
{
  public class Time
  {
    // private member variables
    private int Year;
    private int Month;
    private int Date;
```

*Example 4-9. Overloading the constructor (continued)*

```
  private int Hour;
  private int Minute;
  private int Second;

  // public accessor methods
  public void DisplayCurrentTime( )
  {
    System.Console.WriteLine( "{0}/{1}/{2} {3}:{4}:{5}",
      Month, Date, Year, Hour, Minute, Second );
  }

  // constructors
  public Time( System.DateTime dt )
  {
    Year = dt.Year;
    Month = dt.Month;
    Date = dt.Day;
    Hour = dt.Hour;
    Minute = dt.Minute;
    Second = dt.Second;
  }

  public Time( int Year, int Month, int Date,
    int Hour, int Minute, int Second )
  {
    this.Year = Year;
    this.Month = Month;
    this.Date = Date;
    this.Hour = Hour;
    this.Minute = Minute;
    this.Second = Second;
  }
}

public class Tester
{
  static void Main( )
  {
    System.DateTime currentTime = System.DateTime.Now;

    Time t1= new Time( currentTime );
    t.DisplayCurrentTime( );

    Time t2 = new Time( 2007, 11, 18, 11, 03, 30 );
    t2.DisplayCurrentTime( );

  }
}
}
```

As you can see, the Time class in Example 4-9 has two constructors. If a function's signature consisted only of the function name, the compiler would not know which constructors to call when constructing t1 and t2. However, because the signature includes the function argument types, the compiler is able to match the constructor call for t1 with the constructor whose signature requires a DateTime object. Likewise, the compiler is able to associate the t2 constructor call with the constructor method whose signature specifies six integer arguments.

When you overload a method, you must change the signature (i.e., the name, number, or type of the parameters). You are free, as well, to change the return type, but this is optional. Changing only the return type doesn't overload the method, and creating two methods with the same signature but differing return types will generate a compile error, as you can see in Example 4-10.

*Example 4-10. Varying the return type on overloaded methods*

```
#region Using directives

using System;
using System.Collections.Generic;
using System.Text;

#endregion

namespace VaryingReturnType
{
  public class Tester
  {
    private int Triple( int val )
    {
      return 3 * val;
    }

    private long Triple( long val )
    {
      return 3 * val;
    }

    public void Test()
    {
      int x = 5;
      int y = Triple( x );
      System.Console.WriteLine( "x: {0} y: {1}", x, y );

      long lx = 10;
      long ly = Triple( lx );
      System.Console.WriteLine( "lx: {0} ly: {1}", lx, ly );

    }
    static void Main()
    {
```

*Example 4-10. Varying the return type on overloaded methods (continued)*

```
      Tester t = new Tester();
      t.Test();
    }
  }
}
```

In this example, the Tester class overloads the Triple() method, one to take an integer, the other to take a long. The return type for the two Triple() methods varies. Although this is not required, it is very convenient in this case.

# Encapsulating Data with Properties

Properties allow clients to access class state as though they were accessing member fields directly, while actually implementing that access through a class method.

This is ideal. The client wants direct access to the state of the object and doesn't want to work with methods. The class designer, however, wants to hide the internal state of his class in class members, and provide indirect access through a method.

By decoupling the class state from the method that accesses that state, the designer is free to change the internal state of the object as needed. When the Time class is first created, the Hour value might be stored as a member variable. When the class is redesigned, the Hour value might be computed or retrieved from a database. If the client had direct access to the original Hour member variable, the change to computing the value would break the client. By decoupling and forcing the client to go through a method (or property), the Time class can change how it manages its internal state without breaking client code.

Properties meet both goals: they provide a simple interface to the client, appearing to be a member variable. They are implemented as methods, however, providing the data-hiding required by good object-oriented design, as illustrated in Example 4-11.

*Example 4-11. Using a property*

```
#region Using directives

using System;
using System.Collections.Generic;
using System.Text;

#endregion

namespace UsingAProperty
{
  public class Time
  {
    // private member variables
    private int year;
```

*Example 4-11. Using a property (continued)*

```
    private int month;
    private int date;
    private int hour;
    private int minute;
    private int second;

    // public accessor methods
    public void DisplayCurrentTime( )
    {

      System.Console.WriteLine(
        "Time\t: {0}/{1}/{2} {3}:{4}:{5}",
        month, date, year, hour, minute, second );
    }

    // constructors
    public Time( System.DateTime dt )
    {
      year = dt.Year;
      month = dt.Month;
      date = dt.Day;
      hour = dt.Hour;
      minute = dt.Minute;
      second = dt.Second;
    }

    // create a property

    public int Hour
    {
      get
      {
        return hour;
      }

      set
      {
        hour = value;
      }
    }
  }

  public class Tester
  {
    static void Main( )
    {
      System.DateTime currentTime = System.DateTime.Now;
      Time t = new Time( currentTime );
      t.DisplayCurrentTime( );

      int theHour = t.Hour;
      System.Console.WriteLine( "\nRetrieved the hour: {0}\n",
```

*Example 4-11. Using a property (continued)*

```
      theHour );
    theHour++;
    t.Hour = theHour;
    System.Console.WriteLine( "Updated the hour: {0}\n", theHour );
  }
 }
}
```

To declare a property, write the property type and name followed by a pair of braces. Within the braces you may declare get and set accessors. Neither of these has explicit parameters, though the set( ), accessor has an implicit parameter value, as shown next.

In Example 4-11, Hour is a property. Its declaration creates two accessors: get and set:

```
public int Hour
{
  get
  {
    return hour;
  }

  set
  {
    hour = value;
  }
}
```

Each accessor has an accessor body that does the work of retrieving and setting the property value. The property value might be stored in a database (in which case the accessor body would do whatever work is needed to interact with the database), or it might just be stored in a private member variable:

```
private int hour;
```

## The get Accessor

The body of the get accessor is similar to a class method that returns an object of the type of the property. In the example, the accessor for Hour is similar to a method that returns an int. It returns the value of the private member variable in which the value of the property has been stored:

```
get
{
  return hour;
}
```

In this example, a local int member variable is returned, but you could just as easily retrieve an integer value from a database, or compute it on the fly.

Whenever you read the property, the get accessor is invoked:

```
Time t = new Time(currentTime);
int theHour = t.Hour;
```

In this example, the value of the Time object's Hour property is retrieved, invoking the get accessor to extract the property, which is then assigned to a local variable.

## The set Accessor

The set accessor sets the value of a property and is similar to a method that returns void. When you define a set accessor, you must use the value keyword to represent the argument whose value is passed to and stored by the property:

```
set
{
   hour = value;
}
```

Here, again, a private member variable is used to store the value of the property, but the set accessor could write to a database or update other member variables as needed.

When you assign a value to the property, the set accessor is automatically invoked, and the implicit parameter value is set to the value you assign:

```
theHour++;
t.Hour = theHour;
```

The two main advantages of this approach are that the client can interact with the properties directly, without sacrificing the data-hiding and encapsulation sacrosanct in good object-oriented design, and that the author of the property can ensure that the data provided is valid.

## Property Access Modifiers

It is possible to set an access modifier (protected, internal, private) to modify access to either the get or set accessor. To do so, your property must have both a set and a get accessor, and you may modify only one or the other. Also, the modifier must be more restrictive than the accessibility level already on the property or the indexer (thus, you may add protected to the get or set accessor of a public property, but not to a private property):

```
public string MyString
{
   protected get { return myString; }
   set { myString = value; }
}
```

In this example, access to the get accessor is restricted to methods of this class and classes derived from this class, whereas the set accessor is publicly visible.

Note that you may not put an access modifier on an interface (see Chapter 8) or on explicit interface member implementation. In addition, if you are overriding a virtual property or index (as discussed next), the access modifier *must* match the base property's access modifier.

# readonly Fields

You might want to create a version of the Time class that is responsible for providing public static values representing the current time and date. Example 4-12 illustrates a simple approach to this problem.

*Example 4-12. Using static public constants*

```
#region Using directives

using System;
using System.Collections.Generic;
using System.Text;

#endregion

namespace StaticPublicConstants
{
  public class RightNow
  {
    // public member variables
    public static int Year;
    public static int Month;
    public static int Date;
    public static int Hour;
    public static int Minute;
    public static int Second;

    static RightNow( )
    {
      System.DateTime dt = System.DateTime.Now;
      Year = dt.Year;
      Month = dt.Month;
      Date = dt.Day;
      Hour = dt.Hour;
      Minute = dt.Minute;
      Second = dt.Second;
    }
  }

  public class Tester
  {
    static void Main( )
    {
      System.Console.WriteLine( "This year: {0}",
```

*Example 4-12. Using static public constants (continued)*

```
      RightNow.Year.ToString( ) );
        RightNow.Year = 2008;
        System.Console.WriteLine( "This year: {0}",
          RightNow.Year.ToString( ) );
    }
  }
}
```

```
Output:
This year: 2007
This year: 2008
```

This works well enough, until someone comes along and changes one of these values. As the example shows, the RightNow.Year value can be changed, for example, to 2008. This is clearly not what we'd like.

You'd like to mark the static values as constant, but that is not possible because you don't initialize them until the static constructor is executed. C# provides the keyword readonly for exactly this purpose. If you change the class member variable declarations as follows:

```
    public static readonly int Year;
    public static readonly int Month;
    public static readonly int Date;
    public static readonly int Hour;
    public static readonly int Minute;
    public static readonly int Second;
```

and then comment out the reassignment in Main( ):

```
    // RightNow.Year = 2008; // error!
```

the program will compile and run as intended.

# CHAPTER 5

# Inheritance and Polymorphism

The preceding chapter demonstrated how to create new types by declaring classes. This chapter explores the relationship between objects in the real world and how to model these relationships in your code. This chapter focuses on *specialization*, which is implemented in C# through *inheritance*. This chapter also explains how instances of more specialized types can be treated as though they were instances of more general types, a process known as *polymorphism*. This chapter ends with a consideration of *sealed* classes, which can't be specialized; *abstract* classes, which exist only to be specialized; and the root of all classes, the Object type.

 *VB 6 programmers take note:* like VB.NET, C# provides full object-oriented technology, including inheritance, polymorphism, and encapsulation. These are relatively new topics for VB 6 programmers. You should study them carefully; they affect your class and application design.

## Specialization and Generalization

Classes and their instances (objects) don't exist in a vacuum, but rather in a network of interdependencies and relationships, just as we, as social animals, live in a world of relationships and categories.

The *is-a* relationship is one of *specialization*. When we say that a dog *is-a* mammal, we mean that the dog is a specialized kind of mammal. It has all the characteristics of any mammal (it bears live young, nurses with milk, has hair), but it specializes these characteristics to the familiar characteristics of *Canis domesticus*. A cat is also a mammal. As such, we expect it to share certain characteristics with the dog that are generalized in mammals, but to differ in those characteristics that are specialized in cats.

The specialization and generalization relationships are both reciprocal and hierarchical. They are reciprocal because specialization is the other side of the coin from generalization. Thus, dog and cat specialize mammal, and mammal generalizes from dog and cat.

These relationships are hierarchical because they create a relationship tree, with specialized types branching off from more generalized types. As you move up the hierarchy, you achieve greater *generalization*. You move up toward mammal to generalize that dogs and cats and horses all bear live young. As you move down the hierarchy, you specialize. Thus, the cat specializes mammal in having claws (a characteristic) and purring (a behavior).

Similarly, when you say that ListBox and Button *are* Controls you indicate that there are characteristics and behaviors of Controls that you expect to find in both of these types, as illustrated in Figure 5-1. In other words, Control generalizes the shared characteristics of both ListBox and Button, while each specializes its own particular characteristics and behaviors.

---

### About the Unified Modeling Language

The Unified Modeling Language (UML) is a standardized "language" for describing a system or business. The part of the UML that is useful for the purposes of this chapter is the set of diagrams used to document the relationships between classes.

In the UML, classes are represented as boxes. The name of the class appears at the top of the box, and (optionally) methods and members can be listed in the sections within the box. In the UML, you model (for example) specialization relationships as shown in Figure 5-1. Note that the arrow points from the more specialized class up to the more general class.

---

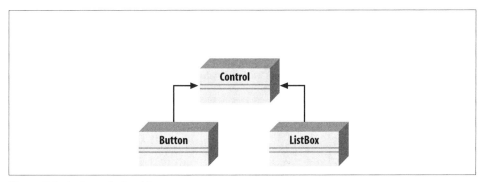

*Figure 5-1. An is-a relationship*

When developing an application, it is common to note that two classes share functionality, and then to factor out these commonalities into a shared base class. This provides you with easier-to-maintain code and greater reuse of common code. For example, suppose you started out creating a series of objects as illustrated in Figure 5-2.

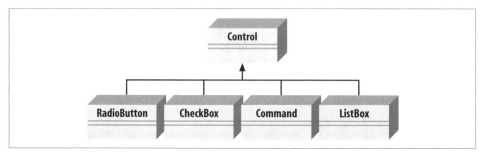

*Figure 5-2. Deriving from Control*

After working with RadioButtons, CheckBoxes, and Command buttons for a while, you realize that they share certain characteristics and behaviors that are more specialized than Control, but more general than any of the three. You might factor these common traits and behaviors into a common base class, Button, and rearrange your inheritance hierarchy as shown in Figure 5-3. This is an example of how generalization is used in object-oriented development.

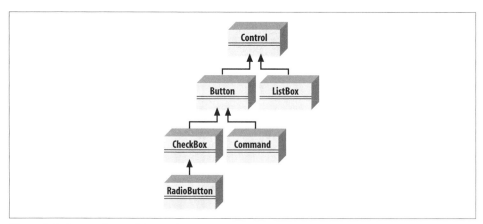

*Figure 5-3. A more factored hierarchy*

This UML diagram depicts the relationship between the factored classes and shows that both ListBox and Button derive from Control, and that Button is in turn specialized into CheckBox and Command. Finally, RadioButton derives from CheckBox. You can thus say that RadioButton is a CheckBox, which in turn is a Button, and that Buttons are Controls.

This is not the only, or even necessarily the best, organization for these objects, but it is a reasonable starting point for understanding how these types (classes) relate to one another.

Actually, although this might reflect how some widget hierarchies are organized, I'm very skeptical of any system in which the model doesn't reflect how we perceive reality. When I find myself saying that a RadioButton is a CheckBox, I have to think long and hard about whether that makes sense. I suppose a RadioButton *is* a kind of checkbox. It is a checkbox that supports the idiom of mutually exclusive choices. With that said, it is a bit of a stretch, and might be a sign of a shaky design.

Microsoft offers a better design in Windows Presentation Foundation, in which ToggleButton serves as a base class for both CheckBox and RadioButton. The ButtonBase class then serves as the common base for Button and ToggleButton, thereby eliminating the artificial (and frankly bizarre) inheritance of RadioButton deriving from CheckBox.

# Inheritance

In C#, the specialization relationship is typically implemented using inheritance. This is not the only way to implement specialization, but it is the most common and most natural way to implement this relationship.

Saying that ListBox inherits from (or derives from) Control indicates that it specializes Control. Control is referred to as the *base* class, and ListBox is referred to as the *derived* class. That is, ListBox derives its characteristics and behaviors from Control, and then specializes to its own particular needs.

## Implementing Inheritance

In C#, you create a derived class by adding a colon after the name of the derived class, followed by the name of the base class:

```
public class ListBox : Control
```

This code declares a new class, ListBox, which derives from Control. You can read the colon as "derives from."

*C++ programmers take note*: C# has no private or protected inheritance, and implements multiple inheritance only for interfaces, not for multiple base types. After eight years of C++ and now eight years of C#, I can honestly say that I see no disadvantage to this limitation.

The derived class inherits all the members of the base class, both member variables and methods.

# Polymorphism

There are two powerful aspects to inheritance. One is code reuse. When you create a ListBox class, you're able to reuse some of the logic in the base (Control) class.

What is arguably more powerful, however, is the second aspect of inheritance: *polymorphism*. *Poly* means "many" and *morph* means "form." Thus, polymorphism refers to being able to use many forms of a type without regard to the details.

When the phone company sends your phone a ring signal, it doesn't know what type of phone is on the other end of the line. You might have an old-fashioned Western Electric phone that energizes a motor to ring a bell, or you might have an electronic phone that plays digital music.

As far as the phone company is concerned, it knows only about the "base type" Phone and expects that any "instance" of this type knows how to ring. When the phone company tells your phone to *ring*, it simply expects the phone to "do the right thing." Thus, the phone company treats your phone polymorphically.

## Creating Polymorphic Types

Because a ListBox *is-a* Control and a Button *is-a* Control, we expect to be able to use either of these types in situations that call for a Control. For example, a form might want to keep a collection of all the instances of Control it manages so that when the form is opened, it can tell each of its Controls to draw itself. For this operation, the form doesn't want to know which elements are listboxes and which are buttons; it just wants to tick through its collection and tell each to "draw." In short, the form wants to treat all its Control objects polymorphically.

## Creating Polymorphic Methods

To create a method that supports polymorphism, you need only mark it as virtual in its base class. For example, to indicate that the method DrawWindow( ) of class Control in Example 5-1 is polymorphic, simply add the keyword virtual to its declaration as follows:

```
public virtual void DrawWindow( )
```

Now, each derived class is free to implement its own version of DrawWindow( ). To do so, simply override the base class virtual method by using the keyword override in the derived class method definition, and then add the new code for that overridden method.

In the following excerpt from Example 5-1 (which appears later in this section), ListBox derives from Control and implements its own version of DrawWindow( ):

```
public override void DrawWindow( )
{
  base.DrawWindow( ); // invoke the base method
  Console.WriteLine ("Writing string to the listbox: {0}",
  listBoxContents);
}
```

The keyword override tells the compiler that this class has intentionally overridden how DrawWindow( ) works. Similarly, you'll override this method in another class, Button, also derived from Control.

In the body of Example 5-1, you'll first create three objects: a Control, a ListBox, and a Button. You'll then call DrawWindow( ) on each:

```
Control win = new Control(1,2);
ListBox lb = new ListBox(3,4,"Stand alone list box");
Button b = new Button(5,6);
win.DrawWindow( );
lb.DrawWindow( );
b.DrawWindow( );
```

This works much as you might expect. The correct DrawWindow( ) object is called for each. So far, nothing polymorphic has been done. The real magic starts when you create an array of Control objects. (Arrays are simple collections, covered in Chapter 9.) Because a ListBox *is-a* Control, you are free to place a ListBox into a Control array. You can also place a Button into an array of Control objects because a Button is also a Control:

```
Control[] winArray = new Control[3]; // declare an array of 3 Controls
winArray[0] = new Control(1,2);
winArray[1] = new ListBox(3,4,"List box in array");
winArray[2] = new Button(5,6);
```

What happens when you call DrawWindow( ) on each object?

```
for (int i = 0;i < 3; i++)
{
  winArray[i].DrawWindow( );
}
```

All the compiler knows is that it has three Control objects, and that you've called DrawWindow( ) on each. If you had not marked DrawWindow as virtual, Control's DrawWindow( ) method would be called three times. However, because you did mark DrawWindow( ) as virtual, and because the derived classes override that method, when you call DrawWindow( ) on the array, the compiler determines the runtime type of the actual objects (a Control, a ListBox, and a Button), and calls the right method on each. This is the essence of polymorphism. Example 5-1 shows the complete code for this example.

*Example 5-1. Using virtual methods*

```
using System;

namespace Using_virtual_methods
{
    public class Control
    {
        // these members are protected and thus visible
        // to derived class methods. We'll examine this
        // later in the chapter
// and then assign/refer to these as this.Top, this.Left in the rest of the code
        protected int Top { get; set; }
        protected int Left { get; set; }
        // constructor takes two integers to
        // fix location on the console
        public Control(int top, int left)
        {
            this.top = top;
            this.left = left;
        }

        // simulates drawing the window
        public virtual void DrawWindow()
        {
            Console.WriteLine("Control: drawing Control at {0}, {1}",
            top, left);
        }
    }

    // ListBox derives from Control
    public class ListBox : Control
    {
        private string listBoxContents; // new member variable

        // constructor adds a parameter
        public ListBox(
        int top,
        int left,
        string contents) :
            base(top, left) // call base constructor
        {

            listBoxContents = contents;
        }

        // an overridden version (note keyword) because in the
        // derived method we change the behavior
        public override void DrawWindow()
        {
            base.DrawWindow(); // invoke the base method
            Console.WriteLine("Writing string to the listbox: {0}",
            listBoxContents);
        }
    }
```

*Example 5-1. Using virtual methods (continued)*

```
    }

    public class Button : Control
    {
        public Button(
        int top,
        int left) :
            base(top, left)
        {
        }


        // an overridden version (note keyword) because in the
        // derived method we change the behavior
        public override void DrawWindow( )
        {
            Console.WriteLine("Drawing a button at {0}, {1}\n",
            top, left);
        }
    }

    class Program
    {
        static void Main(string[] args)
        {
            Control win = new Control(1, 2);
            ListBox lb = new ListBox(3, 4, "Stand alone list box");
            Button b = new Button(5, 6);
            win.DrawWindow( );
            lb.DrawWindow( );
            b.DrawWindow( );

            Control[] winArray = new Control[3];
            winArray[0] = new Control(1, 2);
            winArray[1] = new ListBox(3, 4, "List box in array");
            winArray[2] = new Button(5, 6);

            for (int i = 0; i < 3; i++)
            {
                winArray[i].DrawWindow( );
            }
        }
    }
}


Output:
Control: drawing Control at 1, 2
Control: drawing Control at 3, 4
Writing string to the listbox: Stand alone list box
Drawing a button at 5, 6
```

*Example 5-1. Using virtual methods (continued)*

```
Control: drawing Control at 1, 2
Control: drawing Control at 3, 4
Writing string to the listbox: List box in array
Drawing a button at 5, 6
```

Note that throughout this example we've marked the new overridden methods with the keyword override:

```
public override void DrawWindow( )
```

The compiler now knows to use the overridden method when treating these objects polymorphically. The compiler is responsible for tracking the real type of the object and for ensuring that it is ListBox.DrawWindow( ) that is called when the Control reference really points to a ListBox object.

C++ *programmers take note*: you must explicitly mark the declaration of any method that overrides a virtual method with the keyword override.

## Calling Base Class Constructors

In Example 5-1, the new class ListBox derives from Control and has its own constructor, which takes three parameters. The ListBox constructor invokes the constructor of its parent (Control) by placing a colon (:) after the parameter list and then invoking the base class with the keyword base:

```
public ListBox(
    int theTop,
    int theLeft,
    string theContents):
    base(theTop, theLeft) // call base constructor
```

Because classes can't inherit constructors, a derived class must implement its own constructor and can only make use of the constructor of its base class by calling it explicitly.

If the base class has an accessible (e.g., public) default constructor, the derived constructor is not required to invoke the base constructor explicitly; instead, the default constructor is called implicitly. However, if the base class doesn't have a default constructor, every derived constructor *must* explicitly invoke one of the base class constructors using the base keyword.

As discussed in Chapter 4, if you don't declare a constructor of any kind, the compiler will create a default constructor for you. Whether you write it or you use the one provided "by default" by the compiler, a default constructor is one that takes no parameters. Note, however, that once you do create a constructor of any kind (with or without parameters), the compiler doesn't create a default constructor for you.

## Controlling Access

The visibility of a class and its members can be restricted through the use of access modifiers, such as public, private, protected, internal, and protected internal. (See Chapter 4 for a discussion of access modifiers.)

As you've seen, public allows a member to be accessed by the member methods of other classes, and private indicates that the member is visible only to member methods of its own class. The protected keyword extends visibility to methods of derived classes, whereas internal extends visibility to methods of any class in the same assembly.

The internal protected keyword pair allows access to members of the same assembly (internal) *or* derived classes (protected). You can think of this designation as internal *or* protected.

Classes as well as their members can be designated with any of these accessibility levels. If a class member has an access designation that is different from that of the class, the more restricted access applies. Thus, if you define a class, myClass, as follows:

```
public class myClass
{
  // ...
  protected int myValue;
}
```

the accessibility for myValue is protected even though the class itself is public. A *public class* is one that is visible to any other class that wishes to interact with it. Often, classes are created that exist only to help other classes in an assembly, and these classes might be marked internal rather than public (the default for classes is internal, but it is good programming practice to make the accessibility explicit).

## Versioning with the new and override Keywords

In C#, the programmer's decision to override a virtual method is made explicit with the override keyword. This helps you to release new versions of your code; changes to the base class will not break existing code in the derived classes. The requirement to use the keyword override helps prevent that problem.

Here's how: assume for a moment that the Control base class of the preceding example was written by Company A. Suppose also that the ListBox and RadioButton classes were written by programmers from Company B using a purchased copy of the Company A Control class as a base. The programmers in Company B have little or no control over the design of the Control class, including future changes that Company A might choose to make.

Now, suppose that one of the programmers for Company B decides to add a Sort( )
method to ListBox:

```
public class ListBox : Control
{
  public virtual void Sort() {...}
}
```

This presents no problems until Company A, the author of Control, releases version
2 of its Control class, and it turns out that the programmers in Company A have also
added a Sort( ) method to their public class Control:

```
public class Control
{
  // ...
  public virtual void Sort() {...}
}
```

In other object-oriented languages (such as C++), the new virtual Sort( ) method in
Control would now act as a base method for the virtual Sort( ) method in ListBox.
The compiler would call the Sort( ) method in ListBox when you intend to call the
Sort( ) in Control. In Java, if the Sort( ) in Control has a different return type, the
class loader would consider the Sort( ) in ListBox to be an invalid override and
would fail to load.

C# prevents this confusion. In C#, a virtual function is always considered to be the
root of virtual dispatch; that is, once C# finds a virtual method, it looks no further
up the inheritance hierarchy. If a new virtual Sort( ) function is introduced into
Control, the runtime behavior of ListBox is unchanged.

When ListBox is compiled again, however, the compiler generates a warning:

```
...\class1.cs(54,24): warning CS0114: 'ListBox.Sort()' hides
inherited member 'Control.Sort()'.
To make the current member override that implementation,
add the override keyword. Otherwise add the new keyword.
```

To remove the warning, the programmer must indicate what he intends. He can
mark the ListBox Sort( ) method with new, to indicate that it is *not* an override of the
virtual method in Control:

```
public class ListBox : Control
{
 public new virtual void Sort() {...}
```

This action removes the warning. If, on the other hand, the programmer does want
to override the method in Control, he need only use the override keyword to make
that intention explicit:

```
public class ListBox : Control
{
  public override void Sort() {...}
```

To avoid this warning, it might be tempting to add the keyword new to all your virtual methods. This is a bad idea. When new appears in the code, it ought to document the versioning of code. It points a potential client to the base class to see what you aren't overriding. Using new scattershot undermines this documentation. Further, the warning exists to help identify a real issue.

# Abstract Classes

Every subclass of Control *should* implement its own DrawWindow( ) method—but nothing requires that it do so. To require subclasses to implement a method of their base, you need to designate that method as *abstract*.

An abstract method has no implementation. It creates a method name and signature that must be implemented in all derived classes. Furthermore, making one or more methods of any class abstract has the side effect of making the class abstract.

Abstract classes establish a base for derived classes, but it is not legal to instantiate an object of an abstract class. Once you declare a method to be abstract, you prohibit the creation of any instances of that class.

Thus, if you were to designate DrawWindow( ) as abstract in the Control class, you could derive from Control, but you could not create any Control objects. Each derived class would have to implement DrawWindow( ). If the derived class failed to implement the abstract method, that class would also be abstract, and again no instances would be possible.

Designating a method as abstract is accomplished by placing the keyword abstract at the beginning of the method definition, as follows:

```
abstract public void DrawWindow( );
```

(Because the method can have no implementation, there are no braces; only a semicolon.)

If one or more methods are abstract, the class definition must also be marked abstract, as in the following:

```
abstract public class Control
```

Example 5-2 illustrates the creation of an abstract Control class and an abstract DrawWindow( ) method.

*Example 5-2. Using an abstract method and class*

```
using System;

namespace abstract_method_and_class
{
    abstract public class Control
    {
```

*Example 5-2. Using an abstract method and class (continued)*

```csharp
    protected int top;
    protected int left;

    // constructor takes two integers to
    // fix location on the console
    protected Control(int top, int left)
    {
        this.top = top;
        this.left = left;
    }

    // simulates drawing the window
    // notice: no implementation
    abstract public void DrawWindow();

}

// ListBox derives from Control
public class ListBox : Control
{
    private string listBoxContents; // new member variable

    // constructor adds a parameter
    public ListBox(
    int top,
    int left,
    string contents) :
        base(top, left) // call base constructor
    {

        listBoxContents = contents;
    }

    // an overridden version implementing the
    // abstract method

    public override void DrawWindow()
    {
        Console.WriteLine("Writing string to the listbox: {0}",
        listBoxContents);
    }

}

public class Button : Control
{
    public Button(
    int top,
    int left) :
        base(top, left)
    {
    }
```

*Example 5-2. Using an abstract method and class (continued)*

```
        // implement the abstract method
        public override void DrawWindow( )
        {
            Console.WriteLine("Drawing a button at {0}, {1}\n",
            top, left);
        }

    }


    class Program
    {
        static void Main(string[] args)
        {
            Control[] winArray = new Control[3];
            winArray[0] = new ListBox(1, 2, "First List Box");
            winArray[1] = new ListBox(3, 4, "Second List Box");
            winArray[2] = new Button(5, 6);

            for (int i = 0; i < 3; i++)
            {
                winArray[i].DrawWindow( );
            }

        }
    }
}
```

In Example 5-2, the Control class has been declared abstract and therefore can't be instantiated. If you replace the first array member:

```
    winArray[0] = new ListBox(1,2,"First List Box");
```

with this code:

```
    winArray[0] = new Control(1,2);
```

the program generates the following error:

```
    Cannot create an instance of the abstract class or interface
    'abstractmethods.Control'
```

You can instantiate the ListBox and Button objects because these classes override the abstract method, thus making the classes *concrete* (i.e., not abstract).

## Limitations of Abstract

Although designating DrawWindow( ) as abstract does force all the derived classes to implement the method, this is a very limited solution to the problem. If we derive a class from ListBox (e.g., DropDownListBox), nothing forces that derived class to implement its own DrawWindow( ) method.

*C++ programmers take note*: in C#, it is not possible for `Control.DrawWindow( )` to provide an implementation, so you can't take advantage of the common `DrawWindow( )` routines that might otherwise be shared by the derived classes.

Finally, abstract classes should not just be an implementation trick; they should represent the idea of an abstraction that establishes a "contract" for all derived classes. In other words, abstract classes describe the public methods of the classes that will implement the abstraction.

The idea of an abstract `Control` class ought to lay out the common characteristics and behaviors of all `Control`s, even if you never intend to instantiate the abstraction `Control` itself.

The idea of an abstract class is implied in the word *abstract*. It serves to implement the abstraction of "control" that will be manifest in the various concrete instances of `Control`, such as browser window, frame, button, listbox, or drop-down menu. The abstract class establishes what a `Control` is, even though you never intend to create a control per se. An alternative to using `abstract` is to define an interface, as described in Chapter 8.

## Sealed Class

The obverse side of the design coin from abstract is *sealed*. Although an abstract class is intended to be derived from and to provide a template for its subclasses to follow, a sealed class doesn't allow classes to derive from it at all. Placed before the class declaration, the `sealed` keyword precludes derivation. Classes are most often marked sealed to prevent accidental inheritance.

*Java programmers take note*: a *sealed* class in C# is the equivalent of a *final* class in Java.

If you change the declaration of `Control` in Example 5-2 from `abstract` to `sealed` (eliminating the `abstract` keyword from the `DrawWindow( )` declaration as well), the program will fail to compile. If you try to build this project, the compiler will return the following error message:

```
'ListBox' cannot inherit from sealed class 'Control'
```

among many other complaints (such as that you can't create a new protected member in a sealed class).

# The Root of All Types: Object

All C# classes, of any type, are treated as though they ultimately derive from System. Object. Interestingly, this includes value types.

A base class is the immediate "parent" of a derived class. A derived class can be the base to further derived classes, creating an inheritance "tree" or hierarchy. A root class is the topmost class in an inheritance hierarchy.

In C#, the root class is Object. The nomenclature is a bit confusing until you imagine an upside-down tree, with the root on top, and the derived classes below. Thus, the base class is considered to be "above" the derived class.

*C++ programmers take note*: C# uses single inheritance with a monolithic class hierarchy: every class inherits from a base class of Object, and multiple inheritance is not possible. However, C# interfaces provide many of the benefits of multiple inheritance. (See Chapter 8 for more information.)

Object provides a number of virtual methods that subclasses can and do override. These include Equals() to determine whether two objects are the same; GetType(), which returns the type of the object (discussed in Chapter 8); and ToString(), which returns a string to represent the current object (discussed in Chapter 10). Table 5-1 summarizes the methods of Object.

*Table 5-1. The methods of Object*

| Method | What it does |
| --- | --- |
| Equals() | Evaluates whether two objects are equivalent |
| GetHashCode() | Allows objects to provide their own hash function for use in collections (see Chapter 9) |
| GetType() | Provides access to the type object |
| ToString() | Provides a string representation of the object |
| Finalize() | Cleans up unmanaged resources; implemented by a destructor (see Chapter 4) |
| MemberwiseClone() | Creates copies of the object; should never be implemented by your type |
| ReferenceEquals() | Evaluates whether two objects refer to the same instance |

Example 5-3 illustrates the use of the ToString() method inherited from Object, as well as the fact that primitive datatypes such as int can be treated as though they inherit from Object. Note that the DisplayValue method expects an object, but works perfectly fine if you pass in an integer.

*Example 5-3. Inheriting from Object*

```csharp
using System;

namespace Inheriting_From_Object
{
    public class SomeClass
    {
        private int val;

        public SomeClass(int someVal)
        {
            val = someVal;
        }

        public override string ToString()
        {
            return val.ToString();
        }
    }

    class Program
    {
        static void DisplayValue( object o )
        {
            Console.WriteLine(
                "The value of the object passed in is {0}", o;
        }


        static void Main(string[] args)
        {

            int i = 5;
            Console.WriteLine("The value of i is: {0}", i.ToString());
            DisplayValue(i);

            SomeClass s = new SomeClass(7);
            Console.WriteLine("The value of s is {0}", s.ToString());
            DisplayValue(s);
        }
    }
}
```

```
Output:
The value of i is: 5
The value of the object passed in is 5
The value of s is 7
The value of the object passed in is 7
```

The documentation for Object.ToString( ) reveals its signature:

```csharp
public virtual string ToString( );
```

It is a public virtual method that returns a string and that takes no parameters. All the built-in types, such as int, derive from Object and so can invoke Object's methods. The Write and WriteLine methods of Console will automagically invoke the ToString( ) method on any object provided.

Example 5-3 overrides the virtual function for SomeClass, which is the usual case, so that the class's ToString( ) method will return a meaningful value. If you comment out the overridden function, the base method will be invoked, which will change the output to:

```
The value of s is SomeClass
```

Thus, the default behavior is to return a string with the name of the class itself.

Classes don't need to explicitly declare that they derive from Object; the inheritance is implicit.

# Nesting Classes

Classes have members, and it is entirely possible for the member of a class to be another user-defined type. Thus, a Button class might have a member of type Location, and a Location class might contain members of type Point. Finally, Point might contain members of type int.

At times, the contained class might exist only to serve the outer class, and there might be no reason for it to be otherwise visible. (In short, the contained class acts as a helper class.) You can define the helper class within the definition of the outer class. The contained, inner class is called a *nested* class, and the class that contains it is called, simply, the *outer* class.

Nested classes have the advantage of access to all the members of the outer class. A method of a nested class can access private members of the outer class.

In addition, the nested class can be hidden from all other classes—that is, it can be private to the outer class.

Finally, a nested class that is public is accessed within the scope of the outer class. If Outer is the outer class, and Nested is the (public) inner class, refer to Nested as Outer.Nested, with the outer class acting (more or less) as a namespace or scope.

*Java programmers take note*: nested classes are roughly equivalent to static inner classes; there is no C# equivalent to Java's nonstatic inner classes.

Example 5-4 features a nested class of Fraction named FractionArtist. The job of FractionArtist is to render the fraction on the console. In this example, the rendering is handled by a pair of simple WriteLine( ) statements.

*Example 5-4. Using a nested class*

```
using System;

namespace Nested_Class
{
    public class Fraction
    {
        private int numerator;
        private int denominator;

        public Fraction(int numerator, int denominator)
        {
            this.numerator = numerator;
            this.denominator = denominator;
        }

        public override string ToString()
        {
            return String.Format("{0}/{1}",
                numerator, denominator);
        }

        internal class FractionArtist
        {
            public void Draw(Fraction f)
            {
                Console.WriteLine("Drawing the numerator: {0}",
                    f.numerator);
                Console.WriteLine("Drawing the denominator: {0}",
                    f.denominator);
            }
        }
    }

    class Program
    {
        static void Main(string[] args)
        {
            Fraction f1 = new Fraction(3, 4);
            Console.WriteLine("f1: {0}", f1.ToString());

            Fraction.FractionArtist fa = new Fraction.FractionArtist();
            fa.Draw(f1);

        }
    }
}
```

The nested class is shown in bold. The FractionArtist class provides only a single member, the Draw( ) method. What is particularly interesting is that Draw( ) has access to the private data members f.numerator and f.denominator, to which it wouldn't have had access if it weren't a nested class.

Notice in Main( ) that to declare an instance of this nested class, you must specify the type name of the outer class:

```
Fraction.FractionArtist fa = new Fraction.FractionArtist();
```

FractionArtist is scoped to be within the Fraction class.

# CHAPTER 6

# Operator Overloading

It is a design goal of C# that user-defined classes can have all the functionality of built-in types. For example, suppose you have defined a type to represent fractions. Ensuring that this class has all the functionality of the built-in types means that you must be able to perform arithmetic on instances of your fractions (e.g., add two fractions, multiply, etc.) and convert fractions to and from built-in types such as integer (int). You could, of course, implement methods for each operation and invoke them by writing statements such as:

```
Fraction theSum = firstFraction.Add(secondFraction);
```

Although this will work, it is ugly, and is not how the built-in types are used. It would be much better to write:

```
Fraction theSum = firstFraction + secondFraction;
```

Statements like this are intuitive and consistent with how built-in types, such as int, are added.

In this chapter, you will learn techniques for adding standard operators to your user-defined types. You will also learn how to add conversion operators so that your user-defined types can be implicitly and explicitly converted to other types.

## Using the operator Keyword

In C#, you implement operators by creating static methods whose return values represent the result of an operation and whose parameters are the operands. When you create an operator for a class you say that you have "overloaded" that operator, much as you might overload any member method. Thus, to overload the addition operator (+), you would write:

```
public static Fraction operator+(Fraction lhs, Fraction rhs)
```

It is our convention to name the parameters lhs and rhs. The parameter name lhs stands for "lefthand side," and reminds us that the first parameter represents the lefthand side of the operation. Similarly, rhs stands for "righthand side."

The C# syntax for overloading an operator is to write the word operator followed by the operator to overload. The operator keyword is a method modifier. Thus, to overload the addition operator (+), you write operator+.

The operator then acts as a method, with the body of the operator method implementing the action of the operator (e.g., doing the work of whatever it is you mean by +).

When you write:

```
Fraction theSum = firstFraction + secondFraction;
```

the overloaded + operator is invoked, with the first Fraction passed as the first argument, and the second Fraction passed as the second argument. When the compiler sees the expression:

```
firstFraction + secondFraction
```

it translates that expression into:

```
Fraction.operator+(firstFraction, secondFraction)
```

The result is that a new Fraction is returned, which in this case is assigned to the Fraction object named theSum.

*C++ programmers take note*: it is not possible to create nonstatic operators, and thus binary operators must take two operands.

# Supporting Other .NET Languages

C# provides the ability to overload operators for your classes, even though this is not, strictly speaking, in the Common Language Specification (CLS). Other .NET languages might not support operator overloading, and it is important to ensure that your class supports the alternative methods that these other languages might call to create the same effect.

Thus, if you overload the addition operator (+), you might also want to provide an Add( ) method that does the same work. Operator overloading ought to be a syntactic shortcut, not the only path for your objects to accomplish a given task.

# Creating Useful Operators

Operator overloading can make your code more intuitive and enable it to act more like the built-in types. It can also make your code unmanageable, complex, and obtuse if you break the common idiom for the use of operators. Resist the temptation to use operators in new and idiosyncratic ways.

For example, although it might be tempting to overload the increment operator (++) on an employee class to invoke a method incrementing the employee's pay level, this can create tremendous confusion for clients of your class. It is best to use operator overloading sparingly, and only when its meaning is clear and consistent with how the built-in classes operate.

# Logical Pairs

It is quite common to overload the equality operator (==) to test whether two objects are equal (however equality might be defined for your object). C# insists that if you overload the equals (==) operator, you must also overload the not-equals operator (!=). Similarly, the less-than (<) and greater-than (>) operators must be paired, as must the less-than or equals (<=) and greater-than or equals (>=) operators.

# The Equality Operator

If you overload the equality operator (==), it is recommended that you also override the virtual Equals( ) method provided by Object and route its functionality back to the equals operator. This allows your class to be polymorphic, and provides compatibility with other .NET languages that don't overload operators (but do support method overloading). The .NET Framework classes will not use the overloaded operators, but will expect your classes to implement the underlying methods. The Object class implements the Equals( ) method with this signature:

```
public virtual bool Equals(object o)
```

By overriding this method, you allow your Fraction class to act polymorphically with all other objects. Inside the body of Equals( ), you will need to ensure that you are comparing with another Fraction, and if so, you can pass the implementation along to the equals operator definition that you've written:

```
public override bool Equals(object o)
{
  if (! (o is Fraction) )
  {
     return false;
  }
  return this == (Fraction) o;
}
```

The is operator is used to check whether the runtime type of an object is compatible with the operand (in this case, Fraction). Thus, o is Fraction will evaluate true if o is in fact a type compatible with Fraction.

 The compiler will also expect you to override GetHashCode, as explained shortly.

## Conversion Operators

C# converts int to long implicitly, and allows you to convert long to int explicitly. The conversion from int to long is *implicit* (it happens without requiring any special syntax), and is safe because you know that any int will fit into the memory representation of a long. The reverse operation, from long to int, must be *explicit* (using a cast operator) because it is possible to lose information in the conversion:

```
int myInt = 5;
long myLong;
myLong = myInt; // implicit
myInt = (int) myLong; // explicit
```

You will want to provide the same functionality for your fractions. Given an int, you can support an implicit conversion to a fraction because any whole value is equal to that value over 1 (e.g., 15==15/1).

Given a fraction, you might want to provide an explicit conversion back to an integer, understanding that some value might be lost. Thus, you might convert 9/4 to the integer value 2.

When implementing your own conversions, the keyword implicit is used when the conversion is guaranteed to succeed and no information will be lost; otherwise, explicit is used.

 Make sure to use implicit whenever you don't use explicit!

## Putting Operators to Work

Example 6-1 illustrates how you might implement implicit and explicit conversions, and some of the operators of the Fraction class. (Although we've used Console.WriteLine() to print messages illustrating which method we're entering, the better way to pursue this kind of trace is with the debugger. You can place a breakpoint on each test statement, and then step into the code, watching the invocation of the constructors as they occur.) When you compile this example, it will generate some warnings because GetHashCode() is not implemented (see Chapter 9).

*Example 6-1. Defining conversions and operators for the Fraction class*

```
using System;

namespace Conversions
{

    public class Fraction
    {
        private int numerator;
        private int denominator;

        public Fraction(int numerator, int denominator)
        {
            Console.WriteLine("In Fraction Constructor(int, int)");
            this.numerator = numerator;
            this.denominator = denominator;
        }

        public Fraction(int wholeNumber)
        {
            Console.WriteLine("In Fraction Constructor(int)");
            numerator = wholeNumber;
            denominator = 1;
        }

        public static implicit operator Fraction(int theInt)
        {
            Console.WriteLine("In implicit conversion to Fraction");
            return new Fraction(theInt);
        }

        public static explicit operator int(Fraction theFraction)
        {
            Console.WriteLine("In explicit conversion to int");
              return theFraction.numerator / theFraction.denominator;
        }

        public static bool operator ==(Fraction lhs, Fraction rhs)
        {
            Console.WriteLine("In operator ==");
            if (lhs.denominator == rhs.denominator &&
            lhs.numerator == rhs.numerator)
            {
                return true;
            }
            // code here to handle unlike fractions
            return false;
        }

        public static bool operator !=(Fraction lhs, Fraction rhs)
        {
            Console.WriteLine("In operator !=");
```

```
        return !(lhs == rhs);
    }

    public override bool Equals(object o)
    {
        Console.WriteLine("In method Equals");
        if (!(o is Fraction))
        {
            return false;
        }
        return this == (Fraction)o;
    }

    public static Fraction operator +(Fraction lhs, Fraction rhs)
    {
        Console.WriteLine("In operator+");
        if (lhs.denominator == rhs.denominator)
        {
            return new Fraction(lhs.numerator + rhs.numerator,
            lhs.denominator);
        }

        // simplistic solution for unlike fractions
        // 1/2 + 3/4 == (1*4) + (3*2) / (2*4) == 10/8
        int firstProduct = lhs.numerator * rhs.denominator;
        int secondProduct = rhs.numerator * lhs.denominator;
        return new Fraction(
        firstProduct + secondProduct,
        lhs.denominator * rhs.denominator
        );
    }

    public override string ToString()
    {
        String s = numerator.ToString() + "/" +
        denominator.ToString();
        return s;
    }
}

class Program
{
    static void Main(string[] args)
    {
        Fraction f1 = new Fraction(3, 4);
        Console.WriteLine("f1: {0}", f1.ToString());

        Fraction f2 = new Fraction(2, 4);
        Console.WriteLine("f2: {0}", f2.ToString());

        Fraction f3 = f1 + f2;
        Console.WriteLine("f1 + f2 = f3: {0}", f3.ToString());
```

```
        Fraction f4 = f3 + 5;
        Console.WriteLine("f3 + 5 = f4: {0}", f4.ToString());

        Fraction f5 = new Fraction(2, 4);
        if (f5 == f2)
        {
            Console.WriteLine("F5: {0} == F2: {1}",
            f5.ToString(),
            f2.ToString());
        }
    }
}
}
```

The Fraction class begins with two constructors. One takes a numerator and denominator, and the other takes a whole number. The constructors are followed by the declaration of two conversion operators. The first conversion operator changes an integer into a Fraction:

```
public static implicit operator Fraction(int theInt)
{
  return new Fraction(theInt);
}
```

This conversion is marked implicit because any whole number (int) can be converted to a Fraction by setting the numerator to the int and the denominator to 1. Delegate this responsibility to the constructor that takes an int.

The second conversion operator is for the explicit conversion of Fractions into integers:

```
public static explicit operator int(Fraction theFraction)
{
 return theFraction.numerator /
 theFraction.denominator;
}
```

Because this example uses integer division, it will truncate the value. Thus, if the fraction is 15/16, the resulting integer value will be 0. A more sophisticated conversion operator might accomplish rounding.

The conversion operators are followed by the equals operator (==) and the not equals operator (!=). Remember that if you implement one of these equality operators, you must implement the other.

Value equality has been defined for a Fraction such that the numerators and denominators must match. For this exercise, 3/4 and 6/8 aren't considered equal. Again, a more sophisticated implementation would reduce these fractions and notice the equality.

Include an override of the Object class' Equals() method so that your Fraction objects can be treated polymorphically with any other object. Your implementation is to delegate the evaluation of equality to the equality operator.

A Fraction class would, no doubt, implement all the arithmetic operators (addition, subtraction, multiplication, division). To keep the illustration simple, we'll implement only addition, and even here we'll simplify greatly. Check to see whether the denominators are the same; if so, add the following numerators:

```
public static Fraction operator+(Fraction lhs, Fraction rhs)
{
  if (lhs.denominator == rhs.denominator)
  {
    return new Fraction(lhs.numerator+rhs.numerator,
      lhs.denominator);
  }
```

If the denominators aren't the same, cross multiply:

```
int firstProduct = lhs.numerator * rhs.denominator;
int secondProduct = rhs.numerator * lhs.denominator;
return new Fraction(
  firstProduct + secondProduct,
  lhs.denominator * rhs.denominator
  );
```

This code is best understood with an example. If you were adding 1/2 and 3/4, you can multiply the first numerator (1) by the second denominator (4), and store the result (4) in firstProduct. You can also multiply the second numerator (3) by the first denominator (2) and store that result (6) in secondProduct. You add these products (6+4) to a sum of 10, which is the numerator for the answer. You then multiply the two denominators (2*4) to generate the new denominator (8). The resulting fraction (10/8) is the correct answer.

Finally, you override ToString() so that Fraction can return its value in the format numerator/denominator:

```
public override string ToString()
{
 String s = numerator.ToString() + "/" +
 denominator.ToString();
 return s;
}
```

With your Fraction class in hand, you're ready to test. Your first tests create simple fractions, 3/4 and 2/4:

```
Fraction f1 = new Fraction(3,4);
Console.WriteLine("f1: {0}", f1.ToString());

Fraction f2 = new Fraction(2,4);
Console.WriteLine("f2: {0}", f2.ToString());
```

The output from this is what you would expect—the invocation of the constructors and the value printed in WriteLine( ) looks like this:

```
In Fraction Constructor(int, int)
f1: 3/4
In Fraction Constructor(int, int)
f2: 2/4
```

The next line in Main( ) invokes the static operator+. The purpose of this operator is to add two fractions and return the sum in a new fraction:

```
Fraction f3 = f1 + f2;
Console.WriteLine("f1 + f2 = f3: {0}", f3.ToString( ));
```

Examining the output reveals how operator+ works:

```
In operator+
In Fraction Constructor(int, int)
f1 + f2 = f3: 5/4
```

The operator+ is invoked, and then the constructor for f3, taking the two int values representing the numerator and denominator of the resulting new fraction. The next test in Main( ) adds an int to the Fraction f3, and assigns the resulting value to a new Fraction, f4:

```
Fraction f4 = f3 + 5;
Console.WriteLine("f3 + 5: {0}", f4.ToString( ));
```

The output shows the steps for the various conversions:

```
In implicit conversion to Fraction
In Fraction Constructor(int)
In operator+
In Fraction Constructor(int, int)
f3 + 5 = f4: 25/4
```

Notice that the implicit conversion operator was invoked to convert 5 to a fraction. In the return statement from the implicit conversion operator, the Fraction constructor was called, creating the fraction 5/1. This new fraction was then passed along with Fraction f3 to operator+, and the sum was passed to the constructor for f4. In your final test, a new fraction (f5) is created. Test whether it is equal to f2. If so, print their values:

```
Fraction f5 = new Fraction(2,4);
if (f5 == f2)
{
 Console.WriteLine("F5: {0} == F2: {1}",
 f5.ToString( ),
 f2.ToString( ));
}
```

The output shows the creation of f5, and then the invocation of the overloaded equals operator:

```
In Fraction Constructor(int, int)
In operator ==
F5: 2/4 == F2: 2/4
```

# CHAPTER 7

# Structs

A *struct* is a simple user-defined type, a lightweight alternative to a class. Structs are similar to classes in that they may contain constructors, properties, methods, fields, operators, nested types, and indexers (see Chapter 9).

There are also significant differences between classes and structs. For instance, structs don't support inheritance or destructors. More important, although a class is a reference type, a struct is a *value type*. (See Chapter 3 for more information about classes and types.) Thus, structs are useful for representing objects that don't require reference semantics.

The consensus view is that you ought to use structs only for types that are small, simple, and similar in their behavior and characteristics to built-in types.

 *C++ programmers take note*: the meaning of C#'s struct construct is very different from C++'s. In C++, a struct is exactly like a class, except that the visibility (public versus private) is different by default. In C#, structs are value types, whereas classes are reference types, and C# structs have other limitations, as described in this chapter.

Structs are somewhat more efficient in their use of memory in arrays (see Chapter 9). However, they can be less efficient when used in nongeneric collections. Collections that take objects expect references, and structs must be boxed. There is overhead in boxing and unboxing, and classes might be more efficient in some large collections. This concern is greatly ameliorated by using generic collections (see Chapter 9), and the truth is that many C# programmers go months at a time without using structs at all.

On the other hand, if you have a class that has, as its member variables, 10 structs instead of 10 objects, when that class is created on the heap, one big object is created (the class with its 10 structs) rather than 11 objects. That allows the garbage collector to do much less work when your containing class is ready to be destroyed, making your program more efficient. If you have a lot of classes like that, and you create and destroy them frequently, the performance differences can begin to be noticeable.

In this chapter, you will learn how to define and work with structs, and how to use constructors to initialize their values.

## Defining Structs

The syntax for declaring a struct is almost identical to that for a class:

```
[attributes] [access-modifiers] struct identifier [:interface-list]
{ struct-members }
```

Example 7-1 illustrates the definition of a struct. Location represents a point on a two-dimensional surface. Notice that the struct Location is declared exactly as a class would be, except for the use of the keyword struct. Also notice that the Location constructor takes two integers and assigns their value to the instance members, xVal and yVal. The x and y coordinates of Location are declared as properties.

*Example 7-1. Creating a struct*

```
using System;

namespace CreatingAStruct
{
    public struct Location
    {
        public int X { get; set; }
        public int Y { get; set; }

        public override string ToString()
        {
            return (String.Format("{0}, {1}", X, Y));
        }

    }

    public class Tester
    {
        public void myFunc(Location loc)
        {
            loc.X = 50;
            loc.Y = 100;
            Console.WriteLine("In MyFunc loc: {0}", loc);
        }
        static void Main()
        {
            Location loc1 = new Location();
            loc1.X = 200;
            loc1.Y = 300;
            Console.WriteLine("Loc1 location: {0}", loc1);
```

*Example 7-1. Creating a struct (continued)*

```
        Tester t = new Tester( );
        t.myFunc(loc1);
        Console.WriteLine("Loc1 location: {0}", loc1);
    }
  }
}
```

```
Output:
Loc1 location: 200, 300
In MyFunc loc: 50, 100
Loc1 location: 200, 300
```

Unlike classes, structs don't support inheritance. They implicitly derive from Object (as do all types in C#, including the built-in types), but can't inherit from any other class or struct. Structs are also implicitly *sealed* (i.e., no class or struct can derive from a struct). Like classes, however, structs can implement multiple interfaces. Additional differences include the following:

*No destructor or custom default constructor*
> Structs can't have destructors, nor can they have a custom parameterless (default) constructor; however, the CLR will initialize your structure and zero out all the fields if your object is called as though it had a default constructor, as shown in the example.

*No initialization*
> You can't initialize an instance field in a struct. Thus, it is illegal to write:

>     ```
>     private int xVal = 50;
>     private int yVal = 100;
>     ```

> though that would have been fine had this been a class.

Structs are designed to be simple and lightweight. Although private member data promotes data-hiding and encapsulation, some programmers feel it is overkill for structs. They make the member data public, thus simplifying the implementation of the struct. Other programmers feel that properties provide a clean and simple interface, and that good programming practice demands data-hiding even with simple lightweight objects.

# Creating Structs

You create an instance of a struct by using the new keyword in an assignment statement, just as you would for a class. In Example 7-1, the Tester class creates an instance of Location as follows:

```
Location loc1 = new Location( );
```

Here, the new instance is named loc1, and the fields are initialized to 0. The example then uses the public properties to set the values of the fields to 200 and 300, respectively.

## Structs As Value Types

The definition of the Tester class in Example 7-1 includes a Location object* struct (loc1) created with the values 200 and 300. This line of code calls the Location constructor:

```
Location loc1 = new Location(200,300);
```

Then WriteLine( ) is called:

```
Console.WriteLine("Loc1 location: {0}", loc1);
```

WriteLine( ) is expecting an object, but of course, Location is a struct (a value type). The compiler automatically wraps the struct in an object, a process called boxing (as it would any value type), and it is the boxed object that is passed to WriteLine( ). ToString( ) is called on the boxed object, and because the struct (implicitly) inherits from object, it is able to respond polymorphically, overriding the method just as any other object might:

```
Loc1 location: 200, 300
```

> You can avoid this boxing by changing the preceding snippet to:
> ```
> Console.WriteLine("Loc1 location: {0}",
>     loc1.ToString( ));
> ```
> You avoid the box operation by calling ToString directly on a variable of a value type where the value type provides an override of ToString.

Structs are value objects, however, and when passed to a function, they are passed by value—as seen in the next line of code, in which the loc1 object is passed to the myFunc( ) method:

```
t.myFunc(loc1);
```

In myFunc( ), new values are assigned to x and y, and these new values are printed:

```
Loc1 location: 50, 100
```

When you return to the calling function (Main( )), and call WriteLine( ) again, the values are unchanged:

```
Loc1 location: 200, 300
```

---

* Throughout this book, I use the term *object* to refer to reference and value types. There is some debate in the object-oriented world about this, but I take solace in the fact that Microsoft has implemented the value types as though they inherited from the root class Object (and thus, you may call all of Object's methods on any value type, including the built-in types such as int).

The struct was passed as a value object, and a copy was made in myFunc( ). Try to change the declaration to class:

```
public class Location
```

and run the test again. Here is the output:

```
Loc1 location: 200, 300
In MyFunc loc: 50, 100
Loc1 location: 50, 100
```

This time the Location object has reference semantics. Thus, when the values are changed in myFunc( ), they are changed on the actual object back in Main( ).*

---

* Another way to solve this problem is to use the keyword ref (as explained in the "Passing by Reference" section in Chapter 4), which allows you to pass a value type by reference.

# CHAPTER 8

# Interfaces

An *interface* is a contract that guarantees to a client how a class or struct will behave (I'll just use the term *class* for the rest of this chapter, though everything I say will apply to structs as well).

When a class *implements* an interface, it tells any potential client "I guarantee I'll support *all* the methods, properties, events, and indexers of the named interface." (See Chapter 4 for information about methods and properties, Chapter 12 for information about events, and Chapter 9 for coverage of indexers.) See also the sidebar "Abstract Class Versus Interface Versus Mix-Ins."

These contracts are made manifest using the interface keyword, which declares a reference type that encapsulates the contract.

When you define an interface, you may define methods, properties, indexers, and events that will (and must!) be implemented by any class that implements the interface.

*Java programmers take note*: C# doesn't support the use of constant fields (member constants) in interfaces. The closest analog is the use of enumerated constants (enums).

In this chapter, you will learn how to create, implement, and use interfaces. You'll learn how to implement multiple interfaces, and how to combine and extend interfaces, as well as how to test whether a class has implemented an interface.

## Defining and Implementing an Interface

The syntax for defining an interface is as follows:

```
[attributes] [access-modifier] interface interface-name[:base-list]
{interface-body}
```

Don't worry about attributes for now; I cover them in Chapter 20.

## Abstract Class Versus Interface Versus Mix-Ins

An interface offers an alternative to an abstract class for creating contracts among classes and their clients; the difference is that abstract classes serve as the top of an inheritance hierarchy, whereas interfaces may add their contract to numerous inheritance trees.

Thus, for example, you might have an interface named IPrintable (by convention, interface names begin with a capital *I*, such as IPrintable, IStorable, IClaudius). IPrintable defines all the methods, events, and so on that a class must implement to be printable, and any number of classes (notes, documents, calendar items, email, spreadsheet documents) might implement that interface without having to share a common root element.

Further, because a subset of these IPrintable types might also be IStorable, using interfaces rather than abstract classes keeps your inheritance tree much cleaner. This allows inheritance to define the *is-a* relationship (a note *is a* document) rather than the *implements* relationship (both notes and email implement IPrintable).

Historical Note of Interest to East Coast Geeks: In Somerville, Massachusetts, there was, at one time, an ice cream parlor where you could have candies and other goodies "mixed in" with your chosen ice cream flavor. This seemed like a good metaphor to some of the object-oriented pioneers from nearby MIT who were working on the fortuitously named SCOOPS programming language. They appropriated the term *mix-in* for classes that mixed in additional capabilities. These mix-in—or capability—classes serve much the same role as interfaces do in C#.

I discussed access modifiers, including public, private, protected, internal, and protected internal, in Chapter 4.

The interface keyword is followed by the name of the interface. It is common (but not required) to begin the name of your interface with a capital *I* (thus, IStorable, ICloneable, IClaudius, etc.).

The base-list lists the interfaces that this interface extends (as described in the next section, "Implementing More Than One Interface").

The interface-body describes the methods, properties, and so forth that must be implemented by the implementing class.

Suppose you wish to create an interface that describes the methods and properties a class needs, to be stored to and retrieved from a database or other storage such as a file. You decide to call this interface IStorable.

In this interface, you might specify two methods: Read( ) and Write( ), which appear in the interface-body:

```
interface IStorable
{
```

```
        void Read();
        void Write(object);
    }
```

The purpose of an interface is to define the capabilities you want to have available in a class.

For example, you might create a class, Document. It turns out that Document types can be stored in a database, so you decide to have Document implement the IStorable interface.

To do so, use the same syntax as though the new Document class were inheriting from IStorable—a colon (:), followed by the interface name:

```
    public class Document : IStorable
    {
        public void Read() {...}
        public void Write(object obj) {...}
        // ...
    }
```

It is now your responsibility, as the author of the Document class, to provide a meaningful implementation of the IStorable methods. Having designated Document as implementing IStorable, you must implement all the IStorable methods, or you will generate an error when you compile. I illustrate this in Example 8-1, in which the Document class implements the IStorable interface.

*Example 8-1. Using a simple interface*

```
using System;


namespace SimpleInterface
{
    interface IStorable
    {
        // no access modifiers, methods are public
        // no implementation
        void Read();
        void Write(object obj);
        int Status { get; set; }

    }

    // create a class which implements the IStorable interface
    public class Document : IStorable
    {


        public Document(string s)
        {
            Console.WriteLine("Creating document with: {0}", s);
        }
```

*Example 8-1. Using a simple interface (continued)*

```
        // implement the Read method
        public void Read( )
        {
            Console.WriteLine(
            "Implementing the Read Method for IStorable");
        }

        // implement the Write method
        public void Write(object o)
        {
            Console.WriteLine(
            "Implementing the Write Method for IStorable");
        }

        public int Status  { get; set; }


    }

    // Take our interface out for a spin
    public class Tester
    {

        static void Main( )
        {
            // access the methods in the Document object
            Document doc = new Document("Test Document");
            doc.Status = -1;
            doc.Read( );
            Console.WriteLine("Document Status: {0}", doc.Status);
        }
    }
}
```

```
Output:
Creating document with: Test Document
Implementing the Read Method for IStorable
Document Status: -1
```

Example 8-1 defines a simple interface, IStorable, with two methods (Read( ) and Write( )), and a property (Status) of type integer. Notice that the property declaration doesn't provide an implementation for get and set, but simply designates that there *is* a get and a set:

```
    int Status { get; set; }
```

Notice also that the IStorable method declarations don't include access modifiers (e.g., public, protected, internal, private). In fact, providing an access modifier generates a compile error. Interface methods are implicitly public because an interface is a contract meant to be used by other classes. You can't create an instance of an interface; instead, you instantiate a class that implements the interface.

The class implementing the interface must fulfill the contract exactly and completely. Document must provide both a Read( ) and a Write( ) method and the Status property. *How* it fulfills these requirements, however, is entirely up to the Document class. Although IStorable dictates that Document must have a Status property, it doesn't know or care whether Document stores the actual status as a member variable or looks it up in a database. The details are up to the implementing class.

## Implementing More Than One Interface

Classes can implement more than one interface. For example, if your Document class can be stored and it also can be compressed, you might choose to implement both the IStorable and ICompressible interfaces, shown here:

```
interface ICompressible
{
    void Compress( );
    void Decompress( );
}
```

To do so, change the declaration (in the base list) to indicate that both interfaces are implemented, separating the two interfaces with commas:

```
public class Document : IStorable, ICompressible
```

Having done this, the Document class must also implement the methods specified by the ICompressible interface:

```
public void Compress( )
{
    Console.WriteLine("Implementing the Compress Method");
}

public void Decompress( )
{
    Console.WriteLine("Implementing the Decompress Method");
}
```

## Extending Interfaces

It is possible to extend an existing interface to add new methods or members, or to modify how existing members work. For example, you might extend ICompressible with a new interface, ILoggedCompressible, which extends the original interface with methods to keep track of the bytes saved:

```
interface ILoggedCompressible : ICompressible
{
    void LogSavedBytes( );
}
```

Effectively, by extending ICompressible in this way, you are saying that anything that implements ILoggedCompressible must also implement ICompressible.

Classes are now free to implement either ICompressible or ILoggedCompressible, depending on whether they need the additional functionality. If a class does implement ILoggedCompressible, it must implement all the methods of both ILoggedCompressible and ICompressible. Objects of that type can be cast to ILoggedCompressible or to ICompressible.

## Combining Interfaces

Similarly, you can create new interfaces by combining existing interfaces and, optionally, adding new methods or properties. For example, you might decide to create IStorableCompressible. This interface would combine the methods of each of the other two interfaces, but would also add a new method to store the original size of the precompressed item:

```
interface IStorableCompressible : IStorable, ILoggedCompressible
{
    void LogOriginalSize( );
}
```

Example 8-2 illustrates extending and combining interfaces.

*Example 8-2. Extending and combining interfaces*

```
using System;

namespace ExtendAndCombineInterface
{
    interface IStorable
    {
        void Read( );
        void Write(object obj);
        int Status { get; set; }

    }

    // here's the new interface
    interface ICompressible
    {
        void Compress( );
        void Decompress( );
    }

    // Extend the interface
    interface ILoggedCompressible : ICompressible
    {
        void LogSavedBytes( );
    }
```

*Example 8-2. Extending and combining interfaces (continued)*

```csharp
// Combine Interfaces
interface IStorableCompressible : IStorable, ILoggedCompressible
{
    void LogOriginalSize( );
}

// yet another interface
interface IEncryptable
{
    void Encrypt( );
    void Decrypt( );
}

public class Document : IStorableCompressible, IEncryptable
{

    // hold the data for IStorable's Status property
    private int status = 0;

    // the document constructor
    public Document(string s)
    {
        Console.WriteLine("Creating document with: {0}", s);

    }

    // implement IStorable
    public void Read( )
    {
        Console.WriteLine(
        "Implementing the Read Method for IStorable");
    }

    public void Write(object o)
    {
        Console.WriteLine(
        "Implementing the Write Method for IStorable");
    }

    public int Status { get; set; }

    // implement ICompressible
    public void Compress( )
    {
        Console.WriteLine("Implementing Compress");
    }

    public void Decompress( )
    {
        Console.WriteLine("Implementing Decompress");
    }
```

*Example 8-2. Extending and combining interfaces (continued)*

```csharp
        // implement ILoggedCompressible
        public void LogSavedBytes( )
        {
            Console.WriteLine("Implementing LogSavedBytes");
        }

        // implement IStorableCompressible
        public void LogOriginalSize( )
        {
            Console.WriteLine("Implementing LogOriginalSize");
        }

        // implement IEncryptable
        public void Encrypt( )
        {
            Console.WriteLine("Implementing Encrypt");

        }

        public void Decrypt( )
        {
            Console.WriteLine("Implementing Decrypt");

        }
    }

    public class Tester
    {

        static void Main( )
        {
            // create a document object
            Document doc = new Document("Test Document");
            doc.Read( );
            doc.Compress( );
            doc.LogSavedBytes( );
            doc.Compress( );
            doc.LogOriginalSize( );
            doc.LogSavedBytes( );
            doc.Compress( );
            doc.Read( );
            doc.Encrypt( );
        }
    }
}

Output
Creating document with: Test Document
Implementing the Read Method for IStorable
Implementing Compress
Implementing LogSavedBytes
Implementing Compress
```

*Example 8-2. Extending and combining interfaces (continued)*

```
Implementing LogOriginalSize
Implementing LogSavedBytes
Implementing Compress
Implementing the Read Method for IStorable
Implementing Encrypt
```

## Polymorphism with Interfaces

The problem with the approach we've taken so far is that you could well have a collection of Document objects, some implementing IStorable, some implementing ICompressible, some implementing ILoggedCompressible, some implementing IStorableCompressible, and some implementing IEncryptable. If you just call methods from each interface, sooner or later you're going to throw an exception.

Let's build such an example slowly, because this problem is very real, very confusing, and very likely to cause a nasty bug in your program if it isn't fully understood.

Start by declaring the interfaces just as you did in the previous example (I won't repeat them here). Next, rather than declaring a simple Document class, let's declare an abstract Document class, and two derived Document classes:

```csharp
public abstract class Document { }

public class BigDocument : Document, IStorableCompressible, IEncryptable
{
    //....
}
```

The implementation of BigDocument is identical to the implementation of Document in the previous example. There's no change whatsoever, except that the constructor must be named BigDocument, and note that it now inherits from our abstract class.

Finally, let's add a smaller type of Document:

```csharp
class LittleDocument : Document, IEncryptable
{
    public LittleDocument(string s)
    {
        Console.WriteLine("Creating document with: {0}", s);

    }
    void IEncryptable.Encrypt()
    {
        Console.WriteLine("Implementing Encrypt");
    }

    void IEncryptable.Decrypt()
    {
        Console.WriteLine("Implementing Decrypt");
    }

}
```

Notice that LittleDocument also inherits from Document, but it implements only one interface: IEncryptable.

Let's change Main, now to create a collection of Documents:

```
for (int i = 0; i < 5; i++)
{
    if (i % 2 == 0)
    {
        folder[i] = new BigDocument("Big Document # " + i);
    }
    else
    {
        folder[i] = new LittleDocument("Little Document # " + i);
    }
}
```

We create five documents, with the even-numbered ones being "big" and the odd-numbered ones being "little." If you now iterate through the "folder" (the array of Document objects) and try to call various methods of the interface, you have a problem:

```
foreach (Document doc in folder)
{
    doc.Read();
    doc.Compress();
    doc.LogSavedBytes();
    doc.Compress();
    doc.LogOriginalSize();
    doc.LogSavedBytes();
    doc.Compress();
    doc.Read();
    doc.Encrypt();
}
```

This won't compile—nor should it. The compiler cannot know which kind of Document it has: a BigDocument (which can Read and Compress), or a LittleDocument (which can't).

To solve this problem, we need to see whether the Document in question implements the interface we want to use, as shown in Example 8-3.

*Example 8-3. Collections of Documents*

```
using System;

namespace ExtendAndCombineInterface
{
    interface IStorable
    {
        void Read();
        void Write(object obj);
        int Status { get; set; }

    }
```

*Example 8-3. Collections of Documents (continued)*

```csharp
// here's the new interface
interface ICompressible
{
    void Compress();
    void Decompress();
}

// Extend the interface
interface ILoggedCompressible : ICompressible
{
    void LogSavedBytes();
}

// Combine Interfaces
interface IStorableCompressible : IStorable, ILoggedCompressible
{
    void LogOriginalSize();
}

// yet another interface
interface IEncryptable
{
    void Encrypt();
    void Decrypt();
}

public abstract class Document { }

public class BigDocument : Document, IStorableCompressible, IEncryptable
{

    // hold the data for IStorable's Status property
    private int status = 0;

    // the document constructor
    public BigDocument(string s)
    {
        Console.WriteLine("Creating document with: {0}", s);

    }

    // implement IStorable
    public void Read()
    {
        Console.WriteLine(
        "Implementing the Read Method for IStorable");
    }

    public void Write(object o)
    {
        Console.WriteLine(
        "Implementing the Write Method for IStorable");
```

*Example 8-3. Collections of Documents (continued)*

```
        }

        public int Status { get; set; }

        // implement ICompressible
        public void Compress()
        {
            Console.WriteLine("Implementing Compress");
        }

        public void Decompress()
        {
            Console.WriteLine("Implementing Decompress");
        }

        // implement ILoggedCompressible
        public void LogSavedBytes()
        {
            Console.WriteLine("Implementing LogSavedBytes");
        }

        // implement IStorableCompressible
        public void LogOriginalSize()
        {
            Console.WriteLine("Implementing LogOriginalSize");
        }

        // implement IEncryptable
        public void Encrypt()
        {
            Console.WriteLine("Implementing Encrypt");

        }

        public void Decrypt()
        {
            Console.WriteLine("Implementing Decrypt");

        }
    }

    class LittleDocument : Document, IEncryptable
    {
        public LittleDocument(string s)
        {
            Console.WriteLine("Creating document with: {0}", s);

        }
        void IEncryptable.Encrypt()
        {
            Console.WriteLine("Implementing Encrypt");
        }
```

*Example 8-3. Collections of Documents (continued)*

```
    void IEncryptable.Decrypt( )
    {
        Console.WriteLine("Implementing Decrypt");
    }

}


public class Tester
{

    static void Main( )
    {
        Document[] folder = new Document[5];
        for (int i = 0; i < 5; i++)
        {
            if (i % 2 == 0)
            {
                folder[i] = new BigDocument("Big Document # " + i);
            }
            else
            {
                folder[i] = new LittleDocument("Little Document # " + i);
            }
        }

        foreach (Document doc in folder)
        {
            // cast the document to the various interfaces
            IStorable isStorableDoc = doc as IStorable;
            if (isStorableDoc != null)
            {
                isStorableDoc.Read( );
            }
            else
                Console.WriteLine("IStorable not supported");

            ICompressible icDoc = doc as ICompressible;
            if (icDoc != null)
            {
                icDoc.Compress( );
            }
            else
                Console.WriteLine("Compressible not supported");

            ILoggedCompressible ilcDoc = doc as ILoggedCompressible;
            if (ilcDoc != null)
            {
                ilcDoc.LogSavedBytes( );
                ilcDoc.Compress( );
                // ilcDoc.Read( );
            }
```

*Example 8-3. Collections of Documents (continued)*

```
                else
                    Console.WriteLine("LoggedCompressible not supported");

                IStorableCompressible isc = doc as IStorableCompressible;
                if (isc != null)
                {
                    isc.LogOriginalSize( ); // IStorableCompressible
                    isc.LogSavedBytes( ); // ILoggedCompressible
                    isc.Compress( ); // ICompressible
                    isc.Read( ); // IStorable

                }
                else
                {
                    Console.WriteLine("StorableCompressible not supported");
                }

                IEncryptable ie = doc as IEncryptable;
                if (ie != null)
                {
                    ie.Encrypt( );
                }
                else
                    Console.WriteLine("Encryptable not supported");

            }   // end for
        }       // end main
    }           // end class
}               // end namespace
```

Output:

```
Creating document with: Big Document # 0
Creating document with: Little Document # 1
Creating document with: Big Document # 2
Creating document with: Little Document # 3
Creating document with: Big Document # 4
Implementing the Read Method for IStorable
Implementing Compress
Implementing LogSavedBytes
Implementing Compress
Implementing LogOriginalSize
Implementing LogSavedBytes
Implementing Compress
Implementing the Read Method for IStorable
Implementing Encrypt
IStorable not supported
Compressible not supported
LoggedCompressible not supported
StorableCompressible not supported
Implementing Encrypt
Implementing the Read Method for IStorable
```

*Example 8-3. Collections of Documents (continued)*

```
Implementing Compress
Implementing LogSavedBytes
Implementing Compress
Implementing LogOriginalSize
Implementing LogSavedBytes
Implementing Compress
Implementing the Read Method for IStorable
Implementing Encrypt
IStorable not supported
Compressible not supported
LoggedCompressible not supported
StorableCompressible not supported
Implementing Encrypt
Implementing the Read Method for IStorable
Implementing Compress
Implementing LogSavedBytes
Implementing Compress
Implementing LogOriginalSize
Implementing LogSavedBytes
Implementing Compress
Implementing the Read Method for IStorable
Implementing Encrypt
```

A quick examination of the output shows that we created three big documents and two little ones; that in fact, three of the documents are able to implement the interfaces and two are not; and that with the exception of `Encrypt`, all are able to implement, just as we have every right to expect.

---

### as Operator

Example 8-3 makes use of the as operator to determine whether a document implements the interfaces required for its encryption. The as operator casts the left operand to the type specified by the right operand and returns null if the cast fails.

The as operator is like two operators rolled into one. In Example 8-3, it's used first to check whether doc implements, for example, the `IStorableCompressible` interface, and if it does, it converts doc to an instance of that type.

Otherwise, it returns null. It is a common programming practice to then check whether the result, isc, is null before using it, as demonstrated in this example.

---

## Interface Versus Abstract Class

Interfaces are very similar to abstract classes. In fact, you could change the declaration of IStorable to be an abstract class:

```
abstract class Storable
{
```

```
        abstract public void Read( );
        abstract public void Write( );
    }
```

Document could now inherit from Storable, and there would not be much difference from using the interface.

Suppose, however, that you purchase a List class from a third-party vendor whose capabilities you wish to combine with those specified by Storable. In C++, you could create a StorableList class and inherit from List and Storable. But in C#, you're stuck; you can't inherit from the Storable abstract class and the List class because C# doesn't allow multiple inheritance with classes.

However, C# does allow you to implement any number of interfaces and derive from one base class. Thus, by making Storable an interface, you can inherit from the List class and from IStorable, as StorableList does in the following example:

```
public class StorableList : List, IStorable
{
    // List methods here ...
    public void Read( ) {...}
    public void Write(object obj) {...}
    // ...
}
```

# Overriding Interface Implementations

An implementing class is free to mark any or all of the methods that implement the interface as virtual. Derived classes can override these implementations to achieve polymorphism. For example, a Document class might implement the IStorable interface and mark the Read( ) and Write( ) methods as virtual. The Document might Read( ) and Write( ) its contents to a File type. The developer might later derive new types from Document, such as a Note or EmailMessage type, and he might decide that Note will read and write to a database rather than to a file.

Example 8-4 strips down the complexity of Example 8-3 and illustrates overriding an interface implementation. The Read( ) method is marked as virtual and is implemented by Document. Read( ) is then overridden in a Note type that derives from Document.

*Example 8-4. Overriding an interface implementation*

```
using System;

namespace overridingInterface
{
    interface IStorable
    {
        void Read( );
        void Write( );
    }
```

*Example 8-4. Overriding an interface implementation (continued)*

```csharp
// Simplify Document to implement only IStorable
public class Document : IStorable
{
    // the document constructor
    public Document(string s)
    {
        Console.WriteLine(
        "Creating document with: {0}", s);
    }

    // Make read virtual
    public virtual void Read()
    {
        Console.WriteLine(
        "Document Read Method for IStorable");
    }

    // NB: Not virtual!
    public void Write()
    {
        Console.WriteLine(
        "Document Write Method for IStorable");
    }
}

// Derive from Document
public class Note : Document
{
    public Note(string s) :
        base(s)
    {
        Console.WriteLine(
        "Creating note with: {0}", s);
    }

    // override the Read method

    public override void Read()
    {
        Console.WriteLine(
        "Overriding the Read method for Note!");
    }

    // implement my own Write method
    public new void Write()
    {
        Console.WriteLine(
        "Implementing the Write method for Note!");
    }
}
public class Tester
{

    static void Main()
```

*Example 8-4. Overriding an interface implementation (continued)*

```
        {
            // create a document reference to a Note object
            Document theNote = new Note("Test Note");
            IStorable isNote = theNote as IStorable;
            if (isNote != null)
            {
                isNote.Read();
                isNote.Write();
            }

            Console.WriteLine("\n");

            // direct call to the methods
            theNote.Read();
            theNote.Write();

            Console.WriteLine("\n");

            // create a note object
            Note note2 = new Note("Second Test");
            IStorable isNote2 = note2 as IStorable;
            if (isNote2 != null)
            {
                isNote2.Read();
                isNote2.Write();
            }

            Console.WriteLine("\n");

            // directly call the methods
            note2.Read();
            note2.Write();
        }
    }
}
```

```
Output:
Creating document with: Test Note
Creating note with: Test Note
Overriding the Read method for Note!
Document Write Method for IStorable

Overriding the Read method for Note!
Document Write Method for IStorable

Creating document with: Second Test
Creating note with: Second Test
Overriding the Read method for Note!
Document Write Method for IStorable

Overriding the Read method for Note!
Implementing the Write method for Note!
```

In this example, Document implements a simplified IStorable interface (simplified to make the example clearer):

```
interface IStorable
{
    void Read( );
    void Write( );
}
```

The designer of Document has opted to make the Read( ) method virtual, but not to make the Write( ) method virtual:

```
public virtual void Read( )
```

In a real-world application, if you were to mark one as virtual, you would almost certainly mark both as virtual, but I've differentiated them to demonstrate that the developer is free to pick and choose which methods are made virtual.

The Note class derives from Document:

```
public class Note : Document
```

It's not necessary for Note to override Read( ), but it is free to do so, and has in fact done so here:

```
public override void Read( )
```

In Tester, the Read and Write methods are called in four ways:

- Through the base class reference to a derived object
- Through an interface created from the base class reference to the derived object
- Through a derived object
- Through an interface created from the derived object

To accomplish the first two calls, a Document (base class) reference is created, and the address of a new Note (derived) object created on the heap is assigned to the Document reference:

```
Document theNote = new Note("Test Note");
```

An interface reference is created, and the as operator is used to cast the Document to the IStorable reference:

```
IStorable isNote = theNote as IStorable;
```

You then invoke the Read( ) and Write( ) methods through that interface. The output reveals that the Read( ) method is responded to polymorphically and the Write( ) method is not, just as you would expect:

```
Overriding the Read method for Note!
Document Write Method for IStorable
```

The Read( ) and Write( ) methods are then called directly on the object itself:

```
theNote.Read( );
theNote.Write( );
```

and once again you see the polymorphic implementation has worked:

```
Overriding the Read method for Note!
Document Write Method for IStorable
```

In both cases, the Read( ) method of Note is called and the Write( ) method of Document is called.

To prove to yourself that this is a result of the overriding method, next create a second Note object, this time assigning its address to a reference to a Note. This will be used to illustrate the final cases (i.e., a call through a derived object, and a call through an interface created from the derived object):

```
Note note2 = new Note("Second Test");
```

Once again, when you cast to a reference, the overridden Read( ) method is called. However, when methods are called directly on the Note object:

```
note2.Read( );
note2.Write( );
```

the output reflects that you've called a Note and not an overridden Document:

```
Overriding the Read method for Note!
Implementing the Write method for Note!
```

# Explicit Interface Implementation

In the implementation shown so far, the implementing class (in this case, Document) creates a member method with the same signature and return type as the method detailed in the interface. It is not necessary to explicitly state that this is an implementation of an interface; the compiler understands this implicitly.

What happens, however, if the class implements two interfaces, each of which has a method with the same signature? Example 8-5 creates two interfaces: IStorable and ITalk. The latter implements a Read( ) method that reads a book aloud. Unfortunately, this conflicts with the Read( ) method in IStorable.

Because both IStorable and ITalk have a Read( ) method, the implementing Document class must use *explicit implementation* for at least one of the methods. With explicit implementation, the implementing class (Document) explicitly identifies the interface for the method:

```
void ITalk.Read( )
```

This resolves the conflict, but it creates a series of interesting side effects.

First, there is no need to use explicit implementation with the other method of Talk( ):

```
public void Talk( )
```

Because there is no conflict, this can be declared as usual.

More important, the explicit implementation method can't have an access modifier:

```
void ITalk.Read( )
```

This method is implicitly public.

In fact, a method declared through explicit implementation can't be declared with the abstract, virtual, override, or new modifier.

Most important, you can't access the explicitly implemented method through the object itself. When you write:

```
theDoc.Read( );
```

the compiler assumes you mean the implicitly implemented interface for IStorable. The only way to access an explicitly implemented interface is through a cast to an interface:

```
ITalk itDoc = theDoc;
itDoc.Read( );
```

Example 8-5 demonstrates explicit implementation.

*Example 8-5. Explicit implementation*

```
using System;

namespace ExplicitImplementation
{
    interface IStorable
    {
        void Read( );
        void Write( );
    }

    interface ITalk
    {
        void Talk( );
        void Read( );
    }

    // Modify Document to implement IStorable and ITalk
    public class Document : IStorable, ITalk
    {
        // the document constructor
        public Document(string s)
        {
            Console.WriteLine("Creating document with: {0}", s);

        }

        // Make read virtual
        public virtual void Read( )
        {
            Console.WriteLine("Implementing IStorable.Read");
        }
```

*Example 8-5. Explicit implementation (continued)*

```
    public void Write( )
    {
        Console.WriteLine("Implementing IStorable.Write");

    }

    void ITalk.Read( )
    {
        Console.WriteLine("Implementing ITalk.Read");
    }

    public void Talk( )
    {
        Console.WriteLine("Implementing ITalk.Talk");
    }
}

public class Tester
{

    static void Main( )
    {
        // create a document object
        Document theDoc = new Document("Test Document");
        IStorable isDoc = theDoc;
        isDoc.Read( );

        ITalk itDoc = theDoc;
        itDoc.Read( );

        theDoc.Read( );
        theDoc.Talk( );
    }
}
}
```

Output:
Creating document with: Test Document
Implementing IStorable.Read
Implementing ITalk.Read
Implementing IStorable.Read
Implementing ITalk.Talk

## Selectively Exposing Interface Methods

A class designer can take advantage of the fact that when an interface is implemented through explicit implementation, the interface is not visible to clients of the implementing class except through casting.

Suppose the semantics of your Document object dictate that it implement the IStorable interface, but you don't want the Read( ) and Write( ) methods to be part of the public interface of your Document. You can use explicit implementation to ensure that they aren't available except through casting. This allows you to preserve the public API of your Document class while still having it implement IStorable. If your client wants an object that implements the IStorable interface, it can make a cast, but when using your document as a Document, the API will not include Read( ) and Write( ).

In fact, you can select which methods to make visible through explicit implementation so that you can expose some implementing methods as part of Document but not others. In Example 8-5, the Document object exposes the Talk( ) method as a method of Document, but the ITalk.Read( ) method can be obtained only through a cast. Even if IStorable didn't have a Read( ) method, you might choose to make Read( ) explicitly implemented so that you don't expose Read( ) as a method of Document.

Note that because explicit interface implementation prevents the use of the virtual keyword, a derived class would be forced to reimplement the method. Thus, if Note derived from Document, it would be forced to reimplement ITalk.Read( ) because the Document implementation of ITalk.Read( ) couldn't be virtual.

## Member Hiding

It is possible for an interface member to become hidden. For example, suppose you have an interface IBase that has a property P:

```
interface IBase
{
    int P { get; set; }
}
```

Suppose you derive from that interface a new interface, IDerived, which hides the property P with a new method P( ):

```
interface IDerived : IBase
{
    new int P( );
}
```

Setting aside whether this is a good idea, you have now hidden the property P in the base interface. An implementation of this derived interface will require at least one explicit interface member. You can use explicit implementation for *either* the base property or the derived method, or you can use explicit implementation for both. Thus, any of the following three versions would be legal:

```
class myClass : IDerived
{
    // explicit implementation for the base property
    int IBase.P { get {...} }

    // implicit implementation of the derived method
    public int P() {...}
}
```

```
class myClass : IDerived
{
    // implicit implementation for the base property
    public int P { get {...} }

    // explicit implementation of the derived method
    int IDerived.P() {...}
}

class myClass : IDerived
{
    // explicit implementation for the base property
    int IBase.P { get {...} }

    // explicit implementation of the derived method
    int IDerived.P() {...}
}
```

## CHAPTER 9

# Arrays, Indexers, and Collections

The .NET Framework provides a rich suite of collection classes. With the advent of Generics in .NET 2.0, most of these collection classes are now type-safe, making for a greatly enhanced programming experience. These classes include the Array, List, Dictionary, Sorted Dictionary, Queue, and Stack.

The simplest collection is the Array, the only collection type for which C# provides built-in support. In this chapter, you will learn to work with single, multidimensional, and jagged arrays. Arrays have built-in indexers, allowing you to request the *n*th member of the array. In this chapter, you will also be introduced to creating your own indexers, a bit of C# syntactic sugar that makes it easier to access class properties as though the class were indexed like an array.

The .NET Framework provides a number of interfaces, such as IEnumerable and ICollection, whose implementation provides you with standard ways to interact with collections. In this chapter, you will see how to work with the most essential of these. The chapter concludes with a tour of commonly used .NET collections, including List, Dictionary, Queue, and Stack.

 In previous versions of C#, the collection objects were not type-safe (you could, for example, mix strings and integers in a Dictionary). The nontype-safe versions of List (ArrayList), Dictionary, Queue, and Stack are still available for backward compatibility, but we won't cover them in this book because their use is similar to the Generics-based versions, and because they are obsolete and deprecated.

## Arrays

An *array* is an indexed collection of objects, all of the same type. C# arrays are somewhat different from arrays in C++ because they are objects. This provides them with useful methods and properties.

C# provides native syntax for the declaration of Arrays. What is actually created, however, is an object of type System.Array.* Arrays in C# thus provide you with the best of both worlds: easy-to-use C-style syntax underpinned with an actual class definition so that instances of an array have access to the methods and properties of System.Array. These appear in Table 9-1.

*Table 9-1. System.Array methods and properties*

| Method or property | Purpose |
| --- | --- |
| AsReadOnly( ) | Public static method that returns a read-only instance for a given array |
| BinarySearch( ) | Overloaded public static method that searches a one-dimensional sorted array |
| Clear( ) | Public static method that sets a range of elements in the array either to 0 or to a null reference |
| Clone( ) | Public method that creates a deep copy of the current array |
| ConstrainedCopy( ) | Public static method that copies a section of one array to another array; this method guarantees that the destination array will be modified only if all specified elements are copied successfully |
| ConvertAll( ) | Public static method that converts an array of one type into another type |
| Copy( ) | Overloaded public static method that copies a section of one array to another array |
| CopyTo( ) | Overloaded public method that copies all elements in the current array to another |
| CreateInstance( ) | Overloaded public static method that instantiates a new instance of an array |
| Exists( ) | Overloaded public static method that checks whether an array contains elements that match a condition |
| Find( ) | Public static method that finds the first element that matches a condition |
| FindAll( ) | Public static method that finds all elements that match a condition |
| FindIndex( ) | Overloaded public static method that returns the index of the first element that matches a condition |
| FindLast( ) | Public static method that finds the last element that matches a condition |
| FindLastIndex( ) | Overloaded public static method that returns the index of the last element that matches a condition |
| ForEach( ) | Public static method that performs an action on all elements of an array |
| GetEnumerator( ) | Public method that returns an IEnumerator |
| GetLength( ) | Public method that returns the length of the specified dimension in the array |
| GetLongLength( ) | Public method that returns the length of the specified dimension in the array as a 64-bit integer |
| GetLowerBound( ) | Public method that returns the lower boundary of the specified dimension of the array |
| GetUpperBound( ) | Public method that returns the upper boundary of the specified dimension of the array |
| GetValue( ) | Overloaded public method that returns the value of an element of the array |
| IndexOf( ) | Overloaded public static method that returns the index (offset) of the first instance of a value in a one-dimensional array |

* Of course, when you create an array with int[] myArray = new int[5] what you actually create in the IL code is an instance of System.int32[], but because this derives from the abstract base class System.Array, it is fair to say you've created an instance of a System.Array.

*Table 9-1. System.Array methods and properties (continued)*

| Method or property | Purpose |
|---|---|
| Initialize( ) | Initializes all values in a value type array by calling the default constructor for each value; with reference arrays, all elements in the array are set to null |
| IsFixedSize | Required because Array implements ICollection; with arrays, this will always return true (all arrays are of a fixed size) |
| IsReadOnly | Public property (required because Array implements IList) that returns a Boolean value indicating whether the array is read-only |
| IsSynchronized | Public property (required because Array implements ICollection) that returns a Boolean value indicating whether the array is thread-safe |
| LastIndexOf( ) | Overloaded public static method that returns the index of the last instance of a value in a one-dimensional array |
| Length | Public property that returns the length of the array |
| LongLength | Public property that returns the length of the array as a 64-bit integer |
| Rank | Public property that returns the number of dimensions of the array |
| Resize( ) | Public static method that changes the size of an array |
| Reverse( ) | Overloaded public static method that reverses the order of the elements in a one-dimensional array |
| SetValue( ) | Overloaded public method that sets the specified array elements to a value |
| Sort( ) | Overloaded public static method that sorts the values in a one-dimensional array |
| SyncRoot | Public property that returns an object that can be used to synchronize access to the array |
| TrueForAll( ) | Public static method that checks whether all elements match a condition |

# Declaring Arrays

You declare a C# array with the following syntax:

```
type[] array-name;
```

For example:

```
int[] myIntArray;
```

 You aren't actually declaring an array. Technically, you are declaring a variable (myIntArray) that will hold a reference to an array of integers. As always, we'll use the shorthand and refer to myIntArray as the array, knowing that we really mean a variable that holds a reference to an (unnamed) array.

The square brackets ([]) tell the C# compiler that you are declaring an array, and the type specifies the type of the elements it will contain. In the previous example, myIntArray is an array of integers.

You instantiate an array by using the new keyword. For example:

```
myIntArray = new int[5];
```

This declaration creates and initializes an array of five integers, all of which are initialized to the value 0.

*VB 6 programmers take note*: in C#, the value of the size of the array marks the number of elements in the array, not the upper bound. In fact, there is no way to set the upper or lower bound—with the exception that you can set the lower bounds in multidimensional arrays (discussed later), but even that is not supported by the .NET Framework class library.

Thus, the first element in an array is 0. The following C# statement declares an array of 10 elements, with indexes 0 through 9:

```
string myArray[10];
```

The upper bound is 9, not 10, and you can't change the size of the array (i.e., there is no equivalent to the VB 6 Redim function).

It is important to distinguish between the array (which is a collection of elements) and the elements of the array. myIntArray is the array (or, more accurately, the variable that holds the reference to the array); its elements are the five integers it holds.

C# arrays are reference types, created on the heap. Thus, the array to which myIntArray refers is allocated on the heap. The *elements* of an array are allocated based on their own type. Because integers are value types, the elements in myIntArray will be value types, *not* boxed integers, and thus all the elements will be created inside the block of memory allocated for the array.

The block of memory allocated to an array of reference types will contain references to the actual elements, which are themselves created on the heap in memory separate from that allocated for the array.

## Understanding Default Values

When you create an array of value types, each element initially contains the default value for the type stored in the array (refer back to Table 4-2 in Chapter 4). The statement:

```
myIntArray = new int[5];
```

creates an array of five integers, each whose value is set to 0, which is the default value for integer types.

Unlike with arrays of value types, the reference types in an array aren't initialized to their default value. Instead, the references held in the array are initialized to null. If you attempt to access an element in an array of reference types before you have specifically initialized the elements, you will generate an exception.

Assume that you have created a Button class. You would declare an array of Button objects with the following statement:

```
Button[] myButtonArray;
```

and instantiate the actual array like this:

```
myButtonArray = new Button[3];
```

You can shorten this to:

```
Button[] myButtonArray = new Button[3];
```

This statement doesn't create an array with references to three Button objects. Instead, this creates the array myButtonArray with three null references. To use this array, you must first construct and assign the Button objects for each reference in the array. You can construct the objects in a loop that adds them one by one to the array.

## Accessing Array Elements

You access the elements of an array using the index operator ([ ]). Arrays are zero-based, which means that the index of the first element is always 0—in this case, myArray[0].

As explained previously, arrays are objects and thus have properties. One of the more useful of these is Length, which tells you how many objects are in an array. Array objects can be indexed from 0 to Length-1. That is, if there are five elements in an array, their indexes are 0, 1, 2, 3, 4.

Example 9-1 illustrates the array concepts covered so far. In this example, a class named Tester creates an array of Employees and an array of integers, populates the Employee array, and then prints the values of both.

*Example 9-1. Working with an array*

```
namespace Programming_CSharp
{
    // a simple class to store in the array
    public class Employee
    {
        public Employee(int empID)
        {
            this.empID = empID;
        }
        public override string ToString()
        {
            return empID.ToString();
        }
        private int empID;
    }
    public class Tester
    {
        static void Main()
        {
```

*Example 9-1. Working with an array (continued)*

```
int[] intArray;
Employee[] empArray;
intArray = new int[5];
empArray = new Employee[3];

// populate the array
for (int i = 0; i < empArray.Length; i++)
{
    empArray[i] = new Employee(i + 5);
}

for (int i = 0; i < intArray.Length; i++)
{
    Console.WriteLine(intArray[i].ToString());
}

for (int i = 0; i < empArray.Length; i++)
{
    Console.WriteLine(empArray[i].ToString());
}
        }
    }
}
```

```
Output:
0
0
0
0
0
5
6
7
```

The example starts with the definition of an Employee class that implements a constructor that takes a single integer parameter. The ToString( ) method inherited from Object is overridden to print the value of the Employee object's employee ID.

The test method declares and then instantiates a pair of arrays. The integer array is automatically filled with integers whose values are set to 0. The Employee array contents must be constructed by hand.

Finally, the contents of the arrays are printed to ensure that they are filled as intended. The five integers print their value first, followed by the three Employee objects.

# The foreach Statement

The foreach looping statement is new to the C family of languages, though it is already well known to VB programmers. The foreach statement allows you to iterate through all the items in an array or other collection, examining each item in turn. The syntax for the foreach statement is:

```
foreach (type identifier in expression) statement
```

Thus, you might update Example 9-1 to replace the for statements that iterate over the contents of the populated array with foreach statements, as shown in Example 9-2.

*Example 9-2. Using foreach*

```csharp
using System;
using System.Collections.Generic;
using System.Text;

namespace UsingForEach
{
    // a simple class to store in the array
    public class Employee
    {
        // a simple class to store in the array
        public Employee( int empID )
        {
            this.empID = empID;
        }
        public override string ToString()
        {
            return empID.ToString();
        }
        private int empID;
    }
    public class Tester
    {
        static void Main()
        {
            int[] intArray;
            Employee[] empArray;
            intArray = new int[5];
            empArray = new Employee[3];

            // populate the array
            for ( int i = 0; i < empArray.Length; i++ )
            {
                empArray[i] = new Employee( i + 5 );
            }

            foreach ( int i in intArray )
            {
```

*Example 9-2. Using foreach (continued)*

```
            Console.WriteLine( i.ToString() );
        }

        foreach ( Employee e in empArray )
        {
            Console.WriteLine( e.ToString() );
        }
    }
  }
}
```

The output for Example 9-2 is identical to Example 9-1. In Example 9-1, you created a for statement that measured the size of the array and used a temporary counting variable as an index into the array, as in the following:

```
for (int i = 0; i < empArray.Length; i++)
{
  Console.WriteLine(empArray[i].ToString());
}
```

In Example 9-2, you tried another approach: you iterated over the array with the foreach loop, which automatically extracted the next item from within the array and assigned it to the temporary object you created in the head of the statement:

```
foreach (Employee e in empArray)
{
  Console.WriteLine(e.ToString());
}
```

The object extracted from the array is of the appropriate type; thus, you may call any public method on that object.

## Initializing Array Elements

It is possible to initialize the contents of an array at the time it is instantiated by providing a list of values delimited by curly brackets ({}). C# provides a longer and a shorter syntax:

```
int[] myIntArray = new int[5] { 2, 4, 6, 8, 10 }
int[] myIntArray = { 2, 4, 6, 8, 10 }
```

There is no practical difference between these two statements, and most programmers will use the shorter syntax, but see the note on syntaxes.

 Both syntaxes exist because in some rare circumstances, you have to use the longer syntax—specifically, if the C# compiler is unable to infer the correct type for the array.

# The params Keyword

You can create a method that displays any number of integers to the console by passing in an array of integers and then iterating over the array with a foreach loop.[*] The params keyword allows you to pass in a variable number of parameters without necessarily explicitly creating the array.

In the next example, you create a method, DisplayVals( ), that takes a variable number of integer arguments:

```
public void DisplayVals(params int[] intVals)
```

The method itself can treat the array as though an integer array were explicitly created and passed in as a parameter. You are free to iterate over the array as you would over any other array of integers:

```
foreach (int i in intVals)
{
   Console.WriteLine("DisplayVals {0}",i);
}
```

The calling method, however, need not explicitly create an array: it can simply pass in integers, and the compiler will assemble the parameters into an array for the DisplayVals( ) method:

```
t.DisplayVals(5,6,7,8);
```

You are free to pass in an array if you prefer:

```
int [] explicitArray = new int[5] {1,2,3,4,5};
t.DisplayVals(explicitArray);
```

Example 9-3 provides the complete source code illustrating the params keyword.

*Example 9-3. Using the params keyword*

```
using System;
using System.Collections.Generic;
using System.Text;

namespace UsingParams
{
    public class Tester
    {
        static void Main( )
        {
            Tester t = new Tester( );
            t.DisplayVals(5, 6, 7, 8);
            int[] explicitArray = new int[5] { 1, 2, 3, 4, 5 };
            t.DisplayVals(explicitArray);
```

---

[*] The lifetime of objects declared in the header of a foreach loop is scoped outside the loop, much like the objects declared in a for loop.

*Example 9-3. Using the params keyword (continued)*

```
        }

        public void DisplayVals(params int[] intVals)
        {
            foreach (int i in intVals)
            {
                Console.WriteLine("DisplayVals {0}", i);
            }
        }
    }
}
Output:
DisplayVals 5
DisplayVals 6
DisplayVals 7
DisplayVals 8
DisplayVals 1
DisplayVals 2
DisplayVals 3
DisplayVals 4
DisplayVals 5
```

# Multidimensional Arrays

You can think of an array as a long row of slots into which you can place values. Once you have a picture of a row of slots, imagine 10 rows, one on top of another. This is the classic two-dimensional array of rows and columns. The rows run across the array and the columns run up and down the array.

A third dimension is possible, but somewhat harder to imagine. Make your arrays three-dimensional, with new rows stacked atop the old two-dimensional array. OK, now imagine four dimensions. Now imagine 10.

Those of you who aren't string-theory physicists have probably given up, as have we. Multidimensional arrays are useful, however, even if you can't quite picture what they would look like.

C# supports two types of multidimensional arrays: rectangular and jagged. In a rectangular array, every row is the same length. A jagged array, however, is an array of arrays, each of which can be a different length.

## Rectangular arrays

A *rectangular array* is an array of two (or more) dimensions. In the classic two-dimensional array, the first dimension is the number of rows and the second dimension is the number of columns.

*Java programmers take note:* rectangular arrays don't exist in Java.

To declare a two-dimensional array, use the following syntax:

> *type* [,] *array-name*

For example, to declare and instantiate a two-dimensional rectangular array named myRectangularArray that contains two rows and three columns of integers, you would write:

```
int [,] myRectangularArray = new int[2,3];
```

Example 9-4 declares, instantiates, initializes, and prints the contents of a two-dimensional array. In this example, a for loop is used to initialize the elements of the array.

*Example 9-4. Rectangular array*

```
using System;
using System.Collections.Generic;
using System.Text;

namespace RectangularArray
{
    public class Tester
    {
        static void Main( )
        {
            const int rows = 4;
            const int columns = 3;

            // declare a 4x3 integer array
            int[,] rectangularArray = new int[rows, columns];

            // populate the array
            for (int i = 0; i < rows; i++)
            {
                for (int j = 0; j < columns; j++)
                {
                    rectangularArray[i, j] = i + j;
                }
            }

            // report the contents of the array
            for (int i = 0; i < rows; i++)
            {
                for (int j = 0; j < columns; j++)
                {
                    Console.WriteLine("rectangularArray[{0},{1}] = {2}",
                        i, j, rectangularArray[i, j]);
```

*Example 9-4. Rectangular array (continued)*

```
                    }
                }
            }
        }
    }
}
```

```
Output:
rectangularArray[0,0] = 0
rectangularArray[0,1] = 1
rectangularArray[0,2] = 2
rectangularArray[1,0] = 1
rectangularArray[1,1] = 2
rectangularArray[1,2] = 3
rectangularArray[2,0] = 2
rectangularArray[2,1] = 3
rectangularArray[2,2] = 4
rectangularArray[3,0] = 3
rectangularArray[3,1] = 4
rectangularArray[3,2] = 5
```

In this example, you declare a pair of constant values:

```
const int rows = 4;
const int columns = 3;
```

that are then used to dimension the array:

```
int[,] rectangularArray = new int[rows, columns];
```

Notice the syntax. The brackets in the int[,] declaration indicate that the type is an array of integers, and the comma indicates that the array has two dimensions (two commas would indicate three dimensions, etc.). The actual instantiation of rectangularArray with new int[rows, columns] sets the size of each dimension. Here, the declaration and instantiation have been combined.

The program fills the rectangle with a pair of for loops, iterating through each column in each row. Thus, the first element filled is rectangularArray[0,0], followed by rectangularArray[0,1] and rectangularArray[0,2]. Once this is done, the program moves on to the next rows: rectangularArray[1,0], rectangularArray[1,1], rectangularArray[1,2], and so forth, until all the columns in all the rows are filled.

Just as you can initialize a one-dimensional array using bracketed lists of values, you can initialize a two-dimensional array using similar syntax. Example 9-5 declares a two-dimensional array (rectangularArray), initializes its elements using bracketed lists of values, and then prints the contents.

*Example 9-5. Initializing a multidimensional array*

```
using System;
using System.Collections.Generic;
using System.Text;
```

*Example 9-5. Initializing a multidimensional array (continued)*

```
namespace InitializingMultiDimensionalArray
{
    public class Tester
    {
        static void Main( )
        {
            const int rows = 4;
            const int columns = 3;

            // imply a 4x3 array
            int[,] rectangularArray =
                {
                    {0,1,2}, {3,4,5}, {6,7,8}, {9,10,11}
                };

            for (int i = 0; i < rows; i++)
            {
                for (int j = 0; j < columns; j++)
                {
                    Console.WriteLine("rectangularArray[{0},{1}] = {2}",
                        i, j, rectangularArray[i, j]);
                }
            }
        }
    }
}
```

```
Output:
rectangularArrayrectangularArray[0,0] = 0
rectangularArrayrectangularArray[0,1] = 1
rectangularArrayrectangularArray[0,2] = 2
rectangularArrayrectangularArray[1,0] = 3
rectangularArrayrectangularArray[1,1] = 4
rectangularArrayrectangularArray[1,2] = 5
rectangularArrayrectangularArray[2,0] = 6
rectangularArrayrectangularArray[2,1] = 7
rectangularArrayrectangularArray[2,2] = 8
rectangularArrayrectangularArray[3,0] = 9
rectangularArrayrectangularArray[3,1] = 10
rectangularArrayrectangularArray[3,2] = 11
```

The preceding example is similar to Example 9-4, but this time you *imply* the exact dimensions of the array by how you initialize it:

```
int[,] rectangularArrayrectangularArray =
{
{0,1,2}, {3,4,5}, {6,7,8}, {9,10,11}
};
```

Assigning values in four bracketed lists, each consisting of three elements, implies a 4 × 3 array. Had you written this as:

```
int[,] rectangularArrayrectangularArray =
{
{0,1,2,3}, {4,5,6,7}, {8,9,10,11}
};
```

you would instead have implied a 3 × 4 array.

You can see that the C# compiler understands the implications of your clustering because it can access the objects with the appropriate offsets, as illustrated in the output.

You might guess that because this is a 12-element array, you can just as easily access an element at `rectangularArray[0,3]` (the fourth element in the first row) as at `rectangularArray[1,0]` (the first element in the second row). This works in C++, but if you try it in C#, you will run right into an exception:

```
Exception occurred: System.IndexOutOfRangeException:
Index was outside the bounds of the array.
at Programming_CSharp.Tester.Main() in
csharp\programming csharp\listing0703.cs:line 23
```

C# arrays are smart, and they keep track of their bounds. When you imply a 4 × 3 array, you must treat it as such.

## Jagged arrays

A *jagged array* is an array of arrays. It is called "jagged" because each row need not be the same size as all the others, and thus a graphical representation of the array would not be square.

When you create a jagged array, you declare the number of rows in your array. Each row will hold an array, which can be of any length. These arrays must each be declared. You can then fill in the values for the elements in these "inner" arrays.

In a jagged array, each dimension is a one-dimensional array. To declare a jagged array, use the following syntax, where the number of brackets indicates the number of dimensions of the array:

   *type* [] []...

For example, you would declare a two-dimensional jagged array of integers named `myJaggedArray` as follows:

   `int [] [] myJaggedArray;`

You access the fifth element of the third array by writing `myJaggedArray[2][4]`.

Example 9-6 creates a jagged array named `myJaggedArray`, initializes its elements, and then prints their content. To save space, the program takes advantage of the fact that integer array elements are automatically initialized to 0, and it initializes the values of only some of the elements.

*Example 9-6. Working with a jagged array*

```
using System;
using System.Collections.Generic;
using System.Text;

namespace JaggedArray
{
    public class Tester
    {
        static void Main( )
        {
            const int rows = 4;

            // declare the jagged array as 4 rows high
            int[][] jaggedArray = new int[rows][];

            // the first row has 5 elements
            jaggedArray[0] = new int[5];

            // a row with 2 elements
            jaggedArray[1] = new int[2];

            // a row with 3 elements
            jaggedArray[2] = new int[3];

            // the last row has 5 elements
            jaggedArray[3] = new int[5];

            // Fill some (but not all) elements of the rows
            jaggedArray[0][3] = 15;
            jaggedArray[1][1] = 12;
            jaggedArray[2][1] = 9;
            jaggedArray[2][2] = 99;
            jaggedArray[3][0] = 10;
            jaggedArray[3][1] = 11;
            jaggedArray[3][2] = 12;
            jaggedArray[3][3] = 13;
            jaggedArray[3][4] = 14;

            for (int i = 0; i < 5; i++)
            {
                Console.WriteLine("jaggedArray[0][{0}] = {1}",
                    i, jaggedArray[0][i]);
            }

            for (int i = 0; i < 2; i++)
            {
                Console.WriteLine("jaggedArray[1][{0}] = {1}",
                    i, jaggedArray[1][i]);
            }

            for (int i = 0; i < 3; i++)
            {
```

*Example 9-6. Working with a jagged array (continued)*

```
                Console.WriteLine("jaggedArray[2][{0}] = {1}",
                    i, jaggedArray[2][i]);
            }
            for (int i = 0; i < 5; i++)
            {
                Console.WriteLine("jaggedArray[3][{0}] = {1}",
                    i, jaggedArray[3][i]);
            }
        }
    }
}
```

```
Output:
jaggedArray[0][0] = 0
jaggedArray[0][1] = 0
jaggedArray[0][2] = 0
jaggedArray[0][3] = 15
jaggedArray[0][4] = 0
jaggedArray[1][0] = 0
jaggedArray[1][1] = 12
jaggedArray[2][0] = 0
jaggedArray[2][1] = 9
jaggedArray[2][2] = 99
jaggedArray[3][0] = 10
jaggedArray[3][1] = 11
jaggedArray[3][2] = 12
jaggedArray[3][3] = 13
jaggedArray[3][4] = 14
```

In this example, a jagged array is created with four rows:

```
int[][] jaggedArray = new int[rows][];
```

Notice that the second dimension is not specified. This is set by creating a new array for each row. Each array can have a different size:

```
// the first row has 5 elements
jaggedArray[0] = new int[5];

// a row with 2 elements
jaggedArray[1] = new int[2];

// a row with 3 elements
jaggedArray[2] = new int[3];

// the last row has 5 elements
jaggedArray[3] = new int[5];
```

Once an array is specified for each row, you need only populate the various members of each array and then print their contents to ensure that all went as expected.

Notice that when you access the members of a rectangular array, you put the indexes all within one set of square brackets:

```
rectangularArrayrectangularArray[i,j]
```

whereas with a jagged array you need a pair of brackets:

```
jaggedArray[3][i]
```

You can keep this straight by thinking of the first array as a single array of more than one dimension, and the jagged array as an array *of arrays*.

## Array Bounds

The Array class can also be created by using the overloaded CreateInstance method. One of the overloads allows you to specify the lower bounds (starting index) of each dimension in a multidimensional array. This is a fairly obscure capability, not often used.

Briefly, here is how you do it: you call the static method CreateInstance, which returns an Array and which takes three parameters: an object of type Type (indicating the type of object to hold in the array), an array of integers indicating the length of each dimension in the array, and a second array of integers indicating the lower bound for each dimension. Note that the two arrays of integers must have the same number of elements; that is, you must specify a lower bound for each dimension:

```csharp
using System;
using System.Collections.Generic;
using System.Text;

namespace SettingArrayBounds
{
    public class SettingArrayBounds
    {
        public static void CreateArrayWithBounds()
        {
            // Creates and initializes a multidimensional
            // Array of type String.
            int[] lengthsArray = new int[2] { 3, 5 };
            int[] boundsArray = new int[2] { 2, 3 };
            Array multiDimensionalArray = Array.CreateInstance(
                typeof(String), lengthsArray, boundsArray);

            // Displays the lower bounds and the
            // upper bounds of each dimension.
            Console.WriteLine("Bounds:\tLower\tUpper");
            for (int i = 0; i < multiDimensionalArray.Rank; i++)
                Console.WriteLine("{0}:\t{1}\t{2}", i,
                    multiDimensionalArray.GetLowerBound(i),
                    multiDimensionalArray.GetUpperBound(i));
        }
        static void Main()
        {
```

```
                SettingArrayBounds.CreateArrayWithBounds();
        }
    }
}
```

# Array Conversions

You can convert one array into another, if the dimensions of the two arrays are
equal, and if a conversion is possible between the reference element types. An
implicit conversion can occur if the elements can be implicitly converted; otherwise,
an explicit conversion is required.

You can also convert an array of derived objects to an array of base objects.
Example 9-7 illustrates the conversion of an array of user-defined Employee types to
an array of objects.

*Example 9-7. Converting arrays*

```
using System;
using System.Collections.Generic;
using System.Text;

namespace ConvertingArrays
{
    // create an object we can
    // store in the array
    public class Employee
    {
        // a simple class to store in the array
        public Employee(int empID)
        {
            this.empID = empID;
        }
        public override string ToString()
        {
            return empID.ToString();
        }
        private int empID;
    }

    public class Tester
    {
        // This method takes an array of objects.
        // We'll pass in an array of Employees
        // and then an array of strings.
        // The conversion is implicit since both Employee
        // and string derive (ultimately) from object.
        public static void PrintArray(object[] theArray)
        {
            Console.WriteLine("Contents of the Array {0}",
            theArray.ToString());
```

*Example 9-7. Converting arrays (continued)*

```
                // walk through the array and print
                // the values.
                foreach (object obj in theArray)
                {
                    Console.WriteLine("Value: {0}", obj);
                }
            }

        static void Main( )
        {
            // make an array of Employee objects
            Employee[] myEmployeeArray = new Employee[3];

            // initialize each Employee's value
            for (int i = 0; i < 3; i++)
            {
                myEmployeeArray[i] = new Employee(i + 5);
            }

            // display the values
            PrintArray(myEmployeeArray);

            // create an array of two strings
            string[] array = {"hello", "world"};

            // print the value of the strings
            PrintArray(array);
        }
    }
}
```

```
Output:
Contents of the Array Programming_CSharp.Employee[]
Value: 5
Value: 6
Value: 7
Contents of the Array System.String[]
Value: hello
Value: world
```

Example 9-7 begins by creating a simple Employee class, as seen earlier in the chapter. The Tester class now contains a new static method, PrintArray( ), that takes as a parameter a one-dimensional array of Objects:

```
    public static void PrintArray(object[] theArray)
```

Object is the implicit base class of every object in the .NET Framework, and so is the base class of both String and Employee.

The PrintArray( ) method takes two actions. First, it calls the ToString( ) method on the array itself:

```
Console.WriteLine("Contents of the Array {0}",
  theArray.ToString( ));
```

System.Array overrides the ToString( ) method to your advantage, printing an identifying name of the array:

```
Contents of the Array Programming_CSharp. Employee []
Contents of the Array System.String[]
```

PrintArray( ) then goes on to call ToString( ) on each element in the array it receives
as a parameter. Because ToString( ) is a virtual method in the base class Object, it is
guaranteed to be available in every derived class. You have overridden this method
appropriately in Employee so that the code works properly. Calling ToString( ) on a
String object might not be necessary, but it is harmless, and it allows you to treat
these objects polymorphically.

## Sorting Arrays

Two useful static methods of Array are Sort( ) and Reverse( ). These are fully supported for arrays of the built-in C# types such as string. Making them work with
your own classes is a bit trickier, as you must implement the IComparable interface
(see the section "Implementing IComparable," later in this chapter). Example 9-8
demonstrates the use of these two methods to manipulate String objects.

*Example 9-8. Using Array.Sort and Array.Reverse*

```
using System;
using System.Collections.Generic;
using System.Text;

namespace ArraySortAndReverse
{
    public class Tester
    {
        public static void PrintMyArray(object[] theArray)
        {
            foreach (object obj in theArray)
            {
                Console.WriteLine("Value: {0}", obj);
            }
            Console.WriteLine("\n");
        }

        static void Main( )
        {
            String[] myArray = {"Who", "is", "Douglas", "Adams"};

            PrintMyArray(myArray);
            Array.Reverse(myArray);
            PrintMyArray(myArray);
```

*Example 9-8. Using Array.Sort and Array.Reverse (continued)*

```
        String[] myOtherArray =
               {
                   "We", "Hold", "These", "Truths",
                   "To", "Be", "Self","Evident",
               };

        PrintMyArray(myOtherArray);
        Array.Sort(myOtherArray);
        PrintMyArray(myOtherArray);
    }
  }
}

Output:
Value: Who
Value: is
Value: Douglas
Value: Adams

Value: Adams
Value: Douglas
Value: is
Value: Who

Value: We
Value: Hold
Value: These
Value: Truths
Value: To
Value: Be
Value: Self
Value: Evident

Value: Be
Value: Evident
Value: Hold
Value: Self
Value: These
Value: To
Value: Truths
Value: We
```

The example begins by creating myArray, an array of strings with the words:

```
"Who", "is", "Douglas", "Adams"
```

This array is printed, and then is passed to the Array.Reverse( ) method, where it is printed again to see that the array itself has been reversed:

```
Value: Adams
Value: Douglas
Value: is
Value: Who
```

Similarly, the example creates a second array, `myOtherArray`, containing the words:

```
"We", "Hold", "These", "Truths",
"To", "Be", "Self", "Evident",
```

This is passed to the `Array.Sort()` method. Then `Array.Sort()` happily sorts them alphabetically:

```
Value: Be
Value: Evident
Value: Hold
Value: Self
Value: These
Value: To
Value: Truths
Value: We
```

# Indexers

Sometimes you may need to access a collection within a class as though the class itself were an array. For example, suppose you create a listbox control named `myListBox` that contains a list of strings stored in a one-dimensional array, a private member variable named `myStrings`. A listbox control contains member properties and methods in addition to its array of strings. However, it would be convenient to be able to access the listbox array with an index, just as though the listbox were an array.* For example, such a property would permit statements like the following:

```
string theFirstString = myListBox[0];
string theLastString = myListBox[Length-1];
```

An *indexer* is a C# construct that allows you to access collections contained by a class using the familiar [] syntax of arrays. An indexer is a special kind of property, and includes get and set accessors to specify its behavior.

You declare an indexer property within a class using the following syntax:

```
type this [type argument]{get; set;}
```

The return type determines the type of object that will be returned by the indexer, whereas the type argument specifies what kind of argument will be used to index into the collection that contains the target objects. Although it is common to use integers as index values, you can index a collection on other types as well, including strings. You can even provide an indexer with multiple parameters to create a multi-dimensional array!

The `this` keyword is a reference to the object in which the indexer appears. As with a normal property, you also must define get and set accessors, which determine how the requested object is retrieved from or assigned to its collection.

---

* The actual `ListBox` control provided by Windows Forms and ASP.NET has a collection called `Items`, and it is the `Items` collection that implements the indexer.

Example 9-9 declares a listbox control (ListBoxTest) that contains a simple array (myStrings) and a simple indexer for accessing its contents.

 *C++ programmers take note*: the indexer serves much the same purpose as overloading the C++ index operator ([ ]). The index operator can't be overloaded in C#, which provides the indexer in its place.

*Example 9-9. Using a simple indexer*

```
using System;
using System.Collections.Generic;
using System.Text;

namespace SimpleIndexer
{
    // a simplified ListBox control
    public class ListBoxTest
    {
        private string[] strings;
        private int ctr = 0;

        // initialize the listbox with strings
        public ListBoxTest(params string[] initialStrings)
        {
            // allocate space for the strings
            strings = new String[256];

            // copy the strings passed in to the constructor
            foreach (string s in initialStrings)
            {
                strings[ctr++] = s;
            }
        }

        // add a single string to the end of the listbox
        public void Add(string theString)
        {
            if (ctr >= strings.Length)
            {
                // handle bad index
            }
            else
                strings[ctr++] = theString;
        }

        // allow array-like access

        public string this[int index]
        {
            get
            {
                if (index < 0 || index >= strings.Length)
                {
```

*Example 9-9. Using a simple indexer (continued)*

```
                        // handle bad index
                }
                return strings[index];
        }
        set
        {
                // add only through the add method
                if (index >= ctr)
                {
                        // handle error
                }
                else
                        strings[index] = value;
        }
    }

    // publish how many strings you hold
    public int GetNumEntries()
    {
        return ctr;
    }
}

public class Tester
{
    static void Main()
    {
        // create a new listbox and initialize
        ListBoxTest lbt =
            new ListBoxTest("Hello", "World");

        // add a few strings
        lbt.Add("Who");
        lbt.Add("Is");
        lbt.Add("Douglas");
        lbt.Add("Adams");

        // test the access
        string subst = "Universe";
        lbt[1] = subst;

        // access all the strings
        for (int i = 0; i < lbt.GetNumEntries(); i++)
        {
            Console.WriteLine("lbt[{0}]: {1}", i, lbt[i]);
        }
    }
}
}
```

*Example 9-9. Using a simple indexer (continued)*

```
Output:
lbt[0]: Hello
lbt[1]: Universe
lbt[2]: Who
lbt[3]: Is
lbt[4]: Douglas
lbt[5]: Adams
```

To keep Example 9-9 simple, we strip the listbox control down to the few features we care about. The listing ignores everything having to do with being a user control and focuses only on the list of strings the listbox maintains and methods for manipulating them. In a real application, of course, these are a small fraction of the total methods of a listbox, whose principal job is to display the strings and enable user choice.

The first things to notice are the two private members:

```
private string[] strings;
private int ctr = 0;
```

In this program, the listbox maintains a simple array of strings: `strings`. Again, in a real listbox, you might use a more complex and dynamic container, such as a hash table (described later in this chapter). The member variable `ctr` will keep track of how many strings have been added to this array.

Initialize the array in the constructor with the statement:

```
strings = new String[256];
```

The remainder of the constructor adds the parameters to the array. Again, for simplicity, you add new strings to the array in the order received.

 Because you can't know how many strings will be added, you use the keyword `params`, as described earlier in this chapter.

The `Add()` method of `ListBoxTest` does nothing more than append a new string to the internal array.

The key method of `ListBoxTest`, however, is the indexer. An indexer is unnamed, so use the `this` keyword:

```
public string this[int index]
```

The syntax of the indexer is very similar to that for properties. There is either a `get()` method, a `set()` method, or both. In the case shown, the `get()` method endeavors to implement rudimentary bounds-checking, and assuming the index requested is acceptable, it returns the value requested:

```
get
{
  if (index < 0 || index >= strings.Length)
  {
    // handle bad index
  }
  return strings[index];
}
```

The set( ) method checks to make sure that the index you are setting already has a value in the listbox. If not, it treats the set as an error. (New elements can only be added using Add with this approach.) The set accessor takes advantage of the implicit parameter value that represents whatever is assigned using the index operator:

```
set
{
if (index >= ctr )
  {
    // handle error
  }
  else
   strings[index] = value;
}
```

Thus, if you write:

```
lbt[5] = "Hello World"
```

the compiler will call the indexer set( ) method on your object and pass in the string Hello World as an implicit parameter named value.

## Indexers and Assignment

In Example 9-9, you can't assign to an index that doesn't have a value. So, if you write:

```
lbt[10] = "wow!";
```

you will trigger the error handler in the set( ) method, which will note that the index you've passed in (10) is larger than the counter (6).

Of course, you can use the set( ) method for assignment; you simply have to handle the indexes you receive. To do so, you might change the set( ) method to check the Length of the buffer rather than the current value of counter. If a value was entered for an index that did not yet have a value, you would update ctr:

```
set
{
  // add only through the add method
  if (index >= strings.Length )
  {
    // handle error
  }
  else
  {
```

```
        strings[index] = value;
        if (ctr < index+1)
          ctr = index+1;
    }
  }
```

 This code is kept simple and thus is not robust. There are any number
of other checks you'll want to make on the value passed in (e.g.,
checking that you were not passed a negative index, and that it doesn't
exceed the size of the underlying strings[ ] array).

This allows you to create a "sparse" array in which you can assign to offset 10 without ever having assigned to offset 9. Thus, if you now write:

```
lbt[10] = "wow!";
```

the output will be:

```
lbt[0]: Hello
lbt[1]: Universe
lbt[2]: Who
lbt[3]: Is
lbt[4]: Douglas
lbt[5]: Adams
lbt[6]:
lbt[7]:
lbt[8]:
lbt[9]:
lbt[10]: wow!
```

In Main( ), you create an instance of the ListBoxTest class named lbt and pass in two strings as parameters:

```
ListBoxTest lbt = new ListBoxTest("Hello", "World");
```

Then, call Add( ) to add four more strings:

```
// add a few strings
lbt.Add("Who");
lbt.Add("Is");
lbt.Add("Douglas");
lbt.Add("Adams");
```

Before examining the values, modify the second value (at index 1):

```
string subst = "Universe";
lbt[1] = subst;
```

Finally, display each value in a loop:

```
for (int i = 0;i<lbt.GetNumEntries( );i++)
{
  Console.WriteLine("lbt[{0}]: {1}",i,lbt[i]);
}
```

# Indexing on Other Values

C# doesn't require that you always use an integer value as the index to a collection. When you create a custom collection class and create your indexer, you are free to create indexers that index on strings and other types. In fact, the index value can be overloaded so that a given collection can be indexed, for example, by an integer value or by a string value, depending on the needs of the client.

In the case of your listbox, you might want to be able to index into the listbox based on a string. Example 9-10 illustrates a string index. The indexer calls findString( ), which is a helper method that returns a record based on the value of the string provided. Notice that the overloaded indexer and the indexer from Example 9-9 are able to coexist.

*Example 9-10. Overloading an index*

```
using System;
using System.Collections.Generic;
using System.Text;

namespace OverloadedIndexer
{
    // a simplified ListBox control
    public class ListBoxTest
    {
        private string[] strings;
        private int ctr = 0;

        // initialize the listbox with strings
        public ListBoxTest(params string[] initialStrings)
        {
            // allocate space for the strings
            strings = new String[256];

            // copy the strings passed in to the constructor
            foreach (string s in initialStrings)
            {
                strings[ctr++] = s;
            }
        }

        // add a single string to the end of the listbox
        public void Add(string theString)
        {
            strings[ctr] = theString;
            ctr++;
        }

        // allow array-like access
        public string this[int index]
        {
```

*Example 9-10. Overloading an index (continued)*

```
        get
        {
            if (index < 0 || index >= strings.Length)
            {
                // handle bad index
            }
            return strings[index];
        }
        set
        {
            strings[index] = value;
        }
    }

    private int findString(string searchString)
    {
        for (int i = 0; i < strings.Length; i++)
        {
            if (strings[i].StartsWith(searchString))
            {
                return i;
            }
        }
        return -1;
    }

    // index on string
    public string this[string index]
    {
        get
        {
            if (index.Length == 0)
            {
                // handle bad index
            }

            return this[findString(index)];
        }
        set
        {
            strings[findString(index)] = value;
        }
    }

    // publish how many strings you hold
    public int GetNumEntries()
    {
        return ctr;
    }
}
```

*Example 9-10. Overloading an index (continued)*

```
public class Tester
{
    static void Main()
    {
        // create a new listbox and initialize
        ListBoxTest lbt =
        new ListBoxTest("Hello", "World");

        // add a few strings
        lbt.Add("Who");
        lbt.Add("Is");
        lbt.Add("Douglas");
        lbt.Add("Adams");

        // test the access
        string subst = "Universe";
        lbt[1] = subst;
        lbt["Hel"] = "GoodBye";
        // lbt["xyz"] = "oops";

        // access all the strings
        for (int i = 0; i < lbt.GetNumEntries(); i++)
        {
            Console.WriteLine("lbt[{0}]: {1}", i, lbt[i]);
        } // end for
    } // end main
} // end tester
}
```

```
Output:
lbt[0]: GoodBye
lbt[1]: Universe
lbt[2]: Who
lbt[3]: Is
lbt[4]: Douglas
lbt[5]: Adams
```

Example 9-10 is identical to Example 9-9 except for the addition of an overloaded indexer, which can match a string, and the method findString, created to support that index.

The findString method simply iterates through the strings held in myStrings until it finds a string that starts with the target string you use in the index. If found, it returns the index of that string; otherwise, it returns the value -1.

We see in Main() that the user passes in a string segment to the index, just as with an integer:

```
lbt["Hel"] = "GoodBye";
```

This calls the overloaded index, which does some rudimentary error-checking (in this case, making sure the string passed in has at least one letter), and then passes the value (Hel) to findString. It gets back an index and uses that index to index into myStrings:

```
return this[findString(index)];
```

The set value works in the same way:

```
myStrings[findString(index)] = value;
```

The careful reader will note that if the string doesn't match, a value of -1 is returned, which is then used as an index into myStrings. This action then generates an exception (System.NullReferenceException), as you can see by uncommenting the following line in Main( ):

```
lbt["xyz"] = "oops";
```

The proper handling of not finding a string is, as they say, left as an exercise for the reader. You might consider displaying an error message or otherwise allowing the user to recover from the error.

# Collection Interfaces

The .NET Framework provides two sets of standard interfaces for enumerating and comparing collections: the traditional (nontype-safe) and the new generic type-safe collections. This book focuses only on the new type-safe collection interfaces, as these are far preferable.

You can declare an ICollection of any specific type by substituting the *actual* type (e.g., int or string) for the *generic* type in the interface declaration (<T>).

*C++ programmers take note*: C# Generics are similar in syntax and usage to C++ templates. However, because the generic types are expanded to their specific type at runtime, the JIT compiler is able to share code among different instances, dramatically reducing the code bloat that you may see when using templates in C++.

Table 9-2 lists the key generic collection interfaces.[*]

*Table 9-2. Collection interfaces*

| Interface | Purpose |
| --- | --- |
| ICollection<T> | Base interface for generic collections |
| IEnumerator<T> IEnumerable<T> | Enumerate through a collection using a foreach statement |

---

[*] For backward compatibility, C# also provides nongeneric interfaces (e.g., ICollection, IEnumerator), but they aren't considered here because they are obsolete.

*Table 9-2. Collection interfaces (continued)*

| Interface | Purpose |
|---|---|
| ICollection<T> | Implemented by all collections to provide the CopyTo( ) method as well as the Count, IsSynchronized, and SyncRoot properties |
| IComparer<T> IComparable<T> | Compare two objects held in a collection so that the collection can be sorted |
| IList<T> | Used by array-indexable collections |
| IDictionary<K,V> | Used for key-/value-based collections such as Dictionary |

# The IEnumerable<T> Interface

You can support the foreach statement in ListBoxTest by implementing the
IEnumerable<T> interface (see Example 9-11). IEnumerable<T> has only one method,
GetEnumerator( ), whose job is to return an implementation of IEnumerator<T>. The
C# language provides special help in creating the enumerator, using the new key-
word yield.

*Example 9-11. Making a ListBox an enumerable class*

```
using System;
using System.Collections;
using System.Collections.Generic;
using System.Text;

namespace Enumerable
{
    public class ListBoxTest : IEnumerable<string>
    {
        private string[] strings;
        private int ctr = 0;
        // Enumerable classes can return an enumerator
        public IEnumerator<string> GetEnumerator( )
        {
            foreach (string s in strings)
            {
                yield return s;
            }
        }

        // Explicit interface implementation.
        IEnumerator IEnumerable.GetEnumerator( )
        {
            return GetEnumerator( );
        }

        // initialize the listbox with strings
        public ListBoxTest(params string[] initialStrings)
        {
            // allocate space for the strings
            strings = new String[8];
```

*Example 9-11. Making a ListBox an enumerable class (continued)*

```
        // copy the strings passed in to the constructor
        foreach (string s in initialStrings)
        {
            strings[ctr++] = s;
        }
    }

    // add a single string to the end of the listbox
    public void Add(string theString)
    {
        strings[ctr] = theString;
        ctr++;
    }

    // allow array-like access
    public string this[int index]
    {
        get
        {
            if (index < 0 || index >= strings.Length)
            {
                // handle bad index
            }
            return strings[index];
        }
        set
        {
            strings[index] = value;
        }
    }

    // publish how many strings you hold
    public int GetNumEntries()
    {
        return ctr;
    }
}

public class Tester
{
    static void Main()
    {
        // create a new listbox and initialize
        ListBoxTest lbt =
        new ListBoxTest("Hello", "World");

        // add a few strings
        lbt.Add("Who");
        lbt.Add("Is");
```

*Example 9-11. Making a ListBox an enumerable class (continued)*

```
            lbt.Add("Douglas");
            lbt.Add("Adams");

            // test the access
            string subst = "Universe";
            lbt[1] = subst;

            // access all the strings
            foreach (string s in lbt)
            {
                Console.WriteLine("Value: {0}", s);
            }
        }
    }
}
```

```
Output:
Value: Hello
Value: Universe
Value: Who
Value: Is
Value: Douglas
Value: Adams
Value:
Value:
```

The program begins in Main( ), creating a new ListBoxTest object and passing two strings to the constructor. When the object is created, an array of Strings is created with enough room for eight strings. Four more strings are added using the Add method, and the second string is updated, just as in the previous example.

The big change in this version of the program is that a foreach loop is called, retrieving each string in the listbox. The foreach loop automatically uses the IEnumerable<T> interface, invoking GetEnumerator( ).

The GetEnumerator method is declared to return an IEnumerator of string:

```
    public IEnumerator<string> GetEnumerator( )
```

The implementation iterates through the array of strings, yielding each in turn:

```
    foreach ( string s in strings )
    {
      yield return s;
    }
```

All the bookkeeping for keeping track of which element is next, resetting the iterator, and so forth is provided for you by the Framework.

# Constraints

There are times when you must ensure that the elements you add to a generic list meet certain constraints (e.g., they derive from a given base class, or they implement a specific interface). In the next example, you implement a simplified, singly linked, sortable list. The list consists of Nodes, and each Node must be guaranteed that the types added to it implement IComparer. You do so with the following statement:

```
public class Node<T> :
   IComparable<Node<T>> where T : IComparable<T>
```

This defines a generic Node that holds a type, T. Node of T implements the IComparable<T> interface, which means that two Nodes of T can be compared. The Node class is constrained (where T : IComparable<T>) to hold only types that implement the IComparable interface. Thus, you may substitute any type for T as long as that type implements IComparable.

Example 9-12 illustrates the complete implementation, with analysis to follow.

*Example 9-12. Using constraints*

```
using System;
using System.Collections.Generic;

namespace UsingConstraints
{
    public class Employee : IComparable<Employee>
    {
        private string name;
        public Employee(string name)
        {
            this.name = name;
        }
        public override string ToString()
        {
            return this.name;
        }

        // implement the interface
        public int CompareTo(Employee rhs)
        {
            return this.name.CompareTo(rhs.name);
        }
        public bool Equals(Employee rhs)
        {
            return this.name == rhs.name;
        }
    }

    // node must implement IComparable of Node of T.
    // constrain Nodes to only take items that implement IComparable
    // by using the where keyword.
```

*Example 9-12. Using constraints (continued)*

```csharp
public class Node<T> :
IComparable<Node<T>> where T : IComparable<T>
{
    // member fields
    private T data;
    private Node<T> next = null;
    private Node<T> prev = null;

    // constructor
    public Node(T data)
    {
        this.data = data;
    }

    // properties
    public T Data { get { return this.data; } }

    public Node<T> Next
    {
        get { return this.next; }
    }

    public int CompareTo(Node<T> rhs)
    {
        // this works because of the constraint
        return data.CompareTo(rhs.data);
    }

    public bool Equals(Node<T> rhs)
    {
        return this.data.Equals(rhs.data);
    }

    // methods
    public Node<T> Add(Node<T> newNode)
    {
        if (this.CompareTo(newNode) > 0) // goes before me
        {
            newNode.next = this; // new node points to me

            // if I have a previous, set it to point to
            // the new node as its next
            if (this.prev != null)
            {
                this.prev.next = newNode;
                newNode.prev = this.prev;
            }

            // set prev in current node to point to new node
            this.prev = newNode;
```

*Example 9-12. Using constraints (continued)*

```
                // return the newNode in case it is the new head
                return newNode;
        }
        else // goes after me
        {
                // if I have a next, pass the new node along for
                // comparison
                if (this.next != null)
                {
                    this.next.Add(newNode);
                }

                // I don't have a next so set the new node
                // to be my next and set its prev to point to me.
                else
                {
                    this.next = newNode;
                    newNode.prev = this;
                }

                return this;
        }
    }

    public override string ToString()
    {
        string output = data.ToString();

        if (next != null)
        {
            output += ", " + next.ToString();
        }

        return output;
    }
} // end class

public class LinkedList<T> where T : IComparable<T>
{
    // member fields
    private Node<T> headNode = null;

    // properties

    // indexer
    public T this[int index]
    {
        get
        {
            int ctr = 0;
            Node<T> node = headNode;
```

*Example 9-12. Using constraints (continued)*

```
                while (node != null && ctr <= index)
                {
                    if (ctr == index)
                    {
                        return node.Data;
                    }
                    else
                    {
                        node = node.Next;
                    }

                    ++ctr;
                } // end while
                throw new ArgumentOutOfRangeException();
            } // end get
        } // end indexer

        // constructor
        public LinkedList()
        {
        }

        // methods
        public void Add(T data)
        {
            if (headNode == null)
            {
                headNode = new Node<T>(data);
            }
            else
            {
                headNode = headNode.Add(new Node<T>(data));
            }
        }
        public override string ToString()
        {
            if (this.headNode != null)
            {
                return this.headNode.ToString();
            }
            else
            {
                return string.Empty;
            }
        }
    }

    // Test engine
    class Test
    {
        // entry point
        static void Main(string[] args)
        {
```

*Example 9-12. Using constraints (continued)*

```
            // make an instance, run the method
            Test t = new Test( );
            t.Run( );
        }

        public void Run( )
        {
            LinkedList<int> myLinkedList = new LinkedList<int>( );
            Random rand = new Random( );
            Console.Write("Adding: ");

            for (int i = 0; i < 10; i++)
            {
                int nextInt = rand.Next(10);
                Console.Write("{0} ", nextInt);
                myLinkedList.Add(nextInt);
            }

            LinkedList<Employee> employees = new LinkedList<Employee>( );
            employees.Add(new Employee("Douglas"));
            employees.Add(new Employee("Paul"));
            employees.Add(new Employee("George"));
            employees.Add(new Employee("Ringo"));

            Console.WriteLine("\nRetrieving collections...");

            Console.WriteLine("Integers: " + myLinkedList);
            Console.WriteLine("Employees: " + employees);
        }
    }
}
```

In this example, you begin by declaring a class that can be placed into the linked list:

```
public class Employee : IComparable<Employee>
```

This declaration indicates that Employee objects are comparable, and you see that the Employee class implements the required methods (CompareTo and Equals). Note that these methods are type-safe (they know that the parameter passed to them will be of type Employee). The LinkedList itself is declared to hold only types that implement IComparable:

```
public class LinkedList<T> where T : IComparable<T>
```

so you are guaranteed to be able to sort the list. The LinkedList holds an object of type Node. Node also implements IComparable and requires that the objects it holds as data themselves implement IComparable:

```
public class Node<T> :
    IComparable<Node<T>> where T : IComparable<T>
```

These constraints make it safe and simple to implement the CompareTo method of Node because the Node knows it will be comparing other Nodes whose data is comparable:

```
    public int CompareTo(Node<T> rhs)
    {
        // this works because of the constraint
        return data.CompareTo(rhs.data);
    }
```

Notice that you don't have to test rhs to see whether it implements IComparable; you've already constrained Node to hold only data that implements IComparable.

# List<T>

The classic problem with the Array type is its fixed size. If you don't know in advance how many objects an array will hold, you run the risk of declaring either too small an array (and running out of room), or too large an array (and wasting memory).

Your program might be asking the user for input, or gathering input from a web site. As it finds objects (strings, books, values, etc.), you will add them to the array, but you have no idea how many objects you'll collect in any given session. The classic fixed-size array is not a good choice, as you can't predict how large an array you'll need.

The List class is an array whose size is dynamically increased as required. Lists provide a number of useful methods and properties for their manipulation. Table 9-3 shows some of the most important ones.

*Table 9-3. List methods and properties*

| Method or property | Purpose |
|---|---|
| Capacity | Property to get or set the number of elements the List can contain; this value is increased automatically if count exceeds capacity; you might set this value to reduce the number of reallocations, and you may call Trim( ) to reduce this value to the actual Count |
| Count | Property to get the number of elements currently in the array |
| Item( ) | Gets or sets the element at the specified index; this is the indexer for the List class[a] |
| Add( ) | Public method to add an object to the List |
| AddRange( ) | Public method that adds the elements of an ICollection to the end of the List |
| AsReadOnly( ) | Public method that returns a read-only instance of the current instance |
| BinarySearch( ) | Overloaded public method that uses a binary search to locate a specific element in a sorted List |
| Clear( ) | Removes all elements from the List |
| Contains( ) | Determines whether an element is in the List |
| ConvertAll( ) | Public method that converts all elements in the current list into another type |
| CopyTo( ) | Overloaded public method that copies a List to a one-dimensional array |
| Exists( ) | Determines whether an element is in the List |
| Find( ) | Returns the first occurrence of the element in the List |
| FindAll( ) | Returns all the specified elements in the List |
| FindIndex( ) | Overloaded public method that returns the index of the first element that matches a condition |
| FindLast( ) | Public method that finds the last element that matches a condition |

*Table 9-3. List methods and properties (continued)*

| Method or property | Purpose |
|---|---|
| FindLastIndex( ) | Overloaded public method that returns the index of the last element that matches a condition |
| ForEach( ) | Public static method that performs an action on all elements of an array |
| GetEnumerator( ) | Overloaded public method that returns an enumerator to iterate through a List |
| GetRange( ) | Copies a range of elements to a new List |
| IndexOf( ) | Overloaded public method that returns the index of the first occurrence of a value |
| Insert( ) | Inserts an element into the List |
| InsertRange( ) | Inserts the elements of a collection into the List |
| LastIndexOf( ) | Overloaded public method that returns the index of the last occurrence of a value in the List |
| Remove( ) | Removes the first occurrence of a specific object |
| RemoveAll( ) | Removes all elements that match a specific condition |
| RemoveAt( ) | Removes the element at the specified index |
| RemoveRange( ) | Removes a range of elements |
| Reverse( ) | Reverses the order of elements in the List |
| Sort( ) | Sorts the List |
| ToArray( ) | Copies the elements of the List to a new array |
| TrimExcess( ) | Reduce the current list's capacity to the actual number of elements in the list |
| TrimToSize( ) | Sets the capacity of the actual number of elements in the List |

[a] The idiom in the FCL is to provide an Item element for collection classes that is implemented as an indexer in C#.

When you create a List, you don't define how many objects it will contain. You add to the List using the Add( ) method, and the list takes care of its own internal book-keeping, as illustrated in Example 9-13.

*Example 9-13. Working with List*

```
using System;
using System.Collections.Generic;
using System.Text;

namespace ListCollection
{
    // a simple class to store in the List
    public class Employee
    {
        public Employee(int empID)
        {
            this.EmpID = empID;
        }
        public override string ToString()
        {
            return EmpID.ToString();
        }
        public int EmpID { get; set; }
```

*Example 9-13. Working with List (continued)*

```
    }
    public class Tester
    {
        static void Main( )
        {
            List<Employee> empList = new List<Employee>( );
            List<int> intList = new List<int>( );

            // populate the List
            for (int i = 0; i < 5; i++)
            {
                empList.Add(new Employee(i + 100));
                intList.Add(i * 5);
            }

            // print all the contents
            for (int i = 0; i < intList.Count; i++)
            {
                Console.Write("{0} ", intList[i].ToString( ));
            }

            Console.WriteLine("\n");

            // print all the contents of the Employee List
            for (int i = 0; i < empList.Count; i++)
            {
                Console.Write("{0} ", empList[i].ToString( ));
            }

            Console.WriteLine("\n");
            Console.WriteLine("empList.Capacity: {0}",
                empList.Capacity);
        }
    }
}
```

```
Output:
0 5 10 15 20
100 101 102 103 104
empArray.Capacity: 8
```

With an Array class, you define how many objects the array will hold. If you try to add more than that, the Array class will throw an exception. With a List, you don't declare how many objects the List will hold. The List has a property, Capacity, which is the number of elements that the List is capable of storing:

```
    public int Capacity { get; set; }
```

The default capacity is eight. When you add the 17th element, the capacity is automatically doubled to 16. If you change the for loop to:

```
    for (int i = 0;i < 9;i++)
```

the output looks like this:

```
0 5 10 15 20 25 30 35 40 45 50 55 60 65 70 75 80
5 6 7 8 9 10 11 12 13 14 15 16 17 18 19 20 21
empArray.Capacity: 32
```

You can manually set the capacity to any number equal to or greater than the count. If you set it to a number less than the count, the program will throw an exception of type ArgumentOutOfRangeException.

## Implementing IComparable

Like all collections, the List implements the Sort( ) method, which allows you to sort any objects that implement IComparable. In the next example, you'll modify the Employee object to implement IComparable:

```
public class Employee : IComparable<Employee>
```

To implement the IComparable<Employee> interface, the Employee object must provide a CompareTo( ) method:

```
public int CompareTo(Employee rhs)
{
    return this.empID.CompareTo(rhs.empID);
}
```

The CompareTo( ) method takes an Employee as a parameter. You know this is an Employee because this is a type-safe collection. The current Employee object must compare itself to the Employee passed in as a parameter and return -1 if it is smaller than the parameter, 1 if it is greater than the parameter, and 0 if it is equal to the parameter. It is up to Employee to determine what *smaller than*, *greater than*, and *equal to* mean. In this example, you delegate the comparison to the empId member. The empId member is an int and uses the default CompareTo( ) method for integer types, which will do an integer comparison of the two values.

 The System.Int32 class implements IComparable<Int32>, so you may delegate the comparison responsibility to integers.

You are now ready to sort the array list of employees, empList. To see whether the sort is working, you'll need to add integers and Employee instances to their respective arrays with random values. To create the random values, you'll instantiate an object of class Random; to generate the random values, you'll call the Next( ) method on the Random object, which returns a pseudorandom number. The Next( ) method is overloaded; one version allows you to pass in an integer that represents the largest random number you want. In this case, you'll pass in the value 10 to generate a random number between 0 and 10:

```
Random r = new Random( );
r.Next(10);
```

Example 9-14 creates an integer array and an Employee array, populates them both with random numbers, and prints their values. It then sorts both arrays and prints the new values.

*Example 9-14. Sorting an integer and an employee array*

```
using System;
using System.Collections.Generic;
using System.Text;

namespace IComparable
{
    // a simple class to store in the array
    public class Employee : IComparable<Employee>
    {
        private int empID;

        public Employee(int empID)
        {
            this.empID = empID;
        }

        public override string ToString()
        {
            return empID.ToString();
        }

        public bool Equals(Employee other)
        {
            if (this.empID == other.empID)
            {
                return true;
            }
            else
            {
                return false;
            }
        }

        // Comparer delegates back to Employee
        // Employee uses the integer's default
        // CompareTo method

        public int CompareTo(Employee rhs)
        {
            return this.empID.CompareTo(rhs.empID);
        }
    }
    public class Tester
    {
        static void Main()
        {
            List<Employee> empArray = new List<Employee>();
            List<Int32> intArray = new List<Int32>();
```

*Example 9-14. Sorting an integer and an employee array (continued)*

```
            // generate random numbers for
            // both the integers and the
            // employee IDs

            Random r = new Random( );

            // populate the array
            for (int i = 0; i < 5; i++)
            {
                // add a random employee id
                empArray.Add(new Employee(r.Next(10) + 100));

                // add a random integer
                intArray.Add(r.Next(10));
            }

            // display all the contents of the int array
            for (int i = 0; i < intArray.Count; i++)
            {
                Console.Write("{0} ", intArray[i].ToString( ));
            }
            Console.WriteLine("\n");

            // display all the contents of the Employee array
            for (int i = 0; i < empArray.Count; i++)
            {
                Console.Write("{0} ", empArray[i].ToString( ));
            }
            Console.WriteLine("\n");

            // sort and display the int array
            intArray.Sort( );
            for (int i = 0; i < intArray.Count; i++)
            {
                Console.Write("{0} ", intArray[i].ToString( ));
            }
            Console.WriteLine("\n");

            // sort and display the employee array
            empArray.Sort( );

            // display all the contents of the Employee array
            for (int i = 0; i < empArray.Count; i++)
            {
                Console.Write("{0} ", empArray[i].ToString( ));
            }
            Console.WriteLine("\n");
        }
    }
}
```

*Example 9-14. Sorting an integer and an employee array (continued)*

```
Output:
4 5 6 5 7
108 100 101 103 103
4 5 5 6 7
100 101 103 103 108
```

The output shows that the integer array and Employee array were generated with random numbers. When sorted, the display shows the values have been ordered properly.

## Implementing IComparer

When you call Sort( ) on the List, the default implementation of IComparer is called, which uses QuickSort to call the IComparable implementation of CompareTo( ) on each element in the List.

You are free to create your own implementation of IComparer, which you might want to do if you need control over how the sort ordering is defined. In the next example, you will add a second field to Employee, yearsOfSvc. You want to be able to sort the Employee objects in the List on either field—empID or yearsOfSvc.

To accomplish this, create a custom implementation of IComparer that you pass to the Sort( ) method of the List. This IComparer class, EmployeeComparer, knows about Employee objects and knows how to sort them.

EmployeeComparer has the WhichComparison property, of type Employee. EmployeeComparer.ComparisonType:

```
public Employee.EmployeeComparer.ComparisonType
  WhichComparison
{
  get{return whichComparison;}
  set{whichComparison = value;}
}
```

ComparisonType is an enumeration with two values, empID and yearsOfSvc (indicating that you want to sort by employee ID or years of service, respectively):

```
public enum ComparisonType
{
  EmpID,
  YearsOfService
};
```

Before invoking Sort( ), create an instance of EmployeeComparer, and set its ComparisonType property:

```
Employee.EmployeeComparer c = Employee.GetComparer( );
c.WhichComparison=Employee.EmployeeComparer.ComparisonType.EmpID;
empArray.Sort(c);
```

When you invoke Sort( ), the List calls the Compare method on the EmployeeComparer, which in turn delegates the comparison to the Employee.CompareTo( ) method, passing in its WhichComparison property:

```
public int Compare( Employee lhs, Employee rhs )
{
  return lhs.CompareTo( rhs, WhichComparison );
}
```

The Employee object must implement a custom version of CompareTo( ), which takes the comparison, and compares the objects accordingly:

```
public int CompareTo(
  Employee rhs,
  Employee.EmployeeComparer.ComparisonType which)
{
  switch (which)
  {
    case Employee.EmployeeComparer.ComparisonType.EmpID:
      return this.empID.CompareTo(rhs.empID);
    case Employee.EmployeeComparer.ComparisonType.Yrs:
      return this.yearsOfSvc.CompareTo(rhs.yearsOfSvc);
  }
  return 0;
}
```

Example 9-15 shows the complete source for this example. The integer array has been removed to simplify the example and the output of the employee's ToString( ) method has been enhanced to enable you to see the effects of the sort.

*Example 9-15. Sorting an array by employees' IDs and years of service*

```
using System;
using System.Collections.Generic;
using System.Text;

namespace IComparer
{
    public class Employee : IComparable<Employee>
    {
        private int empID;

        private int yearsOfSvc = 1;

        public Employee(int empID)
        {
            this.empID = empID;
        }

        public Employee(int empID, int yearsOfSvc)
        {
            this.empID = empID;
            this.yearsOfSvc = yearsOfSvc;
        }
```

*Example 9-15. Sorting an array by employees' IDs and years of service (continued)*

```
public override string ToString()
{
    return "ID: " + empID.ToString() +
    ". Years of Svc: " + yearsOfSvc.ToString();
}

public bool Equals(Employee other)
{
    if (this.empID == other.empID)
    {
        return true;
    }
    else
    {
        return false;
    }
}

// static method to get a Comparer object
public static EmployeeComparer GetComparer()
{
    return new Employee.EmployeeComparer();
}

// Comparer delegates back to Employee
// Employee uses the integer's default
// CompareTo method
public int CompareTo(Employee rhs)
{
    return this.empID.CompareTo(rhs.empID);
}

// Special implementation to be called by custom comparer
public int CompareTo(Employee rhs,
        Employee.EmployeeComparer.ComparisonType which)
{
    switch (which)
    {
        case Employee.EmployeeComparer.ComparisonType.EmpID:
            return this.empID.CompareTo(rhs.empID);
        case Employee.EmployeeComparer.ComparisonType.Yrs:
            return this.yearsOfSvc.CompareTo(rhs.yearsOfSvc);
    }
    return 0;

}

// nested class which implements IComparer
public class EmployeeComparer : IComparer<Employee>
{
    // enumeration of comparison types
    public enum ComparisonType
```

*Example 9-15. Sorting an array by employees' IDs and years of service (continued)*

```csharp
    {
        EmpID,
        Yrs
    };

    public bool Equals(Employee lhs, Employee rhs)
    {
        return this.Compare(lhs, rhs) == 0;
    }

    public int GetHashCode(Employee e)
    {
        return e.GetHashCode( );
    }

    // Tell the Employee objects to compare themselves
    public int Compare(Employee lhs, Employee rhs)
    {
        return lhs.CompareTo(rhs, WhichComparison);
    }

    public Employee.EmployeeComparer.ComparisonType
        WhichComparison {get; set;}
    }
}
public class Tester
{
    static void Main( )
    {
        List<Employee> empArray = new List<Employee>( );

        // generate random numbers for
        // both the integers and the
        // employee IDs
        Random r = new Random( );

        // populate the array
        for (int i = 0; i < 5; i++)
        {
            // add a random employee ID

            empArray.Add(
            new Employee(
            r.Next(10) + 100, r.Next(20)
            )
            );
        }

        // display all the contents of the Employee array
        for (int i = 0; i < empArray.Count; i++)
        {
            Console.Write("\n{0} ", empArray[i].ToString( ));
```

*Example 9-15. Sorting an array by employees' IDs and years of service (continued)*

```
        }
        Console.WriteLine("\n");

        // sort and display the employee array
        Employee.EmployeeComparer c = Employee.GetComparer();
        c.WhichComparison =
        Employee.EmployeeComparer.ComparisonType.EmpID;
        empArray.Sort(c);

        // display all the contents of the Employee array
        for (int i = 0; i < empArray.Count; i++)
        {
            Console.Write("\n{0} ", empArray[i].ToString());
        }
        Console.WriteLine("\n");

        c.WhichComparison = Employee.EmployeeComparer.ComparisonType.Yrs;
        empArray.Sort(c);

        for (int i = 0; i < empArray.Count; i++)
        {
            Console.Write("\n{0} ", empArray[i].ToString());
        }
        Console.WriteLine("\n");
    }
  }
}
```

```
Output:
ID: 103. Years of Svc: 11
ID: 101. Years of Svc: 15
ID: 107. Years of Svc: 14
ID: 108. Years of Svc: 5
ID: 102. Years of Svc: 0

ID: 101. Years of Svc: 15
ID: 102. Years of Svc: 0
ID: 103. Years of Svc: 11
ID: 107. Years of Svc: 14
ID: 108. Years of Svc: 15
ID: 108. Years of Svc: 5

ID: 102. Years of Svc: 0
ID: 108. Years of Svc: 5
ID: 103. Years of Svc: 11
ID: 107. Years of Svc: 14
ID: 101. Years of Svc: 15
```

The first block of output shows the Employee objects as they are added to the List. The employee ID values and the years of service are in random order. The second block shows the results of sorting by the employee ID, and the third block shows the results of sorting by years of service.

If you are creating your own collection, as in Example 9-11, and wish to implement IComparer, you may need to ensure that all the types placed in the list implement IComparer (so that they may be sorted), by using constraints, as described earlier. Note that in a production environment, employee ID would always be nonrandom and unique.

# Queues

A *queue* represents a first-in, first-out (FIFO) collection. The classic analogy is to a line (or queue, if you are British) at a ticket window. The first person in line ought to be the first person to come off the line to buy a ticket.

A queue is a good collection to use when you are managing a limited resource. For example, you might want to send messages to a resource that can handle only one message at a time. You would then create a message queue so that you can say to your clients: "Your message is important to us. Messages are handled in the order in which they are received."

The Queue class has a number of member methods and properties, as shown in Table 9-4.

*Table 9-4. Queue methods and properties*

| Method or property | Purpose |
| --- | --- |
| Count | Public property that gets the number of elements in the Queue |
| Clear( ) | Removes all objects from the Queue |
| Contains( ) | Determines whether an element is in the Queue |
| CopyTo( ) | Copies the Queue elements to an existing one-dimensional array |
| Dequeue( ) | Removes and returns the object at the beginning of the Queue |
| Enqueue( ) | Adds an object to the end of the Queue |
| GetEnumerator( ) | Returns an enumerator for the Queue |
| Peek( ) | Returns the object at the beginning of the Queue without removing it |
| ToArray( ) | Copies the elements to a new array |
| TrimExcess( ) | Reduces the current queue's capacity to the actual number of elements in the list |

You add elements to your queue with the Enqueue command, and take them off the queue with Dequeue or by using an enumerator. Example 9-16 illustrates.

*Example 9-16. Working with a queue*

```
using System;
using System.Collections.Generic;
using System.Text;
```

*Example 9-16. Working with a queue (continued)*

```
namespace Queue
{
    public class Tester
    {
        static void Main( )
        {
            Queue<Int32> intQueue = new Queue<Int32>( );

            // populate the array
            for (int i = 0; i < 5; i++)
            {
                intQueue.Enqueue(i * 5);
            }

            // Display the Queue.
            Console.Write("intQueue values:\t");
            PrintValues(intQueue);

            // Remove an element from the queue.
            Console.WriteLine(
            "\n(Dequeue)\t{0}", intQueue.Dequeue( ));

            // Display the Queue.
            Console.Write("intQueue values:\t");
            PrintValues(intQueue);

            // Remove another element from the queue.
            Console.WriteLine(
            "\n(Dequeue)\t{0}", intQueue.Dequeue( ));

            // Display the Queue.
            Console.Write("intQueue values:\t");
            PrintValues(intQueue);

            // View the first element in the
            // Queue but do not remove.
            Console.WriteLine(
            "\n(Peek) \t{0}", intQueue.Peek( ));

            // Display the Queue.
            Console.Write("intQueue values:\t");
            PrintValues(intQueue);
        }

        public static void PrintValues(IEnumerable<Int32> myCollection)
        {
            IEnumerator<Int32> myEnumerator =
            myCollection.GetEnumerator( );
            while (myEnumerator.MoveNext( ))
                Console.Write("{0} ", myEnumerator.Current);
            Console.WriteLine( );
        }
```

*Example 9-16. Working with a queue (continued)*

```
    }
}
```

```
Output:
intQueue values: 0 5 10 15 20

(Dequeue) 0
intQueue values: 5 10 15 20

(Dequeue) 5
intQueue values: 10 15 20

(Peek) 10
intQueue values: 10 15 20
```

In this example, the List is replaced by a Queue. We've dispensed with the Employee class to save room, but of course, you can Enqueue user-defined objects as well.

The output shows that queuing objects adds them to the Queue, and calls to Dequeue return the object as well as remove them from the Queue. The Queue class also provides a Peek( ) method that allows you to see, but not remove, the first element.

Because the Queue class is enumerable, you can pass it to the PrintValues method, which is provided as an IEnumerable interface. The conversion is implicit. In the PrintValues method, you call GetEnumerator, which you will remember is the single method of all IEnumerable classes. This returns an IEnumerator, which you then use to enumerate all the objects in the collection.

# Stacks

A *stack* is a last-in, first-out (LIFO) collection, like a stack of dishes at a buffet table or a stack of coins on your desk. An item added on top is the first item you take off the stack.

The principal methods for adding to and removing from a stack are Push( ) and Pop( ); Stack also offers a Peek( ) method, very much like Queue. Table 9-5 shows the significant methods and properties for Stack.

*Table 9-5. Stack methods and properties*

| Method or property | Purpose |
| --- | --- |
| Count | Public property that gets the number of elements in the Stack |
| Clear( ) | Removes all objects from the Stack |
| Contains( ) | Determines whether an element is in the Stack |
| CopyTo( ) | Copies the Stack elements to an existing one-dimensional array |
| GetEnumerator( ) | Returns an enumerator for the Stack |

*Table 9-5. Stack methods and properties (continued)*

| Method or property | Purpose |
| --- | --- |
| Peek( ) | Returns the object at the top of the Stack without removing it |
| Pop( ) | Removes and returns the object at the top of the Stack |
| Push( ) | Inserts an object at the top of the Stack |
| ToArray( ) | Copies the elements to a new array |
| TrimExcess( ) | If the number of elements in the current stack is less than 90 percent of its capacity, reduces the current stack's capacity to the actual number of elements in the stack |

The List, Queue, and Stack types contain overloaded CopyTo( ) and ToArray( ) methods for copying their elements to an array. In the case of a Stack, the CopyTo( ) method will copy its elements to an existing one-dimensional array, overwriting the contents of the array beginning at the index you specify. The ToArray( ) method returns a new array with the contents of the stack's elements. Example 9-17 illustrates.

*Example 9-17. Working with a stack*

```
using System;
using System.Collections.Generic;
using System.Text;

namespace Stack
{
    public class Tester
    {
        static void Main( )
        {
            Stack<Int32> intStack = new Stack<Int32>( );

            // populate the array
            for (int i = 0; i < 8; i++)
            {
                intStack.Push(i * 5);
            }

            // Display the Stack.
            Console.Write("intStack values:\t");
            PrintValues(intStack);

            // Remove an element from the stack.
            Console.WriteLine("\n(Pop)\t{0}",
                intStack.Pop( ));

            // Display the Stack.
            Console.Write("intStack values:\t");
            PrintValues(intStack);

            // Remove another element from the stack.
            Console.WriteLine("\n(Pop)\t{0}",
                intStack.Pop( ));
```

*Example 9-17. Working with a stack (continued)*

```
            // Display the Stack.
            Console.Write("intStack values:\t");
            PrintValues(intStack);

            // View the first element in the
            // Stack but do not remove.
            Console.WriteLine("\n(Peek) \t{0}",
            intStack.Peek());

            // Display the Stack.
            Console.Write("intStack values:\t");
            PrintValues(intStack);

            // declare an array object which will
            // hold 12 integers
            int[] targetArray = new int[12];

            for (int i = 0; i < targetArray.Length; i++)
            {
                targetArray[i] = i * 100 + 100;
            }
            // Display the values of the target Array instance.
            Console.WriteLine("\nTarget array: ");
            PrintValues(targetArray);

            // Copy the entire source Stack to the
            // target Array instance, starting at index 6.
            intStack.CopyTo(targetArray, 6);

            // Display the values of the target Array instance.
            Console.WriteLine("\nTarget array after copy: ");
            PrintValues(targetArray);
        }

        public static void PrintValues(
        IEnumerable<Int32> myCollection)
        {
            IEnumerator<Int32> enumerator =
            myCollection.GetEnumerator();
            while (enumerator.MoveNext())
                Console.Write("{0} ", enumerator.Current);
            Console.WriteLine();
        }
    }
}

Output:
intStack values: 35 30 25 20 15 10 5 0
```

*Example 9-17. Working with a stack (continued)*

```
(Pop) 35
intStack values: 30 25 20 15 10 5 0

(Pop) 30
intStack values: 25 20 15 10 5 0

(Peek) 25
intStack values: 25 20 15 10 5 0

Target array:
100 200 300 400 500 600 700 800 900 1000 1100 1200

Target array after copy:
100 200 300 400 500 600 25 20 15 10 5 0
```

The output reflects that the items pushed onto the stack were popped in reverse order.

You can see the effect of CopyTo( ) by examining the target array before and after calling CopyTo( ). The array elements are overwritten beginning with the index specified (6).

# Dictionaries

A *dictionary* is a collection that associates a *key* to a *value*. A language dictionary, such as Webster's, associates a word (the key) with its definition (the value).

To see the value of dictionaries, start by imagining that you want to keep a list of the state capitals. One approach might be to put them in an array:

```
string[] stateCapitals = new string[50];
```

The stateCapitals array will hold 50 state capitals. Each capital is accessed as an off-set into the array. For example, to access the capital of Arkansas, you need to know that Arkansas is the fourth state in alphabetical order:

```
string capitalOfArkansas = stateCapitals[3];
```

It is inconvenient, however, to access state capitals using array notation. After all, if we need the capital of Massachusetts, there is no easy way for us to determine that Massachusetts is the 21st state alphabetically.

It would be far more convenient to store the capital with the state name. A dictionary allows you to store a value (in this case, the capital) with a key (in this case, the name of the state).

A .NET Framework dictionary can associate any kind of key (string, integer, object, etc.) with any kind of value (string, integer, object, etc.). Typically, of course, the key is fairly short, the value fairly complex.

The most important attributes of a good dictionary are that it is easy to add and quick to retrieve values (see Table 9-6).

*Table 9-6. Dictionary methods and properties*

| Method or property | Purpose |
| --- | --- |
| Count | Public property that gets the number of elements in the Dictionary |
| Item( ) | The indexer for the Dictionary |
| Keys | Public property that gets a collection containing the keys in the Dictionary (see also Values) |
| Values | Public property that gets a collection containing the values in the Dictionary (see also Keys) |
| Add( ) | Adds an entry with a specified Key and Value |
| Clear( ) | Removes all objects from the Dictionary |
| ContainsKey( ) | Determines whether the Dictionary has a specified key |
| ContainsValue( ) | Determines whether the Dictionary has a specified value |
| GetEnumerator( ) | Returns an enumerator for the Dictionary |
| GetObjectData( ) | Implements ISerializable and returns the data needed to serialize the Dictionary |
| Remove( ) | Removes the entry with the specified Key |
| TryGetValue( ) | Gets the Value associated with the specified Key; if the Key does not exist, gets the default value of the Value type |

The key in a Dictionary can be a primitive type, or it can be an instance of a user-defined type (an object). Objects used as keys for a Dictionary must implement GetHashCode( ) as well as Equals. In most cases, you can simply use the inherited implementation from Object.

# IDictionary<K,V>

Dictionaries implement the IDictionary<K,V> interface (where K is the key type, and V is the value type). IDictionary provides a public property, Item. The Item property retrieves a value with the specified key. In C#, the declaration for the Item property is:

```
V[K key]
{get; set;}
```

The Item property is implemented in C# with the index operator ([ ]). Thus, you access items in any Dictionary object using the offset syntax, as you would with an array.

Example 9-18 demonstrates adding items to a Dictionary and then retrieving them with the Item property.

*Example 9-18. The Item property as offset operators*

```
using System;
using System.Collections.Generic;

namespace Dictionary
{
    public class Tester
    {
        static void Main( )
        {
            // Create and initialize a new Dictionary.
            Dictionary<string, string> Dictionary =
                new Dictionary<string, string>( );
            Dictionary.Add("000440312", "Jesse Liberty");
            Dictionary.Add("000123933", "Stacey Liberty");
            Dictionary.Add("000145938", "Douglas Adams");
            Dictionary.Add("000773394", "Ayn Rand");

            // access a particular item
            Console.WriteLine("myDictionary[\"000145938\"]: {0}",
            Dictionary["000145938"]);
        }
    }
}
```

```
Output:
Dictionary["000145938"]: Douglas Adams
```

Example 9-18 begins by instantiating a new Dictionary. The type of the key and of the value is declared to be string.

Add four key/value pairs. In this example, the Social Security number is tied to the person's full name. (Note that the Social Security numbers here are intentionally bogus.)

Once the items are added, you access a specific entry in the dictionary using the Social Security number as the key.

If you use a reference type as a key, and the type is mutable (strings are immutable), you must not change the value of the key object once you are using it in a dictionary.

If, for example, you use the Employee object as a key, changing the employee ID creates problems if that property is used by the Equals or GetHashCode method because the dictionary consults these methods.

# CHAPTER 10

# Strings and Regular Expressions

There was a time when people thought of computers exclusively as manipulating numeric values. Early computers were first used to calculate missile trajectories (though recently declassified documents suggest that some were used for code-breaking as well). In any case, there was a time that programming was taught in the math department of major universities, and computer science was considered a discipline of mathematics.

Today, most programs are concerned more with strings of characters than with strings of numbers. Typically, these strings are used for word processing, document manipulation, and creation of web pages.

C# provides built-in support for a fully functional string type. More important, C# treats strings as objects that encapsulate all the manipulation, sorting, and searching methods normally applied to strings of characters.

 *C programmers take note*: in C#, string is a first-class type, not an array of characters.

Complex string manipulation and pattern-matching are aided by the use of *regular expressions*. C# combines the power and complexity of regular expression syntax, originally found only in string manipulation languages such as awk and Perl, with a fully object-oriented design.

In this chapter, you will learn to work with the C# string type and the .NET Framework System.String class that it aliases. You will see how to extract substrings, manipulate and concatenate strings, and build new strings with the StringBuilder class. In addition, you will learn how to use the RegEx class to match strings based on complex regular expressions.

# Strings

C# treats strings as first-class types that are flexible, powerful, and easy to use.

 In C# programming, you typically use the C# alias for a Framework type (e.g., int for Int32), but you are always free to use the underlying type. C# programmers thus use string (lowercase) and the underlying Framework type String (uppercase) interchangeably.

The declaration of the String class is:

```
public sealed class String :
    IComparable, IComparable<String>, ICloneable, IConvertible,
    IEnumerable, IEnumerable<char>, IEquatable<String>
```

This declaration reveals that the class is sealed, meaning that it is not possible to derive from the String class. The class also implements seven system interfaces—IComparable, IComparable<String>, ICloneable, IConvertible, IEnumerable, IEnumerable<String>, and IEquatable<String>—that dictate functionality that String shares with other classes in the .NET Framework.

 Each string object is an *immutable* sequence of Unicode characters. The fact that String is immutable means that methods that appear to change the string actually return a modified copy; the original string remains intact in memory until it is garbage-collected. This may have performance implications; if you plan to do significant repeated string manipulation, use a StringBuilder (described later).

As explained in Chapter 9, the IComparable<String> interface is implemented by types whose values can be ordered. Strings, for example, can be alphabetized; any given string can be compared with another string to determine which should come first in an ordered list.* IComparable classes implement the CompareTo method. IEnumerable, also discussed in Chapter 9, lets you use the foreach construct to enumerate a string as a collection of chars.

ICloneable objects can create new instances with the same value as the original instance. In this case, it is possible to clone a string to produce a new string with the same values (characters) as the original. ICloneable classes implement the Clone( ) method.

---

* Ordering the string is one of a number of lexical operations that act on the value of the string and take into account culture-specific information based on the explicitly declared culture or the implicit current culture. Therefore, if the current culture is U.S. English (as is assumed throughout this book), the Compare method considers a less than A. CompareOrdinal performs an ordinal comparison, and thus regardless of culture, a is greater than A.

Actually, because strings are immutable, the Clone( ) method on String just returns a reference to the original string.

If you use that reference to make a change, a new string is created and the reference created by Clone( ) now points to the new (changed) string:

```
string s1 = "One Two Three Four";
string sx = (string)s1.Clone( );Console.WriteLine(
    Object.ReferenceEquals(s1,sx));
sx += " Five";
Console.WriteLine(
    Object.ReferenceEquals(s1, sx));
Console.WriteLine(sx);
```

In this case, sx is created as a clone of s1. The first WriteLine statement will print the word true; the two string variables refer to the same string in memory. When you change sx, you actually create a new string from the first, and when the ReferenceEquals method returns false, the final WriteLine statement returns the contents of the original string with the word Five appended.

IConvertible classes provide methods to facilitate conversion to other primitive types such as ToInt32( ), ToDouble( ), ToDecimal( ), and so on.

## Creating Strings

The most common way to create a string is to assign a quoted string of characters, known as a *string literal*, to a user-defined variable of type string:

```
string newString = "This is a string literal";
```

Quoted strings can include *escape characters*, such as \n or \t, which begin with a backslash character (\). The two shown are used to indicate where line breaks or tabs are to appear, respectively.

Because the backslash is the escape character, if you want to put a backslash into a string (e.g., to create a path listing), you must quote the backslash with a second backslash (\\).

Strings can also be created using *verbatim* string literals, which start with the at (@) symbol. This tells the String constructor that the string should be used verbatim, even if it spans multiple lines or includes escape characters. In a verbatim string literal, backslashes and the characters that follow them are simply considered additional characters of the string. Thus, the following two definitions are equivalent:

```
string literalOne = "\\\\MySystem\\MyDirectory\\ProgrammingC#.cs";
string verbatimLiteralOne = @"\\MySystem\MyDirectory\ProgrammingC#.cs";
```

In the first line, a nonverbatim string literal is used, and so the backslash character (\)
must be *escaped*. This means it must be preceded by a second backslash character. In
the second line, a verbatim literal string is used, so the extra backslash is not needed. A
second example illustrates multiline verbatim strings:

```
string literalTwo = "Line One\nLine Two";
string verbatimLiteralTwo = @"Line One
Line Two";
```

 If you have double quotes within a verbatim string, you must escape
them (with double-double quotes) so that the compiler knows when
the verbatim string ends. For example:

```
String verbatim = @"This is a ""verbatim"" string"
```

will produce the output:

```
This is a "verbatim" string
```

Again, these declarations are interchangeable. Which one you use is a matter of convenience and personal style.

## The ToString( ) Method

Another common way to create a string is to call the ToString( ) method on an
object and assign the result to a string variable. All the built-in types override this
method to simplify the task of converting a value (often a numeric value) to a string
representation of that value. In the following example, the ToString( ) method of an
integer type is called to store its value in a string:

```
int myInteger = 5;
string integerString = myInteger.ToString( );
```

The call to myInteger.ToString( ) returns a String object, which is then assigned to
integerString.

The .NET String class provides a wealth of overloaded constructors that support a
variety of techniques for assigning string values to string types. Some of these constructors enable you to create a string by passing in a character array or character
pointer. Passing in a character array as a parameter to the constructor of the String
creates a CLR-compliant new instance of a string. Passing in a character pointer
requires the unsafe marker, as explained in Chapter 23.

## Manipulating Strings

The string class provides a host of methods for comparing, searching, and manipulating strings, the most important of which appear in Table 10-1.

*Table 10-1. Methods and fields for the string class*

| Method or field | Purpose |
| --- | --- |
| Chars | The string indexer |
| Compare( ) | Overloaded public static method that compares two strings |
| CompareTo( ) | Compares this string with another |
| Concat( ) | Overloaded public static method that creates a new string from one or more strings |
| Copy( ) | Public static method that creates a new string by copying another |
| CopyTo( ) | Copies the specified number of characters to an array of Unicode characters |
| Empty | Public static field that represents the empty string |
| EndsWith( ) | Indicates whether the specified string matches the end of this string |
| Equals( ) | Overloaded public static and instance method that determines whether two strings have the same value |
| Format( ) | Overloaded public static method that formats a string using a format specification |
| Join( ) | Overloaded public static method that concatenates a specified string between each element of a string array |
| Length | The number of characters in the instance |
| Split( ) | Returns the substrings delimited by the specified characters in a string array |
| StartsWith( ) | Indicates whether the string starts with the specified characters |
| Substring( ) | Retrieves a substring |
| ToUpper( ) | Returns a copy of the string in uppercase |
| Trim( ) | Removes all occurrences of a set of specified characters from the beginning and end of the string |
| TrimEnd( ) | Behaves like Trim( ), but only at the end |

Example 10-1 illustrates the use of some of these methods, including Compare( ), Concat( ) (and the overloaded + operator), Copy( ) (and the = operator), Insert( ), EndsWith( ), and IndexOf( ).

*Example 10-1. Working with strings*

```
using System;
using System.Collections.Generic;
using System.Text;

namespace WorkingWithStrings
{
    public static class StringTester
    {
        static void Main()
        {
            // create some strings to work with
            string s1 = "abcd";
            string s2 = "ABCD";
            string s3 = @"Liberty Associates, Inc.
                provides custom .NET development,
                on-site Training and Consulting";
```

*Example 10-1. Working with strings (continued)*

```
int result; // hold the results of comparisons

// compare two strings, case sensitive
result = string.Compare(s1, s2);
Console.WriteLine(
"compare s1: {0}, s2: {1}, result: {2}\n", s1, s2, result);

// overloaded compare, takes boolean "ignore case"
//(true = ignore case)
result = string.Compare(s1, s2, true);
Console.WriteLine("compare insensitive\n");
Console.WriteLine("s4: {0}, s2: {1}, result: {2}\n", s1, s2, result);

// concatenation method
string s6 = string.Concat(s1, s2);
Console.WriteLine("s6 concatenated from s1 and s2: {0}", s6);

// use the overloaded operator
string s7 = s1 + s2;
Console.WriteLine("s7 concatenated from s1 + s2: {0}", s7);

// the string copy method
string s8 = string.Copy(s7);
Console.WriteLine("s8 copied from s7: {0}", s8);

// use the overloaded operator
string s9 = s8;
Console.WriteLine("s9 = s8: {0}", s9);

// three ways to compare.
Console.WriteLine(
"\nDoes s9.Equals(s8)?: {0}", s9.Equals(s8));
Console.WriteLine("Does Equals(s9,s8)?: {0}", string.Equals(s9, s8));
Console.WriteLine("Does s9==s8?: {0}", s9 == s8);

// Two useful properties: the index and the length
Console.WriteLine("\nString s9 is {0} characters long. ", s9.Length);
Console.WriteLine("The 5th character is {0}\n", s9[4]);

// test whether a string ends with a set of characters
Console.WriteLine("s3:{0}\nEnds with Training?: {1}\n", s3,
    s3.EndsWith("Training"));
Console.WriteLine("Ends with Consulting?: {0}",
    s3.EndsWith("Consulting"));

// return the index of the substring
Console.WriteLine("\nThe first occurrence of Training ");
Console.WriteLine("in s3 is {0}\n", s3.IndexOf("Training"));

// insert the word "excellent" before "training"
string s10 = s3.Insert(101, "excellent ");
Console.WriteLine("s10: {0}\n", s10);
```

*Example 10-1. Working with strings (continued)*

```
        // you can combine the two as follows:
        string s11 = s3.Insert(s3.IndexOf("Training"), "excellent ");
        Console.WriteLine("s11: {0}\n", s11);
    }
  }
}
```

```
Output:
compare s1: abcd, s2: ABCD, result: -1

compare insensitive

s4: abcd, s2: ABCD, result: 0

s6 concatenated from s1 and s2: abcdABCD
s7 concatenated from s1 + s2: abcdABCD
s8 copied from s7: abcdABCD
s9 = s8: abcdABCD

Does s9.Equals(s8)?: True
Does Equals(s9,s8)?: True
Does s9==s8?: True

String s9 is 8 characters long.
The 5th character is A

s3:Liberty Associates, Inc.
 provides custom .NET development,
 on-site Training and Consulting
Ends with Training?: False

Ends with Consulting?: True

The first occurrence of Training
in s3 is 101

s10: Liberty Associates, Inc.
            provides custom .NET development,
            on-site excellent Training and Consulting

s11: Liberty Associates, Inc.
            provides custom .NET development,
            on-site excellent Training and Consulting
```

## Example 10-1 begins by declaring three strings:

```
    string s1 = "abcd";
    string s2 = "ABCD";
    string s3 = @"Liberty Associates, Inc.
     provides custom .NET development,
     on-site Training and Consulting";
```

The first two are string literals, and the third is a verbatim string literal. You begin by comparing s1 to s2. The Compare( ) method is a public static method of string, and it is overloaded. The first overloaded version takes two strings and compares them:

```
// compare two strings, case sensitive
result = string.Compare(s1, s2);
Console.WriteLine("compare s1: {0}, s2: {1}, result: {2}\n",
    s1, s2, result);
```

This is a case-sensitive comparison and returns different values, depending on the results of the comparison:

- A negative integer, if the first string is less than the second string
- 0, if the strings are equal
- A positive integer, if the first string is greater than the second string

In this case, the output properly indicates that s1 is "less than" s2. In Unicode (as in ASCII), when evaluating for English, a lowercase letter has a smaller value than an uppercase letter:

```
compare s1: abcd, s2: ABCD, result: -1
```

The second comparison uses an overloaded version of Compare( ) that takes a third, Boolean parameter, whose value determines whether case should be ignored in the comparison. If the value of this "ignore case" parameter is true, the comparison is made without regard to case, as in the following:

```
result = string.Compare(s1,s2, true);
Console.WriteLine("compare insensitive");
Console.WriteLine("s4: {0}, s2: {1}, result: {2}\n", s1, s2, result);
```

 The result is written with two WriteLine( ) statements to keep the lines short enough to print properly in this book.

This time, the case is ignored and the result is 0, indicating that the two strings are identical (without regard to case):

```
compare insensitive

s4: abcd, s2: ABCD, result: 0
```

Example 10-1 then concatenates some strings. There are a couple of ways to accomplish this. You can use the Concat( ) method, which is a static public method of string:

```
string s6 = string.Concat(s1,s2);
```

or, you can simply use the overloaded concatenation (+) operator:

```
string s7 = s1 + s2;
```

In both cases, the output reflects that the concatenation was successful:

```
s6 concatenated from s1 and s2: abcdABCD
s7 concatenated from s1 + s2: abcdABCD
```

Similarly, you can create a new copy of a string in two ways. First, you can use the static Copy( ) method:

```
string s8 = string.Copy(s7);
```

This actually creates two separate strings with the same values. Because strings are immutable, this is wasteful. Better is to use either the overloaded assignment operator or the Clone method (mentioned earlier), both of which leave you with two variables pointing to the same string in memory:

```
string s9 = s8;
```

The .NET String class provides three ways to test for the equality of two strings. First, you can use the overloaded Equals( ) method and ask s9 directly whether s8 is of equal value:

```
Console.WriteLine("\nDoes s9.Equals(s8)?: {0}", s9.Equals(s8));
```

A second technique is to pass both strings to String's static method, Equals( ):

```
Console.WriteLine("Does Equals(s9,s8)?: {0}",
  string.Equals(s9,s8));
```

A final method is to use the equality operator (==) of String:

```
Console.WriteLine("Does s9==s8?: {0}", s9 == s8);
```

In each case, the returned result is a Boolean value, as shown in the output:

```
Does s9.Equals(s8)?: True
Does Equals(s9,s8)?: True
Does s9==s8?: True
```

The next several lines in Example 10-1 use the index operator ([ ]) to find a particular character within a string, and use the Length property to return the length of the entire string:

```
Console.WriteLine("\nString s9 is {0} characters long.", s9.Length);
Console.WriteLine("The 5th character is {1}\n", s9.Length, s9[4]);
```

Here's the output:

```
String s9 is 8 characters long.
The 5th character is A
```

The EndsWith( ) method asks a string whether a substring is found at the end of the string. Thus, you might first ask s3 whether it ends with Training (which it doesn't), and then whether it ends with Consulting (which it does):

```
// test whether a string ends with a set of characters
Console.WriteLine("s3:{0}\nEnds with Training?: {1}\n",
    s3, s3.EndsWith("Training") );
```

```
Console.WriteLine("Ends with Consulting?: {0}",
    s3.EndsWith("Consulting"));
```

The output reflects that the first test fails and the second succeeds:

```
s3:Liberty Associates, Inc.
              provides custom .NET development,
              on-site Training and Consulting
Ends with Training?: False
Ends with Consulting?: True
```

The IndexOf( ) method locates a substring within our string, and the Insert( ) method inserts a new substring into a copy of the original string.

The following code locates the first occurrence of Training in s3:

```
Console.WriteLine("\nThe first occurrence of Training ");
Console.WriteLine ("in s3 is {0}\n", s3.IndexOf("Training"));
```

The output indicates that the offset is 101:

```
The first occurrence of Training in s3 is 101
```

You can then use that value to insert the word excellent, followed by a space, into that string. Actually, the insertion is into a copy of the string returned by the Insert( ) method and assigned to s10:

```
string s10 = s3.Insert(101,"excellent ");
Console.WriteLine("s10: {0}\n",s10);
```

Here's the output:

```
s10: Liberty Associates, Inc.
              provides custom .NET development,
              on-site excellent Training and Consulting
```

Finally, you can combine these operations:

```
string s11 = s3.Insert(s3.IndexOf("Training"),"excellent ");
Console.WriteLine("s11: {0}\n",s11);
```

to obtain the identical output:

```
s11: Liberty Associates, Inc.
              provides custom .NET development,
              on-site excellent Training and Consulting
```

## Finding Substrings

The String type provides an overloaded Substring( ) method for extracting substrings from within strings. Both versions take an index indicating where to begin the extraction, and one of the two versions takes a second index to indicate where to end the operation. Example 10-2 illustrates the Substring( ) method.

*Example 10-2. Using the Substring() method*

```csharp
using System;
using System.Collections.Generic;
using System.Text;

namespace SubString
{
    public class StringTester
    {
        static void Main( )
        {
            // create some strings to work with
            string s1 = "One Two Three Four";

            int ix;

            // get the index of the last space
            ix = s1.LastIndexOf(" ");

            // get the last word.
            string s2 = s1.Substring(ix + 1);

            // set s1 to the substring starting at 0
            // and ending at ix (the start of the last word
            // thus s1 has one two three
            s1 = s1.Substring(0, ix);

            // find the last space in s1 (after two)
            ix = s1.LastIndexOf(" ");

            // set s3 to the substring starting at
            // ix, the space after "two" plus one more
            // thus s3 = "three"
            string s3 = s1.Substring(ix + 1);

            // reset s1 to the substring starting at 0
            // and ending at ix, thus the string "one two"
            s1 = s1.Substring(0, ix);

            // reset ix to the space between
            // "one" and "two"
            ix = s1.LastIndexOf(" ");

            // set s4 to the substring starting one
            // space after ix, thus the substring "two"
            string s4 = s1.Substring(ix + 1);

            // reset s1 to the substring starting at 0
            // and ending at ix, thus "one"
            s1 = s1.Substring(0, ix);

            // set ix to the last space, but there is
            // none, so ix now = -1
            ix = s1.LastIndexOf(" ");
```

*Example 10-2. Using the Substring() method (continued)*

```
                // set s5 to the substring at one past
                // the last space. There was no last space
                // so this sets s5 to the substring starting
                // at zero
                string s5 = s1.Substring(ix + 1);

                Console.WriteLine("s2: {0}\ns3: {1}", s2, s3);
                Console.WriteLine("s4: {0}\ns5: {1}\n", s4, s5);
                Console.WriteLine("s1: {0}\n", s1);
        }
    }
}
```

```
Output:
s2: Four
s3: Three
s4: Two
s5: One

s1: One
```

Example 10-2 is not an elegant solution to the problem of extracting words from a string, but it is a good first approximation, and it illustrates a useful technique. The example begins by creating a string, s1:

```
    string s1 = "One Two Three Four";
```

Next, ix is assigned the value of the *last* space in the string:

```
    ix=s1.LastIndexOf(" ");
```

Then, the substring that begins one space later is assigned to the new string, s2:

```
    string s2 = s1.Substring(ix+1);
```

This extracts ix+1 to the end of the line, assigning to s2 the value Four. The next step is to remove the word Four from s1. You can do this by assigning to s1 the substring of s1, which begins at 0, and ends at ix:

```
    s1 = s1.Substring(0,ix);
```

Reassign ix to the last (remaining) space, which points you to the beginning of the word Three, which we then extract into string s3. Continue like this until s4 and s5 are populated. Finally, print the results:

```
    s2: Four
    s3: Three
    s4: Two
    s5: One

    s1: One
```

This isn't elegant, but it works, and it illustrates the use of Substring. This is not unlike using pointer arithmetic in C++, but without the pointers and unsafe code.

# Splitting Strings

A more effective solution to the problem illustrated in Example 10-2 is to use the Split( ) method of String, whose job is to parse a string into substrings. To use Split( ), pass in an array of delimiters (characters that will indicate a split in the words), and the method returns an array of substrings. Example 10-3 illustrates.

*Example 10-3. Using the Split( ) method*

```
using System;
using System.Collections.Generic;
using System.Text;

namespace StringSplit
{
    public class StringTester
    {
        static void Main( )
        {
            // create some strings to work with
            string s1 = "One,Two,Three Liberty Associates, Inc.";

            // constants for the space and comma characters
            const char Space = ' ';
            const char Comma = ',';

            // array of delimiters to split the sentence with
            char[] delimiters = new char[] {Space, Comma};

            string output = "";
            int ctr = 1;

            // split the string and then iterate over the
            // resulting array of strings
            foreach (string subString in s1.Split(delimiters))
            {
                output += ctr++;
                output += ": ";
                output += subString;
                output += "\n";
            }
            Console.WriteLine(output);
        }
    }
}
Output:
1: One
2: Two
3: Three
4: Liberty
5: Associates
6:
7: Inc.
```

You start by creating a string to parse:

```
string s1 = "One,Two,Three Liberty Associates, Inc.";
```

The delimiters are set to the space and comma characters. You then call `Split()` on this string, and pass the results to the `foreach` loop:

```
foreach (string subString in s1.Split(delimiters))
```

Because `Split` uses the params keyword, you can reduce your code to:
```
foreach (string subString in s1.Split(' ', ','))
```
This eliminates the declaration of the array entirely.

Start by initializing output to an empty string, and then build up the output string in four steps. Concatenate the value of `ctr`. Next add the colon, then the substring returned by `Split()`, then the newline. With each concatenation, a new copy of the string is made, and all four steps are repeated for each substring found by `Split()`. This repeated copying of `string` is terribly inefficient.

The problem is that the string type is not designed for this kind of operation. What you want is to create a new string by appending a formatted string each time through the loop. The class you need is `StringBuilder`.

## Manipulating Dynamic Strings

The `System.Text.StringBuilder` class is used for creating and modifying strings. Table 10-2 summarizes the important members of `StringBuilder`.

*Table 10-2. StringBuilder methods*

| Method | Explanation |
| --- | --- |
| Chars | The indexer |
| Length | Retrieves or assigns the length of the `StringBuilder` |
| Append() | Overloaded public method that appends a string of characters to the end of the current `StringBuilder` |
| AppendFormat() | Overloaded public method that replaces format specifiers with the formatted value of an object |
| Insert() | Overloaded public method that inserts a string of characters at the specified position |
| Remove() | Removes the specified characters |
| Replace() | Overloaded public method that replaces all instances of specified characters with new characters |

Unlike `String`, `StringBuilder` is mutable. Example 10-4 replaces the `String` object in Example 10-3 with a `StringBuilder` object.

*Example 10-4. Using a StringBuilder*

```
using System;
using System.Collections.Generic;
using System.Text;

namespace UsingStringBuilder
{
    public class StringTester
    {
        static void Main()
        {
            // create some strings to work with
            string s1 = "One,Two,Three Liberty Associates, Inc.";

            // constants for the space and comma characters
            const char Space = ' ';
            const char Comma = ',';

            // array of delimiters to split the sentence with
            char[] delimiters = new char[] {Space, Comma};

            // use a StringBuilder class to build the
            // output string
            StringBuilder output = new StringBuilder();
            int ctr = 1;

            // split the string and then iterate over the
            // resulting array of strings
            foreach (string subString in s1.Split(delimiters))
            {
                // AppendFormat appends a formatted string
                output.AppendFormat("{0}: {1}\n", ctr++, subString);
            }
            Console.WriteLine(output);
        }
    }
}
```

Only the last part of the program is modified. Instead of using the concatenation operator to modify the string, use the `AppendFormat()` method of `StringBuilder` to append new, formatted strings as you create them. This is more efficient. The output is identical to that of Example 10-3:

```
1: One
2: Two
3: Three
4: Liberty
5: Associates
6:
7: Inc.
```

---

### Delimiter Limitations

Because you passed in delimiters of both comma and space, the space after the comma between "Associates" and "Inc." is returned as a word, numbered 6 as shown. That is not what you want. To eliminate this, you need to tell `split` to match a comma (as between One, Two, and Three), or a space (as between Liberty and Associates), or a comma followed by a space. It is that last bit that is tricky, and regular expressions provide a ready solution.

---

# Regular Expressions

Regular expressions are a powerful language for describing and manipulating text. A regular expression is *applied* to a string—that is, to a set of characters. Often, that string is an entire text document.

The result of applying a regular expression to a string is one of the following:

- To find out whether the string matches the regular expression
- To return a substring
- To return a new string representing a modification of some part of the original string

(Remember that strings are immutable, and so can't be changed by the regular expression.)

By applying a properly constructed regular expression to the following string:

```
One,Two,Three Liberty Associates, Inc.
```

you can return any or all of its substrings (e.g., Liberty or One), or modified versions of its substrings (e.g., LIBeRtY or OnE). What the regular expression *does* is determined by the syntax of the regular expression itself.

A regular expression consists of two types of characters: *literals* and *metacharacters*. A literal is a character you wish to match in the target string. A metacharacter is a special symbol that acts as a command to the regular expression parser. The parser is the engine responsible for understanding the regular expression. For example, if you create a regular expression:

```
^(From|To|Subject|Date):
```

this will match any substring with the letters From, To, Subject, or Date, as long as those letters start a new line (^) and end with a colon (:).

The caret (^) in this case indicates to the regular expression parser that the string you're searching for must begin a new line. The letters in From and To are literals, and the left and right parentheses (( )) and vertical bar (|) metacharacters are used to group sets of literals and indicate that any of the choices should match. (Note that ^ is a metacharacter as well, used to indicate the start of the line.)

Thus, you would read this line:

```
^(From|To|Subject|Date):
```

as follows: "Match any string that begins a new line followed by any of the four literal strings From, To, Subject, or Date followed by a colon."

A full explanation of regular expressions is beyond the scope of this book, but all the regular expressions used in the examples are explained. For a complete understanding of regular expressions, I highly recommend *Mastering Regular Expressions* by Jeffrey E. F. Friedl (O'Reilly).

## Using Regular Expressions: Regex

The .NET Framework provides an object-oriented approach to regular expression matching and replacement.

C#'s regular expressions are based on Perl 5 *regexp*, including lazy quantifiers (??, *?, +?, {n,m}?), positive and negative look ahead, and conditional evaluation.

The namespace System.Text.RegularExpressions is the home to all the .NET Framework objects associated with regular expressions. The central class for regular expression support is Regex, which represents an immutable, compiled regular expression. Although instances of Regex can be created, the class also provides a number of useful static methods. Example 10-5 illustrates the use of Regex.

*Example 10-5. Using the Regex class for regular expressions*

```
using System;
using System.Collections.Generic;
using System.Text;
using System.Text.RegularExpressions;

namespace UsingRegEx
{
    public class Tester
    {
        static void Main( )
        {
            string s1 = "One,Two,Three Liberty Associates, Inc.";
            Regex theRegex = new Regex(" |, |,");
            StringBuilder sBuilder = new StringBuilder( );
            int id = 1;

            foreach (string subString in theRegex.Split(s1))
```

*Example 10-5. Using the Regex class for regular expressions (continued)*

```
            {
                sBuilder.AppendFormat("{0}: {1}\n", id++, subString);
            }
            Console.WriteLine("{0}", sBuilder);
        }
    }
}
```

```
Output:
1: One
2: Two
3: Three
4: Liberty
5: Associates
6: Inc.
```

Example 10-5 begins by creating a string, s1, which is identical to the string used in Example 10-4:

```
string s1 = "One,Two,Three Liberty Associates, Inc.";
```

It also creates a regular expression, which will be used to search that string, matching any space, comma, or comma followed by a space:

```
Regex theRegex = new Regex(" |,|, ");
```

One of the overloaded constructors for Regex takes a regular expression string as its parameter. This is a bit confusing. In the context of a C# program, which is the regular expression? Is it the text passed in to the constructor, or the Regex object itself? It is true that the text string passed to the constructor is a regular expression in the traditional sense of the term. From an object-oriented C# point of view, however, the argument to the constructor is just a string of characters; it is theRegex that is the regular expression object.

The rest of the program proceeds like the earlier Example 10-4, except that instead of calling Split( ) on string s1, the Split( ) method of Regex is called. Regex.Split( ) acts in much the same way as String.Split( ), returning an array of strings as a result of matching the regular expression pattern within theRegex.

Regex.Split( ) is overloaded. The simplest version is called on an instance of Regex, as shown in Example 10-5. There is also a static version of this method, which takes a string to search and the pattern to search with, as illustrated in Example 10-6.

*Example 10-6. Using static Regex.Split()*

```
using System;
using System.Collections.Generic;
using System.Text;
using System.Text.RegularExpressions;
```

*Example 10-6. Using static Regex.Split( ) (continued)*

```
namespace RegExSplit
{
    public class Tester
    {
        static void Main()
        {
            string s1 = "One,Two,Three Liberty Associates, Inc.";
            StringBuilder sBuilder = new StringBuilder();
            int id = 1;
            foreach (string subStr in Regex.Split(s1, " |, |,"))
            {
                sBuilder.AppendFormat("{0}: {1}\n", id++, subStr);
            }
            Console.WriteLine("{0}", sBuilder);
        }
    }
}
```

Example 10-6 is identical to Example 10-5, except that the latter example doesn't instantiate an object of type Regex. Instead, Example 10-6 uses the static version of Split( ), which takes two arguments: a string to search for, and a regular expression string that represents the pattern to match.

The instance method of Split( ) is also overloaded with versions that limit the number of times the split will occur as well as determine the position within the target string where the search will begin.

## Using Regex Match Collections

Two additional classes in the .NET RegularExpressions namespace allow you to search a string repeatedly, and to return the results in a collection. The collection returned is of type MatchCollection, which consists of zero or more Match objects. Two important properties of a Match object are its length and its value, each of which can be read as illustrated in Example 10-7.

*Example 10-7. Using MatchCollection and Match*

```
using System;
using System.Collections.Generic;
using System.Text;
using System.Text.RegularExpressions;

namespace UsingMatchCollection
{
    class Test
    {
        public static void Main()
        {
            string string1 = "This is a test string";
```

*Example 10-7. Using MatchCollection and Match (continued)*

```
            // find any nonwhitespace followed by whitespace
            Regex theReg = new Regex(@"(\S+)\s");

            // get the collection of matches
            MatchCollection theMatches = theReg.Matches(string1);

            // iterate through the collection
            foreach (Match theMatch in theMatches)
            {
                Console.WriteLine("theMatch.Length: {0}",
                                    theMatch.Length);

                if (theMatch.Length != 0)
                {
                    Console.WriteLine("theMatch: {0}",
                                        theMatch.ToString( ));
                }
            }
        }
    }
}

Output:
theMatch.Length: 5
theMatch: This
theMatch.Length: 3
theMatch: is
theMatch.Length: 2
theMatch: a
theMatch.Length: 5
theMatch: test
```

Example 10-7 creates a simple string to search:

```
    string string1 = "This is a test string";
```

and a trivial regular expression to search it:

```
    Regex theReg = new Regex(@"(\S+)\s");
```

The string \S finds nonwhitespace, and the plus sign indicates one or more. The string \s (note lowercase) indicates whitespace. Thus, together, this string looks for any nonwhitespace characters followed by whitespace.

 Remember that the at (@) symbol before the string creates a verbatim string, which avoids having to escape the backslash (\) character.

The output shows that the first four words were found. The final word wasn't found because it isn't followed by a space. If you insert a space after the word string, and before the closing quotation marks, this program finds that word as well.

The length property is the length of the captured substring, and I discuss it in the section "Using CaptureCollection" later in this chapter.

## Using Regex Groups

It is often convenient to group subexpression matches together so that you can parse out pieces of the matching string. For example, you might want to match on IP addresses and group all IP addresses found anywhere within the string.

 IP addresses are used to locate computers on a network, and typically have the form x.x.x.x, where x is generally any digit between 0 and 255 (such as 192.168.0.1).

The Group class allows you to create groups of matches based on regular expression syntax, and represents the results from a single grouping expression.

A grouping expression names a group and provides a regular expression; any substring matching the regular expression will be added to the group. For example, to create an ip group, you might write:

```
@"(?<ip>(\d|\.)+)\s"
```

The Match class derives from Group, and has a collection called Groups that contains all the groups your Match finds.

Example 10-8 illustrates the creation and use of the Groups collection and Group classes.

*Example 10-8. Using the Group class*

```
using System;
using System.Collections.Generic;
using System.Text;
using System.Text.RegularExpressions;

namespace RegExGroup
{
    class Test
    {
        public static void Main( )
        {
            string string1 = "04:03:27 127.0.0.0 LibertyAssociates.com";

            // group time = one or more digits or colons followed by space
            Regex theReg = new Regex(@"(?<time>(\d|\:)+)\s" +
                // ip address = one or more digits or dots followed by space
                @"(?<ip>(\d|\.)+)\s" +
                // site = one or more characters
                @"(?<site>\S+)");
```

*Example 10-8. Using the Group class (continued)*

```
        // get the collection of matches
        MatchCollection theMatches = theReg.Matches(string1);

        // iterate through the collection
        foreach (Match theMatch in theMatches)
        {
            if (theMatch.Length != 0)
            {
                Console.WriteLine("\ntheMatch: {0}",
                    theMatch.ToString());
                Console.WriteLine("time: {0}",
                    theMatch.Groups["time"]);
                Console.WriteLine("ip: {0}",
                    theMatch.Groups["ip"]);
                Console.WriteLine("site: {0}",
                    theMatch.Groups["site"]);
            }
        }
    }
  }
}
```

Again, Example 10-8 begins by creating a string to search:

```
string string1 = "04:03:27 127.0.0.0 LibertyAssociates.com";
```

This string might be one of many recorded in a web server logfile or produced as the result of a search of the database. In this simple example, there are three columns: one for the time of the log entry, one for an IP address, and one for the site, each separated by spaces. Of course, in an example solving a real-life problem, you might need to do more complex queries and choose to use other delimiters and more complex searches.

In Example 10-8, we want to create a single `Regex` object to search strings of this type and break them into three groups: `time`, `ip address`, and `site`. The regular expression string is fairly simple, so the example is easy to understand. However, keep in mind that in a real search, you would probably use only a part of the source string rather than the entire source string, as shown here:

```
// group time = one or more digits or colons
// followed by space
Regex theReg = new Regex(@"(?<time>(\d|\:)+)\s" +
// ip address = one or more digits or dots
// followed by space
@"(?<ip>(\d|\.)+)\s" +
// site = one or more characters
@"(?<site>\S+)");
```

Let's focus on the characters that create the group:

```
(?<time>(\d|\:)+)
```

The parentheses create a group. Everything between the opening parenthesis (just before the question mark) and the closing parenthesis (in this case, after the + sign) is a single unnamed group.

The string ?<time> names that group time, and the group is associated with the matching text, which is the regular expression (\d|\:)+)\s. This regular expression can be interpreted as "one or more digits or colons followed by a space."

Similarly, the string ?<ip> names the ip group, and ?<site> names the site group. As Example 10-7 does, Example 10-8 asks for a collection of all the matches:

```
MatchCollection theMatches = theReg.Matches(string1);
```

Example 10-8 iterates through the Matches collection, finding each Match object.

If the Length of the Match is greater than 0, a Match was found; it prints the entire match:

```
Console.WriteLine("\ntheMatch: {0}",
    theMatch.ToString( ));
```

Here's the output:

```
theMatch: 04:03:27 127.0.0.0 LibertyAssociates.com
```

It then gets the time group from the theMatch.Groups collection and prints that value:

```
Console.WriteLine("time: {0}",
    theMatch.Groups["time"]);
```

This produces the output:

```
time: 04:03:27
```

The code then obtains ip and site groups:

```
Console.WriteLine("ip: {0}",
    theMatch.Groups["ip"]);
Console.WriteLine("site: {0}",
    theMatch.Groups["site"]);
```

This produces the output:

```
ip: 127.0.0.0
site: LibertyAssociates.com
```

In Example 10-8, the Matches collection has only one Match. It is possible, however, to match more than one expression within a string. To see this, modify string1 in Example 10-8 to provide several logFile entries instead of one, as follows:

```
string string1 = "04:03:27 127.0.0.0 LibertyAssociates.com " +
"04:03:28 127.0.0.0 foo.com " +
"04:03:29 127.0.0.0 bar.com " ;
```

This creates three matches in the MatchCollection, called theMatches. Here's the resulting output:

```
theMatch: 04:03:27 127.0.0.0 LibertyAssociates.com
time: 04:03:27
ip: 127.0.0.0
site: LibertyAssociates.com

theMatch: 04:03:28 127.0.0.0 foo.com
time: 04:03:28
ip: 127.0.0.0
site: foo.com

theMatch: 04:03:29 127.0.0.0 bar.com
time: 04:03:29
ip: 127.0.0.0
site: bar.com
```

In this example, theMatches contains three Match objects. Each time through the outer foreach loop, we find the next Match in the collection and display its contents:

```
foreach (Match theMatch in theMatches)
```

For each Match item found, you can print the entire match, various groups, or both.

## Using CaptureCollection

Please note that we are now venturing into advanced use of regular expressions, which themselves are considered a black art by many programmers. Feel free to skip over this section if it gives you a headache, and come back to it if you need it.

Each time a Regex object matches a subexpression, a Capture instance is created and added to a CaptureCollection collection. Each Capture object represents a single capture.

Each group has its own capture collection of the matches for the subexpression associated with the group.

So, taking that apart, if you don't create Groups, and you match only once, you end up with one CaptureCollection with one Capture object. If you match five times, you end up with one CaptureCollection with five Capture objects in it.

If you don't create groups, but you match on three subexpressions, you will end up with three CaptureCollections, each of which will have Capture objects for each match for that subexpression.

Finally, if you do create groups (e.g., one group for IP addresses, one group for machine names, one group for dates), and each group has a few capture expressions, you'll end up with a hierarchy: each group collection will have a number of capture collections (one per subexpression to match), and each group's capture collection will have a capture object for each match found.

A key property of the Capture object is its length, which is the length of the captured substring. When you ask Match for its length, it is Capture.Length that you retrieve because Match derives from Group, which in turn derives from Capture.

The regular expression inheritance scheme in .NET allows Match to include in its interface the methods and properties of these parent classes. In a sense, a Group *is-a* capture: it is a capture that encapsulates the idea of grouping subexpressions. A Match, in turn, *is-a* Group: it is the encapsulation of all the groups of subexpressions making up the entire match for this regular expression. (See Chapter 5 for more about the *is-a* relationship and other relationships.)

Typically, you will find only a single Capture in a CaptureCollection, but that need not be so. Consider what would happen if you were parsing a string in which the company name might occur in either of two positions. To group these together in a single match, create the ?<company> group in two places in your regular expression pattern:

```
Regex theReg = new Regex(@"(?<time>(\d|\:)+)\s" +
@"(?<company>\S+)\s" +
@"(?<ip>(\d|\.)+)\s" +
@"(?<company>\S+)\s");
```

This regular expression group captures any matching string of characters that follows time, as well as any matching string of characters that follows ip. Given this regular expression, you are ready to parse the following string:

```
string string1 = "04:03:27 Jesse 0.0.0.127 Liberty ";
```

The string includes names in both of the positions specified. Here is the result:

```
theMatch: 04:03:27 Jesse 0.0.0.127 Liberty
time: 04:03:27
ip: 0.0.0.127
Company: Liberty
```

What happened? Why is the Company group showing Liberty? Where is the first term, which also matched? The answer is that the second term overwrote the first. The group, however, has captured both. Its Captures collection can demonstrate, as illustrated in Example 10-9.

*Example 10-9. Examining the Captures collection*

```
using System;
using System.Collections.Generic;
using System.Text;
using System.Text.RegularExpressions;

namespace CaptureCollection
{
    class Test
    {
        public static void Main()
        {
            // the string to parse
            // note that names appear in both
```

*Example 10-9. Examining the Captures collection (continued)*

```csharp
            // searchable positions
            string string1 =
            "04:03:27 Jesse 0.0.0.127 Liberty ";

            // regular expression that groups company twice
            Regex theReg = new Regex(@"(?<time>(\d|\:)+)\s" +
                           @"(?<company>\S+)\s" +
                           @"(?<ip>(\d|\.)+)\s" +
                           @"(?<company>\S+)\s");

            // get the collection of matches
            MatchCollection theMatches =
            theReg.Matches(string1);

            // iterate through the collection
            foreach (Match theMatch in theMatches)
            {
                if (theMatch.Length != 0)
                {
                    Console.WriteLine("theMatch: {0}",
                        theMatch.ToString());
                    Console.WriteLine("time: {0}",
                        theMatch.Groups["time"]);
                    Console.WriteLine("ip: {0}",
                        theMatch.Groups["ip"]);
                    Console.WriteLine("Company: {0}",
                        theMatch.Groups["company"]);

                    // iterate over the captures collection
                    // in the company group within the
                    // groups collection in the match

                    foreach (Capture cap in
                        theMatch.Groups["company"].Captures)
                    {
                        Console.WriteLine("cap: {0}", cap.ToString());
                    }
                }
            }
        }
    }
}
```

```
Output:
theMatch: 04:03:27 Jesse 0.0.0.127 Liberty
time: 04:03:27
ip: 0.0.0.127
Company: Liberty
cap: Jesse
cap: Liberty
```

The code in bold iterates through the Captures collection for the Company group:

```
foreach (Capture cap in
    theMatch.Groups["company"].Captures)
```

Let's review how this line is parsed. The compiler begins by finding the collection that it will iterate over. theMatch is an object that has a collection named Groups. The Groups collection has an indexer that takes a string and returns a single Group object. Thus, the following line returns a single Group object:

```
theMatch.Groups["company"]
```

The Group object has a collection named Captures. Thus, the following line returns a Captures collection for the Group stored at Groups["company"] within the theMatch object:

```
theMatch.Groups["company"].Captures
```

The foreach loop iterates over the Captures collection, extracting each element in turn and assigning it to the local variable cap, which is of type Capture. You can see from the output that there are two capture elements: Jesse and Liberty. The second one overwrites the first in the group, and so the displayed value is just Liberty. However, by examining the Captures collection, you can find both values that were captured.

# CHAPTER 11

# Exceptions

Like many object-oriented languages, C# handles abnormal conditions with *exceptions*. An exception is an object that encapsulates information about an unusual program occurrence.

It is important to distinguish between bugs, errors, and exceptions. A *bug* is a programmer mistake that should be fixed before the code is shipped. Exceptions aren't a protection against bugs. Although a bug might cause an exception to be thrown, you should not rely on exceptions to handle your bugs. Rather, you should fix the bugs.

An *error* is caused by user action. For example, the user might enter a number where a letter is expected. Once again, an error might cause an exception, but you can prevent that by catching errors with validation code. Whenever possible, errors should be anticipated and prevented.

Even if you remove all bugs and anticipate all user errors, you will still run into predictable but unpreventable problems, such as running out of memory or attempting to open a file that no longer exists. You can't prevent exceptions, but you can handle them so that they don't bring down your program.

When your program encounters an exceptional circumstance, such as running out of memory, it *throws* (or "raises") an exception. When an exception is thrown, execution of the current function halts, and the stack is unwound until an appropriate exception handler is found (see the sidebar, "Unwinding the Stack").

This means that if the currently running function doesn't handle the exception, the current function will terminate, and the calling function will get a chance to handle the exception. If none of the calling functions handles it, the exception will ultimately be handled by the CLR, which will abruptly terminate your program.

An *exception handler* is a block of code designed to handle the exception you've thrown. Exception handlers are implemented as catch statements. Ideally, if the exception is caught and handled, the program can fix the problem and continue. Even if your program can't continue, by catching the exception, you have an opportunity to print a meaningful error message and terminate gracefully.

### Unwinding the Stack

When a method is called, an area is set aside on the stack, known as the *stack frame*, which holds the return address of the next instruction in the calling method, the arguments passed into the called method, and all the local variables in the called method.

Because MethodA can call MethodB which can call MethodC which can, in fact, call MethodA (which can even call MethodA!), and so on, "unwinding the stack" refers to the process of finding the return address of the calling method and returning to that method peremptorily, looking for a catch block to handle the exception. The stack may have to "unwind" through a number of called methods before it finds a handler. Ultimately, if it unwinds all the way to main and no handler is found, a default handler is called, and the program exits.

Assuming a handler is found, the program continues from the handler, *not* from where the exception was thrown, or from the method that called the method in which the exception was thrown (unless that method had the handler). Once unwound, the stack frame is lost.

If there is code in your function that must run regardless of whether an exception is encountered (e.g., to release resources you've allocated), you can place that code in a finally block, where it is certain to run, even in the presence of exceptions.

# Throwing and Catching Exceptions

In C#, you can throw only objects of type System.Exception, or objects derived from that type. The CLR System namespace includes a number of exception types that your program can use. These exception types include ArgumentNullException, InvalidCastException, and OverflowException, as well as many others.

 *C++ programmers take note*: in C#, not just any object can be thrown—it must be derived from System.Exception.

## The throw Statement

To signal an abnormal condition in a C# class, you throw an exception. To do this, use the keyword throw. This line of code creates a new instance of System.Exception and then throws it:

```
throw new System.Exception( );
```

Throwing an exception immediately halts execution of the current "thread" (see Chapter 21 for a discussion of threads) while the CLR searches for an exception handler. If an exception handler can't be found in the current method, the runtime unwinds the stack, popping up through the calling methods until a handler is found. If the runtime returns all the way through Main( ) without finding a handler, it terminates the program. Example 11-1 illustrates.

*Example 11-1. Throwing an exception*

```
using System;

namespace Programming_CSharp
{
    public class Test
    {
        public static void Main()
        {
            Console.WriteLine("Enter Main...");
            Test t = new Test();
            t.Func1();
            Console.WriteLine("Exit Main...");
        }

        public void Func1()
        {
            Console.WriteLine("Enter Func1...");
            Func2();
            Console.WriteLine("Exit Func1...");
        }

        public void Func2()
        {
            Console.WriteLine("Enter Func2...");
            throw new System.ApplicationException();
            Console.WriteLine("Exit Func2...");
        }
    }
}
```

```
Output:
Enter Main...
Enter Func1...
Enter Func2...
```

When you run this program in debug mode, an "Exception was unhandled" message box comes up, as shown in Figure 11-1.

If you click View Detail, you find the details of the unhandled exception, as shown in Figure 11-2.

This simple example writes to the console as it enters and exits each method. Main( ) creates an instance of type Test and call Func1( ). After printing out the Enter Func1 message, Func1( ) immediately calls Func2( ). Func2( ) prints out the first message and throws an object of type System.Exception.

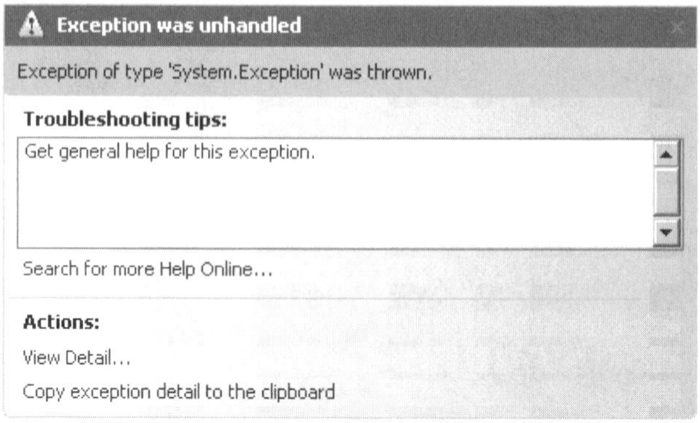

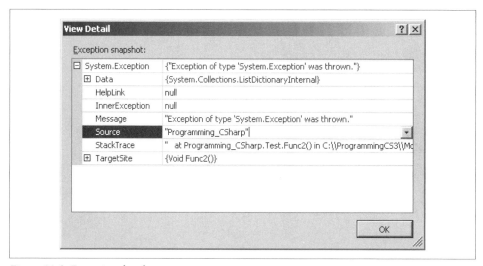

Figure 11-1. Unhandled exception

Figure 11-2. Exception details

Execution immediately shifts to handling the exceptions. The CLR looks to see whether there is a handler in Func2( ). There is not, and so the runtime unwinds the stack (never printing the exit statement) to Func1( ). Again, there is no handler, and the runtime unwinds the stack back to Main( ). With no exception handler there, the default handler is called, which opens the exception message box.

## The catch Statement

In C#, an exception handler is called a *catch block* and is created with the catch keyword.

In Example 11-2, the throw statement is executed within a try block, and a catch block is used to announce that the error has been handled.

---

*Example 11-2. Catching an exception*

```
using System;
using System.Collections.Generic;
using System.Text;

namespace CatchingAnException
{
    public class Test
    {
        public static void Main()
        {
            Console.WriteLine("Enter Main...");
            Test t = new Test();
            t.Func1();
            Console.WriteLine("Exit Main...");
        }

        public void Func1()
        {
            Console.WriteLine("Enter Func1...");
            Func2();
            Console.WriteLine("Exit Func1...");
        }

        public void Func2()
        {
            Console.WriteLine("Enter Func2...");

            try
                {
                Console.WriteLine("Entering try block...");
                throw new System.ApplicationException();
                Console.WriteLine("Exiting try block...");
            }
            catch
            {
                // simplified for this book; typically you would
                // correct (or at least log) the problem
                Console.WriteLine("Exception caught and handled.");
            }

            Console.WriteLine("Exit Func2...");
        }
    }
}
```

```
Output:
Enter Main...
Enter Func1...
Enter Func2...
Entering try block...
Exception caught and handled.
```

*Example 11-2. Catching an exception (continued)*

```
Exit Func2...
Exit Func1...
Exit Main...
```

Example 11-2 is identical to Example 11-1 except that now the program includes a try/catch block.

It is a common mistake to clutter your code with try/catch blocks that don't actually do anything and don't solve the problem that the exception is pointing out. It is good programming practice to use a try/catch block only where your catch has the opportunity to rectify the situation (with the exception of the topmost level where, at a minimum, you want to fail reasonably gracefully).

An exception to this practice is to catch and log the exception, and then rethrow it for it to be handled at a higher level, or to catch the exception, add context information, and then nest that information bundled inside a new exception, as described later in this chapter.

Catch statements can be generic, as shown in the previous example, or can be targeted at specific exceptions, as shown later in this chapter.

### Taking corrective action

One of the most important purposes of a catch statement is to take corrective action. For example, if the user is trying to open a read-only file, you might invoke a method that allows the user to change the attributes of the file. If the program has run out of memory, you might give the user an opportunity to close other applications. If all else fails, the catch block can log the error (or even send out email) so that you know specifically where in your program you are having the problem.

### Unwinding the call stack

Examine the output of Example 11-2 carefully. You see the code enter Main( ), Func1( ), Func2( ), and the try block. You never see it exit the try block, though it does exit Func2( ), Func1( ), and Main( ). What happened?

When the exception is thrown, the normal code path is halted immediately and control is handed to the catch block. It *never* returns to the original code path. It never gets to the line that prints the exit statement for the try block. The catch block handles the error, and then execution falls through to the code following catch.

Without catch, the call stack unwinds, but with catch, it doesn't unwind, as a result of the exception. The exception is now handled; there are no more problems, and the program continues. This becomes a bit clearer if you move the try/catch blocks up to Func1( ), as shown in Example 11-3.

*Example 11-3. Catch in a calling function*

```
using System;

namespace CatchingExceptionInCallingFunc
{
    public class Test
    {
        public static void Main()
        {
            Console.WriteLine("Enter Main...");
            Test t = new Test();
            t.Func1();
            Console.WriteLine("Exit Main...");
        }

        public void Func1()
        {
            Console.WriteLine("Enter Func1...");

            try
            {
                Console.WriteLine("Entering try block...");
                Func2();
                Console.WriteLine("Exiting try block...");
            }
            catch
            {
                Console.WriteLine(
                    "Unknown exception caught when calling Func 2.");
            }

            Console.WriteLine("Exit Func1...");
        }

        public void Func2()
        {
            Console.WriteLine("Enter Func2...");
            throw new System.ApplicationException();
            Console.WriteLine("Exit Func2...");
        }
    }
}
```

```
Output:
Enter Main...
Enter Func1...
Entering try block...
Enter Func2...
Unknown exception caught when calling Func 2.
Exit Func1...
Exit Main...
```

This time the exception is not handled in Func2( ), it is handled in Func1( ). When Func2( ) is called, it prints the Enter statement, and then throws an exception. Execution halts and the runtime looks for a handler, but there isn't one. The stack unwinds, and the runtime finds a handler in Func1( ). The catch statement is called, and execution resumes immediately following the catch statement, printing the Exit statement for Func1( ) and then for Main( ).

Make sure you are comfortable with why the Exiting Try Block statement and the Exit Func2 statement aren't printed. This is a classic case where putting the code into a debugger and then stepping through it can make things very clear.

## Try/Catch Best Practices

So far, you've been working only with generic catch statements. Best practices, however, dictate that you want, whenever possible, to create dedicated catch statements that will handle only some exceptions and not others, based on the type of exception thrown. Example 11-4 illustrates how to specify which exception you'd like to handle.

*Example 11-4. Specifying the exception to catch*

```
using System;

namespace SpecifyingCaughtException
{
    public class Test
    {
        public static void Main()
        {
            Test t = new Test();
            t.TestFunc();
        }

        // try to divide two numbers
        // handle possible exceptions
        public void TestFunc()
        {
            try
            {
                double a = 5;
                double b = 0;
                //double b = 2;
                Console.WriteLine("{0} / {1} = {2}",
                a, b, DoDivide(a, b));
            }

            // most derived exception type first
            catch (System.DivideByZeroException)
            {
                Console.WriteLine(
                "DivideByZeroException caught!");
```

*Example 11-4. Specifying the exception to catch (continued)*

```
            }
            catch (System.ArithmeticException)
            {
                Console.WriteLine(
                "ArithmeticException caught!);
            }

            // generic exception type last
            Catch (Exception e)
            {
                Console.Writeline("Log: " + e.ToString());
            }
        }    // end Test function

        // do the division if legal
        public double DoDivide(double a, double  b)
        {
            if (b == 0)
                throw new System.DivideByZeroException();
            if (a == 0)
                throw new System.ArithmeticException();
            // throw new ApplicationException();
            return a / b;
        }
    }  // end class
}    // end namespace
```

```
Output:
DivideByZeroException caught!
```

In this example, the DoDivide() method doesn't let you divide 0 by another number, nor does it let you divide a number by 0. It throws an instance of DivideByZeroException if you try to divide by 0. If you try to divide 0 by another number, there is no appropriate exception; dividing 0 by another number is a legal mathematical operation, and shouldn't throw an exception at all. For the sake of this example, assume you don't want 0 to be divided by any number and throw an ArithmeticException.

When the exception is thrown, the runtime examines each exception handler *in order* and matches the first one it can. When you run this with a=5 and b=7, the output is:

```
5 / 7 = 0.7142857142857143
```

As you'd expect, no exception is thrown. However, when you change the value of a to 0, the output is:

```
ArithmeticException caught!
```

The exception is thrown, and the runtime examines the first exception, DivideByZeroException. Because this doesn't match, it goes on to the next handler, ArithmeticException, which does match.

In a final pass through, suppose you change a to 7 and b to 0. This throws the DivideByZeroException.

 You have to be particularly careful with the order of the catch statements because the DivideByZeroException is derived from ArithmeticException. If you reverse the catch statements, the DivideByZeroException matches the ArithmeticException handler, and the exception won't get to the DivideByZeroException handler. In fact, if their order is reversed, it's impossible for *any* exception to reach the DivideByZeroException handler. The compiler recognizes that the DivideByZeroException handler can't be reached and reports a compile error!

When catching the generic exception, it is often a good idea to at least log as much about the exception as possible by calling ToString on the exception. To see this at work, make three changes to the previous example:

- Change the declared value of b from 0 to 2.
- Uncomment the penultimate line of code.
- Comment out the final line of code (as it will now be unreachable).

The output will look something like this:

```
Log this: System.SystemException: System error.
    at SpecifyingCaughtException.Test.DoDivide(Double a, Double b) in C:\...\Specified
Exception
s\Program.cs:line 53
```

Notice that among other things, the generic exception tells you the file, the method, and the line number; this can save quite a bit of debugging time.

## The finally Statement

In some instances, throwing an exception and unwinding the stack can create a problem. For example, if you have opened a file or otherwise committed a resource, you might need an opportunity to close the file or flush the buffer.

If there is some action you must take regardless of whether an exception is thrown (such as closing a file), you have two strategies to choose from. One approach is to enclose the dangerous action in a try block, and then to close the file in both the catch and try blocks. However, this is an ugly duplication of code, and it's error-prone. C# provides a better alternative in the finally block.

The code in the finally block is guaranteed to be executed regardless of whether an exception is thrown. The TestFunc( ) method in Example 11-5 simulates opening a file as its first action. The method undertakes some mathematical operations, and the file is closed. It is possible that some time between opening and closing the file an exception will be thrown.

 Keep the code in your finally block simple. If an exception is thrown from within your finally block, your finally block will not complete.

If this were to occur, it would be possible for the file to remain open. The developer knows that no matter what happens, at the end of this method the file should be closed, so the file close function call is moved to a finally block, where it will be executed regardless of whether an exception is thrown.

*Example 11-5. Using a finally block*

```
using System;
using System.Collections.Generic;
using System.Text;

namespace UsingFinally
{
    public class Test
    {
        public static void Main( )
        {
            Test t = new Test( );
            t.TestFunc( );
        }

        // try to divide two numbers
        // handle possible exceptions
        public void TestFunc( )
        {
            try
            {
                Console.WriteLine("Open file here");
                double a = 5;
                double b = 0;
                Console.WriteLine("{0} / {1} = {2}",
                a, b, DoDivide(a, b));
                Console.WriteLine(
                "This line may or may not print");
            }

            // most derived exception type first
            catch (System.DivideByZeroException)
            {
                Console.WriteLine(
                "DivideByZeroException caught!");
```

*Example 11-5. Using a finally block (continued)*

```
            }
            catch
            {
                Console.WriteLine("Unknown exception caught");
            }
            finally
            {
                Console.WriteLine("Close file here.");
            }
        }

        // do the division if legal
        public double DoDivide(double a, double b)
        {
            if (b == 0)
                throw new System.DivideByZeroException( );
            if (a == 0)
                throw new System.ArithmeticException( );
            return a / b;
        }
    }
}
```

```
Output:
Open file here
DivideByZeroException caught!
Close file here.

Output when b = 12:
Open file here
5 / 12 = 0.416666666666667
This line may or may not print
Close file here.
```

In this example, one of the catch blocks is eliminated to save space, and a finally block is added. Whether or not an exception is thrown, the finally block is executed (in both output examples you see the message Close file here.).

 You can create a finally block with or without catch blocks, but a finally block requires a try block to execute. It is an error to exit a finally block with break, continue, return, or goto.

# Exception Objects

So far, you've been using the exception as a sentinel—that is, the presence of the exception signals the error—but you haven't touched or examined the Exception object itself. The System.Exception object provides a number of useful methods and properties. The Message property provides information about the exception, such as why it was thrown. The `Message` property is read-only; the code throwing the exception can set the `Message` property as an argument to the exception constructor.

The `HelpLink` property provides a link to the help file associated with the exception. This property is read/write.

> *VB 6 programmers take note*: in C#, you need to be careful when declaring and instantiating object variables on the same line of code. If there is a possibility that an error could be thrown in the constructor method, you might be tempted to put the variable declaration and instantiation inside the try block. But, if you do that, the variable will only be scoped within the try block, and it can't be referenced within the `catch` or `finally` blocks. The best approach is to *declare* the object variable *before* the try block and *instantiate* it *within* the try block.

The `StackTrace` property is read-only and is set by the runtime. In Example 11-6, the `Exception.HelpLink` property is set and retrieved to provide information to the user about the `DivideByZeroException`. The `StackTrace` property of the exception can provide a stack trace for the error statement. A stack trace displays the *call stack*: the series of method calls that lead to the method in which the exception was thrown.

*Example 11-6. Working with an exception object*

```
using System;

namespace ExceptionObject
{
    public class Test
    {
        public static void Main()
        {
            Test t = new Test();
            t.TestFunc();
        }

        // try to divide two numbers
        // handle possible exceptions
        public void TestFunc()
        {
            try
            {
                Console.WriteLine("Open file here");
                double a = 12;
                double b = 0;
                Console.WriteLine("{0} / {1} = {2}",
                    a, b, DoDivide(a, b));
                Console.WriteLine(
                    "This line may or may not print");
            }
```

*Example 11-6. Working with an exception object (continued)*

```
        // most derived exception type first
        catch (System.DivideByZeroException e)
        {
            Console.WriteLine(
                "DivideByZeroException!" + e);
        }
        catch (System.Exception e)
        {
            Console.WriteLine(
            "Log" + e.Message);
        }
        finally
        {
            Console.WriteLine("Close file here.");
        }
    }

    // do the division if legal
    public double DoDivide(double a, double b)
    {
        if (b == 0)
        {
            DivideByZeroException e =
            new DivideByZeroException();
            e.HelpLink =
                "http://www.libertyassociates.com";
            throw e;
        }
        if (a == 0)
            throw new ArithmeticException();
        return a / b;
    }
  }
}
```

```
Output:
Open file here

DivideByZeroException! Msg: Attempted to divide by zero.

HelpLink: http://www.libertyassociates.com

Here's a stack trace:
at ExceptionObject.Test.DoDivide(Double a, Double b)
 in c:\...exception06.cs:line 56
at ExceptionObject.Test.TestFunc()
in...exception06.cs:line 22

Close file here.
```

In the output, the stack trace lists the methods in the reverse order in which they were called; that is, it shows that the error occurred in DoDivide( ), which was called by TestFunc( ). When methods are deeply nested, the stack trace can help you understand the order of method calls.

In this example, rather than simply throwing a DivideByZeroException, you create a new instance of the exception:

```
DivideByZeroException e = new DivideByZeroException( );
```

You don't pass in a custom message, and so the default message will be printed:

```
DivideByZeroException! Msg: Attempted to divide by zero.
```

You can modify this line of code to pass in a default message:

```
new DivideByZeroException(
    "You tried to divide by zero, which is not meaningful");
```

In this case, the output message will reflect the custom message:

```
DivideByZeroException! Msg:
You tried to divide by zero, which is not meaningful
```

Before throwing the exception, set the HelpLink property:

```
e.HelpLink = "http://www.libertyassociates.com";
```

When this exception is caught, the program prints the message and the HelpLink:

```
catch (System.DivideByZeroException e)
{
    Console.WriteLine("\nDivideByZeroException! Msg: {0}",
    e.Message);
    Console.WriteLine("\nHelpLink: {0}", e.HelpLink);
```

This allows you to provide useful information to the user. In addition, it prints the StackTrace by getting the StackTrace property of the exception object:

```
Console.WriteLine("\nHere's a stack trace: {0}\n",
    e.StackTrace);
```

The output of this call reflects a full StackTrace leading to the moment the exception was thrown:

```
Here's a stack trace:
at ExceptionObject.Test.DoDivide(Double a, Double b)
 in c:\...exception06.cs:line 56
at ExceptionObject.Test.TestFunc( )
in...exception06.cs:line 22
```

Note that we've abbreviated the pathnames, so your printout might look different.

# CHAPTER 12

# Delegates and Events

When a head of state dies, the president of the United States typically doesn't have time to attend the funeral personally. Instead, he dispatches a delegate. Often, this delegate is the vice president, but sometimes the VP is unavailable, and the president must send someone else, such as the secretary of state or even the first lady. He doesn't want to "hardwire" his delegated authority to a single person; he might delegate this responsibility to anyone who is able to execute the correct international protocol.

The president defines in advance what responsibility will be delegated (attend the funeral), what parameters will be passed (condolences, kind words), and what value he hopes to get back (good will). He then assigns a particular person to that delegated responsibility at "runtime" as the course of his presidency progresses.

## Events

In programming, you are often faced with situations where you need to execute a particular action, but you don't know in advance which method, or even which object, you'll want to call upon to execute it. The classic example of this is the method called to handle a button press, a menu selection, or some other "event."

An *event*, in event-driven programming (like Windows!), is when something happens—often as a result of user action, but at times as a result of a change in system state or a result of a message begin received from outside the system (e.g., via the Internet).

You must imagine that the person who creates a button (or listbox or other control) will not necessarily be the programmer who *uses* the control. The control inventor knows that when the button is clicked, the programmer using the button will want something to happen, but the inventor can't know what!

The solution to this dilemma is for the creator of the button to say, in effect, "My button publishes a series of events, such as click. My listbox has other events, such as selection changed, entry added, and so on. You programmers who want to use my controls, you can hook up whatever method you want to these events when you use my controls." You hook up to these events using *delegates*.

A delegate is an object that contains the address of a method. That makes them useful for many purposes, but ideal for two:

- "Call this method when this event happens" (event handling).
- "Call this method when you're done doing this work" (callbacks, discussed later in this chapter).

In C#, delegates are first-class members of the language (to a C++ programmer, they are Pointers To Member Functions on steroids!), and they are used to hook up an event to a method that will handle that event. In fact, events are just a restricted kind of delegate, as you'll see later in this chapter.

## Events and Delegates

In C#, delegates are fully supported by the language. Technically, a delegate is a reference type used to encapsulate a method with a specific signature and return type.[*] You can encapsulate any matching method in that delegate.

You create a delegate with the delegate keyword, followed by a return type and the signature of the methods that can be delegated to it, as in the following:

```
public delegate void ButtonClick(object sender, EventArgs e);
```

This declaration defines a delegate named ButtonClick, which will encapsulate any method that takes an object of type Object (the base class for everything in C#) as its first parameter and an object of type EventArgs (or anything derived from EventArgs) as its second parameter. The method will return void. The delegate itself is public.

Once the delegate is defined, you can encapsulate a member method with that delegate by instantiating the delegate, passing in a method that matches the return type and signature.

For example, you might define this delegate:

```
public delegate void buttonPressedHandler(object sender, EventArgs e);
```

That delegate could encapsulate either of these two methods:

```
public void onButtonPressed(object sender, EventArgs e)
{
    MessageBox.Show("the button was pressed!");
}
```

---

[*] If the method is an instance method, the delegate encapsulates the target object as well.

or:

```
public void myFunkyMethod(object s, EventArgs x)
{
    MessageBoxShow("Ouch!");
}
```

As you'll see later, it can even encapsulate both at the same time! The key is that both methods return void and take two properties, an object and an EventArgs, as specified by the delegate.

## Indirect Invocation

As an alternative, you can use anonymous methods as described later. In either case, the delegate can then be used to invoke that encapsulated method. In short, delegates *decouple* the class that declares the delegate from the class that uses the delegate: that is, the creator of the Button does not need to know how the Button will be used in every program that places a button on the page.

## Publish and Subscribe/Observer

One very common "design pattern" in programming is that the creator of a control (such as a button) "publishes" (documents) the events to which the button will respond (such as click). Programmers who use the button (such as those who put a button on their form) may choose to "subscribe" to one or more of the button's events. Thus, if you're implementing a web form that uses a button, you might choose to subscribe (be notified) when someone clicks the button, but not when a mouse hovers over the button.

A closely related "pattern" is the observer pattern, in which the form is said to be the observer, and the button is said to be observed.

In any case, the mechanism for publishing is to create a delegate. The mechanism for subscribing is to create a method that matches the signature and return type of the delegate and then to subscribe your matching method with the syntax shown in Example 12-1.

The subscribing method is typically called an *event handler*, because it handles the event raised by the publishing class. That is, the form might *handle* the "click" event raised by the button.

By convention, event handlers in the .NET Framework return void and take two parameters. The first parameter is the "source" of the event (i.e., the publishing object). The second parameter is an object derived from EventArgs.

EventArgs is the base class for all event data. Other than its constructor, the EventArgs class inherits all its methods from Object, though it does add a public static field named Empty, which represents an event with no state (to allow for the efficient use of events with no state). The EventArgs derived class contains information about the event.

To make this less theoretical and more concrete, let's look at Example 12-1, and then take it apart.

*Example 12-1. Publish and subscribe with delegates*

```
using System;
using System.Collections.Generic;
using System.Text;
using System.Threading;

namespace EventsWithDelegates
{
    // a class to hold the information about the event
    // in this case it will hold only information
    // available in the clock class, but could hold
    // additional state information
    public class TimeInfoEventArgs : EventArgs
    {
        public TimeInfoEventArgs(int hour, int minute, int second)
        {
            this.Hour = hour;
            this.Minute = minute;
            this.Second = second;
        }
        public readonly int Hour;
        public readonly int Minute;
        public readonly int Second;
    }

    // our subject -- it is this class that other classes
    // will observe. This class publishes one delegate:
    // OnSecondChange.
    public class Clock
    {
        private int hour;
        private int minute;
        private int second;

        // the delegate
        public delegate void SecondChangeHandler
        (
            object clock,
            TimeInfoEventArgs timeInformation
        );

        // an instance of the delegate
        public SecondChangeHandler SecondChanged;
```

*Example 12-1. Publish and subscribe with delegates (continued)*

```
        protected virtual void OnSecondChanged(TimeInfoEventArgs e)
        {
            if (SecondChanged != null)
            {
                SecondChanged(this, e);
            }
        }



        // set the clock running
        // it will raise an event for each new second
        public void Run( )
        {
            for (; ; )
            {
                // sleep 10 milliseconds
                Thread.Sleep(10);

                // get the current time
                System.DateTime dt = System.DateTime.Now;

                // if the second has changed
                // notify the subscribers
                if (dt.Second != second)
                {
                    // create the TimeInfoEventArgs object
                    // to pass to the subscriber
                    TimeInfoEventArgs timeInformation =
                    new TimeInfoEventArgs(
                    dt.Hour, dt.Minute, dt.Second);
                    OnSecondChanged(timeInformation);

                }

                // update the state
                this.second = dt.Second;
                this.minute = dt.Minute;
                this.hour = dt.Hour;
            }
        }
    }

    // an observer. DisplayClock subscribes to the
    // clock's events. The job of DisplayClock is
    // to display the current time
    public class DisplayClock
    {
        // given a clock, subscribe to
        // its SecondChangeHandler event
        public void Subscribe(Clock theClock)
        {
```

*Example 12-1. Publish and subscribe with delegates (continued)*

```
            theClock.SecondChanged +=
                new Clock.SecondChangeHandler(TimeHasChanged);
    }

    // the method that implements the
    // delegated functionality
    public void TimeHasChanged(
        object theClock, TimeInfoEventArgs ti)
    {
        Console.WriteLine("Current Time: {0}:{1}:{2}",
                          ti.Hour.ToString(),
                          ti.Minute.ToString(),
                          ti.Second.ToString());
    }
}

// a second subscriber whose job is to write to a file
public class LogCurrentTime
{
    public void Subscribe(Clock theClock)
    {
        theClock.SecondChanged +=
            new Clock.SecondChangeHandler(WriteLogEntry);
    }

    // This method should write to a file.
    // We write to the console to see the effect.
    // This object keeps no state.
    public void WriteLogEntry(
    object theClock, TimeInfoEventArgs ti)
    {
        Console.WriteLine("Logging to file: {0}:{1}:{2}",
                          ti.Hour.ToString(),
                          ti.Minute.ToString(),
                          ti.Second.ToString());
    }
}

public class Test
{
    public static void Main()
    {
        // create a new clock
        Clock theClock = new Clock();

        // create the display and tell it to
        // subscribe to the clock just created
        DisplayClock dc = new DisplayClock();
        dc.Subscribe(theClock);

        // create a Log object and tell it
        // to subscribe to the clock
```

*Example 12-1. Publish and subscribe with delegates (continued)*

```
            LogCurrentTime lct = new LogCurrentTime( );
            lct.Subscribe(theClock);

            // Get the clock started
            theClock.Run( );
        }
    }
}
```

```
Partial Output...
Current Time: 16:0:7
Logging to file: 16:0:7
Current Time: 16:0:8
Logging to file: 16:0:8
Current Time: 16:0:9
Logging to file: 16:0:9
Current Time: 16:0:10
Logging to file: 16:0:10
Current Time: 16:0:11
Logging to file: 16:0:11
Current Time: 16:0:12
Logging to file: 16:0:12
```

## The Publishing Class: Clock

The class that we will be observing is Clock. It publishes one event, SecondChanged. The syntax for publishing that event is that it declares a delegate, SecondChangedHandler, that must be subscribed to by anyone interested in being notified when the second changes:

```
public delegate void SecondChangeHandler
(
    object clock,
    TimeInfoEventArgs timeInformation
);
```

As is typical for all event handlers in .NET, this delegate returns void and takes two arguments: the first of type void, and the second of type EventArgs (or, as in this case, of a type derived from EventArgs).

Let's delay looking at TimeInfoEventArgs for just a bit and continue on.

The Clock class must then create an instance of this delegate, which it does on the following line:

```
public SecondChangeHandler SecondChanged;
```

You read this as "The member variable SecondChanged is an instance of the delegate SecondChangeHandler."

The third thing that the Clock will do is to provide a protected method for invoking its event. The event will be invoked only if there are subscribers (again, I'll show how other classes subscribe in just a moment):

```
protected virtual void OnSecondChanged(TimeInfoEventArgs e)
{
    if (SecondChanged != null)
    {
        SecondChanged(this, e);
    }
}
```

You can infer from this that if no one has subscribed, the instance SecondChanged will be null, but if any other class has subscribed, it will not be null, and the method that the other classes have registered will be invoked *through the delegate* by calling the instance of the delegate and passing in the Clock (this) and the instance of TimeInfoEventArgs that was passed into OnSecondChanged.

So, who calls OnSecondChanged?

It turns out that Clock has another method, Run, that keeps an eye on the clock, and every time the seconds change, it makes a new instance of TimeInfoEventArgs and calls OnSecondChanged:

```
public void Run( )
{
    for (; ; )
    {
        // sleep 10 milliseconds
        Thread.Sleep(10);

        // get the current time
        System.DateTime dt = System.DateTime.Now;

        // if the second has changed
        // notify the subscribers
        if (dt.Second != second)
        {
            // create the TimeInfoEventArgs object
            // to pass to the subscriber
            TimeInfoEventArgs timeInformation =
            new TimeInfoEventArgs(
            dt.Hour, dt.Minute, dt.Second);

            OnSecondChanged(timeInformation);

        }

        // update the state
        this.second = dt.Second;
        this.minute = dt.Minute;
        this.hour = dt.Hour;
    }
}
```

Run consists of a "forever" loop (it never stops until you shut down the program). It sleeps for 10 milliseconds (so as not to bring your computer to a complete halt), and then checks the system time against the hour, minute, and second that it stores in member variables. If there is a change, it creates a new instance of the TimeInfoEventArgs object, and then invokes OnSecondChanged, passing in that object.

OK, here's the definition of TimeInfoEventArgs:

```
public class TimeInfoEventArgs : EventArgs
{
    public readonly int Hour;
    public readonly int Minute;
    public readonly int Second;
    public TimeInfoEventArgs(int hour, int minute, int second)
    {
        this.Hour = hour;
        this.Minute = minute;
        this.Second = second;
    }

}
```

## Registering to Be Notified

We're almost ready to walk through the scenario, but we still don't know how classes register to be notified. To see this, we need to create two subscribers, DisplayClock and LogCurrentTime.

DisplayClock, we'll pretend, is a nice digital clock that sits on your desktop, and LogCurrentTime is a nifty utility you can invoke when you want to log an error and have it timestamped. Cool, eh? Wish we were really going to write that.

But we're not:

```
public class DisplayClock
{
    public void Subscribe(Clock theClock)
    {
        theClock.SecondChanged +=
            new Clock.SecondChangeHandler(TimeHasChanged);
    }

    public void TimeHasChanged(
        object theClock, TimeInfoEventArgs ti)
    {
        Console.WriteLine("Current Time: {0}:{1}:{2}",
                            ti.Hour.ToString(),
                            ti.Minute.ToString(),
                            ti.Second.ToString());
    }
}
```

You pass a Clock object into the Subscribe method of DisplayClock, and it registers itself to be notified. How? It uses the += operator on the delegate it wants to register with (secondChanged), creating a new instance of the delegate, passing to the constructor the name of a method within DisplayClock that matches the return value (void) and the parameters (object, TimeEventArgs). DisplayClock just happens to have such a method: TimeHasChanged.

This serendipitous method does not display the time nicely on your computer, but it does display it, using the Hour, Minute, and Second it retrieves from the TimeInfoEventArgs it gets back when notified that the time has changed!

The second subscriber is much more sophisticated:

```
public class LogCurrentTime
{
    public void Subscribe(Clock theClock)
    {
        theClock.SecondChanged +=
            new Clock.SecondChangeHandler(WriteLogEntry);
    }

    public void WriteLogEntry(
    object theClock, TimeInfoEventArgs ti)
    {
        Console.WriteLine("Logging to file: {0}:{1}:{2}",
                        ti.Hour.ToString( ),
                        ti.Minute.ToString( ),
                        ti.Second.ToString( ));
    }
}
```

Here, we pretend to write to a logfile the Hour, Minute, and Second that we get from the TimeInfoEventArgs object, but we don't really do that either; we just write it to the screen.

So, how do our two subscribers get their clock instances? Easy—we pass the Clock object in right after we create them, in Main( ):

```
public static void Main( )
{
    // create a new clock
    Clock theClock = new Clock( );

    // create the display and tell it to
    // subscribe to the clock just created
    DisplayClock dc = new DisplayClock( );
    dc.Subscribe(theClock);

    // create a Log object and tell it
    // to subscribe to the clock
    LogCurrentTime lct = new LogCurrentTime( );
    lct.Subscribe(theClock);
```

```
        // Get the clock started
        theClock.Run( );
    }
```

## Sequence of Events

Here is the sequence of events (which, as you might suspect already, is the reverse order of that in which I explained them!).

In `Main( )`, we create a `Clock`, cleverly named `theClock`. A clock knows how to publish the time, if anyone subscribes.

We then create an instance of a `DisplayClock` (named dc), which is quite good at subscribing to the `Clock`, and we tell it to `Subscribe`, passing in our new `Clock` so that it may do so.

We also create an instance of a `LogCurrentTime` class (lct), and tell it to `Subscribe` to theClock, which it does.

Finally, now that two listeners are paying attention, we tell `theClock` to Run. Every second, `theClock` realizes that a second has passed, so it creates a new `TimeInfoEventArgs` object and calls `OnSecondChanged`. `OnSecondChanged` tests whether the delegate is null, which it is not because two listeners have registered, so it fires the delegate:

```
        SecondChanged(this, e);
```

This is exactly as though it had reached into `DisplayClock` and called `TimeHasChanged`, passing in a copy of itself and a copy of the newly minted `TimeInfoEventArgs`, and then reached into `LogCurrentTime` and called `WriteLogEntry`, passing in the same two arguments!

## The Danger with Delegates

There is a problem with Example 12-1, however. What if the `LogCurrentTime` class was not so considerate, and it used the assignment operator (=) rather than the subscribe operator (+=), as in the following:

```
    public void Subscribe(Clock theClock)
    {
        theClock.OnSecondChange =
        new Clock.SecondChangeHandler(WriteLogEntry);
    }
```

If you make that one tiny change to the example, you'll find that the `Logger( )` method is called, but the `DisplayClock` method is *not* called. The assignment operator *replaced* the delegate held in the `OnSecondChange` multicast delegate. The technical term for this is *bad*.

A second problem is that other methods can call `SecondChangeHandler` directly. For example, you might add the following code to the `Main( )` method of your `Test` class:

```
Console.WriteLine("Calling the method directly!");
System.DateTime dt = System.DateTime.Now.AddHours(2);

TimeInfoEventArgs timeInformation =
    new TimeInfoEventArgs(
    dt.Hour,dt.Minute,dt.Second);

theClock.OnSecondChange(theClock, timeInformation);
```

Here, Main( ) has created its own TimeInfoEventArgs object and invoked OnSecondChange directly. This runs fine, even though it is not what the designer of the Clock class intended. Here is the output:

```
Calling the method directly!
Current Time: 18:36:7
Logging to file: 18:36:7
Current Time: 16:36:7
Logging to file: 16:36:7
```

The problem is that the designer of the Clock class intended the methods encapsulated by the delegate to be invoked only when the event is fired. Here, Main( ) has gone around through the back door and invoked those methods itself. What is more, it has passed in bogus data (passing in a time construct set to two hours into the future!).

How can you, as the designer of the Clock class, ensure that no one calls the delegated method directly? You can make the delegate private, but then it won't be possible for clients to register with your delegate at all. What you need is a way to say, "This delegate is designed for event handling: you may subscribe and unsubscribe, but you may not invoke it directly."

## The event Keyword

The solution to this dilemma is to use the event keyword. The event keyword indicates to the compiler that the delegate can be invoked only by the defining class, and that other classes can only subscribe to and unsubscribe from the delegate using the appropriate += and -= operators, respectively.

To fix your program, change your definition of OnSecondChange from:

```
public SecondChangeHandler OnSecondChange;
```

to the following:

```
public event SecondChangeHandler OnSecondChange;
```

Adding the event keyword fixes both problems. Classes can no longer attempt to subscribe to the event using the assignment operator (=), as they could previously, nor can they invoke the event directly, as was done in Main( ) in the preceding example. Either of these attempts will now generate a compile error:

```
The event 'Programming_CSharp.Clock.OnSecondChange' can only appear on
the left hand side of += or -= (except when used from within the type
'Programming_CSharp.Clock')
```

There are two ways to look at OnSecondChange now that you've modified it. In one sense, it is simply a delegate instance to which you've restricted access using the keyword event. In another, more important sense, OnSecondChange *is* an event, implemented by a delegate of type SecondChangeHandler. These two statements mean the same thing, but the latter is a more object-oriented way to look at it and better reflects the intent of this keyword: to create an event that your object can raise, and to which other objects can respond.

Example 12-2 shows the complete source, modified to use the event rather than the unrestricted delegate.

*Example 12-2. Using the event keyword*

```csharp
using System;
using System.Collections.Generic;
using System.Text;
using System.Threading;

namespace EventsWithDelegates
{
    public class TimeInfoEventArgs : EventArgs
    {
        public readonly int Hour;
        public readonly int Minute;
        public readonly int Second;
        public TimeInfoEventArgs(int hour, int minute, int second)
        {
            this.Hour = hour;
            this.Minute = minute;
            this.Second = second;
        }
    }

    public class Clock
    {
        private int hour;
        private int minute;
        private int second;

        public delegate void SecondChangeHandler
        (
            object clock,
            TimeInfoEventArgs timeInformation
        );

        // public SecondChangeHandler SecondChanged;
        public event SecondChangeHandler SecondChanged;
```

*Example 12-2. Using the event keyword (continued)*

```csharp
    protected virtual void OnSecondChanged(TimeInfoEventArgs e)
    {
        if (SecondChanged != null)
        {
            SecondChanged(this, e);
        }
    }

    public void Run( )
    {
        for (; ; )
        {
            Thread.Sleep(10);

            System.DateTime dt = System.DateTime.Now;

            if (dt.Second != second)
            {
                TimeInfoEventArgs timeInformation =
                new TimeInfoEventArgs(
                dt.Hour, dt.Minute, dt.Second);
                OnSecondChanged(timeInformation);
            }

            this.second = dt.Second;
            this.minute = dt.Minute;
            this.hour = dt.Hour;
        }
    }
}

public class DisplayClock
{
    public void Subscribe(Clock theClock)
    {
        theClock.SecondChanged +=
            new Clock.SecondChangeHandler(TimeHasChanged);
    }

    public void TimeHasChanged(
        object theClock, TimeInfoEventArgs ti)
    {
        Console.WriteLine("Current Time: {0}:{1}:{2}",
            ti.Hour.ToString( ),
            ti.Minute.ToString( ),
            ti.Second.ToString( ));
    }
}

public class LogCurrentTime
{
```

*Example 12-2. Using the event keyword (continued)*

```
    public void Subscribe(Clock theClock)
    {
        //theClock.SecondChanged =
        //    new Clock.SecondChangeHandler(WriteLogEntry);

        theClock.SecondChanged +=
            new Clock.SecondChangeHandler(WriteLogEntry);


    }

    public void WriteLogEntry(
    object theClock, TimeInfoEventArgs ti)
    {
        Console.WriteLine("Logging to file: {0}:{1}:{2}",
                ti.Hour.ToString( ),
                ti.Minute.ToString( ),
                ti.Second.ToString( ));
    }
}

public class Test
{
    public static void Main( )
    {
        Clock theClock = new Clock( );


        DisplayClock dc = new DisplayClock( );
        dc.Subscribe(theClock);


        LogCurrentTime lct = new LogCurrentTime( );
        lct.Subscribe(theClock);


        //Console.WriteLine("Calling the method directly!");
        //System.DateTime dt = System.DateTime.Now.AddHours(2);

        //TimeInfoEventArgs timeInformation =
        //    new TimeInfoEventArgs(
        //    dt.Hour, dt.Minute, dt.Second);

        //theClock.SecondChanged(theClock, timeInformation);


        theClock.Run( );
    }
}
}
```

# Anonymous Methods

In the preceding example, you subscribed to the event by invoking a new instance of the delegate, passing in the name of a method that implements the event:

```
theClock.OnSecondChange +=
    new Clock.SecondChangeHandler(TimeHasChanged);
```

You can also assign this delegate by writing the shortened version:

```
theClock.OnSecondChange += TimeHasChanged;
```

Later in the code, you must define `TimeHasChanged` as a method that matches the signature of the `SecondChangeHandler` delegate:

```
public void TimeHasChanged(object theClock, TimeInfoEventArgs ti)
{
    Console.WriteLine("Current Time: {0}:{1}:{2}",
                      ti.Hour.ToString(),
                      ti.Minute.ToString(),
                      ti.=Second.ToString());
}
```

C# offers *anonymous methods* that allow you to pass a code block rather than the name of the method. This can make for more efficient and easier-to-maintain code, and the anonymous method has access to the variables in the scope in which they are defined:

```
clock.OnSecondChange += delegate( object theClock, TimeInfoEventArgs ti )
{
    Console.WriteLine( "Current Time: {0}:{1}:{2}",
                      ti.Hour.ToString(),
                      ti.Minute.ToString(),
                      ti.Second.ToString() );
};
```

 Overused, this can also make for cut-and-paste code that is *harder* to maintain.

Notice that instead of registering an instance of a delegate, you use the keyword delegate, followed by the parameters that would be passed to your method, followed by the body of your method encased in braces and terminated by a semicolon.

This "method" has no name; hence, it is anonymous. You can invoke the method only through the delegate, but that is exactly what you want.

## Lambda Expressions

C# 3.0 extends the concept of anonymous methods and introduces *lambda expressions*, which are more powerful and flexible than anonymous methods.

 Lambda expressions are designed to provide not only inline delegate definitions, but also a framework for Language-Integrated Query (LINQ). We discuss LINQ in detail in Chapters 13 and 15.

You define a lambda expression using this syntax:

```
(input parameters) => {expression or statement block};
```

The lambda operator, =>, is newly introduced in C# 3.0 and is read as "goes to." The left operand is a list of zero or more input parameters, and the right operand is the body of the lambda expression.

You can thus rewrite the delegate definition as follows:

```
theClock.OnSecondChange +=
    (aClock, ti) =>
    {
        Console.WriteLine("Current Time: {0}:{1}:{2}",
                          ti.hour.ToString(),
                          ti.minute.ToString(),
                          ti.second.ToString());
    };
```

You read this as "theClock's OnSecondChange delegate adds an anonymous delegate defined by this lambda expression. The two parameters, aClock and ti, go to the WriteLine expression that writes out the hour and minute and second from ti."

The two input parameters, aClock and ti, are of type Clock and TimeInfoEventArgs, respectively. Their types are not specified because the C# compiler infers their types from the OnSecondChange delegate definition. If the compiler is unable to infer the types of your operands, you may specify them explicitly:

```
(Clock aClock, TimeInfoEventArgs ti) => {...};
```

If there is no input parameter, you write a pair of empty parentheses:

```
() => {expression or statement block};
```

If there is only one input parameter, the parentheses can be omitted:

```
n => n * n;
```

## Callback Methods

The second classic use for a delegate is a *callback*. When you go to your favorite restaurant at 8 p.m. on a Saturday, the wait may be quite long. You give your name and they give you a pager. When your table is ready, they dial a number that buzzes your pager, and that signals you that your table is ready. Callbacks work the same way, only this time, the table is your data, the pager is a method, and the phone number they call to make the pager buzz is a delegate!

Let's say you reach a place in your program where you need to get data from a web service (a program running on another computer that you do not control, and that is out there on the Internet "somewhere"). You can't know how long it will take to get your data, but it might be a very long time, a second or more. Rather than having your program wait in the crowded lobby, listening to annoying muzak, you hand over a delegate to the method that should be called when your table (excuse me, when your data) is ready. When the web service returns with the data, your delegate is invoked, and because it has the address of your method, the method is called, which takes action on the data returned.

You implement callbacks with the `AsyncCallback` delegate, which allows the main work of your program to continue until "your table is ready":

```
[Serializable]
public delegate void AsyncCallback
(
    IAsyncResult ar
);
```

The attribute (`Serializable`) is covered in Chapter 22. You can see here, however, that `AsyncCallback` is a delegate for a method that returns `void` and takes a single argument, an object of type `IAsyncResult`. The Framework defines this interface, and the CLR will be calling your method with an object that implements `IAsyncResult`, so you don't need to know the details of the interface; you can just use the object provided to you.

Here's how it works. You will ask the delegate for its invocation list, and you will call `BeginInvoke` on each delegate in that list. `BeginInvoke` will take two parameters. The first will be a delegate of type `AsyncCallback`, and the second will be your own delegate that invokes the method you want to call:

```
del.BeginInvoke(new AsyncCallback(ResultsReturned),del);
```

In the preceding line of code, you are calling the method encapsulated by `del` (e.g., `DisplayCounter`), and when that method completes, you want to be notified via your method `ResultsReturned`.

The method to be called back (`ResultsReturned`) must match the return type and signature of the `AsyncCallback` delegate: it must return `void`, and must take an object of type `IAsyncResult`:

```
private void ResultsReturned(IAsyncResult iar)
{
```

When that method is called back, the .NET Framework passes in the `IAsyncResult` object. The second parameter to `BeginInvoke` is your delegate, and that delegate is stashed away for you in the `AsyncState` property of the `IAsyncResult` as an `Object`. Inside the `ResultsReturned` callback method, you can extract that `Object` and cast it to its original type:

```
DelegateThatReturnsInt del = (DelegateThatReturnsInt)iar.AsyncState;
```

You can now use that delegate to call the EndInvoke( ) method, passing in the IAsyncResult object you received as a parameter:

```
int result = del.EndInvoke(iar);
```

EndInvoke( ) returns the value of the called (and now completed) method, which you assign to a local variable named result, and which you are now free to display to the user.

The net effect is that in Run( ), you get each registered method in turn (first FirstSubscriber.DisplayCounter and then SecondSubscriber.Doubler), and you invoke each asynchronously. There is no delay between the call to the first and the call to the second, as you aren't waiting for DisplayCounter to return.

When DisplayCounter (or Doubler) has results, your callback method (ResultsReturned) is invoked, and you use the IAsyncResult object provided as a parameter to get the actual results back from these methods. Example 12-3 shows the complete implementation.

*Example 12-3. Asynchronous invocation of delegates*

```
using System;
using System.Collections.Generic;
using System.Text;
using System.Threading;

namespace AsyncDelegates
{
    public class ClassWithDelegate
    {
        // a multicast delegate that encapsulates a method
        // that returns an int
        public delegate int DelegateThatReturnsInt( );
        public DelegateThatReturnsInt theDelegate;

        public void Run( )
        {
            for (; ; )
            {
                // sleep for a half second
                Thread.Sleep(500);

                if (theDelegate != null)
                {
                    // explicitly invoke each delegated method
                    foreach (
                    DelegateThatReturnsInt del in
                    theDelegate.GetInvocationList( ))
                    {
                        // invoke asynchronously
                        // pass the delegate in as a state object
                        del.BeginInvoke(new AsyncCallback(ResultsReturned),
                        del);
```

*Example 12-3. Asynchronous invocation of delegates (continued)*

```
                } // end foreach
            } // end if
        } // end for ;;
    } // end run

    // callback method to capture results
    private void ResultsReturned(IAsyncResult iar)
    {
        // cast the state object back to the delegate type
        DelegateThatReturnsInt del =
        (DelegateThatReturnsInt)iar.AsyncState;

        // call EndInvoke on the delegate to get the results
        int result = del.EndInvoke(iar);

        // display the results
        Console.WriteLine("Delegate returned result: {0}", result);
    }
} // end class

public class FirstSubscriber
{
    private int myCounter = 0;

    public void Subscribe(ClassWithDelegate theClassWithDelegate)
    {
        theClassWithDelegate.theDelegate +=
        new ClassWithDelegate.DelegateThatReturnsInt(DisplayCounter);
    }

    public int DisplayCounter()
    {
        Console.WriteLine("Busy in DisplayCounter...");
        Thread.Sleep(10000);
        Console.WriteLine("Done with work in DisplayCounter...");
        return ++myCounter;
    }
}

public class SecondSubscriber
{
    private int myCounter = 0;

    public void Subscribe(ClassWithDelegate theClassWithDelegate)
    {
        theClassWithDelegate.theDelegate +=
        new ClassWithDelegate.DelegateThatReturnsInt(Doubler);
    }

    public int Doubler()
    {
        return myCounter += 2;
```

*Example 12-3. Asynchronous invocation of delegates (continued)*

```
        }
    }

    public class Test
    {
        public static void Main( )
        {
            ClassWithDelegate theClassWithDelegate =
            new ClassWithDelegate( );

            FirstSubscriber fs = new FirstSubscriber( );
            fs.Subscribe(theClassWithDelegate);

            SecondSubscriber ss = new SecondSubscriber( );
            ss.Subscribe(theClassWithDelegate);

            theClassWithDelegate.Run( );
        }
    }
}
```

# PART II

# C# and Data

Chapter 13, *Introducing LINQ*
Chapter 14, *Working with XML*
Chapter 15, *Putting LINQ to Work*
Chapter 16, *ADO.NET and Relational Databases*

# Introducing LINQ

One of the common programming tasks C# programmers perform every day is finding and retrieving objects in memory, a database, or an XML file. For example, you may be developing a cell phone customer support system that will allow a customer to see how much each member of the family has spent in phone calls. To do so, you'll need to retrieve records from various sources (phone company records online, phone books kept locally, etc.), filtered by various criteria (by name or by month), and sorted in various ways (e.g., by date, by family member).

One way you might have implemented this in the past would be to search a database by address, returning all the records to the user, perhaps presenting them in a listbox. The user would pick the name she was interested in and the data of interest (e.g., the number of ringtones downloaded in the past three months), and you would go back to the database (or perhaps to a different database) and retrieve that information, using the chosen family member's unique ID as a key, retrieving the required data.

Although C# provides support for in-memory searches such as finding a name in a collection, traditionally, you were required to turn to another technology (such as ADO.NET) to retrieve data from a database. Although ADO.NET made this fairly easy, a sharp distinction was drawn between retrieving data from in-memory collections and retrieving data from persistent storage.

In-memory searches lacked the powerful and flexible query capabilities of SQL, whereas ADO.NET was not integrated into C#, and SQL itself was not object-oriented (in fact, the point of ADO.NET was to bridge the object-to-relational model). LINQ is an integrated feature of C# 3.0 itself, and thus (at long last) brings an object-oriented bridge over the impedance mismatch between object-oriented languages and relational databases.

The goal of LINQ (Language-INtegrated Query) is to integrate extensive query capabilities into the C# language, to make SQL-like capabilities part of the language, and to remove the distinctions among searching a database, an XML document, or an in-memory data collection.

This chapter will introduce LINQ and show how it fits into C# and into your programming. Subsequent chapters will dive into the details of using LINQ to retrieve and manipulate data in databases and in other data repositories. You'll learn about ADO.NET in Chapter 16.

# Defining and Executing a Query

In previous versions of C#, if you wanted to find an object in a database you had to leave C# and turn to the Framework (most often ADO.NET). With LINQ, you can stay within C#, and thus within a fully class-based perspective.

 Many books start with anonymous methods, then introduce Lambda expressions, and finally introduce LINQ. It is my experience that it is far easier to understand each of these concepts by going in the opposite direction, starting with queries and introducing Lambda expressions for what they are: enabling technologies. Each of these topics will, however, be covered here and in subsequent chapters.

Let's start simply by searching a collection for objects that match a given criterion, as demonstrated in Example 13-1.

*Example 13-1. A simple LINQ query*

```
using System;
using System.Collections.Generic;
using System.Linq;
namespace Programming_CSharp
{
    // Simple customer class
    public class Customer
    {
        public string FirstName { get; set; }
        public string LastName { get; set; }
        public string EmailAddress { get; set; }

        // Overrides the Object.ToString() to provide a
        // string representation of the object properties.
        public override string ToString()
        {
            return string.Format("{0} {1}\nEmail:   {2}",
                    FirstName, LastName, EmailAddress);
        }
    }

    // Main program
    public class Tester
    {
        static void Main()
        {
            List<Customer> customers = CreateCustomerList();
```

*Example 13-1. A simple LINQ query (continued)*

```
            // Find customer by first name
            IEnumerable<Customer> result =
                from   customer in customers
                where  customer.FirstName == "Donna"
                select customer;
            Console.WriteLine("FirstName == \"Donna\"");
            foreach (Customer customer in result)
                Console.WriteLine(customer.ToString( ));

            customers[3].FirstName = "Donna";
            Console.WriteLine("FirstName == \"Donna\" (take two)");
            foreach (Customer customer in result)
                Console.WriteLine(customer.ToString( ));
        }

        // Create a customer list with sample data
        private static List<Customer> CreateCustomerList( )
        {
            List<Customer> customers = new List<Customer>
                {
                    new Customer { FirstName = "Orlando",
                                   LastName = "Gee",
                                   EmailAddress = "orlando0@adventure-works.com"},
                    new Customer { FirstName = "Keith",
                                   LastName = "Harris",
                                   EmailAddress = "keith0@adventure-works.com" },
                    new Customer { FirstName = "Donna",
                                   LastName = "Carreras",
                                   EmailAddress = "donna0@adventure-works.com" },
                    new Customer { FirstName = "Janet",
                                   LastName = "Gates",
                                   EmailAddress = "janet1@adventure-works.com" },
                    new Customer { FirstName = "Lucy",
                                   LastName = "Harrington",
                                   EmailAddress = "lucy0@adventure-works.com" }
                };
            return customers;
        }
    }
}

Output:
FirstName == "Donna"
Donna Carreras
Email:   donna0@adventure-works.com
FirstName == "Donna" (take two)
Donna Carreras
Email:   donna0@adventure-works.com
Donna Gates
Email:   janet1@adventure-works.com
```

Example 13-1 defines a simple Customer class with three properties: FirstName, LastName, and EmailAddress. It overrides the Object.ToString( ) method to provide a string representation of its instances.

## Creating the Query

The program starts by creating a customer list with some sample data, taking advantage of object initialization as discussed in Chapter 4. Once the list of customers is created, Example 13-1 defines a LINQ query:

```
IEnumerable<Customer> result =
            from    customer in customers
            where   customer.FirstName == "Donna"
            select customer;
```

The result variable is initialized with a query expression. In this example, the query will retrieve all Customer objects whose first name is "Donna" from the customer list. The result of such a query is a collection that implements IEnumerable<T>, where T is the type of the result object. In this example, because the query result is a set of Customer objects, the type of the result variable is IEnumerable<Customer>.

Let's dissect the query and look at each part in more detail.

### The from clause

The first part of a LINQ query is the from clause:

```
from    customer in customers
```

The generator of a LINQ query specifies the data source and a range variable. A LINQ data source can be any collection that implements the System.Collections. Generic.IEnumerable<T> interface. In this example, the data source is customers, an instance of List<Customer> that implements IEnumerable<T>.

 You'll see how to do the same query against a SQL database in Chapter 15.

A LINQ *range variable* is like an iteration variable in a foreach loop, iterating over the data source. Because the data source implements IEnumerable<T>, the C# compiler can infer the type of the range variable from the data source. In this example, because the type of the data source is List<Customer>, the range variable customer is of type Customer.

### Filtering

The second part of this LINQ query is the where clause, which is also called a *filter*. This portion of the clause is optional:

```
where   customer.FirstName == "Donna"
```

The filter is a Boolean expression. It is common to use the range variable in a `where` clause to filter the objects in the data source. Because `customer` in this example is of type `Customer`, you use one of its properties, in this case `FirstName`, to apply the filter for your query.

Of course, you may use any Boolean expression as your filter. For instance, you can invoke the `String.StartsWith( )` method to filter customers by the first letter of their last name:

```
where  customer.LastName.StartsWith("G")
```

You can also use composite expressions to construct more complex queries. In addition, you can use nested queries where the result of one query (the inner query) is used to filter another query (the outer query).

### Projection (or select)

The last part of a LINQ query is the `select` clause (known to database geeks as the "projection"), which defines (or projects) the results:

```
select customer;
```

In this example, the query returns the customer objects that satisfy the query condition. You may constrain which fields you project, much as you would with SQL. For instance, you can return only the qualified customers' email addresses only:

```
select customer.EmailAddress;
```

## Deferred Query Evaluation

LINQ implements deferred query evaluation, meaning that the declaration and initialization of a query expression do not actually execute the query. Instead, a LINQ query is executed, or evaluated, when you iterate through the query result:

```
foreach (Customer customer in result)
    Console.WriteLine(customer.ToString( ));
```

Because the query returns a collection of `Customer` objects, the iteration variable is an instance of the `Customer` class. You can use it as you would any `Customer` object. This example simply calls each `Customer` object's `ToString( )` method to output its property values to the console.

Each time you iterate through this `foreach` loop, the query will be reevaluated. If the data source has changed between executions, the result will be different. This is demonstrated in the next code section:

```
customers[3].FirstName = "Donna";
```

Here, you modify the first name of the customer "Janet Gates" to "Donna" and then iterate through the result again:

```
Console.WriteLine("FirstName == \"Donna\" (take two)");
```

```
    foreach (Customer customer in result)
        Console.WriteLine(customer.ToString( ));
```

As shown in the sample output, you can see that the result now includes Donna Gates as well.

In most situations, deferred query evaluation is desired because you want to obtain the most recent data in the data source each time you run the query. However, if you want to cache the result so that it can be processed later without having to reexecute the query, you can call either the ToList( ) or the ToArray( ) method to save a copy of the result. Example 13-2 demonstrates this technique as well.

*Example 13-2. A simple LINQ query with cached results*

```
using System;
using System.Collections.Generic;
using System.Linq;
namespace Programming_CSharp
{
    // Simple customer class
    public class Customer
    {
        // Same as in Example 13-1
    }

    // Main program
    public class Tester
    {
        static void Main( )
        {
            List<Customer> customers = CreateCustomerList( );

            // Find customer by first name
            IEnumerable<Customer> result =
                from customer in customers
                where customer.FirstName == "Donna"
                select customer;
            List<Customer> cachedResult = result.ToList<Customer>( );

            Console.WriteLine("FirstName == \"Donna\"");
            foreach (Customer customer in cachedResult)
                Console.WriteLine(customer.ToString( ));

            customers[3].FirstName = "Donna";
            Console.WriteLine("FirstName == \"Donna\" (take two)");
            foreach (Customer customer in cachedResult)
                Console.WriteLine(customer.ToString( ));
        }

        // Create a customer list with sample data
        private static List<Customer> CreateCustomerList( )
        {
            // Same as in Example 13-1
```

*Example 13-2. A simple LINQ query with cached results (continued)*

```
        }
    }
}
```

```
Output:
FirstName == "Donna"
Donna Carreras
Email:   donna0@adventure-works.com
FirstName == "Donna" (take two)
Donna Carreras
Email:   donna0@adventure-works.com
```

In this example, you call the ToList<T> method of the result collection to cache the result. Note that calling this method causes the query to be evaluated immediately. If the data source is changed after this, the change will not be reflected in the cached result. You can see from the output that there is no Donna Gates in the result.

One interesting point here is that the ToList<T> and ToArray<T> methods are not actually methods of IEnumerable; that is, if you look in the documentation for IEnumerable, you will not see them in the methods list. They are actually extension methods provided by LINQ. We will look at extension methods in more detail later in this chapter.

If you are familiar with SQL, you will notice a striking similarity between LINQ and SQL, at least in their syntax. The only odd-one-out at this stage is that the select statement in LINQ appears at the end of LINQ query expressions, instead of at the beginning, as in SQL. Because the generator, or the from clause, defines the range variable, it must be stated first. Therefore, the projection part is pushed back.

# LINQ and C#

LINQ provides many of the common SQL operations, such as join queries, grouping, aggregation, and sorting of results. In addition, it allows you to use the object-oriented features of C# in query expressions and processing, such as hierarchical query results.

## Joining

You will often want to search for objects from more than one data source. LINQ provides the join clause that offers the ability to join many data sources, not all of which need be databases. Suppose you have a list of customers containing customer names and email addresses, and a list of customer home addresses. You can use LINQ to combine both lists to produce a list of customers, with access to both their email and home addresses:

```
        from customer in customers
            join address in addresses on
```

```
customer.Name equals address.Name
    ...
```

The join condition is specified in the on subclause, similar to SQL, except that the objects joined need not be tables or views in a database. The join class syntax is:

```
[data source 1] join [data source 2] on [join condition]
```

Here, we are joining two data sources, customers and addresses, based on the customer name properties in each object. In fact, you can join more than two data sources using a combination of join clauses:

```
from customer in customers
    join address in addresses on
        customer.Name equals address.Name
    join invoice in invoices  on
        customer.Id   equals invoice.CustomerId
    join invoiceItem in invoiceItems on
        invoice.Id    equals invoiceItem.invoiceId
```

A LINQ join clause returns a result only when objects satisfying the join condition exist in all data sources. For instance, if a customer has no invoice, the query will not return anything for that customer, not even her name and email address. This is the equivalent of a SQL inner join clause.

 LINQ cannot perform an outer join (which returns a result if either of the data sources contains objects that meet the join condition).

## Ordering and the var Keyword

You can also specify the sort order in LINQ queries with the orderby clause:

```
from customer in Customers
    orderby customer.LastName
    select customer;
```

This sorts the result by customer last name in ascending order. Example 13-3 shows how you can sort the results of a join query.

*Example 13-3. A sorted join query*

```
using System;
using System.Collections.Generic;
using System.Linq;

namespace Programming_CSharp
{
    // Simple customer class
    public class Customer
    {
        // Same as in Example 13-1
    }
```

*Example 13-3. A sorted join query (continued)*

```csharp
// Customer address class
public class Address
{
    public string Name   { get; set; }
    public string Street { get; set; }
    public string City   { get; set; }

    // Overrides the Object.ToString() to provide a
    // string representation of the object properties.
    public override string ToString()
    {
        return string.Format("{0}, {1}", Street, City);
    }
}

// Main program
public class Tester
{
    static void Main()
    {
        List<Customer> customers = CreateCustomerList();
        List<Address>  addresses = CreateAddressList();

        // Find all addresses of a customer
        var result =
            from customer in customers
            join address in addresses on
                string.Format("{0} {1}", customer.FirstName,
                    customer.LastName)
                equals address.Name
            orderby customer.LastName, address.Street descending
            select new { Customer = customer, Address = address };

        foreach (var ca in result)
        {
            Console.WriteLine(string.Format("{0}\nAddress: {1}",
                ca.Customer, ca.Address));
        }
    }

    // Create a customer list with sample data
    private static List<Customer> CreateCustomerList()
    {
        // Same as in Example 13-1
    }

    // Create a customer list with sample data
    private static List<Address> CreateAddressList()
    {
        List<Address> addresses = new List<Address>
            {
```

*Example 13-3. A sorted join query (continued)*

```
                  new Address { Name   = "Janet Gates",
                                Street = "165 North Main",
                                City = "Austin" },
                  new Address { Name   = "Keith Harris",
                                Street = "3207 S Grady Way",
                                City = "Renton" },
                  new Address { Name   = "Janet Gates",
                                Street = "800 Interchange Blvd.",
                                City = "Austin" },
                  new Address { Name   = "Keith Harris",
                                Street = "7943 Walnut Ave",
                                City = "Renton" },
                  new Address { Name   = "Orlando Gee",
                                Street = "2251 Elliot Avenue",
                                City = "Seattle" }
            };
        return addresses;
    }
  }
}
```

```
Output:
Janet Gates
Email:   janet1@adventure-works.com
Address: 800 Interchange Blvd., Austin
Janet Gates
Email:   janet1@adventure-works.com
Address: 165 North Main, Austin
Orlando Gee
Email:   orlando0@adventure-works.com
Address: 2251 Elliot Avenue, Seattle
Keith Harris
Email:   keith0@adventure-works.com
Address: 7943 Walnut Ave, Renton
Keith Harris
Email:   keith0@adventure-works.com
Address: 3207 S Grady Way, Renton
```

The Customer class is identical to the one used in Example 13-1. The address is also very simple, with a customer name field containing customer names in the <first name> <last name> form, and the street and city of customer addresses.

The CreateCustomerList() and CreateAddressList() methods are just helper functions to create sample data for this example. This example also uses the new C# object and collection initializers, as explained in Chapter 4.

The query definition, however, looks quite different from the last example:

```
var result =
    from   customer in customers
           join address in addresses on
               string.Format("{0} {1}", customer.FirstName, customer.LastName)
               equals address.Name
```

```
orderby customer.LastName, address.Street descending
select new { Customer = customer, Address = address.Street };
```

The first difference is the declaration of the result. Instead of declaring the result as an explicitly typed IEnumerable<Customer> instance, this example declares the result as an implicitly typed variable using the new var keyword. We will leave this for just a moment, and jump to the query definition itself.

The generator now contains a join clause to signify that the query is to be operated on two data sources: customers and addresses. Because the customer name property in the Address class is a concatenation of customer first and last names, you construct the names in Customer objects to the same format:

```
string.Format("{0} {1}", customer.FirstName, customer.LastName)
```

The dynamically constructed customer full name is then compared with the customer name property in the Address objects using the equals operator:

```
string.Format("{0} {1}", customer.FirstName, customer.LastName)
equals address.Name
```

The orderby clause indicates the order in which the result should be sorted:

```
orderby customer.LastName, address.Street descending
```

In the example, the result will be sorted first by customer last name in ascending order, then by street address in descending order.

The combined customer name, email address, and home address are returned. Here you have a problem—LINQ can return a collection of objects of any type, but it can't return multiple objects of different types in the same query, unless they are encapsulated in one type. For instance, you can select either an instance of the Customer class or an instance of the Address class, but you cannot select both, like this:

```
select customer, address
```

The solution is to define a new type containing both objects. An obvious way is to define a CustomerAddress class:

```
public class CustomerAddress
{
    public Customer Customer { get; set; }
    public Address Address   { get; set; }
}
```

You can then return customers and their addresses from the query in a collection of CustomerAddress objects:

```
var result =
    from    customer in customers
            join address in addresses on
                string.Format("{0} {1}", customer.FirstName, customer.LastName)
                equals address.Name
    orderby customer.LastName, address.Street descending
    Select new CustomerAddress { Customer = customer, Address = address };
```

# Grouping and the group Keyword

Another powerful feature of LINQ, commonly used by SQL programmers but now integrated into the language itself, is grouping, as shown in Example 13-4.

*Example 13-4. A group query*

```
using System;
using System.Collections.Generic;
using System.Linq;

namespace Programming_CSharp
{
    // Customer address class
    public class Address
    {
        // Same as in Example 13-3
    }

    // Main program
    public class Tester
    {
        static void Main( )
        {
            List<Address>  addresses = CreateAddressList( );

            // Find addresses grouped by customer name
            var result =
                from address in addresses
                group address by address.Name;
            foreach (var group in result)
            {
                Console.WriteLine("{0}", group.Key);
                foreach (var a in group)
                    Console.WriteLine("\t{0}", a);
            }
                }

        // Create a customer list with sample data
        private static List<Address> CreateAddressList( )
        {
        // Same as in Example 13-3
        }
    }
}

Output:
Janet Gates
        165 North Main, Austin
        800 Interchange Blvd., Austin
Keith Harris
        3207 S Grady Way, Renton
        7943 Walnut Ave, Renton
Orlando Gee
        2251 Elliot Avenue, Seattle
```

Example 13-4 makes use of the group keyword, a query operator that splits a sequence into a group given a key value—in this case, customer name (address.Name). The result is a collection of groups, and you'll need to enumerate each group to get the objects belonging to it.

## Anonymous Types

Often, you do not want to create a new class just for storing the result of a query. C# 3.0 provides *anonymous types* that allow us to declare both an *anonymous class* and an instance of that class using *object initializers*. For instance, we can initialize an anonymous customer address object:

```
new { Customer = customer, Address = address }
```

This declares an anonymous class with two properties, Customer and Address, and initializes it with an instance of the Customer class and an instance of the Address class. The C# compiler can infer the property types with the types of assigned values, so here, the Customer property type is the Customer class, and the Address property type is the Address class. As a normal, named class, anonymous classes can have properties of any type.

Behind the scenes, the C# compiler generates a unique name for the new type. This name cannot be referenced in application code; therefore, it is considered nameless.

## Implicitly Typed Local Variables

Now, let's go back to the declaration of query results where you declare the result as type var:

```
var result = ...
```

Because the select clause returns an instance of an anonymous type, you cannot define an explicit type IEnumerable<T>. Fortunately, C# 3.0 provides another feature—*implicitly typed local variables*—that solves this problem.

You can declare an implicitly typed local variable by specifying its type as var:

```
var id = 1;
var name = "Keith";
var customers = new List<Customer>();
var person = new {FirstName = "Donna", LastName = "Gates", Phone="123-456-7890" };
```

The C# compiler infers the type of an implicitly typed local variable from its initialized value. Therefore, you must initialize such a variable when you declare it. In the preceding code snippet, the type of id will be set as an integer, the type of name as a string, and the type of customers as a strongly typed List<T> of Customer objects. The type of the last variable, person, is an anonymous type containing three properties: FirstName, LastName, and Phone. Although this type has no name in our code, the C#

compiler secretly assigns it one and keeps track of its instances. In fact, the Visual Studio IDE IntelliSense is also aware of anonymous types, as shown in Figure 13-1.

*Figure 13-1. Visual Studio IntelliSense recognizes anonymous types*

Back in Example 13-3, result is an instance of the constructed IEnumerable<T> that contains query results, where the type of the argument T is the anonymous type that contains two properties: Customer and Address.

Now that the query is defined, the next statement executes it using the foreach loop:

```
foreach (var ca in result)
{
    Console.WriteLine(string.Format("{0}\nAddress: {1}",
        ca.Customer, ca.Address));
}
```

As the result is an implicitly typed IEnumerable<T> of the anonymous class {Customer, Address}, the iteration variable is also implicitly typed to the same class. For each object in the result list, this example simply prints its properties.

# Extension Methods

If you already know a little SQL, the query expressions introduced in previous sections are quite intuitive and easy to understand because LINQ is similar to SQL. As C# code is ultimately executed by the .NET CLR, the C# compiler has to translate query expressions to the format understandable by .NET. Because the .NET runtime understands method calls that can be executed, the LINQ query expressions written in C# are translated into a series of method calls. Such methods are called *extension methods*, and they are defined in a slightly different way than normal methods.

Example 13-5 is identical to Example 13-1 except it uses query operator *extension methods* instead of query expressions. The parts of the code that have not changed are omitted for brevity.

*Example 13-5. Using query operator extension methods*

```
using System;
using System.Collections.Generic;
using System.Linq;
namespace Programming_CSharp
```

*Example 13-5. Using query operator extension methods (continued)*

```
{
    // Simple customer class
    public class Customer
    {
        // Same as in Example 13-1
    }

    // Main program
    public class Tester
    {
        static void Main( )
        {
            List<Customer> customers = CreateCustomerList( );

            // Find customer by first name
            IEnumerable<Customer> result =
                customers.Where(customer => customer.FirstName == "Donna");
            Console.WriteLine("FirstName == \"Donna\"");
            foreach (Customer customer in result)
                Console.WriteLine(customer.ToString( ));
        }

        // Create a customer list with sample data
        private static List<Customer> CreateCustomerList( )
        {
            // Same as in Example 13-1
        }
    }
}
```

```
Output:
(Same as in Example 13-1)
```

Example 13-5 searches for customers whose first name is "Donna" using a query expression with a where clause. Here's the original code from Example 13-1:

```
IEnumerable<Customer> result =
    from    customer in customers
    where   customer.FirstName == "Donna"
    select customer;
```

Here is the extension Where( ) method:

```
IEnumerable<Customer> result =
    customers.Where(customer => customer.FirstName == "Donna");
```

You may have noticed that the select clause seems to have vanished in this example. For details on this, please see the sidebar, "Whither the select Clause?" (And try to remember, as Chico Marx reminded us, "There ain't no such thing as a Sanity Clause.")

## Whither the select Clause?

The select is omitted because we use the resulting customer object without projecting it into a different form. Therefore, the Where( ) method from Example 13-4 is the same as this:

```
IEnumerable<Customer> result =
    customers.Where(customer => customer.FirstName ==
        "Donna").Select(customer => customer);
```

If a projection of results is required, you will need to use the Select method. For instance, if you want to retrieve Donna's email address instead of the whole customer object, you can use the following statement:

```
IEnumerable<string> result =
    customers.Where(customer => customer.FirstName ==
                "Donna")
            .Select(customer => customer.EmailAddress);
```

Recall that Customers is of type List<Customer>, which might lead you to think that List<T> must have implemented the Where method to support LINQ. It does not. The Where method is called an *extension method* because it extends an existing type. Before we go into more details in this example, let's take a closer look at extension methods.

## Defining and Using Extension Methods

C# 3.0 introduces extension methods that provide the ability for programmers to add methods to existing types. For instance, System.String does not provide a Right( ) function that returns the rightmost *n* characters of a string. If you use this functionality a lot in your application, you may have considered building and adding it to your library. However, System.String is defined as sealed, so you can't subclass it. It is not a partial class, so you can't extend it using that feature.

Of course, you can't modify the .NET core library directly either. Therefore, you would have to define your own helper method outside of System.String and call it with syntax such as this:

```
MyHelperClass.GetRight(aString, n)
```

This is not exactly intuitive. With C# 3.0, however, there is a more elegant solution. You can actually add a method to the System.String class; in other words, you can extend the System.String class without having to modify the class itself. Such a method is called an extension method. Example 13-6 demonstrates how to define and use an extension method.

*Example 13-6. Defining and using extension methods*

```
using System;

namespace Programming_CSharp_Extensions
{
    // Container class for extension methods.
    public static class ExtensionMethods
    {
        // Returns a substring containing the rightmost
        // n characters in a specific string.
        public static string Right(this string s, int n)
        {
            if (n < 0 || n > s.Length)
                return s;
            else
                return s.Substring(s.Length - n);
        }
    }

    public class Tester
    {
        public static void Main( )
        {
            string hello = "Hello";
            Console.WriteLine("hello.Right(-1) = {0}", hello.Right(-1));
            Console.WriteLine("hello.Right(0) = {0}", hello.Right(0));
            Console.WriteLine("hello.Right(3) = {0}", hello.Right(3));
            Console.WriteLine("hello.Right(5) = {0}", hello.Right(5));
            Console.WriteLine("hello.Right(6) = {0}", hello.Right(6));
        }
    }
}

Output:
hello.Right(-1) = Hello
hello.Right(0) =
hello.Right(3) = llo
hello.Right(5) = Hello
hello.Right(6) = Hello
```

The first parameter of an extension method is always the target type, which is the string class in this example. Therefore, this example effectively defines a Right( ) function for the string class. You want to be able to call this method on any string, just like calling a normal System.String member method:

```
aString.Right(n)
```

In C#, an extension method must be defined as a static method in a static class. Therefore, this example defines a static class, ExtensionMethods, and a static method in this class:

```
public static string Right(this string s, int n)
{
    if (n < 0 || n > s.Length)
```

```
            return s;
        else
            return s.Substring(s.Length - n);
    }
```

Compared to a regular method, the only notable difference is that the first parameter of an extension method always consists of the this keyword, followed by the target type, and finally an instance of the target type:

```
this string s
```

The subsequent parameters are just normal parameters of the extension method. The method body has no special treatment compared to regular methods either. Here, this function simply returns the desired substring or, if the length argument n is invalid, the original string.

To use an extension method, it must be in the same scope as the client code. If the extension method is defined in another namespace, you should add a "using" directive to import the namespace where the extension method is defined. You can't use fully qualified extension method names as you do with a normal method. The use of extension methods is otherwise identical to any built-in methods of the target type. In this example, you simply call it like a regular System.String method:

```
hello.Right(3)
```

## Extension Method Restrictions

It is worth mentioning, however, that extension methods are somewhat more restrictive than regular member methods—extension methods can only access public members of target types. This prevents the breach of encapsulation of the target types.

Another restriction is that if an extension method conflicts with a member method in the target class, the member method is always used instead of the extension method, as you can see in Example 13-7.

*Example 13-7. Conflicting extension methods*

```
using System;

namespace Programming_CSharp_Extensions
{
    // Container class for extension methods.
    public static class ExtensionMethods
    {
        // Returns a substring between the specific
        // start and end index of a string.
        public static string Substring(this string s, int startIndex, int endIndex)
        {
            if (startIndex >= 0 && startIndex <= endIndex && endIndex < s.Length)
                return s.Substring(startIndex, endIndex - startIndex);
```

*Example 13-7. Conflicting extension methods (continued)*

```
            else
                return s;
        }
    }

    public class Tester
    {
        public static void Main()
        {
            string hello = "Hello";
            Console.WriteLine("hello.Substring(2, 3) = {0}",
                            hello.Substring(2, 3));
        }
    }
}
```

```
Output:
hello.Substring(2, 3) = llo
```

The Substring( ) extension method in this example has exactly the same signature as the built-in String.Substring(int startIndex, int length) method. As you can see from the output, it is the built-in Substring( ) method that is executed in this example. Now, we'll go back to Example 13-4, where we used the LINQ extension method, Where, to search a customer list:

```
    IEnumerable<Customer> result =
        customers.Where(customer => customer.FirstName == "Donna");
```

This method takes a predicate as an input argument.

 In C# and LINQ, a *predicate* is a delegate that examines certain conditions and returns a Boolean value indicating whether the conditions are met.

The predicate performs a filtering operation on queries. The argument to this method is quite different from a normal method argument. In fact, it's a lambda expression, which I introduced in Chapter 12.

# Lambda Expressions in LINQ

In Chapter 12, I mentioned that you can use *lambda expressions* to define inline delegate definitions. In the following expression:

```
    customer => customer.FirstName == "Donna"
```

the left operand, customer, is the input parameter. The right operand is the lambda expression that checks whether the customer's FirstName property is equal to "Donna." Therefore, for a given customer object, you're checking whether its first name is Donna. This lambda expression is then passed into the Where method to perform this comparison operation on each customer in the customer list.

Queries defined using extension methods are called *method-based queries*. Although the query and method syntaxes are different, they are semantically identical, and the compiler translates them into the same IL code. You can use either of them based on your preference.

Let's start with a very simple query, as shown in Example 13-8.

*Example 13-8. A simple method-based query*

```
using System;
using System.Linq;

namespace SimpleLamda
{
  class Program
  {
    static void Main(string[] args)
    {

      string[] names = { "Jesse", "Donald", "Douglas" };
      var dNames = names.Where(n => n.StartsWith("D"));
      foreach (string foundName in dNames)
      {
        Console.WriteLine("Found: " + foundName);
      }

    }
  }
}
Output:
Found: Donald
Found: Douglas
```

The statement names.Where is shorthand for:

```
System.Linq.Enumerable.Where(names,n=>n.StartsWith("D"));
```

Where is an extension method and so you can leave out the object (names) as the first argument, and by including the namespace System.Linq, you can call upon Where directly on the names object rather than through Enumerable.

Further, the *type* of dNames is Ienumerable<string>; we are using the new ability of the compiler to infer this by using the keyword var. This does not undermine type-safety, however, because var is compiled into the type Ienumerable<string> through that inference.

Thus, you can read this line:

```
var dNames = names.Where(n => n.StartsWith("D"));
```

as "fill the IEnumerable collection dNames from the collection names with each member where the member starts with the letter D."

As the method syntax is closer to how the C# compiler processes queries, it is worth spending a little more time to look at how a more complex query is expressed to gain a better understanding of LINQ. Let's translate Example 13-3 into a method-based query to see how it would look (see Example 13-9).

*Example 13-9. Complex query in method syntax*

```
namespace Programming_CSharp
{
    // Simple customer class
    public class Customer
    {
        // Same as in Example 13-1
    }

    // Customer address class
    public class Address
    {
        // Same as in Example 13-3
    }

    // Main program
    public class Tester
    {
        static void Main( )
        {
            List<Customer> customers = CreateCustomerList( );
            List<Address> addresses = CreateAddressList( );

            var result = customers.Join(addresses,
                customer => string.Format("{0} {1}", customer.FirstName,
                            customer.LastName),
                address => address.Name,
                (customer, address) => new { Customer = customer, Address =
                 address })
                .OrderBy(ca => ca.Customer.LastName)
                .ThenByDescending(ca => ca.Address.Street);

            foreach (var ca in result)
            {
                Console.WriteLine(string.Format("{0}\nAddress: {1}",
                    ca.Customer, ca.Address));
            }
        }

        // Create a customer list with sample data
        private static List<Customer> CreateCustomerList( )
        {
            // Same as in Example 13-3
        }
```

*Example 13-9. Complex query in method syntax (continued)*

```
    // Create a customer list with sample data
    private static List<Address> CreateAddressList()
    {
        // Same as in Example 13-3
    }
  }
}
```

```
Output:
Janet Gates
Email:   janet1@adventure-works.com
Address: 800 Interchange Blvd., Austin
Janet Gates
Email:   janet1@adventure-works.com
Address: 165 North Main, Austin
Orlando Gee
Email:   orlando0@adventure-works.com
Address: 2251 Elliot Avenue, Seattle
Keith Harris
Email:   keith0@adventure-works.com
Address: 7943 Walnut Ave, Renton
Keith Harris
Email:   keith0@adventure-works.com
Address: 3207 S Grady Way, Renton
```

In Example 13-3, the query is written in query syntax:

```
var result =
    from   customer in customers
           join address in addresses on
                string.Format("{0} {1}", customer.FirstName, customer.LastName)
                equals address.Name
    orderby customer.LastName, address.Street descending
    select new { Customer = customer, Address = address.Street };
```

It is translated into the method syntax:

```
var result = customers.Join(addresses,
    customer => string.Format("{0} {1}", customer.FirstName,
                    customer.LastName),
    address => address.Name,
    (customer, address) => new { Customer = customer, Address = address })
    .OrderBy(ca => ca.Customer.LastName)
    .ThenByDescending(ca => ca.Address.Street);
```

The lambda expression takes some getting used to. Start with the OrderBy clause; you read that as "Order in this way: for each customerAddress, get the Customer's LastName." You read the entire statement as, "start with customers and join to addresses as follows, for customers concatenate the First.Name and Last.Name, and then for address fetch each Address.Name and join the two, then for the resulting record create a CustomerAddress object where the customer matches the Customer and the address matches the Address; now order these first by each customer's LastName and then by each Address' Street name."

The main data source, the customers collection, is still the main target object. The extension method, Join( ), is applied to it to perform the join operation. Its first argument is the second data source, addresses. The next two arguments are join condition fields in each data source. The final argument is the result of the join condition, which is in fact the select clause in the query.

The OrderBy clauses in the query expression indicate that you want to order by the customers' last name in ascending order, and then by their street address in descending order. In the method syntax, you must specify this preference by using the OrderBy and the ThenBy methods.

You can just call OrderBy methods in sequence, but the methods must be in reverse order. That is, you must invoke the method to order the last field in the query OrderBy list first, and order the first field in the query OrderBy list last. In this example, you will need to invoke the order by street method first, followed by the order by name method:

```
var result = customers.Join(addresses,
        customer => string.Format("{0} {1}", customer.FirstName,
                    customer.LastName),
        address => address.Name,
        (customer, address) => new { Customer = customer, Address = address })
        .OrderByDescending(ca => ca.Address.Street)
        .OrderBy(ca => ca.Customer.LastName);
```

As you can see from the result, the results for both examples are identical. Therefore, you can choose either based on your own preference.

Ian Griffiths, one of the smarter C# programmers on Earth, who blogs at IanG on Tap (*http://www.interact-sw.co.uk/iangblog/*), makes the following point, which I will illustrate in Chapter 15, but which I did not want to leave hanging here: "You can use exactly these same two syntaxes on a variety of different sources, but the behavior *isn't always the same*. The meaning of a lambda expression varies according to the signature of the function it is passed to. In these examples, it's a succinct syntax for a delegate. But if you were to use *exactly the same form of queries* against a SQL data source, the lambda expression is turned into something else."

All the LINQ extension methods—Join, Select, Where, and so on—have multiple implementations, each with different target types. Here, we're looking at the ones that operate over IEnumerable. The ones that operate over IQueryable are subtly different. Rather than taking delegates for the join, projection, where, and other clauses, they take expressions. Those are wonderful and magical things that enable the C# source code to be transformed into an equivalent SQL query.

# CHAPTER 14

# Working with XML

XML, or eXtensible Markup Language, provides an industry-standard method for encoding information so that it is easily understandable by different software applications. It contains data and the description of data, which enables software applications to interpret and process that data.

XML specifications are defined and maintained by the World Wide Web Consortium (W3C). The latest version is XML 1.1 (Second Edition). However, XML 1.0 (currently in its fourth edition) is the most popular version, and is supported by all XML parsers. W3C states that:

> You are encouraged to create or generate XML 1.0 documents if you do not need the new features in XML 1.1; XML Parsers are expected to understand both XML 1.0 and XML 1.1.[*]

This chapter will introduce XML 1.0 only, and in fact, will focus on just the most commonly used XML features. I'll introduce you to the XMLDocument and XMLElement classes first, and you'll learn how to create and manipulate XML documents.

Of course, once you have a large document, you'll want to be able to find substrings, and I'll show you two different ways to do that, using XPath and XPath Navigator. XML also forms a key component of the Service Oriented Architecture (SOA), which allows you to access remote objects across applications and platforms. The .NET Framework allows you to *serialize* your objects as XML, and deserialize them at their destination. I'll cover those methods at the end of the chapter.

## XML Basics (A Quick Review)

XML is a markup language, not unlike HTML, except that it is *extensible*—that is, the user of XML can (and does!) create new elements and properties.

---

[*] *http://www.w3.org/XML/Core/#Publications*

# Elements

In XML, a document is composed of a hierarchy of elements. An *element* is defined by a pair of *tags*, called the start and end tags. In the following example, FirstName is an element:

```
<FirstName>Orlando</FirstName>
```

A start tag is composed of the element name surrounded by a pair of angle brackets:

```
<FirstName>
```

An end tag is similar to the start tag, except that the element name is preceded by a forward slash:

```
</FirstName>
```

The content between the start and end tags is the element text, which may consist of a set of *child elements*. The FirstName element's text is simply a string. On the other hand, the Customer element has three child elements:

```
<Customer>
  <FirstName>Orlando</FirstName>
  <LastName>Gee</LastName>
  <EmailAddress>orlando0@hotmail.com</EmailAddress>
</Customer>
```

The top-level element in an XML document is called its *root element*. Every document has exactly one root element.

An element can have zero or more child elements, and (except for the root element) every element has exactly one *parent element*. Elements with the same parent element are called sibling elements.

In this example, Customers (plural) is the root. The children of the root element, Customers, are the three Customer (singular) elements:

```
<Customers>
  <Customer>
    ...
  </Customer>
  <Customer>
    ...
  </Customer>
  <Customer>
    ...
  </Customer>
</Customers>
```

Each Customer has one parent (Customers) and three children (FirstName, LastName, and EmailAddress). Each of these, in turn, has one parent (Customer) and zero children.

## XHTML

XHTML is an enhanced standard of HTML that follows the stricter rules of XML validity. The two most important (and most often overlooked) rules follow:

- No elements may overlap, though they may nest. Thus:

    ```
    <element 1>
       <element2>
          <...>
       </element 2>
    </element 1>
    ```

    You may *not* write:

    ```
    <element 1>
       <element2>
          <...>
       </element 1>
    </element 2>
    ```

    because in the latter case, `element2` overlaps `element1` rather than being neatly nested within it.

- Every element must be closed, which means that for each opened element, you must have a closing tag (or the element tag must be self-closing). Thus, for those of you who cut your teeth on forgiving browsers, it is time to stop writing:

    ```
    <br>
    ```

    and replace it with:

    ```
    <br />
    ```

# X Stands for eXtensible

The key point of XML is to provide an *extensible* markup language. An incredibly short pop-history lesson: HTML was derived from the Structured Query Markup Language (SQML). HTML has many wonderful attributes (pardon), but if you want to add a new element to HTML, you have two choices: apply to the W3C and wait awhile, or strike out on your own and be "nonstandard."

There was a strong need for the ability for two organizations to get together and specify tags that they could use for data exchange. Hey! Presto! XML was born as a more general-purpose markup language that allows users to *define their own tags*. This last point is the critical distinction of XML.

# Creating XML Documents

Because XML documents are structured text documents, you can create them using a text editor and process them using string manipulation functions. To paraphrase David Platt, you can also have an appendectomy through your mouth, but it takes longer and hurts more.

---

To make the job easier, .NET implements a collection of classes and utilities that provide XML functionality, including the streaming XML APIs (which support XmlReader and XmlWriter), and another set of XML APIs that use the XML Document Object Model (DOM).

In Chapter 13, we used a list of customers in our examples. We will use the same customer list in this chapter, starting with Example 14-1, in which we'll write the list of customers to an XML document.

*Example 14-1. Creating an XML document*

```
using System;
using System.Collections.Generic;
using System.Xml;

namespace Programming_CSharp
{
    // Simple customer class
    public class Customer
    {
        public string FirstName    { get; set; }
        public string LastName     { get; set; }
        public string EmailAddress { get; set; }

        // Overrides the Object.ToString() to provide a
        // string representation of the object properties.
        public override string ToString()
        {
            return string.Format("{0} {1}\nEmail:   {2}",
                        FirstName, LastName, EmailAddress);
        }
    }

    // Main program
    public class Tester
    {
        static void Main()
        {
            List<Customer> customers = CreateCustomerList();

            XmlDocument customerXml = new XmlDocument();
            XmlElement rootElem = customerXml.CreateElement("Customers");
            customerXml.AppendChild(rootElem);
            foreach (Customer customer in customers)
            {
                // Create new element representing the customer object.
                XmlElement customerElem = customerXml.CreateElement("Customer");

                // Add element representing the FirstName property
                // to the customer element.
                XmlElement firstNameElem = customerXml.CreateElement("FirstName");
                firstNameElem.InnerText  = customer.FirstName;
                customerElem.AppendChild(firstNameElem);
```

*Example 14-1. Creating an XML document (continued)*

```
        // Add element representing the LastName property
        // to the customer element.
        XmlElement lastNameElem = customerXml.CreateElement("LastName");
        lastNameElem.InnerText = customer.LastName;
        customerElem.AppendChild(lastNameElem);

        // Add element representing the EmailAddress property
        // to the customer element.
        XmlElement emailAddress =
            customerXml.CreateElement("EmailAddress");
        emailAddress.InnerText = customer.EmailAddress;
        customerElem.AppendChild(emailAddress);

        // Finally add the customer element to the XML document
        rootElem.AppendChild(customerElem);
    }

    Console.WriteLine(customerXml.OuterXml);
    Console.Read( );
}

// Create a customer list with sample data
private static List<Customer> CreateCustomerList( )
{
    List<Customer> customers = new List<Customer>
        {
            new Customer { FirstName = "Orlando",
                           LastName = "Gee",
                           EmailAddress = "orlando0@hotmail.com"},
            new Customer { FirstName = "Keith",
                           LastName = "Harris",
                           EmailAddress = "keith0@hotmail.com" },
            new Customer { FirstName = "Donna",
                           LastName = "Carreras",
                           EmailAddress = "donna0@hotmail.com" },
            new Customer { FirstName = "Janet",
                           LastName = "Gates",
                           EmailAddress = "janet1@hotmail.com" },
            new Customer { FirstName = "Lucy",
                           LastName = "Harrington",
                           EmailAddress = "lucy0@hotmail.com" }
        };
    return customers;
    }
  }
}
```

 I've formatted the output here to make it easier to read; your actual format will be in a continuous string:

---

```
Output:
<Customers>
  <Customer>
    <FirstName>Orlando</FirstName>
    <LastName>Gee</LastName>
    <EmailAddress>orlando0@hotmail.com</EmailAddress>
  </Customer>
  <Customer>
    <FirstName>Keith</FirstName>
    <LastName>Harris</LastName>
    <EmailAddress>keith0@hotmail.com</EmailAddress>
  </Customer>
  <Customer>
    <FirstName>Donna</FirstName>
    <LastName>Carreras</LastName>
    <EmailAddress>donna0@hotmail.com</EmailAddress>
  </Customer>
  <Customer>
    <FirstName>Janet</FirstName>
    <LastName>Gates</LastName>
    <EmailAddress>janet1@hotmail.com</EmailAddress>
  </Customer>
  <Customer>
    <FirstName>Lucy</FirstName>
    <LastName>Harrington</LastName>
    <EmailAddress>lucy0@hotmail.com</EmailAddress>
  </Customer>
</Customers>
```

 We could rewrite this example with less code using LINQ to XML, which I cover in Chapter 15.

In .NET, the System.Xml namespace contains all XML-related classes that provide support to creating and processing XML documents. It is convenient to add a using directive to any code files that use classes from this namespace.

The Customer class and the CreateCustomerList function in the main Tester class are identical to those used in Chapter 13, so I will not go over them again here.

The main attraction in this example is the XML creation in the main function. First, a new XML document object is created:

```
XmlDocument customerXml = new XmlDocument();
```

Next, you create the root element:

```
XmlElement rootElem = customerXml.CreateElement("Customers");
customerXml.AppendChild(rootElem);
```

Creating XML elements and other objects in the XML DOM is slightly different from conventional object instantiation. The idiom is to call the CreateElement method of the XML document object to create a new element in the document, and then call its parent element's `AppendChild` method to attach it to the parent. After these two operations, the `customerXML` document will contain an empty element:

```
<Customers></Customers>
```

or:

```
<Customers />
```

In the XML DOM, the root element is also called the *document element*. You can access it through the `DocumentElement` property of the document object:

```
XmlElement rootElem = customerXml.DocumentElement;
```

## XML Elements

With the root element in hand, you can add each customer as a child node:

```
foreach (Customer customer in customers)
{
    // Create new element representing the customer object.
    XmlElement customerElem = customerXml.CreateElement("Customer");
```

In this example, you make each property of the customer object a child element of the customer element:

```
    // Add element representing the FirstName property to the customer element.
    XmlElement firstNameElem = customerXml.CreateElement("FirstName");
    firstNameElem.InnerText  = customer.FirstName;
    cstomerElem.AppendChild(firstNameElem);
```

This adds the `FirstName` child element and assigns the customer's first name to its `InnerText` property. The result will look like this:

```
<FirstName>Orlando</FirstName>
```

The other two properties, `LastName` and `EmailAddress`, are added to the customer element in exactly the same way. Here's an example of the complete customer element:

```
<Customer>
  <FirstName>Orlando</FirstName>
  <LastName>Gee</LastName>
  <EmailAddress>orlando0@hotmail.com</EmailAddress>
</Customer>
```

Finally, the newly created customer element is added to the XML document as a child of the root element:

```
    // Finally add the customer element to the XML document
    rootElem.AppendChild(customerElem);
}
```

Once all customer elements are created, this example prints the XML document:

```
Console.WriteLine(customerXml.OuterXml);
```

When you run the code, the result is just a long string containing the whole XML document and its elements. You can import it into an XML editor and format it into a more human-readable form, as in the example output shown earlier. Visual Studio includes an XML editor, so you can just paste the string into an XML file, and open it in Visual Studio. You can then use the "Format the whole document" command on the XML Editor toolbar to format the string, as shown in Figure 14-1.

*Figure 14-1. Formatting the XML document in Visual Studio*

## XML Attributes

An XML element may have a set of *attributes*, which store additional information about the element. An attribute is a key/value pair contained in the start tag of an XML element:

```
<Customer FirstName="Orlando" LastName="Gee"></Customer>
```

The next example demonstrates how you can mix the use of child elements and attributes. This example creates customer elements with the customer's name stored in attributes and the email address stored as a child element:

```
<Customer FirstName="Orlando" LastName="Gee">
  <EmailAddress>orlando0@hotmail.com</EmailAddress>
</Customer>
```

The only difference between this and Example 14-1 is that you store the `FirstName` and `LastName` properties as attributes to the customer elements here:

```
// Add an attribute representing the FirstName property
// to the customer element.
XmlAttribute firstNameAttr = customerXml.CreateAttribute("FirstName");
firstNameAttr.Value = customer.FirstName;
customerElem.Attributes.Append(firstNameAttr);
```

Similar to creating an element, you call the document object's `CreateAttribute` method to create an `XmlAttribute` object in the document. Assigning the value to an attribute is a little more intuitive than assigning the element text because an attribute has no child nodes; therefore, you can simply assign a value to its `Value` property. For attributes, the `Value` property is identical to the `InnerText` property.

> You will also need to append the attribute to an element's `Attributes` property, which represents a collection of all attributes of the element. Unlike adding child elements, you cannot call the `AppendChild` function of elements to add attributes.

Example 14-2 shows the sample code and output.

*Example 14-2. Creating an XML document containing elements and attributes*

```
using System;
using System.Collections.Generic;
using System.IO;
using System.Xml;

namespace Programming_CSharp
{
    // Simple customer class
    public class Customer
    {
        // Same as in Example 14-1
    }

    // Main program
    public class Tester
    {
        static void Main( )
        {
            List<Customer> customers = CreateCustomerList( );

            XmlDocument customerXml = new XmlDocument( );
            XmlElement rootElem = customerXml.CreateElement("Customers");
            customerXml.AppendChild(rootElem);
            foreach (Customer customer in customers)
            {
                // Create new element representing the customer object.
                XmlElement customerElem = customerXml.CreateElement("Customer");

                // Add an attribute representing the FirstName property
                // to the customer element.
                XmlAttribute firstNameAttr =
                    customerXml.CreateAttribute("FirstName");
                firstNameAttr.Value = customer.FirstName;
                customerElem.Attributes.Append(firstNameAttr);

                // Add an attribute representing the LastName property
                // to the customer element.
                XmlAttribute lastNameAttr =
                    customerXml.CreateAttribute("LastName");
                lastNameAttr.Value = customer.LastName;
                customerElem.Attributes.Append(lastNameAttr);

                // Add element representing the EmailAddress property
                // to the customer element.
                XmlElement emailAddress =
                    customerXml.CreateElement("EmailAddress");
                emailAddress.InnerText = customer.EmailAddress;
                customerElem.AppendChild(emailAddress);
```

*Example 14-2. Creating an XML document containing elements and attributes (continued)*

```
            // Finally add the customer element to the XML document
            rootElem.AppendChild(customerElem);
        }

        Console.WriteLine(customerXml.OuterXml);
        Console.Read( );
    }

    // Create a customer list with sample data
    private static List<Customer> CreateCustomerList( )
    {
        // Same as in Example 14-1
    }
  }
}
```

```
Output:
<Customers>
  <Customer FirstName="Orlando" LastName="Gee">
    <EmailAddress>orlando0@hotmail.com</EmailAddress>
  </Customer>
  <Customer FirstName="Keith" LastName="Harris">
    <EmailAddress>keith0@hotmail.com</EmailAddress>
  </Customer>
  <Customer FirstName="Donna" LastName="Carreras">
    <EmailAddress>donna0@hotmail.com</EmailAddress>
  </Customer>
  <Customer FirstName="Janet" LastName="Gates">
    <EmailAddress>janet1@hotmail.com</EmailAddress>
  </Customer>
  <Customer FirstName="Lucy" LastName="Harrington">
    <EmailAddress>lucy0@hotmail.com</EmailAddress>
  </Customer>
</Customers>
```

Being able to create XML documents to store data to be processed or exchanged is great, but it would not be of much use if you could not find information in them easily. The System.Xml.XPath namespace contains classes and utilities that provide XPath (search) support to C# programmers.

# Searching in XML with XPath

In its simplest form, XPath may look similar to directory file paths. Here's an example using the XML document containing a customer list. This document is shown in Example 14-2 and is reproduced here for convenience:

```
<Customers>
  <Customer FirstName="Orlando" LastName="Gee">
    <EmailAddress>orlando0@hotmail.com</EmailAddress>
```

```
      </Customer>
      <Customer FirstName="Keith" LastName="Harris">
        <EmailAddress>keith0@hotmail.com</EmailAddress>
      </Customer>
      <Customer FirstName="Donna" LastName="Carreras">
        <EmailAddress>donna0@hotmail.com</EmailAddress>
      </Customer>
      <Customer FirstName="Janet" LastName="Gates">
        <EmailAddress>janet1@hotmail.com</EmailAddress>
      </Customer>
      <Customer FirstName="Lucy" LastName="Harrington">
        <EmailAddress>lucy0@hotmail.com</EmailAddress>
      </Customer>
  </Customers>
```

Example 14-3 lists the code for the example.

*Example 14-3. Searching an XML document using XPath*

```csharp
using System;
using System.Collections.Generic;
using System.Xml;

namespace Programming_CSharp
{
    public class Customer
    {
        public string FirstName { get; set; }
        public string LastName { get; set; }
        public string EmailAddress { get; set; }

        // Overrides the Object.ToString() to provide a
        // string representation of the object properties.
        public override string ToString()
        {
            return string.Format("{0} {1}\nEmail:   {2}",
                    FirstName, LastName, EmailAddress);
        }
    }

    public class Tester
    {
        private static XmlDocument CreateCustomerListXml()
        {
            List<Customer> customers = CreateCustomerList();
            XmlDocument customerXml = new XmlDocument();
            XmlElement rootElem = customerXml.CreateElement("Customers");
            customerXml.AppendChild(rootElem);
            foreach (Customer customer in customers)
            {
                XmlElement customerElem = customerXml.CreateElement("Customer");

                XmlAttribute firstNameAttr =
                    customerXml.CreateAttribute("FirstName");
```

*Example 14-3. Searching an XML document using XPath (continued)*

```
            firstNameAttr.Value = customer.FirstName;
            customerElem.Attributes.Append(firstNameAttr);

            XmlAttribute lastNameAttr =
                customerXml.CreateAttribute("LastName");
            lastNameAttr.Value = customer.LastName;
            customerElem.Attributes.Append(lastNameAttr);

            XmlElement emailAddress =
                customerXml.CreateElement("EmailAddress");
            emailAddress.InnerText = customer.EmailAddress;
            customerElem.AppendChild(emailAddress);

            rootElem.AppendChild(customerElem);
        }

        return customerXml;
    }

    private static List<Customer> CreateCustomerList()
    {
        List<Customer> customers = new List<Customer>
            {
                new Customer {FirstName = "Douglas",
                              LastName = "Adams",
                              EmailAddress = "dAdams@foo.com"},
                new Customer {FirstName = "Richard",
                              LastName = "Dawkins",
                              EmailAddress = "rDawkins@foo.com"},
                new Customer {FirstName = "Kenji",
                              LastName = "Yoshino",
                              EmailAddress = "kYoshino@foo.com"},
                new Customer {FirstName = "Ian",
                              LastName = "McEwan",
                              EmailAddress = "iMcEwan@foo.com"},
                new Customer {FirstName = "Neal",
                              LastName = "Stephenson",
                              EmailAddress = "nStephenson@foo.com"},
                new Customer {FirstName = "Randy",
                              LastName = "Shilts",
                              EmailAddress = "rShilts@foo.com"},
                new Customer {FirstName = "Michelangelo",
                              LastName = "Signorile ",
                              EmailAddress = "mSignorile@foo.com"},
                new Customer {FirstName = "Larry",
                              LastName = "Kramer",
                              EmailAddress = "lKramer@foo.com"},
                new Customer {FirstName = "Jennifer",
                              LastName = "Baumgardner",
                              EmailAddress = "jBaumgardner@foo.com"}
            };
        return customers;
```

*Example 14-3. Searching an XML document using XPath (continued)*

```
    }

    static void Main()
    {
        XmlDocument customerXml = CreateCustomerListXml();

        Console.WriteLine("Search for single node...");
        string xPath = "/Customers/Customer[@FirstName='Douglas']";
        XmlNode oneCustomer = customerXml.SelectSingleNode(xPath);

        Console.WriteLine("\nSelectSingleNode(\"{0}\")...", xPath);
        if (oneCustomer != null)
        {
            Console.WriteLine(oneCustomer.OuterXml);
        }
        else
        {
            Console.WriteLine("Not found");
        }

        Console.WriteLine("\nSearch for a single element... ");
        xPath = "/Customers/Customer[@FirstName='Douglas']";
        XmlElement customerElem = customerXml.SelectSingleNode(xPath)
                                 as XmlElement;

        Console.WriteLine("\nSelectSingleNode(\"{0}\")...", xPath);
        if (customerElem != null)
        {
            Console.WriteLine(customerElem.OuterXml);
            Console.WriteLine("customerElem.HasAttributes = {0}",
                        customerElem.HasAttributes);
        }
        else
        {
            Console.WriteLine("Not found");
        }


        Console.WriteLine("\nSearch using descendant axis... ");
        xPath = "descendant::Customer[@FirstName='Douglas']";
        oneCustomer = customerXml.SelectSingleNode(xPath);
        Console.WriteLine("\nSelectSingleNode(\"{0}\")...", xPath);
        if (oneCustomer != null)
        {
            Console.WriteLine(oneCustomer.OuterXml);
        }
        else
        {
            Console.WriteLine("Not found");
        }

        xPath = "descendant::Customer[attribute::FirstName='Douglas']";
        oneCustomer = customerXml.SelectSingleNode(xPath);
```

*Example 14-3. Searching an XML document using XPath (continued)*

```
            Console.WriteLine("\nSelectSingleNode(\"{0}\")...", xPath);
            if (oneCustomer != null)
            {
                Console.WriteLine(oneCustomer.OuterXml);
            }
            else
            {
                Console.WriteLine("Not found");
            }

            Console.WriteLine("\nSearch using node values... ");
            xPath = "descendant::EmailAddress[text( )='dAdams@foo.com']";
            XmlNode oneEmail = customerXml.SelectSingleNode(xPath);
            Console.WriteLine("\nSelectSingleNode(\"{0}\")...", xPath);
            if (oneEmail != null)
            {
                Console.WriteLine(oneEmail.OuterXml);
            }
            else
            {
                Console.WriteLine("Not found");
            }

        xPath = "descendant::Customer[EmailAddress ='dAdams@foo.com']";
        oneCustomer = customerXml.SelectSingleNode(xPath);
        Console.WriteLine("\nSelectSingleNode(\"{0}\")...", xPath);
        if (oneCustomer != null)
        {
            Console.WriteLine(oneCustomer.OuterXml);
        }
        else
        {
            Console.WriteLine("Not found");
        }
            Console.WriteLine("\nSearch using XPath Functions... ");
            xPath = "descendant::Customer[contains(EmailAddress, 'foo.com')]";
            XmlNodeList customers = customerXml.SelectNodes(xPath);
            Console.WriteLine("\nSelectNodes(\"{0}\")...", xPath);
            if (customers != null)
            {
                foreach (XmlNode customer in customers)
                    Console.WriteLine(customer.OuterXml);
            }
            else
            {
                Console.WriteLine("Not found");
            }

        xPath = "descendant::Customer[starts-with(@LastName, 'A') " +
                "and contains(EmailAddress, 'foo.com')]";
        customers = customerXml.SelectNodes(xPath);
        Console.WriteLine("\nSelectNodes(\"{0}\")...", xPath);
        if (customers != null)
```

*Example 14-3. Searching an XML document using XPath (continued)*

```
            {
                foreach (XmlNode customer in customers)
                    Console.WriteLine(customer.OuterXml);
            }
            else
            {
                Console.WriteLine("Not found");
            }   // end else
        }       // end main
    }           // end class
}               // end namespace
```

```
Output:
Search for single node...

SelectSingleNode("/Customers/Customer[@FirstName='Douglas']")...
<Customer FirstName="Douglas" LastName="Adams">
<EmailAddress>dAdams@foo.com</EmailAddress></Customer>

Search for a single element...

SelectSingleNode("/Customers/Customer[@FirstName='Douglas']")...
<Customer FirstName="Douglas" LastName="Adams">
<EmailAddress>dAdams@foo.com</EmailAddress></Customer>
customerElem.HasAttributes = True

Search using descendant axis...

SelectSingleNode("descendant::Customer[@FirstName='Douglas']")...
<Customer FirstName="Douglas" LastName="Adams">
<EmailAddress>dAdams@foo.com</EmailAddress></Customer>

SelectSingleNode("descendant::Customer[attribute::FirstName='Douglas']")...
<Customer FirstName="Douglas" LastName="Adams">
<EmailAddress>dAdams@foo.com</EmailAddress></Customer>

Search using node values...

SelectSingleNode("descendant::EmailAddress[text( )='dAdams@foo.com']")...
<EmailAddress>dAdams@foo.com</EmailAddress>

SelectSingleNode("descendant::EmailAddress[text( )='dAdams@foo.com']")...
<EmailAddress>dAdams@foo.com</EmailAddress>

Search using XPath Functions...

SelectNodes("descendant::Customer[contains(EmailAddress, 'foo.com')]")...
<Customer FirstName="Douglas" LastName="Adams">
<EmailAddress>dAdams@foo.com</EmailAddress></Customer>

<Customer FirstName="Richard" LastName="Dawkins">
<EmailAddress>rDawkins@foo.com</EmailAddress></Customer>
```

*Example 14-3. Searching an XML document using XPath (continued)*

```
<Customer FirstName="Kenji" LastName="Yoshino">
<EmailAddress>kYoshino@foo.com</EmailAddress></Customer>

<Customer FirstName="Ian" LastName="McEwan">
<EmailAddress>iMcEwan@foo.com</EmailAddress></Customer>

<Customer FirstName="Neal" LastName="Stephenson">
<EmailAddress>nStephenson@foo.com</EmailAddress></Customer>

<Customer FirstName="Randy" LastName="Shilts">
<EmailAddress>rShilts@foo.com</EmailAddress></Customer>

<Customer FirstName="Michelangelo" LastName="Signorile ">
<EmailAddress>mSignorile@foo.com</EmailAddress></Customer>

<Customer FirstName="Larry" LastName="Kramer">
<EmailAddress>lKramer@foo.com</EmailAddress></Customer>

<Customer FirstName="Jennifer" LastName="Baumgardner">
<EmailAddress>jBaumgardner@foo.com</EmailAddress></Customer>

<Customer FirstName="Jennifer" LastName="Baumgardner">
<EmailAddress>jBaumgardner@foo.com</EmailAddress></Customer>

SelectNodes("descendant::Customer[starts-with(@LastName, 'A')
and contains(EmailAddress, 'foo.com')]")...
<Customer FirstName="Douglas" LastName="Adams">
<EmailAddress>dAdams@foo.com</EmailAddress></Customer>
```

This example refactors Example 14-2 by extracting the creation of the sample customer list XML document into the CreateCustomerListXml( ) method. You can now simply call this function in the main( ) function to create the XML document.

There are a couple of things to notice about this code. The first is that although most of the code in this book has what I would consider excessive commenting, I took the liberty™ of stripping this one listing down to the level of commenting that I use in my own code: that is, "next to none." I believe in commenting only when the code can't speak for itself, and when it can't I take that as a failure, typically a failure of variable or method naming, often a failure of structure. That's not to say I never comment; just that I do so a lot less than other folks (except when I'm writing books!).

The second thing to note is that I've placed a lot more output statements whose entire purpose is to help you understand what you are seeing in the output; this is the kind of commenting that I think actually is helpful, and was the only kind of debugging available before the days of IDEs and breakpoints. It is good to get back to our roots.

Finally, note that for this example, I changed the names in the listing to some of my favorite writers. I did this as a tribute to them, and I hope that you will note their names and run out and buy everything they've written.

# Searching for a Single Node

The first search is to find a customer whose first name is "Douglas":

```
string xPath = "/Customers/Customer[@FirstName='Douglas']";
XmlNode oneCustomer = customerXml.SelectSingleNode(xPath);
Console.WriteLine("\nSelectSingleNode(\"{0}\")...", xPath);
if (oneCustomer != null)
{
    Console.WriteLine(oneCustomer.OuterXml);
}
else
{
    Console.WriteLine("Not found");
}
```

In general, you will have some ideas about the structure of XML documents you are going to process; otherwise, it will be difficult to find the information you want. Here we know the node we are looking for sits just one level below the root element. This makes it quite easy to construct the XPath using the absolute path:

```
/Customers/Customer[@FirstName='Douglas']
```

The beginning forward slash / indicates that the search should start from the top of the document. You then specify the top-level element, which is always the root element if you start from the top of the document, as in this case. Next, the target element, Customer, is specified. If the target element is a few more levels down, you can just specify the full path including all those levels, much like you do with filesystems.

Once the target element is reached, you specify the search conditions, or *predicates*, which are always enclosed in a pair of square brackets. In this case, you want to search for the value of the FirstName attribute, which is represented in XPath as @FirstName, where the @ prefix denotes that it is an attribute instead of an element. The value is then given to complete the condition expression.

There are many ways to execute an XPath in .NET. Here, you start with the SelectSingleNode method from the XmlDocument class. I cover other execution methods later in this example and in the next example:

```
XmlNode oneCustomer = customerXml.SelectSingleNode(xPath);
```

The SelectSingleNode method searches for nodes starting from the context node, which is the node from which the call is initiated. In this case, the context node is the XmlDocument itself, customerXml. If this method finds a node that satisfies the search condition, it returns an instance of XmlNode. In the XML DOM, XmlNode is the base class representing any nodes in XML document hierarchy. Specialized node classes such as XmlElement and XmlAttribute are all derived from this class. Even the XmlDocument itself is derived from XmlNode, because it just happens to be the top node.

If the method fails to find any node, it returns a null object. Therefore, you should always test the result against null before attempt to use it:

```
if (oneCustomer != null)
    Console.WriteLine(oneCustomer.OuterXml);
else
    Console.WriteLine("Not found");
```

In this example, the method is successful, and the resulting element is displayed. Because XmlNode is a base class, you can access common properties such as Name, Value, InnerXml, OuterXml, and ParentNode, and methods such as AppendChild. If you need to access more specialized properties such as XmlAttribute.Specified, or methods such as XmlElement.RemoveAttribute, you should cast the result to the appropriate specialized type. In such cases, you can combine the testing and casting of search results to save yourself a little bit of typing using the C# as operator:

```
xPath = "/Customers/Customer[@FirstName='Douglas']";
XmlElement customerElem =
    customerXml.SelectSingleNode(xPath) as XmlElement;
Console.WriteLine("\nSelectSingleNode(\"{0}\")...", xPath);
if (customerElem != null)
{
    Console.WriteLine(customerElem.OuterXml);
    Console.WriteLine("customerElem.HasAttributes = {0}",
        customerElem.HasAttributes);
}
else
    Console.WriteLine("Not found");
```

Because the result here is cased into an instance of XmlElement, you can check its HasAttributes property which is not available through XmlNode.

## Searching Using Axes

In practice, you don't always know the absolute path at design time. In such cases, you will need to use one of the XPath *axes* (pronounced as the plural of *axis*), which specify the relationship between the context node and the search target nodes.

Because you call the SelectSingleNode method through the XML document, the target nodes are the children of the document. You should therefore use the descendant axis, which specifies the immediate children and their children, and their children's children, and so on:

```
xPath = "descendant::Customer[@FirstName='Douglas']";
oneCustomer = customerXml.SelectSingleNode(xPath);
Console.WriteLine("\nSelectSingleNode(\"{0}\")...", xPath);
if (oneCustomer != null)
    Console.WriteLine(oneCustomer.OuterXml);
else
    Console.WriteLine("Not found");
```

The descendant axis in this XPath expression means that the `SelectSingleNode` method will search for nodes anywhere, not just those on a specific level, in the document. The result is the same in this case. You can also use a shorthand notation, `//`, for the descendant axis. For instance, in the preceding example, you can also use:

```
xPath = "//Customer[@FirstName='Douglas']";
```

In addition to the descendant axis explained earlier, other types of axes are defined in XPath. You can find more details in the XPath references at *http://www.w3.org/TR/xpath#axes*.

## Predicates

The condition expression in XPath expressions is called a *predicate*. When an XPath search is performed, the predicate is evaluated against each node. In this example, each node is evaluated according to the specific predicate defined in the XPath. Here, the @ prefix is used to indicate that the evaluation will be against an attribute. This is actually an abbreviated form of the `attribute` *axis*. For instance, the following XPath expression is semantically identical to the predicate mentioned earlier, and produces the same search result:

```
xPath = "descendant::Customer[attribute::FirstName='Douglas']";
oneCustomer = customerXml.SelectSingleNode(xPath);
Console.WriteLine("\nSelectSingleNode(\"{0}\")...", xPath);
if (oneCustomer != null)
    Console.WriteLine(oneCustomer.OuterXml);
else
    Console.WriteLine("Not found");
```

If no axis is specified, XPath defaults to the element. Therefore, the following code snippet finds the customer who has a specific email address:

```
xPath = "descendant::Customer[EmailAddress ='dAdams@foo.com']";
oneCustomer = customerXml.SelectSingleNode(xPath);
Console.WriteLine("\nSelectSingleNode(\"{0}\")...", xPath);
if (oneCustomer != null)
{
    Console.WriteLine(oneCustomer.OuterXml);
}
else
{
    Console.WriteLine("Not found");
}
```

What if you want to find a node with specific text—for instance, instead of finding the customer element containing a given email address, we want to find the email address element itself? Unfortunately, because XPath and the XML DOM are separate standards, they don't always provide the same features in the same manner. For instance, `InnerText` or `InnerXml` defined in the XML DOM cannot be used in XPath predicates. Instead, the text of an element is returned with the XPath `text()` function:

```
xPath = "descendant::EmailAddress[text( )='dAdams@foo.com']";
XmlNode oneEmail = customerXml.SelectSingleNode(xPath);
Console.WriteLine("\nSelectSingleNode(\"{0}\")...", xPath);
if (oneEmail != null)
    Console.WriteLine(oneEmail.OuterXml);
else
    Console.WriteLine("Not found");
```

XPath provides a comprehensive list of functions, including string, numeric, and Boolean functions, which you can use to build your queries. So, be sure to read the documentation to understand what they can do for you.

So far, all the queries return a single node, but often, the search result contains a collection of nodes. Therefore, instead of using the SelectSingleNode method, you could use the SelectNodes method:

```
xPath = "descendant::Customer[contains(EmailAddress, 'foo.com')]";
XmlNodeList customers = customerXml.SelectNodes(xPath);
Console.WriteLine("\nSelectNodes(\"{0}\")...", xPath);
if (customers != null)
{
    foreach (XmlNode customer in customers)
        Console.WriteLine(customer.OuterXml);
}
else
    Console.WriteLine("Not found");
```

This query finds all customers whose email address is from the same domain. As you would expect, this method returns a collection of XmlNode objects, which is contained in an instance of the XmlNodeList collection. You can iterate the result collection to see all nodes returned.

## XPath Functions

The next code block shows a more complex predicate to find customers whose last name starts with *A* and whose email is from the same domain:

```
xPath = "descendant::Customer[starts-with(@LastName, 'A') " +
        "and contains(EmailAddress, 'foo.com')]";
customers = customerXml.SelectNodes(xPath);
Console.WriteLine("\nSelectNodes(\"{0}\")...", xPath);
if (customers != null)
{
    foreach (XmlNode customer in customers)
        Console.WriteLine(customer.OuterXml);
}
else
    Console.WriteLine("Not found");
```

The predicate here is composed of evaluation against attributes and child elements. The first part checks whether the LastName attribute value starts with the letter *A* using the XPath starts-with(string1, string2) function, which checks whether string1 starts with string2. The two parts of the predicate are joined using the XPath and operator.

Many functions are defined in XPath; you can obtain a complete list of XPath functions from *http://www.w3.org/TR/xpath#corelib*.

# Searching Using XPathNavigator

Another way to query XML documents using XPath is to use the .NET XPathNavigator class, which is defined in the System.Xml.XPath namespace. This namespace contains a set of classes that provide optimized operations for searching and iterating XML data using XPath.

To demonstrate the use of these functions, we will use the same set of customer data as in the previous examples, as shown in Example 14-4.

*Example 14-4. Searching an XML document using XPathNavigator*

```
using System;
using System.Collections.Generic;
using System.IO;
using System.Xml;
using System.Xml.XPath;

namespace Programming_CSharp
{
    public class Customer
    {
        public string FirstName { get; set; }
        public string LastName { get; set; }
        public string EmailAddress { get; set; }

        // Overrides the Object.ToString() to provide a
        // string representation of the object properties.
        public override string ToString()
        {
            return string.Format("{0} {1}\nEmail:   {2}",
                        FirstName, LastName, EmailAddress);
        }
    }
    // Main program
    public class Tester
    {
        static void Main()
        {
            XmlDocument customerXml = CreateCustomerXml();
            XPathNavigator nav = customerXml.CreateNavigator();

            string xPath = "descendant::Customer[@FirstName='Douglas']";
            XPathNavigator navNode = nav.SelectSingleNode(xPath);
            Console.WriteLine("\nSelectSingleNode(\"{0}\")...", xPath);
            if (navNode != null)
            {
                Console.WriteLine(navNode.OuterXml);
```

*Example 14-4. Searching an XML document using XPathNavigator (continued)*

```
                XmlElement elem = navNode.UnderlyingObject as XmlElement;
                if (elem != null)
                    Console.WriteLine(elem.OuterXml);
                else
                    Console.WriteLine("Found the wrong node!");
            }
            else
                Console.WriteLine("Customer not found");

            xPath = "descendant::Customer[starts-with(@LastName, 'A') " +
                    "and contains(EmailAddress, 'foo.com')]";
            Console.WriteLine("\nSelect(\"{0}\")...", xPath);
            XPathNodeIterator iter = nav.Select(xPath);
            if (iter.Count > 0)
            {
                while (iter.MoveNext())
                    Console.WriteLine(iter.Current.OuterXml);
            }
            else
                Console.WriteLine("Customer not found");

            Console.WriteLine("\nNow sort by FirstName...");
            XPathExpression expr = nav.Compile(xPath);
            expr.AddSort("@FirstName", Comparer<String>.Default);
            iter = nav.Select(expr);
            while (iter.MoveNext())
                Console.WriteLine(iter.Current.OuterXml);

            XPathExpression expr2 = nav.Compile(xPath);
            Console.WriteLine("\nAnd again...");
            expr2.AddSort("@FirstName", XmlSortOrder.Ascending,
                XmlCaseOrder.None, string.Empty, XmlDataType.Text);
            iter = nav.Select(expr2);
            while (iter.MoveNext())
                Console.WriteLine(iter.Current.OuterXml);
        }

        // Create an XML document containing a customer list.
        private static XmlDocument CreateCustomerXml()
        {

            List<Customer> customers = CreateCustomerList();
            XmlDocument customerXml = new XmlDocument();
            XmlElement rootElem = customerXml.CreateElement("Customers");
            customerXml.AppendChild(rootElem);
            foreach (Customer customer in customers)
            {
                XmlElement customerElem = customerXml.CreateElement("Customer");

                XmlAttribute firstNameAttr =
                    customerXml.CreateAttribute("FirstName");
                firstNameAttr.Value = customer.FirstName;
                customerElem.Attributes.Append(firstNameAttr);
```

*Example 14-4. Searching an XML document using XPathNavigator (continued)*

```
            XmlAttribute lastNameAttr =
                customerXml.CreateAttribute("LastName");
            lastNameAttr.Value = customer.LastName;
            customerElem.Attributes.Append(lastNameAttr);

            XmlElement emailAddress =
                customerXml.CreateElement("EmailAddress");
            emailAddress.InnerText = customer.EmailAddress;
            customerElem.AppendChild(emailAddress);

            rootElem.AppendChild(customerElem);
        }

        return customerXml;
    }
    private static List<Customer> CreateCustomerList( )
    {
        List<Customer> customers = new List<Customer>
            {
                new Customer { FirstName = "Douglas",
                               LastName = "Adams",
                               EmailAddress = "dAdams@foo.com"},
                new Customer { FirstName = "Richard",
                               LastName = "Adawkins",
                               EmailAddress = "rDawkins@foo.com" },
                new Customer { FirstName = "Kenji",
                               LastName = "Ayoshino",
                               EmailAddress = "kYoshino@foo.com" },
                new Customer { FirstName = "Ian",
                               LastName = "AmcEwan",
                               EmailAddress = "iMcEwan@foo.com" },
                new Customer { FirstName = "Neal",
                               LastName = "Astephenson",
                               EmailAddress = "nStephenson@foo.com" },
                new Customer { FirstName = "Randy",
                               LastName = "Ashilts",
                               EmailAddress = "rShilts@foo.com" },
                new Customer { FirstName = "Michelangelo",
                               LastName = "Asignorile ",
                               EmailAddress = "mSignorile@foo.com" },
                new Customer { FirstName = "Larry",
                               LastName = "Akramer",
                               EmailAddress = "lKramer@foo.com" },
                new Customer { FirstName = "Jennifer",
                               LastName = "Abaumgardner",
                               EmailAddress = "jBaumgardner@foo.com" }

            };
        return customers;
    }
  }
}
```

*Example 14-4. Searching an XML document using XPathNavigator (continued)*

Output:

```
<Customer FirstName="Kenji" LastName="Ayoshino">
  <EmailAddress>kYoshino@foo.com</EmailAddress>
</Customer>
<Customer FirstName="Ian" LastName="AmcEwan">
  <EmailAddress>iMcEwan@foo.com</EmailAddress>
</Customer>
<Customer FirstName="Neal" LastName="Astephenson">
  <EmailAddress>nStephenson@foo.com</EmailAddress>
</Customer>
<Customer FirstName="Randy" LastName="Ashilts">
  <EmailAddress>rShilts@foo.com</EmailAddress>
</Customer>
<Customer FirstName="Michelangelo" LastName="Asignorile ">
  <EmailAddress>mSignorile@foo.com</EmailAddress>
</Customer>
<Customer FirstName="Larry" LastName="Akramer">
  <EmailAddress>lKramer@foo.com</EmailAddress>
</Customer>
<Customer FirstName="Jennifer" LastName="Abaumgardner">
  <EmailAddress>jBaumgardner@foo.com</EmailAddress>
</Customer>

Now sort by FirstName...
<Customer FirstName="Douglas" LastName="Adams">
  <EmailAddress>dAdams@foo.com</EmailAddress>
</Customer>
<Customer FirstName="Ian" LastName="AmcEwan">
  <EmailAddress>iMcEwan@foo.com</EmailAddress>
</Customer>
<Customer FirstName="Jennifer" LastName="Abaumgardner">
  <EmailAddress>jBaumgardner@foo.com</EmailAddress>
</Customer>
<Customer FirstName="Kenji" LastName="Ayoshino">
  <EmailAddress>kYoshino@foo.com</EmailAddress>
</Customer>
<Customer FirstName="Larry" LastName="Akramer">
  <EmailAddress>lKramer@foo.com</EmailAddress>
</Customer>
<Customer FirstName="Michelangelo" LastName="Asignorile ">
  <EmailAddress>mSignorile@foo.com</EmailAddress>
</Customer>
<Customer FirstName="Neal" LastName="Astephenson">
  <EmailAddress>nStephenson@foo.com</EmailAddress>
</Customer>
<Customer FirstName="Randy" LastName="Ashilts">
  <EmailAddress>rShilts@foo.com</EmailAddress>
</Customer>
<Customer FirstName="Richard" LastName="Adawkins">
  <EmailAddress>rDawkins@foo.com</EmailAddress>
</Customer>
```

*Example 14-4. Searching an XML document using XPathNavigator (continued)*

```
And again...
<Customer FirstName="Douglas" LastName="Adams">
  <EmailAddress>dAdams@foo.com</EmailAddress>
</Customer>
<Customer FirstName="Ian" LastName="AmcEwan">
  <EmailAddress>iMcEwan@foo.com</EmailAddress>
</Customer>
<Customer FirstName="Jennifer" LastName="Abaumgardner">
  <EmailAddress>jBaumgardner@foo.com</EmailAddress>
</Customer>
<Customer FirstName="Kenji" LastName="Ayoshino">
  <EmailAddress>kYoshino@foo.com</EmailAddress>
</Customer>
<Customer FirstName="Larry" LastName="Akramer">
  <EmailAddress>lKramer@foo.com</EmailAddress>
</Customer>
<Customer FirstName="Michelangelo" LastName="Asignorile ">
  <EmailAddress>mSignorile@foo.com</EmailAddress>
</Customer>
<Customer FirstName="Neal" LastName="Astephenson">
  <EmailAddress>nStephenson@foo.com</EmailAddress>
</Customer>
<Customer FirstName="Randy" LastName="Ashilts">
  <EmailAddress>rShilts@foo.com</EmailAddress>
</Customer>
<Customer FirstName="Richard" LastName="Adawkins">
  <EmailAddress>rDawkins@foo.com</EmailAddress>
</Customer>
```

 We had to take some horrible liberties with the last names of some wonderful writers to get this example to work. For that, I apologize.

This example added the using System.Xml.XPath directive to include the required classes. The customer XML document is created in the same way as in previous examples:

```
XmlDocument customerXml = CreateCustomerXml( );
XPathNavigator nav = customerXml.CreateNavigator( );
```

Here, it also creates an instance of the XPathNavigator class, which you can create only by calling the CreateNavigator method of the target XmlDocument instance. Instead of calling the methods of the XML document, you now use the navigator object to execute queries:

```
string xPath = "descendant::Customer[@FirstName='Donna']";
XPathNavigator navNode = nav.SelectSingleNode(xPath);
```

The SelectSingleNode( ) method also returns a single node. However, it returns another XPathNavigator object from which you can query further.

You can access many of the node properties, such as InnerXml, from the navigator object. However, if you need to access properties or methods of the specific node type, you should retrieve the underlying node using the UnderlyingObject property of XPathNavigator:

```
Console.WriteLine("\nSelectSingleNode(\"{0}\")...", xPath);
if (navNode != null)
{
    Console.WriteLine(navNode.OuterXml);

    XmlElement elem = navNode.UnderlyingObject as XmlElement;
    if (elem != null)
        Console.WriteLine(elem.OuterXml);
    else
        Console.WriteLine("Found the wrong node!");
}
else
    Console.WriteLine("Customer not found");
```

## Using XPathNodeIterator

For queries that may return more than one node, you should call the Select method of the XPathNavigator class:

```
xPath = "descendant::Customer[starts-with(@LastName, 'A') " +
        "and contains(EmailAddress, 'foo.com')]";
Console.WriteLine("\nSelect(\"{0}\")...", xPath);
XPathNodeIterator iter = nav.Select(xPath);
if (iter.Count > 0)
{
    while (iter.MoveNext())
        Console.WriteLine(iter.Current.OuterXml);
}
else
{
    Console.WriteLine("Customer not found");
}
```

The Select method returns an XPathNodeIterator instance, which allows you to iterate through the results. One important feature of this approach is that the query is not executed on this line:

```
XPathNodeIterator iter = nav.Select(xPath);
```

The query is executed only when you go through the result by calling the iterator's MoveNext() method. This reduces the initial hit, especially when the document is large. This is one of the performance advantages you gain by using XPathNavigator instead of searching through the XmlDocument directly.

This delayed query execution means that it's not always a good idea to access the iterator's Count property because this causes the query to be executed. Therefore, the code in this example is not very efficient, especially if the document or the result is large. However, it is useful when checking whether the query returns anything.

## Using XPathExpression

Although the `SelectNodes` and `SelectSingleNode` methods of the `XmlDocument` and `XPathNavigator` classes accept an XPath expression as plain text, they actually compile the input expression into a state in which the XML query engine can execute it before the query is actually executed. If you call any of the `SelectXXX` methods with the same XPath expression again, the expression is compiled again.

If you anticipate that you may run the same query many times, it would be beneficial to compile the XPath expression yourself and use the compiled form whenever needed. In XPath, you can do this by calling the `XPathNavigator`'s `Compile` method. The result is an `XPathExpression` object that can be cached for later use:

```
XPathExpression expr = nav.Compile(xPath);
iter = nav.Select(expr);
```

An additional benefit of creating a compiled expression is that you can use it to sort the query results. You can add a sort condition to a compiled expression using its `AddSort` method:

```
expr.AddSort("@FirstName", Comparer<String>.Default);
```

The first argument is the sort key, and the second is an instance of a comparer class that implements `IComparer`. The .NET Framework provides a predefined generic `Comparer<T>` class using the singleton pattern. Therefore, if the sort key is a string, as in this example, you can use default string comparison by passing in the singleton `Comparer<String>.Default` instance to the `AddSort` method. You can also indicate a case-insensitive comparison using the `System.Collections.CaseInsensitiveComparer` class.

The `AddSort` method is overloaded, with the second version taking more arguments to specify detailed sorting requirements and to perform either a numeric or a text comparison:

```
expr2.AddSort(sortKey, sortOrder, caseOrder, language, dataType);
```

You can decide to sort in ascending or descending order, whether the lowercase or uppercase should come first, the language to use for comparison, and whether it should be a numeric or a text search:

```
expr2.AddSort("@FirstName", XmlSortOrder.Ascending,
              XmlCaseOrder.None, string.Empty, XmlDataType.Text);
```

After adding the sort condition in this example, you can see from the preceding result that the returned nodes are now ordered by their `FirstName` attribute.

# XML Serialization

So far, you have constructed the XML representing the Customer objects by hand. As XML is becoming popular, especially with the acceptance of web services as a central component of the SOA, it is increasingly common to serialize objects into XML, transmit them across process and application boundaries, and deserialize them back into conventional objects.

 For more information about SOA, see *Programming WCF Services* by Juval Löwy (O'Reilly).

It is therefore natural for the .NET Framework to provide a built-in serialization mechanism, as a part of the Windows Communication Foundation (WCF), to reduce the coding efforts by application developers. The System.Xml.Serialization namespace defines the classes and utilities that implement methods required for serializing and deserializing objects. Example 14-5 illustrates this.

*Example 14-5. Simple XML serialization and deserialization*

```
using System;
using System.IO;
using System.Xml.Serialization;

namespace Programming_CSharp
{
    // Simple customer class
    public class Customer
    {
        public string FirstName { get; set; }
        public string LastName { get; set; }
        public string EmailAddress { get; set; }

        // Overrides the Object.ToString( ) to provide a
        // string representation of the object properties.
        public override string ToString( )
        {
            return string.Format("{0} {1}\nEmail:    {2}",
                    FirstName, LastName, EmailAddress);
        }
    }

    // Main program
    public class Tester
    {
        static void Main( )
        {
            Customer c1 = new Customer
                        {
                            FirstName = "Orlando",
```

*Example 14-5. Simple XML serialization and deserialization (continued)*

```
                            LastName = "Gee",
                            EmailAddress = "orlando0@hotmail.com"
                    };

        XmlSerializer serializer = new XmlSerializer(typeof(Customer));
        StringWriter writer = new StringWriter();

        serializer.Serialize(writer, c1);
        string xml = writer.ToString();
        Console.WriteLine("Customer in XML:\n{0}\n", xml);

        Customer c2 = serializer.Deserialize(new StringReader(xml))
                    as Customer;
        Console.WriteLine("Customer in Object:\n{0}", c2.ToString());

        Console.ReadKey();
        }
    }
}

Output:
Customer in XML:
<?xml version="1.0" encoding="utf-16"?>
<Customer xmlns:xsi="http://www.w3.org/2001/XMLSchema-instance"
xmlns:xsd="http://www.w3.org/2001/XMLSchema">
  <FirstName>Orlando</FirstName>
  <LastName>Gee</LastName>
  <EmailAddress>orlando0@hotmail.com</EmailAddress>
</Customer>

Customer in Object:
Orlando Gee
Email:   orlando0@hotmail.com
```

To serialize an object using .NET XML serialization, you need to create an XmlSerializer object:

```
XmlSerializer serializer = new XmlSerializer(typeof(Customer));
```

You must pass in the type of the object to be serialized to the XmlSerializer constructor. If you don't know the object type at design time, you can discover it by calling its GetType( ) method:

```
XmlSerializer serializer = new XmlSerializer(c1.GetType());
```

You also need to decide where the serialized XML document should be stored. In this example, you simply send it to a StringWriter:

```
StringWriter writer = new StringWriter();

serializer.Serialize(writer, c1);
string xml = writer.ToString();
Console.WriteLine("Customer in XML:\n{0}\n", xml);
```

The resulting XML string is then displayed on the console:

```
<?xml version="1.0" encoding="utf-16"?>
<Customer xmlns:xsi="http://www.w3.org/2001/XMLSchema-instance" xmlns:xsd="http://
www.w3.org/2001/XMLSchema">
  <FirstName>Orlando</FirstName>
  <LastName>Gee</LastName>
  <EmailAddress>orlando0@hotmail.com</EmailAddress>
</Customer>
```

The first line is an XML declaration. This is to let the consumers (human users and software applications) of this document know that this is an XML file, the official version to which this file conforms, and the encoding format used. This is optional in XML, but it is generated by .NET XML Serialization.

The root element is the Customer element, with each property represented as a child element. The xmlns:xsi and xmlns:xsd attributes specify the XML schema definition used by this document. They are optional, so I will not explain them further. If you are interested, please read the XML specification or other documentation, such as the MSDN Library, for more details.

Aside from those optional parts, this XML representation of the Customer object is identical to the one created in Example 14-1. However, instead of writing tens of lines of code, you need only three lines using .NET XML Serialization classes.

Furthermore, it is just as easy to reconstruct an object from its XML form:

```
Customer c2 = serializer.Deserialize(new StringReader(xml))
            as Customer;
Console.WriteLine("Customer in Object:\n{0}", c2.ToString());
```

All it needs is to call the XmlSerializer.Deserialize method. It has several overloaded versions, one of which takes a TextReader instance as an input parameter. Because StringReader is derived from TextReader, you just pass an instance of StringReader to read from the XML string. The Deserialize method returns an object, so it is necessary to cast it to the correct type.

## Customizing XML Serialization Using Attributes

By default, all public read/write properties are serialized as child elements. You can customize your classes by specifying the type of XML node you want for each of your public properties, as shown in Example 14-6.

*Example 14-6. Customizing XML serialization with attributes*

```
using System;
using System.IO;
using System.Xml.Serialization;

namespace Programming_CSharp
{
```

*Example 14-6. Customizing XML serialization with attributes (continued)*

```
    // Simple customer class
    public class Customer
    {
        [XmlAttribute()]
        public string FirstName { get; set; }

        [XmlIgnore()]
        public string LastName { get; set; }

        public string EmailAddress { get; set; }

        // Overrides the Object.ToString() to provide a
        // string representation of the object properties.
        public override string ToString()
        {
            return string.Format("{0} {1}\nEmail:   {2}",
                        FirstName, LastName, EmailAddress);
        }
    }

    // Main program
    public class Tester
    {
        static void Main()
        {
            Customer c1 = new Customer
                        {
                            FirstName = "Orlando",
                            LastName = "Gee",
                            EmailAddress = "orlando0@hotmail.com"
                        };

            //XmlSerializer serializer = new XmlSerializer(c1.GetType());
            XmlSerializer serializer = new XmlSerializer(typeof(Customer));
            StringWriter writer = new StringWriter();

            serializer.Serialize(writer, c1);
            string xml = writer.ToString();
            Console.WriteLine("Customer in XML:\n{0}\n", xml);

            Customer c2 = serializer.Deserialize(new StringReader(xml)) as
                        Customer;
            Console.WriteLine("Customer in Object:\n{0}", c2.ToString());

            Console.ReadKey();
        }
    }
}

Output:
Customer in XML:
<?xml version="1.0" encoding="utf-16"?>
```

*Example 14-6. Customizing XML serialization with attributes (continued)*

```
<Customer xmlns:xsi="http://www.w3.org/2001/XMLSchema-instance"
          xmlns:xsd="http://www.w3.org/2001/XMLSchema"
          FirstName="Orlando">
  <EmailAddress>orlandoO@hotmail.com</EmailAddress>
</Customer>

Customer in Object:
Orlando
Email:   orlandoO@hotmail.com
```

The only changes in this example are a couple of added XML serialization attributes in the Customer class:

```
[XmlAttribute( )]
public string FirstName { get; set; }
```

The first change is to specify that you want to serialize the FirstName property into an attribute of the Customer element by adding the XmlAttributeAttribute to the property:

```
[XmlIgnore( )]
public string LastName { get; set; }
```

The other change is to tell XML serialization that you in fact do not want the LastName property to be serialized at all. You do this by adding the XmlIgnoreAttribute to the property. As you can see from the sample output, the Customer object is serialized exactly as we asked.

However, you have probably noticed that when the object is deserialized, its LastName property is lost. Because it is not serialized, the XmlSerializer is unable to assign it any value. Therefore, its value is left as the default, which is an empty string.

The goal is to exclude from serialization only those properties you don't need or can compute or can retrieve in other ways.

## Runtime XML Serialization Customization

Sometimes it may be necessary to customize the serialization of objects at runtime. For instance, your class may contain an instance of another class. The contained class may be serialized with all its properties as child elements. However, you may want to have them serialized into attributes to save some space. Example 14-7 illustrates how you can achieve this.

*Example 14-7. Customizing XML serialization at runtime*

```
using System;
using System.IO;
using System.Reflection;
using System.Xml.Serialization;
```

*Example 14-7. Customizing XML serialization at runtime (continued)*

```
namespace Programming_CSharp
{
    // Simple customer class
    public class Customer
    {
        public string FirstName { get; set; }
        public string LastName { get; set; }
        public string EmailAddress { get; set; }

        // Overrides the Object.ToString( ) to provide a
        // string representation of the object properties.
        public override string ToString( )
        {
            return string.Format("{0} {1}\nEmail:    {2}",
                        FirstName, LastName, EmailAddress);
        }
    }

    // Main program
    public class Tester
    {
        static void Main( )
        {
            Customer c1 = new Customer
                            {
                                FirstName = "Orlando",
                                LastName = "Gee",
                                EmailAddress = "orlandoO@hotmail.com"
                            };

            Type customerType = typeof(Customer);
            XmlAttributeOverrides overrides = new XmlAttributeOverrides( );
            foreach (PropertyInfo prop in customerType.GetProperties( ))
            {
                XmlAttributes attrs = new XmlAttributes( );
                attrs.XmlAttribute = new XmlAttributeAttribute( );
                overrides.Add(customerType, prop.Name, attrs);
            }

            XmlSerializer serializer = new XmlSerializer(customerType, overrides);
            StringWriter writer = new StringWriter( );

            serializer.Serialize(writer, c1);
            string xml = writer.ToString( );
            Console.WriteLine("Customer in XML:\n{0}\n", xml);

            Customer c2 = serializer.Deserialize(new StringReader(xml)) as
                            Customer;
            Console.WriteLine("Customer in Object:\n{0}", c2.ToString( ));
```

*Example 14-7. Customizing XML serialization at runtime (continued)*

```
            Console.ReadKey();
        }
    }
}
```

```
Output:
Customer in XML:
<?xml version="1.0" encoding="utf-16"?>
<Customer xmlns:xsi="http://www.w3.org/2001/XMLSchema-instance"
xmlns:xsd="http://www.w3.org/2001/XMLSchema" FirstName="
Orlando" LastName="Gee" EmailAddress="orlandoO@hotmail.com" />

Customer in Object:
Orlando Gee
Email:   orlandoO@hotmail.com
```

The Customer class in this example has no custom XML serialization attributes. Therefore, all its properties are serialized into child elements, as you have seen in previous examples. When an instance of it is serialized at runtime in the main function, we use a combination of reflection and advanced serialization techniques to ensure that the properties are serialized into attributes instead.

In .NET XML serialization, you instruct the serialization engine to override its default behavior with your custom requirements. Because you are going to use the Customer type a lot, you store it locally so that it you can use it later:

```
    Type customerType = typeof(Customer);
```

To specify your custom requirements, you use the XmlAttributeOverrides class:

```
    XmlAttributeOverrides overrides = new XmlAttributeOverrides();
    foreach (PropertyInfo prop in customerType.GetProperties())
    {
        XmlAttributes attrs = new XmlAttributes();
        attrs.XmlAttribute = new XmlAttributeAttribute();
        overrides.Add(customerType, prop.Name, attrs);
    }
```

The first step is to create a new XmlAttributeOverrides instance. You can now use .NET reflection to go through all the properties of the target class, using its GetProperties method. For each property, you override its default serialization behavior by adding an XmlAttributes object to the XmlAttributeOverrides object. To specify that you want to serialize the property as an attribute, you assign an XmlAttributeAttribute object to the XmlAttributes.XmlAttribute property. This is the equivalent of adding the XmlAttributeAttribute to a property at design time, as you did in the last example.

The XmlAttributeOverrides.Add method takes three input parameters. The first is the type of the object, the second is the name of the property, and the last is the customer serialization behavior.

To ensure that the XML serializer use the customer serialization overrides, you must pass in the overrides object to its constructor:

```
XmlSerializer serializer = new XmlSerializer(customerType, overrides);
```

The rest of this example stays unchanged from the last example. You can see from the sample output that all the properties are indeed serialized into attributes instead of child elements. When the object is deserialized, the customer overrides are also recognized and the object is reconstructed correctly.

# CHAPTER 15

# Putting LINQ to Work

LINQ may be the most anticipated, most exciting (and to some, most feared) feature in C# 3.0. The previous two chapters were, in large measure, a necessary introduction, an appetizer to whet your appetite and get you ready for the main meal: using LINQ to retrieve meaningful data in production applications.

Before we begin, let's be clear: your DBA is terrified of LINQ, and not just as a matter of job security. Improperly used, LINQ has the ability to put queries into the hands of inexperienced, untrained goofballs (us) who know little or nothing about writing efficient queries, and who will bring carefully honed data-intensive enterprise systems to their knees (fun, eh?). OK, I said it out loud, so let's all stop panicking.

As with all programming, the trick is to write the program, get it working, and *then* optimize. It may be that after you have your program up and working (and profiled), you'll discover that there are some places that you've used LINQ that you'd be better off using stored procedures running within your database (that's what databases do for a living), but we don't know that a priori, and the advantages of LINQ are so tremendous (e.g., the ability to use an object-oriented unified syntax to access all your data regardless of source) that it cries out for a "code now, optimize later *if needed*" approach.

The two most common sources you'll use LINQ with are, no doubt, SQL and XML, but they are certainly not the only sources of data. You may well find yourself retrieving data from:

- Files
- Flat databases
- Mail messages
- Web services
- Legacy systems
- In memory data structures

And most exciting are sources you haven't anticipated yet. With the understanding of LINQ fundamentals you gained in Chapter 13, and the grounding in XML you gained in Chapter 14, you are now just about ready to dig in and put LINQ to work.

# Getting Set Up

Examples in this section use the SQL Server 2005 Adventure Works LT sample database. To set up this database, download it from:

*http://www.codeplex.com/MSFTDBProdSamples/Release/ProjectReleases. aspx?ReleaseId=4004*

 Please note that although this database is a simplified version of the more comprehensive AdventureWorks, the two are quite different, and the examples in this chapter will *not* work with the full AdventureWorks database. Please select the AdventureWorks*LT* MSI package applicable for your platform—32-bit, x64, or IA64. If SQL Server is installed in the default directory, install the sample database to *C:\Program Files\ Microsoft SQL Server\MSSQL.1\MSSQL\Data\*. Otherwise, install the database to the Data subdirectory under its installation directory.

If you are using SQL Server Express included in Visual Studio 2008, you will need to enable the Named Pipes protocol:

1. Open SQL Server Configuration Manager under Start → All Programs → Microsoft SQL Server 2005 → Configuration Tools → SQL Server Configuration Manager.

2. In the left pane, select SQL Server Configuration Manager (Local) → SQL Server 2005 Network Configuration → Protocols for SQLEXPRESS.

3. In the right pane, right-click the Named Pipes protocol and select Enable, as shown in Figure 15-1.

4. In the left pane, select SQL Server 2005 Services, then right-click SQL Server (SQLEXPRESS), and select Restart to restart SQL Server, as shown in Figure 15-2.

5. Attach the sample database to SQL Server Express using one of the following methods:

   a. If you already have SQL Server Client tools installed, open SQL Server Management Studio under Start → All Programs → Microsoft SQL Server 2005 → SQL Server Management Studio and connect to the local SQL Server Express database.

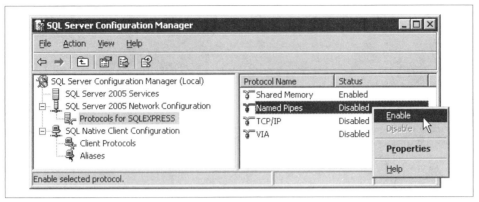

Figure 15-1. Enabling the Named Pipes protocol in SQL Server 2005 Express

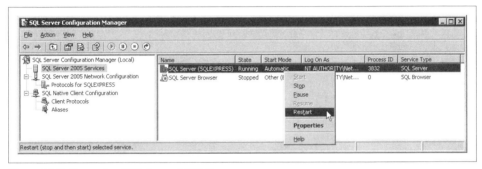

Figure 15-2. Restarting SQL Server 2005 Express

    b. Download SQL Server Express Management Studio from the Microsoft SQL Server Express page (*http://msdn2.microsoft.com/en-us/express/bb410792.aspx*), and install it on your machine. Then, open it and connect to the local SQL Server Express database.

6. In the left pane, right-click Databases and select Attach (see Figure 15-3).

7. On the Attach Databases dialog click Add.

8. Click OK to close this dialog, and OK again to close the Attach Database dialog.

# LINQ to SQL Fundamentals

To begin, open Visual Studio, and create a new application named "Simple Linq to SQL" as a console application. Once the IDE is open, click on View, and open the Server Explorer and make a connection to the AdventureWorksLT database, and test that connection.

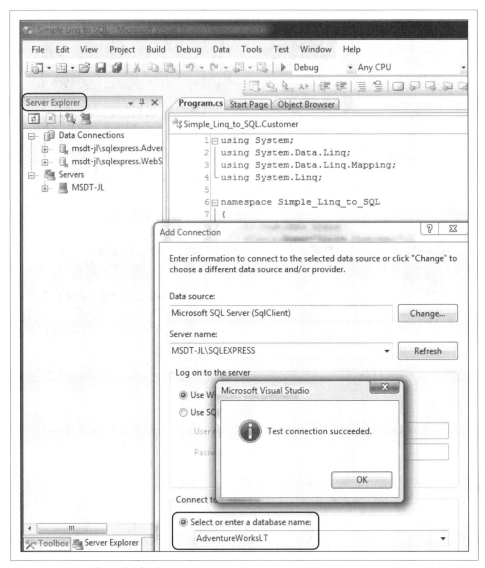

*Figure 15-3. Attaching the database to SQL Server 2005 Express*

With that in place, you are ready to create a program that uses LINQ to connect your SQL database. You'll need to include the System.Data.Linq namespace in the references for your project as shown in Figure 15-4 so that the last two using statements will compile.

This will also create the mapping between each class property and the corresponding database column:

```
public class Customer
  {
```

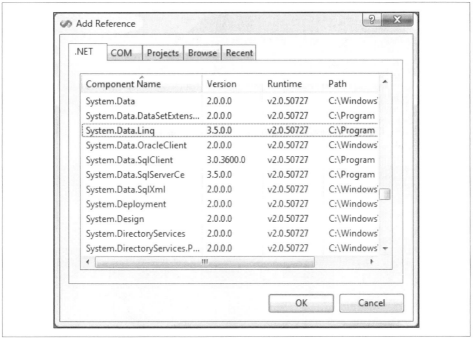

*Figure 15-4. Adding a reference to System.Data.Linq*

```
[Column] public string FirstName      { get; set; }
[Column] public string LastName       { get; set; }
[Column] public string EmailAddress   { get; set; }
```

Complete analysis follows Example 15-1.

*Example 15-1. Simple LINQ to SQL*

```
using System;
using System.Data.Linq;
using System.Data.Linq.Mapping;
using System.Linq;

namespace Simple_Linq_to_SQL
{
    // customer class
    [Table(Name="SalesLT.Customer")]
    public class Customer
    {
        [Column] public string FirstName    { get; set; }
        [Column] public string LastName      { get; set; }
        [Column] public string EmailAddress { get; set; }

        // Overrides the Object.ToString() to provide a
        // string representation of the object properties.
        public override string ToString( )
```

*Example 15-1. Simple LINQ to SQL (continued)*

```
        {
            return string.Format("{0} {1}\nEmail:    {2}",
                    FirstName, LastName, EmailAddress);
        }
    }


    public class Tester
    {
        static void Main( )
        {
            DataContext db = new DataContext(
                @"Data Source=.\SqlExpress;
                    Initial Catalog=AdventureWorksLT;
                    Integrated Security=True");

            Table<Customer> customers = db.GetTable<Customer>( );
            var query =
                from customer in customers
                where customer.FirstName == "Donna"
                select customer;

            foreach(var c in query)
                Console.WriteLine(c.ToString( ));

            Console.ReadKey( );
        }
    }
}
```

```
Output:
Donna Carreras
Email:   donna0@adventure-works.com
```

The key to this program is in the first line of Main( ), where you define db to be of type DataContext. A DataContext object is the entry point for the LINQ to SQL framework, providing a bridge between the application code and database-specific commands. Its job is to translate high-level C# LINQ to SQL code to corresponding database commands and execute them behind the scenes. It maintains a connection to the underlying database, fetches data from the database when requested, tracks changes made to every entity retrieved from the database, and updates the database as needed. It maintains an "identity cache" to guarantee that if you retrieve an entity more than once, all duplicate retrievals will be represented by the same object instance (thereby preventing database corruption; for more information, see the "Database Corruption" sidebar).

Once the DataContext is instantiated, you can access the objects contained in the underlying database. This example uses the Customer table in the AdventureWorksLT database using the DataContext's GetTable( ) function:

```
        Table<Customer> customers = db.GetTable<Customer>( );
```

## Database Corruption

The data in a large database can be "corrupted" in many ways—that is, the data can inadvertently come to misrepresent the information you hoped to keep accurate.

A typical scenario would be this: you have data representing the books in your store and how many are available. When you make a query about a book, the data is retrieved from the database into a temporary record (or object) that is no longer connected to the database until you "write it back"—any changes to the database are not reflected in the record you are looking at unless you refresh the data (this is necessary to keep a busy database responsive).

Suppose that Joe takes a call asking how many copies of *Programming C#* are on hand. He calls up the record in his database and finds to his horror that they are down to a single copy. While he is talking with his customer, Jane, a second seller, takes a call looking for the same book. She sees one book available and sells it to her customer, while Joe is discussing the merits of the book with his customer. Joe's customer decides to make the purchase, but by the time he does it is too late; Jane has already sold the last copy. Joe tries to put the sale through, but the book that quite clearly is showing as available is no longer there. You now have one very unhappy customer and a salesperson that has been made to look like an idiot. Oops.

I mention in the text that LINQ ensures that multiple retrievals of a database record are represented by the *same* object instance; this makes it much harder for the aforementioned scenario to occur, as both Joe and Jane are working on the same record in memory; thus, if Jane were to change the "number on hand," that would be reflected in Joe's representation of the object—they are looking at the same data, not at independent snapshots.

This function is a generic function so that you can specify that the table should be mapped to a collection of Customer objects.

DataContext has a great many methods and properties, one of which is a Log. This property allows you to specify the destination where it logs the SQL queries and commands executed. By redirecting it to where you can access it, you can see how LINQ does its magic. For instance, you can redirect the Log to Console.Out so that you can see the output on the system console:

```
Output:
SELECT [t0].[FirstName], [t0].[LastName], [t0].[EmailAddress]
FROM [SalesLT].[Customer] AS [t0]
WHERE [t0].[FirstName] = @p0
-- @p0: Input String (Size = 5; Prec = 0; Scale = 0) [Donna]
-- Context: SqlProvider(Sql2005) Model: AttributedMetaModel Build: 3.5.20706.1
```

# Using Visual Studio LINQ to SQL Designer

Rather than working out the data relationships in the underlying database and mapping them in the DataContext manually, you can use the designer built into Visual Studio. This is a very powerful mechanism that makes working with LINQ painfully simple. To see how this works, first open the AdventureWorksLT database in SQL Server Management Studio Express and examine the Customer, CustomerAddress, and Address tables so that you feel comfortable you understand their relationship, as illustrated by the Entity-Relationship diagram shown in Figure 15-5.

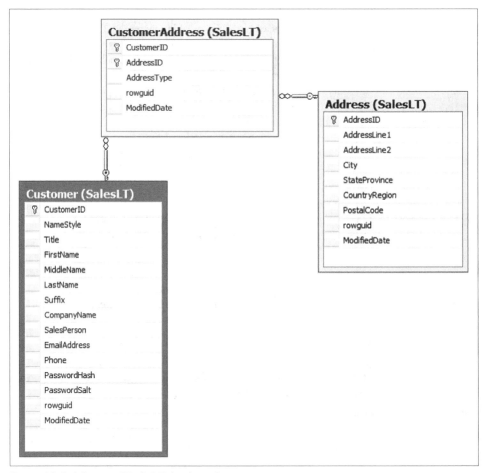

*Figure 15-5. AdventureWorksLT database diagram*

Create a new Visual Studio console application called AdventureWorksDBML. Make sure the Server Explorer is visible and you have a connection to AdventureWorksLT, as shown in Figure 15-6. If the connection is not available, follow the instructions mentioned earlier to create it.

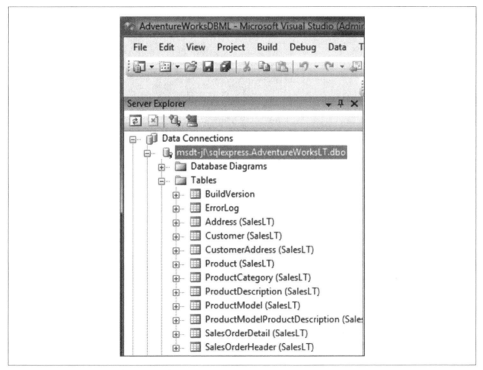

*Figure 15-6. Server Explorer window*

To create your LINQ to SQL classes, right-click on the project, and choose Add → New Item, as shown in Figure 15-7.

When the New Item dialog opens, choose LINQ to SQL Classes. You can use the default name (probably DataClasses1), or replace it with a more meaningful name. In this case, replace it with AdventureWorksAddress, and click Add. The name you select will become the name of your `DataContext` object with the word *DataContext* appended. Therefore, the data context name in this case will be `AdventureWorksAddressDataContext`.

The center window shows changes to the Object Relational Designer. You can now drag tables from Server Explorer or Toolbox to the designer. Drag the Address, Customer, and CustomerAddress tables from the Server Explorer onto this space, as shown in Figure 15-8.

In the image, two tables have been dragged on, and the third is about to be dropped. Once your tables are dropped, Visual Studio 2008 automatically retrieves and displays the relationship between the tables. You can arrange them to ensure that the relationships between the tables are displayed clearly.

*Figure 15-7. Selecting Add→New Item*

Once you've done that, two new files have been created: *AdventureWorksAddress.dbml.
layout* and *AdventureWorksAddress.designer.cs*. The former has the XML representation of the tables you've put on the surface, a short segment of which is shown here:

```
<?xml version="1.0" encoding="utf-8"?>
<ordesignerObjectsDiagram dslVersion="1.0.0.0" absoluteBounds="0, 0, 11, 8.5"
name="AdventureWorksAddress">
  <DataContextMoniker Name="/AdventureWorksAddressDataContext" />
  <nestedChildShapes>
    <classShape Id="4a893188-c5cd-44db-a114-0444cced4057" absoluteBounds="1.125,
1.375, 2, 2.5401025390625">
      <DataClassMoniker Name="/AdventureWorksAddressDataContext/Address" />
      <nestedChildShapes>
        <elementListCompartment Id="d59f1bc4-752e-41db-a940-4a9938014ca7"
absoluteBounds="1.1400000000000001, 1.835, 1.9700000000000002, 1.9801025390625"
name="DataPropertiesCompartment" titleTextColor="Black" itemTextColor="Black" />
      </nestedChildShapes>
    </classShape>
    <classShape Id="c432968b-f644-4ca3-b26b-61dfe4292884" absoluteBounds="5.875, 1,
2, 3.6939111328124996">
      <DataClassMoniker Name="/AdventureWorksAddressDataContext/Customer" />
      <nestedChildShapes>
        <elementListCompartment Id="c240ad98-f162-4921-927a-c87781db6ac4"
absoluteBounds="5.8900000000000006, 1.46, 1.9700000000000002, 3.1339111328125"
name="DataPropertiesCompartment" titleTextColor="Black" itemTextColor="Black" />
```

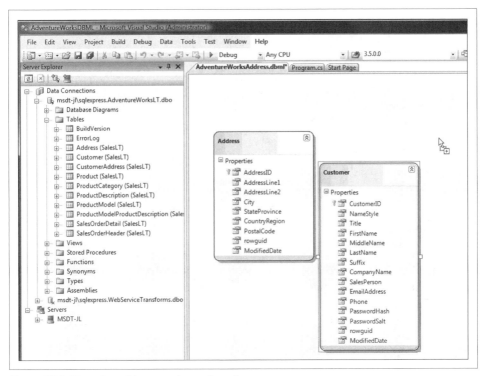

Figure 15-8. Dragging tables onto the work surface

```
    </nestedChildShapes>
  </classShape>
```

The .cs file has the code to handle all the LINQ to SQL calls that you otherwise would have to write by hand. Like all machine-generated code, it is terribly verbose; here is a very brief excerpt:

```csharp
public Address()
{
    OnCreated();
    this._CustomerAddresses = new EntitySet<CustomerAddress>(new
      Action<CustomerAddress>(this.attach_CustomerAddresses),
      new Action<CustomerAddress>(this.detach_CustomerAddresses));
}

[Column(Storage="_AddressID", AutoSync=AutoSync.OnInsert,
DbType="Int NOT NULL IDENTITY", IsPrimaryKey=true, IsDbGenerated=true)]
public int AddressID
{
    get
    {
        return this._AddressID;
    }
    set
    {
```

```
        if ((this._AddressID != value))
        {
            this.OnAddressIDChanging(value);
            this.SendPropertyChanging( );
            this._AddressID = value;
            this.SendPropertyChanged("AddressID");
            this.OnAddressIDChanged( );
        }
    }
}
```

The classes that are generated are strongly typed, and a class is generated for each table you place in the designer.

For a review of strongly typed versus loosely typed classes, see Chapter 9, particularly the section on Generics.

The DataContext class exposes each table as a property, and the relationships between the tables are represented by properties of the classes representing data records. For example, the CustomerAddress table is mapped to the CustomerAddresses property, which is a strongly typed collection (LINQ table) of CustomerAddress objects. You can access the parent Customer and Address objects of a CustomerAddress object through its Customer and Address properties, respectively. This makes it quite easy to write the code to retrieve data.

---

## Appending a Method to a Generated Class

One of the wonderful things about the partial class keyword added in C# 2.0 is that you can add a method to the classes generated by the designer. In this case, we are overriding the ToString method of the Customer class to have it display all its members in a relatively easy-to-read manner:

```
public partial class Customer
{
    public override string ToString( )
    {
        StringBuilder sb = new StringBuilder( );
        sb.AppendFormat("{0} {1} {2}",
                FirstName, LastName, EmailAddress);
        foreach (CustomerAddress ca in CustomerAddresses)
        {
            sb.AppendFormat("\n\t{0}, {1}",
                ca.Address.AddressLine1,
                ca.Address.City);
        }
        sb.AppendLine( );
        return sb.ToString( );
    }
}
```

---

# Retrieving Data

Replace the contents of *Program.cs* with the code shown in Example 15-2 to use the generated LINQ to SQL code to retrieve data from the three tables you've mapped using the designer.

*Example 15-2. Using LINQ to SQL designer-generated classes*

```
using System;
using System.Linq;
using System.Text;

namespace AdventureWorksDBML
{
    // Main program
    public class Tester
    {
        static void Main( )
        {
            AdventureWorksAddressDataContext dc = new
                AdventureWorksAddressDataContext( );
            // Uncomment the statement below to show the
            // SQL statement generated by LINQ to SQL.
            // dc.Log = Console.Out;

            // Find one customer record.
            Customer donna = dc.Customers.Single(c => c.FirstName == "Donna");");
            Console.WriteLine(donna);

            // Find a list of customer records.
            var customerDs =
                from customer in dc.Customers
                where customer.FirstName.StartsWith("D")
                orderby customer.FirstName, customer.LastName
                select customer;

            foreach (Customer customer in customerDs)
            {
                Console.WriteLine(customer);
            }
        }
    }

    // Add a method to the generated Customer class to
    // show formatted customer properties.
    public partial class Customer
    {
        public override string ToString( )
        {
            StringBuilder sb = new StringBuilder( );
            sb.AppendFormat("{0} {1} {2}",
                    FirstName, LastName, EmailAddress);
            foreach (CustomerAddress ca in CustomerAddresses)
```

*Example 15-2. Using LINQ to SQL designer-generated classes (continued)*

```
            {
                sb.AppendFormat("\n\t{0}, {1}",
                    ca.Address.AddressLine1,
                    ca.Address.City);
            }
            sb.AppendLine( );
            return sb.ToString( );
        }
    }
}
```

```
Output:
Donna Carreras donna0@adventure-works.com
      12345 Sterling Avenue, Irving

(only showing the first 5 customers):
Daniel Blanco daniel0@adventure-works.com
        Suite 800 2530 Slater Street, Ottawa
Daniel Thompson daniel2@adventure-works.com
        755 Nw Grandstand, Issaquah
Danielle Johnson danielle1@adventure-works.com
        955 Green Valley Crescent, Ottawa
Darrell Banks darrell0@adventure-works.com
        Norwalk Square, Norwalk
Darren Gehring darren0@adventure-works.com
        509 Nafta Boulevard, Laredo
```

## Creating Properties for Each Table

As you can see, you begin by creating an instance of the DataContext object you asked the tool to generate:

```
    AdventureWorksAddressDataContext dc = new AdventureWorksAddressDataContext( );
```

When you use the designer, one of the things it does, besides creating the DataContext class, is define a property for each table you've placed in the designer (in this case, Customer, Address, and CustomerAddress). It names those properties by making them plural. Therefore, the properties of AdventureWorksAddressDataContext include Customers, Addresses, and CustomerAddresses.

> One side effect of this convention is that it would be a good idea to name your database tables in singular form to avoid potential confusion in your code. By default, the LINQ to SQL designer names the generated data classes the same as the table names. If you use plural table names, the class names will be the same as the DataContext property names. Therefore, you will need to manually modify the generated class names to avoid such naming conflicts.

You can access these properties through the DataContext instance:

```
dc.Customers
```

These properties are themselves table objects that implement the IQueryable interface, which itself has a number of very useful methods that allow you to filter, traverse, and project operations over the data in a LINQ table.

Most of these methods are *extension methods* of the LINQ types, which means they can be called just as though they were instance methods of the object that implements IQueryable<T> (in this case, the tables in the DataContext). Therefore, because Single is a method of IQueryable that returns the only element in a collection that meets a given set of criteria, we'll use that to find the one customer whose first name is Donna. If there is more than one customer with that specific first name, only the first customer record is returned:

```
Customer donna = dc.Customers.Single(c => c.FirstName == "Donna");
```

Let's unpack this line of code.

You begin by getting the Customers property of the DataContext instance, dc:

```
dc.Customers
```

What you get back is a Customer table object, which implements IQueryable. You can therefore call the method Single on this object:

```
dc.Customers.Single(condition);
```

The result will be to return a Customer object, which you can assign to a local variable of type Customer:

```
Customer donna = dc.Customers.Single(condition);
```

 Notice that everything we are doing here is strongly typed. This is goodness.

Inside the parentheses, you must place the expression that will filter for the one record we need, and this is a *great* opportunity to use lambda expressions:

```
c => c.FirstName == "Donna"
```

 You read this as "c goes to c.FirstName where c.FirstName equals Donna."

In this notation, c is an implicitly typed variable (of type Customer). LINQ to SQL translates this expression into a SQL statement similar to the following:

*Select \* from Customer where FirstName = 'Donna';*

Please note that this is just an arbitrary sample SQL. You can see the exact SQL as generated by LINQ to SQL by redirecting the `DataContext` log and examining the output, as described earlier in this chapter.

This SQL statement is executed when the `Single` method is executed:

```
Customer donna = dc.Customers.Single(c => c.FirstName == "Donna");
```

This `Customer` object (donna) is then printed to the console:

```
Console.WriteLine(donna);
```

The output is:

```
Donna Carreras donna0@adventure-works.com
        12345 Sterling Avenue, Irving,
```

Note that although you searched only by first name, what you retrieved was a complete record, including the address information. Also note that the output is created just by passing in the object, using the overridden method we created for the tool-generated class (see the earlier sidebar, "Appending a Method to a Generated Class").

## A LINQ Query

The next block uses the new-to-C# 3.0 keyword var to declare a variable customerDS which is implicitly typed by the compiler, based on the information returned by the LINQ query:

```
var customerDs =
    from customer in dc.Customers
    where customer.FirstName.StartsWith("D")
    orderby customer.FirstName, customer.LastName
    select customer;
```

This query is similar to a SQL query (as noted in the previous chapter), and as you can see, you are selecting from the `DataContext` Customers property (e.g., the Customer table) each customer whose `FirstName` property (e.g., the FirstName column) begins with *D*. You are ordering by `FirstName` and then `LastName`, and returning all of the results into customerDs, whose implicit type is a `TypedCollection` of Customers.

With that in hand, you can iterate through the collection and print the data about these customers to the console, treating them as `Customer` objects rather than as data records:

```
foreach (Customer customer in customerDs)
{
    Console.WriteLine(customer);
}
```

This is reflected in this excerpt of the output:

```
Delia Toone delia0@adventure-works.com
        755 Columbia Ctr Blvd, Kennewick
```

Della Demott Jr della0@adventure-works.com
        25575 The Queensway, Etobicoke

Denean Ison denean0@adventure-works.com
        586 Fulham Road,, London

Denise Maccietto denise1@adventure-works.com
        Port Huron, Port Huron

Derek Graham derek0@adventure-works.com
        655-4th Ave S.W., Calgary

Derik Stenerson derik0@adventure-works.com
        Factory Merchants, Branson

Diane Glimp diane3@adventure-works.com
        4400 March Road, Kanata

# Updating Data Using LINQ to SQL

To add or modify data to the database using LINQ, you interact with objects in C#, make your changes, and then tell the DataContext to SubmitChanges, allowing LINQ to take care of the details. This is an extremely object-oriented way to approach data storage. Your code remains strongly typed and yet decoupled from the underlying persistence mechanism.

If you want to add new data to the database, you instantiate a new object and then save it. If you want to modify data already persisted (stored) in the database, you retrieve the object, modify it, and then store it. The key to Example 15-3 is that from a C# perspective, you are interacting with objects and letting LINQ worry about the details of interacting with SQL Server.

*Example 15-3. Modifying data using LINQ to SQL*

```
using System;
using System.Collections.Generic;
using System.Data.Linq;
using System.Data.Linq.Mapping;
using System.Linq;
using System.Text;

namespace Modifying_Data_Using_Linq_To_SQL
{
    // Main program
    public class Tester
    {
        static void Main()
        {
            AddCustomer();
            UpdateCustomer();
            Console.ReadKey();
```

*Example 15-3. Modifying data using LINQ to SQL (continued)*

```
    }

private static void AddCustomer()
{
    Console.WriteLine("Adding a new customer...");
    AdventureWorksDataContext dc = new AdventureWorksDataContext();
    // Uncomment the statement below to show the
    // SQL statement generated by LINQ to SQL.
    // dc.Log = Console.Out;

    // Add a new customer with address
    Customer douglas = new Customer();
    douglas.FirstName = "Douglas";
    douglas.LastName = "Adams";
    douglas.EmailAddress = "douglas0@adventureworks.com";
    douglas.PasswordHash = "fake";
    douglas.PasswordSalt = "fake";
    douglas.ModifiedDate = DateTime.Today;
    douglas.rowguid = Guid.NewGuid();

    Address addr = new Address();
    addr.AddressLine1 = "1c Sharp Way";
    addr.City = "Seattle";
    addr.PostalCode = "98011";
    addr.StateProvince = "Washington";
    addr.CountryRegion = "United States";
    addr.ModifiedDate = DateTime.Today;
    addr.rowguid = Guid.NewGuid();

    CustomerAddress ca = new CustomerAddress();
    ca.AddressType = "Main Office";
    ca.Address = addr;
    ca.Customer = douglas;
    ca.ModifiedDate = DateTime.Today;
    ca.rowguid = Guid.NewGuid();

    dc.Customers.Add(douglas);
    dc.SubmitChanges();

    ShowCustomersByFirstName("Douglas");
}

// Update a customer record
private static void UpdateCustomer()
{
    Console.WriteLine("Updating a customer...");
    AdventureWorksDataContext dc = new AdventureWorksDataContext();
    // Uncomment the statement below to show the
    // SQL statement generated by LINQ to SQL.
    //dc.Log = Console.Out;
```

*Example 15-3. Modifying data using LINQ to SQL (continued)*

```
        Customer dAdams = dc.Customers.Single(
            c => (c.FirstName == "Douglas" && c.LastName == "Adams"));
        Console.WriteLine("Before:\n{0}", dAdams);

        dAdams.Title = "Mr.";

        // Add a new shipping address
        Address addr = new Address();
        addr.AddressLine1 = "1 Warehouse Place";
        addr.City = "Los Angeles";
        addr.PostalCode = "30210";
        addr.StateProvince = "California";
        addr.CountryRegion = "United States";
        addr.ModifiedDate = DateTime.Today;
        addr.rowguid = Guid.NewGuid();

        CustomerAddress ca = new CustomerAddress();
        ca.AddressType = "Shipping";
        ca.Address = addr;
        ca.Customer = dAdams;
        ca.ModifiedDate = DateTime.Today;
        ca.rowguid = Guid.NewGuid();

        dc.SubmitChanges();

        Customer dAdams1 = dc.Customers.Single(
            c => (c.FirstName == "Douglas" && c.LastName == "Adams"));
        Console.WriteLine("After:\n{0}", dAdams);
    }

    // Find a list of customer records with a specific first name.
    private static void ShowCustomersByFirstName(string firstName)
    {
        AdventureWorksDataContext dc = new AdventureWorksDataContext();
        var customers =
            from customer in dc.Customers
            where customer.FirstName == "Douglas"
            orderby customer.FirstName, customer.LastName
            select customer;

        Console.WriteLine("Customers whose first name is {0}:", firstName);
        foreach (Customer customer in customers)
            Console.WriteLine(customer);
    }
}

// Add a method to the generated Customer class to
// show formatted customer properties.
public partial class Customer
{
    public override string ToString()
    {
```

*Example 15-3. Modifying data using LINQ to SQL (continued)*

```
            StringBuilder sb = new StringBuilder( );
            sb.AppendFormat("{0} {1} {2} {3}",
                    Title, FirstName, LastName, EmailAddress);
            foreach (CustomerAddress ca in CustomerAddresses)
            {
                sb.AppendFormat("\n\t{0}: {1}, {2}",
                    ca.AddressType,
                    ca.Address.AddressLine1,
                    ca.Address.City);
            }
            sb.AppendLine( );
            return sb.ToString( );
        }
    }
}
```

The test program takes two actions: AddCustomer and then UpdateCustomer, each of which is encapsulated in a method call.

## Adding a Customer Record

AddCustomer begins by creating an instance of the Customer class and populating its properties:

```
Customer douglas = new Customer( );
douglas.FirstName = "Douglas";
douglas.LastName = "Adams";
douglas.EmailAddress = "douglas0@adventureworks.com";
douglas.PasswordHash = "fake";
douglas.PasswordSalt = "fake";
douglas.ModifiedDate = DateTime.Today;
douglas.rowguid = Guid.NewGuid( );
```

It does the same for the Address class:

```
Address addr = new Address( );
addr.AddressLine1 = "1c Sharp Way";
addr.City = "Seattle";
addr.PostalCode = "98011";
addr.StateProvince = "Washington";
addr.CountryRegion = "United States";
addr.ModifiedDate = DateTime.Today;
addr.rowguid = Guid.NewGuid( );
```

Finally, the class that joins an address to a customer is created:

```
CustomerAddress ca = new CustomerAddress( );
ca.AddressType = "Main Office";
ca.Address = addr;
ca.Customer = douglas;
ca.ModifiedDate = DateTime.Today;
ca.rowguid = Guid.NewGuid( );
```

Notice that the relationship among these three objects is created through the properties of the `CustomerAddress` object (highlighted).

 The advantage to this approach is that the customer may have more than one address (e.g., work, home, vacation home, etc.).

With all three new objects created, you can add them to the database just by adding the new `Customer` object to the Customers table and then telling the `DataContext` to submit the changes:

```
dc.Customers.Add(douglas);
dc.SubmitChanges();
```

Because the `Customer` "has" an address, the `Address` and the joining table that represents the "has-a" relationship come along for the ride.

When `ShowCustomersByFirstName("Douglas")` is called, you find every customer whose first name is Douglas and display the object:

```
private static void ShowCustomersByFirstName(string firstName)
{
    AdventureWorksDataContext dc = new AdventureWorksDataContext();
    var customers =
        from customer in dc.Customers
        where customer.FirstName == "Douglas"
        orderby customer.FirstName, customer.LastName
        select customer;

    Console.WriteLine("Customers whose first name is {0}:", firstName);
    foreach (Customer customer in customers)
        Console.WriteLine(customer);
}
```

The newly added `Customer` (complete with its address) is displayed appropriately:

```
Douglas Adams douglas0@adventureworks.com
  Main Office: 1c Sharp Way, Seattle
```

## Modifying a Customer Record

Modifying the customer involves finding the record you want to modify, retrieving it, modifying it as an object, and then storing it back in the database.

You retrieve Douglas Adams' record much as you saw earlier:

```
Customer dAdams = dc.Customers.Single(
    c => (c.FirstName == "Douglas" && c.LastName == "Adams"));
```

With the record in hand, you add a new shipping address, which requires creating an address record and a `CustomerAddress` record (to tie the new `Address` record to the existing `Customer` record):

```
Address addr = new Address();
addr.AddressLine1 = "1 Warehouse Place";
addr.City = "Los Angeles";
addr.PostalCode = "30210";
addr.StateProvince = "California";
addr.CountryRegion = "United States";
addr.ModifiedDate = DateTime.Today;
addr.rowguid = Guid.NewGuid();

CustomerAddress ca = new CustomerAddress();
ca.AddressType = "Shipping";
ca.Address = addr;
ca.Customer = dAdams;
ca.ModifiedDate = DateTime.Today;
ca.rowguid = Guid.NewGuid();
```

For a bit of sport, you also change his title, with all due respect, from blank to "Mr.":

```
dAdams.Title = "Mr.";
```

By using `Console.WriteLine` statements before and after the modification, you can see the changes:

```
Updating a customer...
Before:
 Douglas Adams douglas0@adventureworks.com
        Main Office: 1c Sharp Way, Seattle

After:
Mr. Douglas Adams douglas0@adventureworks.com
        Main Office: 1c Sharp Way, Seattle
        Shipping: 1 Warehouse Place, Los Angeles
```

You should also now see one record in the Customer table, and two each in the CustomerAddress and Address tables, as shown in Figure 15-9.

# Deleting Relational Data

Deleting a customer is a bit trickier than adding or modifying one, because the relational database is going to enforce referential integrity. That is, to avoid data inconsistency, the relational database (e.g., SQL Server) is going to ensure that the rows in CustomerAddress be deleted before the rows in Address or Customer are deleted. Ideally, in fact, you'd like the entire deletion of all the related rows, in all the related tables, to be within a transaction so that if any of the deletions fail, the entire set is "rolled back" to its initial state. That way, you don't end up with orphaned address records, or customers who have somehow lost data. (See the sidebar "Data Consistency" later in this chapter.)

The easiest way to do this is to ask the database to help you. After all, this is what databases do for a living. One solution they offer is stored procedures (they offer others,

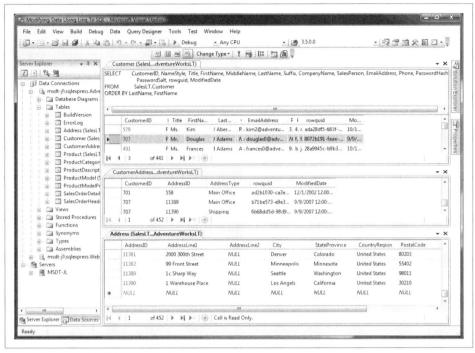

Figure 15-9. Modified data in the database

such as cascading deletes, etc.). To create a stored procedure, begin by right-clicking on the Stored Procedures file folder of your data connection and choose Add New Stored Procedure, as shown in Figure 15-10.

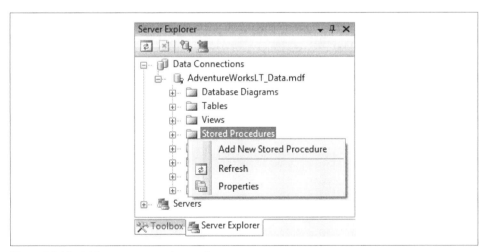

Figure 15-10. Adding a new stored procedure

Replace the code in the prototype stored procedure with that shown in Example 15-4. You don't need to fully understand the SQL at this point; you can trust that it will properly delete customers with the given first and last names and all related address records. With that said, I've added some comments (after a double dash) to help you along with what it is we're doing in the SPROC (geek speak for Stored PROCedure).

*Example 15-4. Stored procedure*

```
Create PROCEDURE [SalesLT].[DeleteCustomer]
    @firstName Name, -- parameters with their type
    @lastName   Name
AS
BEGIN
    SET NOCOUNT ON;      --- administrative stuff
    SET ANSI_NULLS ON
    SET QUOTED_IDENTIFIER ON
    declare @customerId   int;  -- local variable
    declare @addressId    int;
    declare addressCursor cursor for  -- keep track of where we're up to
            select  CustomerId, AddressId  -- find this record
              from  CustomerAddress   -- fromt this table
             where  CustomerId in   -- where this column is found in these results:
                   (
                       select  CustomerId - find this column
                         from  Customer  -- in this table
                        where  FirstName = @firstName   -- where this is true
                          and  LastName  = @lastName -- and this is also true
                   );

    begin transaction; -- start a transaction
    open addressCursor;  -- go get that cursor
      -- get the next record and put results into our variables
    fetch next from addressCursor into @customerId, @addressId;
       -- start a while loop
    while @@fetch_status = 0 begin
        -- delete the matching records
        delete CustomerAddress where customerId = @customerId
          and addressId =  @addressId
              --delete these matching records too
        delete Address where addressId = @addressId;
    loop
        fetch next from addressCursor into @customerId, @addressId;
    end;  -- end the while
    close addressCursor;  -- close the cursor
    deallocate addressCursor;  -- clean up the resource

    delete  Customer  -- delete where you have a match
     where  FirstName = @firstName
       and  LastName  = @lastName;

    commit;  -- once everything worked, commit it all
          -- (implicit - if anything fails, roll back to your starting point)
END
```

Open the Stored Procedures folder and locate your new stored procedure (DeleteCustomer). Next, double-click on *Adventureworks.dbml* in the Solution Explorer, which will reopen the designer.

Drag the new stored procedure onto the designer. It is now registered with the designer and will appear in the righthand window of the designer, as shown in Figure 15-11.

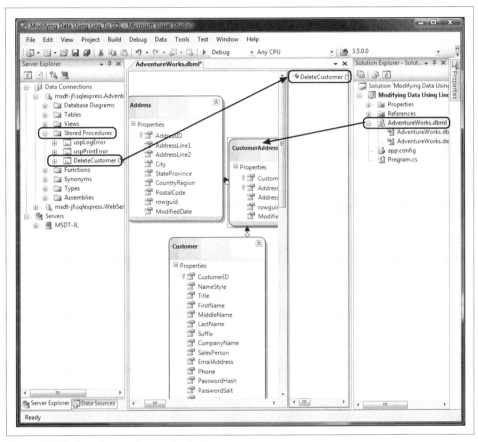

*Figure 15-11. Stored procedure in the designer*

You now have access to that stored procedure from within your DataContext, as shown in Example 15-5.

*Example 15-5. Calling stored procedures using LINQ to SQL: C# code*

```
private static void DeleteCustomer( )
{
    Console.WriteLine("Deleting a customer...");
    Console.Write("Before: ");
    ShowCustomersByFirstName("Douglas");

    AdventureWorksDataContext dc = new AdventureWorksDataContext( );
    // Uncomment the statement below to show the
    // SQL statement generated by LINQ to SQL.
    // dc.Log = Console.Out;

    dc.DeleteCustomer("Douglas", "Adams");
    Console.Write("After: ");
    ShowCustomersByFirstName("Douglas");
}
```

Output:

```
Deleting a customer...
Before: Customers whose first name is Douglas:
Mr. Douglas Adams douglas0@adventureworks.com
        Main Office: 1c Sharp Way, Seattle
        Shipping: 1 Warehouse Place, Los Angeles

Mr. Douglas Baldwin douglas1@adventure-works.com
        Main Office: Horizon Outlet Center, Holland

Mr. Douglas Groncki douglas2@adventure-works.com
        Main Office: 70259 West Sunnyview Ave, Visalia

After: Customers whose first name is Douglas:
Mr. Douglas Baldwin douglas1@adventure-works.com
        Main Office: Horizon Outlet Center, Holland

Mr. Douglas Groncki douglas2@adventure-works.com
        Main Office: 70259 West Sunnyview Ave, Visalia
```

The code is unchanged from the previous example, except for a new method (which you must call from Main( )), named DeleteCustomer( ). This method gets the AdventureWorksDataContext, but then just calls DeleteCustomer, passing in the two parameters of the first and last names. That's it!

Because DeleteCustomer is a stored procedure registered with the DataContext, the DataContext knows just what to do: it calls the stored procedure, and the Sproc does all the work. Wicked cool.

**Data Consistency**

One issue for database managers is that of data consistency. To understand how this works, you must first understand the concept of "normalization," which, among other things, implies that data is not unnecessarily duplicated in a relational database.

Thus, for example, if you have a database that tracks customers and their orders, rather than duplicate the information about each customer (the customer's name, address, phone, etc.) in each order, you would create a customer record and assign each customer a unique `CustomerID`. Each order would then contain a `CustomerID` that would identify the customer who "owns" that order.

This has many advantages, one of which is that if you change the customer's phone number, you need to change it only in the customer record, not in every order record.

The data would be inconsistent, however, if the `CustomerID` in an order did not refer to any customer at all (or worse, if it referred to the wrong customer!). To avoid this, database administers like databases that enforce consistency rules, such as that you cannot delete a customer record unless you've deleted all the orders for that customer first (thus, not leaving any "orphan" orders that have no associated customer) and never reusing a `CustomerID`.

# LINQ to XML

If you would like the output of your work to go to an XML document rather than to a SQL database, you have only to create a new XML element for each object in the Customers table, and a new XML attribute for each property representing a column in the table. To do this, you use the LINQ to XML API, as illustrated in Example 15-6.

Note carefully that this code takes advantage of the new LINQ to XML classes, such as XElement, XAttribute, and XDocument. Working with XAttributes, for example, is very similar to working with standard XML elements. However, note carefully that, for example, XAttributes are not nodes in an XML tree, but instead are name/value pairs associated with an actual XML element. This is also quite different from what you are used to in working with the DOM.

The XElement object represents an actual XML element and can be used to create elements. It interoperates cleanly with System.XML, and makes for a terrific transition class between LINQ to XML and XML itself.

Finally, the XDocument class derives from XContainer and has exactly one child node (you guessed it: an XElement). It can also have an XDeclaration, zero or more XProcessingInstructions, XComments, and one XDocumentType (for the DTD), but that is more detail than we need.

In the next example, we're going to create some XElements and assign some XAttributes. This should be very familiar to anyone comfortable with XML and a relatively easy first glimpse for those who are totally new to raw XML (see Chapter 14).

*Example 15-6. Constructing an XML document using LINQ to XML*

```
using System;
using System.Data.Linq;
using System.Linq;
using System.Xml.Linq;

namespace LinqToXML
{
    // Main program
    public class Tester
    {
        static void Main()
        {
            XElement customerXml = CreateCustomerListXml();
            Console.WriteLine(customerXml);
        }

        /// <summary>
        /// Create an XML document containing a list of customers.
        /// </summary>
        /// <returns>XML document containing a list of customers.</returns>
        private static XElement CreateCustomerListXml()
        {
            AdventureWorksDataContext dc = new AdventureWorksDataContext();
            // Uncomment the statement below to show the
            // SQL statement generated by LINQ to SQL.
            // dc.Log = Console.Out;

            // Find a list of customer records.
            var customerDs =
                from customer in dc.Customers
                where customer.FirstName.StartsWith("D")
                orderby customer.FirstName, customer.LastName
                select customer;

            XElement customerXml = new XElement("Customers");
            foreach (Customer customer in customerDs)
            {
                customerXml.Add(new XElement("Customer",
                    new XAttribute("FirstName", customer.FirstName),
                    new XAttribute("LastName", customer.LastName),
                    new XElement("EmailAddress", customer.EmailAddress)));
            }
            return customerXml;
        }
    }
}
```

In this example, rather than simply writing out the values of the CustomerDS that we've retrieved from the database, we convert the object to an XML file by using the LINQ to XML API. It is so straightforward as to be almost startling.

Let's take this example apart. We begin by calling CreateCustomerListXml and assigning the results to an XElement named customerXml. CreateCustomerListXml begins by creating a LINQ statement (those of us who grew up with SQL will take a few years to get used to having the select statement come at the end!):

```
var customerDs =
    from customer in dc.Customers
    where customer.FirstName.StartsWith("D")
    orderby customer.FirstName, customer.LastName
    select customer;
```

Let me remind you that even though we use the keyword var here, which in JavaScript is not type-safe, in C#, this is entirely type-safe; the compiler imputes the type based on the query.

Next, we create an XElement named customerXml:

```
XElement customerXml = new XElement("Customers");
```

Here's another potentially confusing aspect. We've given the C# XElement an identifier, customerXml, so that we can refer to it in C# code, but when we instantiated the XElement, we passed a name to the constructor (Customers). It is that name (Customers) that will appear in the XML file.

Next, we iterate through the CustomerDS collection that we retrieved earlier, pulling out each Customer object in turn, and create a new XElement based on the Customer object, adding an XAttribute for the FirstName, LastName, and EmailAddress "columns":

```
foreach (Customer customer in customerDs)
{
    XElement cust = new XElement("Customer",
        new XAttribute("FirstName", customer.FirstName),
        new XAttribute("LastName", customer.LastName),
        new XElement("EmailAddress", customer.EmailAddress));
```

As we iterate through each customer, we also iterate through each customer's associated CustomerAddress collection (customer.Addresses). These return an object of type Customer.Address, and we add to the XElement cust the Attributes for the Address, beginning with a new XElement named Address. This gives our Customer element a subelement of Addresses, with attributes for AddressLine1, AddressLine2, City, and so on.

Thus, a single Address object in the XML will look like this:

```
<Customer FirstName="Dora" LastName="Verdad">
  <EmailAddress>dora0@adventure-works.com</EmailAddress>
  <Address AddressLine1="Suite 2502 410 Albert Street" AddressLine2=""
    City="Waterloo" StateProvince="Ontario" PostalCode="N2V" />
</Customer>
```

Finally, we want each of these `Customer` elements (with their child `Address` elements) to be child elements of the `Customers` (plural) element that we created earlier. We accomplish this by opening the C# object and adding the new customer to the element after each iteration of the loop:

```
customerXml.Add(cust);
```

Notice that because we're doing this in the C#, we access the `Element` through its C# identifier, not through its XML identifier. In the resulting XML document, the name of the outer element will be `Customers` and within `Customers` will be a series of `Customer` elements, each of which will contain `Address` elements:

```
<Customers>
  <Customer ...
    <Address ....     </Address>
    <EmailAddress ...  /EmailAddress/>
  </Customer>
  <Customer ...
    <Address ....     </Address>
    <EmailAddress ...  /EmailAddress/>
  </Customer>
</Customers>
```

Once we've iterated through the lot, we return the `customerXml` (the `Customers` element) which contains all the `Customer` elements, which in turn contain all the address elements; that is, the entire tree:

```
return customerXml;
```

Piece of pie; easy as cake.

Here is an excerpt from the complete output (slightly reformatted to fit the page):

```
<Customers>
  <Customer FirstName="Daniel" LastName="Blanco">
    <EmailAddress>daniel0@adventure-works.com</EmailAddress>
    <Address AddressLine1="Suite 800 2530 Slater Street"
        AddressLine2="" City="Ottawa"
    StateProvince="Ontario" PostalCode="K4B 1T7" />
  </Customer>
  <Customer FirstName="Daniel" LastName="Thompson">
    <EmailAddress>daniel2@adventure-works.com</EmailAddress>
    <Address AddressLine1="755 Nw Grandstand" AddressLine2="" City="Issaquah"
      StateProvince="Washington" PostalCode="98027" />
  </Customer>
  <Customer FirstName="Danielle" LastName="Johnson">
    <EmailAddress>danielle1@adventure-works.com</EmailAddress>
    <Address AddressLine1="955 Green Valley Crescent" AddressLine2=""
      City="Ottawa" StateProvince="Ontario" PostalCode="K4B 1S1" />
  </Customer>
  <Customer FirstName="Darrell" LastName="Banks">
    <EmailAddress>darrell0@adventure-works.com</EmailAddress>
    <Address AddressLine1="Norwalk Square" AddressLine2=""
      City="Norwalk" StateProvince="California" PostalCode="90650" />
```

```
    </Customer>
    <Customer FirstName="Darren" LastName="Gehring">
      <EmailAddress>darren0@adventure-works.com</EmailAddress>
      <Address AddressLine1="509 Nafta Boulevard" AddressLine2=""
          City="Laredo" StateProvince="Texas" PostalCode="78040" />
    </Customer>
    <Customer FirstName="David" LastName="Givens">
      <EmailAddress>david15@adventure-works.com</EmailAddress>
      <Address AddressLine1="#500-75 O'Connor Street" AddressLine2=""
          City="Ottawa" StateProvince="Ontario" PostalCode="K4B 1S2" />
    </Customer>
</Customers>
```

# CHAPTER 16

# ADO.NET and Relational Databases

If you are working with a relational database, you have the option of accessing your data with LINQ, with LINQ and ADO.NET, or directly with ADO.NET. ADO.NET was designed to provide a *disconnected* data architecture (as database connections are typically considered "precious resources"), though it does have a connected alternative.

In a disconnected architecture, data is retrieved from a database and cached on your local machine. You manipulate the data on your local computer and connect to the database only when you wish to alter records or acquire new data.

There are significant advantages to disconnecting your data architecture from your database. The biggest advantage is that your application, whether running on the Web or on a local machine, will create a reduced burden on the database server, which may help your application to scale well. Database connections are resource-intensive, and it is difficult to have thousands (or hundreds of thousands) of simultaneous continuous connections. A disconnected architecture is resource-frugal, though there are times that all you want to do is connect to the database, suck out a stream of data, and disconnect; and ADO.NET has a Reader class that allows for that as well.

ADO.NET typically connects to the database to retrieve data, and connects again to update data when you've made changes. Most applications spend most of their time simply reading through data and displaying it; ADO.NET provides a disconnected subset of the data for your use while reading and displaying, but it is up to you as the developer to keep in mind that the data in the database may change while you are disconnected, and to plan accordingly. I cover this in some detail later in this chapter.

## Relational Databases and SQL

Although one can certainly write an entire book on relational databases, and another on SQL, the essentials of these technologies aren't hard to understand. A *database* is a repository of data. A *relational database* organizes your data into tables. Consider the Northwind database.

Microsoft provides the Northwind database as a free download on Microsoft.com (just search on "Northwind database"; the first link should take you to the download page), or you can download the file (*SQL200SampleDb.msi*) from my site (*http://www.JesseLiberty.com*) by clicking on Books, then again on Books, and then scrolling down to *this* book and clicking on Northwind Database. Unzip the file, and double-click on the *.msi* file to install it.

## Tables, Records, and Columns

The Northwind database describes a fictional company buying and selling food products. The data for Northwind is divided into 13 tables, including Customers, Employees, Orders, Order Details, Products, and so forth.

Every table in a relational database is organized into rows, where each row represents a single record. The rows are organized into columns. All the rows in a table have the same column structure. For example, the Orders table has these columns: OrderID, CustomerID, EmployeeID, OrderDate, and so on.

For any given order, you need to know the customer's name, address, contact name, and so forth. You could store that information with each order, but that would be very inefficient. Instead, you use a second table called Customers, in which each row represents a single customer. In the Customers table is a column for the CustomerID. Each customer has a unique ID, and that field is marked as the *primary key* for that table. A primary key is the column or combination of columns that uniquely identifies a record in a given table.

---

### For VB 6 Programmers Moving to ADO.NET

ADO.NET is somewhat different from ADO. While learning how to implement the new functionality found in ADO.NET, you are probably going to keep asking yourself such questions as "Where is the MoveNext( ) method?" and "How do I test for the end-of-file?"

In ADO.NET, the functionality that was in Record Sets now resides in two places. Navigation and retrieval are in the IDataReader interface, and support for disconnected operation is in the (tremendously more powerful) DataSet and DataTables.

You can think of DataTables as an array of DataRows. Calling the MoveFirst( ) method in ADO.NET would be the same as going to the first index of the array. Testing for the end-of-file is the same as testing whether the current index matches the array's upper bound. Want to set a bookmark for a particular record? Just create a variable and assign it the index of the current record—you don't need a special BookMark property.

---

The Orders table uses the CustomerID as a *foreign key*. A foreign key is a column (or combination of columns) that is a primary (or otherwise unique) key from a different table. The Orders table uses the CustomerID (the primary key used in the Customers table) to identify which customer has placed the order. To determine the address for the order, you can use the CustomerID to look up the customer record in the Customers table.

This use of foreign keys is particularly helpful in representing one-to-many or many-to-one relationships between tables. By separating information into tables that are linked by foreign keys, you avoid having to repeat information in records. A single customer, for example, can have multiple orders, but it is inefficient to place the same customer information (name, phone number, credit limit, etc.) in every order record. The process of removing redundant information from your records and shifting it to separate tables is called *normalization*.

## Normalization

Normalization not only makes your use of the database more efficient, but it also reduces the likelihood of data corruption. If you kept the customer's name in both the Customers table and the Orders table, you would run the risk that a change in one table might not be reflected in the other. Thus, if you changed the customer's address in the Customers table, that change might not be reflected in every row in the Orders table (and a lot of work would be necessary to make sure that it was reflected). By keeping only the CustomerID in Orders, you are free to change the address in Customers, and the change is automatically reflected for each order.

Just as C# programmers want the compiler to catch bugs at compile time rather than at runtime, database programmers want the database to help them avoid data corruption. The compiler helps avoid bugs in C# by enforcing the rules of the language (e.g., you can't use a variable you've not defined). SQL Server and other modern relational databases avoid bugs by enforcing constraints that you request. For example, the Customers database marks the CustomerID as a primary key. This creates a primary key constraint in the database, which ensures that each CustomerID is unique. If you were to enter a customer named Liberty Associates, Inc., with the CustomerID of LIBE, and then tried to add Liberty Mutual Funds with a CustomerID of LIBE, the database would reject the second record because of the primary key constraint.

## Declarative Referential Integrity

Relational databases use *declarative referential integrity* (DRI) to establish constraints on the relationships among the various tables. For example, you might declare a constraint on the Orders table that dictates that no order can have a CustomerID unless that CustomerID represents a valid record in Customers. This helps avoid two types of mistakes. First, you can't enter a record with an invalid

CustomerID. Second, you can't delete a customer record if that CustomerID is used in any order. The integrity of your data and its relationships is thus protected.

## SQL

The most popular language for querying and manipulating databases is Structured Query Language (SQL), usually pronounced "sequel." SQL is a declarative language, as opposed to a procedural language, and it can take awhile to get used to working with a declarative language when you are used to languages such as C#.

The heart of SQL is the *query*. A query is a statement that returns a set of records from the database. The queries in Transact-SQL (the version used by SQL Server) are very similar to the queries used in LINQ, though the actual syntax is slightly different.

For example, you might like to see all the CompanyNames and CustomerIDs of every record in the Customers table in which the customer's address is in London. To do so, write:

```
Select CustomerID, CompanyName from Customers where city = 'London'
```

This returns the following six records as output:

```
CustomerID CompanyName
---------- ---------------------------------------
AROUT      Around the Horn
BSBEV      B's Beverages
CONSH      Consolidated Holdings
EASTC      Eastern Connection
NORTS      North/South
SEVES      Seven Seas Imports
```

SQL is capable of much more powerful queries. For example, suppose the Northwind manager would like to know what products were purchased in July 1996 by the customer "Vins et alcools Chevalier." This turns out to be somewhat complicated. The Order Details table knows the ProductID for all the products in any given order. The Orders table knows which CustomerIDs are associated with an order. The Customers table knows the CustomerID for a customer, and the Products table knows the product name for the ProductID. How do you tie all this together? Here's the query:

```
select o.OrderID, productName
from [Order Details] od
join orders o on o.OrderID = od.OrderID
join products p on p.ProductID = od.ProductID
join customers c on o.CustomerID = c.CustomerID
where c.CompanyName = 'Vins et alcools Chevalier'
and orderDate >= '7/1/1996' and orderDate <= '7/31/1996'
```

This asks the database to get the OrderID and the product name from the relevant tables. First, look at Order Details (which we've called od for short), and then join that with the Orders table for every record in which the OrderID in the Order Details table is the same as the OrderID in the Orders table.

When you join two tables, you can say, "Get every record that exists in either table" (this is called an *outer join*), or, as we've done here, "Get only those records that exist in both tables" (called an *inner join*). That is, an inner join states to get only the records in Orders that match the records in Order Details by having the same value in the OrderID field (on o.Orderid = od.Orderid).

 SQL joins are inner joins by default. Writing join orders is the same as writing inner join orders.

The SQL statement goes on to ask the database to create an inner join with Products, getting every row in which the ProductID in the Products table is the same as the ProductID in the Order Details table.

Then, create an inner join with customers for those rows where the CustomerID is the same in both the Orders table and the Customers table.

Finally, tell the database to constrain the results to only those rows in which the CompanyName is the one you want, and the dates are in July.

The collection of constraints finds only three records that match:

```
OrderID ProductName
----------- ----------------------------------------
10248 Queso Cabrales
10248 Singaporean Hokkien Fried Mee
10248 Mozzarella di Giovanni
```

This output shows that there was only one order (10248) in which the customer had the right ID and in which the date of the order was July 1996. That order produced three records in the Order Details table, and using the product IDs in these three records, you got the product names from the Products table.

You can use SQL not only for searching for and retrieving data, but also for creating, updating, and deleting tables, and generally managing and manipulating both the content and the structure of the database.

# The ADO.NET Object Model

The ADO.NET object model is rich, but at its heart it is a fairly straightforward set of classes. The most important of these is the DataSet. The DataSet represents a subset of the entire database, cached on your machine without a continuous connection to the database.

Periodically, you'll reconnect the DataSet to its parent database, update the database with changes you've made to the DataSet, and update the DataSet with changes in the database made by other processes.

This is highly efficient, but to be effective, the DataSet must be a robust subset of the database, capturing not just a few rows from a single table, but also a set of tables with all the metadata necessary to represent the relationships and constraints of the original database. This is, not surprisingly, what ADO.NET provides.

The DataSet is composed of DataTable objects as well as DataRelation objects. These are accessed as properties of the DataSet object. The Tables property returns a DataTableCollection, which in turn contains all the DataTable objects.

## DataTables and DataColumns

The DataTable can be created programmatically or as a result of a query against the database. The DataTable has a number of public properties, including the Columns collection, which returns the DataColumnCollection object, which in turn consists of DataColumn objects. Each DataColumn object represents a column in a table.

## DataRelations

In addition to the Tables collection, the DataSet has a Relations property, which returns a DataRelationCollection consisting of DataRelation objects. Each DataRelation represents a relationship between two tables through DataColumn objects. For example, in the Northwind database, the Customers table is in a relationship with the Orders table through the CustomerID column.

The nature of this relationship is one-to-many, or parent-to-child. For any given order, there will be exactly one customer, but any given customer might be represented in any number of orders.

## Rows

DataTable's Rows collection returns a set of rows for that table. Use this collection to examine the results of queries against the database, iterating through the rows to examine each record in turn. Programmers experienced with ADO are often confused by the absence of the RecordSet with its moveNext and movePrevious commands. With ADO.NET, you don't iterate through the DataSet; instead, you access the table you need, and then you can iterate through the Rows collection, typically with a foreach loop. You'll see this in the example in this chapter.

## Data Adapter

The DataSet is an abstraction of a relational database. ADO.NET uses a DataAdapter as a bridge between the DataSet and the data source, which is the underlying database. DataAdapter provides the Fill( ) method to retrieve data from the database and populate the DataSet.

Instead of tying the DataSet object too closely to your database architecture, ADO.NET uses a DataAdapter object to mediate between the DataSet object and the database. This decouples the DataSet from the database and allows a single DataSet to represent more than one database or other data source.

## DBCommand and DBConnection

The DBConnection object represents a connection to a data source. This connection can be shared among different command objects. The DBCommand object allows you to send a command (typically, a SQL statement or a stored procedure) to the database. Often, these objects are implicitly created when you create a DataAdapter, but you can explicitly access these objects; for example, you can declare a connection as follows:

```
string connectionString = "server=.\\sqlexpress;" +
"Trusted_Connection=yes; database=Northwind";
```

You can then use this connection string to create a connection object or to create a DataAdapter object.

## DataReader

An alternative to creating a DataSet (and DataAdapter) is to create a DataReader. The DataReader provides connected, forward-only, read-only access to a collection of tables by executing either a SQL statement or stored procedures. DataReaders are lightweight objects that are ideally suited for filling controls with data and then breaking the connection to the backend database.

# Getting Started with ADO.NET

Enough theory! Let's write some code and see how this works. Working with ADO. NET can be complex, but for many queries, the model is surprisingly simple.

In this example, we'll create a console application, and we'll list out bits of information from the Customers table in the Northwind database.

Begin by creating a (SQL Server-specific) DataAdapter object:

```
SqlDataAdapter DataAdapter =
new SqlDataAdapter(
commandString, connectionString);
```

The two parameters are commandString and connectionString. The commandString is the SQL statement that will generate the data you want in your DataSet:

```
string commandString =
  "Select CompanyName, ContactName from Customers";
```

The connectionString is whatever string is needed to connect to the database. Typically, this will be SQL Server Express, which is installed with Visual Studio.

With the DataAdapter in hand, you're ready to create the DataSet and fill it with the data that you obtain from the SQL select statement:

```
DataSet DataSet = new DataSet();
DataAdapter.Fill(DataSet,"Customers");
```

That's it. You now have a DataSet, and you can query, manipulate, and otherwise manage the data. The DataSet has a collection of tables; you care only about the first one because you've retrieved only a single table:

```
DataTable dataTable = DataSet.Tables[0];
```

You can extract the rows you've retrieved with the SQL statement and add the data to the listbox:

```
foreach (DataRow dataRow in dataTable.Rows)
{
    lbCustomers.Items.Add(
    dataRow["CompanyName"] +
    " (" + dataRow["ContactName"] + ")" );
}
```

The listbox is filled with the company name and contact name from the table in the database, according to the SQL statement we passed in. Example 16-1 contains the complete source code for this example.

*Example 16-1. Working with ADO.NET*

```
using System;
using System.Data;
using System.Data.SqlClient;

namespace Working_With_ADO.NET
{
    class Program
    {
        static void Main(string[] args)
        {
            string connectionString = "server=.\\sqlexpress;" +
            "Trusted_Connection=yes; database=Northwind";

            // get records from the Customers table
            string commandString =
            "Select CompanyName, ContactName from Customers";

            // create the data set command object
            // and the DataSet
            SqlDataAdapter DataAdapter =
            new SqlDataAdapter(
            commandString, connectionString);

            DataSet DataSet = new DataSet();
```

*Example 16-1. Working with ADO.NET (continued)*

```
            // fill the DataSet object
            DataAdapter.Fill(DataSet, "Customers");

            // Get the one table from the DataSet
            DataTable dataTable = DataSet.Tables[0];

            // for each row in the table, display the info
            foreach (DataRow dataRow in dataTable.Rows)
            {
                Console.WriteLine("CompanyName: {0}. Contact: {1}",
dataRow["CompanyName"],
                    dataRow["ContactName"]);
            }
        }
    }
}
```

```
Output (partial)
CompanyName: Centro comercial Moctezuma. Contact: Francisco Chang
CompanyName: Chop-suey Chinese. Contact: Yang Wang
CompanyName: Comércio Mineiro. Contact: Pedro Afonso
CompanyName: Consolidated Holdings. Contact: Elizabeth Brown
CompanyName: Drachenblut Delikatessen. Contact: Sven Ottlieb
CompanyName: Du monde entier. Contact: Janine Labrune
CompanyName: Eastern Connection. Contact: Ann Devon
CompanyName: Ernst Handel. Contact: Roland Mendel
CompanyName: Familia Arquibaldo. Contact: Aria Cruz
CompanyName: FISSA Fabrica Inter. Salchichas S.A.. Contact: Diego Roel
CompanyName: Folies gourmandes. Contact: Martine Rancé
CompanyName: Folk och fä HB. Contact: Maria Larsson
CompanyName: Frankenversand. Contact: Peter Franken
CompanyName: France restauration. Contact: Carine Schmitt
CompanyName: Franchi S.p.A.. Contact: Paolo Accorti
CompanyName: Furia Bacalhau e Frutos do Mar. Contact: Lino Rodriguez
CompanyName: Galería del gastrónomo. Contact: Eduardo Saavedra
CompanyName: Godos Cocina Típica. Contact: José Pedro Freyre
CompanyName: Gourmet Lanchonetes. Contact: André Fonseca
CompanyName: Great Lakes Food Market. Contact: Howard Snyder
CompanyName: GROSELLA-Restaurante. Contact: Manuel Pereira
CompanyName: Hanari Carnes. Contact: Mario Pontes
CompanyName: HILARION-Abastos. Contact: Carlos Hernández
CompanyName: Hungry Coyote Import Store. Contact: Yoshi Latimer
CompanyName: Hungry Owl All-Night Grocers. Contact: Patricia McKenna
CompanyName: Island Trading. Contact: Helen Bennett
CompanyName: Königlich Essen. Contact: Philip Cramer
CompanyName: La corne d'abondance. Contact: Daniel Tonini
CompanyName: La maison d'Asie. Contact: Annette Roulet
CompanyName: Laughing Bacchus Wine Cellars. Contact: Yoshi Tannamuri
CompanyName: Lazy K Kountry Store. Contact: John Steel
```

With just a few lines of code, you have extracted a set of data from the database and displayed it. This code will:

- Create the string for the connection:

```
string connectionString = "server=.\\sqlexpress;" +
"Trusted_Connection=yes; database=northwind";
```

- Create the string for the select statement:

```
string commandString =
"Select CompanyName, ContactName from Customers";
```

- Create the DataAdapter and pass in the select and connection strings:

```
SqlDataAdapter DataAdapter =
new SqlDataAdapter(
commandString, connectionString);
```

- Create a new DataSet object:

```
DataSet DataSet = new DataSet();
```

- Fill the DataSet from the Customers table using the DataAdapter:

```
DataAdapter.Fill(DataSet,"Customers");
```

- Extract the DataTable from the DataSet:

```
DataTable dataTable = DataSet.Tables[0];
```

- Use the DataTable to fill the listbox:

```
foreach (DataRow dataRow in dataTable.Rows)
{
 lbCustomers.Items.Add(
 dataRow["CompanyName"] +
 " (" + dataRow["ContactName"] + ")" );
}
```

# PART III

# Programming with C#

Chapter 17, *Programming ASP.NET Applications*

Chapter 18, *Programming WPF Applications*

Chapter 19, *Programming Windows Forms Applications*

# Programming ASP.NET Applications

Developers are writing more and more of their applications to run over the Web and to be seen in a browser. The most popular technology for doing so is ASP.NET, and with AJAX (and now Silverlight), much of the application can be run client-side.

There are many obvious advantages to web-based applications. For one, you don't have to create as much of the user interface; you can let Internet Explorer and other browsers handle a lot of the work for you. Another advantage is that distribution of the application and of revisions is often faster, easier, and less expensive. Most important, a web application can be run on any platform by any user at any location, which is harder to do (though not impossible) with smart-client applications.

Another advantage of web applications is distributed processing (though smart-client applications are making inroads). With a web-based application, it is easy to provide server-side processing, and the Web provides standardized protocols (e.g., HTTP, HTML, and XML) to facilitate building *n*-tier applications.

The focus of this chapter is where ASP.NET and C# programming intersect: the creation of Web Forms and their event handlers. For intensive coverage of ASP.NET, please see either *Programming ASP.NET* by myself and Dan Hurwitz or *Learning ASP.NET 2.0 with AJAX* by Jesse Liberty et al. (both published by O'Reilly).

## Web Forms Fundamentals

Web Forms bring Rapid Application Development (RAD) to the creation of web applications. From within Visual Studio or Visual Web Developer, you drag-and-drop controls onto a form and write the supporting code in *code-behind* pages. The application is deployed to a web server (typically IIS, which is shipped with most versions of Windows, and Cassini, which is built into Visual Studio for testing your application), and users interact with the application through a standard browser.

Web Forms implement a programming model in which web pages are dynamically generated on a web server for delivery to a browser over the Internet. With Web Forms, you create an ASPX page with more or less static content consisting of HTML and web controls, as well as AJAX and Silverlight, and you write C# code to add additional dynamic content. The C# code *runs on the server* for the standard ASPX event handlers and on the client for the Silverlight event handlers (JavaScript is used for standard AJAX event handlers), and the data produced is integrated with the declared objects on your page to create an HTML page that is sent to the browser.

You should pick up the following three critical points from the preceding paragraph and keep them in mind for this entire chapter:

- Web pages can have both HTML and web controls (described later).
- Processing may be done on the server or on the client, in managed code or in unmanaged code, or via a combination.
- Typical ASP.NET controls produce standard HTML for the browser.

Web Forms divide the user interface into two parts: the visual part or user interface (UI), and the logic that lies behind it. This is called *code separation*; and it is a good thing.

 From version 2.0 of ASP.NET, Visual Studio takes advantage of partial classes, allowing the code-separation page to be far simpler than it was in version 1.*x*. Because the code-separation and declarative pages are part of the same class, there is no longer a need to have protected variables to reference the controls of the page, and the designer can hide its initialization code in a separate file.

The UI page for ASP.NET pages is stored in a file with the extension *.aspx*. When you run the form, the server generates HTML sent to the client browser. This code uses the rich Web Forms types found in the System.Web and System.Web.UI namespaces of the .NET FCL, and the System.Web.Extension namespace in Microsoft ASP.NET AJAX.

With Visual Studio, Web Forms programming couldn't be simpler: open a form, drag some controls onto it, and write the code to handle events. Presto! You've written a web application.

On the other hand, even with Visual Studio, writing a robust and complete web application can be a daunting task. Web Forms offer a very rich UI; the number and complexity of web controls have greatly multiplied in recent years, and user expectations about the look and feel of web applications have risen accordingly.

In addition, web applications are inherently distributed. Typically, the client will not be in the same building as the server. For most web applications, you must take network latency, bandwidth, and network server performance into account when creating the UI; a round trip from client to host might take a few seconds.

 To simplify this discussion, and to keep the focus on C#, we'll ignore client-side processing for the rest of this chapter, and focus on server-side ASP.NET controls.

# Web Forms Events

Web Forms are event-driven. An *event* represents the idea that "something happened" (see Chapter 12 for a full discussion of events).

An event is generated (or *raised*) when the user clicks a button, or selects from a list-box, or otherwise interacts with the UI. Events can also be generated by the system starting or finishing work. For example, if you open a file for reading, the system raises an event when the file has been read into memory.

The method that responds to the event is called the *event handler*. Event handlers are written in C#, and are associated with controls in the HTML page through control attributes.

By convention, ASP.NET event handlers return void and take two parameters. The first parameter represents the object raising the event. The second, called the *event argument*, contains information specific to the event, if any. For most events, the event argument is of type EventArgs, which doesn't expose any properties. For some controls, the event argument might be of a type derived from EventArgs that can expose properties specific to that event type.

In web applications, most events are typically handled on the server and, therefore, require a round trip. ASP.NET supports only a limited set of events, such as button clicks and text changes. These are events that the user might expect to cause a significant change, as opposed to Windows events (such as mouse-over) that might happen many times during a single user-driven task.

## Postback versus nonpostback events

*Postback* events are those that cause the form to be posted back to the server immediately. These include click-type events, such as the button Click event. In contrast, many events (typically change events) are considered *nonpostback* in that the form isn't posted back to the server immediately. Instead, the control caches these events until the next time a postback event occurs.

 You can force controls with nonpostback events to behave in a postback manner by setting their AutoPostBack property to true.

## State

A web application's *state* is the current value of all the controls and variables for the current user in the current session. The Web is inherently a "stateless" environment. This means that every post to the server loses the state from previous posts, unless the developer takes great pains to preserve this session knowledge. ASP.NET, however, provides support for maintaining the state of a user's session.

Whenever a page is posted to the server, the server re-creates it from scratch before it is returned to the browser. ASP.NET provides a mechanism that automatically maintains state for server controls (ViewState) independent of the HTTP session. Thus, if you provide a list, and the user has made a selection, that selection is preserved after the page is posted back to the server and redrawn on the client.

 The HTTP session maintains the illusion of a connection between the user and the web application, despite the fact that the Web is a stateless, connectionless environment.

# Web Forms Life Cycle

Every request for a page made to a web server causes a chain of events at the server. These events, from beginning to end, constitute the *life cycle* of the page and all its components. The life cycle begins with a request for the page, which causes the server to load it. When the request is complete, the page is unloaded. From one end of the life cycle to the other, the goal is to render appropriate HTML output back to the requesting browser. The life cycle of a page is marked by the following events, each of which you can handle yourself or leave to default handling by the ASP.NET server:

*Initialize*
> Initialize is the first phase in the life cycle for any page or control. It is here that any settings needed for the duration of the incoming request are initialized.

*Load* ViewState
> The ViewState property of the control is populated. The ViewState information comes from a hidden variable on the control, used to persist the state across round trips to the server. The input string from this hidden variable is parsed by the page framework, and the ViewState property is set. You can modify this via the LoadViewState( ) method. This allows ASP.NET to manage the state of your control across page loads so that each control isn't reset to its default state each time the page is posted.

*Process Postback Data*
> During this phase, the data sent to the server in the posting is processed. If any of this data results in a requirement to update the ViewState, that update is performed via the LoadPostData( ) method.

*Load*

> CreateChildControls() is called, if necessary, to create and initialize server controls in the control tree. State is restored, and the form controls contain client-side data. You can modify the load phase by handling the Load event with the OnLoad() method.

*Send Postback Change Modifications*

> If there are any state changes between the current state and the previous state, change events are raised via the RaisePostDataChangedEvent() method.

*Handle Postback Events*

> The client-side event that caused the postback is handled.

*PreRender*

> This is your last chance to modify the output prior to rendering, using the OnPreRender() method.

*Save State*

> Near the beginning of the life cycle, the persisted view state was loaded from the hidden variable. Now it is saved back to the hidden variable, persisting as a string object that will complete the round trip to the client. You can override this using the SaveViewState() method.

*Render*

> This is where the output to be sent back to the client browser is generated. You can override it using the Render method. CreateChildControls() is called, if necessary, to create and initialize server controls in the control tree.

*Dispose*

> This is the last phase of the life cycle. It gives you an opportunity to do any final cleanup and release references to any expensive resources, such as database connections. You can modify it using the Dispose() method.

# Creating a Web Form

To create the simple Web Form that we will use in the next example, start up Visual Studio .NET and select File → New Web Site. In the New Web Site dialog, choose ASP.NET Web Site from the templates, File System for the location (you can also create web sites remotely using HTTP or FTP), and Visual C# as your language. Give your web site a location and a name and choose your .NET Framework, as shown in Figure 17-1.

Visual Studio creates a folder named *ProgrammingCSharpWeb* in the directory you've indicated, and within that directory it creates your *Default.aspx* page (for the user interface), *Default.aspx.cs* file (for your code), *web.config* file (for web site configuration settings), and an *App_Data* directory (currently empty but often used to hold *.mdb* files or other data-specific files).

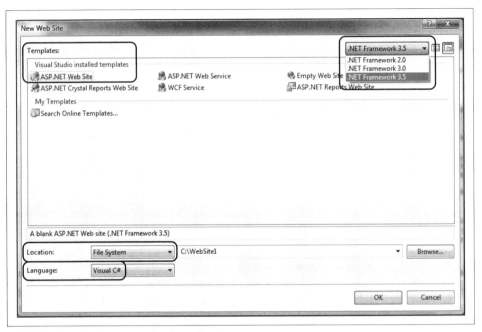

Figure 17-1. Creating your new web application

 Although Visual Studio no longer uses projects for web applications, it does keep solution files to allow you to quickly return to a web site or desktop application you've been developing. The solution files are kept in a directory you can designate through the Tools → Options window, as shown in Figure 17-2.

## Code-Behind Files

Let's take a closer look at the *.aspx* and code-behind files that Visual Studio creates. Start by renaming *Default.aspx* to *HelloWeb.aspx*. To do this, close *Default.aspx* and then right-click its name in the Solution Explorer. Choose Rename, and enter the name **HelloWeb.aspx**. That renames the file, but not the class. To rename the class, right-click the *.aspx* page, choose View Code in the code page, and then rename the class **HelloWeb_aspx**. You'll see a small line next to the name. Click it, and you'll open the smart tag that allows you to rename the class. Click "Rename '_Default' to 'HelloWeb_aspx'" and Visual Studio ensures that every occurrence of Default_aspx is replaced with its real name, as shown in Figure 17-3.

Within the HTML view of *HelloWeb.aspx*, you see that a form has been specified in the body of the page using the standard HTML form tag:

```
<form id="form1" runat="server">
```

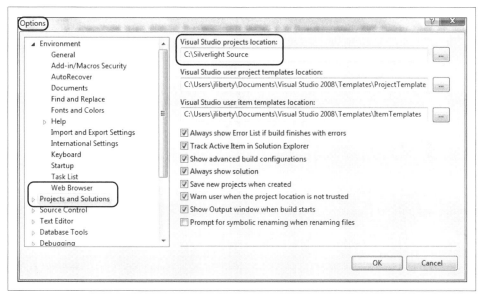

*Figure 17-2. Project location options*

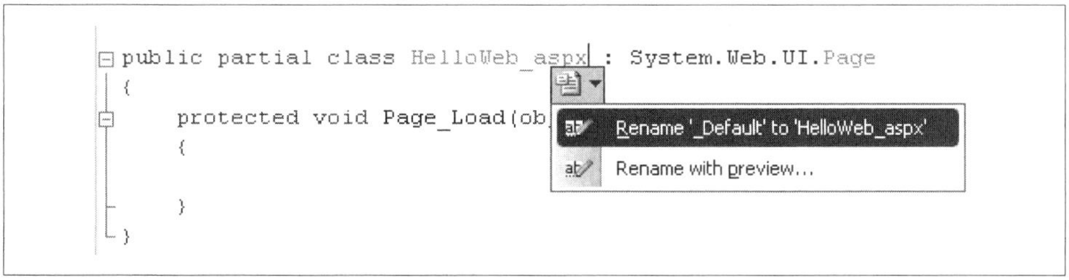

*Figure 17-3. Renaming the class*

Web Forms assume that you need at least one form to manage the user interaction, and it creates one when you open a project. The attribute runat="server" is the key to the server-side magic. Any tag that includes this attribute is considered a server-side control to be executed by the ASP.NET Framework on the server. Within the form, Visual Studio has opened div tags to facilitate placing your controls and text.

Having created an empty Web Form, the first thing you might want to do is add some text to the page. By switching to the Source view, you can add script and HTML directly to the file just as you could with classic ASP. Adding to the body segment of the *.aspx* page the highlighted line in the following code snippet:

```
<%@ Page Language="C#" AutoEventWireup="true"  CodeFile="HelloWeb.aspx.cs"
Inherits="HelloWeb_aspx" %>

<!DOCTYPE html PUBLIC "-//W3C//DTD XHTML 1.0 Transitional//EN"
"http://www.w3.org/TR/xhtml1/DTD/xhtml1-transitional.dtd">
```

```
<html xmlns="http://www.w3.org/1999/xhtml">
<head runat="server">
    <title>Hello Web Page</title>
</head>
<body>
    <form id="form1" runat="server">
    Hello World! It is now <% = DateTime.Now.ToString( ) %>
    <div>

    </div>
    </form>
</body>
</html>
```

will cause it to display a greeting and the current local time:

```
Hello World! It is now 9/9/2009 5:24:16 PM
```

The <% and %> marks work just as they did in classic ASP, indicating that code falls between them (in this case, C#). The = sign immediately following the opening tag causes ASP.NET to display the value, just like a call to Response.Write( ). You could just as easily write the line as:

```
Hello World! It is now
<% Response.Write(DateTime.Now.ToString( )); %>
```

Run the page by pressing F5.

---

### Enabling Debugging

When you press F5, you begin the debugger. It's likely that Visual Studio will notice that debugging is not enabled in the *Web.config* file for this application, and the Debugging Not Enabled dialog box will appear, as shown in Figure 17-4.

The default in this dialog box is to modify (and, if needed, create) the *Web.config* file. Go ahead and click OK to enable debugging for your application.

---

## Adding Controls

You can add server-side controls to a Web Form in three ways: by writing HTML into the HTML page, by dragging controls from the toolbox to the Design page, or by programmatically adding them at runtime. For example, suppose you want to use buttons to let the user choose one of three shippers provided in the Northwind database. You can write the following HTML into the <form> element in the HTML window:

```
<asp:RadioButton GroupName="Shipper" id="Speedy"
    text = "Speedy Express" Checked="True" runat="server">
</asp:RadioButton>
<asp:RadioButton GroupName="Shipper" id="United"
    text = "United Package" runat="server">
```

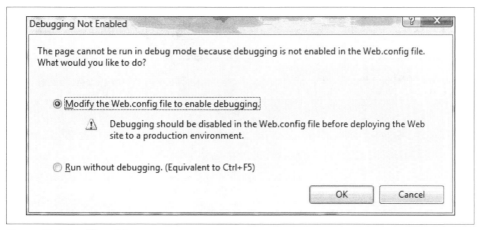

*Figure 17-4. Enabling debugging*

```
    </asp:RadioButton>
    <asp:RadioButton GroupName="Shipper" id="Federal"
        text = "Federal Shipping" runat="server">
    </asp:RadioButton>
```

The asp tags declare server-side ASP.NET controls that are replaced with normal HTML when the server processes the page. When you run the application, the browser displays three radio buttons in a button group; selecting one deselects the others.

You can create the same effect more easily by dragging three buttons from the Visual Studio toolbox onto the form, or to make life even easier, you can drag a radio button list onto the form, which will manage a set of radio buttons declaratively. When you do, the smart tag is opened, and you are prompted to choose a data source (which allows you to bind to a collection; perhaps one you've obtained from a database) or to edit items. Clicking Edit Items opens the ListItem Collection Editor, where you can add three radio buttons.

Each radio button is given the default name ListItem, but you may edit its text and value in the ListItem properties, where you can also decide which of the radio buttons is selected, as shown in Figure 17-5.

You can improve the look of your radio button list by changing properties in the Properties window, including the font, colors, number of columns, repeat direction (vertical is the default), and so forth, as well as by utilizing Visual Studio's extensive support for CSS styling, as shown in Figure 17-6.

In Figure 17-6, you can just see that in the lower-righthand corner you can switch between the Properties window and the Styles window. Here, we've used the Properties window to set the tool tip, and the Styles window to create and apply the ListBox style, which creates the border around our listbox and sets the font and font color. We're also using the split screen option to look at Design and Source at the same time.

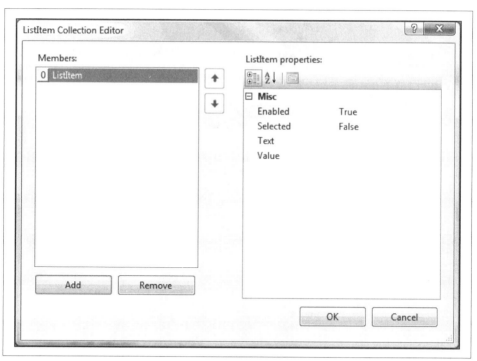

*Figure 17-5. List item collection*

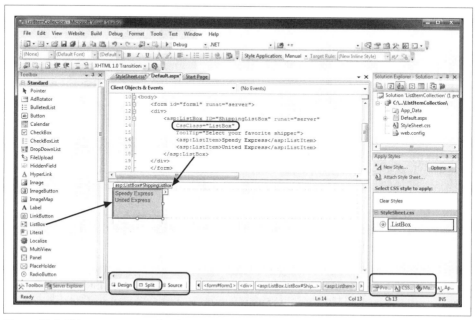

*Figure 17-6. Using properties and styles*

The tag indications (provided automatically at the bottom of the window) show us our location in the document; specifically, inside a ListItem, within the ListBox which is inside a div which itself is inside form1. Very nice.

## Server Controls

Web Forms offer two types of server-side controls. The first is server-side HTML controls. These are HTML controls that you tag with the attribute runat=Server.

The alternative to marking HTML controls as server-side controls is to use ASP.NET Server Controls, also called ASP controls or web controls. ASP controls have been designed to augment and replace the standard HTML controls. ASP controls provide a more consistent object model and more consistently named attributes. For example, with HTML controls, there are myriad ways to handle input:

```
<input type="radio">
<input type="checkbox">
<input type="button">
<input type="text">
<textarea>
```

Each behaves differently and takes different attributes. The ASP controls try to normalize the set of controls, using attributes consistently throughout the ASP control object model. Here are the ASP controls that correspond to the preceding HTML server-side controls:

```
<asp:RadioButton>
<asp:CheckBox>
<asp:Button>
<asp:TextBox rows="1">
<asp:TextBox rows="5">
```

The remainder of this chapter focuses on ASP controls.

# Data Binding

Various technologies have offered programmers the opportunity to bind controls to data so that as the data was modified, the controls responded automatically. However, as Rocky used to say to Bullwinkle, "That trick never works." Bound controls often provided the developer with severe limitations in how the control looked and performed.

The ASP.NET designers set out to solve these problems and provide a suite of robust data-bound controls, which simplify display and modification of data, sacrificing neither performance nor control over the UI. From version 2.0, they have expanded the list of bindable controls and provided even more out-of-the-box functionality.

In the previous section, you hardcoded radio buttons onto a form, one for each of three shippers in the Northwind database. That can't be the best way to do it; if you change the shippers in the database, you have to go back and rewire the controls. This section shows you how you can create these controls dynamically and then bind them to data in the database.

You might want to create the radio buttons based on data in the database because you can't know at design time what text the buttons will have, or even how many buttons you'll need. To accomplish this, you'll bind your `RadioButtonList` to a data source.

Create a new page (right-click on the project, and choose Add New Item; put your form in split view; from the dialog box, choose Web Form). Name the new Web Form *DisplayShippers.aspx*.

From the toolbox, drag a `RadioButtonList` onto the new form, either onto the design pane, or within the `<div>` in the Source view.

If you don't see the radio buttons on the left of your work space, try clicking on View → Toolbox to open the toolbox, and then clicking on the Standard tab of the toolbox. Right-click on any control in the toolbox, and choose Sort Items Alphabetically.

In the Design pane, click on the new control's smart tag. Then, select Choose Data Source. The Choose a Data Source dialog opens, as shown in Figure 17-7.

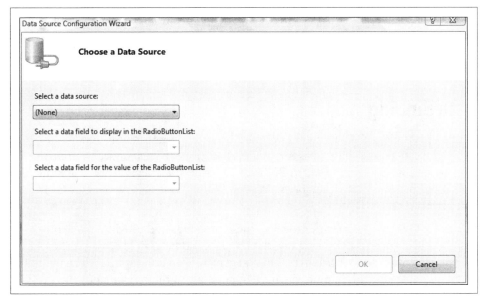

*Figure 17-7. Choose a Data Source dialog*

Drop down the "Select a data source" menu and choose <New Data Source>. You are then prompted to choose a data source from the datatypes on your machine. Select Database, assign it an ID, and click OK. The Configure Data Source dialog box opens, as shown in Figure 17-8.

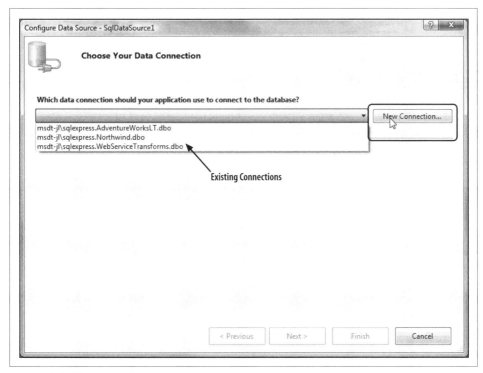

*Figure 17-8. Choosing a data connection*

Choose an existing connection, or in this case, choose New Connection to configure a new data source, and the Add Connection dialog opens.

Fill in the fields: choose your server name, how you want to log in to the server (if in doubt, choose Windows Authentication), and the name of the database (for this example, Northwind). Be sure to click Test Connection to test the connection. When everything is working, click OK, as shown in Figure 17-9.

After you click OK, the connection properties will be filled in for the Configure Data Source dialog. Review them, and if they are OK, click Next. On the next wizard page, name your connection (e.g., NorthWindConnectionString) if you want to save it to your *web.config* file.

When you click Next, you'll have the opportunity to specify the tables and columns you want to retrieve, or to specify a custom SQL statement or stored procedure for retrieving the data.

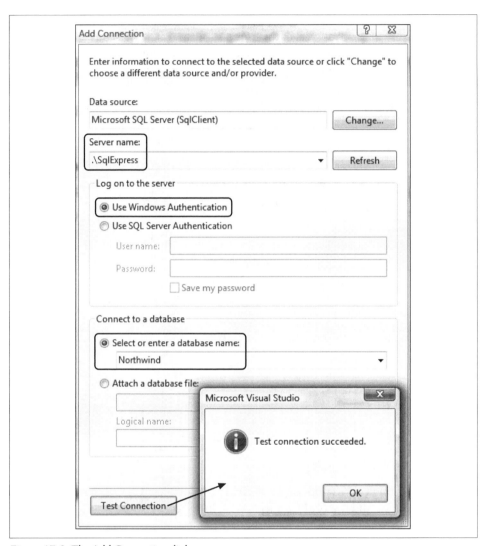

*Figure 17-9. The Add Connection dialog*

Open the Table list, and scroll down to Shippers. Select the ShipperID and CompanyName fields, as shown in Figure 17-10.

While you are here, you may want to click the Advanced button just to see what other options are available to you.

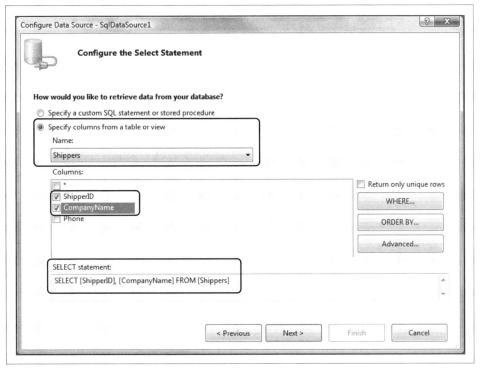

*Figure 17-10. Configuring the Select statement*

Click Next, and test your query to see that you are getting back the values you expected, as shown in Figure 17-11.

It is now time to attach the data source you've just built to the RadioButtonList. A RadioButtonList (like most lists) distinguishes between the value to display (e.g., the name of the delivery service) and the value of that selection (e.g., the delivery service ID). Set these fields in the wizard, using the drop down, as shown in Figure 17-12.

You can improve the look and feel of the radio buttons by binding to the Shippers table, clicking the Radio Button list, and then setting the list's properties and CSS styles, as shown in Figure 17-13.

## Examining the Code

Before moving on, there are a few things to notice. When you press F5 to run this application, it appears in a web browser, and the radio buttons come up as expected. Choose View → Source, and you'll see that what is being sent to the browser is simple HTML, as shown in Example 17-1.

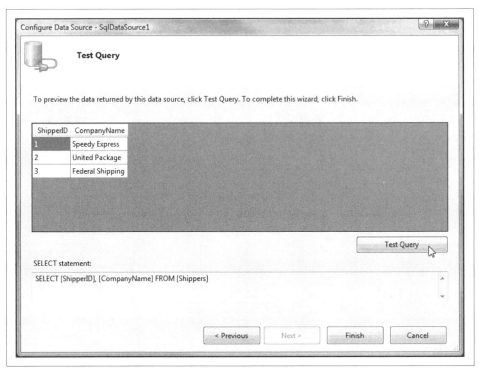

*Figure 17-11. Testing the query*

*Figure 17-12. Binding radio buttons to the data source*

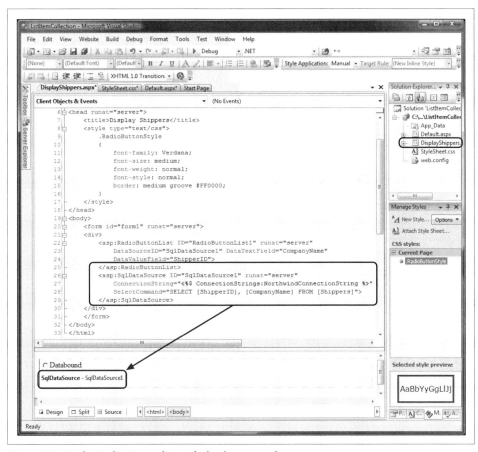

*Figure 17-13. The Radio Button list with the data control*

*Example 17-1. HTML Source view*

```
<!DOCTYPE html PUBLIC "-//W3C//DTD XHTML 1.0 Transitional//EN" "http://www.w3.org/TR/
xhtml1/DTD/xhtml1-transitional.dtd">

<html xmlns="http://www.w3.org/1999/xhtml">
<head><title>
    Display Shippers
</title>
    <style type="text/css">
        .RadioButtonStyle
        {
            font-family: Verdana;
            font-size: medium;
            font-weight: normal;
            font-style: normal;
            border: medium groove #FF0000;
        }
    </style>
```

*Example 17-1. HTML Source view (continued)*

```
</head>
<body>
    <form name="form1" method="post" action="DisplayShippers.aspx" id="form1">
<div>
<input type="hidden" name="__VIEWSTATE" id="__VIEWSTATE"
value="/wEPDwUJMzU1NzcyMDkoD2QWAgIDD2QWAgIBDxAPFgIeC18hRGF0YUJvdW5kZ2QQFQMOU3BlZWR5
IEV4cHJlc3MOVW5pdGVkIFBhY2thZ2UORmVkZXJhbCBTaGlwcGluZxUDATEBMgEzFCsDA2dnZ2RkZA9Nylp
g2l0bProKzM1NvwXJoMBn" />
</div>

    <div>
        <table id="RadioButtonList1" border="0">
            <tr>
                <td><input id="RadioButtonList1_0" type="radio"
                    name="RadioButtonList1" value="1" />
                    <label for="RadioButtonList1_0">Speedy Express</label></td>
            </tr>
            <tr>
                <td><input id="RadioButtonList1_1" type="radio"
                    name="RadioButtonList1" value="2" />
                    <label for="RadioButtonList1_1">United Package</label></td>
            </tr>
            <tr>
                <td><input id="RadioButtonList1_2" type="radio"
                    name="RadioButtonList1" value="3" />
                    <label for="RadioButtonList1_2">Federal Shipping</label></td>
            </tr>
        </table>

    </div>

<div>

<input type="hidden" name="__EVENTVALIDATION" id="__EVENTVALIDATION"
value="/wEWBQLIyMfLBQL444i9AQL544i9AQL644i9AQL3jKLTDcEXOHLsO/LFFixl7k4g2taGl6Qy" />
</div></form>
</body>
</html>
```

Notice that the HTML has no RadioButtonList; it has a table, with cells, within which are standard HTML input objects and labels. ASP.NET has translated the developer controls to HTML understandable by any browser.

 A malicious user may create a message that looks like a valid post from your form, but in which he has set a value for a field you never provided in your form. This may enable him to choose an option not properly available (e.g., a Premier-customer option), or even to launch a SQL injection attack. You want to be especially careful about exposing important data such as primary keys in your HTML, and take care that what you receive from the user may not be restricted to what you provide in your form. For more information on secure coding in .NET, see *http://msdn.microsoft.com/security/*.

## Adding Controls and Events

By adding just a few more controls, you can create a complete form with which users can interact. You will do this by adding a more appropriate greeting ("Welcome to NorthWind"), a text box to accept the name of the user, two new buttons (Order and Cancel), and text that provides feedback to the user. Figure 17-14 shows the finished form.

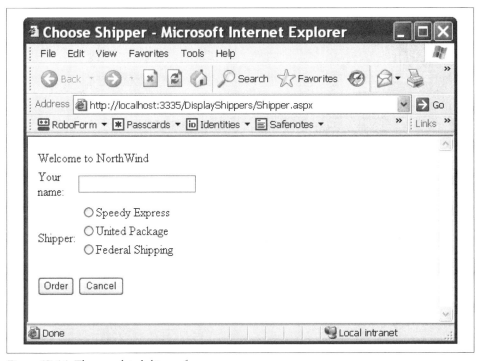

*Figure 17-14. The completed shipper form*

This form won't win any awards for design, but its use will illustrate a number of key points about Web Forms.

 I've never known a developer who didn't think he could design a perfectly fine UI. At the same time, I never knew one who actually could. UI design is one of those skills (such as teaching) that we all think we possess, but only a few very talented folks are good at it. As developers, we know our limitations: we write the code, and someone else lays it out on the page and ensures that usability issues are reviewed. For more on this, I highly recommend every programmer read *Don't Make Me Think: A Common Sense Approach to Web Usability* by Steve Krug (New Riders Press) and *Why Software Sucks...and What You Can Do About It* by David Platt (Addison-Wesley).

Example 17-2 is the complete HTML for the *.aspx* file.

*Example 17-2. The .aspx file*

```
<%@ Page Language="C#" AutoEventWireup="true" CodeFile="DisplayShippers.aspx.cs"
Inherits="DisplayShippers" %>

<!DOCTYPE html PUBLIC "-//W3C//DTD XHTML 1.0 Transitional//EN"
"http://www.w3.org/TR/xhtml1/DTD/xhtml1-transitional.dtd">

<html xmlns="http://www.w3.org/1999/xhtml">
<head runat="server">
    <title>Choose Shippers</title>
    <style type="text/css">
        .RadioButtonStyle
        {
            font-family: Verdana;
            font-size: medium;
            font-weight: normal;
            font-style: normal;
            border: medium groove #FF0000;
        }
    </style>
</head>
<body>
    <form id="form1" runat="server">
    <table style="width: 300px; height: 33px">
        <tr>
            <td colspan="2" style="height: 20px">Welcome to NorthWind</td>
        </tr>
        <tr>
            <td>Your name:</td>
            <td><asp:TextBox ID="txtName" Runat=server></asp:TextBox></td>
        </tr>
        <tr>
            <td>Shipper:</td>
            <td>
                <asp:RadioButtonList ID="rblShippers" runat="server"
                    DataSourceID="SqlDataSource1" DataTextField="CompanyName"
                    DataValueField="ShipperID">
                </asp:RadioButtonList>
            </td>
        </tr>
        <tr>
            <td><asp:Button ID="btnOrder"  Runat=server Text="Order"
                    onclick="btnOrder_Click" /></td>
            <td><asp:Button ID="btnCancel" Runat=server Text="Cancel" /></td>
        </tr>
        <tr>
            <td colspan="2"><asp:Label id="lblMsg" runat=server></asp:Label></td>
        </tr>


    </table>
```

*Example 17-2. The .aspx file (continued)*

```
        <asp:SqlDataSource ID="SqlDataSource1" runat="server"
            ConnectionString="<%$ ConnectionStrings:NorthwindConnectionString %>"
            SelectCommand="SELECT [ShipperID], [CompanyName] FROM [Shippers]">
        </asp:SqlDataSource>
    </form>
</body>
</html>
```

When the user clicks the Order button, you'll check that the user has filled in his name, and you'll also provide feedback on which shipper was chosen. Remember, at design time, you can't know the name of the shipper (this is obtained from the database), so you'll have to ask the Listbox for the chosen name (and ID).

To accomplish all of this, switch to Design mode, and double-click the Order button. Visual Studio will put you in the code-behind page, and will create an event handler for the button's Click event.

 To simplify this code, we will not validate that the user has entered a name in the text box. For more on the controls that make such validation simple, please see *Programming ASP.NET*.

You add the event-handling code, setting the text of the label to pick up the text from the text box, and the text and value from the RadioButtonList:

```
protected void btnOrder_Click(object sender, EventArgs e)
{
    lblMsg.Text = "Thank you " + txtName.Text.Trim( ) +
        ". You chose " + rblShippers.SelectedItem.Text +
        " whose ID is " + rblShippers.SelectedValue;
}
```

When you run this program, you'll notice that none of the radio buttons are selected. Binding the list did not specify which one is the default. There are a number of ways to do this, but the easiest is to add a single line in the Page_Load method that Visual Studio created:

```
protected void Page_Load(object sender, EventArgs e)
{
    rblShippers.SelectedIndex = 0;
}
```

This sets the RadioButtonList's first radio button to Selected. The problem with this solution is subtle. If you run the application, you'll see that the first button is selected, but if you choose the second (or third) button and click OK, you'll find that the first button is reset. You can't seem to choose any but the first selection. This is because each time the page is loaded, the OnLoad event is run, and in that event handler you are (re-)setting the selected index.

The fact is that you only want to set this button the first time the page is selected, not when it is posted back to the browser as a result of the OK button being clicked.

To solve this, wrap the setting in an if statement that tests whether the page has been posted back:

```
protected override void OnLoad(EventArgs e)
{
    if (!IsPostBack)
    {
        rblShippers.SelectedIndex = 0;
    }
}
```

When you run the page, the IsPostBack property is checked. The first time the page is posted, this value is false, and the radio button is set. If you click a radio button and then click OK, the page is sent to the server for processing (where the btnOrder_Click handler is run), and then the page is posted back to the user. This time, the IsPostBack property is true, and thus the code within the if statement isn't run, and the user's choice is preserved, as shown in Figure 17-15.

*Figure 17-15. The user's choices preserved on postback*

Example 17-3 shows the complete code-behind form.

*Example 17-3. Code-behind form for DisplayShippers aspx.cs*

```
using System;

public partial class DisplayShippers : System.Web.UI.Page
{
    protected void Page_Load(object sender, EventArgs e)
    {
        if (!IsPostBack)
        {
            rblShippers.SelectedIndex = 0;
        }
    }

    protected void btnOrder_Click(object sender, EventArgs e)
    {
        lblMsg.Text = "Thank you " + txtName.Text.Trim( ) +
        ". You chose " + rblShippers.SelectedItem.Text +
        " whose ID is " + rblShippers.SelectedValue;
    }
}
```

# CHAPTER 18

# Programming WPF Applications

Microsoft currently offers two ways to create desktop applications: Windows Forms (the technology in use since .NET 1.0) and Windows Presentation Foundation, or WPF (new to .NET 3.5).

It is useful to see that regardless of the technology involved, the C# is very much the same, so I will cover WPF in this chapter and Windows Forms in the next.

In this chapter, I'll show you how to create a relatively straightforward (though nontrivial) WPF application with C# event handlers. In the next chapter, I'll show you another nontrivial application, written in Windows Forms, and again, we'll use C# to implement the event handlers.

Everything about the two applications will be different, except for the C#; the language remains unchanged whether you are writing WPF, Windows Forms, ASP. NET, or Silverlight.

## WPF in a Very Small Nutshell

 It isn't possible or reasonable to teach all of WPF in a single chapter, and I won't try. For a more reasonable introduction, please see *Programming .NET 3.5* by myself and Alex Horovitz (O'Reilly), and for a complete and comprehensive review of WPF please see the truly wonderful *Programming WPF* by Ian Griffiths and Chris Sells (O'Reilly), which may be one of the best technical books I've ever read.

WPF is written, in large part, using a declarative language: XAML (pronounced *zamel*, to rhyme with camel). XAML stands for eXtensible Application Markup Language, which is a dialect of the industry-standard XML and thus is easily read and manipulated by tools such as Visual Studio.

## Creating a WPF Example

WPF does a lot of things well, but what sets it apart from previous Windows frameworks is its command of rich text and rich graphics. WPF uses a different model from the form-centric approach that many of us have (overly?) focused on with Windows Forms.

 Any sweeping generalization about WPF versus Windows Forms is bound to fail, as one can always find a counterexample. What I'm describing here is what I've seen in practice in many development organizations, not what can be done in theory. As my old boss, Pat Johnson, used to say (and as I've quoted before), "In theory, theory and practice are the same, but in practice, they never are."

Because this is a book about C# and not WPF, I'm going to start by showing you the example we're going to build, and I'll teach only enough to get us there, with an emphasis on the C# needed to make it work.

## The Example Program

The example program we're going to use is a variant on an example I've used in a number of other places (varied here to emphasize the C#, to keep you interested, and to stop my editor from yelling at me).

In this example, we're going to reach out to the White House's web site, and pull down the images of the first 20 presidents of the United States and present them in a custom WPF control.

The control will not be wide enough to show all 20, so we'll provide a horizontal scroll bar, and as the user mouses over an image, we'll provide feedback by enlarging that image (from 75 to 85) and increasing its opacity from 75 percent to 100 percent. As the user mouses off, we'll return the image to its smaller, dimmer starting point.

This will show off declarative animation (we'll write no procedural code to accomplish these changes in the images!). In addition, when the user clicks on an image, we'll capture the click and display the name of the president using a C# event handler, and we'll reach into the control and place the president's name into the title bar of the control.

Figure 18-1 shows the result of scrolling to the 16th president and clicking on the image. Note that the name of the president is displayed in the title bar, and that the image of President Lincoln is both larger and brighter than the surrounding images.

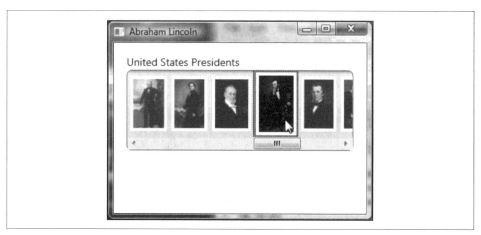

*Figure 18-1. Clicking on Abraham Lincoln*

# Building the Application

To create this application, open Visual Studio 2008, and select Create → Project. In the New Project dialog select .NET Framework 3.5, and choose Visual C# in the Project Types window and WPF Application in the Templates window. Select a location for your program and give your program a name (I'll be naming mine Presidential Browser), as shown in Figure 18-2.

Visual Studio will create a starter application with a window, inside of which it will place an empty grid. It will present you with a split window, with the designer on top, and the XAML on the bottom. We can work with this (we're easy).

Because we know that we want two items in our grid—the text block that says "United States Presidents" and our sideways listbox of photographs—we can make a start at a layout.

## Grids and Stack Panels

Two of the layout objects WPF provides are stack panels and grids (not to be confused with data grids!). A *stack panel* lets you stack a set of objects one on top of (or next to) another set of objects. That turns out to be very useful.

At times, you'd like to set up a stack that is both horizontal and vertical—essentially a table, which is what a *grid* is for. A grid has columns and rows, both counting from zero.

We'll create a simple grid of two rows and one column, and inside each row, we'll place a stack panel. The top stack panel will hold the text, and the bottom stack panel will hold the listbox that will, in turn, hold the photos. (Don't panic! We'll take this one step at a time.)

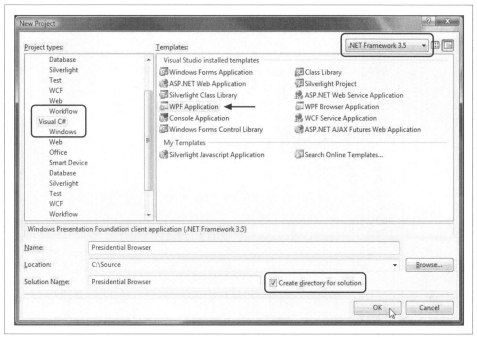

*Figure 18-2. The New Project dialog box*

To begin, let's give the grid some dimensions: a width of 300 and a height of 190 should do it (I know this because I'm a stud programmer, and because I tried some values until I found two that worked pretty well).

As a matter of good programming practice, every time we open a tag, we immediately create its closing tag and then fill in its contents. This is not required, but you'd be amazed at how much debugging time it saves. IntelliSense will help with this, as shown in Figure 18-3.

*Figure 18-3. IntelliSense helping to find the closing tag*

Fill in your code until it looks like Example 18-1.

*Example 18-1. Starter XAML*

```
<Window x:Class="Presidential_Browser.Window1"
    xmlns="http://schemas.microsoft.com/winfx/2006/xaml/presentation"
    xmlns:x="http://schemas.microsoft.com/winfx/2006/xaml"
    Title="Window1" Height="300" Width="300">
    <Grid Width="300" Height="180">
        <Grid.RowDefinitions>
            <RowDefinition Height="70" />
            <RowDefinition Height="*" />
        </Grid.RowDefinitions>
        <StackPanel Grid.Row="0">
            <TextBlock Text="Top Stack Panel" VerticalAlignment="Center"/>
        </StackPanel>
        <StackPanel Grid.Row="1">
            <TextBlock Text="Bottom Stack Panel" VerticalAlignment="Center"/>
        </StackPanel>
    </Grid>
</Window>
```

Let's take this apart. The first three lines declare the standard namespaces for WPF. This is followed by the title of the window (cleverly named Window1), and the height and width of the window.

The next line has the declaration of the grid and its height (note that the grid is only 300 wide).

Within the grid, I've added a Grid.RowDefinition declaration that lets me divide the grid so that I can take precise control over the distribution of the spacing of the rows, allocating 7/18 of the space to the first row. I could compute the remaining space for the bottom row (120), or use the asterisk to let the grid do the math.

Next, I define two stack panels, telling the first that it is to occupy the first row of the grid (and you do have such familiar attributes as RowSpan and ColumnSpan!), and within each of the two StackPanels, I place a TextBlock. TextBlocks are very powerful and flexible controls for text that we are using here just to display simple text and to align that text to the center of the panel, which we see immediately in the Design view, as shown in Figure 18-4.

Change the text block in the first stack panel to the following:

```
<TextBlock FontSize="14" Grid.Row="0" >United States Presidents</TextBlock>
```

Note that the TextBlock has a property for FontSize. You may also want to play with font weight and font family and a host of other features in the TextBlock. While you're tinkering, let's fix the apportionment of the rows, allocating only 20 to the first row, and the remainder to the second row, and setting the grid to 170.

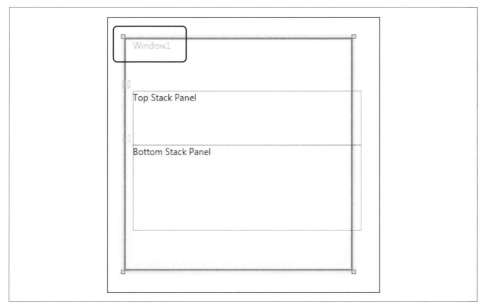

*Figure 18-4. Grid and stack panels*

## Sucking on a Fire Hose

Now I'm going to do something evil. If this were a book on WPF, I'd walk you through how we do data access on groups of data in a number of small steps. Instead, because this is a book on C#, I'm going to throw it at you all at once.

You have a couple of choices. You can struggle through what is admittedly a somewhat superficial and fast explanation so that you can see how the C# is used, and come back to WPF when you are ready, or you can go off and read a couple of chapters in a good WPF book (see the earlier note; I'll wait right here, I promise).

The problem is that if I take you through the WPF in the kind of detail I'd like, this will become a long diversion that really has little to do with C#, so forgive me while I just throw a Nolan Ryan speedball directly between your eyes.

### Our goals

Our first goal is to get the pictures into a listbox and to turn the listbox sideways so that the pictures scroll along, as shown in Figure 18-1.

To accomplish that, we need to do two things: we need to work with the style of the listbox, and we need to work with its data. Yes, you can separate these two aspects, but it is faster and easier if I show you both at once, so fasten your seatbelts.

We're going to jump to the top of the XAML file and start by creating some resources. The first is a LinearGradientBrush, which we will name ListBoxGradient.

We'll be able to use this brush anywhere we want to draw a fill (rather than a color, as this will give us a nice linear gradient, which is a color that changes gradually as it moves through the colors identified in the gradient stops):

```
<Window.Resources>
    <LinearGradientBrush x:Key="ListBoxGradient"
            StartPoint="0,0"
            EndPoint="0,1">
        <GradientStop Color="#90000000"
        Offset="0" />
        <GradientStop Color="#40000000"
        Offset="0.005" />
        <GradientStop Color="#10000000"
        Offset="0.04" />
        <GradientStop Color="#20000000"
        Offset="0.945" />
        <GradientStop Color="#60FFFFFF"
        Offset="1" />
    </LinearGradientBrush>
```

Briefly, all linear gradients are perceived to occur on a line ranging from 0 to 1. You can set the start points and endpoints (traditionally, the start point 0,0 is the upper-left corner, and the endpoint 1,1 is the lower-right corner, making the linear gradient run on an angle). Here, we've set the linear gradient to end at 0,1, making the gradient run from top to bottom, giving a horizontal gradient, moving through five colors, unevenly spaced.

Still within the resources, we next define a Style object, and we define its TargetType to be an object of type ListBox:

```
<Style x:Key="SpecialListStyle"
        TargetType="{x:Type ListBox}">
    <Setter Property="Template">
        <Setter.Value>
            <ControlTemplate TargetType="{x:Type ListBox}" >
                <Border BorderBrush="Gray"
                    BorderThickness="1"
                    CornerRadius="6"
                    Background="{DynamicResource ListBoxGradient}" >
                    <ScrollViewer VerticalScrollBarVisibility="Disabled"
                        HorizontalScrollBarVisibility="Visible">
                            <StackPanel IsItemsHost="True"
                            Orientation="Horizontal"
                            HorizontalAlignment="Left" />
                    </ScrollViewer>
                </Border>
            </ControlTemplate>
        </Setter.Value>
    </Setter>
</Style>
```

The net effect of this code is to allow you to apply this style to a listbox to create a gray border using the ListBoxGradient that will have no vertical scroll bar but will have a horizontal scroll bar, and that will make the listbox itself horizontal.

Having created a style for the listbox, we need a style for the items in the listbox:

```
<Style x:Key="SpecialListItem"
    TargetType="{x:Type ListBoxItem}">
        <Setter Property="MaxHeight"  Value="75" />
        <Setter Property="MinHeight"  Value="75" />
        <Setter Property="Opacity"    Value=".75" />
    <Style.Triggers>
        <EventTrigger RoutedEvent="Mouse.MouseEnter">
            <EventTrigger.Actions>
                <BeginStoryboard>
                    <Storyboard>
                        <DoubleAnimation Duration="0:0:0.2"
                            Storyboard.TargetProperty="MaxHeight"  To="85" />
                        <DoubleAnimation Duration="0:0:0.2"
                            Storyboard.TargetProperty="Opacity" To="1.0" />
                    </Storyboard>
                </BeginStoryboard>
            </EventTrigger.Actions>
        </EventTrigger>

        <EventTrigger RoutedEvent="Mouse.MouseLeave">
            <EventTrigger.Actions>
                <BeginStoryboard>
                    <Storyboard>
                        <DoubleAnimation Duration="0:0:1"
                            Storyboard.TargetProperty="MaxHeight" />
                        <DoubleAnimation Duration="0:0:0.2"
                                Storyboard.TargetProperty="Opacity" />
                    </Storyboard>
                </BeginStoryboard>
            </EventTrigger.Actions>
        </EventTrigger>
    </Style.Triggers>
</Style>
```

This style begins by setting its target type (ListBoxItems) and three properties (MaxHeight, MinHeight, and Opacity). It then sets *triggers*. As you might imagine, triggers are events that will set off a change; the change that a trigger sets off is the beginning of an animation. Animations are defined in storyboards.

There are a number of ways to tie animations and storyboards to events, but one way (and the way used here) is to tie an EventTrigger to a RoutedEvent. Let's unpack the first one:

```
<EventTrigger RoutedEvent="Mouse.MouseEnter">
```

Pretty clear: the following will be kicked off when the mouse enters the object that is associated with this EventTrigger (that object will be the listbox item).

Within that `EventTrigger` are defined one or more `EventTrigger.Actions`. In this case, the action is `BeginStoryBoard`, and there is a single, unnamed `Storyboard`:

```
<EventTrigger RoutedEvent="Mouse.MouseEnter">
    <EventTrigger.Actions>
        <BeginStoryboard>
            <Storyboard>
                <DoubleAnimation Duration="0:0:0.2"
                    Storyboard.TargetProperty="MaxHeight"  To="85" />
                <DoubleAnimation Duration="0:0:0.2"
                    Storyboard.TargetProperty="Opacity" To="1.0" />
            </Storyboard>
        </BeginStoryboard>
    </EventTrigger.Actions>
</EventTrigger>
```

The action is inside the storyboard, where we find two animations. There are various kinds of animations, named for the kind of value they act upon. The two we see here act upon *doubles* (nonintegral numeric values). These two animations are defined to have a duration of 2/10 of a second. The `TargetProperty` refers to the property of the object to be animated (that is the listbox item)—in the first case, the height of the listbox item, which will be animated to a height of 85 (from a starting point of 75). The second animation will change the opacity from its starting point of .75 to 1 (making it appear to brighten).

## Adding Data

We're now going to cheat very badly, and rather than getting our data from a web service or from a database, we're going to put it right into our resources (please don't tell!). The data will consist of a generic list of `ImageURL` objects. You've not heard of such objects because we haven't created them yet. Right-click on the project and choose Add → Class, and in your new class add the code in Example 18-2.

*Example 18-2. ImageURL class*

```
using System;
using System.Collections.Generic;
using System.Windows.Media.Imaging;

namespace PhotoCatalog
{
    public class ImageURL
    {
        public string Path { get; private set; }
        public Uri ImageURI { get; set; }
        public BitmapFrame Image { get; private set; }
        public string Name { get;  set; }

        public ImageURL( ) { }

        public ImageURL(string path, string name)
```

*Example 18-2. ImageURL class (continued)*

```
    {
        Path = path;
        ImageURI = new Uri(Path);
        Image = BitmapFrame.Create(ImageURI);
        Name = name;
    }
    public override string ToString( )
    {
        return Path;
    }
}

public class Images : List<ImageURL> { }
}
```

OK, I lied—we created two classes. The first, ImageURL, is designed to act as a wrapper for an image that we retrieve given the path to an image or a URI from which we can create an image. Note that we use the new C# Automatic Properties syntax (isn't that wicked cool!), and we override ToString( ) to return the Path property even though we haven't explicitly created the backing variable; gotta love that.

The second class is at the very bottom: Images derives from (*is-a*) generic list of ImageURL objects. The implementation is empty, so it serves as an alias for List<ImageURL>.

### Instantiating objects declaratively

What takes awhile to get your head around is that now that we've declared these classes, we can create instances of them in our resources section! To do so, we must first include our class in our XAML file by creating a namespace for our project; we'll call that namespace local, as shown in Figure 18-5.

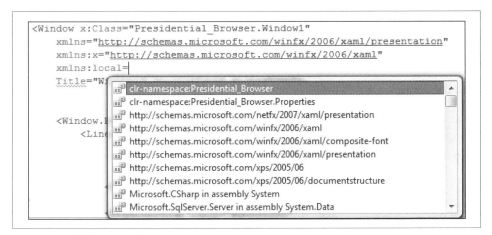

*Figure 18-5. Adding a local namespace*

We create an instance of the Images class like this:

```
<local:Images x:Key="Presidents">
```

This is the XAML equivalent of writing:

```
List<ImageURL> Presidents = new List<ImageURL>();
```

We then add to that list by creating instances of ImageURL between the opening and closing tags of the Images declaration:

```
<local:ImageURL ImageURI="http://www.whitehouse.gov/history/ presidents/images/gw1.
gif" Name="George Washington" />
```

Again, this is the XAML equivalent of writing:

```
ImageURL newImage = new ImageURL(
    "http://www.whitehouse.gov/history/ presidents/images/gw1.gif,
    "George Washington");
Presidents.Add(newImage)";
```

We do that 20 times, once for each of the first 20 presidents. That creates a static data resource we can refer to in the rest of our XAML file, completing the resources section.

## Using the Data in the XAML

Our next step is to provide a DataContext for the Grid:

```
<Grid Width="300" Height="170"
    DataContext="{StaticResource Presidents}">
```

Every Framework object has a DataContext object, usually null. If you don't instruct the object otherwise, it will look up the tree from where it is defined until it finds an object that does have a DataContext defined, and then it will use that DataContext as its data source (you can use virtually anything as a DataSource—a LINQ statement, a connection to a database, or, as in this case, a static resource).

## Defining the Listbox

We are now ready to define the listbox and the template for its contents in the second StackPanel:

```
<StackPanel Grid.Row="1" Grid.ColumnSpan="3" >
  <ListBox Style="{StaticResource SpecialListStyle}"
      Name="PresPhotoListBox" Margin="0,0,0,20"
      SelectionChanged="PresPhotoListBox_SelectionChanged"
      ItemsSource="{Binding }"
      IsSynchronizedWithCurrentItem="True" SelectedIndex="0"
      ItemContainerStyle="{StaticResource SpecialListItem}" >
```

The first line shown here places the stack panel into the grid at row offset 1 (the second row). The ListBox itself has its style set to a StaticResource (i.e., a resource we defined earlier in the resources section). The listbox is named:

```
Name="PresPhotoListBox"
```

And an event handler is defined for anytime an image is clicked:

```
SelectionChanged="PresPhotoListBox_SelectionChanged"
```

The source for each item is set to `Binding`, indicating that we are binding to the source in the parent element (defined in the grid). Finally, the `ItemContainerStyle` is set, again, to the style defined earlier in the resources section.

Each item in the listbox will be drawn from the (unknown) number of items in the data (which in this case happens to be statically placed in the resources, but could well be dynamically drawn from a web service). To do this, we'll need a template for how to draw each item:

```
<ListBox.ItemTemplate>
    <DataTemplate>
        <Border VerticalAlignment="Center"
          HorizontalAlignment="Center" Padding="4"
            Margin="2" Background="White">
            <Image Source="{Binding Path=ImageURI}" />
        </Border>
    </DataTemplate>
</ListBox.ItemTemplate>
```

Within the `ListBox.ItemTemplate` we place a `DataTemplate`; this is necessary if you want to show anything more than simple text derived from the data retrieved. In this case, we place a `Border` object within the `DataTemplate`, and within the `Border` object, we place the `Image` object. It is the `Image` object we really care about (though the `Border` object helps with placement). The `Image` requires a source, and here, we add `Binding` (indicating that we are binding to the current source), and we add the helpful information that we'll be using the `ImageURI` property to set the `Path`. Because the source we bind to is a list of `ImageURL` objects, and each `ImageURL` has four public properties (`Path`, `ImageURI`, `Image`, and `Name`), this is the critical piece of data required to tell the `DataTemplate` how to get the information necessary to create the image in the listbox.

## The Complete XAML File

For those of you who are not sitting in front of a computer, Example 18-3 has the complete XAML listing, truncated a bit so as not to take up too much room in the chapter.

*Example 18-3. Complete XAML listing*

```
<Window x:Class="PhotoCatalog.Window1"
    xmlns="http://schemas.microsoft.com/winfx/2006/xaml/presentation"
    xmlns:x="http://schemas.microsoft.com/winfx/2006/xaml"
    xmlns:local="clr-namespace:PhotoCatalog"
    Title="President Identifier"  ShowInTaskbar="False" Height="256" Width="253">

    <Window.Resources>
    <LinearGradientBrush x:Key="ListBoxGradient"
```

*Example 18-3. Complete XAML listing (continued)*

```xaml
      StartPoint="0,0"
      EndPoint="0,1">

      <GradientStop Color="#90000000"
       Offset="0" />
      <GradientStop Color="#40000000"
       Offset="0.005" />
      <GradientStop Color="#10000000"
       Offset="0.04" />
      <GradientStop Color="#20000000"
       Offset="0.945" />
      <GradientStop Color="#60FFFFFF"
       Offset="1" />

  </LinearGradientBrush>

  <Style x:Key="SpecialListStyle"
    TargetType="{x:Type ListBox}">
    <Setter Property="Template">
     <Setter.Value>
      <ControlTemplate TargetType="{x:Type ListBox}" >
        <Border    BorderBrush="Gray"
          BorderThickness="1" CornerRadius="6"
          Background="{DynamicResource ListBoxGradient}" >
            <ScrollViewer VerticalScrollBarVisibility="Disabled"
            HorizontalScrollBarVisibility="Visible">
              <StackPanel    IsItemsHost="True"
               Orientation="Horizontal"
               HorizontalAlignment="Left" />
          </ScrollViewer>
        </Border>
      </ControlTemplate>
     </Setter.Value>
    </Setter>
  </Style>

  <Style x:Key="SpecialListItem"
    TargetType="{x:Type ListBoxItem}">
    <Setter Property="MaxHeight"  Value="75" />
    <Setter Property="MinHeight"  Value="75" />
    <Setter Property="Opacity"    Value=".75" />
  <Style.Triggers>
   <EventTrigger RoutedEvent="Mouse.MouseEnter">
    <EventTrigger.Actions>
     <BeginStoryboard>
        <Storyboard>
          <DoubleAnimation Duration="0:0:0.2"
          Storyboard.TargetProperty="MaxHeight"  To="85" />
          <DoubleAnimation Duration="0:0:0.2"
          Storyboard.TargetProperty="Opacity" To="1.0" />
        </Storyboard>
     </BeginStoryboard>
```

*Example 18-3. Complete XAML listing (continued)*

```
      </EventTrigger.Actions>
     </EventTrigger>

     <EventTrigger RoutedEvent="Mouse.MouseLeave">
      <EventTrigger.Actions>
       <BeginStoryboard>
        <Storyboard>
          <DoubleAnimation Duration="0:0:1"
         Storyboard.TargetProperty="MaxHeight" />
          <DoubleAnimation Duration="0:0:0.2"
         Storyboard.TargetProperty="Opacity" />
        </Storyboard>
       </BeginStoryboard>
      </EventTrigger.Actions>
     </EventTrigger>
    </Style.Triggers>
   </Style>

   <local:Images x:Key="Presidents">
   <local:ImageURL
ImageURI="http://www.whitehouse.gov/history/presidents/images/gw1.gif"
Name="George Washington" />
   <local:ImageURL ImageURI=".../ja2.gif" Name="John Adams" />
   <local:ImageURL ImageURI=".../tj3.gif" Name="Thomas Jefferson" />
   <local:ImageURL ImageURI=".../jm4.gif" Name="James Madison" />
   <local:ImageURL ImageURI=".../jm5.gif" Name="James Monroe" />
   <local:ImageURL ImageURI=".../ja6.gif" Name="John Quincy Adams" />
   <local:ImageURL ImageURI=".../aj7.gif" Name="Andrew Jackson" />
   <local:ImageURL ImageURI=".../mb8.gif" Name="Martin Van Buren" />
   <local:ImageURL ImageURI=".../wh9.gif" Name="William H. Harrison" />
   <local:ImageURL ImageURI=".../jt10.gif" Name="John Tyler" />
   <local:ImageURL ImageURI=".../jp11.gif" Name="James K. Polk" />
   <local:ImageURL ImageURI=".../zt12.gif" Name="Zachary Taylor" />
   <local:ImageURL ImageURI=".../mf13.gif" Name="Millard Fillmore" />
   <local:ImageURL ImageURI=".../fp14.gif" Name="Franklin Pierce" />
   <local:ImageURL ImageURI=".../jb15.gif" Name="James Buchanan" />
   <local:ImageURL ImageURI=".../al16.gif" Name="Abraham Lincoln" />
   <local:ImageURL ImageURI=".../aj17.gif" Name="Andrew Johnson" />
   <local:ImageURL ImageURI=".../ug18.gif" Name="Ulysses S. Grant" />
   <local:ImageURL ImageURI=".../rh19.gif" Name="Rutherford B. Hayes" />
   <local:ImageURL ImageURI=".../jp11.gif" Name="James Garfield" />
   <local:ImageURL ImageURI=".../jg20.gif" Name="Chester A. Arthur" />
   </local:Images>
  </Window.Resources>

  <Grid Width="300" Height="170"
      DataContext="{StaticResource Presidents}">
   <Grid.RowDefinitions>
    <RowDefinition Height="20" />
    <RowDefinition Height="*" />
   </Grid.RowDefinitions>
   <StackPanel >
```

*Example 18-3. Complete XAML listing (continued)*

```
            <TextBlock FontSize="14" Grid.Row="0" >
                United States Presidents
            </TextBlock>
        </StackPanel>
        <StackPanel Grid.Row="1" Grid.ColumnSpan="3" >
            <ListBox Style="{StaticResource SpecialListStyle}"
              Name="PresPhotoListBox" Margin="0,0,0,20"
              SelectionChanged="PresPhotoListBox_SelectionChanged"
              ItemsSource="{Binding }"
              IsSynchronizedWithCurrentItem="True" SelectedIndex="0"
               ItemContainerStyle="{StaticResource SpecialListItem}" >

            <ListBox.ItemTemplate>
              <DataTemplate>
               <Border VerticalAlignment="Center"
                 HorizontalAlignment="Center" Padding="4"
                 Margin="2" Background="White">
                     <Image Source="{Binding Path=ImageURI}" />
                </Border>
              </DataTemplate>
            </ListBox.ItemTemplate>
          </ListBox>
        </StackPanel>
      </Grid>
</Window>
```

## Event Handling (Finally!)

Note carefully that we did, in fact, wire up an event handler for when the user changes the selected item in the listbox:

```
SelectionChanged="PresPhotoListBox_SelectionChanged"
```

This is typically done by clicking on an image (though you can accomplish this with the arrow keys as well!). This will fire the event handler in the code-behind file, which is, finally, C#. Remember C#? This is a book about C# (apologies to Arlo Guthrie).

The event handler is, as you would expect, in the code-behind file, *Window1.xaml.cs*:

```csharp
private void PresPhotoListBox_SelectionChanged(
            object sender, SelectionChangedEventArgs e)
{
    ListBox lb = sender as ListBox;
    if (lb != null)
    {

        if (lb.SelectedItem != null)
        {

            string chosenName =  (lb.SelectedItem as ImageURL).Name.ToString( );
            Title = chosenName;
```

---

```
        }
    }
    else
    {
        throw new ArgumentException(
                "Expected ListBox to call selection changed in
                    PresPhotoListBox_SelectionChanged");
    }

}
```

Like all event handlers in .NET, you receive two parameters: the sender (in this case, the listbox), and an object derived from `EventArgs`.

In the code shown, we cast the sender to the listbox (and consider it an exception if the sender is not a listbox, as that is the only type of object that should be sending to this event handler).

We then check to make sure that the `selectedItem` is not null (during startup it is possible that it can be null). Assuming it is not null, we cast the `selectedItem` to an `ImageURL`, extract the `Name` property, and assign it to a temporary variable, `chosenName`, which we then in turn assign to the title of the window.

The interim variable is useful only for debugging; there is no other reason not to write:

```
Title = (lb.SelectedItem as ImageURL).Name.ToString();
```

 You can also get at both the currently selected president's `ImageURL` and the previously selected `ImageURL` through the `SelectionChangedEventArgs` parameter.

# What Have You Learned, Dorothy?

WPF is heavily declarative, and although it is true that you will still be writing your event handlers (and your business classes) in C#, many of the challenges in your program will (at least at first) be in the XAML.

What we didn't do in this program, of course, is integrate LINQ to access data, nor did we build an entire business layer (though one can argue that the business layer in many applications should be written in WF, which also uses XAML!).

Pick up a good book on WPF. You'll find a fair amount of C#, but you'll be surprised at how many of the listings are in XAML compared to C#. C# hasn't receded in importance, but declarative programming has certainly supplemented object-oriented programming as another arrow in our quiver.

# CHAPTER 19

# Programming Windows Forms Applications

When .NET first came to life, there were two ways to create applications: ASP.NET for web applications, and Windows Forms for Windows applications. Although WPF offers many advantages over Windows Forms, Microsoft realizes that there are a great many Windows Forms applications already up, tested, and working, and that many companies will choose to maintain and extend them.

Our interest in this book is how we can use C# to interact with Windows Forms, and in this chapter we'll look at building a nontrivial application using this technology. Figure 19-1 shows the application we're going to build. It is a Windows application for copying files from one or more directories to a target directory, written in Windows Forms and designed to be run on a Windows computer (this application has been tested on Windows XP, 2000, and Vista).

Once again, because this is a C# book and not a Windows programming book, we're going to make fast work of the UI and focus on the code-behind file and the event handlers—that is, on the C#. Unlike with WPF, however, there is no declarative aspect to Windows Forms; you create the UI by dragging objects onto a form, and then interacting with those objects by clicking on them and setting their properties, either in the Properties window at design time, or programmatically at runtime.

## Creating the Application

Open Visual Studio 2008, and choose Create → Project. In the New Project window, create a new Visual C# application, and from the Templates window, choose Windows Forms Application. Name it Windows Form File Copier, as shown in Figure 19-2.

Visual Studio responds by creating a Windows Forms application and, best of all, putting you into a design environment and opening a toolbox with controls sorted by the type of work you might want to do. The user interface for `FileCopier` consists of the following controls:

- Labels (source files and target files)
- Buttons (Clear, Copy, Delete, and Cancel)

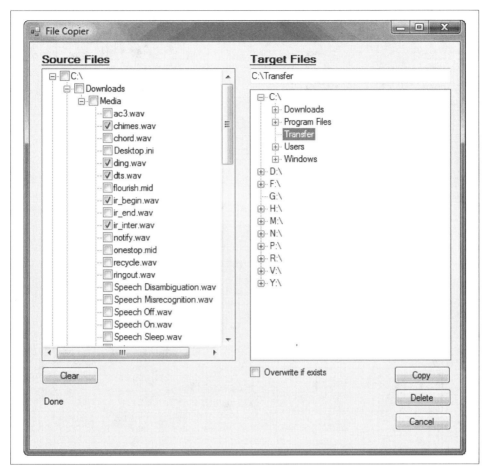

*Figure 19-1. The File Copier application*

- An "Overwrite if exists" checkbox
- A text box displaying the path of the selected target directory
- Two large tree-view controls, one for available source directories, and one for available target devices and directories

To create the UI, click on the form and click in the Properties window. Expand the Size property and set the Width to 585 and the Height to 561. Change the Text property to File Copier, change the name to frmFileCopier, and change the AutoSizeMode to GrowOnly. You can leave the remaining properties alone.

Drag two tree-view controls onto the form, placing them as shown in Figure 19-3. Note that the left tree-view control is taller than the right, allowing room for a text box above the right tree-view control. Continue to drag controls onto the form and then name them, as shown in Table 19-1.

Table 19-1 shows the names we assigned to the controls on this form.

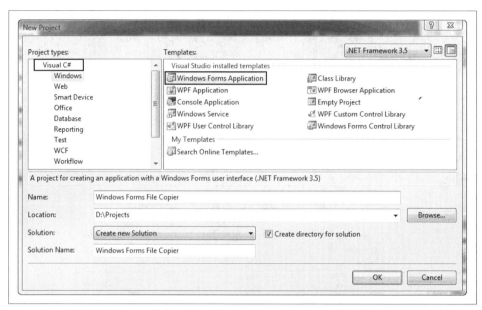

Figure 19-2. The New Project dialog

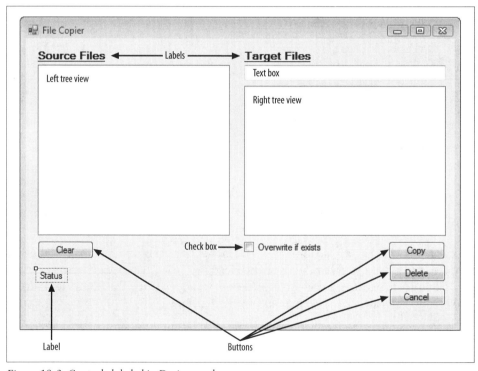

Figure 19-3. Controls labeled in Design mode

*Table 19-1. Controls on form*

| Control type | Control name |
|---|---|
| Tree view (left) | tvwSource |
| Tree view (right) | tvwDestination |
| Text box | txtTargetDir |
| Label | lblSource |
| Label | lblTarget |
| Label | lblStatus |
| Button | btnClear |
| Button | btnCopy |
| Button | btnDelete |
| Button | btnCancel |
| Checkbox | chkOverwrite |

## Creating Event Handlers

There are four common ways to create event handlers in Visual Studio. One is to click on a control, and then to name the event handler in the Properties window. You can switch the Properties window into Events mode by clicking on the lightning bolt button. Find the event you want to hook up, click in the box next to the event, and type a name, as shown in Figure 19-4.

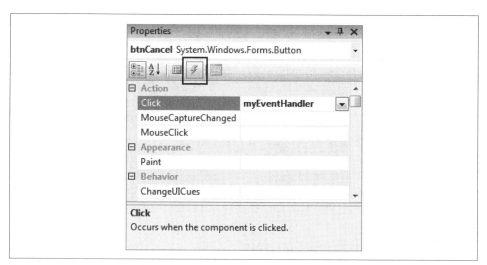

*Figure 19-4. Naming event handlers*

When you press the Enter key, Visual Studio 2008 will create an event handler stub and place you in the source code to fill in the details.

The second option is to do the same thing, but rather than typing in a name, just double-click in the space next to the property name in the Properties window. This instructs Visual Studio to create a name for you, which it does by concatenating the name of the control and the name of the event. Thus, were you to have double-clicked in the space next to Click in Figure 19-4, Visual Studio would have created an event handler named btnCancel_Click, and placed you in the stub of that event handler:

```
private void btnCancel_Click(object sender, EventArgs e)
{

}
```

The third option is to drop down a list of existing event handlers and thus instruct Visual Studio that the Click event for this button will share an already existing event handling method, as shown in Figure 19-5.

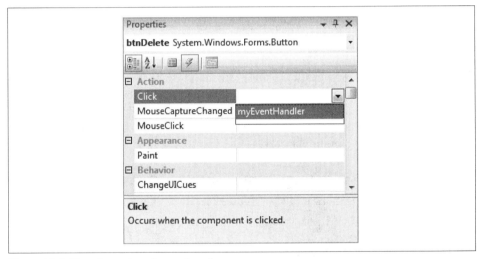

*Figure 19-5. Choosing a shared event handler*

The fourth and fastest way to wire up an event handler is to double-click on a control. Each control has a default event (the most common event for that control). With a button, that event is, of course, Click, and double-clicking on a button is exactly like navigating to the Click event and double-clicking in the event name area: an event handler is created for you with the name btnCancel_Click.

## Populating the TreeView Controls

The two TreeView controls work identically, except that the left control, tvwSource, lists the directories and files, whereas the right control, tvwTargetDir, lists only directories. The CheckBoxes property on tvwSource is set to true, and on tvwTargetDir it is set to false. Also, although tvwSource will allow multiselection, which is the default for TreeView controls, you will enforce single selection for tvwTargetDir.

# .NET Windows Forms Tips for VB 6 Programmers

It's great that the basic .NET Windows controls have a lot in common with their VB 6 ancestors. But there are some changes that could catch you off guard. Keep these tips in mind when designing forms.

In VB 6, some controls display text using the Text property and some use the Caption property. With .NET, all text-related properties are now simply called Text.

VB 6 CommandButtons use the properties Default and Cancel so that the user could effectively select them by pressing the Enter or the Escape key. With .NET, these properties are now part of the Form object. The AcceptButton and CancelButton properties are used to reference which button on the form assumes each responsibility.

You display a VB 6 form by calling the Show( ) method. If you want the form to be displayed as a modal dialog box, you pass the vbModal enumerator to the Show( ) method. In .NET, these two functions have been separated into two different method calls: Show( ) and ShowModal( ).

You'll factor the common code for both TreeView controls into a shared method, FillDirectoryTree, and pass in the control with a flag indicating whether to get the files. You'll call this method from the form's constructor, once for each of the two controls:

```
FillDirectoryTree(tvwSource, true);
FillDirectoryTree(tvwTargetDir, false);
```

The FillDirectoryTree implementation names the TreeView parameter tvw. This will represent the source TreeView and the destination TreeView in turn. You'll need some classes from System.IO, so add a using System.IO; statement at the top of *Form1.cs*. Next, add the method declaration to *Form1.cs*:

```
private void FillDirectoryTree(TreeView tvw, bool isSource)
```

### TreeNode objects

The TreeView control has a property, Nodes, which gets a TreeNodeCollection object. The TreeNodeCollection is a collection of TreeNode objects, each of which represents a node in the tree. Start by emptying that collection:

```
tvw.Nodes.Clear();
```

You are ready to fill the TreeView's Nodes collection by recursing through the directories of all the drives. First, get all the logical drives on the system. To do so, call a static method of the Environment object, GetLogicalDrives( ). The Environment class provides information about and access to the current platform environment. You can use the Environment object to get the machine name, OS version, system directory, and so forth, from the computer on which you are running your program:

```
string[] strDrives = Environment.GetLogicalDrives();
```

GetLogicalDrives( ) returns an array of strings, each of which represents the root directory of one of the logical drives. You will iterate over that collection, adding nodes to the TreeView control as you go:

```
foreach (string rootDirectoryName in strDrives)
{
```

You process each drive within the foreach loop.

The very first thing you need to determine is whether the drive is ready. Our hack for that is to get the list of top-level directories from the drive by calling GetDirectories( ) on a DirectoryInfo object we created for the root directory:

```
DirectoryInfo dir = new DirectoryInfo(rootDirectoryName);
dir.GetDirectories( );
```

The DirectoryInfo class exposes instance methods for creating, moving, and enumerating through directories, their files, and their subdirectories. I cover the DirectoryInfo class in detail in Chapter 22.

The GetDirectories( ) method returns a list of directories, but actually, this code throws the list away. You are calling it here only to generate an exception if the drive is not ready.

Wrap the call in a try block and take no action in the catch block. The effect is that if an exception is thrown, the drive is skipped.

Once you know that the drive is ready, create a TreeNode to hold the root directory of the drive and add that node to the TreeView control:

```
TreeNode ndRoot = new TreeNode(rootDirectoryName);
tvw.Nodes.Add(ndRoot);
```

To get the plus (+) signs right in the TreeView, you must find at least two levels of directories (so that the TreeView knows which directories have subdirectories and can write the + next to them). You don't want to recurse through all the subdirectories, however, because that would be too slow.

The job of the GetSubDirectoryNodes( ) method is to recurse two levels deep, passing in the root node, the name of the root directory, a flag indicating whether you want files, and the current level (you always start at level 1):

```
if ( isSource )
{

  GetSubDirectoryNodes( ndRoot, ndRoot.Text, true,1 );
}
else
{
  GetSubDirectoryNodes( ndRoot, ndRoot.Text, false,1 );
}
```

You are probably wondering why you need to pass in ndRoot.Text if you're already passing in ndRoot. Patience—you will see why this is needed when you recurse back into GetSubDirectoryNodes. You are now finished with FillDirectoryTree( ). See Example 19-1, later in this chapter, for a complete listing of this method.

### Recursing through the subdirectories

GetSubDirectoryNodes( ) begins by once again calling GetDirectories( ), this time stashing away the resulting array of DirectoryInfo objects:

```
private void GetSubDireoctoryNodes(
  TreeNode parentNode, string fullName, bool getFileNames)
{
    DirectoryInfo dir = new DirectoryInfo(fullName);
    DirectoryInfo[] dirSubs = dir.GetDirectories();
```

Notice that the node passed in is named parentNode. The current level of nodes will be considered children to the node passed in. This is how you map the directory structure to the hierarchy of the tree view.

Iterate over each subdirectory, skipping any that are marked Hidden:

```
foreach (DirectoryInfo dirSub in dirSubs)
{
  if ( (dirSub.Attributes & FileAttributes.Hidden) != 0 )
  {
    continue;
  }
}
```

FileAttributes is an enum; other possible values include Archive, Compressed, Directory, Encrypted, Hidden, Normal, ReadOnly, and so on.

The property dirSub.Attributes is the bit pattern of the current attributes of the directory. If you logically AND that value with the bit pattern FileAttributes.Hidden, a bit is set if the file has the hidden attribute; otherwise, all the bits are cleared. You can check for any hidden bit by testing whether the resulting int is something other than 0.

Create a TreeNode with the directory name, and add it to the Nodes collection of the node passed in to the method (parentNode):

```
TreeNode subNode = new TreeNode(dirSub.Name);
parentNode.Nodes.Add(subNode);
```

Now you check the current level (passed in by the calling method) against a constant defined for the class:

```
private const int MaxLevel = 2;
```

so as to recurse only two levels deep:

```
if ( level < MaxLevel )
{
 GetSubDirectoryNodes(
 subNode, dirSub.FullName, getFileNames, level+1 );
}
```

You pass in the node you just created as the new parent, the full path as the full name of the parent, and the flag you received, along with one greater than the current level (thus, if you started at level 1, this next call will set the level to 2).

 The call to the TreeNode constructor uses the Name property of the DirectoryInfo object, whereas the call to GetSubDirectoryNodes() uses the FullName property. If your directory is *C:\Windows\Media\Sounds*, the FullName property returns the full path, and the Name property returns just *Sounds*. Pass in only the name to the node because that is what you want displayed in the tree view. Pass in the full name with the path to the GetSubDirectoryNodes() method so that the method can locate all the subdirectories on the disk. This answers the question asked earlier regarding why you need to pass in the root node's name the first time you call this method. What is passed in isn't the name of the node; it is the full path to the directory represented by the node!

### Getting the files in the directory

Once you've recursed through the subdirectories, it is time to get the files for the directory if the getFileNames flag is true. To do so, call the GetFiles() method on the DirectoryInfo object. An array of FileInfo objects is returned:

```
if (getFileNames)
{
 // Get any files for this node.
 FileInfo[] files = dir.GetFiles();
```

The FileInfo class provides instance methods for manipulating files.

You can now iterate over this collection, accessing the Name property of the FileInfo object, and passing that name to the constructor of a TreeNode, which you then add to the parent node's Nodes collection (thus creating a child node). There is no recursion this time because files don't have subdirectories:

```
foreach (FileInfo file in files)
{
    TreeNode fileNode = new TreeNode(file.Name);
    parentNode.Nodes.Add(fileNode);
}
```

That's all it takes to fill the two tree views. See Example 19-1 for a complete listing of this method.

 If you found any of this confusing, I highly recommend putting the code into your debugger and stepping through the recursion; you can watch the TreeView build its nodes.

# Handling TreeView Events

You must handle a number of events in this example. First, the user might click Cancel, Copy, Clear, or Delete. Second, the user might click one of the checkboxes in the left TreeView, one of the nodes in the right TreeView, or one of the plus signs in either view.

Let's consider the clicks on the TreeViews first, as they are the more interesting, and potentially the more challenging.

### Clicking the source TreeView

There are two TreeView objects, each with its own event handler. Consider the source TreeView object first. The user checks the files and directories he wants to copy from. Each time the user clicks the checkbox indicating a file or directory, a number of events are raised. The event you must handle is AfterCheck.

To do so, implement a custom event handler method you will create and name tvwSource_AfterCheck( ). Visual Studio will wire this to the event handler, or if you aren't using the IDE, you must do so yourself:

```
tvwSource.AfterCheck +=
new System.Windows.Forms.TreeViewEventHandler
  (this.tvwSource_AfterCheck);
```

The implementation of AfterCheck( ) delegates the work to a recursable method named SetCheck( ) that you'll also write. The SetCheck method will recursively set the checkmark for all the contained folders.

To add the AfterCheck event, select the tvwSource control, click the Events icon in the Properties window, and then double-click AfterCheck. This will add the event, wire it up, and place you in the code editor where you can add the body of the method:

```
private void tvwSource_AfterCheck (
object sender, System.Windows.Forms.TreeViewEventArgs e)
{
  SetCheck(e.Node,e.Node.Checked);
}
```

The event handler passes in the sender object and an object of type TreeViewEventArgs. It turns out that you can get the node from this TreeViewEventArgs object (e). Call SetCheck( ), passing in the node and the state of whether the node has been checked.

Each node has a Nodes property, which gets a TreeNodeCollection containing all the subnodes. SetCheck( ) recurses through the current node's Nodes collection, setting each subnode's checkmark to match that of the node that was checked. In other words, when you check a directory, all its files and subdirectories are checked, recursively, all the way down.

## It's Turtles, All the Way Down

Here's my favorite story on recursion, as told by Stephen Hawking: it happened that a famous scientist was telling a story about primitive creation myths. "Some peoples," he said, "believe the world rests on the back of a great turtle. Of course, that raises the question: on what does the turtle rest?"

An elderly woman from the back of the room stood up and said, "Very clever, Sonny, but it's turtles, all the way down."

For each `TreeNode` in the `Nodes` collection, check to see whether it is a leaf. A node is a leaf if its own `Nodes` collection has a count of 0. If it is a leaf, set its `check` property to whatever was passed in as a parameter. If it isn't a leaf, recurse:

```
private void SetCheck(TreeNode node, bool check)
{
    // find all the child nodes from this node
    foreach (TreeNode n in node.Nodes)
    {
        n.Checked = check; // check the node

        // if this is a node in the tree, recurse
        if (n.Nodes.Count != 0)
        {
            SetCheck(n,check);
        }
    }
}
```

This propagates the checkmark (or clears the checkmark) down through the entire structure. In this way, the user can indicate that he wants to select all the files in all the subdirectories by clicking a single directory.

### Expanding a directory

Each time you click a + next to a directory in the source (or in the target), you want to expand that directory. To do so, you'll need an event handler for the `BeforeExpand` event. Because the event handlers will be identical for both the source and the target tree views, you'll create a shared event handler (assigning the same event handler to both):

```
private void tvwExpand(object sender, TreeViewCancelEventArgs e)
{
    TreeView tvw = ( TreeView ) sender;
    bool getFiles = tvw == tvwSource;
    TreeNode currentNode = e.Node;
```

```
    string fullName = currentNode.FullPath;
    currentNode.Nodes.Clear( );
    GetSubDirectoryNodes( currentNode, fullName, getFiles, 1 );
}
```

The first line of this code casts the object passed in by the delegate from object to TreeView, which is safe because you know that only a TreeView can trigger this event.

Your second task is to determine whether you want to get the files in the directory you are opening, and you do only if the name of the TreeView that triggered the event is tvwSource.

You determine which node's + was checked by getting the Node property from the TreeViewCancelEventArgs that is passed in by the event:

**TreeNode** currentNode = e.Node;

Once you have the current node, you get its full pathname (which you will need as a parameter to GetSubDirectoryNodes), and then you must clear its collection of subnodes because you are going to refill that collection by calling in to GetSubDirectoryNodes:

    currentNode.Nodes.Clear( );

Why do you clear the subnodes and then refill them? Because this time you will go another level deep so that the subnodes know whether *they* in turn have subnodes, and thus will know whether they should draw a + next to their subdirectories.

### Clicking the target TreeView

The second event handler for the target TreeView (in addition to BeforeExpand) is somewhat trickier. The event itself is AfterSelect. (Remember that the target TreeView doesn't have checkboxes.) This time, you want to take the one directory chosen and put its full path into the text box at the upper-left corner of the form.

To do so, you must work your way up through the nodes, finding the name of each parent directory, and building the full path:

```
private void tvwTargetDir_AfterSelect (
  object sender, System.Windows.Forms.TreeViewEventArgs e)
{

  string theFullPath = GetParentString(e.Node);
```

We'll look at GetParentString( ) in just a moment. Once you have the full path, you must lop off the backslash (if any) on the end, and then you can fill the text box:

```
if (theFullPath.EndsWith("\\"))
{
    theFullPath =
    theFullPath.Substring(0,theFullPath.Length-1);
}
txtTargetDir.Text = theFullPath;
```

The `GetParentString( )` method takes a node and returns a string with the full path. To do so, it recurses upward through the path, adding the backslash after any node that is not a leaf:

```
private string GetParentString( TreeNode node )
{
    if ( node.Parent == null )
    {
        return node.Text;
    }
    else
    {
        return GetParentString( node.Parent ) + node.Text +
            ( node.Nodes.Count == 0 ? "" : "\\" );
    }
}
```

 The conditional operator (?) is the only ternary operator in C# (a *ternary operator* takes three terms). The logic is "Test whether node. Nodes.Count is 0; if so, return the value before the colon (in this case, an empty string). Otherwise, return the value after the colon (in this case, a backslash)."

The recursion stops when there is no parent; that is, when you hit the root directory.

### Handling the Clear button event

Given the `SetCheck( )` method developed earlier, handling the Clear button's `Click` event is trivial:

```
private void btnClear_Click( object sender, System.EventArgs e )
{
    foreach ( TreeNode node in tvwSource.Nodes )
    {
        SetCheck( node, false );
    }
}
```

Just call the `SetCheck( )` method on the root nodes, and tell them to recursively uncheck all their contained nodes.

## Implementing the Copy Button Event

Now that you can check the files and pick the target directory, you're ready to handle the Copy button-click event. The very first thing you need to do is to get a list of which files were selected. What you want is an array of `FileInfo` objects, but you have no idea how many objects will be in the list. This is a perfect job for `ArrayList`. Delegate responsibility for filling the list to a method called `GetFileList( )`:

---

```
private void btnCopy_Click (object sender, System.EventArgs e)
{
    List<FileInfo> fileList = GetFileList();
```

Let's pick that method apart before returning to the event handler.

### Getting the selected files

Start by instantiating a new List object to hold the strings representing the names of all the files selected:

```
private List<FileInfo> GetFileList()
{
    List<string> fileNames = new List<string>();
```

To get the selected filenames, you can walk through the source TreeView control:

```
foreach (TreeNode theNode in tvwSource.Nodes)
{
    GetCheckedFiles(theNode, fileNames);
}
```

To see how this works, step into the GetCheckedFiles() method. This method is pretty simple: it examines the node it was handed. If that node has no children (node. Nodes.Count == 0), it is a leaf. If that leaf is checked, get the full path (by calling GetParentString() on the node), and add it to the ArrayList passed in as a parameter:

```
private void GetCheckedFiles( TreeNode node, List<string> fileNames )
{
    if ( node.Nodes.Count == 0 )
    {
        if ( node.Checked )
        {
            string fullPath = GetParentString( node );
            fileNames.Add( fullPath );
        }
    }
```

If the node is *not* a leaf, recurse down the tree, finding the child nodes:

```
    else
    {
        foreach ( TreeNode n in node.Nodes )
        {
            GetCheckedFiles( n, fileNames );
        }
    }
}
```

This returns the List filled with all the filenames. Back in GetFileList(), use this List of filenames to create a second List, this time to hold the actual FileInfo objects:

```
List<FileInfo> fileList = new List<FileInfo>();
```

Notice the use of type-safe List objects to ensure that the compiler flags any objects added to the collection that aren't of type FileInfo.

You can now iterate through the filenames in fileList, picking out each name and instantiating a FileInfo object with it. You can detect whether it is a file or a directory by calling the Exists property, which will return false if the File object you created is actually a directory. If it is a File, you can add it to the new ArrayList:

```
foreach (string fileName in fileNames)
{
   FileInfo file = new FileInfo(fileName);

   if (file.Exists)
   {
      fileList.Add(file);
   }
}
```

### Sorting the list of selected files

You want to work your way through the list of selected files in large to small order so that you can pack the target disk as tightly as possible. You must therefore sort the ArrayList. You can call its Sort( ) method, but how will it know how to sort FileInfo objects?

To solve this, you must pass in an IComparer<T> interface. We'll create a class called FileComparer that will implement this generic interface for FileInfo objects:

```
public class FileComparer : IComparer<FileInfo>
{
```

This class has only one method, Compare( ), which takes two FileInfo objects as arguments:

```
public int Compare(FileInfo file1, FileInfo file2){
```

The normal approach is to return 1 if the first object (file1) is larger than the second (file2), to return -1 if the opposite is true, and to return 0 if they are equal. In this case, however, you want the list sorted from big to small, so you should reverse the return values.

 Because this is the only use of the compare method, it is reasonable to put this special knowledge that the sort is from big to small right into the compare method itself. The alternative is to sort small to big, and have the *calling* method reverse the results.

To test the length of the FileInfo object, you must cast the Object parameters to FileInfo objects (which is safe because you know this method will never receive anything else):

---

```
    public int Compare(FileInfo file1, FileInfo file2)
    {

      if ( file1.Length > file2.Length )
      {
        return -1;
      }
      if ( file1.Length < file2.Length )
      {
        return 1;
      }
      return 0;
    }
```

Returning to GetFileList( ), you were about to instantiate the IComparer reference and pass it to the Sort( ) method of fileList:

```
    IComparer<FileInfo> comparer = ( IComparer<FileInfo> ) new FileComparer( );
    fileList.Sort(comparer);
```

With that done, you can return fileList to the calling method:

```
    return fileList;
```

The calling method was btnCopy_Click. Remember, you went off to GetFileList( ) in the first line of the event handler:

```
    protected void btnCopy_Click (object sender, System.EventArgs e)
    {
      List<FileInfo> fileList = GetFileList( );
```

At this point, you've returned with a sorted list of File objects, each representing a file selected in the source TreeView.

You can now iterate through the list, copying the files and updating the UI:

```
    foreach ( FileInfo file in fileList )
    {
      try
      {
        lblStatus.Text = "Copying " + txtTargetDir.Text +
          "\\" + file.Name + "...";
        Application.DoEvents( );

        file.CopyTo( txtTargetDir.Text + "\\" +
          file.Name, chkOverwrite.Checked );
      }

      catch ( Exception ex )
      {
        MessageBox.Show( ex.Message );
      }
    }
    lblStatus.Text = "Done.";
```

As you go, write the progress to the lblStatus label and call Application.DoEvents( ) to give the UI an opportunity to redraw. Then, call CopyTo( ) on the file, passing in the target directory obtained from the text field, and a Boolean flag indicating whether the file should be overwritten if it already exists.

You'll notice that the flag you pass in is the value of the chkOverWrite checkbox. The Checked property evaluates true if the checkbox is checked and false if not.

The copy is wrapped in a try block because you can anticipate any number of things going wrong when copying files. For now, handle all exceptions by popping up a dialog box with the error; you might want to take corrective action in a commercial application.

That's it; you've implemented file copying!

## Handling the Delete Button Event

The code to handle the Delete event is even simpler. The very first thing you do is ask the user whether she is sure she wants to delete the files:

```
private void btnDelete_Click( object sender, System.EventArgs e )
{
   System.Windows.Forms.DialogResult result =
       MessageBox.Show(
        "Are you quite sure?",              // msg
       "Delete Files",                      // caption
       MessageBoxButtons.OKCancel,          // buttons
       MessageBoxIcon.Exclamation,          // icons
       MessageBoxDefaultButton.Button2 );   // default button

   if ( result == System.Windows.Forms.DialogResult.OK )
   {
      List<FileInfo> fileNames = GetFileList( );

      foreach ( FileInfo file in fileNames )
      {
         try
         {
             lblStatus.Text = "Deleting " +
              txtTargetDir.Text + "\\" +
              file.Name + "...";
            Application.DoEvents( );

            // Danger Will Robinson!
            file.Delete( );
         }

         catch ( Exception ex )
         {
            MessageBox.Show( ex.Message );
         }
```

```
      }
      lblStatus.Text = "Done.";
      Application.DoEvents();
   }

}
```

You can use the MessageBox static Show() method, passing in the message you want to display, the title "Delete Files" as a string, and flags, as follows:

- MessageBox.OKCancel asks for two buttons: OK and Cancel.

- MessageBox.IconExclamation indicates that you want to display an exclamation mark icon.

- MessageBox.DefaultButton.Button2 sets the second button (Cancel) as the default choice.

When the user chooses OK or Cancel, the result is passed back as a System.Windows. Forms.DialogResult enumerated value. You can test this value to see whether the user selected OK:

```
if (result == System.Windows.Forms.DialogResult.OK)
{
```

If so, you can get the list of fileNames and iterate through it, deleting each as you go.

This code is identical to the copy code, except that the method that is called on the file is Delete().

Example 19-1 provides the commented source code for this example.

*Example 19-1. FileCopier source code*

```
using System;
using System.Collections;
using System.Collections.Generic;
using System.IO;
using System.Windows.Forms;


/// <remarks>
///    File Copier - Windows Forms demonstration program
///    (c) Copyright 2007 O'Reilly Media
/// </remarks>
namespace FileCopier
{


   /// <summary>
   /// Form demonstrating Windows Forms implementation
   /// </summary>
   partial class frmFileCopier : Form
   {
      private const int MaxLevel = 2;
      public frmFileCopier()
```

*Example 19-1. FileCopier source code (continued)*

```csharp
{
    InitializeComponent( );
    FillDirectoryTree( tvwSource, true );
    FillDirectoryTree( tvwTarget, false );
}

/// <summary>
///     nested class which knows how to compare
///     two files we want to sort large to small,
///     so reverse the normal return values.
/// </summary>
public class FileComparer : IComparer<FileInfo>
{


    public int Compare(FileInfo file1, FileInfo file2)
    {

        if ( file1.Length > file2.Length )
        {
            return -1;
        }
        if ( file1.Length < file2.Length )
        {
            return 1;
        }
        return 0;
    }

    public bool Equals(FileInfo x, FileInfo y) { throw new NotImplementedException( );}
    public int GetHashCode(FileInfo x) {throw new NotImplementedException( ); }

}



private void FillDirectoryTree( TreeView tvw, bool isSource )
{
    //  Populate tvwSource, the Source TreeView,
    //  with the contents of
    //  the local hard drive.
    //  First clear all the nodes.
    tvw.Nodes.Clear( );

    //  Get the logical drives and put them into the
    //  root nodes. Fill an array with all the
    //  logical drives on the machine.
    string[] strDrives = Environment.GetLogicalDrives( );

    //  Iterate through the drives, adding them to the tree.
    //  Use a try/catch block, so if a drive is not ready,
    //  e.g., an empty floppy or CD,
```

*Example 19-1. FileCopier source code (continued)*

```
    //     it will not be added to the tree.
    foreach ( string rootDirectoryName in strDrives )
    {

        try
        {

            // Fill an array with all the first level
            // subdirectories. If the drive is
            // not ready, this will throw an exception.
            DirectoryInfo dir =
                new DirectoryInfo( rootDirectoryName );

            dir.GetDirectories();      // force exception if drive not ready

            TreeNode ndRoot = new TreeNode( rootDirectoryName );

            // Add a node for each root directory.
            tvw.Nodes.Add( ndRoot );

            // Add subdirectory nodes.
            // If Treeview is the source,
            // then also get the filenames.
            if ( isSource )
            {

                GetSubDirectoryNodes(
                    ndRoot, ndRoot.Text, true,1 );
            }
            else
            {
                GetSubDirectoryNodes(
                    ndRoot, ndRoot.Text, false,1 );
            }
        }
        // Catch any errors such as
            // Drive not ready.
        catch
        {
        }
        Application.DoEvents();
    }
} //  close for FillSourceDirectoryTree

/// <summary>
/// Gets all the subdirectories below the
/// passed-in directory node.
/// Adds to the directory tree.
/// The parameters passed in are the parent node
/// for this subdirectory,
/// the full pathname of this subdirectory,
/// and a Boolean to indicate
```

*Example 19-1. FileCopier source code (continued)*

```
/// whether or not to get the files in the subdirectory.
/// </summary>
private void GetSubDirectoryNodes(
    TreeNode parentNode, string fullName, bool getFileNames, int level )
{
    DirectoryInfo dir = new DirectoryInfo( fullName );
    DirectoryInfo[] dirSubs = dir.GetDirectories();

    //  Add a child node for each subdirectory.
    foreach ( DirectoryInfo dirSub in dirSubs )
    {

        // do not show hidden folders
        if ( ( dirSub.Attributes & FileAttributes.Hidden )
          != 0 )
        {
            continue;
        }

        /// <summary>
        ///     Each directory contains the full path.
        ///     We need to split it on the backslashes,
        ///     and only use
        ///     the last node in the tree.
        ///     Need to double the backslash since it
        ///     is normally
        ///     an escape character
        /// </summary>
        TreeNode subNode = new TreeNode( dirSub.Name );
        parentNode.Nodes.Add( subNode );

        //  Call GetSubDirectoryNodes recursively.

        if ( level < MaxLevel )
        {
            GetSubDirectoryNodes(
              subNode, dirSub.FullName, getFileNames, level+1 );
        }

    }
    if ( getFileNames )
    {
        //  Get any files for this node.
        FileInfo[] files = dir.GetFiles();

        // After placing the nodes,
        // now place the files in that subdirectory.
        foreach ( FileInfo file in files )
        {
            TreeNode fileNode = new TreeNode( file.Name );
            parentNode.Nodes.Add( fileNode );
        }
```

*Example 19-1. FileCopier source code (continued)*

```
      }
}


/// <summary>
///     Create an ordered list of all
///     the selected files, copy to the
///     target directory
/// </summary>
private void btnCopy_Click( object sender,
    System.EventArgs e )
{
   // get the list
   List<FileInfo> fileList = GetFileList( );

   // copy the files
   foreach ( FileInfo file in fileList )
   {
      try
      {
         // update the label to show progress
         lblStatus.Text = "Copying " + txtTargetDir.Text +
            "\\" + file.Name + "...";
         Application.DoEvents( );

         // copy the file to its destination location
         file.CopyTo( txtTargetDir.Text + "\\" +
            file.Name, chkOverwrite.Checked );
      }

      catch ( Exception ex )
      {
         // you may want to do more than
         // just show the message
         MessageBox.Show( ex.Message );
      }
   }
   lblStatus.Text = "Done.";

}


/// <summary>
///     Tell the root of each tree to uncheck
///     all the nodes below
/// </summary>
private void btnClear_Click( object sender, System.EventArgs e )
{
   // get the topmost node for each drive
   // and tell it to clear recursively
   foreach ( TreeNode node in tvwSource.Nodes )
   {
```

*Example 19-1. FileCopier source code (continued)*

```csharp
            SetCheck( node, false );
        }
    }

    /// <summary>
    ///     on cancel,  exit
    /// </summary>
    private void btnCancel_Click(object sender, EventArgs e)
    {
        Application.Exit( );
    }


    /// <summary>
    ///     Given a node and an array list
    ///     fill the list with the names of
    ///     all the checked files
    /// </summary>
    // Fill the ArrayList with the full paths of
    // all the files checked
    private void GetCheckedFiles( TreeNode node,
        List<string> fileNames )
    {
        // if this is a leaf...
        if ( node.Nodes.Count == 0 )
        {
            // if the node was checked...
            if ( node.Checked )
            {
                // get the full path and add it to the arrayList
                string fullPath = GetParentString( node );
                fileNames.Add( fullPath );
            }
        }
        else  // if this node is not a leaf
        {
            // if this node is not a leaf
            foreach ( TreeNode n in node.Nodes )
            {
                GetCheckedFiles( n, fileNames );
            }
        }
    }

    /// <summary>
    ///     Given a node, return the
    ///     full pathname
    /// </summary>
    private string GetParentString( TreeNode node )
    {
        // if this is the root node (c:\) return the text
        if ( node.Parent == null )
```

*Example 19-1. FileCopier source code (continued)*

```
      {
         return node.Text;
      }
      else
      {
         // recurse up and get the path then
         // add this node and a slash
         // if this node is the leaf, don't add the slash
         return GetParentString( node.Parent ) + node.Text +
            ( node.Nodes.Count == 0 ? "" : "\\" );
      }
   }


   /// <summary>
   ///     shared by delete and copy
   ///     creates an ordered list of all
   ///     the selected files
   /// </summary>
   private List<FileInfo> GetFileList()
   {
      // create an unsorted array list of the full filenames
       List<string> fileNames = new List<string>();

      // ArrayList fileNames = new ArrayList();

      // fill the fileNames ArrayList with the
      // full path of each file to copy
      foreach ( TreeNode theNode in tvwSource.Nodes )
      {
         GetCheckedFiles( theNode, fileNames );
      }

      // Create a list to hold the FileInfo objects
      List<FileInfo> fileList = new List<FileInfo>();
       // ArrayList fileList = new ArrayList();

      // for each of the filenames we have in our unsorted list
      // if the name corresponds to a file (and not a directory)
      // add it to the file list
      foreach ( string fileName in fileNames )
      {
         // create a file with the name
         FileInfo file = new FileInfo( fileName );

         // see if it exists on the disk
         // this fails if it was a directory
         if ( file.Exists )
         {
            // both the key and the value are the file
            // would it be easier to have an empty value?
            fileList.Add( file );
         }
```

*Example 19-1. FileCopier source code (continued)*

```
      }

      // Create an instance of the IComparer interface
      IComparer<FileInfo> comparer = ( IComparer<FileInfo> ) new FileComparer( );

      // pass the comparer to the sort method so that the list
      // is sorted by the compare method of comparer.
      fileList.Sort( comparer );
      return fileList;
   }


   /// <summary>
   ///     check that the user does want to delete
   ///     Make a list and delete each in turn
   /// </summary>
   private void btnDelete_Click( object sender, System.EventArgs e )
   {
      // ask them if they are sure
      System.Windows.Forms.DialogResult result =
          MessageBox.Show(
           "Are you quite sure?",              // msg
          "Delete Files",                      // caption
          MessageBoxButtons.OKCancel,          // buttons
          MessageBoxIcon.Exclamation,          // icons
          MessageBoxDefaultButton.Button2 );   // default button

      // if they are sure...
      if ( result == System.Windows.Forms.DialogResult.OK )
      {
         // iterate through the list and delete them.
         // get the list of selected files
        List<FileInfo> fileNames = GetFileList( );

        foreach ( FileInfo file in fileNames )
         {
            try
            {
               // update the label to show progress
               lblStatus.Text = "Deleting " +
                   txtTargetDir.Text + "\\" +
                   file.Name + "...";
               Application.DoEvents( );

               // Danger Will Robinson!
               file.Delete( );
            }

            catch ( Exception ex )
            {
               // you may want to do more than
               // just show the message
               MessageBox.Show( ex.Message );
```

*Example 19-1. FileCopier source code (continued)*

```
            }
        }
        lblStatus.Text = "Done.";
        Application.DoEvents( );
    }

}

/// <summary>
///    Get the full path of the chosen directory
///    copy it to txtTargetDir
/// </summary>
private void tvwTargetDir_AfterSelect(
    object sender,
    System.Windows.Forms.TreeViewEventArgs e )
{
    // get the full path for the selected directory
    string theFullPath = GetParentString( e.Node );

    // if it is not a leaf, it will end with a backslash
    // remove the backslash
    if ( theFullPath.EndsWith( "\\" ) )
    {
        theFullPath =
            theFullPath.Substring( 0, theFullPath.Length - 1 );
    }
    // insert the path in the text box
    txtTargetDir.Text = theFullPath;
}

/// <summary>
///    Mark each node below the current
///    one with the current value of checked
/// </summary>
private void tvwSource_AfterCheck( object sender,
    System.Windows.Forms.TreeViewEventArgs e )
{
    // Call a recursible method.
    // e.node is the node which was checked by the user.
    // The state of the checkmark is already
    // changed by the time you get here.
    // Therefore, we want to pass along
    // the state of e.node.Checked.
     SetCheck( e.Node, e.Node.Checked );
}

/// <summary>
///    recursively set or clear checkmarks
/// </summary>
private void SetCheck( TreeNode node, bool check )
{
    // find all the child nodes from this node
```

*Example 19-1. FileCopier source code (continued)*

```
        foreach ( TreeNode n in node.Nodes )
        {
            n.Checked = check;    // check the node

            // if this is a node in the tree, recurse
            if ( n.Nodes.Count != 0 )
            {
                SetCheck( n, check );
            }
        }
    }


    private void tvwExpand(object sender, TreeViewCancelEventArgs e)
    {

        TreeView tvw = ( TreeView ) sender;
        bool getFiles = tvw == tvwSource;
        TreeNode currentNode = e.Node;
        string fullName = currentNode.FullPath;
        currentNode.Nodes.Clear( );
        GetSubDirectoryNodes( currentNode, fullName, getFiles, 1 );

    }

}           // end class frmFileCopier
}           // end namespace FileCopier
```

# PART IV

# The CLR and the .NET Framework

Chapter 20, *Attributes and Reflection*

Chapter 21, *Threads and Synchronization*

Chapter 22, *Streams*

Chapter 23, *Programming .NET and COM*

# Attributes and Reflection

Throughout this book, I have emphasized that a .NET application contains code, data, and metadata. *Metadata* is information about the data—that is, information about the types, code, assembly, and so forth—stored along with your program. This chapter explores how some of that metadata is created and used.

*Attributes* are a mechanism for adding metadata, such as compiler instructions and other data about your data, methods, and classes to the program itself. Attributes are inserted into the metadata and are visible through ILDASM and other metadata-reading tools.

*Reflection* is the process by which a program can read its own metadata, or metadata from another program. A program is said to reflect on itself or on another program, extracting metadata from the reflected assembly and using that metadata either to inform the user or to modify the program's behavior.

## Attributes

An *attribute* is an object that represents data you want to associate with an element in your program. The element to which you attach an attribute is referred to as the *target* of that attribute. For example, the attribute:

```
[NoIDispatch]
```

is associated with a class or an interface to indicate that the target class should derive from IUnknown rather than IDispatch when exporting to COM. I discuss COM interface programming in detail in Chapter 23.

# Types of Attributes

Some attributes are supplied as part of the CLR, or by the framework. In addition, you are free to create your own custom attributes for your own purposes.

Most programmers will use only the attributes provided by the framework, though creating your own custom attributes can be a powerful tool when combined with reflection, as described later in this chapter.

### Attribute targets

If you search through the CLR, you'll find a great many attributes. Some attributes are applied to an assembly, others to a class or interface, and some, such as [WebMethod], are applied to class members. These are called the *attribute targets*. The possible attributes are declared in the AttributeTargets enumeration, and are detailed in Table 20-1.

*Table 20-1. Possible attribute targets*

| Member name | Usage |
| --- | --- |
| All | Applied to any of the following elements: assembly, class, constructor, delegate, enum, event, field, interface, method, module, parameter, property, return value, or struct |
| Assembly | Applied to the assembly itself |
| Class | Applied to a class |
| Constructor | Applied to a given constructor |
| Delegate | Applied to a delegate |
| Enum | Applied to an enumeration |
| Event | Applied to an event |
| Field | Applied to a field |
| Interface | Applied to an interface |
| Method | Applied to a method |
| Module | Applied to a single module |
| Parameter | Applied to a parameter of a method |
| Property | Applied to a property (both get and set, if implemented) |
| ReturnValue | Applied to a return value |
| Struct | Applied to a struct |

### Applying attributes

You apply attributes to their targets by placing them in square brackets immediately before the target item (except in the case of assemblies, in which case you place them at the top of the file).

You can combine attributes by stacking one on top of another:

```
[assembly: AssemblyDelaySign(false)]
[assembly: AssemblyKeyFile(".\\keyFile.snk")]
```

You can also do this by separating the attributes with commas:

```
[assembly: AssemblyDelaySign(false),
 assembly: AssemblyKeyFile(".\\keyFile.snk")]
```

 You must place assembly attributes after all using statements and before any code.

Many attributes are used for interoperating with COM, as discussed in detail in Chapter 23. You've already seen use of one attribute ([WebMethod]) in Chapter 16. You'll see other attributes, such as the [Serializable] attribute, used in the discussion of serialization in Chapter 22.

The System.Reflection namespace offers a number of attributes, including attributes for assemblies (such as the AssemblyKeyFileAttribute), for configuration, and for version attributes.

One of the attributes you are most likely to use in your everyday C# programming (if you aren't interacting with COM) is [Serializable]. As you'll see in Chapter 22, all you need to do to ensure that your class can be serialized to disk or to the Internet is add the [Serializable] attribute to the class:

```
[Serializable]
class MySerializableClass
```

The attribute tag is put in square brackets immediately before its target—in this case, the class declaration.

The key fact about attributes is that you know when you need them; the task will dictate their use.

## Custom Attributes

You are free to create your own custom attributes and use them at runtime as you see fit. Suppose, for example, that your development organization wants to keep track of bug fixes. You already keep a database of all your bugs, but you'd like to tie your bug reports to specific fixes in the code.

You might add comments to your code along the lines of:

```
// Bug 323 fixed by Jesse Liberty 1/1/2008.
```

This would make it easy to see in your source code, but there is no enforced connection to Bug 323 in the database. A custom attribute might be just what you need. You would replace your comment with something like this:

```
[BugFixAttribute(323,"Jesse Liberty","1/1/2008",
Comment="Off by one error")]
```

You could then write a program to read through the metadata to find these bug-fix notations and update the database. The attribute would serve the purposes of a comment, but would also allow you to retrieve the information programmatically through tools you'd create.

 This may be a somewhat artificial example, however, because these attributes would be compiled into the shipping code.

### Declaring an attribute

Attributes, like most things in C#, are embodied in classes. To create a custom attribute, derive your new custom attribute class from System.Attribute:

```
public class BugFixAttribute : System.Attribute
```

You need to tell the compiler which kinds of elements this attribute can be used with (the attribute target). Specify this with (what else?) an attribute:

```
[AttributeUsage(AttributeTargets.Class |
    AttributeTargets.Constructor |
    AttributeTargets.Field |
    AttributeTargets.Method |
    AttributeTargets.Property,
    AllowMultiple = true)]
```

AttributeUsage is an attribute applied to attributes: a *meta-attribute*. It provides, if you will, meta-metadata—that is, data about the metadata. For the AttributeUsage attribute constructor, you pass two arguments.

The first argument is a set of flags that indicate the target—in this case, the class and its constructor, fields, methods, and properties. The second argument is a flag that indicates whether a given element might receive more than one such attribute. In this example, AllowMultiple is set to true, indicating that class members can have more than one BugFixAttribute assigned.

### Naming an attribute

The new custom attribute in this example is named BugFixAttribute. The convention is to append the word *Attribute* to your attribute name. The compiler supports this by allowing you to call the attribute with the shorter version of the name. Thus, you can write:

```
[BugFix(123, "Jesse Liberty", "01/01/08", Comment="Off by one")]
```

The compiler will first look for an attribute named BugFix and, if it doesn't find that, will then look for BugFixAttribute.

## Constructing an attribute

Attributes take two types of parameters: *positional* and *named*. In the BugFix example, the programmer's name, the bug ID, and the date are positional parameters, and comment is a named parameter. Positional parameters are passed in through the constructor, and must be passed in the order declared in the constructor:

```
public BugFixAttribute(int bugID, string programmer,
string date)
{
    this.BugID = bugID;
    this.Programmer = programmer;
    this.Date = date;
}
```

Named parameters are implemented as fields or as properties:

```
public string Comment    { get; set; }
```

It is common to create read-only properties for the positional parameters:

```
public int BugID     { get; private set; }
```

## Using an attribute

Once you have defined an attribute, you can put it to work by placing it immediately before its target. To test the BugFixAttribute of the preceding example, the following program creates a simple class named MyMath and gives it two functions. Assign BugFixAttributes to the class to record its code-maintenance history:

```
[BugFixAttribute(121,"Jesse Liberty","01/03/08")]
[BugFixAttribute(107,"Jesse Liberty","01/04/08",
                Comment="Fixed off by one errors")]
public class MyMath
```

These attributes are stored with the metadata. Example 20-1 shows the complete program.

*Example 20-1. Working with custom attributes*

```
using System;

namespace CustomAttributes
{
    // create custom attribute to be assigned to class members
    [AttributeUsage(AttributeTargets.Class |
                AttributeTargets.Constructor |
                AttributeTargets.Field |
                AttributeTargets.Method |
                AttributeTargets.Property,
                AllowMultiple = true)]
    public class BugFixAttribute : System.Attribute
    {
        // attribute constructor for positional parameters
        public BugFixAttribute
```

*Example 20-1. Working with custom attributes (continued)*

```csharp
        (
            int bugID,
            string programmer,
            string date
        )
        {
            this.BugID = bugID;
            this.Programmer = programmer;
            this.Date = date;
        }

        // accessors
        public int BugID { get; private set; }
        public string Date { get; private set; }
        public string Programmer { get; private set; }

        // property for named parameter
        public string Comment { get; set; }
    }

    // ********* assign the attributes to the class ********

    [BugFixAttribute(121, "Jesse Liberty", "01/03/08")]
    [BugFixAttribute(107, "Jesse Liberty", "01/04/08",
                     Comment = "Fixed off by one errors")]
    public class MyMath
    {
        public double DoFunc1(double param1)
        {
            return param1 + DoFunc2(param1);
        }

        public double DoFunc2(double param1)
        {
            return param1 / 3;
        }
    }

    public class Tester
    {
        static void Main(string[] args)
        {
            MyMath mm = new MyMath();
            Console.WriteLine("Calling DoFunc(7). Result: {0}",
            mm.DoFunc1(7));
        }
    }
}

Output:
Calling DoFunc(7). Result: 9.3333333333333333
```

As you can see, the attributes had absolutely no impact on the output. In fact, for the moment, you have only my word that the attributes exist at all. A quick look at the metadata using ILDASM does reveal that the attributes are in place, however, as shown in Figure 20-1. You'll see how to get at this metadata and use it in your program in the next section.

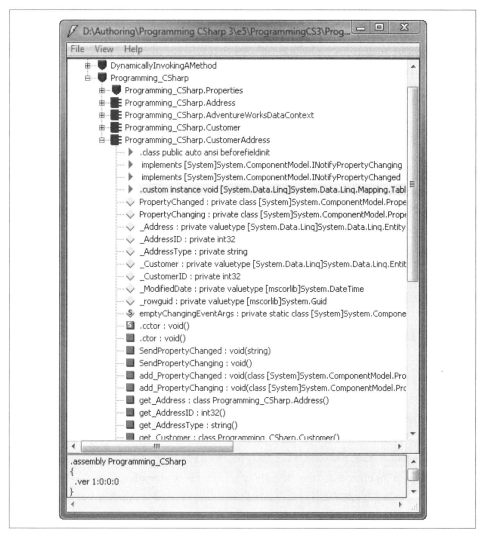

*Figure 20-1. The metadata in the assembly*

# Reflection

For the attributes in the metadata to be useful, you need a way to access them, ideally during runtime. The classes in the Reflection namespace, along with the System.Type class, provide support for examining and interacting with the metadata.

Reflection is generally used for any of four tasks:

*Viewing metadata*
> This might be used by tools and utilities that wish to display metadata.

*Performing type discovery*
> This allows you to examine the types in an assembly and interact with or instantiate those types. This can be useful in creating custom scripts. For example, you might want to allow your users to interact with your program using a script language, such as JavaScript, or a scripting language you create yourself.

*Late binding to methods and properties*
> This allows the programmer to invoke properties and methods on objects dynamically instantiated, based on type discovery. This is also known as *dynamic invocation*.

*Creating types at runtime (reflection emit)*
> The ultimate use of reflection is to create new types at runtime and then to use those types to perform tasks. You might do this when a custom class, created at runtime, will run significantly faster than more generic code created at compile time.

## Viewing Metadata

In this section, you will use the C# reflection support to read the metadata in the MyMath class.

Start by obtaining an object of the type MemberInfo. This object, in the System. Reflection namespace, is provided to discover the attributes of a member and to provide access to the metadata:

```
System.Reflection.MemberInfo inf = typeof(MyMath);
```

Call the typeof operator on the MyMath type, which returns an object of type Type, which derives from MemberInfo.

 The Type class is the heart of the reflection classes. Type encapsulates a representation of the type of an object. The Type class is the primary way to access metadata. Type derives from MemberInfo and encapsulates information about the members of a class (e.g., methods, properties, fields, events, etc.).

---

The next step is to call GetCustomAttributes on this MemberInfo object, passing in the type of the attribute you want to find. You get back an array of objects, each of type BugFixAttribute:

```
object[] attributes;
attributes =
    inf.GetCustomAttributes(typeof(BugFixAttribute),false);
```

You can now iterate through this array, printing out the properties of the BugFixAttribute object. Example 20-2 replaces the Tester class from Example 20-1.

*Example 20-2. Using reflection*

```
public static void Main(string[] args)
{
    MyMath mm = new MyMath( );
    Console.WriteLine("Calling DoFunc(7). Result: {0}",
                        mm.DoFunc1(7));

    // get the member information and use it to
    // retrieve the custom attributes
    System.Reflection.MemberInfo inf = typeof(MyMath);
    object[] attributes;
    attributes = inf.GetCustomAttributes(
                    typeof(BugFixAttribute), false);

    // iterate through the attributes, retrieving the
    // properties
    foreach (Object attribute in attributes)
    {
        BugFixAttribute bfa = (BugFixAttribute)attribute;
        Console.WriteLine("\nBugID: {0}", bfa.BugID);
        Console.WriteLine("Programmer: {0}", bfa.Programmer);
        Console.WriteLine("Date: {0}", bfa.Date);
        Console.WriteLine("Comment: {0}", bfa.Comment);
    }
}

Output:
Calling DoFunc(7). Result: 9.33333333333333

BugID: 121
Programmer: Jesse Liberty
Date: 01/03/08
Comment:

BugID: 107
Programmer: Jesse Liberty
Date: 01/04/08
Comment: Fixed off by one errors
```

When you put this replacement code into Example 20-1 and run it, you can see the metadata printed as you'd expect.

# Type Discovery

You can use reflection to explore and examine the contents of an assembly. You can find the types associated with a module; the methods, fields, properties, and events associated with a type, as well as the signatures of each of the type's methods; the interfaces supported by the type; and the type's base class.

To start, you load an assembly dynamically with the `Assembly.Load()` static method. The `Assembly` class encapsulates the actual assembly itself, for purposes of reflection. One signature for the `Load` method is:

```
public static Assembly.Load(AssemblyName)
```

For the next example, pass in the core library to the `Load()` method. *Mscorlib.dll* has the core classes of the .NET Framework:

```
Assembly a = Assembly.Load("Mscorlib");
```

Once the assembly is loaded, you can call `GetTypes()` to return an array of `Type` objects. The `Type` object is the heart of reflection. `Type` represents type declarations (classes, interfaces, arrays, values, and enumerations):

```
Type[] types = a.GetTypes();
```

The assembly returns an array of types that you can display in a `foreach` loop, as shown in Example 20-3. Because this example uses the `Type` class, you will want to add a `using` directive for the `System.Reflection` namespace.

*Example 20-3. Reflecting on an assembly*

```
using System;
using System.Reflection;

namespace ReflectingAnAssembly
{
    public class Tester
    {
        public static void Main()
        {
            // what is in the assembly
            Assembly a = Assembly.Load("Mscorlib");
            Type[] types = a.GetTypes();
            foreach (Type t in types)
            {
                Console.WriteLine("Type is {0}", t);
            }
            Console.WriteLine(
                "{0} types found", types.Length);
        }
    }
}
```

The output from this would fill many pages. Here is a short excerpt:

```
Type is System.Object
Type is ThisAssembly
Type is AssemblyRef
Type is System.ICloneable
Type is System.Collections.IEnumerable
Type is System.Collections.ICollection
Type is System.Collections.IList
Type is System.Array
2373 types found
```

This example obtained an array filled with the types from the core library and printed them one by one. The array contained 2,373 entries on my machine.

 In version 1.1, I found 1,426 entries on my machine. Microsoft has been busy!

## Reflecting on a Type

You can reflect on a single type in the Mscorlib assembly as well. To do so, you extract a type from the assembly with either typeOf or the GetType( ) method, as shown in Example 20-4.

*Example 20-4. Reflecting on a type*

```
using System;

namespace ReflectingOnAType
{
    public class Tester
    {
        public static void Main( )
        {
            // examine a type
            Type theType = Type.GetType("System.Reflection.Assembly");
            Console.WriteLine("\nSingle Type is {0}\n", theType);
        }
    }
}

Output:
Single Type is System.Reflection.Assembly
```

### Finding all type members

You can ask the Assembly type for all its members using the GetMembers( ) method of the Type class, which lists all the methods, properties, and fields, as shown in Example 20-5.

*Example 20-5. Reflecting on the members of a type*

```
using System;
using System.Reflection;

namespace ReflectingOnMembersOfAType
{
    public class Tester
    {
        public static void Main( )
        {
            // examine a single object
            Type theType = Type.GetType("System.Reflection.Assembly");
            Console.WriteLine("\nSingle Type is {0}\n", theType);

            // get all the members
            MemberInfo[] mbrInfoArray = theType.GetMembers( );
            foreach (MemberInfo mbrInfo in mbrInfoArray)
            {
                Console.WriteLine("{0} is a {1}",
                        mbrInfo, mbrInfo.MemberType);
            }
        }
    }
}
```

Once again, the output is quite lengthy, but within the output you see fields, methods, constructors, and properties, as shown in this excerpt:

```
System.Type GetType(System.String, Boolean, Boolean) is a Method
System.Type[] GetExportedTypes( ) is a Method
System.Reflection.Module GetModule(System.String) is a Method
System.String get_FullName( ) is a Method
```

### Finding type methods

You might want to focus on methods only, excluding the fields, properties, and so forth. To do so, remove the call to GetMembers( ):

```
MemberInfo[] mbrInfoArray =
    theType.GetMembers( );
```

and add a call to GetMethods( ):

```
mbrInfoArray = theType.GetMethods( );
```

The output now contains nothing but the methods:

```
Output (excerpt):
Boolean Equals(System.Object) is a Method
System.String ToString( ) is a Method
System.String CreateQualifiedName(
System.String, System.String) is a Method
Boolean get_GlobalAssemblyCache( ) is a Method
```

## Finding particular type members

Finally, to narrow it down even further, you can use the `FindMembers` method to find particular members of the type. For example, you can narrow your search to methods whose names begin with "Get."

To narrow the search, use the `FindMembers` method, which takes four parameters:

MemberTypes

A `MemberTypes` object that indicates the type of the member to search for. These include `All`, `Constructor`, `Custom`, `Event`, `Field`, `Method`, `Nestedtype`, `Property`, and `TypeInfo`. You will also use the `MemberTypes.Method` to find a method.

BindingFlags

An enumeration that controls the way searches are conducted by reflection. There are a great many `BindingFlags` values, including `IgnoreCase`, `Instance`, `Public`, `Static`, and so forth.

MemberFilter

A delegate (see Chapter 12) that filters the list of members in the `MemberInfo` array of objects. You use a `Type.FilterName` filter, which is a field of the `Type` class that filters on a name.

Object

A string value used by the filter. In this case, you pass in `Get*` to match only those methods that begin with "Get."

The complete listing for filtering on these methods is shown in Example 20-6.

*Example 20-6. Finding particular members*

```
using System;
using System.Reflection;

namespace FindingParticularMembers
{
    public class Tester
    {
        public static void Main()
        {
            // examine a single object
            Type theType = Type.GetType("System.Reflection.Assembly");

            // just members which are methods beginning with Get
            MemberInfo[] mbrInfoArray = theType.FindMembers(
                            MemberTypes.Method,
                            BindingFlags.Public |
                            BindingFlags.Static |
                            BindingFlags.NonPublic |
                            BindingFlags.Instance |
                            BindingFlags.DeclaredOnly,
                            Type.FilterName, "Get*");
            foreach (MemberInfo mbrInfo in mbrInfoArray)
```

*Example 20-6. Finding particular members (continued)*

```
        {
            Console.WriteLine("{0} is a {1}",
                        mbrInfo, mbrInfo.MemberType);
        }
    }
}
}
```

```
Output (excerpt):
System.Type GetType(System.String, Boolean, Boolean) is a Method
System.Type[] GetExportedTypes() is a Method
System.Reflection.Module GetModule(System.String) is a Method
System.Reflection.AssemblyName[] GetReferencedAssemblies() is a Method
Int64 GetHostContext() is a Method
System.String GetLocation() is a Method
System.String GetFullName() is a Method
```

# Late Binding

Once you find a method, you can invoke it using reflection. For example, you might like to invoke the Cos( ) method of System.Math, which returns the cosine of an angle.

 You can, of course, call Cos( ) in the normal course of your code, but reflection allows you to bind to that method at runtime. This is called *late binding*, and offers the flexibility of choosing at runtime which object to bind to and invoking it programmatically. This can be useful when creating a custom script to be run by the user or when working with objects that might not be available at compile time. For example, by using late binding, your program can interact with the spellchecker or other components of a running commercial word processing program such as Microsoft Word.

To invoke Cos( ), first get the Type information for the System.Math class:

```
Type theMathType = Type.GetType("System.Math");
```

With that type information, you can dynamically load an instance of a class using a static method of the Activator class. Because Cos( ) is static, you don't need to construct an instance of System.Math (and you can't because System.Math has no public constructor).

The Activator class contains four methods, all static, which you can use to create objects locally or remotely, or to obtain references to existing objects. The four methods are as follows:

CreateComInstanceFrom
    Creates instances of COM objects.

CreateInstanceFrom

Creates a reference to an object from a particular assembly and type name.

GetObject

Used when marshaling objects.

CreateInstance

Creates local or remote instances of an object. For example:

```
Object theObj = Activator.CreateInstance(someType);
```

Back to the Cos( ) example. You now have one object in hand: a Type object named theMathType, which you created by calling GetType.

Before you can invoke a method on the object, you must get the method you need from the Type object, theMathType. To do so, you'll call GetMethod( ), and you'll pass in the signature of the Cos method.

The signature, you will remember, is the name of the method (Cos) and its parameter types. In the case of Cos( ), there is only one parameter: a double. However, Type. GetMethod takes two parameters. The first represents the name of the method you want, and the second represents the parameters. The name is passed as a string; the parameters are passed as an array of types:

```
MethodInfo CosineInfo =
  theMathType.GetMethod("Cos",paramTypes);
```

Before calling GetMethod( ), you must prepare the array of types:

```
Type[] paramTypes = new Type[1];
paramTypes[0]= Type.GetType("System.Double");
```

This code declares the array of Type objects, and then fills the first element (paramTypes[0]) with a type representing a double. Obtain the type representing a double by calling the static method Type.GetType( ), and passing in the string System.Double.

You now have an object of type MethodInfo on which you can invoke the method. To do so, you must pass in the object on which to invoke the method and the actual value of the parameters, again in an array. Because this is a static method, pass in theMathType (if Cos( ) were an instance method, you could use theObj instead of theMathType):

```
Object[] parameters = new Object[1];
parameters[0] = 45 * (Math.PI/180); // 45 degrees in radians
Object returnVal = CosineInfo.Invoke(theMathType,parameters);
```

Note that you've created two arrays. The first, paramTypes, holds the type of the parameters. The second, parameters, holds the actual value. If the method had taken two arguments, you'd have declared these arrays to hold two values. If the method didn't take any values, you can still create the array, but you give it a size of zero:

```
Type[] paramTypes = new Type[0];
```

Odd as this looks, it is correct.

Example 20-7 illustrates dynamically calling the Cos( ) method.

*Example 20-7. Dynamically invoking a method*

```
using System;
using System.Reflection;

namespace DynamicallyInvokingAMethod
{
    public class Tester
    {
        public static void Main()
        {
            Type theMathType = Type.GetType("System.Math");
            // Since System.Math has no public constructor, this
            // would throw an exception.
            // Object theObj =
            //     Activator.CreateInstance(theMathType);

            // array with one member
            Type[] paramTypes = new Type[1];
            paramTypes[0] = Type.GetType("System.Double");

            // Get method info for Cos()
            MethodInfo CosineInfo =
                theMathType.GetMethod("Cos", paramTypes);

            // fill an array with the actual parameters
            Object[] parameters = new Object[1];
            parameters[0] = 45 * (Math.PI / 180); // 45 degrees in radians
            Object returnVal =
                CosineInfo.Invoke(theMathType, parameters);
            Console.WriteLine(
                "The cosine of a 45 degree angle {0}",
                returnVal);
        }
    }
}
```

```
Output:
The cosine of a 45 degree angle 0.707106781186548
```

That was a lot of work just to invoke a single method. The power, however, is that you can use reflection to discover an assembly on the user's machine, to query what methods are available, and to invoke one of those members dynamically.

# CHAPTER 21

# Threads and Synchronization

*Threads* are responsible for multitasking within a single application. The System. Threading namespace provides a wealth of classes and interfaces to manage multi-threaded programming. The majority of programmers might never need to manage threads explicitly, however, because the CLR abstracts much of the threading support into classes that simplify most threading tasks.

The first part of this chapter shows you how to create, manage, and kill threads. Even if you don't create your own threads explicitly, you'll want to ensure that your code can handle multiple threads if it's run in a multithreading environment. This concern is especially important if you are creating components that other programmers might use in a program that supports multithreading.

The second part of this chapter focuses on synchronization. When you have a limited resource (such as a database connection) you may need to restrict access to that resource to one thread at a time. A classic analogy is to a restroom on an airplane. You want to allow access to the restroom for only one person at a time. You do this by putting a lock on the door. When passengers want to use the restroom, they try the door handle; if it is locked, they either go away and do something else, or wait patiently in line with others who want access to the resource. When the resource becomes free, one person is taken off the line and given the resource, which is then locked again.

At times, various threads might want to access a resource in your program, such as a file. It might be important to ensure that only one thread has access to your resource at a time, and so you will lock the resource, allow a thread access, and then unlock the resource. Programming locks can be fairly sophisticated, ensuring a fair distribution of resources.

# Threads

Threads are typically created when you want a program to do two things at once. For example, assume you are calculating *pi* (3.141592653589…) to the 10 billionth place. The processor will happily begin to compute this, but nothing will write to the user interface while it is working. Because computing *pi* to the 10 billionth place will take a few million years, you might like the processor to provide an update as it goes. In addition, you might want to provide a Stop button so that the user can cancel the operation at any time. To allow the program to handle the click on the Stop button, you will need a second thread of execution.

Another common place to use threading is when you must wait for an event, such as user input, a read from a file, or receipt of data over the network. Freeing the processor to turn its attention to another task while you wait (such as computing another 10,000 values of *pi*) is a good idea, and it makes your program appear to run more quickly.

On the flip side, note that in some circumstances, threading can actually slow you down. Assume that in addition to calculating *pi*, you also want to calculate the Fibonacci series (1,1,2,3,5,8,13,21,…). If you have a multiprocessor machine, this will run faster if each computation is in its own thread. If you have a single-processor machine (as most users do), computing these values in multiple threads will certainly run *slower* than computing one and then the other in a single thread because the processor must switch back and forth between the two threads. This incurs some overhead.

## Starting Threads

The simplest way to create a thread is to create a new instance of the Thread class. The Thread constructor takes a single argument: a delegate instance. The CLR provides the ThreadStart delegate class specifically for this purpose, which points to a method you designate. This allows you to construct a thread and to say to it, "When you start, run this method." The ThreadStart delegate declaration is:

```
public delegate void ThreadStart();
```

As you can see, the method you attach to this delegate must take no parameters and must return void. Thus, you might create a new thread like this:

```
Thread myThread = new Thread( new ThreadStart(myFunc) );
```

For example, you might create two worker threads, one that counts up from zero:

```
public void Incrementer()
{
    for (int i =0;i<1000;i++)
    {
        Console.WriteLine("Incrementer: {0}", i);
    }
}
```

and one that counts down from 1,000:

```
public void Decrementer( )
{
    for (int i = 1000;i>=0;i--)
    {
        Console.WriteLine("Decrementer: {0}", i);
    }
}
```

To run these in threads, create two new threads, each initialized with a `ThreadStart` delegate. These in turn would be initialized to the respective member functions:

```
Thread t1 = new Thread( new ThreadStart(Incrementer) );
Thread t2 = new Thread( new ThreadStart(Decrementer) );
```

Instantiation of these threads doesn't start them running. To do so, you must call the Start method on the `Thread` object itself:

```
t1.Start( );
t2.Start( );
```

 If you don't take further action, the thread stops when the function returns. You'll see how to stop a thread before the function ends later in this chapter.

Example 21-1 is the full program and its output. You will need to add a `using` statement for `System.Threading` to make the compiler aware of the `Thread` class. Notice the output, where you can see the processor switching from t1 to t2.

*Example 21-1. Using threads*

```
using System;
using System.Threading;

namespace UsingThreads
{
    class Tester
    {
        static void Main( )
        {
            // make an instance of this class
            Tester t = new Tester( );

            Console.WriteLine("Hello");
            // run outside static Main
            t.DoTest( );
        }

        public void DoTest( )
        {
            // create a thread for the Incrementer
            // pass in a ThreadStart delegate
```

*Example 21-1. Using threads (continued)*

```
            // with the address of Incrementer
            Thread t1 = new Thread(
                new ThreadStart(Incrementer));

            // create a thread for the Decrementer
            // pass in a ThreadStart delegate
            // with the address of Decrementer
            Thread t2 = new Thread(
                new ThreadStart(Decrementer));

            // start the threads
            t1.Start();
            t2.Start();
        }

        // demo function, counts up to 1K
        public void Incrementer()
        {
            for (int i = 0; i < 1000; i++)
            {
                System.Console.WriteLine(
                    "Incrementer: {0}", i);
            }
        }

        // demo function, counts down from 1k
        public void Decrementer()
        {
            for (int i = 1000; i >= 0; i--)
            {
                System.Console.WriteLine(
                    "Decrementer: {0}", i);
            }
        }
    }
}

Output (excerpt):
Incrementer: 102
Incrementer: 103
Incrementer: 104
Incrementer: 105
Incrementer: 106
Decrementer: 1000
Decrementer: 999
Decrementer: 998
Decrementer: 997
```

The processor allows the first thread to run long enough to count up to 106. Next, the second thread kicks in, counting down from 1,000 for a while. Then, the first thread is allowed to run. When I run this with larger numbers, I've noticed that each thread is allowed to run for about 100 numbers before switching.

The actual amount of time devoted to any given thread is handled by the thread scheduler and depends on many factors, such as the processor speed, demands on the processor from other programs, and so on.

## Joining Threads

When you tell a thread to stop processing and wait until a second thread completes its work, you are said to be joining the first thread to the second. It is as though you tied the tip of the first thread onto the tail of the second, hence "joining" them.

To join thread 1 (t1) onto thread 2 (t2), write:

```
t2.Join();
```

If this statement is executed in a method in thread t1, t1 will halt and wait until t2 completes and exits. For example, you might ask the thread in which Main() executes to wait for all your other threads to end before it writes its concluding message. In this next code snippet, assume you've created a collection of threads named myThreads. Iterate over the collection, joining the current thread to each thread in the collection in turn:

```
foreach (Thread myThread in myThreads)
{
    myThread.Join();
}

Console.WriteLine("All my threads are done.");
```

The final message, All my threads are done., isn't printed until all the threads have ended. In a production environment, you might start up a series of threads to accomplish some task (e.g., printing, updating the display, etc.) and not want to continue the main thread of execution until the worker threads are completed.

## Blocking Threads with Sleep

At times, you want to suspend your thread for a short while. You might, for example, like your clock thread to suspend for about a second in between testing the system time. This lets you display the new time about once a second without devoting hundreds of millions of machine cycles to the effort.

The Thread class offers a public static method, Sleep, for just this purpose. The method is overloaded; one version takes an int, the other a timeSpan object.

Each represents the number of milliseconds you want the thread suspended for, expressed either as an int (e.g., 2,000 = 2,000 milliseconds or two seconds), or as a timeSpan.

Although timeSpan objects can measure *ticks* (100 nanoseconds), the Sleep() method's granularity is in milliseconds (1 million nanoseconds).

To cause your thread to sleep for one second, you can invoke the static method of Thread.Sleep, which suspends the thread in which it is invoked:

```
Thread.Sleep(1000);
```

At times, you'll pass zero for the amount of time to sleep; this signals the thread scheduler that you'd like your thread to yield to another thread, even if the thread scheduler might otherwise give your thread a bit more time.

If you modify Example 21-1 to add a Thread.Sleep(1) statement after each WriteLine( ), the output changes significantly:

```
for (int i =0;i<1000;i++)
{
    Console.WriteLine(
    "Incrementer: {0}", i);
    Thread.Sleep(1);
}
```

This small change is sufficient to give each thread an opportunity to run once the other thread prints one value. The output reflects this change:

```
Incrementer: 0
Incrementer: 1
Decrementer: 1000
Incrementer: 2
Decrementer: 999
Incrementer: 3
Decrementer: 998
Incrementer: 4
Decrementer: 997
Incrementer: 5
Decrementer: 996
Incrementer: 6
Decrementer: 995
```

## Killing Threads

Typically, threads die after running their course. You can, however, ask a thread to kill itself. The cleanest way is to set a KeepAlive Boolean flag that the thread can check periodically. When the flag changes state (e.g., goes from true to false), the thread can stop itself.

An alternative is to call Thread.Interrupt, which asks the thread to kill itself. Finally, in desperation, and if you are shutting down your application in any case, you may call Thread.Abort. This causes a ThreadAbortException exception to be thrown, which the thread can catch.

The thread ought to treat the ThreadAbortException exception as a signal that it is time to exit immediately. In any case, you don't so much kill a thread as politely request that it commit suicide.

You might wish to kill a thread in reaction to an event, such as the user clicking the Cancel button. The event handler for the Cancel button might be in thread t1, and the event it is canceling might be in thread t2. In your event handler, you can call Abort on t1:

```
t2.Abort( );
```

An exception will be raised in t1's currently running method that t1 can catch.

In Example 21-2, three threads are created and stored in an array of Thread objects. Before the Threads are started, the IsBackground property is set to true (background threads are exactly like foreground threads, except that they don't stop a process from terminating). Each thread is then started and named (e.g., Thread1, Thread2, etc.). A message is displayed indicating that the thread is started, and then the main thread sleeps for 50 milliseconds before starting up the next thread.

After all three threads are started, and another 50 milliseconds have passed, the first thread is aborted by calling Abort( ). The main thread then joins all three of the running threads. The effect of this is that the main thread will not resume until all the other threads have completed. When they do complete, the main thread prints a message: All my threads are done.. Example 21-2 displays the complete source.

*Example 21-2. Interrupting a thread*

```
using System;
using System.Threading;

namespace InterruptingThreads
{
    class Tester
    {
        static void Main( )
        {
            // make an instance of this class
            Tester t = new Tester( );

            // run outside static Main
            t.DoTest( );
        }

        public void DoTest( )
        {
            // create an array of unnamed threads
            Thread[] myThreads =
             {
                new Thread( new ThreadStart(Decrementer) ),
                new Thread( new ThreadStart(Incrementer) ),
                new Thread( new ThreadStart(Decrementer) ),
                new Thread( new ThreadStart(Incrementer) )
             };
```

*Example 21-2. Interrupting a thread (continued)*

```
        // start each thread
        int ctr = 1;
        foreach (Thread myThread in myThreads)
        {
            myThread.IsBackground = true;
            myThread.Start();
            myThread.Name = "Thread" + ctr.ToString();
            ctr++;
            Console.WriteLine("Started thread {0}",
            myThread.Name);
            Thread.Sleep(50);
        }

        // ask the first thread to stop
        myThreads[0].Interrupt();

        // tell the second thread to abort immediately
        myThreads[1].Abort();

        // wait for all threads to end before continuing
        foreach (Thread myThread in myThreads)
        {
            myThread.Join();
        }

        // after all threads end, print a message
        Console.WriteLine("All my threads are done.");
    }

    // demo function, counts down from 100
    public void Decrementer()
    {
        try
        {
            for (int i = 100; i >= 0; i--)
            {
                Console.WriteLine(
                    "Thread {0}. Decrementer: {1}",
                    Thread.CurrentThread.Name, i);
                Thread.Sleep(1);
            }
        }
        catch (ThreadAbortException)
        {
            Console.WriteLine(
                "Thread {0} aborted! Cleaning up...",
            Thread.CurrentThread.Name);
        }
        catch (System.Exception e)
        {
            Console.WriteLine(
                "Thread has been interrupted ");
```

*Example 21-2. Interrupting a thread (continued)*

```
            }
        finally
        {
            Console.WriteLine(
                "Thread {0} Exiting. ",
                Thread.CurrentThread.Name);
        }
    }

    // demo function, counts up to 100
    public void Incrementer( )
    {
        try
        {
            for (int i = 0; i < 100; i++)
            {
                Console.WriteLine(
                    "Thread {0}. Incrementer: {1}",
                    Thread.CurrentThread.Name, i);
                Thread.Sleep(1);
            }
        }
        catch (ThreadAbortException)
        {
            Console.WriteLine(
                "Thread {0} aborted!",
                Thread.CurrentThread.Name);
        }
        catch (System.Exception e)
        {
            Console.WriteLine(
                "Thread has been interrupted");
        }
        finally
        {
            Console.WriteLine(
                "Thread {0} Exiting. ",
                Thread.CurrentThread.Name);
        }
    }
    }
}
```

```
Output (excerpt):
Thread Thread2. Incrementer: 42
Thread Thread1. Decrementer: 7
Thread Thread2. Incrementer: 43
Thread Thread1. Decrementer: 6
Thread Thread2. Incrementer: 44
Thread Thread1. Decrementer: 5
```

*Example 21-2. Interrupting a thread (continued)*

```
Thread Thread2. Incrementer: 45
Thread Thread1. Decrementer: 4
Thread Thread2. Incrementer: 46
Started thread Thread3
Thread Thread3. Decrementer: 100
Thread Thread2. Incrementer: 47
Thread Thread1. Decrementer: 3
Thread Thread2. Incrementer: 48
Thread Thread1. Decrementer: 2
Thread Thread3. Decrementer: 99
Thread Thread2. Incrementer: 49
Thread Thread3. Decrementer: 98
Thread Thread1. Decrementer: 1
Thread Thread1. Decrementer: 0
Thread Thread2. Incrementer: 50
Thread Thread3. Decrementer: 97
Thread Thread2. Incrementer: 51
Thread Thread1 Exiting.
Thread Thread3. Decrementer: 96
...
Thread Thread4. Incrementer: 99
Thread Thread4 Exiting.
All my threads are done.
```

You see the first thread start and decrement from 100 to 99. The second thread starts, and the two threads are interleaved for a while until the third and fourth threads start. After a short while, however, Thread2 reports that it has been aborted, and then it reports that it is exiting. A little while later, Thread1 reports that it was interrupted. Because the interrupt waits for the thread to be in a wait state, this can be a bit less immediate than a call to Abort. The two remaining threads continue until they are done. They then exit naturally, and the main thread, which was joined on all three, resumes to print its exit message.

# Synchronization

At times, you might want to control access to a resource, such as an object's properties or methods, so that only one thread at a time can modify or use that resource. Your object is similar to the airplane restroom discussed earlier, and the various threads are like the people waiting in line. Synchronization is provided by a lock on the object, which helps the developer avoid having a second thread barge in on your object until the first thread is finished with it.

This section examines three synchronization mechanisms: the Interlock class, the C# lock statement, and the Monitor class. But first, you need to create a shared resource (often a file or printer); in this case, a simple integer variable: counter. You will increment counter from each of two threads.

To start, declare the member variable and initialize it to 0:

```
int counter = 0;
```

Modify the Incrementer method to increment the counter member variable:

```
public void Incrementer( )
{
  try
  {
    while (counter < 1000)
    {
      int temp = counter;
      temp++; // increment

      // simulate some work in this method
      Thread.Sleep(1);

      // assign the Incremented value
      // to the counter variable
      // and display the results
      counter = temp;
      Console.WriteLine(
      "Thread {0}. Incrementer: {1}",
      Thread.CurrentThread.Name,
      counter);
    }
  }
}
```

The idea here is to simulate the work that might be done with a controlled resource. Just as you might open a file, manipulate its contents, and then close it, here, you read the value of counter into a temporary variable, increment the temporary variable, sleep for one millisecond to simulate work, and then assign the incremented value back to counter.

The problem is that your first thread reads the value of counter (0) and assigns that to a temporary variable. Then, it increments the temporary variable. While it is doing its work, the second thread reads the value of counter (still 0), and assigns that value to a temporary variable. The first thread finishes its work, and then assigns the temporary value (1) back to counter and displays it. The second thread does the same. What is printed is 1,1. In the next go around, the same thing happens. Rather than having the two threads count 1,2,3,4, you'll see 1,2,3,3,4,4. Example 21-3 shows the complete source code and output for this example.

*Example 21-3. Simulating a shared resource*

```
using System;
using System.Threading;

namespace SharedResource
{
    class Tester
```

*Example 21-3. Simulating a shared resource (continued)*

```csharp
{
    private int counter = 0;

    static void Main( )
    {
        // make an instance of this class
        Tester t = new Tester( );

        // run outside static Main
        t.DoTest( );
    }

    public void DoTest( )
    {
        Thread t1 = new Thread(new ThreadStart(Incrementer));
        t1.IsBackground = true;
        t1.Name = "ThreadOne";
        t1.Start( );
        Console.WriteLine("Started thread {0}",
        t1.Name);

        Thread t2 = new Thread(new ThreadStart(Incrementer));
        t2.IsBackground = true;
        t2.Name = "ThreadTwo";
        t2.Start( );
        Console.WriteLine("Started thread {0}",
        t2.Name);
        t1.Join( );
        t2.Join( );

        // after all threads end, print a message
        Console.WriteLine("All my threads are done.");
    }

    // demo function, counts up to 1K
    public void Incrementer( )
    {
        try
        {
            while (counter < 1000)
            {
                int temp = counter;
                temp++; // increment

                // simulate some work in this method
                Thread.Sleep(1);

                // assign the decremented value
                // and display the results
                counter = temp;
                Console.WriteLine(
```

*Example 21-3. Simulating a shared resource (continued)*

```
                    "Thread {0}. Incrementer: {1}",
                    Thread.CurrentThread.Name,
                    counter);
            }
        }
        catch (ThreadInterruptedException)
        {
            Console.WriteLine(
                "Thread {0} interrupted! Cleaning up...",
                Thread.CurrentThread.Name);
        }
        finally
        {
            Console.WriteLine(
                "Thread {0} Exiting. ",
                Thread.CurrentThread.Name);
        }
    }
}
}
```

```
Output:
Started thread ThreadOne
Started thread ThreadTwo
Thread ThreadOne. Incrementer: 1
Thread ThreadOne. Incrementer: 2
Thread ThreadOne. Incrementer: 3
Thread ThreadTwo. Incrementer: 3
Thread ThreadTwo. Incrementer: 4
Thread ThreadOne. Incrementer: 4
Thread ThreadTwo. Incrementer: 5
Thread ThreadOne. Incrementer: 5
Thread ThreadTwo. Incrementer: 6
Thread ThreadOne. Incrementer: 6
```

# Using Interlocked

The CLR provides a number of synchronization mechanisms. These include the common synchronization tools such as critical sections (called *locks* in .NET), as well as the Monitor class. Each is discussed later in this chapter.

Incrementing and decrementing a value is such a common programming pattern, and one which needs synchronization protection so often that the CLR offers a special class, Interlocked, just for this purpose. Interlocked has two methods, Increment and Decrement, which not only increment or decrement a value, but also do so under synchronization control.

Modify the Incrementer method from Example 21-3 as follows:

```
public void Incrementer( )
{
```

```
try
{
    while (counter < 1000)
    {
        int temp = Interlocked.Increment(ref counter);

        // simulate some work in this method
        Thread.Sleep(0);

        // display the incremented value
        Console.WriteLine(
            "Thread {0}. Incrementer: {1}",
            Thread.CurrentThread.Name, temp);

    }
}
```

The catch and finally blocks and the remainder of the program are unchanged from the previous example.

Interlocked.Increment() expects a single parameter: a reference to an int. Because int values are passed by value, use the ref keyword, as described in Chapter 4.

 The Increment() method is overloaded and can take a reference to a long rather than to an int, if that is what you need.

Once this change is made, access to the counter member is synchronized, and the output is what we'd expect:

```
Output (excerpts):
Started thread ThreadOne
Started thread ThreadTwo
Thread ThreadOne. Incrementer: 1
Thread ThreadTwo. Incrementer: 2
Thread ThreadOne. Incrementer: 3
Thread ThreadTwo. Incrementer: 4
Thread ThreadOne. Incrementer: 5
Thread ThreadTwo. Incrementer: 6
Thread ThreadOne. Incrementer: 7
Thread ThreadTwo. Incrementer: 8
Thread ThreadOne. Incrementer: 9
Thread ThreadTwo. Incrementer: 10
Thread ThreadOne. Incrementer: 11
Thread ThreadTwo. Incrementer: 12
Thread ThreadOne. Incrementer: 13
Thread ThreadTwo. Incrementer: 14
Thread ThreadOne. Incrementer: 15
Thread ThreadTwo. Incrementer: 16
Thread ThreadOne. Incrementer: 17
```

```
Thread ThreadTwo. Incrementer: 18
Thread ThreadOne. Incrementer: 19
Thread ThreadTwo. Incrementer: 20
```

# Using Locks

Although the `Interlocked` object is fine if you want to increment or decrement a value, there will be times when you want to control access to other objects as well. What is needed is a more general synchronization mechanism. This is provided by the C# lock feature.

A lock marks a critical section of your code, providing synchronization to an object you designate while the lock is in effect. The syntax of using a `lock` is to request a lock on an object and then to execute a statement or block of statements. The lock is removed at the end of the statement block.

C# provides direct support for locks through the `lock` keyword. Pass in a reference to an object, and follow the keyword with a statement block:

```
lock(expression) statement-block
```

For example, you can modify `Incrementer` again to use a `lock` statement, as follows:

```
public void Incrementer( )
{
    try
    {
        while (counter < 1000)
        {
            int temp;
            lock (this)
            {
                temp = counter;
                temp++;
                Thread.Sleep(1);
                counter = temp;
            }

            // assign the decremented value
            // and display the results
            Console.WriteLine(
                "Thread {0}. Incrementer: {1}",
                Thread.CurrentThread.Name, temp);

        }
    }
```

The catch and `finally` blocks and the remainder of the program are unchanged from the previous example.

The output from this code is identical to that produced using `Interlocked`.

## Using Monitors

The objects used so far will be sufficient for most needs. For the most sophisticated control over resources, you might want to use a *monitor*. A monitor lets you decide when to enter and exit the synchronization, and it lets you wait for another area of your code to become free.

When you want to begin synchronization, call the Enter() method of the monitor, passing in the object you want to lock:

```
Monitor.Enter(this);
```

If the monitor is unavailable, the object protected by the monitor is presumed to be in use. You can do other work while you wait for the monitor to become available, and then try again. You can also explicitly choose to Wait(), suspending your thread until the moment the monitor is free and the developer calls Pulse (discussed in a bit). Wait() helps you control thread ordering.

For example, suppose you are downloading and printing an article from the Web. For efficiency, you'd like to print in a background thread, but you want to ensure that at least 10 pages have downloaded before you begin.

Your printing thread will wait until the get-file thread signals that enough of the file has been read. You don't want to Join the get-file thread because the file might be hundreds of pages. You don't want to wait until it has completely finished downloading, but you do want to ensure that at least 10 pages have been read before your print thread begins. The Wait() method is just the ticket.

To simulate this, rewrite Tester, and add back the decrementer method. Your incrementer counts up to 10. The decrementer method counts down to zero. It turns out you don't want to start decrementing unless the value of counter is at least 5.

In decrementer, call Enter on the monitor. Then, check the value of counter, and if it is less than 5, call Wait on the monitor:

```
if (counter < 5)
{
    Monitor.Wait(this);
}
```

This call to Wait() frees the monitor, but signals the CLR that you want the monitor back the next time it is free. Waiting threads are notified of a chance to run again if the active thread calls Pulse():

```
Monitor.Pulse(this);
```

Pulse() signals the CLR that there has been a change in state that might free a thread that is waiting.

When a thread is finished with the monitor, it must mark the end of its controlled area of code with a call to Exit():

```
Monitor.Exit(this);
```

---

Example 21-4 continues the simulation, providing synchronized access to a counter variable using a Monitor.

*Example 21-4. Using a Monitor object*

```
using System;
using System.Threading;

namespace UsingAMonitor
{
    class Tester
    {
        private long counter = 0;

        static void Main( )
        {
            // make an instance of this class
            Tester t = new Tester( );

            // run outside static Main
            t.DoTest( );
        }

        public void DoTest( )
        {
            // create an array of unnamed threads
            Thread[] myThreads =
             {
                 new Thread( new ThreadStart(Decrementer) ),
                 new Thread( new ThreadStart(Incrementer) )
             };

            // start each thread
            int ctr = 1;
            foreach (Thread myThread in myThreads)
            {
                myThread.IsBackground = true;
                myThread.Start( );
                myThread.Name = "Thread" + ctr.ToString( );
                ctr++;
                Console.WriteLine("Started thread {0}", myThread.Name);
                Thread.Sleep(50);
            }

            // wait for all threads to end before continuing
            foreach (Thread myThread in myThreads)
            {
                myThread.Join( );
            }

            // after all threads end, print a message
            Console.WriteLine("All my threads are done.");
        }
```

*Example 21-4. Using a Monitor object (continued)*

```
void Decrementer( )
{
    try
    {
        // synchronize this area of code
        Monitor.Enter(this);

        // if counter is not yet 10
        // then free the monitor to other waiting
        // threads, but wait in line for your turn
        if (counter < 10)
        {
            Console.WriteLine(
                "[{0}] In Decrementer. Counter: {1}. Gotta Wait!",
                Thread.CurrentThread.Name, counter);
            Monitor.Wait(this);
        }

        while (counter > 0)
        {
            long temp = counter;
            temp--;
            Thread.Sleep(1);
            counter = temp;
            Console.WriteLine(
                "[{0}] In Decrementer. Counter: {1}. ",
                Thread.CurrentThread.Name, counter);
        }
    }
    finally
    {
        Monitor.Exit(this);
    }
}

void Incrementer( )
{
    try
    {
        Monitor.Enter(this);
        while (counter < 10)
        {
            long temp = counter;
            temp++;
            Thread.Sleep(1);
            counter = temp;
            Console.WriteLine(
                "[{0}] In Incrementer. Counter: {1}",
                Thread.CurrentThread.Name, counter);
        }
```

*Example 21-4. Using a Monitor object (continued)*

```
                    // I'm done incrementing for now, let another
                    // thread have the Monitor
                    Monitor.Pulse(this);
                }
                finally
                {
                    Console.WriteLine("[{0}] Exiting...",
                        Thread.CurrentThread.Name);
                    Monitor.Exit(this);
                }
            }
        }
    }
}
```

```
Output:
Started thread Thread1
[Thread1] In Decrementer. Counter: 0. Gotta Wait!
Started thread Thread2
[Thread2] In Incrementer. Counter: 1
[Thread2] In Incrementer. Counter: 2
[Thread2] In Incrementer. Counter: 3
[Thread2] In Incrementer. Counter: 4
[Thread2] In Incrementer. Counter: 5
[Thread2] In Incrementer. Counter: 6
[Thread2] In Incrementer. Counter: 7
[Thread2] In Incrementer. Counter: 8
[Thread2] In Incrementer. Counter: 9
[Thread2] In Incrementer. Counter: 10
[Thread2] Exiting...
[Thread1] In Decrementer. Counter: 9.
[Thread1] In Decrementer. Counter: 8.
[Thread1] In Decrementer. Counter: 7.
[Thread1] In Decrementer. Counter: 6.
[Thread1] In Decrementer. Counter: 5.
[Thread1] In Decrementer. Counter: 4.
[Thread1] In Decrementer. Counter: 3.
[Thread1] In Decrementer. Counter: 2.
[Thread1] In Decrementer. Counter: 1.
[Thread1] In Decrementer. Counter: 0.
All my threads are done.
```

In this example, decrementer is started first. In the output, you see Thread1 (the decrementer) start up and then realize that it has to wait. You then see Thread2 start up. Only when Thread2 pulses does Thread1 begin its work.

Try some experiments with this code. First, comment out the call to Pulse( ); you'll find that Thread1 never resumes. Without Pulse( ), there is no signal to the waiting threads.

As a second experiment, rewrite Incrementer to pulse and exit the monitor after each increment:

```
void Incrementer()
{
    try
    {
        while (counter < 10)
        {
            Monitor.Enter(this);
            long temp = counter;
            temp++;
            Thread.Sleep(1);
            counter = temp;
            Console.WriteLine(
                "[{0}] In Incrementer. Counter: {1}",
                Thread.CurrentThread.Name, counter);
            Monitor.Pulse(this);
            Monitor.Exit(this);
        }
    }
    Catch {}
```

Rewrite Decrementer as well, changing the if statement to a while statement, and knocking down the value from 10 to 5:

```
//if (counter < 10)
while (counter < 5)
```

The net effect of these two changes is to cause Thread2, the Incrementer, to pulse the Decrementer after each increment. While the value is smaller than five, the Decrementer must continue to wait; once the value goes over five, the Decrementer runs to completion. When it is done, the Incrementer thread can run again. The output is shown here:

```
[Thread2] In Incrementer. Counter: 2
[Thread1] In Decrementer. Counter: 2. Gotta Wait!
[Thread2] In Incrementer. Counter: 3
[Thread1] In Decrementer. Counter: 3. Gotta Wait!
[Thread2] In Incrementer. Counter: 4
[Thread1] In Decrementer. Counter: 4. Gotta Wait!
[Thread2] In Incrementer. Counter: 5
[Thread1] In Decrementer. Counter: 4.
[Thread1] In Decrementer. Counter: 3.
[Thread1] In Decrementer. Counter: 2.
[Thread1] In Decrementer. Counter: 1.
[Thread1] In Decrementer. Counter: 0.
[Thread2] In Incrementer. Counter: 1
[Thread2] In Incrementer. Counter: 2
[Thread2] In Incrementer. Counter: 3
[Thread2] In Incrementer. Counter: 4
[Thread2] In Incrementer. Counter: 5
[Thread2] In Incrementer. Counter: 6
[Thread2] In Incrementer. Counter: 7
```

```
[Thread2] In Incrementer. Counter: 8
[Thread2] In Incrementer. Counter: 9
[Thread2] In Incrementer. Counter: 10
```

# Race Conditions and Deadlocks

The .NET library provides sufficient thread support such that you will rarely find yourself creating your own threads or managing synchronization manually.

Thread synchronization can be tricky, especially in complex programs. If you do decide to create your own threads, you must confront and solve all the traditional problems of thread synchronization, such as race conditions and deadlock.

## Race Conditions

A race condition exists when the success of your program depends on the uncontrolled order of completion of two independent threads.

Suppose, for example, that you have two threads—one is responsible for opening a file, and the other is responsible for writing to the file. It is important that you control the second thread so that it's assured that the first thread has opened the file. If not, under some conditions, the first thread will open the file, and the second thread will work fine; under other unpredictable conditions, the first thread won't finish opening the file before the second thread tries to write to it, and you'll throw an exception (or worse, your program will simply seize up and die). This is a race condition, and race conditions can be very difficult to debug.

You can't leave these two threads to operate independently; you must ensure that Thread1 will have completed before Thread2 begins. To accomplish this, you might Join( ) Thread2 on Thread1. As an alternative, you can use a Monitor and Wait( ) for the appropriate conditions before resuming Thread2.

## Deadlocks

When you wait for a resource to become free, you are at risk of a *deadlock*, also called a *deadly embrace*. In a deadlock, two or more threads are waiting for each other, and neither can become free.

Suppose you have two threads, ThreadA and ThreadB. ThreadA locks down an Employee object, and then tries to get a lock on a row in the database. It turns out that ThreadB already has that row locked, so ThreadA waits.

Unfortunately, ThreadB can't update the row until it locks down the Employee object, which is already locked down by ThreadA. Neither thread can proceed; neither thread will unlock its own resource. They are waiting for each other in a deadly embrace.

As described, a deadlock is fairly easy to spot—and to correct. In a program running many threads, a deadlock can be very difficult to diagnose, let alone solve. One guideline is to get all the locks you need or to release all the locks you have. That is, as soon as ThreadA realizes that it can't lock the Row, it should release its lock on the Employee object. Similarly, when ThreadB can't lock the Employee, it should release the Row. A second important guideline is to lock as small a section of code as possible, and to hold the lock as briefly as possible.

# CHAPTER 22

# Streams

For many applications, data is held in memory and accessed as though it were a three-dimensional solid; when you need to access a variable or an object, use its name, and, presto, it is available to you. When you want to move your data into or out of a file, across the network, or over the Internet, however, your data must be *streamed*.\* In a *stream*, data flows much like bubbles in a stream of water.

Typically, the endpoint of a stream is a backing store. The backing store provides a source for the stream, like a lake provides a source for a river. Typically, the backing store is a file, but it is also possible for the backing store to be a network or web connection.

Files and directories are abstracted by classes in the .NET Framework. These classes provide methods and properties for creating, naming, manipulating, and deleting files and directories on your disk.

The .NET Framework provides buffered and unbuffered streams, as well as classes for asynchronous I/O. With asynchronous I/O, you can instruct the .NET classes to read your file; while they are busy getting the bits off the disk, your program can be working on other tasks. The asynchronous I/O tasks notify you when their work is done. The asynchronous classes are sufficiently powerful and robust that you might be able to avoid creating threads explicitly (see Chapter 21).

Streaming into and out of files is no different from streaming across the network, and the second part of this chapter will describe streaming using both TCP/IP and web protocols.

To create a stream of data, your object will typically be *serialized*, or written to the stream as a series of bits. The .NET Framework provides extensive support for serialization, and the final part of this chapter walks you through the details of taking control of the serialization of your object.

---

\* Internet data may also be sent in datagrams.

# Files and Directories

Before looking at how you can get data into and out of files, let's start by examining the support provided for file and directory manipulation.

The classes you need are in the System.IO namespace. These include the File class, which represents a file on disk, and the Directory class, which represents a directory (also known in Windows as a *folder*).

## Working with Directories

The Directory class exposes static methods for creating, moving, and exploring directories. All the methods of the Directory class are static; therefore, you can call them all without having an instance of the class.

The DirectoryInfo class is a similar class, but one that has nothing but instance members (i.e., no static members at all). DirectoryInfo derives from FileSystemInfo, which in turn derives from MarshalByRefObject. The FileSystemInfo class has a number of properties and methods that provide information about a file or directory.

Table 22-1 lists the principal methods of the Directory class, and Table 22-2 lists the principal methods of the DirectoryInfo class, including important properties and methods inherited from FileSystemInfo.

*Table 22-1. Principal methods of the Directory class*

| Method | Use |
| --- | --- |
| CreateDirectory( ) | Creates all directories and subdirectories specified by its path parameter |
| GetCreationTime( ) | Returns and sets the time the specified directory was created |
| GetDirectories( ) | Gets named directories |
| GetLogicalDrives( ) | Returns the names of all the logical drives in the form <drive>:\ |
| GetFiles( ) | Returns the names of files matching a pattern |
| GetParent( ) | Returns the parent directory for the specified path |
| Move( ) | Moves a directory and its contents to a specified path |

*Table 22-2. Principal methods and properties of the DirectoryInfo class*

| Method or property | Use |
| --- | --- |
| Attributes | Inherits from FileSystemInfo; gets or sets the attributes of the current file |
| CreationTime | Inherits from FileSystemInfo; gets or sets the creation time of the current file |
| Exists | Public property Boolean value, which is true if the directory exists |
| Extension | Public property inherited from FileSystemInfo; that is, the file extension |
| FullName | Public property inherited from FileSystemInfo; that is, the full path of the file or directory |
| LastAccessTime | Public property inherited from FileSystemInfo; gets or sets the last access time |

*Table 22-2. Principal methods and properties of the DirectoryInfo class (continued)*

| Method or property | Use |
|---|---|
| LastWriteTime | Public property inherited from FileSystemInfo; gets or sets the time when the current file or directory was last written to |
| Name | Public property name of this instance of DirectoryInfo |
| Parent | Public property parent directory of the specified directory |
| Root | Public property root portion of the path |
| Create( ) | Public method that creates a directory |
| CreateSubdirectory( ) | Public method that creates a subdirectory on the specified path |
| Delete( ) | Public method that deletes a DirectoryInfo and its contents from the path |
| GetDirectories( ) | Public method that returns a DirectoryInfo array with subdirectories |
| GetFiles( ) | Public method that returns a list of files in the directory |
| GetFileSystemInfos( ) | Public method that retrieves an array of FileSystemInfo objects |
| MoveTo( ) | Public method that moves a DirectoryInfo and its contents to a new path |
| Refresh( ) | Public method inherited from FileSystemInfo; refreshes the state of the object |

## Creating a DirectoryInfo Object

To explore a directory hierarchy, you need to instantiate a DirectoryInfo object. The DirectoryInfo class provides methods for getting not just the names of contained files and directories, but also FileInfo and DirectoryInfo objects, allowing you to dive into the hierarchical structure, extracting subdirectories and exploring these recursively.

You instantiate a DirectoryInfo object with the name of the directory you want to explore:

```
string path = Environment.GetEnvironmentVariable("SystemRoot");
DirectoryInfo dir = new DirectoryInfo(path);
```

 Remember that the at (@) sign before a string creates a verbatim string literal in which it isn't necessary to escape characters such as the backslash. I covered this in Chapter 10.

You can ask that DirectoryInfo object for information about itself, including its name, full path, attributes, the time it was last accessed, and so forth. To explore the subdirectory hierarchy, ask the current directory for its list of subdirectories:

```
DirectoryInfo[] directories = dir.GetDirectories();
```

This returns an array of DirectoryInfo objects, each of which represents a directory. You can then recurse into the same method, passing in each DirectoryInfo object in turn:

```
foreach (DirectoryInfo newDir in directories)
```

```
        {
            dirCounter++;
            ExploreDirectory(newDir);
        }
```

The dirCounter static int member variable keeps track of how many subdirectories have been found altogether. To make the display more interesting, add a second static int member variable, indentLevel, which will be incremented each time you recurse into a subdirectory, and will be decremented when you pop out. This will allow you to display the subdirectories indented under the parent directories. Example 22-1 shows the complete listing.

*Example 22-1. Recursing through subdirectories*

```
using System;
using System.IO;

namespace RecursingDirectories
{
    class Tester
    {
        // static member variables to keep track of totals
        // and indentation level
        static int dirCounter = 1;
        static int indentLevel = -1; // so first push = 0

        public static void Main( )
        {
            Tester t = new Tester( );

            // choose the initial subdirectory
            string theDirectory =
            Environment.GetEnvironmentVariable("SystemRoot");
            // Mono and Shared Source CLI users on Linux, Unix or
            // Mac OS X should comment out the preceding two lines
            // of code and uncomment the following:
            //string theDirectory = "/tmp";

            // call the method to explore the directory,
            // displaying its access date and all
            // subdirectories

            DirectoryInfo dir = new DirectoryInfo(theDirectory);

            t.ExploreDirectory(dir);

            // completed. print the statistics
            Console.WriteLine(
                "\n\n{0} directories found.\n",
                    dirCounter);
        }
```

*Example 22-1. Recursing through subdirectories (continued)*

```
        // Set it running with a directoryInfo object
        // for each directory it finds, it will call
        // itself recursively

        private void ExploreDirectory(DirectoryInfo dir)
        {
            indentLevel++; // push a directory level

            // create indentation for subdirectories
            for (int i = 0; i < indentLevel; i++)
                Console.Write("  "); // two spaces per level

            // print the directory and the time last accessed
            Console.WriteLine("[{0}] {1} [{2}]\n",
                indentLevel, dir.Name, dir.LastAccessTime);

            // get all the directories in the current directory
            // and call this method recursively on each
            DirectoryInfo[] directories = dir.GetDirectories();
            foreach (DirectoryInfo newDir in directories)
            {
                dirCounter++; // increment the counter
                ExploreDirectory(newDir);
            }
            indentLevel--; // pop a directory level
        }
    }
}
```

```
Output (excerpt):
    [2] logiscan [5/1/2001 3:06:41 PM]

    [2] miitwain [5/1/2001 3:06:41 PM]

  [1] Web [5/1/2001 3:06:41 PM]

    [2] printers [5/1/2001 3:06:41 PM]

      [3] images [5/1/2001 3:06:41 PM]

    [2] Wallpaper [5/1/2001 3:06:41 PM]

363 directories found.
```

You must add using System.IO; to the top of your file; Visual Studio
2008 doesn't do this automatically.

This program will throw an exception in Vista as you attempt to read into directories that are protected by the operating system. That is a good thing; it means Vista is doing what it should.

The program begins by identifying a directory (*SystemRoot*, usually *C:\WinNT* or *C:\Windows*) and creating a `DirectoryInfo` object for that directory. It then calls `ExploreDirectory`, passing in that `DirectoryInfo` object. `ExploreDirectory` displays information about the directory, and then retrieves all the subdirectories.

The list of all the subdirectories of the current directory is obtained by calling `GetDirectories`. This returns an array of `DirectoryInfo` objects. `ExploreDirectory` is the recursive method; each `DirectoryInfo` object is passed into `ExploreDirectory` in turn. The effect is to push recursively into each subdirectory, and then to pop back out to explore sister directories until all the subdirectories of *%SystemRoot%* are displayed. When `ExploreDirectory` finally returns, the calling method prints a summary.

## Working with Files

The `DirectoryInfo` object can also return a collection of all the files in each subdirectory found. The `GetFiles( )` method returns an array of `FileInfo` objects, each of which describes a file in that directory. The `FileInfo` and `File` objects relate to one another, much as `DirectoryInfo` and `Directory` do. Like the methods of `Directory`, all the `File` methods are static; like `DirectoryInfo`, all the methods of `FileInfo` are instance methods.

Table 22-3 lists the principal methods of the `File` class; Table 22-4 lists the important members of the `FileInfo` class.

*Table 22-3. Principal public static methods of the File class*

| Method | Use |
| --- | --- |
| AppendText( ) | Creates a `StreamWriter` that appends text to the specified file |
| Copy( ) | Copies an existing file to a new file |
| Create( ) | Creates a file in the specified path |
| CreateText( ) | Creates a `StreamWriter` that writes a new text file to the specified file |
| Delete( ) | Deletes the specified file |
| Exists( ) | Returns `true` if the specified file exists |
| GetAttributes( ), SetAttributes( ) | Gets or sets the `FileAttributes` of the specified file |
| GetCreationTime( ), SetCreationTime( ) | Returns or sets the creation date and time of the file |
| GetLastAccessTime( ), SetLastAccessTime( ) | Returns or sets the last time the specified file was accessed |

*Table 22-3. Principal public static methods of the File class (continued)*

| Method | Use |
|---|---|
| GetLastWriteTime( ),<br>SetLastWriteTime( ) | Returns or sets the last time the specified file was written to |
| Move( ) | Moves a file to a new location; can be used to rename a file |
| OpenRead( ) | Public static method that opens a FileStream on the file |
| OpenWrite( ) | Creates a read/write Stream on the specified path |

*Table 22-4. Methods and properties of the FileInfo class*

| Method or property | Use |
|---|---|
| Attributes( ) | Inherits from FileSystemInfo; gets or sets the attributes of the current file |
| CreationTime | Inherits from FileSystemInfo; gets or sets the creation time of the current file |
| Directory | Public property that gets an instance of the parent directory |
| Exists | Public property Boolean value that is true if the directory exists |
| Extension | Public property inherited from FileSystemInfo; that is, the file extension |
| FullName | Public property inherited from FileSystemInfo; that is, the full path of the file or directory |
| LastAccessTime | Public property inherited from FileSystemInfo; gets or sets the last access time |
| LastWriteTime | Public property inherited from FileSystemInfo; gets or sets the time when the current file or directory was last written to |
| Length | Public property that gets the size of the current file |
| Name | Public property Name of this DirectoryInfo instance |
| AppendText( ) | Public method that creates a StreamWriter that appends text to a file |
| CopyTo( ) | Public method that copies an existing file to a new file |
| Create( ) | Public method that creates a new file |
| Delete( ) | Public method that permanently deletes a file |
| MoveTo( ) | Public method to move a file to a new location; can be used to rename a file |
| Open( ) | Public method that opens a file with various read/write and sharing privileges |
| OpenRead( ) | Public method that creates a read-only FileStream |
| OpenText( ) | Public method that creates a StreamReader that reads from an existing text file |
| OpenWrite( ) | Public method that creates a write-only FileStream |

Example 22-2 modifies Example 22-1, adding code to get a FileInfo object for each file in each subdirectory. That object is used to display the name of the file, along with its length and the date and time it was last accessed.

*Example 22-2. Exploring files and subdirectories*

```
using System;
using System.IO;

using System.Collections;

namespace ExploringFilesAndSubdirectories
```

*Example 22-2. Exploring files and subdirectories (continued)*

```
{
    class Tester
    {
        // static member variables to keep track of totals
        // and indentation level
        static int dirCounter = 1;
        static int indentLevel = -1; // so first push = 0
        static int fileCounter = 0;

        public static void Main( )
        {
            Tester t = new Tester( );
            //Console.WriteLine("GetEnvironmentVariables: ");
            //IDictionary    environmentVariables =
            //   Environment.GetEnvironmentVariables( );
            //foreach (DictionaryEntry de in environmentVariables)
            //   {
            //        Console.WriteLine("  {0} = {1}", de.Key, de.Value);
            //   }


            //return;


            // choose the initial subdirectory
            string theDirectory =
                Environment.GetEnvironmentVariable("SystemRoot");
            // Mono and Shared Source CLI users on Linux, Unix or
            // Mac OS X should comment out the preceding two lines
            // of code and uncomment the following:
            //string theDirectory = "/tmp";

            // call the method to explore the directory,
            // displaying its access date and all
            // subdirectories
            DirectoryInfo dir = new DirectoryInfo(theDirectory);

            t.ExploreDirectory(dir);

            // completed. print the statistics

            Console.WriteLine(
                "\n\n{0} files in {1} directories found.\n",
                fileCounter, dirCounter);
        }

        // Set it running with a directoryInfo object
        // for each directory it finds, it will call
        // itself recursively
        private void ExploreDirectory(DirectoryInfo dir)
        {
            indentLevel++; // push a directory level
```

*Example 22-2. Exploring files and subdirectories (continued)*

```
            // create indentation for subdirectories
            for (int i = 0; i < indentLevel; i++)
                Console.Write("  "); // two spaces per level

            // print the directory and the time last accessed
            Console.WriteLine("[{0}] {1} [{2}]\n",
                indentLevel, dir.Name, dir.LastAccessTime);

            // get all the files in the directory and
            // print their name, last access time, and size
            try
            {
                FileInfo[] filesInDir = dir.GetFiles();

                foreach (FileInfo file in filesInDir)
                {
                    // indent once more to put files
                    // under their directory
                    for (int i = 0; i < indentLevel + 1; i++)
                        Console.Write("  "); // two spaces per level

                    Console.WriteLine("{0} [{1}] Size: {2} bytes",
                    file.Name,
                    file.LastWriteTime,
                    file.Length);
                    fileCounter++;
                }
                // get all the directories in the current directory
                // and call this method recursively on each
                DirectoryInfo[] directories = dir.GetDirectories();
                foreach (DirectoryInfo newDir in directories)
                {
                    dirCounter++; // increment the counter
                    ExploreDirectory(newDir);
                }
                indentLevel--; // pop a directory level
            }
            catch { }  // skip over the ones Vista doesn't like

        }
    }
}
```

Output (excerpt):

```
 0.LOG [8/30/2007 8:26:05 PM] Size: 0 bytes
 AC3API.INI [1/14/1999 2:04:06 PM] Size: 231 bytes
 actsetup.log [7/1/2004 11:13:11 AM] Size: 3848 bytes
 Blue Lace 16.bmp [8/29/2002 6:00:00 AM] Size: 1272 bytes
 BOOTSTAT.DAT [8/30/2007 8:25:03 PM] Size: 2048 bytes
44760 files in 8251 directories found.
```

The example is initialized with the name of the *SystemRoot* directory. It prints information about all the files in that directory, and then recursively explores all the subdirectories and all their subdirectories (your output might differ). This can take quite a while to run because the *SystemRoot* directory tree is rather large (in this case, 44,760 files in 8,251 directories).

In this version, we used a try/catch block to catch the exception thrown when we tried to get information about directories that are protected by Vista, and so the program was able to run to completion (though the count of files and directories is diminished by the uncounted secured directories):

```
try
{
    FileInfo[] filesInDir = dir.GetFiles();
    //...
    indentLevel--; // pop a directory level
}
catch { }
```

## Modifying Files

As you saw from Tables 22-3 and 22-4, you can use the `FileInfo` class to create, copy, rename, and delete files. The next example creates a new subdirectory, copies files in, renames some, deletes others, and then deletes the entire directory.

To set up these examples, create a *\test* directory and copy the media directory from WinNT or Windows into the *\test* directory. Don't work on files in the system root directly; when working with system files, you want to be extraordinarily careful.

The first step is to create a `DirectoryInfo` object for the test directory (adjust theDirectory appropriately if you are on a Mac OS X, Linux, or Unix system):

```
string theDirectory = @"c:\test\media";
DirectoryInfo dir = new DirectoryInfo(theDirectory);
```

Next, create a subdirectory within the test directory by calling `CreateSubDirectory` on the `DirectoryInfo` object. You get back a new `DirectoryInfo` object, representing the newly created subdirectory:

```
string newDirectory = "newTest";
DirectoryInfo newSubDir =
    dir.CreateSubdirectory(newDirectory);
```

You can now iterate over the test and copy files to the newly created subdirectory:

```
FileInfo[] filesInDir = dir.GetFiles();
foreach (FileInfo file in filesInDir)
{
    string fullName = newSubDir.FullName +
                "\\" + file.Name;
```

```
        file.CopyTo(fullName);
        Console.WriteLine("{0} copied to newTest",
            file.FullName);
    }
```

Notice the syntax of the CopyTo method. This is a method of the FileInfo object. Pass in the full path of the new file, including its full name and extension.

Once you've copied the files, you can get a list of the files in the new subdirectory and work with them directly:

```
filesInDir = newSubDir.GetFiles();
foreach (FileInfo file in filesInDir)
{
```

Create a simple integer variable named counter, and use it to rename every other file:

```
if (counter++ %2 == 0)
{
    file.MoveTo(fullName + ".bak");
    Console.WriteLine("{0} renamed to {1}",
        fullName,file.FullName);
}
```

You rename a file by "moving" it to the same directory, but with a new name. You can, of course, move a file to a new directory with its original name, or you can move and rename at the same time.

Rename every other file, and delete the ones you don't rename:

```
file.Delete();
Console.WriteLine("{0} deleted.", fullName);
```

Once you're done manipulating the files, you can clean up by deleting the entire subdirectory:

```
newSubDir.Delete(true);
```

The Boolean parameter determines whether this is a recursive delete. If you pass in false, and if this directory has subdirectories with files in it, it throws an exception.

Example 22-3 lists the source code for the complete program. Be careful when running this: when it is done, the subdirectory is gone. To see the renaming and deletions, put a breakpoint on or remove the last line.

*Example 22-3. Creating a subdirectory and manipulating files*

```
using System;
using System.IO;

namespace CreatingSubdirectoryManipulatingFile
{
    class Tester
    {
        public static void Main()
        {
```

*Example 22-3. Creating a subdirectory and manipulating files (continued)*

```csharp
        // make an instance and run it
        Tester t = new Tester( );
        string theDirectory = @"c:\test\media";
        DirectoryInfo dir = new DirectoryInfo(theDirectory);
        t.ExploreDirectory(dir);
    }

    // Set it running with a directory name
    private void ExploreDirectory(DirectoryInfo dir)
    {

        // make a new subdirectory
        string newDirectory = "newTest";
        DirectoryInfo newSubDir =
            dir.CreateSubdirectory(newDirectory);

        // get all the files in the directory and
        // copy them to the new directory
        FileInfo[] filesInDir = dir.GetFiles( );
        foreach (FileInfo file in filesInDir)
        {
            string fullName = newSubDir.FullName +
                        "\\" + file.Name;
            file.CopyTo(fullName);
            Console.WriteLine("{0} copied to newTest",
                        file.FullName);
        }

        // get a collection of the files copied in
        filesInDir = newSubDir.GetFiles( );

        // delete some and rename others
        int counter = 0;
        foreach (FileInfo file in filesInDir)
        {
            string fullName = file.FullName;

            if (counter++ % 2 == 0)
            {
                file.MoveTo(fullName + ".bak");
                Console.WriteLine("{0} renamed to {1}",
                    fullName, file.FullName);
            }
            else
            {
                file.Delete( );
                Console.WriteLine("{0} deleted.", fullName);
            }
        }

        newSubDir.Delete(true); // delete the subdirectory
    }
```

*Example 22-3. Creating a subdirectory and manipulating files (continued)*

```
    }
}
Output (excerpts):
c:\test\media\Bach's Brandenburg Concerto No. 3.RMI
 copied to newTest
c:\test\media\Beethoven's 5th Symphony.RMI copied to newTest
c:\test\media\Beethoven's Fur Elise.RMI copied to newTest
c:\test\media\canyon.mid copied to newTest
c:\test\media\newTest\Bach's Brandenburg Concerto
 No. 3.RMI renamed to
c:\test\media\newTest\Bach's Brandenburg Concerto
 No. 3.RMI.bak
c:\test\media\newTest\Beethoven's 5th Symphony.RMI deleted.
c:\test\media\newTest\Beethoven's Fur Elise.RMI renamed to
c:\test\media\newTest\Beethoven's Fur Elise.RMI.bak
c:\test\media\newTest\canyon.mid deleted.
```

# Reading and Writing Data

Reading and writing data is accomplished with the Stream class. Remember streams? This is a chapter about streams.[*]

Stream supports synchronous and asynchronous reads and writes. The .NET Framework provides a number of classes derived from Stream, including FileStream, MemoryStream, and NetworkStream. In addition, there is a BufferedStream class that provides buffered I/O, and can be used with any of the other stream classes. Table 22-5 summarizes the principal classes involved with I/O.

*Table 22-5. Principal I/O classes of the .NET Framework*

| Class | Use |
| --- | --- |
| Stream | Abstract class that supports reading and writing bytes |
| BinaryReader/BinaryWriter | Read and write encoded strings and primitive datatypes to and from streams |
| File, FileInfo, Directory, DirectoryInfo | Provide implementations for the abstract FileSystemInfo classes, including creating, moving, renaming, and deleting files and directories |
| FileStream | For reading to and from File objects; supports random access to files; opens files synchronously by default; supports asynchronous file access |
| TextReader, TextWriter, StringReader, StringWriter | TextReader and TextWriter are abstract classes designed for Unicode character I/O; StringReader and StringWriter write to and from strings, allowing your input and output to be either a stream or a string |
| BufferedStream | A stream that adds buffering to another stream such as a NetworkStream; BufferedStreams can improve the performance of the stream to which they are attached, but note that FileStream has buffering built in |

---

[*] With a tip of the hat to Arlo Guthrie.

*Table 22-5. Principal I/O classes of the .NET Framework (continued)*

| Class | Use |
|---|---|
| MemoryStream | A nonbuffered stream whose encapsulated data is directly accessible in memory, and is most useful as a temporary buffer |
| NetworkStream | A stream over a network connection |

# Binary Files

This section starts by using the basic Stream class to perform a binary read of a file. The term *binary read* is used to distinguish from a *text read*. If you don't know for certain that a file is just text, it is safest to treat it as a stream of bytes, known as a *binary* file.

The Stream class is chock-a-block with methods, but the most important are Read( ), Write( ), BeginRead( ), BeginWrite( ), and Flush( ). We will cover all of these in the next few sections.

To perform a binary read, begin by creating a pair of Stream objects, one for reading and one for writing:

```
Stream inputStream = File.OpenRead(
    @"C:\test\source\test1.cs");

Stream outputStream = File.OpenWrite(
    @"C:\test\source\test1.bak");
```

To open the files to read and write, you use the static OpenRead( ) and OpenWrite( ) methods of the File class. The static overload of these methods takes the path for the file as an argument, as shown previously.

Binary reads work by reading into a buffer. A buffer is just an array of bytes that will hold the data read by the Read( ) method.

Pass in the buffer, the offset in the buffer at which to begin storing the data read in, and the number of bytes to read. InputStream.Read reads bytes from the backing store into the buffer and returns the total number of bytes read.

It continues reading until no more bytes remain:

```
while ( (bytesRead =
        inputStream.Read(buffer,0,SIZE_BUFF)) > 0 )
{
    outputStream.Write(buffer,0,bytesRead);
}
```

Each bufferful of bytes is written to the output file. The arguments to Write( ) are the buffer from which to read, the offset into that buffer at which to start reading, and the number of bytes to write. Notice that you write the same number of bytes as you just read.

Example 22-4 provides the complete listing.

---

*Example 22-4. Implementing a binary read and write to a file*

```csharp
using System;
using System.IO;


namespace ImplementingBinaryReadWriteToFile
{
    class Tester
    {
        const int SizeBuff = 1024;

        public static void Main( )
        {
            // make an instance and run it
            Tester t = new Tester( );
            t.Run( );
        }

        // Set it running with a directory name
        private void Run( )
        {
            // the file to read from
            Stream inputStream = File.OpenRead(
                @"C:\test\source\test1.cs");

            // the file to write to
            Stream outputStream = File.OpenWrite(
                @"C:\test\source\test1.bak");

            // create a buffer to hold the bytes
            byte[] buffer = new Byte[SizeBuff];
            int bytesRead;

            // while the read method returns bytes
            // keep writing them to the output stream
            while ((bytesRead =
            inputStream.Read(buffer, 0, SizeBuff)) > 0)
            {
                outputStream.Write(buffer, 0, bytesRead);
            }

            // tidy up before exiting
            inputStream.Close( );
            outputStream.Close( );
        }
    }
}
```

 Before you run this program, create the *C:\test\source* subdirectory and add a file (containing the source to this program) named *test1.cs*. As with previous examples, Unix, Linux, and Mac OS X readers should adjust the paths appropriately.

The result of running this program is that a copy of the input file (*test1.cs*) is made in the same directory and is named *test1.bak*. You can compare these files using your favorite file comparison tool; they are identical, as shown in Figure 22-1.[*]

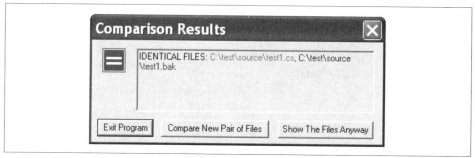

*Figure 22-1. File comparison showing the two files are identical*

## Buffered Streams

In the previous example, you created a buffer to read into. When you called Read( ), a bufferful was read from disk. It might be, however, that the operating system can be much more efficient if it reads a larger (or smaller) number of bytes at once.

A *buffered stream* object creates an internal buffer, and reads bytes to and from the backing store in whatever increments it thinks are most efficient. It will still fill your buffer in the increments you dictate, but your buffer is filled from the in-memory buffer, not from the backing store. The net effect is that the input and output are more efficient and thus faster.

A BufferedStream object is composed around an existing Stream object that you already have created. To use a BufferedStream, start by creating a normal stream class as you did in Example 22-4:

```
Stream inputStream = File.OpenRead(
    @"C:\test\source\folder3.cs");

Stream outputStream = File.OpenWrite(
    @"C:\test\source\folder3.bak");
```

Once you have the normal stream, pass that stream object to the buffered stream's constructor:

```
BufferedStream bufferedInput =
    new BufferedStream(inputStream);

BufferedStream bufferedOutput =
    new BufferedStream(outputStream);
```

---

[*] My favorite file comparison utility, as shown here, is ExamDiff Pro (*http://www.prestosoft.com/ps. asp?page=edp_examdiffpro*).

You can then use the BufferedStream as a normal stream, calling Read( ) and Write( ) just as you did before. The operating system handles the buffering:

```
while ( (bytesRead =
    bufferedInput.Read(buffer,0,SIZE_BUFF)) > 0 )
{
    bufferedOutput.Write(buffer,0,bytesRead);
}
```

Remember to *flush* the buffer when you want to ensure that the data is written out to the file:

```
bufferedOutput.Flush( );
```

This essentially tells the in-memory buffer to flush out its contents.

 Note that all streams should be closed, though the finalizer will eventually close them for you if you just let them go out of scope. In a robust program, you should always explicitly close the buffer.

Example 22-5 provides the complete listing.

*Example 22-5. Implementing buffered I/O*

```
using System;
using System.IO;

namespace Programming_CSharp
{
    class Tester
    {
        const int SizeBuff = 1024;

        public static void Main( )
        {
            // make an instance and run it
            Tester t = new Tester( );
            t.Run( );
        }

        // Set it running with a directory name
        private void Run( )
        {
            // create binary streams
            Stream inputStream = File.OpenRead(
                @"C:\test\source\folder3.cs");

            Stream outputStream = File.OpenWrite(
                @"C:\test\source\folder3.bak");

            // add buffered streams on top of the
            // binary streams
```

*Example 22-5. Implementing buffered I/O (continued)*

```
        BufferedStream bufferedInput =
            new BufferedStream(inputStream);

        BufferedStream bufferedOutput =
            new BufferedStream(outputStream);
        byte[] buffer = new Byte[SizeBuff];
        int bytesRead;

        while ((bytesRead =
        bufferedInput.Read(buffer, 0, SizeBuff)) > 0)
        {
            bufferedOutput.Write(buffer, 0, bytesRead);
        }

        bufferedOutput.Flush();
        bufferedInput.Close();
        bufferedOutput.Close();
    }
  }
}
```

With larger files, this example should run more quickly than Example 22-4 did.

## Working with Text Files

If you know that the file you are reading (and writing) contains nothing but text, you might want to use the StreamReader and StreamWriter classes. These classes are designed to make text manipulation easier. For example, they support the ReadLine( ) and WriteLine( ) methods that read and write a line of text at a time. You've already used WriteLine( ) with the Console object.

To create a StreamReader instance, start by creating a FileInfo object, and then call the OpenText( ) method on that object:

```
    FileInfo theSourceFile =
        new FileInfo (@"C:\test\source\test1.cs");

    StreamReader stream = theSourceFile.OpenText();
```

OpenText( ) returns a StreamReader for the file. With the StreamReader in hand, you can now read the file, line by line:

```
    do
    {
        text = stream.ReadLine();
    } while (text != null);
```

ReadLine( ) reads a line at a time until it reaches the end of the file. The StreamReader will return null at the end of the file.

To create the `StreamWriter` class, call the `StreamWriter` constructor, passing in the full name of the file you want to write to:

```
StreamWriter writer = new
StreamWriter(@"C:\test\source\folder3.bak",false);
```

The second parameter is the Boolean argument append. If the file already exists, true will cause the new data to be appended to the end of the file, and `false` will cause the file to be overwritten. In this case, pass in `false`, overwriting the file if it exists.

You can now create a loop to write out the contents of each line of the old file into the new file, and while you're at it, to print the line to the console as well:

```
do
{
    text = reader.ReadLine( );
    writer.WriteLine(text);
    Console.WriteLine(text);
} while (text != null);
```

Example 22-6 provides the complete source code.

*Example 22-6. Reading and writing to a text file*

```
using System;
using System.Collections.Generic;
using System.IO;
using System.Text;

namespace ReadingWritingToTextFile
{
    class Tester
    {
        public static void Main( )
        {
            // make an instance and run it
            Tester t = new Tester( );
            t.Run( );
        }

        // Set it running with a directory name
        private void Run( )
        {
            // open a file
            FileInfo theSourceFile = new FileInfo(
                @"C:\test\source\test.cs");

            // create a text reader for that file
            StreamReader reader = theSourceFile.OpenText( );

            // create a text writer to the new file
            StreamWriter writer = new StreamWriter(
                @"C:\test\source\test.bak", false);
```

*Example 22-6. Reading and writing to a text file (continued)*

```
            // create a text variable to hold each line
            string text;

            // walk the file and read every line
            // writing both to the console
            // and to the file
            do
            {
                text = reader.ReadLine( );
                writer.WriteLine(text);
                Console.WriteLine(text);
            } while (text != null);

            // tidy up
            reader.Close( );
            writer.Close( );
        }
    }
}
```

When this program is run, the contents of the original file are written both to the screen and to the new file. Notice the syntax for writing to the console:

```
Console.WriteLine(text);
```

This syntax is nearly identical to that used to write to the file:

```
writer.WriteLine(text);
```

The key difference is that the `WriteLine( )` method of `Console` is static, and the `WriteLine( )` method of `StreamWriter`, which is inherited from `TextWriter`, is an instance method, and thus must be called on an object rather than on the class itself.

# Asynchronous I/O

All the programs you've looked at so far perform *synchronous I/O*, meaning that while your program is reading or writing, all other activity is stopped. It can take a long time (relatively speaking) to read data to or from the backing store, especially if the backing store is a slow disk or (horrors!) a source on the Internet.

With large files, or when reading or writing across the network, you'll want *asynchronous I/O*, which allows you to begin a read and then turn your attention to other matters while the CLR fulfills your request. The .NET Framework provides asynchronous I/O through the `BeginRead( )` and `BeginWrite( )` methods of `Stream`.

The sequence is to call `BeginRead( )` on your file and then to go on to other, unrelated work while the read continues, possibly in another thread. When the read completes, you are notified via a callback method. You can then process the data that was read, kick off another read, and then go back to your other work.

In addition to the three parameters you've used in the binary read (the buffer, the off-set, and how many bytes to read), BeginRead( ) asks for a *delegate* and a *state object*.

 This is an instance of the more general async pattern seen through-out .NET (e.g., async stream I/O, async socket operations, async delegate invocation, etc.).

The delegate is an optional callback method, which, if provided, is called when the data is read. The state object is also optional. In this example, pass in null for the state object. The state of the object is kept in the member variables of the test class.

You are free to put any object you like in the state parameter, and you can retrieve it when you are called back. Typically (as you might guess from the name), you stash away state values that you'll need on retrieval. The developer can use the state parameter to hold the state of the call (paused, pending, running, etc.).

In this example, create the buffer and the Stream object as private member variables of the class:

```
public class AsynchIOTester
{
    private Stream inputStream;
    private byte[] buffer;
    const int BufferSize = 256;
```

In addition, create your delegate as a private member of the class:

```
private AsyncCallback myCallBack; // delegated method
```

The delegate is declared to be of type AsyncCallback, which is what the BeginRead( ) method of Stream expects.

An AsyncCallback delegate is declared in the System namespace as follows:

```
public delegate void AsyncCallback (IAsyncResult ar);
```

Thus, this delegate can be associated with any method that returns void and that takes an IAsyncResult interface as a parameter. The CLR will pass in the IAsyncResult interface object at runtime when the method is called. You only have to declare the method:

```
void OnCompletedRead(IAsyncResult asyncResult)
```

and then hook up the delegate in the constructor:

```
AsynchIOTester( )
{
    //...
    myCallBack = new AsyncCallback(this.OnCompletedRead);
}
```

Here's how it works, step by step. In Main( ), create an instance of the class and tell it to run:

```
public static void Main( )
{
    AsynchIOTester theApp = new AsynchIOTester( );
    theApp.Run( );
}
```

The call to new invokes the constructor. In the constructor, open a file and get a Stream object back. Then, allocate space in the buffer, and hook up the callback mechanism:

```
AsynchIOTester( )
{
    inputStream = File.OpenRead(@"C:\test\source\AskTim.txt");
    buffer = new byte[BufferSize];
    myCallBack = new AsyncCallback(this.OnCompletedRead);
}
```

 This example needs a large text file. I've copied a column written by Tim O'Reilly ("Ask Tim") from *http://www.oreilly.com* into a text file named *AskTim.txt*. I placed that in the subdirectory *test\source* on my C: drive. You can use any text file in any subdirectory.

In the Run( ) method, call BeginRead( ), which causes an asynchronous read of the file:

```
inputStream.BeginRead(
    buffer, // where to put the results
    0, // offset
    buffer.Length, // BufferSize
    myCallBack, // call back delegate
    null); // local state object
```

Then, go on to do other work. In this case, simulate useful work by counting up to 500,000, displaying your progress every 1,000 iterations:

```
for (long i = 0; i < 500000; i++)
{
    if (i%1000 == 0)
    {
        Console.WriteLine("i: {0}", i);
    }
}
```

When the read completes, the CLR will call your callback method:

```
void OnCompletedRead(IAsyncResult asyncResult)
{
```

The first thing to do when notified that the read has completed is to find out how many bytes were actually read. Do so by calling the EndRead( ) method of the Stream object, passing in the IAsyncResult interface object passed in by the CLR:

```
int bytesRead = inputStream.EndRead(asyncResult);
```

EndRead( ) returns the number of bytes read. If the number is greater than zero, you'll convert the buffer into a string, and write it to the console, and then call BeginRead( ) again, for another asynchronous read:

```
if (bytesRead > 0)
{
    String s =
    Encoding.ASCII.GetString (buffer, 0, bytesRead);
    Console.WriteLine(s);
    inputStream.BeginRead(
        buffer, 0, buffer.Length,
        myCallBack, null);
}
```

The effect is that you can do other work while the reads are taking place, but you can handle the read data (in this case, by outputting it to the console) each time a bufferful is ready. Example 22-7 provides the complete program.

*Example 22-7. Implementing asynchronous I/O*

```
using System;
using System.IO;

namespace AsynchronousIO
{
    public class AsynchIOTester
    {
        private Stream inputStream;

        // delegated method
        private AsyncCallback myCallBack;

        // buffer to hold the read data
        private byte[] buffer;

        // the size of the buffer
        const int BufferSize = 256;

        // constructor
        AsynchIOTester( )
        {
            // open the input stream
            inputStream = File.OpenRead(
                @"C:\test\source\AskTim.txt");

            // allocate a buffer
            buffer = new byte[BufferSize];

            // assign the callback
            myCallBack =
                new AsyncCallback(this.OnCompletedRead);
        }
```

*Example 22-7. Implementing asynchronous I/O (continued)*

```
public static void Main( )
{
    // create an instance of AsynchIOTester
    // which invokes the constructor
    AsynchIOTester theApp = new AsynchIOTester( );

    // call the instance method
    theApp.Run( );
}

void Run( )
{
    inputStream.BeginRead(
        buffer, // holds the results
        0, // offset
        buffer.Length, // (BufferSize)
        myCallBack, // callback delegate
        null); // local state object

    // do some work while data is read
    for (long i = 0; i < 500000; i++)
    {
        if (i % 1000 == 0)
        {
            Console.WriteLine("i: {0}", i);
        }
    }
}

// callback method
void OnCompletedRead(IAsyncResult asyncResult)
{
    int bytesRead =
        inputStream.EndRead(asyncResult);

    // if we got bytes, make them a string
    // and display them, then start up again.
    // Otherwise, we're done.
    if (bytesRead > 0)
    {
        String s =
            Encoding.ASCII.GetString(buffer, 0, bytesRead);
        Console.WriteLine(s);
        inputStream.BeginRead(
            buffer, 0, buffer.Length, myCallBack, null);
    }
}
}
}
```

*Example 22-7. Implementing asynchronous I/O (continued)*

```
Output (excerpt):
i: 47000
i: 48000
i: 49000
Date: January 2001
From: Dave Heisler
To: Ask Tim
Subject: Questions About O'Reilly
Dear Tim,
I've been a programmer for about ten years. I had heard of
O'Reilly books,then...
Dave,
You might be amazed at how many requests for help with
school projects I get;
i: 50000
i: 51000
i: 52000
```

The output reveals that the program is working on the two threads concurrently. The reads are done in the background while the other thread is counting and printing out every one-thousandth iteration. As the reads complete, they are printed to the console, and then you go back to counting. (I've shortened the listings to illustrate the output.)

In a real-world application, you might process user requests or compute values while the asynchronous I/O is busy retrieving or storing to a file or database.

# Network I/O

Writing to a remote object on the Internet isn't very different from writing to a file on your local machine. You might want to do this if your program needs to store its data to a file on a machine on your network, or if you are creating a program that displays information on a monitor connected to another computer on your network.

Network I/O is based on the use of streams created with sockets. Sockets are very useful for client/server and peer-to-peer (P2P) applications, and when making remote procedure calls.

A *socket* is an object that represents an endpoint for communication between processes communicating across a network. Sockets can work with various protocols, including UDP and TCP. In this section, we will create a TCP/IP connection between a server and a client. TCP/IP is a connection-based stream-like protocol for network communication. *Connection-based* means that with TCP/IP, once a connection is made, the two processes can talk with one another as though they were connected by a direct phone line.

Although TCP/IP is designed to talk across a network, you can simulate network communication by running the two processes on the same machine.

It is possible for more than one application on a given computer to be talking to various clients all at the same time (e.g., you might be running a web server, an FTP server, and a program that provides calculation support). Therefore, each application must have a unique ID so that the client can indicate which application it is looking for. That ID is known as a *port*. Think of the IP address as a phone number and the port as an extension.

The server instantiates a TcpListener and tells the listener to listen for connections on a specific port. The constructor for the TcpListener has two parameters, an IP address and an int representing the port on which that listener should listen.

Client applications connect to a specific IP address. For example, Yahoo!'s IP address is 66.94.234.13. Clients must also connect to a specific port. All web browsers connect to port 80 by default. Port numbers range from 0 to 65535 (e.g., 216); however, some numbers are reserved.*

 Ports are divided into the following ranges:
- 0–1023: well-known ports
- 1024–49151: registered ports
- 49152–65535: dynamic and/or private ports

For a list of all the well-known and registered ports, look at *http://www.iana.org/assignments/port-numbers*.

Once the listener is created, call Start( ) on it, telling the listener to begin accepting network connections. When the server is ready to start responding to calls from clients, call AcceptSocket( ). The thread in which you've called AcceptSocket( ) blocks (waiting sadly by the phone, wringing its virtual hands, hoping for a call).

You can imagine creating the world's simplest listener. It waits patiently for a client to call. When it gets a call, it interacts with that client to the exclusion of all other clients. The next few clients to call will connect, but they will automatically be put on hold. While they are listening to the music and being told their call is important and will be handled in the order received, they will block in their own threads. Once the backlog (hold) queue fills, subsequent callers will get the equivalent of a busy signal. They must hang up and wait for our simple socket to finish with its current client. This model works fine for servers that take only one or two requests a week, but it

---

* If you run your program on a network with a firewall, talk to your network administrator about which ports are closed.

doesn't scale well for real-world applications. Most servers need to handle thousands, even tens of thousands, of connections a minute!

To handle a high volume of connections, applications use asynchronous I/O to accept a call and create a socket with the connection to the client. The original listener then returns to listening, waiting for the next client. This way, your application can handle many calls; each time a call is accepted, a new socket is created.

The client is unaware of this sleight of hand in which a new socket is created. As far as the client is concerned, he has connected with the IP address and port he requested. Note that the new socket establishes a connection with the client. This is quite different from UDP, which uses a connectionless protocol. With TCP/IP, once the connection is made, the client and server know how to talk with each other without having to readdress each packet.

## Creating a Network Streaming Server

To create a network server for TCP/IP streaming, start by creating a `TcpListener` object to listen to the TCP/IP port you've chosen. I've arbitrarily chosen port 65000 from the available port IDs:

```
IPAddress localAddr = IPAddress.Parse("127.0.0.1");
TcpListener tcpListener = new TcpListener(localAddr, 65000);
```

Once the `TcpListener` object is constructed, you can ask it to start listening:

```
tcpListener.Start();
```

Now, wait for a client to request a connection:

```
Socket socketForClient = tcpListener.AcceptSocket();
```

The `AcceptSocket` method of the `TcpListener` object returns a `Socket` object that represents a *Berkeley socket interface* and is bound to a specific endpoint. `AcceptSocket()` is a synchronous method that will not return until it receives a connection request.

 Because the model is widely accepted by computer vendors, *Berkeley sockets* simplify the task of porting existing socket-based source code from Windows and Unix environments.

Once you have a socket you're ready to send the file to the client. Create a `NetworkStream` class, passing the socket into the constructor:

```
NetworkStream networkStream = new NetworkStream(socketForClient);
```

Then create a `StreamWriter` object much as you did before, except this time not on a file, but rather on the `NetworkStream` you just created:

```
System.IO.StreamWriter streamWriter = new
    System.IO.StreamWriter(networkStream);
```

When you write to this stream, the stream is sent over the network to the client. Example 22-8 shows the entire server. (I've stripped this server down to its bare essentials. With a production server, you almost certainly would run the request processing code in a thread, and you'd want to enclose the logic in try blocks to handle network problems.)

*Example 22-8. Implementing a network streaming server*

```
using System;
using System.Collections.Generic;
using System.Net;
using System.Net.Sockets;
using System.Text;

namespace NetworkStreamingServer
{
    public class NetworkIOServer
    {
        public static void Main()
        {
            NetworkIOServer app = new NetworkIOServer();
            app.Run();
        }

        private void Run()
        {
            // create a new TcpListener and start it up
            // listening on port 65000

            IPAddress localAddr = IPAddress.Parse("127.0.0.1");
            TcpListener tcpListener = new TcpListener(localAddr, 65000);
            tcpListener.Start();

            // keep listening until you send the file
            for (; ; )
            {
                // if a client connects, accept the connection
                // and return a new socket named socketForClient
                // while tcpListener keeps listening
                Socket socketForClient =
                tcpListener.AcceptSocket();
                Console.WriteLine("Client connected");

                // call the helper method to send the file
                SendFileToClient(socketForClient);

                Console.WriteLine("Disconnecting from client...");

                // clean up and go home
                socketForClient.Close();
                Console.WriteLine("Exiting...");
                break;
            }
```

*Example 22-8. Implementing a network streaming server (continued)*

```
        }

        // helper method to send the file
        private void SendFileToClient(
        Socket socketForClient)
        {
            // create a network stream and a stream writer
            // on that network stream
            NetworkStream networkStream =
            new NetworkStream(socketForClient);
            System.IO.StreamWriter streamWriter =
            new System.IO.StreamWriter(networkStream);

            // create a stream reader for the file
            System.IO.StreamReader streamReader =
                new System.IO.StreamReader(
                    @"C:\test\source\myTest.txt");

            string theString;

            // iterate through the file, sending it
            // line by line to the client
            do
            {
                theString = streamReader.ReadLine();

                if (theString != null)
                {
                    Console.WriteLine(
                        "Sending {0}", theString);
                    streamWriter.WriteLine(theString);
                    streamWriter.Flush();
                }
            }
            while (theString != null);

            // tidy up
            streamReader.Close();
            networkStream.Close();
            streamWriter.Close();
        }
    }
}
```

## Creating a Streaming Network Client

The client instantiates a TcpClient class, which represents a TCP/IP client connection to a host:

```
TcpClient socketForServer;
socketForServer = new TcpClient("localHost", 65000);
```

With this TcpClient, you can create a NetworkStream, and on that stream, you can create a StreamReader:

```
NetworkStream networkStream = socketForServer.GetStream( );
System.IO.StreamReader streamReader =
    new System.IO.StreamReader(networkStream);
```

Now, read the stream as long as there is data on it, outputting the results to the console:

```
do
{
    outputString = streamReader.ReadLine( );

    if( outputString != null )
    {
        Console.WriteLine(outputString);
    }
}
while( outputString != null );
```

Example 22-9 is the complete client.

*Example 22-9. Implementing a network streaming client*

```
using System;
using System.Collections.Generic;
using System.Net.Sockets;
using System.Text;

namespace NetworkStreamingClient
{
    public class Client
    {
        static public void Main(string[] Args)
        {
            // create a TcpClient to talk to the server
            TcpClient socketForServer;
            try
            {
                socketForServer =
                    new TcpClient("localHost", 65000);
            }
            catch
            {
                Console.WriteLine(
                    "Failed to connect to server at {0}:65000",
                    "localhost");
                return;
            }

            // create the Network Stream and the Stream Reader object
            NetworkStream networkStream =
                socketForServer.GetStream( );
```

*Example 22-9. Implementing a network streaming client (continued)*

```
            System.IO.StreamReader streamReader =
                new System.IO.StreamReader(networkStream);

            try
            {
                string outputString;

                // read the data from the host and display it
                do
                {
                    outputString = streamReader.ReadLine( );

                    if (outputString != null)
                    {
                        Console.WriteLine(outputString);
                    }
                }
                while (outputString != null);
            }
            catch
            {
                Console.WriteLine(
                "Exception reading from Server");
            }

            // tidy up
            networkStream.Close( );
        }
    }
}
```

To test this, I created a simple test file named *myTest.txt*:

```
This is line one
This is line two
This is line three
This is line four
```

Here is the output from the server and the client:

```
Output (Server):

Client connected
Sending This is line one
Sending This is line two
Sending This is line three
Sending This is line four
Disconnecting from client...
Exiting...
Output (Client):

This is line one
This is line two
```

```
This is line three
This is line four
Press any key to continue
```

 If you are testing this on a single machine, run the client and server in separate command windows or individual instances of the development environment. You need to start the server first, or the client will fail, saying it can't connect. If you aren't running this on a single machine, you need to replace occurrences of 127.0.0.1 and localhost with the IP address of the machine running the server. If you are running Windows XP Service Pack 2 with the default settings, you will get a Windows Security Alert asking whether you want to unblock the port.

## Handling Multiple Connections

As I mentioned earlier, this example doesn't scale well. Each client demands the entire attention of the server. A server is needed that can accept the connection and then pass the connection to overlapped I/O, providing the same asynchronous solution that you used earlier for reading from a file.

To manage this, create a new server, AsynchNetworkServer, which will nest within it a new class, ClientHandler. When your AsynchNetworkServer receives a client connection, it instantiates a ClientHandler, and passes the socket to that ClientHandler instance.

The ClientHandler constructor will create a copy of the socket and a buffer and open a new NetworkStream on that socket. It then uses overlapped I/O to asynchronously read and write to that socket. For this demonstration, it simply echoes whatever text the client sends back to the client and also to the console.

To create the asynchronous I/O, ClientHandler defines two delegate methods, OnReadComplete( ) and OnWriteComplete( ), that manage the overlapped I/O of the strings sent by the client.

The body of the Run( ) method for the server is very similar to what you saw in Example 22-8. First, create a listener and then call Start( ). Then, create a forever loop and call AcceptSocket( ). Once the socket is connected, instead of handling the connection, create a new ClientHandler and call StartRead( ) on that object.

Example 22-10 shows the complete source for the server.

*Example 22-10. Implementing an asynchronous network streaming server*

```
using System;
using System.Collections.Generic;
using System.Net;
using System.Net.Sockets;
using System.Text;
```

*Example 22-10. Implementing an asynchronous network streaming server (continued)*

```
namespace AsynchNetworkServer
{
    public class AsynchNetworkServer
    {
        class ClientHandler
        {
            private byte[] buffer;
            private Socket socket;
            private NetworkStream networkStream;
            private AsyncCallback callbackRead;
            private AsyncCallback callbackWrite;

            public ClientHandler(Socket socketForClient)
            {
                socket = socketForClient;
                buffer = new byte[256];
                networkStream =
                    new NetworkStream(socketForClient);

                callbackRead =
                    new AsyncCallback(this.OnReadComplete);

                callbackWrite =
                    new AsyncCallback(this.OnWriteComplete);
            }

            // begin reading the string from the client
            public void StartRead( )
            {
                networkStream.BeginRead(
                    buffer, 0, buffer.Length,
                    callbackRead, null);
            }

            // when called back by the read, display the string
            // and echo it back to the client
            private void OnReadComplete(IAsyncResult ar)
            {
                int bytesRead = networkStream.EndRead(ar);

                if (bytesRead > 0)
                {
                    string s =
                        System.Text.Encoding.ASCII.GetString(
                            buffer, 0, bytesRead);
                    Console.Write(
                        "Received {0} bytes from client: {1}",
                        bytesRead, s);
                    networkStream.BeginWrite(
                        buffer, 0, bytesRead, callbackWrite, null);
                }
                else
```

```
            {
                Console.WriteLine("Read connection dropped");
                networkStream.Close( );
                socket.Close( );
                networkStream = null;
                socket = null;
            }
        }

        // after writing the string, print a message and resume reading
        private void OnWriteComplete(IAsyncResult ar)
        {
            networkStream.EndWrite(ar);
            Console.WriteLine("Write complete");
            networkStream.BeginRead(
                buffer, 0, buffer.Length,
                callbackRead, null);
        }
    }

    public static void Main( )
    {
        AsynchNetworkServer app = new AsynchNetworkServer( );
        app.Run( );
    }

    private void Run( )
    {
        // create a new TcpListener and start it up
        // listening on port 65000

        IPAddress localAddr = IPAddress.Parse("127.0.0.1");
        TcpListener tcpListener = new TcpListener(localAddr, 65000);
        tcpListener.Start( );

        // keep listening until you send the file
        for (; ; )
        {
            // if a client connects, accept the connection
            // and return a new socket named socketForClient
            // while tcpListener keeps listening
            Socket socketForClient = tcpListener.AcceptSocket( );
            Console.WriteLine("Client connected");
            ClientHandler handler =
                new ClientHandler(socketForClient);
            handler.StartRead( );
        }
    }
}
```

The server starts up and listens to port 65000. If a client connects, the server instanti-ates a `ClientHandler` that will manage the I/O with the client while the server listens for the next client.

> In this example, you write the string received from the client to the console in `OnReadComplete()` and `OnWriteComplete()`. Writing to the console can block your thread until the write completes. In a produc-tion program, you don't want to take any blocking action in these methods because you are using a pooled thread. If you block in `OnReadComplete()` or `OnWriteComplete()`, you may cause more threads to be added to the thread pool, which is inefficient and will harm per-formance and scalability.

The client code is very simple. The client creates a `tcpSocket` for the port on which the server will listen (65000), and creates a `NetworkStream` object for that socket. It then writes a message to that stream and flushes the buffer. The client creates a `StreamReader` to read on that stream, and writes whatever it receives to the console. Example 22-11 shows the complete source for the client.

*Example 22-11. Implementing a client for asynchronous network I/O*

```
using System;
using System.Collections.Generic;
using System.Net.Sockets;
using System.Text;

namespace AsynchNetworkClient
{
    public class AsynchNetworkClient
    {
        private NetworkStream streamToServer;

        static public int Main()
        {
            AsynchNetworkClient client =
                new AsynchNetworkClient();
            return client.Run();
        }

        AsynchNetworkClient()
        {
            string serverName = "localhost";
            Console.WriteLine("Connecting to {0}", serverName);
            TcpClient tcpSocket = new TcpClient(serverName, 65000);
            streamToServer = tcpSocket.GetStream();
        }

        private int Run()
        {
            string message = "Hello Programming C#";
```

```
        Console.WriteLine(
            "Sending {0} to server.", message);

        // create a streamWriter and use it to
        // write a string to the server
        System.IO.StreamWriter writer =
            new System.IO.StreamWriter(streamToServer);
        writer.WriteLine(message);
        writer.Flush( );

        // Read response
        System.IO.StreamReader reader =
            new System.IO.StreamReader(streamToServer);
        string strResponse = reader.ReadLine( );
        Console.WriteLine("Received: {0}", strResponse);
        streamToServer.Close( );
        return 0;
      }
   }
}


Output (Server):
Client connected
Received 22 bytes from client: Hello Programming C#
Write complete
Read connection dropped

Output (Client):
Connecting to localhost
Sending Hello Programming C# to server.
Received: Hello Programming C#
```

In this example, the network server doesn't block while it is handling client connections, but rather, it delegates the management of those connections to instances of ClientHandler. Clients should not experience a delay waiting for the server to handle their connections.

## Asynchronous Network File Streaming

You can now combine the skills you learned for asynchronous file reads with asynchronous network streaming to produce a program that serves a file to a client on demand.

Your server will begin with an asynchronous read on the socket, waiting to get a filename from the client. Once you have the filename, you can kick off an asynchronous read of that file on the server. As each bufferful of the file becomes available, you can begin an asynchronous write back to the client. When the asynchronous write to the client finishes, you can kick off another read of the file; in this way, you ping-pong back and forth, filling the buffer from the file and writing the buffer out to the client. The client need do nothing but read the stream from the server. In the next example, the client will write the contents of the file to the console, but you could easily begin an asynchronous write to a new file on the client, thereby creating a network-based file copy program.

The structure of the server isn't unlike that shown in Example 22-10. Once again you will create a ClientHandler class, but this time, you will add an AsyncCallback named myFileCallBack, which you initialize in the constructor along with the callbacks for the network read and write:

```
myFileCallBack =
    new AsyncCallback(this.OnFileCompletedRead);

callbackRead =
    new AsyncCallback(this.OnReadComplete);

callbackWrite =
    new AsyncCallback(this.OnWriteComplete);
```

The Run( ) function of the outer class, now named AsynchNetworkFileServer, is unchanged. Once again you create and start the TcpListener class as well as create a forever loop in which you call AcceptSocket( ). If you have a socket, instantiate the ClientHandler and call StartRead( ). As in the previous example, StartRead( ) kicks off a BeginRead( ), passing in the buffer and the delegate to OnReadComplete.

When the read from the network stream completes, your delegated method OnReadComplete( ) is called and it retrieves the filename from the buffer. If text is returned, OnReadComplete( ) retrieves a string from the buffer using the static System.Text.Encoding.ASCII.GetString( ) method:

```
if( bytesRead > 0 )
{
    string fileName =
        System.Text.Encoding.ASCII.GetString(
        buffer, 0, bytesRead);
```

You now have a filename; with that, you can open a stream to the file and use the exact same asynchronous file read used in Example 22-7:

```
inputStream =
    File.OpenRead(fileName);

inputStream.BeginRead(
    buffer, // holds the results
    0, // offset
    buffer.Length, // Buffer Size
    myFileCallBack, // callback delegate
    null); // local state object
```

This read of the file has its own callback that will be invoked when the input stream has read a bufferful from the file on the server disk drive.

As noted earlier, you normally shouldn't take any action in an over-lapped I/O method that might block the thread for any appreciable time. The call to open the file and begin reading it is normally pushed off to a helper thread instead of doing this work in OnReadComplete( ). I simplified it for this example to avoid distracting from the issues at hand.

When the buffer is full, OnFileCompletedRead( ) is called, which checks to see whether any bytes were read from the file. If so, it begins an asynchronous write to the network:

```
if (bytesRead > 0)
{
    // write it out to the client
    networkStream.BeginWrite(
        buffer, 0, bytesRead, callbackWrite, null);
}
```

If OnFileCompletedRead was called, and no bytes were read, this signifies that the entire file has been sent. The server reacts by closing the NetworkStream and socket, thus letting the client know that the transaction is complete:

```
networkStream.Close( );
socket.Close( );
networkStream = null;
socket = null;
```

When the network write completes, the OnWriteComplete( ) method is called, and this kicks off another read from the file:

```
private void OnWriteComplete( IAsyncResult ar )
{
    networkStream.EndWrite(ar);
    Console.WriteLine( "Write complete");

    inputStream.BeginRead(
        buffer, // holds the results
        0, // offset
        buffer.Length, // (BufferSize)
        myFileCallBack, // callback delegate
        null); // local state object

}
```

The cycle begins again with another read of the file, and the cycle continues until the file has been completely read and transmitted to the client. The client code simply writes a filename to the network stream to kick off the file read:

```
string message = @"C:\test\source\AskTim.txt";
System.IO.StreamWriter writer =
    new System.IO.StreamWriter(streamToServer);
writer.Write(message);
writer.Flush( );
```

The client then begins a loop, reading from the network stream until no bytes are sent by the server. When the server is done, the network stream is closed. Start by initializing a Boolean value to false and creating a buffer to hold the bytes sent by the server:

```
bool fQuit = false;
while (!fQuit)
{
    char[] buffer = new char[BufferSize];
```

You are now ready to create a new StreamReader from the NetworkStream member variable streamToServer:

```
System.IO.StreamReader reader =
    new System.IO.StreamReader(streamToServer);
```

The call to Read( ) takes three parameters—the buffer, the offset at which to begin reading, and the size of the buffer:

```
int bytesRead = reader.Read(buffer,0, BufferSize);
```

Check to see whether the Read( ) returned any bytes; if not, you are done, and you can set the Boolean value fQuit to true, causing the loop to terminate:

```
if (bytesRead == 0)
    fQuit = true;
```

If you did receive bytes, you can write them to the console, or write them to a file, or do whatever it is you will do with the values sent from the server:

```
else
{
    string theString = new String(buffer);
    Console.WriteLine(theString);
}
}
```

Once you break out of the loop, close the NetworkStream:

```
streamToServer.Close( );
```

Example 22-12 shows the complete annotated source for the server, with the client following later in Example 22-13.

*Example 22-12. Implementing a client for an asynchronous network file server*

```
using System;
using System.Net.Sockets;
using System.Threading;
using System.Text;

public class AsynchNetworkClient
{
    private const int BufferSize = 256;
    private NetworkStream streamToServer;
```

*Example 22-12. Implementing a client for an asynchronous network file server (continued)*

```
static public int Main( )
{
    AsynchNetworkClient client =
        new AsynchNetworkClient( );
    return client.Run( );
}

AsynchNetworkClient( )
{
    string serverName = "localhost";
    Console.WriteLine("Connecting to {0}", serverName);
    TcpClient tcpSocket = new TcpClient(serverName, 65000);
    streamToServer = tcpSocket.GetStream( );
}

private int Run( )
{
    string message = @"C:\test\source\AskTim.txt";
    Console.Write("Sending {0} to server.", message);

    // create a streamWriter and use it to
    // write a string to the server
    System.IO.StreamWriter writer =
        new System.IO.StreamWriter(streamToServer);
    writer.Write(message);
    writer.Flush( );

    bool fQuit = false;

    // while there is data coming
    // from the server, keep reading
    while (!fQuit)
    {
        // buffer to hold the response
        char[] buffer = new char[BufferSize];

        // Read response
        System.IO.StreamReader reader =
            new System.IO.StreamReader(streamToServer);

        // see how many bytes are
        // retrieved to the buffer
        int bytesRead = reader.Read(buffer, 0, BufferSize);
        if (bytesRead == 0) // none? quite
            fQuit = true;
        else // got some?
        {
            // display it as a string
            string theString = new String(buffer);
            Console.WriteLine(theString);
        }
    }
```

```
        streamToServer.Close( ); // tidy up
        return 0;
    }
}
```

By combining the asynchronous file read with the asynchronous network read, you have created a scalable application that can handle requests from a number of clients.

# Web Streams

Instead of reading from a stream provided by a custom server, you can just as easily read from any web page on the Internet.

A WebRequest is an object that requests a resource identified by a URI, such as the URL for a web page. You can use a WebRequest object to create a WebResponse object that will encapsulate the object pointed to by the URI. That is, you can call GetResponse( ) on your WebRequest object to get access to the object pointed to by the URI. What is returned is encapsulated in a WebResponse object. You can then ask that WebResponse object for a Stream object by calling GetResponseStream( ). GetResponseStream( ) returns a stream that encapsulates the contents of the web object (e.g., a stream with the web page).

The next example retrieves the contents of a web page as a stream. To get a web page, you'll want to use HttpWebRequest. HttpWebRequest derives from WebRequest and provides additional support for interacting with the HTTP protocol.

To create the HttpWebRequest, cast the WebRequest returned from the static Create( ) method of the WebRequestFactory:

```
HttpWebRequest webRequest =
    (HttpWebRequest) WebRequest.Create
    ("http://www.libertyassociates.com/book_edit.htm");
```

Create( ) is a static method of WebRequest. When you pass in a URI, an instance of HttpWebRequest is created.

> The method is overloaded on the type of the parameter. It returns different derived types depending on what is passed in. For example, if you pass in a URI, an object of type HttpWebRequest is created. The return type, however, is WebRequest, and so you must cast the returned value to HttpWebRequest.

Creating the HttpWebRequest establishes a connection to a page on your web site. What you get back from the host is encapsulated in an HttpWebResponse object, which is an HTTP protocol-specific subclass of the more general WebResponse class:

```
HttpWebResponse webResponse =
    (HttpWebResponse) webRequest.GetResponse( );
```

You can now open a StreamReader on that page by calling the GetResponseStream( ) method of the WebResponse object:

```
StreamReader streamReader = new StreamReader(
    webResponse.GetResponseStream( ), Encoding.ASCII);
```

You can read from that stream exactly as you read from the network stream. Example 22-13 shows the complete listing.

*Example 22-13. Reading a web page as an HTML stream*

```
using System;
using System.Collections.Generic;
using System.IO;
using System.Net;
using System.Net.Sockets;
using System.Text;

namespace ReadingWebPageAsHTML
{
    public class Client
    {
        static public void Main(string[] Args)
        {
            // create a webRequest for a particular page
            HttpWebRequest webRequest =
                (HttpWebRequest)WebRequest.Create
                    ("http://www.jesseliberty.com/");

            // ask the web request for a webResponse encapsulating
            // that page
            HttpWebResponse webResponse =
                (HttpWebResponse)webRequest.GetResponse( );

            // get the streamReader from the response
            StreamReader streamReader = new StreamReader(
                webResponse.GetResponseStream( ), Encoding.ASCII);

            try
            {
                string outputString;
                outputString = streamReader.ReadToEnd( );
                Console.WriteLine(outputString);
            }
            catch
            {
                Console.WriteLine("Exception reading from web page");
            }
            streamReader.Close( );
        }
    }
}
Output (excerpt):
<html>
```

*Example 22-13. Reading a web page as an HTML stream (continued)*

```
<head>
<title>Liberty Associates</title>
<meta http-equiv="Content-Type" content="text/html; charset=iso-8859-1">
<script language="JavaScript">
<!--
isNS=(navigator.appName=="Netscape");
activeMenu="";
activeIndex=-1;
activeImg="";

window.onError = null;

function setImage(imgName,index) {
 if(activeImg==imgName)
 return true;
 document.images[imgName].src = rolloverImg[index].src;
 return true;
}

rolloverImg=new Array();
```

The output shows that what is sent through the stream is the HTML of the page you requested. You might use this capability for *screen scraping*: reading a page from a site into a buffer and then extracting the information you need.

 All examples of screen scraping in this book assume that you are reading a site for which you have copyright permission.

# Serialization

When an object is streamed to disk, its various member data must be *serialized*—that is, written out to the stream as a series of bytes. The object will also be serialized when stored in a database or when marshaled across a context, app domain, process, or machine boundary.

The CLR provides support for serializing an *object graph*—an object and all the member data of that object. By default, types aren't serializable. To be able to serialize an object, you must explicitly mark it with the [Serializable] attribute.

The CLR will do the work of serializing your object for you. Because the CLR knows how to serialize all the primitive types, if your object consists of nothing but primitive types (all your member data consists of integers, longs, strings, etc.), you're all set. If your object consists of other user-defined types (classes), you must ensure that these types are also serializable. The CLR will try to serialize each object contained by your object (and all their contained objects as well), but these objects themselves must be either primitive types or serializable, or else they will not be serialized.

When an object is marshaled, either by value or by reference, it must be serialized. The difference is only whether a copy is made or a proxy is provided to the client. Objects marked with the [Serializable] attribute are marshaled by value; those that derive from MarshalByRefObject are marshaled by reference, but both are serialized.

## Using a Formatter

When data is serialized, it is eventually read by the same program or another program on the same or a different computer. In any case, the code reading the data expects that data to be in a particular format. Most of the time in a .NET application, the expected format is the native binary format or SOAP.

 SOAP is a simple, lightweight, XML-based protocol for exchanging information across the Web. SOAP is highly modular and very extensible. It also leverages existing Internet technologies, such as HTTP and SMTP.

When data is serialized, the format of the serialization is determined by the formatter you apply. Formatter classes implement the interface IFormatter; you are also free to create your own formatter, though very few programmers will ever need or want to! The CLR provides a SoapFormatter for use with web services and a BinaryFormatter that is useful for fast local storage or remoting.

You can instantiate these objects with their default constructors:

```
BinaryFormatter binaryFormatter =
    new BinaryFormatter( );
```

Once you have an instance of a formatter, you can invoke its Serialize( ) method, passing in a stream and an object to serialize. You'll see how this is done in the next example.

## Working with Serialization

To see serialization at work, you need a sample class that you can serialize and then deserialize. You can start by creating a class named SumOf. SumOf has three member variables:

```
private int startNumber = 1;
private int endNumber;
private int[] theSums;
```

The member array theSums represents the value of the sums of all the numbers from startNumber through endNumber. Thus, if startNumber is 1 and endNumber is 10, the array will have the values:

```
1,3,6,10,15,21,28,36,45,55
```

Each value is the sum of the previous value plus the next in the series. Thus, if the series is 1,2,3,4, the first value in theSums will be 1. The second value is the previous value (1) plus the next in the series (2); thus, theSums[1] will hold the value 3. Likewise, the third value is the previous value (3) plus the next in the series, so theSums[2] is 6. Finally, the fourth value in theSums is the previous value (6) plus the next in the series (4), for a value of 10.

The constructor for the SumOf object takes two integers: the starting number and the ending number. It assigns these to the local values, and then calls a helper function to compute the contents of the array:

```
public SumOf(int start, int end)
{
    startNumber = start;
    endNumber = end;
    ComputeSums();
}
```

The ComputeSums helper function fills in the contents of the array by computing the sums in the series from startNumber through endNumber:

```
private void ComputeSums()
{
    int count = endNumber - startNumber + 1;
    theSums = new int[count];
    theSums[0] = startNumber;
    for (int i=1,j=startNumber + 1;i<count;i++,j++)
    {
        theSums[i] = j + theSums[i-1];
    }
}
```

You can display the contents of the array at any time by using a foreach loop:

```
private void DisplaySums()
{
    foreach(int i in theSums)
    {
        Console.WriteLine("{0}, ",i);
    }
}
```

## Serializing the object

Now, mark the class as eligible for serialization with the [Serializable] attribute:

```
[Serializable]
class SumOf
```

To invoke serialization, you first need a fileStream object into which you'll serialize the SumOf object:

```
FileStream fileStream =
  new FileStream("DoSum.out",FileMode.Create);
```

You are now ready to call the formatter's `Serialize( )` method, passing in the stream and the object to serialize. Because this is done in a method of `SumOf`, you can pass in the this object, which points to the current object:

```
binaryFormatter.Serialize(fileStream,this);
```

This serializes the `SumOf` object to disk.

### Deserializing the object

To reconstitute the object, open the file, and ask a binary formatter to `DeSerialize` it:

```
public static SumOf DeSerialize( ){
    FileStream fileStream =
        new FileStream("DoSum.out",FileMode.Open);
    BinaryFormatter binaryFormatter =
        new BinaryFormatter( );
    SumOf retVal = (SumOf) binaryFormatter.Deserialize(fileStream);
    fileStream.Close( );
    return retVal;}
```

To make sure all this works, first, instantiate a new object of type `SumOf` and tell it to serialize itself. Then, create a new instance of type `SumOf` by calling the static deserializer and asking it to display its values:

```
public static void Main( )
{
    Console.WriteLine("Creating first one with new...");
    SumOf app = new SumOf(1,10);

    Console.WriteLine(
        "Creating second one with deserialize...");
    SumOf newInstance = SumOf.DeSerialize( );
    newInstance.DisplaySums( );
}
```

Example 22-14 provides the complete source code to illustrate serialization and deserialization.

*Example 22-14. Serializing and deserializing an object*

```
using System;
using System.Collections.Generic;
using System.IO;
using System.Runtime.Serialization;
using System.Runtime.Serialization.Formatters.Binary;
using System.Text;

namespace SerializingDeserializingAnObject
{
    [Serializable]
    class SumOf
    {
```

*Example 22-14. Serializing and deserializing an object (continued)*

```csharp
    private int startNumber = 1;
    private int endNumber;
    private int[] theSums;

    public static void Main()
    {
        Console.WriteLine("Creating first one with new...");
        SumOf app = new SumOf(1, 10);

        Console.WriteLine("Creating second one with deserialize...");
        SumOf newInstance = SumOf.DeSerialize();
        newInstance.DisplaySums();
    }

    public SumOf(int start, int end)
    {
        startNumber = start;
        endNumber = end;
        ComputeSums();
        DisplaySums();
        Serialize();
    }

    private void ComputeSums()
    {
        int count = endNumber - startNumber + 1;
        theSums = new int[count];
        theSums[0] = startNumber;
        for (int i = 1, j = startNumber + 1; i < count; i++, j++)
        {
            theSums[i] = j + theSums[i - 1];
        }
    }

    private void DisplaySums()
    {
        foreach (int i in theSums)
        {
            Console.WriteLine("{0}, ", i);
        }
    }

    private void Serialize()
    {
        Console.Write("Serializing...");
        // create a file stream to write the file
        FileStream fileStream =
            new FileStream("DoSum.out", FileMode.Create);
        // use the CLR binary formatter
        BinaryFormatter binaryFormatter =
            new BinaryFormatter();
```

*Example 22-14. Serializing and deserializing an object (continued)*

```
            // serialize to disk
            binaryFormatter.Serialize(fileStream, this);
            Console.WriteLine("...completed");
            fileStream.Close( );
        }

        public static SumOf DeSerialize( )
        {
            FileStream fileStream =
                new FileStream("DoSum.out", FileMode.Open);
            BinaryFormatter binaryFormatter =
                new BinaryFormatter( );
            SumOf retVal = (SumOf)binaryFormatter.Deserialize(fileStream);
            fileStream.Close( );
            return retVal;
        }
    }
}


Output:
Creating first one with new...
1,
3,
6,
10,
15,
21,
28,
36,
45,
55,
Serializing......completed
Creating second one with deserialize...
1,
3,
6,
10,
15,
21,
28,
36,
45,
55,
```

The output shows that the object was created, displayed, and then serialized. The object was then deserialized and output again, with no loss of data.

# Handling Transient Data

In some ways, the approach to serialization demonstrated in Example 22-14 is very wasteful. Because you can compute the contents of the array given its starting and ending numbers, there really is no reason to store its elements to disk. Although the operation might be inexpensive with a small array, it could become costly with a very large one.

You can tell the serializer not to serialize some data by marking it with the [NonSerialized] attribute:

```
[NonSerialized] private int[] theSums;
```

If you don't serialize the array, however, the object you create will not be correct when you deserialize it. The array will be empty. Remember, when you deserialize the object, you simply read it up from its serialized form; no methods are run.

To fix the object before you return it to the caller, implement the IDeserializationCallback interface:

```
[Serializable]
class SumOf : IDeserializationCallback
```

Also, implement the one method of this interface: OnDeserialization(). The CLR promises that if you implement this interface, your class' OnDeserialization() method will be called when the entire object graph has been deserialized. This is just what you want: the CLR will reconstitute what you've serialized, and then you have the opportunity to fix up the parts that were not serialized.

This implementation can be very simple. Just ask the object to recompute the series:

```
public virtual void OnDeserialization (Object sender)
{
    ComputeSums();
}
```

This is a classic space/time trade-off; by not serializing the array, you may make deserialization somewhat slower (because you must take the time to recompute the array), and you make the file somewhat smaller. To see whether not serializing the array had any effect, I ran the program with the digits 1–5,000. Before setting [NonSerialized] on the array, the serialized file was 20 KB. After setting [NonSerialized], the file was 1 KB. Not bad. Example 22-15 shows the source code using the digits 1–5 as input (to simplify the output).

*Example 22-15. Working with a nonserialized object*

```
using System;
using System.Collections.Generic;
using System.IO;
using System.Runtime.Serialization;
using System.Runtime.Serialization.Formatters.Binary;
using System.Text;
```

*Example 22-15. Working with a nonserialized object (continued)*

```
namespace WorkingWithNonSerializedObject
{
    [Serializable]
    class SumOf : IDeserializationCallback
    {
        private int startNumber = 1;
        private int endNumber;
        [NonSerialized]
        private int[] theSums;

        public static void Main()
        {
            Console.WriteLine("Creating first one with new...");
            SumOf app = new SumOf(1, 5);

            Console.WriteLine("Creating second one with deserialize...");
            SumOf newInstance = SumOf.DeSerialize();
            newInstance.DisplaySums();
        }

        public SumOf(int start, int end)
        {
            startNumber = start;
            endNumber = end;
            ComputeSums();
            DisplaySums();
            Serialize();
        }

        private void ComputeSums()
        {
            int count = endNumber - startNumber + 1;
            theSums = new int[count];
            theSums[0] = startNumber;
            for (int i = 1, j = startNumber + 1; i < count; i++, j++)
            {
                theSums[i] = j + theSums[i - 1];
            }
        }

        private void DisplaySums()
        {
            foreach (int i in theSums)
            {
                Console.WriteLine("{0}, ", i);
            }
        }

        private void Serialize()
        {
            Console.Write("Serializing...");
            // create a file stream to write the file
```

*Example 22-15. Working with a nonserialized object (continued)*

```
            FileStream fileStream =
                new FileStream("DoSum.out", FileMode.Create);
            // use the CLR binary formatter
            BinaryFormatter binaryFormatter =
                new BinaryFormatter( );
            // serialize to disk
            binaryFormatter.Serialize(fileStream, this);
            Console.WriteLine("...completed");
            fileStream.Close( );
        }

        public static SumOf DeSerialize( )
        {
            FileStream fileStream =
                new FileStream("DoSum.out", FileMode.Open);
            BinaryFormatter binaryFormatter =
                new BinaryFormatter( );
            SumOf retVal = (SumOf)binaryFormatter.Deserialize(fileStream);
            fileStream.Close( );
            return retVal;
        }

        // fix up the nonserialized data

        public virtual void OnDeserialization(Object sender)
        {
            ComputeSums( );
        }
    }
}
```

```
Output:
Creating first one with new...
1,
3,
6,
10,
15,
Serializing......completed
Creating second one with deserialize...
1,
3,
6,
10,
15,
```

You can see in the output that the data was successfully serialized to disk and then reconstituted by deserialization. The trade-off of disk storage space versus time doesn't make a lot of sense with five values, but it makes a great deal of sense with five million values.

So far, you've streamed your data to disk for storage and across the network for easy communication with distant programs. There is one other time you might create a stream: to store permanent configuration and status data on a per-user basis. For this purpose, the .NET Framework offers *isolated storage*.

# Isolated Storage

The .NET CLR provides isolated storage to allow the application developer to store data on a *per-user* basis. Isolated storage provides much of the functionality of traditional Windows *.ini* files, or the more recent HKEY_CURRENT_USER key in the Windows Registry.

Applications save data to a unique *data compartment* associated with the application. The CLR implements the data compartment with a *data store*, which is typically a directory on the filesystem.

Administrators are free to limit how much isolated storage individual applications can use. They can also use security so that less-trusted code can't call more highly trusted code to write to isolated storage.

What is important about isolated storage is that the CLR provides a standard place to store your application's data, but it doesn't impose (or support) any particular layout or syntax for that data. In short, you can store anything you like in isolated storage.

Typically, you will store text, often in the form of name-value pairs. Isolated storage is a good mechanism for saving user configuration information such as login name, the position of various windows and widgets, and other application-specific, user-specific information. The data is stored in a separate file for each user, but the files can be isolated even further by distinguishing among different aspects of the identity of the code (by assembly or by originating application domain).

Using isolated storage is fairly straightforward. To write to isolated storage, create an instance of an IsolatedStorageFileStream, which you initialize with a filename and a file mode (create, append, etc.):

```
IsolatedStorageFileStream configFile =
 new IsolatedStorageFileStream
 ("Tester.cfg",FileMode.Create);
```

Now, create a StreamWriter on that file:

```
StreamWriter writer =
 new StreamWriter(configFile);
```

Then, write to that stream as you would to any other. Example 22-16 illustrates.

*Example 22-16. Writing to isolated storage*

```
using System;
using System.Collections.Generic;
using System.IO;
using System.IO.IsolatedStorage;
using System.Text;

namespace WritingToIsolatedStorage
{
    public class Tester
    {
        public static void Main( )
        {
            Tester app = new Tester( );
            app.Run( );
        }

        private void Run( )
        {
            // create the configuration file stream
            IsolatedStorageFileStream configFile =
                new IsolatedStorageFileStream
                    ("Tester.cfg", FileMode.Create);

            // create a writer to write to the stream
            StreamWriter writer =
                new StreamWriter(configFile);

            // write some data to the config. file
            String output;
            System.DateTime currentTime = System.DateTime.Now;
            output = "Last access: " + currentTime.ToString( );
            writer.WriteLine(output);
            output = "Last position = 27,35";
            writer.WriteLine(output);

            // flush the buffer and clean up
            writer.Close( );
            configFile.Close( );
        }
    }
}
```

After running this code, search your hard disk for *Tester.cfg*. On my machine, this file is found in:

```
C:\Documents and Settings\Jesse\Local Settings\Application Data\
IsolatedStorage\mipjwcsz.iir\2hzvpjcc.pOy\StrongName.
mwoxzllzqpx3uOtaclp1dti11kpddwyo\Url.a2f4v2g3ytucslmvlpt2wmdxhrhqg1pz\
Files
```

You can read this file with Notepad if what you've written is just text:

```
Last access: 8/26/2007 10:00:57 AM
Last position = 27,35
```

Or, you can access this data programmatically. To do so, reopen the file:

```
IsolatedStorageFileStream configFile =
    new IsolatedStorageFileStream
    ("Tester.cfg",FileMode.Open);
```

Create a StreamReader object:

```
StreamReader reader =
    new StreamReader(configFile);
```

Use the standard stream idiom to read through the file:

```
string theEntry;
do
{
    theEntry = reader.ReadLine( );
    Console.WriteLine(theEntry);
} while (theEntry != null);
Console.WriteLine(theEntry);
```

Isolated storage is scoped by assembly (so if you shut down your program and start it later, you can read the configuration file you created, but you can't read the configuration of any other assembly). Example 22-17 provides the method needed to read the file. Replace the Run( ) method in the previous example, recompile it, and run it (but don't change its name, or it won't be able to access the isolated storage you created previously).

*Example 22-17. Reading from isolated storage*

```
private void Run( )
{
    // open the configuration file stream
    IsolatedStorageFileStream configFile =
        new IsolatedStorageFileStream
            ("Tester.cfg", FileMode.Open);

    // create a standard stream reader
    StreamReader reader =
        new StreamReader(configFile);

    // read through the file and display
    string theEntry;
    do
    {
        theEntry = reader.ReadLine( );
        Console.WriteLine(theEntry);
    } while (theEntry != null);
```

*Example 22-17. Reading from isolated storage (continued)*

```
            reader.Close( );
            configFile.Close( );
        }
    }
```

Output:

```
Last access: 8/26/2007 11:19:51 PM
Last position = 27,35
```

# CHAPTER 23

# Programming .NET and COM

Programmers love a clean slate. Although it would be nice if we could throw away all the code we've ever written and start over, this typically isn't a viable option for most companies. Over the past decade, many development organizations have made a substantial investment in developing and purchasing COM components and ActiveX controls. Microsoft has made a commitment to ensure that these legacy components are usable from within .NET applications, and (perhaps less important) that .NET components are easily callable from COM.

This chapter describes the support .NET provides for importing ActiveX controls and COM components into your application, exposing .NET classes to COM-based applications, and making direct calls to Win32 APIs. You'll also learn about C# pointers and keywords for accessing memory directly; this may be crucial in some applications.

## Importing ActiveX Controls

ActiveX controls are COM components typically dropped into a form, which might or might not have a user interface. When Microsoft developed the OCX standard, which allowed developers to build ActiveX controls in VB and use them with C++ (and vice versa), the ActiveX control revolution began. Over the past few years, thousands of such controls have been developed, sold, and used. They are small, easy to work with, and an effective example of binary reuse. Importing ActiveX controls into .NET is surprisingly easy, considering how different COM objects are from .NET objects. Visual Studio 2008 is able to import ActiveX controls automagically. As an alternative to using Visual Studio, Microsoft has developed a command-line utility, Aximp, which will create the assemblies necessary for the control to be used in a .NET application.

### Creating an ActiveX Control

To demonstrate the ability to use classic ActiveX controls in a .NET application, you'll first develop a simple four-function calculator as an ActiveX control and then invoke that ActiveX control from within a C# application. You'll build the control in

VB 6, and test it in a VB 6 application. If you don't have VB 6 or don't want to bother creating the control, you can download the control from *http://www. JesseLiberty.com*. (Click on the Book site, then click on Books. Navigate to *this* book, and click on the source code.) Once the control is working in the standard Windows environment, you'll import it into your Windows Forms application.

To create the control, open VB 6 and choose ActiveX control as the new project type. Make the project form as small as possible because this control will not have a user interface. Right-click UserControl1 and choose Properties. Rename it Calculator in the Properties window. Click the Project in the Project Explorer, and in the Properties window, rename it CalcControl. Immediately save the project and name both the file and the project CalcControl, as shown in Figure 23-1.

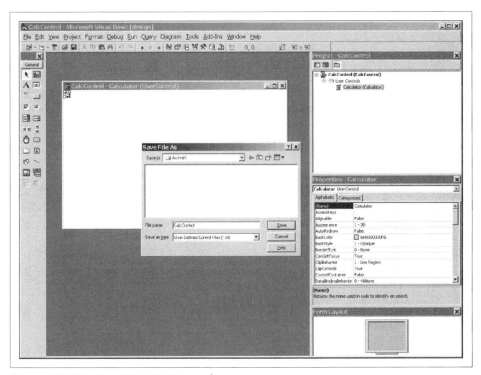

*Figure 23-1. Creating a VB ActiveX control*

You can add the four calculator functions by right-clicking the CalcControl form, selecting View Code from the pop-up menu, and typing the VB code shown in Example 23-1.

*Example 23-1. Implementing the CalcControl ActiveX control*

```
Public Function _
Add(left As Double, right As Double) _
    As Double
    Add = left + right
End Function
```

*Example 23-1. Implementing the CalcControl ActiveX control (continued)*

```
Public Function _
Subtract(left As Double, right As Double) _
    As Double
    Subtract = left - right
End Function

Public Function _
Multiply(left As Double, right As Double) _
    As Double
    Multiply = left * right
End Function

Public Function _
Divide(left As Double, right As Double) _
    As Double
    Divide = left / right
End Function
```

This is the entire code for the control. Compile this to the *CalcControl.ocx* file by choosing File → Make CalcControl.ocx on the VB 6 menu bar. Open a second project in VB as a standard executable (EXE). Name the form TestForm, and name the project CalcTest. Save the file and project as CalcTest. Add the ActiveX control as a component by pressing Ctrl-T and choosing CalcControl from the Controls tab, shown in Figure 23-2.

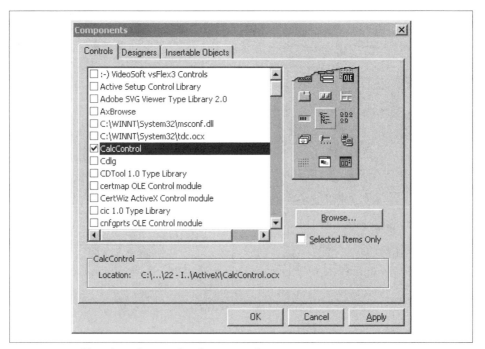

*Figure 23-2. Adding the CalcControl to the VB 6 toolbox*

This action puts a new control on the toolbox, as shown circled in Figure 23-3.

*Figure 23-3. Locating CalcControl in the VB 6 toolbox*

Drag the new control onto the form `TestForm` and name it `CalcControl`. Note that the new control will not be visible. This control has no user interface. Add two text boxes, four buttons, and one label, as shown in Figure 23-4.

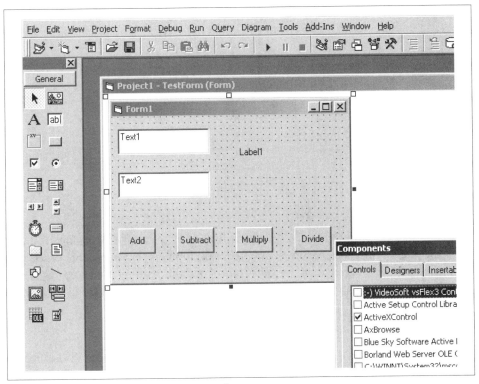

*Figure 23-4. Building the TestForm user interface*

Name the buttons `btnAdd`, `btnSubtract`, `btnMultiply`, and `btnDivide`. All that is left is for you to implement methods for handling the button-click events of the calculator buttons.

Each time a button is clicked, you want to get the values in the two text boxes, cast them to double (as required by CalcControl) using the VB 6 CDbl function, invoke a CalcControl function, and print the result in the label control. Example 23-2 provides the complete source code.

*Example 23-2. Using the CalcControl ActiveX control in a VB program (TestForm)*

```
Private Sub btnAdd_Click( )
    Label1.Caption = _
        calcControl.Add(CDbl(Text1.Text), _
        CDbl(Text2.Text))
End Sub

Private Sub btnDivide_Click( )
    Label1.Caption = _
        calcControl.Divide(CDbl(Text1.Text), _
        CDbl(Text2.Text))
End Sub

Private Sub btnMultiply_Click( )
    Label1.Caption = _
        calcControl.Multiply(CDbl(Text1.Text), _
        CDbl(Text2.Text))
End Sub

Private Sub btnSubtract_Click( )
    Label1.Caption = _
        calcControl.Subtract(CDbl(Text1.Text), _
        CDbl(Text2.Text))
End Sub
```

## Importing a Control in .NET

Now that you've shown that the CalcControl ActiveX control is working, you can copy the *CalcControl.ocx* file to your .NET development environment. Once you have copied it, remember that the *CalcControl.ocx* file requires that you register it using Regsvr32 (if you are running Vista, you'll need to do this as an administrator):

```
Regsvr32 CalcControl.ocx
```

You're now ready to build a test program in .NET to use the calculator.

To get started, create a Visual C# Windows Forms application in Visual Studio 2008, name the application InteropTest, and design a form (such as the TestForm form you created in VB in the preceding section) by dragging and dropping controls onto it. Name the form TestForm. Figure 23-5 shows a complete sample form.

*Figure 23-5. Building a Windows Form to test the CalcControl ActiveX control*

## Importing a control

There are two ways to import an ActiveX control into the Visual Studio 2008 development environment: you can use the Visual Studio 2008 tools themselves, or you can import the control manually using the Aximp utility that ships with the .NET Framework SDK. To use Visual Studio 2008, right-click on the toolbox and add a tab named COM. Then right-click again and select Choose Items. This will bring up the Choose Toolbox Items dialog box. Select the COM Components tab, as shown in Figure 23-6.

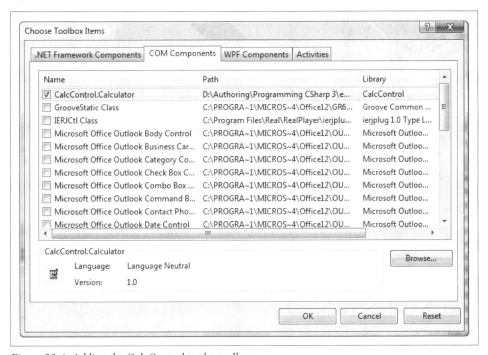

*Figure 23-6. Adding the CalcControl to the toolbox*

### Manually importing the control

Alternatively, you can open a command box and import the control manually using the Aximp.exe utility, as shown in Figure 23-7.

*Figure 23-7. Running Aximp*

Aximp.exe takes one argument, the ActiveX control you want to import (*CalcControl. ocx*). It produces three files:

*AxCalcControl.dll*
    A .NET Windows control

*CalcControl.dll*
    A proxy .NET class library

*AxCalcControl.pdb*
    A debug file

Once this is done, you can return to the Choose Toolbox Items window, but this time, select .NET Framework Components. You can now browse to the location at which the .NET Windows control *AxCalcControl.dll* was generated and import that file into the toolbox, as shown in Figure 23-8.

### Adding the control to the form

Once imported, the control appears on the toolbox menu, as shown in Figure 23-9.

Now, you can drag this control onto your Windows Form and make use of its functions, just as you did in the VB 6 example.

Add event handlers for each of the four buttons. The event handlers will delegate their work to the ActiveX control you wrote in VB 6 and imported into .NET.

Example 23-3 shows the source code for the event handlers.

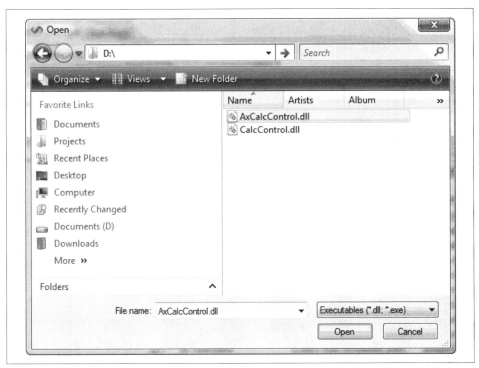

Figure 23-8. Browsing for the imported control

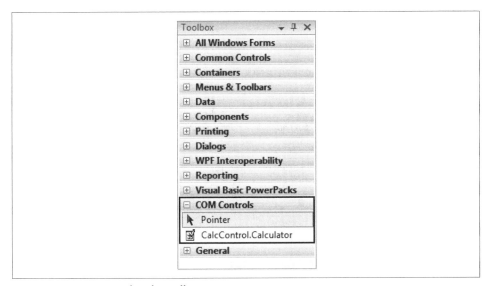

Figure 23-9. New control in the toolbox

*Example 23-3. Implementing the event handlers*

```
using System;
using System.Windows.Forms;

namespace InteropTest
{
    public partial class Form1 : Form
    {
        public Form1( )
        {
            InitializeComponent( );
        }

        private void btnAdd_Click(object sender, EventArgs e)
        {
            double left = double.Parse(textBox1.Text);
            double right = double.Parse(textBox2.Text);
            label1.Text = axCalculator1.Add(ref left, ref right).ToString( );

        }

        private void btnSubtract_Click(object sender, EventArgs e)
        {
            double left = double.Parse(textBox1.Text);
            double right = double.Parse(textBox2.Text);
            label1.Text = axCalculator1.Subtract(ref left, ref right).ToString( );

        }

        private void btnMultiply_Click(object sender, EventArgs e)
        {
            double left = double.Parse(textBox1.Text);
            double right = double.Parse(textBox2.Text);
            label1.Text = axCalculator1.Multiply(ref left, ref right).ToString( );

        }

        private void btnDivide_Click(object sender, EventArgs e)
        {
            double left = double.Parse(textBox1.Text);
            double right = double.Parse(textBox2.Text);
            label1.Text = axCalculator1.Divide(ref left, ref right).ToString( );

        }
    }
}
```

Each implementing method obtains the values in the text fields, converts them to double using the static method double.Parse( ), and passes those values to the calculator's methods. The results are cast back to a string and inserted in the label, as shown in Figure 23-10.

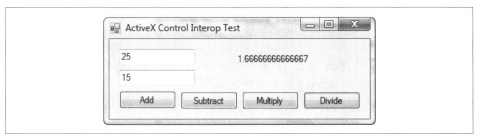

*Figure 23-10. Testing the Interop control*

# P/Invoke

It is possible to invoke unmanaged code from within C#. Typically, you would do this if you needed to accomplish something you couldn't accomplish through the FCL. With the 2.0 version of .NET, the use of P/Invoke will become relatively rare.

The .NET *platform invoke facility* (*P/Invoke*) was originally intended only to provide access to the Windows API, but you can use it to call functions in any DLL.

To see how this works, let's revisit Example 22-3 from Chapter 22. You will recall that you used the FileInfo class to rename files by invoking the MoveTo( ) method:

```
file.MoveTo(fullName + ".bak");
```

You can accomplish the same thing by using the Windows *kernel32.dll* and invoking the MoveFile method.[*] To do so, you need to declare the method as a static extern and use the DllImport attribute:

```
[DllImport("kernel32.dll", EntryPoint="MoveFile",
 ExactSpelling=false, CharSet=CharSet.Unicode,
 SetLastError=true)]
static extern bool MoveFile(
 string sourceFile, string destinationFile);
```

The DllImport attribute class is used to indicate that an unmanaged method will be invoked through P/Invoke. The parameters are as follows:

*DLL name*
    The name of the DLL you are invoking.

EntryPoint
    Indicates the name of the DLL entry point (the method) to call.

ExactSpelling
    Allows the CLR to match methods with slightly different names based on the CLR's knowledge of naming conventions.

---

[*] In fact, this is what Fileinfo.Move( ) is doing itself.

CharSet

Indicates how the string arguments to the method should be marshaled.

SetLastError

Setting this to true allows you to call Marshal.GetLastWin32 Error, and check whether an error occurred when invoking this method.

The rest of the code is virtually unchanged, except for the invocation of the MoveFile( ) method itself. Notice that MoveFile( ) is declared to be a static method of the class, so use static method semantics:

```
Tester.MoveFile(file.FullName,file.FullName + ".bak");
```

Pass in the original filename and the new name, and the file is moved, just as it was when calling file.MoveTo( ). In this example, there is no advantage—and actually considerable disadvantage—to using P/Invoke. You have left managed code, and the result is that you've abandoned type safety and your code will no longer run in "partial-trusted" scenarios. Example 23-4 shows the complete source code for using P/Invoke to move the files.

*Example 23-4. Using P/Invoke to call a Win32 API method*

```
using System;
using System.IO;
using System.Runtime.InteropServices;

namespace UsingPInvoke
{
    class Tester
    {

        // declare the WinAPI method you wish to P/Invoke
        [DllImport("kernel32.dll", EntryPoint = "MoveFile",
        ExactSpelling = false, CharSet = CharSet.Unicode,
        SetLastError = true)]
        static extern bool MoveFile(
        string sourceFile, string destinationFile);

        public static void Main( )
        {
            // make an instance and run it
            Tester t = new Tester( );
            string theDirectory = @"c:\test\media";
            DirectoryInfo dir =
            new DirectoryInfo(theDirectory);
            t.ExploreDirectory(dir);
        }

        // Set it running with a directory name
        private void ExploreDirectory(DirectoryInfo dir)
        {
```

*Example 23-4. Using P/Invoke to call a Win32 API method (continued)*

```
            // make a new subdirectory
            string newDirectory = "newTest";
            DirectoryInfo newSubDir =
            dir.CreateSubdirectory(newDirectory);

            // get all the files in the directory and
            // copy them to the new directory
            FileInfo[] filesInDir = dir.GetFiles( );
            foreach (FileInfo file in filesInDir)
            {
                string fullName = newSubDir.FullName +
                "\\" + file.Name;
                file.CopyTo(fullName);
                Console.WriteLine("{0} copied to newTest",
                file.FullName);
            }

            // get a collection of the files copied in
            filesInDir = newSubDir.GetFiles( );

            // delete some and rename others
            int counter = 0;
            foreach (FileInfo file in filesInDir)
            {
                string fullName = file.FullName;

                if (counter++ % 2 == 0)
                {
                    // P/Invoke the Win API
                    Tester.MoveFile(fullName, fullName + ".bak");

                    Console.WriteLine("{0} renamed to {1}",
                    fullName, file.FullName);
                }
                else
                {
                    file.Delete( );
                    Console.WriteLine("{0} deleted.",
                    fullName);
                }
            }
            // delete the subdirectory
            newSubDir.Delete(true);
        }
    }
}

Output:

c:\test\media\chimes.wav copied to newTest
c:\test\media\chord.wav copied to newTest
c:\test\media\desktop.ini copied to newTest
```

*Example 23-4. Using P/Invoke to call a Win32 API method (continued)*

```
c:\test\media\ding.wav copied to newTest
c:\test\media\dts.wav copied to newTest
c:\test\media\flourish.mid copied to newTest
c:\test\media\ir_begin.wav copied to newTest
c:\test\media\ir_end.wav copied to newTest
c:\test\media\ir_inter.wav copied to newTest
c:\test\media\notify.wav copied to newTest
c:\test\media\onestop.mid copied to newTest
c:\test\media\recycle.wav copied to newTest
c:\test\media\ringout.wav copied to newTest
c:\test\media\Speech Disambiguation.wav copied to newTest
c:\test\media\Speech Misrecognition.wav copied to newTest
c:\test\media\newTest\chimes.wav renamed to c:\test\media\newTest\chimes.wav
c:\test\media\newTest\chord.wav deleted.
c:\test\media\newTest\desktop.ini renamed to c:\test\media\newTest\desktop.ini
c:\test\media\newTest\ding.wav deleted.
c:\test\media\newTest\dts.wav renamed to c:\test\media\newTest\dts.wav
c:\test\media\newTest\flourish.mid deleted.
c:\test\media\newTest\ir_begin.wav renamed to c:\test\media\newTest\ir_begin.wav
c:\test\media\newTest\ir_end.wav deleted.
c:\test\media\newTest\ir_inter.wav renamed to c:\test\media\newTest\ir_inter.wav
c:\test\media\newTest\notify.wav deleted.
c:\test\media\newTest\onestop.mid renamed to c:\test\media\newTest\onestop.mid
c:\test\media\newTest\recycle.wav deleted.
c:\test\media\newTest\ringout.wav renamed to c:\test\media\newTest\ringout.wav
c:\test\media\newTest\Speech Disambiguation.wav deleted.
```

# Pointers

Until now, you've seen no code using C-/C++-style pointers. Only here, in the final paragraphs of the final pages of the book, does this topic arise, even though pointers are central to the C family of languages. In C#, pointers are relegated to unusual and advanced programming; typically, they are used only with P/Invoke.

C# supports the usual C pointer operators, listed in Table 23-1.

*Table 23-1. C# pointer operators*

| Operator | Meaning |
| --- | --- |
| & | The address-of operator returns a pointer to the address of a value |
| * | The dereference operator returns the value at the address of a pointer |
| -> | The member access operator is used to access the members of a type |

The use of pointers is almost never required, and is nearly always discouraged. When you do use pointers, you must mark your code with the C# unsafe modifier. The code is marked unsafe because you can manipulate memory locations directly with pointers. This is a feat that is otherwise impossible within a C# program. In unsafe code, you can directly access memory, perform conversions between pointers and integral types, take the address of variables, and so forth. In exchange, you give up garbage collection and protection against uninitialized variables, dangling pointers, and accessing memory beyond the bounds of an array. In essence, unsafe code creates an island of C++ code within your otherwise safe C# application, and your code will not work in partial-trust scenarios.

As an example of when this might be useful, read a file to the console by invoking two Win32 API calls: CreateFile and ReadFile. ReadFile takes, as its second parameter, a pointer to a buffer. The declaration of the two imported methods is straightforward:

```
[DllImport("kernel32", SetLastError=true)]
static extern unsafe int CreateFile(
    string filename,
    uint desiredAccess,
    uint shareMode,
    uint attributes,
    uint creationDisposition,
    uint flagsAndAttributes,
    uint templateFile);

[DllImport("kernel32", SetLastError=true)]
static extern unsafe bool ReadFile(
    int hFile,
    void* lpBuffer,
    int nBytesToRead,
    int* nBytesRead,
    int overlapped);
```

You will create a new class, APIFileReader, whose constructor will invoke the CreateFile() method. The constructor takes a filename as a parameter, and passes that filename to the CreateFile() method:

```
public APIFileReader(string filename)
{
    fileHandle = CreateFile(
        filename, // filename
        GenericRead, // desiredAccess
        UseDefault, // shareMode
        UseDefault, // attributes
        OpenExisting, // creationDisposition
        UseDefault, // flagsAndAttributes
        UseDefault); // templateFile
}
```

The APIFileReader class implements only one other method, Read(), which invokes ReadFile(). It passes in the file handle created in the class constructor, along with a pointer into a buffer, a count of bytes to retrieve, and a reference to a variable that will hold the number of bytes read. It is the pointer to the buffer that is of interest to us here. To invoke this API call, you must use a pointer.

Because you will access it with a pointer, the buffer needs to be pinned in memory; the .NET Framework can't be allowed to move the buffer during garbage collection. To accomplish this, use the C# fixed keyword. fixed allows you to get a pointer to the memory used by the buffer, and to mark that instance so that the garbage collector won't move it.

The block of statements following the fixed keyword creates a scope, within which the memory will be pinned. At the end of the fixed block, the instance will be unmarked so that it can be moved. This is known as *declarative pinning*:

```
public unsafe int Read(byte[] buffer, int index, int count)
{
    int bytesRead = 0;
    fixed (byte* bytePointer = buffer)
    {
        ReadFile(
            fileHandle,
            bytePointer + index,
            count,
            &bytesRead, 0);
    }
    return bytesRead;
}
```

Notice that the method must be marked with the unsafe keyword. This creates an unsafe context and allows you to create pointers. To compile this you must use the /unsafe compiler option. The easiest way to do so is to open the project properties, click the Build tab, and check the "Allow unsafe code" checkbox, as shown in Figure 23-11.

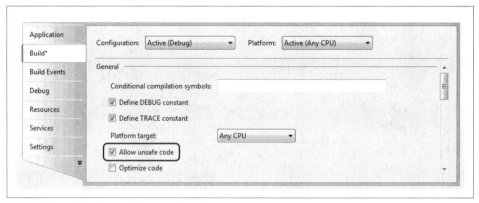

*Figure 23-11. Checking "Allow unsafe code"*

The test program instantiates the APIFileReader and an ASCIIEncoding object. It passes the filename (*8Swnn10.txt*) to the constructor of the APIFileReader and then creates a loop to repeatedly fill its buffer by calling the Read() method, which invokes the ReadFile API call. An array of bytes is returned, which is converted to a string using the ASCIIEncoding object's GetString( ) method. That string is passed to the Console.Write( ) method, to be displayed on the console. Example 23-5 shows the complete source.

 The text that it will read is a short excerpt of *Swann's Way* (by Marcel Proust), currently in the public domain and downloaded as text from Project Gutenberg (*http://www.gutenberg.org/wiki/Main_Page*).

*Example 23-5. Using pointers in a C# program*

```
using System;
using System.Runtime.InteropServices;
using System.Text;

namespace UsingPointers
{
    class APIFileReader
    {
        const uint GenericRead = 0x80000000;
        const uint OpenExisting = 3;
        const uint UseDefault = 0;
        int fileHandle;

        [DllImport("kernel32", SetLastError = true)]
        static extern unsafe int CreateFile(
        string filename,
        uint desiredAccess,
        uint shareMode,
        uint attributes,
        uint creationDisposition,
        uint flagsAndAttributes,
        uint templateFile);

        [DllImport("kernel32", SetLastError = true)]
        static extern unsafe bool ReadFile(
        int hFile,
        void* lpBuffer,
        int nBytesToRead,
        int* nBytesRead,
        int overlapped);

        // constructor opens an existing file
        // and sets the file handle member
        public APIFileReader(string filename)
        {
            fileHandle = CreateFile(
            filename, // filename
            GenericRead, // desiredAccess
            UseDefault, // shareMode
            UseDefault, // attributes
```

*Example 23-5. Using pointers in a C# program (continued)*

```
            OpenExisting, // creationDisposition
            UseDefault, // flagsAndAttributes
            UseDefault); // templateFile
    }

    public unsafe int Read(byte[] buffer, int index, int count)
    {
        int bytesRead = 0;
        fixed (byte* bytePointer = buffer)
        {
            ReadFile(
            fileHandle, // hfile
            bytePointer + index, // lpBuffer
            count, // nBytesToRead
            &bytesRead, // nBytesRead
            0); // overlapped
        }
        return bytesRead;
    }
}

class Test
{
    public static void Main( )
    {
        // create an instance of the APIFileReader,
        // pass in the name of an existing file
        APIFileReader fileReader =
        new APIFileReader("8Swnn10.txt");

        // create a buffer and an ASCII coder
        const int BuffSize = 128;
        byte[] buffer = new byte[BuffSize];
        ASCIIEncoding asciiEncoder = new ASCIIEncoding( );

        // read the file into the buffer and display to console
        while (fileReader.Read(buffer, 0, BuffSize) != 0)
        {
            Console.Write("{0}", asciiEncoder.GetString(buffer));
        }
    }
}
}
```

The key section of code where you create a pointer to the buffer and fix that buffer in memory using the `fixed` keyword is shown in bold. You need to use a pointer here because the API call demands it.

Output:

Altogether, my aunt used to treat him with scant ceremony. Since she was of the opinion that he ought to feel flattered by our invitations, she thought it only right and proper that he should never come to see us in summer without a basket of peaches or raspberries from his garden, and that from each of his visits to Italy he should bring back some photographs of old masters for me.

It seemed quite natural, therefore, to send to him whenever we wanted a recipe for some special sauce or for a pineapple salad for one of our big dinner-parties, to which he himself would not be invited, not seeming of sufficient importance to be served up to new friends who might be in our house for the first time. If the conversation turned upon the Princes of the House of France, "Gentlemen, you and I will never know, will we, and don't want to, do we?" my great-aunt would say tartly to Swann, who had, perhaps, a letter from Twickenham in his pocket; she would make him play accompaniments and turn over music on evenings when my grandmother's sister sang; manipulating this creature, so rare and refined at other times and in other places, with the rough simplicity of a child who will play with some curio from the cabinet no more carefully than if it were a penny toy. Certainly the Swann who was a familiar figure in all the clubs of those days differed hugely from, the Swann created in my great-aunt's mind when, of an evening, in our little garden at Combray, after the two shy peals had sounded from the gate, she would vitalise, by injecting into it everything she had ever heard about the Swann family, the vague and unrecognisable shape which began to appear, with my grandmother in its wake, against a background of shadows, and could at last be identified by the sound of its voice. But then, even in the most insignificant details of our daily life, none of us can be said to constitute a material whole, which is identical for everyone, and need only be turned up like a page in an account-book or the record of a will; our social personality is created by the thoughts of other people. Even the simple act which we describe as "seeing some one we know" is, to some extent, an intellectual process. We pack the physical outline of the creature we see with all the ideas we have already formed about him, and in the complete picture of him which we compose in our minds those ideas have certainly the principal place. In the end they come to fill out so completely the curve of his cheeks, to follow so exactly the line of his nose, they blend so harmoniously in the sound of his voice that these seem to be no more than a transparent envelope, so that each time we see the face or hear the voice it is our own ideas of him which we recognise and to which we listen. And so, no doubt, from the Swann they had built up for their own purposes my family had left out, in their ignorance, a whole crowd of the details of his daily life in the world of fashion, details by means of which other people, when they met him, saw all the Graces enthroned in his face and stopping at the line of his arched nose as at a natural frontier; but they contrived also to put into a face from which its distinction had been evicted, a face vacant and roomy as an untenanted house, to plant in the depths of its unvalued eyes a lingering sense, uncertain but not unpleasing, half-memory and half-oblivion, of idle hours spent together after our weekly dinners, round the card-table or in the garden, during our companionable country life. Our friend's bodily frame had been so well lined with this sense, and with various earlier memories of his family, that their own special Swann had become to my people a complete and living creature; so that even now I have the feeling of leaving some one I know for another quite different person when, going back in memory, I pass from the Swann whom I knew later and more intimately to this early Swann--this early Swann in whom I can distinguish the charming mistakes of my childhood, and who, incidentally, is less like his successor than he is like the other people I knew at that time, as though one's life were a series of galleries in which all the portraits of any one period had a marked family likeness, the same (so to speak) tonality--this early Swann abounding in leisure, fragrant with the scent of the great chestnut-tree, of baskets of raspberries and of a sprig of tarragon.

And yet one day, when my grandmother had gone to ask some favour of a lady whom she had known at the Sacré Coeur (and with whom, because of our caste theory, she had not cared to keep up any degree of intimacy in spite of several common interests), the Marquise de Villeparisis, of the famous house of Bouillon, this lady had said to her:

"I think you know M. Swann very well; he is a great friend of my nephews, the des Laumes."

# C# Keywords

**abstract**

A class modifier that specifies a class cannot be instantiated and the full implementation will be provided by a subclass.

A method modifier that specifies a method is implicitly virtual and without an implementation.

**alias**

Suffixes an extern directive.

**as**

A binary operator that casts the left operand to the type specified by the right operand and returns `null` rather than throwing an exception if the cast fails.

**ascending**

A query comprehension operator used in conjunction with `orderby`.

**base**

A variable with the same meaning as `this`, except that it accesses a base-class implementation of a member.

**bool**

A logical datatype that can be `true` or `false`.

**break**

A jump statement that exits a loop or `switch` statement block.

**by**

A query comprehension operator used in conjunction with `group`.

**byte**

A 1-byte, unsigned integral data type.

**case**

A selection statement that defines a particular choice in a `switch` statement.

catch
> A keyword for the clause in a try statement to catch exceptions of a specific type.

char
> A 2-byte, Unicode character data type.

checked
> A statement or operator that enforces arithmetic bounds checking on an expression or statement block.

class
> A type declaration keyword for a custom reference type; typically used as a blueprint for creating objects.
>
> A generic type constraint, indicating the generic type must be a reference type.

const
> A modifier for a local variable or field declaration that indicates that the value is statically evaluated and immutable.

continue
> A jump statement that skips the remaining statements in a statement block and continues to the next iteration in a loop.

decimal
> A 16-byte precise decimal datatype.

default
> A special label in a switch statement specifying the action to take when no case statements match the switch expression.
>
> An operator that returns the default value for a type.

delegate
> A type declaration keyword for a type that defines a protocol for a method.

descending
> A query comprehension operator used in conjunction with orderby.

do
> A loop statement to iterate a statement block until an expression at the end of the loop evaluates to false.

double
> An 8-byte, floating-point data type.

else
> A conditional statement that defines the action to take when a preceding if expression evaluates to false.

enum

A type declaration keyword that defines a value type representing a group of named numeric constants.

equals

A query comprehension operator that performs an equijoin, used in conjunction with join.

event

A member modifier for a field or property of a delegate type that indicates that only the += and -= methods of the delegate can be accessed.

explicit

An operator that defines an explicit conversion.

extern

A method modifier that indicates that the method is implemented with unmanaged code.

A directive that declares a reference to an external namespace, which must correspond to an argument passed to the C# compiler.

false

A literal of the bool type.

finally

The keyword in the clause of a try statement that executes whenever control leaves the scope of the try block.

fixed

A statement to pin down a reference type so the garbage collector won't move it during pointer arithmetic operations.

A field modifier within an unsafe struct to declare a fixed length array.

float

A 4-byte, floating-point data type.

for

A loop statement that combines an initialization statement, continuation condition, and iterative statement into one statement.

foreach

A loop statement that iterates over collections that implement IEnumerable.

from

A query comprehension operator that specifies the sequence from which to query.

get

The name of the accessor that returns the value of a property.

global

> A keyword placed in front of an identifier to indicate the identifier is qualified with the global namespace.

goto

> A jump statement that jumps to a label within the same method and same scope as the jump point.

group

> A query comprehension operator that splits a sequence into a group given a key value to group by.

if

> A conditional statement that executes its statement block if its expression evaluates to true.

implicit

> An operator that defines an implicit conversion.

in

> The operator between a type and an IEnumerable in a foreach statement.

> A query comprehension operator used in conjunction with from.

int

> A 4-byte, signed integral data type.

into

> A query comprehension operator that specifies a name for an output sequence.

interface

> A type declaration keyword for a custom reference type that defines a contract for a type comprising a set of implicitly abstract members.

internal

> An access modifier that indicates that a type or type member is accessible only to other types in the same assembly.

is

> A relational operator that evaluates to true if the left operand's type matches, is derived from, or implements the type specified by the right operand.

let

> A query comprehension operator that introduces a new variable into each element in a sequence.

lock

> A statement that acquires a lock on a reference-type object to help multiple threads cooperate.

long

> An 8-byte, signed integral data type.

namespace
> A keyword for defining a name that encloses a set of types in a hierarchical name.

new
> An operator that calls a constructor on a type, allocating a new object on the heap if the type is a reference type or initializing the object if the type is a value type.
>
> A type member modifier that hides an inherited member with a new member with the same signature.

null
> A reference-type literal meaning no object is referenced.

object
> A predefined type that is the ultimate base class for all types.

on
> A query comprehension operator used in conjunction with join or group.

operator
> A method modifier that overloads operators.

orderby
> A query comprehension operator that sorts a sequence.

out
> A parameter and argument modifier that specifies that the variable is passed by reference and must be assigned by the method being called.

override
> A method modifier that indicates that a method of a class overrides a virtual method defined by a base class.

params
> A parameter modifier that specifies that the last parameter of a method may accept multiple parameters of the same type.

partial
> A class or method modifier that indicates the definition of the class or method is split (typically across files).

private
> An access modifier that indicates that only the containing type can access the member.

protected
> An access modifier that indicates that only the containing type or derived types can access the member.

public
: An access modifier that indicates that a type or type member is accessible to all other types.

readonly
: A field modifier specifying that a field can be assigned only once, either in its declaration or in its containing type's constructor.

ref
: A parameter and argument modifier that specifies that the variable is passed by reference and is assigned before being passed to the method.

return
: A jump statement that that exits a method, specifying a return value when the method is not void.

sbyte
: A 1-byte, signed integral data type.

sealed
: A class modifier that indicates a class cannot be derived from.

set
: The name of the accessor that sets the value of a property.

short
: A 2-byte, signed integral data type.

sizeof
: An operator that returns the size in bytes of a struct.

stackalloc
: An operator that returns a pointer to a specified number of value types allocated on the stack.

static
: A type member modifier that indicates that the member applies to the type rather than to an instance of the type.

: A class modifier indicating the class is comprised of only static members and cannot be instantiated.

string
: A predefined reference type that represents an immutable sequence of Unicode characters.

struct
: A type declaration keyword for a custom value type; typically used as a blueprint for creating light-weight instances.

: A generic type constraint, indicating the generic type must be a value type.

switch
> A selection statement that allows a selection of choices to be made based on the value of a predefined type.

this
> A variable that references the current instance of a class or struct.

> A parameter modifier for the first parameter in a static method, making the method an extension method.

throw
> A `jump` statement that throws an exception when an abnormal condition has occurred.

true
> A literal of the `bool` type.

try
> A statement that defines a statement block where errors can be caught and handled.

typeof
> An operator that returns the type of an object as a `System.Type` object.

uint
> A 4-byte, unsigned integral data type.

ulong
> An 8-byte, unsigned integral data type.

unchecked
> A statement or operator that prevents arithmetic bounds checking on an expression.

unsafe
> A type modifier, member modifier, or statement that permits executing code that is not type-safe (notably, that uses pointer arithmetic).

ushort
> A 2-byte, unsigned integral data type.

using
> A directive that specifies that types in a particular namespace can be referred to without requiring their fully qualified type names.

> A statement that allows an object implementing `IDisposable` to be disposed of at the end of the statement's scope.

value
> A name used for the implicit variable set by the set accessor of a property.

virtual
> A class method modifier that indicates that a method can be overridden by a derived class.

void
> A keyword used in place of a type for methods that don't have a return value.

volatile
> A field modifier indicating that a field's value may be modified in a multi-threaded scenario; neither the compiler nor runtime should perform optimizations with that field.

while
> A loop statement to iterate a statement block while an expression at the start of each iteration evaluates to `false`.

yield
> A statement that yields the next element from an iterator block.

# Index

## Symbols

+ (addition operator), 50
+= (addition self-assignment operator), 52
& (address-of operator), 554
&& (and operator) in conditionals, 55, 57
<> (angle brackets), around XML tags, 303
<% ... %> (angle brackets, percent sign), in ASP.NET, 388
= (assignment operator), 49
   confusing with equals operator, 39
   using instead of subscribe operator, 266
@ (at sign)
   beginning string literal, 216
   in XPath, 318, 320
\ (backslash)
   escape character for, 24
   in string literals, 24, 216
{} (braces)
   around statement blocks, 37
   in array element initialization, 163, 168
   in class declarations, 8
[] (brackets)
   in array declarations, 158, 166, 169
   in indexers, 177
   in metadata attributes, 450
   in syntax, 35
: (colon), in base class constructor invocation, 106
+ (concatenation operator), 221
-- (decrement operator), 53
* (dereference operator), 554
/ (division operator), 50
/= (division self-assignment operator), 52
. (dot operator), 11, 12
" (double quotes)
   escape character for, 24
   in string literals, 217
= (equal sign), in ASP.NET, 388
== (equals operator), 54
   confusing with assignment operator, 39
   overloading, requirements for, 120, 124
   with strings, 222
> (greater than operator), 54
>= (greater than or equals operator), 54
++ (increment operator), 53
[] (index operator)
   for arrays, 160
   for strings, 222
=> (lambda operator), 272
< (less than operator), 54
<= (less than or equals operator), 54
& (logical AND operator), 57
| (logical OR operator), 57
^ (logical XOR operator), 57
-> (member access operator), 554
% (modulus operator), 50
%= (modulus self-assignment operator), 52
* (multiplication operator), 50
*= (multiplication self-assignment operator), 52
!= (not equals operator), 54
! (not operator) in conditionals, 55
|| (or operator) in conditionals, 55, 57
() (parentheses)
   in if...else statement, 35
   in switch statement, 39

We'd like to hear your suggestions for improving our indexes. Send email to *index@oreilly.com*.

+ (plus sign), in debugger, 19
# (pound sign), preceding directives, 59
; (semicolon)
    ending statements, 33
    not ending class definitions, 63
<<>> (shift operator), 57
' (single quotes), escape character for, 24
/ (slash), in XPath, 318
/* ... */ (slash asterisk), enclosing
    comments, 10
// (slash, double), preceding comments, 9
+= (subscribe operator), 265, 266
- (subtraction operator), 50
-= (subtraction self-assignment operator), 52
?: (ternary operator), 58
-= (unsubscribe operator), 267

**A**

abstract classes, 109–112, 146
abstract keyword, 109
abstract modifier, 561
AcceptSocket() method, TcpListener, 512,
    513
access modifiers, 107
    for classes, 65
    for properties, 95
    for static member variables, 79
    not allowed in explicit
        implementations, 152
ActiveX controls
    adding to form after importing, 548
    creating, 542–546
    importing, 542–550
Add() method
    Dictionary, 212
    List, 195, 196
    XmlAttributeOverrides, 335
addition operator (+), 50
addition self-assignment operator (+=), 52
AddRange() method, List, 195
address-of operator (&), 554
AddSort() method, XPathExpression, 328
ADO, compared to ADO.NET, 369
ADO.NET, 368
    compared to ADO, 369
    connecting to database, 374, 377
    disconnected architecture of, 368
    object model of, 372–374
    querying data, 375, 377
Adventure Works LT sample database, 338

AJAX, 6
    (see also Silverlight)
alert, escape character for, 24
and operator (&&) in conditionals, 55, 57
angle brackets (<>), around XML tags, 303
angle brackets, percent sign (<% ... %>), in
    ASP.NET, 388
anonymous class, 291
anonymous methods, 258, 271
anonymous types, 291
Append() method, StringBuilder, 227
AppendChild() method, XML, 308
AppendFormat() method,
    StringBuilder, 227, 228
AppendText() method
    File, 492
    FileInfo, 493
applications
    console applications, 11
    web-based (see web-based applications)
    Windows Forms (see Windows Forms
        applications)
    WPF applications (see WPF)
arguments of methods (see parameters of
    methods)
arithmetical operators, 50
arrays, 156
    as object of type System.Array, 157
    collections accessed as (see indexers)
    conversions of, 173–175
    declaring, 158
    default values for, 159
    elements of
        accessing, 160–161
        initializing, 163
    instantiating, 158
    iterating over, 162, 164
    jagged, 169–172
    methods for, 157
    multidimensional, 165–172
    passing as parameter without
        creating, 164
    properties for, 157
    rectangular, 165–169
    sorting, 175–177
    upper and lower bounds of, 159, 160,
        172
as operator, 146
ASP (web) controls, 391
asp tag, 389

ASP.NET, 381
    books about, 381
    debugging, enabling, 388
    (see also Web Forms)
.aspx file extension, 382
AsReadOnly() method
    List, 195
    System.Array, 157
assemblies, 5
assignment
    definite, 27, 86–89
    operator precedence for, 57
assignment operator (=), 49
    confusing with equals operator, 39
    using instead of subscribe operator, 266
AsyncCallback delegate, 273–276, 507, 523
AsynchNetworkServe class, 518
asynchronous I/O, 487, 506–511
asynchronous network file
            streaming, 522–527
at sign (@)
    beginning string literal, 216
    in XPath, 318, 320
Attributes property, DirectoryInfo, 488
Attributes() method, FileInfo, 493
attributes, in metadata, 449
    accessing (see reflection)
    custom, 451–455
    naming conventions for, 452
    parameters of, 453
    targets of, 450
        applying to attributes, 450
        list of, 449
    types of, 450
attributes, of files, 488, 493
attributes, of XML elements, 309–311
AttributeTargets enumeration, 450
AutoComplete feature, fixing case errors
            with, 14
axes, XPath searches using, 319
Aximp utility, 542, 547, 548

B

backing store, 487
backslash (\)
    escape character for, 24
    in string literals, 24, 216
backspace, escape character for, 24
base class constructors, 106

base classes, 101, 113
    (see also abstract classes)
base keyword, 106, 561
BeginRead() method, Stream, 506, 508
BeginWrite() method, Stream, 506
Berkeley socket interface, 513
binary files, 500–502
BinaryFormatter class, 530
BinaryReader class, 499
BinarySearch() method
    List, 195
    System.Array, 157
BinaryWriter class, 499
binding
    late binding, using reflection, 456,
            462–464
    server-side controls to data, 391–398
books
    Learning ASP.NET 2.0 with AJAX
            (Liberty et al.), 381
    Programming .NET 3.5 (Liberty,
            Horovitz), x, 6, 404
    Programming ASP.NET (Liberty,
            Hurwitz), 381, 401
    Programming Silverlight (Liberty), 6
    Programming WCF Services (Lowy), 329
    Programming WPF (Sells, Griffiths), 404
    Swann's Way (Proust), 557
bool type, 22
boolean type, 22
braces ({})
    around statement blocks, 37
    in array element initialization, 163, 168
    in class declarations, 8
brackets ([])
    in array declarations, 158, 166, 169
    in indexers, 177
    in metadata attributes, 450
    in syntax, 35
    (see also index operator ([]))
branching
    conditional branching statements, 35–42
    unconditional branching statements, 34
    (see also jump statements)
break statement
    in loops, 47
    in switch statement, 39, 41
breakpoints, in debugger, 18
buffered streams, 502–504
BufferedStream class, 499, 502

bugs, compared to exceptions, 241
built-in types, 21, 22–25
   choosing, 23
   conversion of, 24
   list of, 22
button controls, Windows Forms, 432–437
byte type, 22

## C

C
   strings, differences in, 214
   switch statement differences, 41
C#, x, 3
   book about, x
   features of, 4–6
   history of, 4
   invoking unmanaged code from, 551–554
   new features in, 3, 4
C++
   copy constructor, equivalent for, 73
   indexer operator, overloading, equivalent
      to, 178
   multiple inheritance, equivalent for, 101
   nonstatic operators, no equivalent
      for, 119
   object types that can be thrown,
      limitations to, 242
   private and protected inheritance, no
      equivalent for, 101
   structs, differences in, 127
   switch statement differences, 41
   templates, equivalent for, 186
C++-style comments, 9
call stack
   displaying, with stack trace, 253–255
   unwinding, 242, 246
callback methods, 272–276
camel notation, 14
Capacity property, List, 195, 197
capture collections, for regular
      expressions, 237–240
Capture object, 237
CaptureCollection collection, 237
carriage return, escape character for, 24
case sensitivity, 14
case statement (see switch statement)
casting (explicit conversions), 25, 121, 124
catch block, 244, 246
catch statement, 241, 244–250
char keyword, 562
char literals, 24
   (see also string literals)

char type, 22, 24
   (see also strings)
Chars property
   String, 218
   StringBuilder, 227
checked keyword, 562
child elements, XML, 303, 308
class keyword, 62, 562
class members (see members of a class)
classes, 4, 8, 61
   abstract classes, 109–112, 146
   access modifiers for, 65
   anonymous, 291
   base classes, 101, 113
   behaviors of (see methods)
   concrete classes, 111
   declarations of, 4, 8
   defining, 62–65
   derived classes, 101, 113
   generated, adding methods to, 348
   instantiating (see objects)
   metadata stored with, 5
   named by Visual Studio, 16
   naming conventions for, 14
   nesting, 115–117
   partial classes, 382
   sealed classes, 112
   static, 78
Clear() method
   Dictionary, 212
   List, 195
   Queue, 206
   Stack, 208
   System.Array, 157
ClientHandler class, 518, 523
Clone() method
   ICloneable, 73
   System.Array, 157
Close() method, implementing, 82
code examples, xvi
code reuse, inheritance used for, 102
code separation, 382
code style guidelines by Microsoft, 14
code, commenting out, 10
code-behind pages, 381, 386–388
collection interfaces, 186
   IComparable interface, 198–201
   IComparer interface, 201–205
   IEnumerable interface, 187–189
   list of, 186
   type safety of, 186

collections, 156
    accessing as arrays (see indexers)
    dictionaries, 211–213
    hash function for, 113
    Item element for, 196
    queues, 206–208
    stacks, 208–211
    type safety of, 156
    (see also arrays; lists)
colon (:), in base class constructor
        invocation, 106
columns, relational database, 369
COM components (see ActiveX controls)
comments, 9
    around code, 10
    author's guidelines for, 317
    for XML-based documentation, 11
    nesting, 10
Compare() method, String, 218, 221
CompareTo() method
    IComparable, 198
    String, 218
comparison operators (see relational
        operators)
Compile() method, XPathNavigator, 328
compiling programs, 17
component-oriented programming, with
        C#, 5
Concat() method, String, 218, 221
concatenation operator (+), 221
concrete classes, 111
conditional branching statements, 35–42
    Boolean expressions required for, 35
    if...else statement, 35–37
    nested if statements, 37
    switch statement, 38–42
conditional directives, 60
console applications, 11
Console object, 11
const keyword, 562
constants, 28
    naming conventions for, 14
    (see also enumerations)
ConstrainedCopy() method,
        System.Array, 157
constraints
    for lists, 190–195
    for relational database, 370
constructors, 68–70
    base class constructors, 106
    copy constructors, 73
    default, 68

defining, 69
    overloaded, 71, 89–92
    static, 76–77
contact information for this book, xvi
Contains() method
    List, 195
    Queue, 206
    Stack, 208
ContainsKey() method, Dictionary, 212
ContainsValue() method, Dictionary, 212
continue keyword, 562
continue statement, 47
controls, ActiveX (see ActiveX controls)
controls, server-side (see server-side controls)
controls, Windows Forms
    button controls, 432–437
    creating, 421
    populating, 424–428
    TreeView controls, 424–432
conventions used in this book, xiv
conversions (see type conversion)
ConvertAll() method
    List, 195
    System.Array, 157
copy constructors, 73
Copy() method
    File, 492
    String, 218, 222
    System.Array, 157
CopyTo() method
    FileInfo, 493, 497
    List, 195
    Queue, 206
    Stack, 208, 209, 211
    String, 218
    System.Array, 157
corruption of databases, 343
Count property
    Dictionary, 212
    List, 195
    Queue, 206
    Stack, 208
Create() method
    DirectoryInfo, 489
    File, 492
    FileInfo, 493
CreateAttribute() method, XML, 309
CreateChildControls() method, 385
CreateDirectory() method, Directory, 488
CreateElement() method, XML, 307
CreateInstance() method, System.Array, 157,
        172

CreateNavigator() method,
XmlDocument, 326
CreateSubdirectory() method,
DirectoryInfo, 489, 496
CreateText() method, File, 492
CreationTime property
DirectoryInfo, 488
FileInfo, 493
C-style comments, 10
curly braces (see braces)

# D

data binding, 391–398
data compartment for application, 538
data store, 538
DataAdapter class, ADO.NET, 373, 374,
377
databases, 368
Adventure Works LT sample
database, 338
connecting to, with ADO.NET, 374, 377
connecting to, with LINQ (see LINQ)
corruption of, 343
relational databases, 368–371
searching
LINQ for (see LINQ)
methodologies for, 279
DataColumn class, ADO.NET, 373
DataColumnCollection class,
ADO.NET, 373
DataContext object, 342, 345, 348, 350
DataReader class, ADO.NET, 374
DataRelation class, ADO.NET, 373
DataRelationCollection class,
ADO.NET, 373
DataSet class, ADO.NET, 372, 375, 377
DataTable class, ADO.NET, 373, 377
DBCommand class, ADO.NET, 374
DBConnection class, ADO.NET, 374
deadlocks, 485
debugger, Visual Studio, 18–20
breakpoints in, 18
examining object values, 19
stepping through program, 19
debugging, ASP.NET, 388
decimal keyword, 562
decimal type, 22, 23
declarative pinning, 556
declarative programming, 419
declarative referential integrity (DRI), 370
decrement operator (--), 53

decrement operators, 52–53
default keyword, 562
#define directive, 59
definite assignment, 27, 86–89
delegate keyword, 257, 562
delegates, 5, 257
asynchronous I/O, 507
callbacks using, 272–276
creating, 257
methods called directly,
preventing, 266–271
potential problems with, 266
publish and subscribe pattern
using, 258–266
uses of, 257
Delete() method
DirectoryInfo, 489
File, 492
FileInfo, 493
Dequeue() method, Queue, 206
dereference operator (*), 554
derived classes, 101, 113
deserialization, 532–534
Deserialize() method, XmlSerializer, 331
destructors, 79
defining, 80
Finalize() implemented using, 113
dictionaries, 211–213
Dictionary class, 212
directives, preprocessor, 59–60
directories, 488
listing files in, 492–496
traversing subdirectories of, 489–492
Directory class, 488, 499
Directory property, FileInfo, 493
DirectoryInfo class, 488, 499
instantiating, 489
methods of, 488
properties of, 488
subdirectories
returning files for, 492
traversing, 489–492
Dispose() method, IDisposable, 80–83, 385
division operator (/), 50
division self-assignment operator (/=), 52
do...while loop, 44
document element (see root element)
documentation
this keyword used as, 74
(see also comments)
DocumentElement property, XML, 308
dot operator (.), 11, 12

double keyword,  562
double quotes (")
    escape character for,  24
    in string literals,  217
double type,  22, 23
DRI (declarative referential integrity),  370
dynamic invocation (see late binding, using
        reflection)
dynamic strings (see StringBuilder class)

# E

elements, XML
    attributes of,  309–311
    defining,  303
#elif directive,  60
#else directive,  60
else statement (see if...else statement)
Empty property, String,  218
encapsulation,  61, 92–96
#endif directive,  60
EndRead(), method, Stream,  509
EndsWith() method, String,  218, 222
Enqueue() method, Queue,  206
enumerations,  30–31
equal sign (=), in ASP.NET,  388
    (see also assignment operator (=))
equals operator (==),  54
    confusing with assignment operator,  39
    overloading, requirements for,  120, 124
    with strings,  222
Equals() method
    Object,  113, 120, 125
    String,  218, 222
errors, compared to exceptions,  241
escape characters,  24, 216
event handlers,  258
    Web Forms,  382, 383
    Windows Forms,  423, 429–437
    WPF,  418
event keyword,  267–271
event triggers, WPF,  411
EventArgs class,  258
events,  256
    observing of,  258
    publishing of,  258, 262–264
    subscribing to,  258, 264
    unsubscribing from,  267
    Web Forms,  383, 399–403
examples, source code for,  xi
exception handler,  241
Exception objects,  252–255

exceptions,  241
    actions performed regardless of,  250–252
    catching,  241, 244–250
    throwing,  241, 242–244
Exists property
    DirectoryInfo,  488
    FileInfo,  493
Exists() method
    File,  492
    List,  195
    System.Array,  157
explicit conversions (casting),  25, 121, 124
explicit interface implementation,  151–154
expressions,  49
eXtensible Application Markup Language
        (XAML),  404
eXtensible Markup Language (see XML)
extension methods, LINQ,  3, 292–294, 351
    defining and using,  294–296
    multiple implementations of, on different
        targets,  301
    queries using, as method-based
        queries,  298
    restrictions on,  296
Extension property
    DirectoryInfo,  488
    FileInfo,  493
extern keyword,  563
extra whitespace,  33

# F

"f" suffix on a number,  24
fields (see member variables)
FIFO (first-in, first-out) collection (see
        queues)
File class,  488, 499
    methods for,  492
    relationship to FileInfo class,  492
FileInfo class,  496, 499
    methods for,  493
    properties for,  493
    relationship to File class,  492
files
    accessing in Vista, exceptions caused
        by,  492, 496
    asynchronous I/O for (see asynchronous
        I/O)
    binary files,  500–502
    listing for subdirectories,  492–496
    modifying,  496–499
    reading and writing (see streaming)
    text files,  504–506

FileStream class, 499
FileSystemInfo class, 488
filter, of query, 282
Finalize() method, Object, 113
finally block, 242, 250–252
finally keyword, 563
finally statement, 250–252
Find() method
    List, 195
    System.Array, 157
FindAll() method
    List, 195
    System.Array, 157
FindIndex() method
    List, 195
    System.Array, 157
FindLast() method
    List, 195
    System.Array, 157
FindLastIndex() method
    List, 196
    System.Array, 157
first-in, first-out (FIFO) collection (see
        queues)
fixed keyword, 556
float type, 22, 23
folders (see directories)
fonts used in this book, xiv
for keyword, 563
for loop, 44–47
foreach keyword, 563
foreach loop, 162, 164
ForEach() method
    List, 196
    System.Array, 157
foreign key, relational database, 370
form feed, escape character for, 24
Format() method, String, 218
formatter for serialization, 530
forms (see Web Forms; Windows Forms
        applications)
forward slash (see slash)
from clause of query, 282
FullName property
    DirectoryInfo, 488
    FileInfo, 493
functions, C# (see methods)
functions, XPath, 321

**G**

garbage collection, 23, 79
generalization, 98–101
generic collection interfaces (see collection
        interfaces)
generics, 186
get accessor, 94
get keyword, 563
get() method, for indexers, 180
GetAttributes() method, File, 492
GetCreationTime() method
    Directory, 488
    File, 492
GetDirectories() method
    Directory, 488, 492
    DirectoryInfo, 489
GetEnumerator() method
    Dictionary, 212
    List, 196
    Queue, 206
    Stack, 208
    System.Array, 157
GetFiles() method
    Directory, 488
    DirectoryInfo, 489, 492
GetFileSystemInfos() method,
        DirectoryInfo, 489
GetHashCode() method, Object, 113
GetLastAccessTime() method, File, 492
GetLastWriteTime() method, File, 493
GetLength() method, System.Array, 157
GetLogicalDrives() method, Directory, 488
GetLongLength() method,
        System.Array, 157
GetLowerBound() method,
        System.Array, 157
GetObjectData() method, Dictionary, 212
GetParent() method, Directory, 488
GetProperties() method,
        XmlAttributeOverrides, 335
GetRange() method, List, 196
GetResponse(), WebRequest, 527
GetResponseStream() method,
        WebResponse, 527
GetType() method
    Object, 113
    XmlSerializer, 330
GetUpperBound() method,
        System.Array, 157

GetValue() method, System.Array,  157
global methods, equivalent to,  75
"goes to" operator (see lambda operator)
goto keyword,  564
goto statement,  42
    in switch statement,  39, 41
    reasons to avoid,  42
graphical user interface (see GUI)
greater than operator (>),  54
greater than or equals operator (>=),  54
grids, WPF,  406–408, 414
Griffiths, Ian
    blog for,  301
    Programming WPF,  404
Group class,  234
grouping in query,  290
Groups collection,  234
groups, regular expressions,  234–237
GUI (graphical user interface)
    programs without (see console
        applications)

H

HasAttributes property, XmlElement,  319
hash function for collections,  113
heap,  23
Hejlsberg, Anders (C# creator),  4
"Hello World" example,  7, 14–18
HelpLink property, Exception,  253
HKEY_CURRENT_USER key,  538
Horovitz, Alex (Programming .NET 3.5),  x,
        6, 404
HTML controls,  391
HttpWebRequest class,  527
Hungarian notation,  32
Hurwitz, Dan (Programming
        ASP.NET),  381, 401

I

IAsyncResult interface,  507
ICloneable interface,  73
ICollection interface,  186, 187
IComparable interface,  187, 198–201
IComparer interface,  187, 201–205
identifiers (names),  32
    (see also naming conventions)
identifiers, preprocessor,  59

IDeserializationCallback interface,  535
IDictionary interface,  187, 212
IDisposable interface,  81
IEnumerable interface,  186, 187–189
IEnumerator interface,  186
#if directive,  60
if...else statement,  35–37
IFormatter interface,  530
IList interface,  187
implicit conversions,  24, 121, 124
implicit types,  22
implicitly typed local variables,  291
increment operator (++),  53
increment operators,  52–53
index operator ([])
    for arrays,  160
    for strings,  222
indexers,  177–181
    assignment to,  181–183
    based on strings,  183–186
    declaring,  177
    get() and set() methods for,  180
IndexOf() method
    List,  196
    String,  223
    System.Array,  157
information
    contact information for this book,  xvi
    (see also books; web site resources)
inheritance,  98, 101
.ini files,  538
Initialize() method, System.Array,  158
initializers,  70–73, 79
inline documentation,  5
inner join, SQL,  372
Insert() method
    List,  196
    String,  223
    StringBuilder,  227
InsertRange() method, List,  196
instance members of a class,  75
int keyword,  564
int type,  22, 23
int16 type,  22
int32 type,  22
int64 type,  23
interface keyword,  132

interfaces, 5, 132
    combining, 137–140
    compared to abstract classes, 146
    defining, 132–134
    extending, 136
    hiding members of, 154
    implementing, 134–136
        explicitly, 151–154
        multiple interfaces, 136
    naming, 133
    overriding, 147–151
    polymorphism and, potential problems
        with, 140–146
Interlocked class, 477
internal access modifier, 65
IP address, 512
is-a relationship (see specialization)
IsFixedSize property, System.Array, 158
isolated storage, 538–541
IsolatedStorageFileStream object, 538
IsReadOnly property, System.Array, 158
IsSynchronized property, System.Array, 158
Item element for collection classes, 196
Item property, IDictionary, 212
Item() method
    Dictionary, 212
    List, 195
iteration statements, 42–49
    do...while loop, 44
    for loop, 44–47
    foreach loop, 162, 164
    while loop, 43

**J**

jagged arrays, 169–172
Java
    constant fields, no equivalent for, 132
    final class, equivalent for, 112
    wrapper classes, equivalent for, 83
join clause of query, 285
Join() method
    LINQ, 301
    String, 218
jump statements
    break statement, 47
    continue statement, 47
    goto statement, 42
    in switch statement, 39, 41
    return statement, 35, 126
    (see also unconditional branching
        statements)

**K**

keyboard shortcuts, 17
Keys property, Dictionary, 212
keywords
    reference, 561–568

**L**

lambda expressions
    for delegate definitions, 271
    in LINQ, 297–301
lambda operator (=>), 272
Language-INtegrated Query (see LINQ)
LastAccessTime property
    DirectoryInfo, 488
    FileInfo, 493
last-in, first-out (LIFO) collections (see
        stacks)
LastIndexOf() method
    List, 196
    System.Array, 158
LastWriteTime property
    DirectoryInfo, 489
    FileInfo, 493
late binding, using reflection, 456, 462–464
Learning ASP.NET 2.0 with AJAX (Liberty et
        al.), 381
Length property
    FileInfo, 493
    String, 218, 222
    StringBuilder, 227
    System.Array, 158, 160
less than operator (<), 54
less than or equals operator (<=), 54
Liberty, Jesse (author), x
    Learning ASP.NET 2.0 with AJAX, 381
    Programming .NET 3.5, x, 6, 404
    Programming ASP.NET, 381, 401
    Programming Silverlight, 6
    support provided by, xv
    web site for, xi
life cycle, Web Forms, 384
LIFO (last-in, first-out) collections (see
        stacks)
line break, in string literals, 216
LINQ (Language-INtegrated Query), 279
    compared to SQL, 285
    connecting to SQL database, 339
    deleting data, 358–362
    extension methods of, 3, 285, 292–297,
        298, 301, 351

lambda expressions in, 297–301
mapping class properties to database
        columns
    manually, 340–343
    with Visual Studio, 344–348
queries
    caching results of, 284
    creating, 280–283, 352
    deferred execution of, 283
retrieving data, 349–353
table properties, creating, 350
updating data, 353–358
XML output from, 363–367
List class, 195
lists, 195
    adding items to, 196
    capacity of, 197
    constraints for, 190–195
    methods for, 195
    properties for, 195
literal values, 50
literals, 28
    char literals, 24
    string literals, 32, 216
Load event, 385
LoadPostData() method, 384
LoadViewState() method, 384
lock statement, 479
locking resources (see synchronization)
logical AND operator (&), 57
logical operators, 55, 57
logical OR operator (|), 57
logical XOR operator (^), 57
long type, 23
LongLength property, System.Array, 158
loop variable, scope of, 46
loops (see iteration statements)
Lowy, Juval (Programming WCF
        Services), 329


**M**

"m" suffix on a number, 24
Main() method, 8
manifest types, 22
Match objects, 232–234
MatchCollection type, 232–234
mathematical operators, 50
member access operator (->), 554
member variables
    accessibility by other classes (see access
        modifiers)
    readonly, 96

static, 78
(see also properties)
members of a class, 75–79
    (see also events; indexers; methods;
        properties; variables)
MemberwiseClone() method, Object, 113
MemoryStream class, 500
Message property, Exception, 252
metadata, 5, 449
    attributes of (see attributes, in metadata)
    reading (see reflection)
method-based queries, 298
methods, 8
    accessibility by other classes (see access
        modifiers)
    adding to generated classes, 348
    anonymous, 258, 271
    callback methods, 272–276
    constructors (see constructors)
    declarations of, 8, 65
    encapsulated in delegates (see delegates)
    encapsulating data using, 92–96
    for arrays, 157
    global, equivalent to, 75
    initializers for, 70–73
    invoking
        as unconditional branching, 34
        with dot operator, 11
    LINQ extension methods (see extension
        methods, LINQ)
    naming conventions for, 8, 14
    overloaded, 89–92
    overriding, 102–106, 147–151
    parameters of, 8, 9, 66–67
    polymorphic, 102–106
    return value of, 8, 9
        multiple values, 9
        void, 9
    selectively exposing in interface, 153
    signature of, 89
    stack frame allocated for, 23
    static
        as global methods, 75
        invoking, 75, 76
        passing instance members to, 76
    with same signature, in two implemented
        interfaces, 151
Microsoft code style guidelines, 14
modulus operator (%), 50
modulus self-assignment operator (%=), 52
monitors, 480–485

Move() method
   Directory, 488
   File, 493
MoveNext() method,
      XPathNodeIterator, 327
MoveTo() method
   DirectoryInfo, 489
   FileInfo, 493
multidimensional arrays, 165–172
multiplication operator (*), 50
multiplication self-assignment operator
     (*=), 52

## N

\n escape character, in string literal, 216
Name property
   DirectoryInfo, 489
   FileInfo, 493
Named Pipes protocol, enabling, 338
names (identifiers), 32
   (see also naming conventions)
namespaces, 11
   dot operator for, 12
   naming conventions for, 14
   using directive for, 13
   (see also specific namespaces)
naming conventions, 14, 32, 452
nested classes, 115–117
nested comments, 10
nested if statements, 37
.NET platform, 6
   book about, 6
   new features in, 6
network I/O, 511–513
   asynchronous network file
      streaming, 522–527
   multiple connections, handling, 518–522
   streaming network client for, 515–518
   streaming network server for, 513–515
   testing on single machine, 518
NetworkStream class, 500, 513
new keyword
   for array instantiation, 158
   for methods not overridden, 108
   for object instantiation, 67
new operator, 565
newlines
   escape character for, 24
   in string literals, 216
   (see also whitespace)
nondeterministic finalization, 79

nonpostback events, Web Forms, 383
NonSerialized attribute, 535
normalization, relational database, 370
Northwind database, 369
not equals operator (!=), 54
not operator (!) in conditionals, 55
null keyword, 565
null, escape character for, 24

## O

object graph, 529
object initializers, 291
Object type, 113–115
object type, 565
object-oriented languages, C# as, 4
objects, 8, 61
   as reference and value types, 130
   as reference types, 23
   copying, 113
   created by instantiation, 63, 67
   current instance of (this keyword), 73–74
   destroying (freeing resources), 79–83
   equivalence of, determining, 113
   on the heap, 23, 67
   passing to another method as a
      parameter, 74
   referring to same instance,
      determining, 113
   string representation of, 113
observer design pattern, 258
OCX standard, 542
OnDeserialization() method,
      IDeserializationCallback, 535
OnLoad() method, 385
OnPreRender() method, 385
OnReadComplete() method,
      ClientHandler, 518, 521
OnWriteComplete() method,
      ClientHandler, 518, 521
Open() method, FileInfo, 493
OpenRead() method
   File, 493, 500
   FileInfo, 493
OpenText() method, FileInfo, 493, 504
OpenWrite() method
   File, 493, 500
   FileInfo, 493
operator keyword, 118, 565
operators, 49
   arithmetical operators, 50
   assignment operator (=), 49

decrement operators, 52–53
increment operators, 52–53
logical operators, 55
mathematical operators, 50
overloading, 118
   alternatives for other languages, 119
   cautions regarding, 120
   examples of, 124
   required pairs of, 120
postfix operators, 53
precedence of, 55–58
prefix operators, 53
relational operators, 54
self-assignment operators, 52
short-circuit evaluation of, 56
ternary operator, 58
(see also specific operators)
or operator (||) in conditionals, 55, 57
orderby clause of query, 286–289, 301
OrderBy() method, LINQ, 301
out keyword, 565
out parameter, 86
outer join, SQL, 372
overloaded constructors, 71, 74, 89–92
overloaded methods, 89–92
override keyword, 102, 107, 565
overriding Equals() method, 120
overriding interface
     implementations, 147–151
overriding methods, 102–106

**P**

P/Invoke (platform invoke facility), 551–554
parameters of methods, 8, 9
   defining, 66–67
   optional, 67
   passing by reference, 9, 83–85
   passing by value, 9, 83
   with same name as member variable, 73
params keyword, 164, 565
parent elements, XML, 303
Parent property, DirectoryInfo, 489
parentheses (())
   in if...else statement, 35
   in switch statement, 39
partial classes, 382
partial classes and methods
   partial keyword, 565
partial keyword, 348
Pascal notation, 14
passing by reference, 9

passing by value, 9
Peek() method
   Queue, 206, 208
   Stack, 208, 209
platform invoke facility (P/Invoke), 551–554
plus sign (+), in debugger, 19
   (see also addition operator (+))
pointer operators, 554
pointers, 5, 554–560
   avoiding, 6
   compared to this keyword, 73
polymorphism, 98, 102
   base class constructors, calling, 106
   polymorphic methods, 102–106
   polymorphic types, 102
Pop() method, Stack, 208, 209
ports, 512
postback events, Web Forms, 383
postfix operators, 53
pound sign (#), preceding directives, 59
precedence of operator evaluation, 55–58
predicates (search conditions), XPath, 318,
     320–321
prefix operators, 53
preprocessor directives, 59–60
preprocessor identifiers, 59, 60
primary key, relational database, 369
private (access modifier), 565
private access modifier, 65
Programming .NET 3.5 (Liberty,
     Horovitz), x, 6, 404
Programming ASP.NET (Liberty,
     Hurwitz), 381, 401
Programming Silverlight (Liberty), 6
Programming WCF Services (Lowy), 329
Programming WPF (Sells, Griffiths), 404
programs
   compiling and running, 17
   creating, 15
Project Gutenberg, 557
projection of query, 283, 294
properties, 92
   access modifiers for, 95
   encapsulating data using, 92–96
   for arrays, 157
   get accessor for, 94
   mapping to database columns
     manually, 340–343
     with Visual Studio, 344–348
   naming conventions for, 14
   set accessor for, 95
protected access modifier, 65, 565

protected internal access modifier, 65
public access modifier, 65, 66, 566
publish and subscribe design
        pattern, 258–266
publishing events, 258, 262–264
Push() method, Stack, 208, 209

## Q

queries, ADO.NET, 375, 377
queries, LINQ
    caching results of, 284
    creating, 280–283, 352
    deferred execution of, 283
    from clause, 282
    grouping, 290
    join clause, 285
    method-based queries, 298
    orderby clause, 286–289
    range variable for, 282
    select clause (projection), 283, 294
    storing results with anonymous
            types, 291
    where clause (filter), 282
queries, SQL, 371
Queue class, 206
queues, 206–208
quotes (see double quotes; single quotes)

## R

race conditions, 485
RAD (Rapid Application Development)
    Web Forms for, 381
RaisePostDataChangedEvent() method, 385
range variable, LINQ, 282
Rank property, System.Array, 158
Rapid Application Development (RAD)
    Web Forms for, 381
Read() method, Stream, 500
Reader class, ADO.NET, 368
ReadLine() method
    Console, 47
    StreamReader, 504
readonly fields, 96
readonly modifier, 566
records, relational database, 369
rectangular arrays, 165–169
ref modifier, 566
ref parameter modifier, 83
reference types, objects as, 23, 130
ReferenceEquals() method, Object, 113

reflection, 449, 456
    creating types at runtime using, 456
    late binding using, 456, 462–464
    type discovery using, 456, 458–462
    viewing metadata using, 456–457
reflection emit (see types, creating at runtime
        using reflection)
Refresh() method, DirectoryInfo, 489
Regex class, 230
Regsvr32 utility, 546
regular expressions, 214, 229–232
    capture collections for, 237–240
    grouping subexpression matches
        of, 234–237
    match collections for, 232–234
relational databases, 368–371
    constraints, 370
    declarative referential integrity (DRI), 370
    normalization of, 370
    querying with SQL, 371
relational operators, 54
    operator precedence for, 57
    overloading, required pairs for, 120
remainders in division (see modulus operator
        (%))
Remove() method
    Dictionary, 212
    List, 196
    StringBuilder, 227
RemoveAll() method, List, 196
RemoveAt() method, List, 196
RemoveRange() method, List, 196
Render() method, 385
Replace() method, StringBuilder, 227
Resize() method, System.Array, 158
resources
    creating, in WPF, 409
    freeing, 79–83
    locking (see synchronization)
    unmanaged, cleaning up, 79, 113
resources (information)
    contact information for this book, xvi
    (see also books; web site resources)
return statement, 35, 126
return value of methods, 8
Reverse() method
    List, 196
    System.Array, 158, 175
root element, XML, 303, 307
Root property, DirectoryInfo, 489
Rows collection, ADO.NET, 373
rows, relational database, 369
runat=Server attribute, 391

# S

SaveViewState() method, 385
sbyte keyword, 566
sbyte type, 22
screen scraping, 529
sealed classes, 112
sealed keyword, 112
sealed modifier, 566
search conditions (predicates), XPath, 318, 320–321
searching database (see LINQ)
security, with data binding, 398
select clause of query, 283, 294
Select() method, XPathNavigator, 327
SelectNodes() method, XPath, 321
SelectSingleNode() method, XPath, 318, 319, 326
self-assignment operators, 52
Sells, Chris (Programming WPF), 404
semicolon (;)
    ending statements, 33
    not ending class definitions, 63
Serializable attribute, 529, 531
serialization, 487, 529–538
    formatter for, 530
    transient data, handling, 535
serialization, XML, 329–331
    customizing using attributes, 331–333
    deserialization, 331
    runtime customization of, 333–336
Serialize() method, formatter, 532
server-side controls
    adding to Web Form, 388–391, 399–403
    ASP (web) controls, 391
    binding to data, 391–398
    HTML controls, 391
    validation controls, 401
set accessor, 95
set() method, for indexers, 180
SetAttributes() method, File, 492
SetCreationTime() method, File, 492
SetLastAccessTime() method, File, 492
SetLastWriteTime() method, File, 493
SetValue() method, System.Array, 158
shift operator (<<>>), 57
short type, 22
short-circuit evaluation, 56
signature of a method, 89
Silverlight, information about, 6
Simonyi, Charles (inventor of Hungarian notation), 32

single quotes ('), escape character for, 24
single type, 22
slash (/), in XPath, 318
    (see also division operator (/))
slash asterisk (/* ... */), enclosing comments, 10
slash, double (//), preceding comments, 9
SOA, book about, 329
SOAP, 530
SoapFormatter class, 530
sockets, 511
software requirements, x
Sort() method
    List, 196, 198
    System.Array, 158, 175
sorting arrays, 175–177
sorting query results, 286–289
source code for examples, xi
spaces (see whitespace)
specialization, 98–101
Split() method
    Regex, 231
    String, 218, 226
SQL (Structured Query Language), 371
    connecting to database with LINQ (see LINQ)
    LINQ syntax compared to, 285
SQL injection attack, 398
SQL Server 2005 Adventure Works LT sample database, 338
SQL Server, version used for this book, x
SQML (Structured Query Markup Language), 304
square brackets (see brackets)
stack (in memory), 23
    (see also call stack)
Stack class, 208
stack frame, 23, 242
stack panels, WPF, 406–408, 414
stack trace, 253–255
stackalloc keyword, 566
stacks, 208–211
StackTrace property, Exception, 253
standard output, 11
Start() method, TcpListener, 512, 513
StartRead() method, ClientHandler, 518, 523
starts-with() function, XPath, 321
StartsWith() method, String, 218
state object, asynchronous I/O, 507
state of web application, 384

statement blocks, 37
statements, 33
    conditional branching statements, 35–42
    iteration statements, 42–49
    unconditional branching statements, 34
    (see also specific statements)
static classes, 78
static keyword, 14
static members of a class, 14, 75–79
    constructors, 76–77
    initializers for, 79
    member variables
        accessibility of, 79
        tracking instances using, 78
    methods
        as global, 75
        invoking, 75, 76
        passing instance members to, 76
static modifier, 566
statically typed, 21
storage, isolated, 538–541
Stream class, 499
streaming
    asynchronous network files, 522–527
    network client, 515–518
    network server, 513–515
    web streams, 527–529
StreamReader class, 504
streams, 487
    backing store for, 487
    buffered, 502–504
    serialization of data for (see serialization)
StreamWriter class, 504, 513
String class, 215
string keyword, 32
string literals, 32, 216
    (see also char literals)
string representation of object, 113
StringBuilder class, 227–228
StringReader class, 499
strings, 32, 215, 566
    comparing, 221
    concatenating, 221
    copying, 222
    creating with literals, 216
    creating with ToString() method, 217
    delimiters in, problems with, 229
    equality of, testing, 222
    finding specific character in, 222
    immutable (String class), 215
    indexers based on, 183–186

    length of, 222
    manipulating, 217–223
    methods and properties for, 217
    mutable (StringBuilder class), 227–228
    ordering, 215
    parsing into substrings, 226
    String type compared to string type, 215
    switch statement using, 42
    (see also regular expressions; substrings)
StringWriter class, 499
strongly typed, 22
structs, 5, 127, 566
    creating, 129–131
    defining, 128
    performance of, 127
Structured Query Markup Language
    (SQML), 304
style guidelines for code, by Microsoft, 14
subdirectories
    creating, 496
    listing files in, 492–496
    traversing, 489–492
subscribe operator (+=), 265, 266
subscribing to events, 258, 264
Substring() method, String, 218, 223–225
substrings
    finding at end of string, 222
    finding location of, within string, 223
    finding within string, 223–225
    inserting into a string, 223
    parsing string into, 226
subtraction operator (-), 50
subtraction self-assignment operator (-=), 52
support for this book, xv
SuppressFinalize() method, GC, 81
Swann's Way (Proust), 557
switch keyword, 567
switch statement, 38–42
    C and C++ differences in, 41
    default case for, 41
    on strings, 42
    Visual Basic 6 equivalents to, 40
symbolic constants, 28
symbolic values, 50
synchronization, 465, 474–477
    Interlocked class for, 477
    lock statement for, 479
    monitors for, 480–485
    (see also thread synchronization)
synchronous I/O, 506
SyncRoot property, System.Array, 158

System.Array type, 157
System.Attribute class, 452
System.IO namespace, 488
System.Object type, 113–115
System.Reflection namespace, 451
System.Threading namespace, 465
System.Web namespace, 382
System.Web.Extension namespace, 382
System.Web.UI namespace, 382
System.Xml namespace, 307
System.Xml.Serialization namespace, 329
System.Xml.XPath namespace, 311, 322
SystemRoot directory, 496

**T**

\t escape character, in string literal, 216
tables, relational database, 369
tabs
    escape characters for, 24
    in string literals, 216
    (see also whitespace)
tags, XML, 303
targets, of metadata attributes, 450
    applying to attributes, 450
    list of, 449
TCP/IP protocol, 511
TcpClient class, 515
TcpListener object, 512, 513
ternary operator (?:), 58
text files, 504–506
TextReader class, 499
TextWriter class, 499
ThenBy() method, LINQ, 301
this keyword, 73–74
    as documentation, 74
    for passing objects as parameters, 74
    in indexer declarations, 177, 180
    to call overloaded constructors, 74
    to qualify instance members, 73
Thread class, 466
thread synchronization, 485
threads, 465
    creating, 466
    joining, 469
    killing, 470–474
    scheduling of, 469
    starting, 467
    suspending (sleeping), 469
    uses of, 466

ThreadStart delegate class, 466
throw statement, 242–244
ToArray() method
    LINQ, 284
    List, 196
    Queue, 206
    Stack, 209
ToArray() method, Stack, 209
ToList() method, LINQ, 284
ToString() method, Object, 113, 115, 125, 217
ToUpper() method, String, 218
TreeView controls, Windows Forms
    event handling for, 429–432
    populating, 424–428
triggers, WPF, 411
Trim() method, String, 218
TrimEnd() method, String, 218
TrimExcess() method
    List, 196
    Queue, 206
    Stack, 209
TrimToSize() method, List, 196
TrueForAll() method, System.Array, 158
try block, 244, 246
TryGetValue() method, Dictionary, 212
type conversion
    implementing operators for, 121, 124
    of built-in types, 24
type discovery, using reflection, 456, 458–462
types, 7, 21
    built-in types, 22–25
    creating at runtime using reflection, 456
    suffixes of numbers indicating, 24

**U**

uint type, 22, 23
uint16 type, 22
uint32 type, 22
uint64 type, 23
ulong type, 23
UML (Unified Modeling Language), 99
unconditional branching statements, 34
    (see also jump statements)
#undef directive, 60
UnderlyingObject property, XPathNavigator, 327
Unified Modeling Language (UML), 99

unmanaged code, invoking from
  C#,  551–554
unmanaged resources, cleaning up,  79, 113
unsafe keyword,  554, 556, 567
unsubscribe operator (-=),  267
unwinding the stack,  242, 246
user-defined types,  21
ushort type,  22, 23
using directive,  13
using keyword,  567
using statement,  82

**V**

validation controls,  401
value types,  130
Values property, Dictionary,  212
variables,  25–26
    assigning values to,  25, 27, 49
    declaring,  25
    implicitly types local variables,  291
    initialization of, avoiding,  86–89
    initializing,  25, 27
    naming conventions for,  14
    on the stack,  23
    (see also member variables)
verbatim string literals,  216
versioning,  107
ViewState property, web control,  384
virtual keyword,  102, 567
    (see also overriding methods)
Visual Basic 6
    ADO compared to ADO.NET,  369
    array size, differences in,  159
    controls, differences in,  425
    Dim and New performance penalty, no
        equivalent to,  68
    loop variable differences,  46
    optional parameter equivalents,  67
    pointers in, compared to this keyword,  73
    Static keyword, compared to C# static
        keyword,  75
    switch statement eqivalents in,  40
    variables in try blocks, restrictions
        on,  253

Visual Studio
    compiling programs,  17
    creating projects,  15
    debugger (see debugger)
    importing ActiveX controls using,  547
    LINQ to SQL designer,  344–348
    namespaces included by default,  13, 16
    version used for this book,  x
    web-based applications created
        using,  382, 385

**W**

web controls (see ASP controls)
Web Forms,  381–383
    code separation used by,  382
    code-behind pages for,  381, 386–388
    controls for (see server-side controls)
    creating,  385–391
    event handlers for,  383
    events in,  383, 399–403
    life cycle of,  384
web site resources
    Adventure Works LT sample
        database,  338
    author,  xi, xv
    code style guidelines by Microsoft,  14
    for this book,  xvi
    Griffiths, Ian, blog for,  301
    Hungarian notation,  32
    Northwind database,  369
    port numbers,  512
    Project Gutenberg,  557
    security,  398
    Silverlight,  6
    source code for examples,  xi
    support,  xv
    XPath,  320
    XPath functions,  322
web streams,  527–529
web-based applications
    advantages of,  381
    state of,  384
    Visual Studio used for,  382
    (see also ASP.NET; Web Forms)

WebRequest object, 527
WebResponse object, 527
where clause of query, 282
Where() method, LINQ, 293
while keyword, 568
while loop, 43
whitespace, 33, 47
Wiltamuth, Scott (C# creator), 4
Windows Forms applications
    controls
        button, 432–437
        creating, 421
        populating, 424–428
        TreeView, 424–432
    creating, 420–421
    event handlers for, 423, 429–437
Windows Presentation Foundation (see
        WPF)
Windows Vista
    protected files, accessing, 492, 496
    version used for this book, x
WPF (Windows Presentation
        Foundation), 101
    books about, 404
    creating applications, 405–408
    data for application, 412, 414
    declarative nature of, 419
    event handling in, 418
    grids, 406–408, 414
    instantiating objects declaratively, 413
    resources, creating, 409
    stack panels, 406–408, 414
    triggers in, 411
    Windows version required for, x
Write() method, Console, 46
WriteLine() method
    Console, 11, 26, 506
    StreamWriter, 504, 506

## X

XAML (eXtensible Application Markup
        Language), 6, 404
XAttribute class, 363
XDocument class, 363
XElement class, 363
XHTML, 304
Xie, Donald (author), x
XML (eXtensible Markup Language), 302,
        304
    creating documents, 304–311
    elements in, 303
    LINQ output to, 363–367
    tags in, 303
    versions of, 302
XML editor, 309
XML serialization, 329–331
    customizing using attributes, 331–333
    deserialization, 331
    runtime customization of, 333–336
XmlAttribute object, 309
XmlAttributeAttribute object, 333, 335
XmlAttributeOverrides class, 335
XML-based documentation, comments
        for, 11
XmlNode class, 318
XmlSerializer object, 330
XPath, 311–317
    functions for, 321
    search conditions (predicates) for, 318,
        320–321
    searching for a node, 318–319
    searching using axes, 319
    searching using
        XPathNavigator, 322–328
    web site about, 320, 322
XPathExpression object, 328
XPathNavigator class, 322, 326
XPathNodeIterator object, 327

## About the Authors

**Jesse Liberty**, currently a senior program manager on the Silverlight Development Team at Microsoft, is the author of *Programming .NET 3.5*, *Learning ASP.NET with AJAX* (both for O'Reilly), and many other books. He is a recognized .NET expert whose experience includes working as a software architect at PBS and as a distinguished software engineer at AT&T. He can be reached at *http://www.JesseLiberty.com*.

**Donald Xie** has been programming since Apple II was known as state of the art. He has written a lot of applications using different languages and technologies. Since the late 90s, Donald has focused on developing enterprise-strength business applications using Microsoft technologies—especially with .NET—from the very first beta.

Donald is a coauthor of several books, including *Pro Visual Studio .NET* (Apress), and *Fast Track ADO.NET* and *Data-Centric .NET Programming with C#* (both for Peer Information, Inc.). He has also written books on C++ and Visual Basic. Currently, Donald works as a business analyst for Chevron.

## Colophon

The animal on the cover of *Programming C# 3.0*, Fifth Edition, is an African crowned crane. This tall, skinny bird wanders the marshes and grasslands of West and East Africa (the Western and Eastern African crowned cranes are known as *Balearica pavonia pavonia* and *Balearica regulorum gibbericeps*, respectively).

Adult birds stand about three feet tall and weigh six to nine pounds. Inside their long necks is a five-foot long windpipe—part of which is coiled inside their breastbone—giving voice to loud calls that can carry for miles. They live for about 22 years, spending most of their waking hours looking for the various plants, small animals, and insects they like to eat. (One crowned crane food-finding technique, perfected during the 38 to 54 million years these birds have existed, is to stamp their feet as they walk, flushing out tasty bugs.) They are the only type of crane to perch in trees, which they do at night when sleeping.

Social and talkative, African crowned cranes group together in pairs or families, and the smaller groups band together in flocks of more than 100 birds. Their elaborate mating dance has served as a model for some of the dances of local people.

The cover image is an original engraving from the 19th century. The cover font is Adobe ITC Garamond. The text font is Linotype Birka; the heading font is Adobe Myriad Condensed; and the code font is LucasFont's TheSans Mono Condensed.

# Try the online edition free for 45 days

Get the information you need when you need it, with Safari Books Online. Safari Books Online contains the complete version of the print book in your hands plus thousands of titles from the best technical publishers, with sample code ready to cut and paste into your applications.

Safari is designed for people in a hurry to get the answers they need so they can get the job done. You can find what you need in the morning, and put it to work in the afternoon. As simple as cut, paste, and program.

**To try out Safari and the online edition of the above title FREE for 45 days, go to www.oreilly.com/go/safarienabled and enter the coupon code FWJYTYG.**

To see the complete Safari Library visit:
safari.oreilly.com

70502